"Wonderful."

—*The Atlantic*

"Gould . . . sets sky-high aspirations for his book, attempting not to merely chronicle Redding's meteoric life but to use him as the backdrop for a larger story about race in America, the history of soul music, and the rise of Memphis's small but powerful Stax Records. He does that gracefully."

—*Dallas News*

"Jonathan Gould's much-heralded biography . . . builds beautifully, more like a great soul ballad than the dance hall hit so many music biographies aim at becoming. One feels the time that's gone into the book's organization, its exegesis, its every insightful and often quite funny sentences."

—*Hudson Valley One*

"Some of the best parts of Gould's book are his incisive descriptions of Redding's live performances and recording sessions. . . . But even more than his vivid re-creations of Redding's composing and recording work, it's Gould's insightful portrayal of the Segregated South's racial climate that makes *Otis Redding: An Unfinished Life* so compelling."

—*Paste*

"An excellent and definitive biography . . . A master storyteller, Gould tackles Redding's life by planting his flag firmly at the crossroads of individual genius and social and cultural context. . . . [His] fabulous portrait . . . provides Redding with the "Respect" he richly deserves. Highly recommended."

—*Library Journal* (starred review)

"A music biography with the depth to do its subject justice. Otis Redding (1941–1967) ranks high in the pantheon of 1960s musical luminaries, so it's fitting that [*Otis Redding*] ranks equally high among such work focusing on popular musical artists. . . . Better late than never, the soul master receives his considerable due in this superbly researched and written biography."

—*Kirkus Reviews* (starred review)

"Nuanced and well-researched . . . [*Otis Redding*] belongs in the hands of anyone who cares about soul music in the sixties."

—*Booklist*

Praise for *Otis Redding*

"An absorbing and ambitious book . . . [that] succeeds in making [Redding] seem a good deal more remarkable by taking the measure of the historical circumstances he emerged from . . . Among the great pleasures . . . are [Gould's] very considered assessments of each of Otis's albums, track by track."

—*The New York Review of Books*

"[An] impressive biography . . . Access to Redding's surviving family members helps Gould flesh out his upbringing and offstage personality."

—*The New York Times Book Review*

"Magisterial . . . With meticulous scholarship, lively prose, and a tale that uses a singular musician as a springboard into interrogating America's political and popular cultures, Gould has created a vital book that helps contextualize one of the most important figures in pop music."

—*Boston Globe*

"Perceptive . . . An incisive and deeply humanistic portrait."

—*Wall Street Journal*

"The beloved '60s soul titan . . . comes alive in Gould's insightful, well-researched biography."

—*People*

"Gould vividly brings to life the man Stax Records boss Jim Stewart called 'a walking inspiration' . . . From his supreme triumphs to his one last heartbreaking phone call to Zelma, devotees and soul scholars alike could not wish for a more thorough and sensitive portrait."

—*Mojo*

"A rich picture of [Redding's] world . . . illuminating."

—*Rolling Stone*

OTIS REDDING

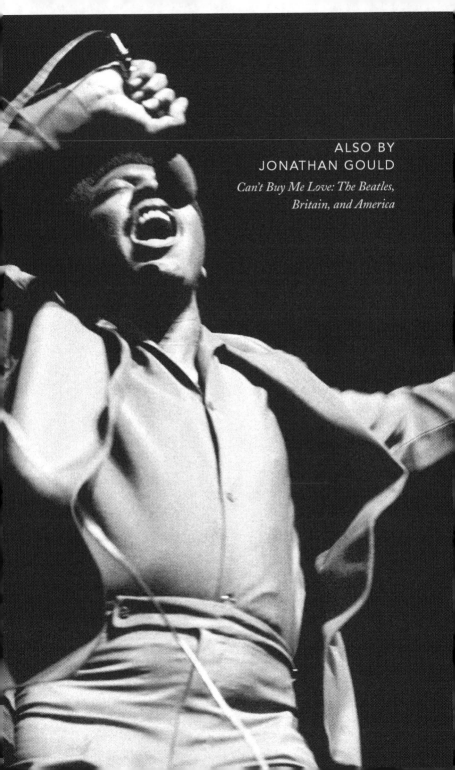

ALSO BY
JONATHAN GOULD

*Can't Buy Me Love: The Beatles,
Britain, and America*

OTIS REDDING

AN UNFINISHED LIFE

JONATHAN GOULD

THREE RIVERS PRESS
NEW YORK

FOR LISA, WITH LOVE

Library of Congress Cataloging-in-Publication Data
Names: Gould, Jonathan, 1951–
Title: Otis Redding / Jonathan Gould.
Description: First edition. | New York : Crown Archetype, [2017] | Includes
bibliographical references.
Identifiers: LCCN 2016043388
Subjects: LCSH: Redding, Otis, 1941–1967. | Soul musicians—United States—
Biography.
Classification: LCC ML420.R295 G68 2017 | DDC 782.421644092 [B]—dc23
LC record available at https://lccn.loc.gov/2016043388

ISBN 978-0-307-45395-2
Ebook ISBN 978-0-307-45396-9

Book design by Lauren Dong
Cover design by Christopher Brand
Cover photograph by Tony Frank/Contributor/Sygma Premium/Getty Images

First Paperback Edition

146119709

CONTENTS

OTIS REDDING

MONTEREY

I was pretty sure that I'd seen God onstage.

—BOB WEIR

Late on the evening of June 18, 1967, as Saturday night turned to Sunday morning, the San Francisco–based rock group known as the Jefferson Airplane concluded their forty-minute set to rousing applause from the 7,500 fans who filled the fairgrounds arena in the resort town of Monterey, California, on the second night of an event billed as the First International Pop Festival. The Airplane were local heroes to the crowd at Monterey, many of whom lived in the Bay Area and had followed the band's career from its inception in 1965. Along with other whimsically named groups like the Charlatans, Big Brother and the Holding Company, and the Grateful Dead, they had gotten their start in the folk coffeehouses and rock ballrooms of the Haight-Ashbury, a neighborhood on the eastern edge of San Francisco's Golden Gate Park whose recent emergence as a bohemian enclave had captured the imagination of young people across America. During the first half of 1967, a series of sensationalistic articles had appeared in newspapers and national magazines describing this self-styled "psychedelic city-state" and the long-haired, hedonistic "hippies" who populated it. This rash of publicity had inspired tens of thousands of footloose college students, college dropouts, teenaged runaways, and "flower children" of all ages to converge on San Francisco in anticipation of an idyllic "Summer of Love."

The Monterey Pop Festival was timed to coincide with the start of that summer. The idea for the festival had originated a few months before as a gleam in the eye of a neophyte Los Angeles promoter named Alan Pariser, who envisioned it as a pop-oriented version of the seaside jazz and folk festivals at Newport and Monterey that had served as a fashionable form of summertime entertainment since the 1950s. After booking the fairgrounds and enlisting a well-connected Hollywood Brit named Derek Taylor (who had previously worked for the Beatles) as their publicist, Pariser and his partner, a talent agent named Ben Shapiro, approached the Los Angeles folk-rock group The Mamas and the Papas with the intent of hiring them as headliners. The group's leader, John Phillips, and their producer, Lou Adler, responded with a vision of their own. They proposed expanding the size and scope of the festival and using it to showcase the explosion of creative energy that had enveloped the world of popular music in the three years since the arrival of the Beatles in America in 1964. They also proposed staging the festival on a nonprofit basis, with the performers donating their services and the proceeds going to charity.

When Shapiro balked at this idea, Phillips and Adler bought out his interest and formed a new partnership with Pariser. They then set out to assemble a roster of some thirty acts, enough to fill three nights and two days of music. Toward this end, they established a tony-sounding "board of governors" that included such prominent pop stars as Paul McCartney, Mick Jagger, Smokey Robinson, and Brian Wilson. Though none of these luminaries actually attended or performed, they gave the festival enough cachet to ensure that most of the artists the promoters contacted accepted their invitation to appear. In the deft hands of Derek Taylor, the advance publicity for the festival also attracted some twelve hundred loosely cre-dentialed representatives of the press, as well as enough agents, managers, and record company executives to lend the proceedings the feeling of an open-air music business trade fair.

Phillips and Adler recognized that staging the festival on a nonprofit basis was essential to realizing their more parochial goal, which was to celebrate California's sudden ascendancy in the world of popular music, with Los Angeles now recognized as the pop recording center of America and San Francisco as the home of the country's most dynamic under-ground music scene. (Fully half the acts that performed came from the West Coast, with the balance drawn from points east, including the new pop capital of London.) Yet bridging the gap between the Northern and Southern Californian nodes of musical sensibility was no simple matter, for the two factions approached one another with the suspicion of rival tribes, vying over their respective notions of the California Dream. The music business in Los Angeles was just that—a branch of the entertainment industry governed by conventional Hollywood standards of stardom and success. The music scene in San Francisco, by contrast, subscribed to a bohemian ethos whose insularity and self-regard had been supercharged by the grandiosity of the psychedelic drug culture. Bay Area bands that could barely sing or play in tune professed to disdain the "commercialism" and "slick professionalism" of their counterparts in L.A. At this point, the music of the Haight-Ashbury was a hodgepodge of strident folk harmonies, impressionistic lyrics, modal improvisation, and sophomoric electric blues. But the purported affinities of this music with the effects of hallucinogenic drugs had earned it the label *acid rock* and generated a formidable mystique.

By the time of their appearance at Monterey, the Jefferson Airplane had established themselves as the most musically accomplished and commercially successful exponents of the San Francisco Sound. Their second album, *Surrealistic Pillow,* stood high on the *Billboard* charts, while their latest single, an anthem of alienation called "Somebody to Love," had attained a saturation-level presence on the airwaves of America's Top 40 radio stations. Onstage and off, the group dressed with a theatrical flair that erased the lines between clothing and costume. All five of the men wore Beatlesque helmets of shoulder-length hair; the one woman, a former fashion model named Grace Slick, had the pale skin, luminous eyes, and flowing kaftan robes of a pagan priestess. Yet, unlike the Beatles and their fellow "British Invasion" bands, who had institutionalized the "rock group" as an autonomous musical unit, the members of the Jefferson Airplane did not project an almost familial uniformity of appearance. They looked instead like a patchwork of different types—a Western gunslinger, a Regency dandy, a bespectacled Sioux—drawn from the collective unconscious of a generation of television babies, raised on a diet of half-hour period dramas. In this the members of the band were indistinguishable from the members of their audience. "At times, our audience was more outrageous than the people onstage," recalled Paul Kantner, the group's rhythm guitarist.

Though the Jefferson Airplane were hometown heroes to the crowd at Monterey, they were not the headlining act on the second night of the festival. No sooner had they finished their set than the harried stage crew, pressed by a midnight curfew that had already expired, began replacing their banks of amplifiers with the more modest gear of a four-piece rhythm section called Booker T. and the MGs and a two-piece horn section called the Mar-Keys. Their presence at Monterey owed to their role as the studio band for Stax Records, a small Memphis label that specialized in a distinctive brand of earthy, gospel-tinged rhythm and blues whose roots in the fervent emotionalism of the black church had earned it the label "soul music." The most prominent and charismatic artist associated with Stax was the singer Otis Redding, and it was as the prelude and accompaniment to Redding's eagerly anticipated performance that the MGs and the Mar-Keys now prepared to take the stage.

Whereas the members of the Jefferson Airplane blended easily into the crowd of predominantly white, long-haired, flamboyantly dressed young people who filled the fairgrounds arena, the MGs and Mar-Keys—three of them white, three of them black—could well have arrived there, as one of them later said, "from another planet." To a man, their hair was cut short and, in the case of the white musicians, swept back into the sort of sculpted pompadour that was commonly associated in 1967 with television evangelists and country music stars. Even more anomalous was the fact that the six of them were dressed in matching, double-breasted, lime-green and electric-blue stage suits from Lansky Brothers, a local institution in Memphis whose most famous client, Elvis Presley, could be said to stand for everything in the realm of contemporary American popular music that the West Coast bands were not.

From his seat in the VIP section, just behind the photographers' pit that ran in front of the stage, Jerry Wexler awaited the start of Otis Redding's set with mounting trepidation. A vice-president of Atlantic Records, Wexler was a renowned music executive and producer, best known for his work with Ray Charles and, more recently, Aretha Franklin. He was also a notorious worrier, and he felt a sense of personal responsibility for Redding's presence at Monterey. It was Wexler who had nurtured the relationship between Atlantic and Stax that put the fledgling Memphis label on the map, and who had assured Redding's manager, Phil Walden, that the festival would be a prime opportunity for his client to connect with the burgeoning audience for progressive rock.

Yet Wexler himself was unnerved by the countercultural pageant he encountered at Monterey. It was not the thick haze of marijuana smoke hovering over the fairgrounds that gave him pause; Wexler had been smoking "reefer" since his club-hopping days in Harlem in the 1930s. It was rather that much of the music he had heard during the afternoon and evening concerts on Saturday had impressed him as amateurish, bombastic, and banal, and he was now consumed with doubt about how this crowd of wide-eyed dilettantes would respond to the raw emotional intensity and high-energy stagecraft of Otis Redding's performance. To make matters worse, a cold drizzle was beginning to fall, and as Booker T. and the MGs launched into their opening number, Wexler's expert ears told him that the group, known for their impeccable timing, was sounding slightly off. When Phil Walden emerged from the backstage area to pay his respects, Wexler told his young protégé that he was afraid they had made a mistake.

By the time Walden returned backstage, Booker T. and the MGs had overcome the effects of the late hour, the cold night, and whatever nervousness they may have felt at performing in such unfamiliar surroundings and were setting up an enormous groove behind the saxophonist Andrew Love as he scorched through his solo on the Mar-Keys' showcase "Philly Dog." As for Otis Redding, the very real apprehension he felt was imperceptible to all but his closest associates. A tall, thick-featured, powerfully built man whose imposing physical presence made him seem considerably older than his age of twenty-five, Redding waited in the wings with his usual air of restless energy. Earlier, when Phil Walden asked him what songs he planned to sing, Redding had teasingly pretended that he hadn't given the matter much thought. (In fact, he had determined his set with the band the day before.) His feigned nonchalance was entirely in character, for one of the traits that had distinguished Redding throughout his five-year professional career was his seemingly boundless confidence in his ability to win people over.

Notwithstanding Jerry Wexler's doubts, Redding had gained a great deal of experience performing in front of nominally hip white audiences during the year that preceded his appearance at Monterey. In the spring of 1966, he had wowed the Hollywood in-crowd with his shows at the Whisky a Go Go, a nightclub on the Sunset Strip. In the fall he had toured in England and France and played a three-night engagement in San Francisco at Bill Graham's Fillmore Auditorium, the Carnegie Hall of acid rock. (Twenty-five years later, Graham would remember it simply as "the best gig I ever put on in my entire life.") More recently, in the spring of 1967, Redding had returned to Europe, where he was rapturously received by fans in Britain, France, and Scandinavia, and afforded a royal welcome by the Beatles, the Rolling Stones, and the other members of London's pop aristocracy who had revered him from afar.

At the conclusion of "Philly Dog," the television host Tommy Smothers came onstage and encouraged the crowd to give a warm welcome to "*Mister* Otis Redding." The MG's initial downbeat was answered by a syncopated fanfare from the horns and a fusillade of accents from the drums as Redding, resplendent in a teal-green silk suit, strode to the microphone, snatched it off its stand, flashed an enormous smile, and issued what was very likely the first unequivocal *command* to come from the stage at Monterey since the festival began. "SHAKE!" he demanded. "Everybody say it." And again: "SHAKE! Let me hear the *whole crowd*." Between the honorific tone of Tommy Smothers's introduction and the note of total authority in the singer's voice and the band's accompaniment, for the 7,500 astonished young listeners who leapt to their feet and surged toward the stage, it was as if the grown-ups had arrived.

THE FIVE SONGS Otis Redding performed in his rain- and curfew-shortened set at Monterey comprised an overview of his brief career. The incendiary opening number, "Shake," had been a posthumous hit for Sam Cooke, the gospel singer turned pop star whose supple voice, clean-cut good looks, and consistent "crossover" success (with white and black listeners alike) had made him, along with Ray Charles, a role model for every soul artist of the 1960s. Following Cooke's untimely death in a shooting incident in 1964, Redding had consciously sought to assume his mantle by recording his songs and emulating his determination to be his own man in the music business.

Otis's second number, "Respect," was one of the three hit singles he released in 1965, the year he emerged as a full-fledged R&B recording star. "Respect" was a prototype of the sort of driving dance tune with a stamping beat and a syncopated chorus of horns that defined the sound of the Stax label, but it had recently gained a new and greater significance as a vehicle for Aretha Franklin, who recorded it as part of her stunning debut on Atlantic Records in the spring of 1967. Franklin turned Redding's song—in which "respect" served as a euphemism ("*give* it to me") for sexual attention—into a woman's demand for the real thing, complete with a newly written release in which she literally spelled out the meaning of the word. By the time of Monterey, this feminist reprise of "Respect" stood at #1 on the *Billboard* Pop charts. "This is a song that a girl took away from me," Otis told the crowd. "But I'm still going to do it anyway."

"I've Been Loving You Too Long (To Stop Now)" was another of Redding's breakthrough hits from 1965, and another hallmark of his style: a slow, imploring ballad in 12/8 time, paced by wistful arpeggios on the guitar and stately crescendos from the horns. "This is the Love Crowd, right?" Otis asked, alluding to the hippies' atmospheric embrace of love (advertised by a banner reading "Music, Love, and Flowers" that ran the length of the stage). He then launched into a romantic testimonial of excruciating intensity, addressed to a woman whose "love is growing cold . . . as our affair grows old." Phrasing tremulously behind the beat, edging into the song like a man edging into a difficult conversation, Otis couched his appeal in expressions of empathy ("you are tired, and you want to be free") and gratitude ("with you my life has been so wonderful"), before plunging into an ad-libbed coda in which he searched and strained for the words that might persuade her to change her mind: pleading ("I'm down on my *knees*"), protesting ("*No!* Don't make me stop"), and finally culminating in a thunderous declaration of "Good God Almighty! I *love* you." In the nuanced emotionality of his singing on this song, Otis seemed to be drawing on a different dimension of feeling and experience than that of any other performer who would be heard at Monterey, and it dramatized the tension that lay at the core of his appeal: that a man so physically imposing and overtly self-possessed could indeed be so consumed, so utterly undone, by the force of his yearning, his desire, and his need.

Finally, with the rain coming down, the crowd in an uproar ("he had the audience spinning like a chicken on a spit," one reviewer wrote), and the local authorities demanding an immediate end to the evening, Redding concluded his performance with a pair of "cover" tunes. The first was a frenetic rendition of the Rolling Stones' hit "(I Can't Get No) Satisfaction," whose presence in his repertoire reflected a conscious effort to cater to a rock audience—the impulse that brought him to Monterey in the first place. By stripping the song down to its bare essentials of title, hook, and groove (and dispensing with the lyrics' pretensions to social commentary), Redding recast "Satisfaction" as a swaggering carnal comedy that took his hypersexualized stage presence nearly to the point of self-parody. In addition to earning him an R&B hit in 1966, the song had served as a familiar crowd pleaser on his European tours, where many fans, aware of the usual pattern of white appropriation, mistakenly assumed that the Stones' version must have been a cover of Redding's original.

The finale, "Try a Little Tenderness," was something else again. The song itself was a Tin Pan Alley standard, written in the early 1930s by a one-handed American pianist named Harry Woods and a pair of English lyricists, Jimmy Campbell and Reg Connelly, and recorded over the years by the likes of Bing Crosby, Frank Sinatra, and Perry Como. The Depression-era lyric carried an economic subtext with its account of a woman who gets "weary wearing the same shabby dress." Redding's version, released as a single in the fall of 1966, was a seamless synthesis of the two strains of sensibility—soft and hard, seductive and aggressive—that ran through the body of his work. Otis retained the ballad tempo of the original in the opening verses, which he sang with an exaggerated tenderness over the bare accompaniment of whole notes on the bass. (For the crowd at Monterey, he ad-libbed an appreciative reference to "that same old *miniskirt* dress.") The instruments drifted in as the song progressed—a looping sax, a distant trill of organ, a thin spine of drums—until the arrival of a jaunty rhythm guitar caused the meter to shift, the beat to solidify, and the entire arrangement to assume the form of one long musical and emotional crescendo. Marching in place, waving his arms, jerking his torso like a man possessed, Otis punctuated his appeal to "*hold* her, *squeeze* her, never *leave* her" with strings of percussive scat syllables, extolling the need for "tenderness" with a ferocious insistence that defied the meaning of the word. When at last he had taken this exhortation as far as it could go—though not before the band had contrived a false ending, generating a dense cloud of sound from which Otis reemerged to sing a final chorus before leaving the stage for good—he had done to "Try a Little Tenderness" what black artists like Louis Armstrong, Billie Holiday, and Ray Charles had been doing for half a century to the genteel conventions and coy platitudes with which Tin Pan Alley composers had sought to sing the praises of love: he had cured the song of its cant and sentimentality, transforming it with a startling infusion of urgency and energy into something inextricably real. "I've got to go. I don't want to go," Otis announced as he walked offstage. And the crowd, which had been standing on its collective feet since the opening number, responded by filling the cold, wet Northern California night with an ovation that lasted nearly ten minutes.

THE LONG AND remarkably diverse history of commercial popular music in America has been marked at regular intervals by moments in which a particular artist has connected with a particular audience in a way that would serve to redefine the parameters of popular taste. Famous examples of this during the first half of the twentieth century include such landmarks as the 1924 debut of George Gershwin's "Rhapsody in Blue" before a gathering of black-tie culturati at New York's Aeolian Hall; the Benny Goodman Band's extended engagement before throngs of jitterbugging Angelenos at the Palomar Ballroom in 1935; and Frank Sinatra's appearances before swarms of swooning bobby-soxers at the Paramount Theater in Times Square in 1943. Each of these performances symbolized a larger shift in the popular music and popular culture of the time: Gershwin's "Rhapsody" heralded the arrival of the Jazz Age; Goodman's triumph the start of the Swing Era; Sinatra's success the emergence of the teen-aged audience and the return of the solo singer to primacy in pop. In the decades after World War II, the capacity of network television to command the simultaneous attention of tens of millions of viewers brought an entirely new dimension to these signal musical moments, as demonstrated by the spectacular debuts of Elvis Presley in 1956 and the Beatles in 1964, both of whom were encountered by vast national audiences whose shared experience lent a revelatory quality to these performers' arrival in the public eye.

By the standards of Presley and the Beatles, certainly, the Monterey Pop Festival was a localized affair, its initial impact confined to the roughly 35,000 people who attended the event (many of whom never actually saw the performers onstage). But the conjunction of not one but three breakthrough performances—by Otis Redding, Jimi Hendrix, and Janis Joplin—combined with a host of other factors to turn the festival into exactly the sort of countercultural watershed its promoters had envisioned. As always, timing played a part: two weeks before, at the beginning of June, the Beatles had released their long-awaited eighth album, an ambitious collection of songs called *Sgt. Pepper's Lonely Hearts Club Band*. The record was widely hailed as the most sophisticated expression to date of the expansive musical genre that would henceforth be known simply as "rock," and it received an unprecedented amount of coverage in the press, inspiring reviews and commentary in newspapers, magazines, and even scholarly journals that had rarely paid serious attention to popular music before. With *Sgt. Pepper* as their touchstone, the twelve hundred practicing and aspiring journalists who attended Monterey incorporated the festival into a larger narrative that centered on the emergence of rock music as a legitimate and transformative cultural force.

Equally influential was the impact of Monterey on the contingent of agents, managers, and record company executives who attended the festival, checkbooks in hand, for whom the spectacle of 35,000 long-haired, pot-smoking, music-loving hippies served as a crash course in the new demographics of the music business. On the eve of the Beatles' arrival in the winter of 1964, one marketing study found that 60 percent of the pop singles sold in America were purchased by teenage girls. Now, three years later, pop was evolving into rock; long-playing albums were replacing three-minute singles as the recording medium of choice; free-form, high-fidelity FM radio stations were breaking the stranglehold of Top 40 programming; and the core audience for popular music had expanded from the squealing "teenyboppers" of 1964 into a broad-based coalition of teenagers, college students, and young adults, a great many of whom associated themselves with the lucrative and seminally American phenomenon of mass-market bohemianism, of which the scene in the Haight-Ashbury was but the tip of a vast psychedelic iceberg.

A defining feature of this new rock audience was that its members belonged to the first generation of white Americans in history who had grown up listening, as a matter of course, to black music on records and radio. Stylistically, American popular music had been in thrall to African American influences since the rise of blackface minstrelsy in the middle of the nineteenth century. Gershwin, Goodman, Sinatra, and Presley—all were avid students of the black music of their time, and all of them owed their careers to the African American models on which they based their styles. They belonged to the small minority of white Americans and Europeans who had always provided an appreciative audience for black folk songs, spirituals, ragtime, blues, gospel, jazz, and swing. But the great majority of Americans had always partaken of this music secondhand, relying on white imitators and emulators, impersonators and appropriators, to translate the sounds and styles of African American music and dance into forms that were aesthetically and commercially compatible with the standards of white sensibility and the doctrines of white supremacy that had prevailed since the days of "Yankee Doodle Dandy."

It was not until the late 1940s, when radio stations and independent record labels began to cater in earnest to the new commercial market represented by the millions of blacks who had migrated from the farms and towns of the South to cities across America, that large numbers of white listeners could access the latest styles of black popular music at the click of a dial or the push of a button. And while the booming postwar population of white teenagers still showed an overall preference for bland appropriators like Pat Boone and gifted emulators like Elvis Presley, growing numbers of them began to seek out what they construed as the Real Thing. From the mid-fifties onward, black singers like Fats Domino, Little Richard, and Chuck Berry sold millions of records to black and white listeners alike. Together with the simultaneous entry of black athletes into the realm of professional team sports, this marked the start of a cultural revolution in America, as black faces, black voices, black style, and black prowess gradually became an inescapable presence on the nation's airwaves, concert stages, and playing fields. It was a cultural revolution whose impact on the consciousness of the nation was compounded, in the wake of the 1955 Montgomery Bus Boycott, by its close affinities with the social revolution known as the civil rights movement.

The Monterey Pop Festival was a product of this cultural revolution. The older members of the audience at Monterey had experienced their musical awakening as teenagers in the 1950s with the advent of rhythm and blues and its mixed-race offspring, rock 'n' roll. Many of them were drawn in their college years to the folk revival movement of the late 1950s, when the advent of long-playing records prompted the reissue of classic prewar blues recordings by artists like Bessie Smith and Robert Johnson and drew attention to contemporary bluesmen like Muddy Waters and John Lee Hooker. The younger members of the audience at Monterey had come of age in the early 1960s listening and dancing to crossover stars like Sam Cooke and Chubby Checker, vocal groups like the Drifters and the Shirelles, and the vanguard of a long parade of talent from Detroit's Motown label. And from 1964 onward, virtually everyone in attendance at Monterey had been swept up in the excitement surrounding the Beatles, the Rolling Stones, and their fellow British bands, who had not only learned the lessons of contemporary black music better than their white American counterparts, but were forthright in paying homage to the black artists they had modeled themselves on.

The promoters of the Monterey Pop Festival were as enthralled by the sounds of black music as the rest of their contemporaries, and they had gone to some lengths to attract a cross section of black talent. Smokey Robinson was placed on the festival's Board of Governors in hopes of drawing some Motown acts, but Motown's president Berry Gordy declined the offer, and a number of major black artists followed suit, skeptical of an invitation to play for free in front of 7,500 paying customers.

In the end, the only three African American performers at Monterey were Otis Redding, Jimi Hendrix, and Lou Rawls, but their impact was disproportional, for Redding and Hendrix were among the acknowledged sensations of the festival. Like Redding, Hendrix had cut his teeth on the so-called "chitlin' circuit" of southern clubs and auditoriums, working as a journeyman guitarist with R&B revues. But his path to Monterey had taken him on a circuitous route through the Greenwich Village folk scene and the Swinging London pop scene, in the course of which he had affected the persona of a psychedelic gypsy to complement his virtuoso synthesis of blues, soul, and acid rock. Hendrix's performance—a ragged, rambling, theatrical set in which he famously set fire to his guitar—came on the final night of the festival, and it did more to showcase his persona than his musical genius. Otis Redding's appearance, by contrast, came at the end of a long day and evening of music that consisted mainly of white blues and blues-based acid rock. It fell to Redding and his incomparable band to embody the standard of authenticity that was aspired to by all of the music that preceded them at Monterey. His overpowering performance came as a vivid reminder that black music, dance, humor, dialect, and religion had served as America's *true* "counterculture" for more than a hundred years. When Bob Weir of the Grateful Dead observed that it was like seeing God onstage, he was speaking for a generation of young people who would seek to base a religion of their own on the hedonistic creed of "sex, drugs, and rock 'n' roll."

IN THE LONG RUN, the cultural legacy of Monterey was assured by the promoters' decision to have the entire festival documented by a team of filmmakers led by D. A. Pennebaker, who was hired on the basis of his recent cinéma vérité portrait of Bob Dylan, *Don't Look Back*. Shooting in color with handheld cameras, Pennebaker and his crew divided their attention between the performers onstage, the promoters backstage, the audience in the arena, and the carnivalesque army of camp followers who filled the festival grounds. Their film was originally intended to be aired as an hour-long television special, but an early screening proved much too much for the ABC executives who had paid the promoters a half million dollars for the broadcast rights. Freed from the editorial constraints of network television, Pennebaker spent more than a year editing the footage into a ninety-minute feature for theatrical release.

By the time *Monterey Pop* reached theaters in January 1969, the Summer of Love was ancient history, the utopian scene in the Haight-Ashbury had collapsed in a Malthusian crisis of indigence and drug crime, and the entire tenor of public life in America had taken a Shakespearean turn. In the intervening eighteen months, the war in Vietnam had spiraled wildly out of control; the moral momentum of the civil rights movement had been sapped by the polarized forces of Black Power and White Backlash and the assassination of Dr. Martin Luther King Jr.; and the American political landscape had been transformed by the abdication of Lyndon Johnson, the assassination of Robert Kennedy, the fiasco of the Democratic Convention in Chicago, and the election of Richard Nixon as president in November 1968.

In the world of popular music, much had changed as well. The Mamas and the Papas had disbanded, Janis Joplin and Jimi Hendrix had become international stars, the Jefferson Airplane had appeared on the cover of *Life* magazine, Fillmore-style rock ballrooms had opened across the country, and *all* of the San Francisco bands that performed at the festival had overcome their scruples about "commercialism" and signed with major corporate record labels. Having reached the economic milestone of a billion dollars in annual sales, the record industry was well on its way to surpassing the film industry as the most profitable and, in the minds of the young, glamorous branch of American show business. A major component of this ascendancy involved the unprecedented levels of crossover success and recognition that were now being attained by African American artists. In January 1969, black singers and groups accounted for seven of the Top 10 and half of the Top 40 singles on the *Billboard* Pop charts.

Yet the most poignant change in the world of popular music between the time of the Monterey festival and the release of *Monterey Pop* was that Otis Redding was dead, killed along with his pilot, his valet, and four members of his touring band in the crash of their private plane into a lake near Madison, Wisconsin, on December 10, 1967. In the weeks before this tragedy, Redding had recorded a spate of new songs, the most distinctive of which, a contemplative ballad called "(Sittin' on) The Dock of the Bay," reflected a major leap in both the style and content of his music. Following its release in January 1968, "Dock of the Bay" sold more than two million copies, posthumously earning Redding his first #1 single, his first Top 10 album, and precisely the sort of mainstream success he had sought at Monterey.

Redding's death turned "(Sittin' On) The Dock of the Bay" and his appearance in *Monterey Pop* into memorials to his singular talent, and it added his name to a roster of distinguished popular musicians that included Bix Beiderbecke, Robert Johnson, Charlie Christian, Hank Williams, Buddy Holly, Patsy Cline, and Sam Cooke—artists whose careers ended not only before their time, but in their absolute prime, when there was every reason to expect that their finest work was yet to come. (Eerily, within a few years, he would be joined in this company by both of his costars at Monterey, Jimi Hendrix and Janis Joplin.) Redding's labels, Stax and Atlantic, culled enough material from the unfinished tracks he recorded in the fall of 1967 to release a series of singles and albums in the three years after his death. Some of these records ranked with his very best work. But they still only hinted at what might have been, for Redding was preparing to make significant changes in his approach to recording and performing during the last months of his life. His final entry on the record charts came in the fall of 1970, when Reprise Records released a live album of his and Jimi Hendrix's "historic performances" at Monterey.

Otis Redding lived and died before the advent of rock journalism in America, in an era when the mainstream press paid little attention to the careers of most black music stars. (*Rolling Stone* magazine, which would serve as the house organ of the rock scene, was founded in San Francisco a month before his death.) Few of Redding's records or live performances were reviewed in any depth, and the only substantial interview with him was published in the teen magazine *Hit Parader* in 1967. As a result, the most basic biographical information about him went largely unreported during his lifetime. For many years, what little the public knew of his life came from the flurry of obituaries, articles, and tributes that appeared in the wake of his death.

The outlines of Redding's biography were first drawn by the music historian Peter Guralnick in his classic chronicle *Sweet Soul Music*, published in 1986. Writing twenty years after the fact, Guralnick spoke with many of the principal figures who played a part in Redding's career, including his former managers Phil and Alan Walden, whose own version of events both enlivened and dominated the narrative. (Both Walden brothers went on to boom-and-bust careers as promoters of Southern rock, Phil as the president of Capricorn Records and the manager of the Allman Brothers Band, Alan as the manager of Lynyrd Skynyrd.) Yet Redding was only a part of the story that Guralnick had to tell, and the relevant chapters in his book presented more of a sketch than a full portrait. Fifteen years later, in 2001, the Atlanta journalist Scott Freeman set out to complete the picture by attempting a full-length biography. But Freeman's efforts were compromised from the start by an earlier book he had written about the Allman Brothers that had earned him the animosity of Phil Walden, who saw to it that none of the Waldens, the Reddings, nor any of the other principal sources would cooperate with his research.

This book is an effort to do justice to Otis Redding's remarkable musical career, and to the life and times of the gifted and determined young man who was both its author and its protagonist. It has benefited from the cooperation of people who knew him intimately, including his widow, Zelma, members of the Redding and Walden families, and numerous colleagues, friends, and associates. It has drawn as well on historical records, contemporary sources, and a trove of published and unpublished interviews and reminiscences that have accumulated over the years. It is further informed by works of history and literature that illuminate the period, places, and circumstances of Otis Redding's life.

At the same time, this account is respectful of the fact that aspects of Redding's story can never be fully told, for he was born into a form of official obscurity that was shared by generations of Americans descended from the 600,000 Africans who were brought to this country as slaves. Much of their history is unknown and unknowable, for while records were kept, they were records of property, not kinship or lineage, and the only specific information they yield relates to the gender and approximate age of the human beings whose existence was noted anonymously in the slave ledgers, probate records, and census figures of the antebellum South. This anonymity endured well into the twentieth century, abetted by isolation, illiteracy, and willful disregard. There were few birth certificates or marriage licenses issued for rural African Americans of Redding's par-

ents' and grandparents' generations, no report cards or high school year-
books, no pay stubs, utility bills, or rent receipts. Otis Redding was born
into a world whose parameters had been determined by the cotton gin,
not the printing press, and it was not until his family migrated to the city
of Macon when he was an infant that traces of their everyday existence
began to impinge on the official records of the time.

Otis Redding's life was a passage from that kind of obscurity to a form
of recognition and renown that reached around the world. By any measure, his was one of the preeminent voices in what may have been the
greatest generation of African American voices in the history of popular music. In 2007, forty years after his death, a panel of artists, critics,
and music business professionals assembled by *Rolling Stone* ranked Redding eighth among the 100 Greatest Singers of All Time, placing him
in a constellation of contemporaries that included Aretha Franklin, Ray
Charles, Sam Cooke, Marvin Gaye, Stevie Wonder, and James Brown.

Fortunately, though the written record is thin, the musical record
could hardly be more robust, consisting of scores of studio recordings,
three live albums, and nearly eighty original songs. Scripture tells us, "By
their fruits ye shall know them." Those recordings, sounding as vital and
fresh as the day they were made, form the heart and soul of this book, and
they will endure for decades to come as Otis Redding's indelible gift to
the world.

GEORGIA ON MY MIND

All up and down the whole creation, sadly I roam,
Still longing for the old plantation,
And for the Old Folks at Home.

—STEPHEN FOSTER

T HE UNITED STATES IS A VAST COUNTRY, AND GEOGRAPHY HAS AL-
ways played a part in the saga of its popular music. Broadway and Tin
Pan Alley are recognized the world over as both real and mythic Manhattan addresses. New Orleans, Chicago, Kansas City, and New York loom
large in the narrative history of jazz. The blues, which flourished in many
places, is commonly associated with the Mississippi Delta and its regional
capital, Memphis, whose intrastate rival, Nashville, is synonymous with
the sound of country music. Numerous cities, including Los Angeles,
Chicago, Cincinnati, Houston, and New York, were home to the independent record labels that helped to turn rhythm and blues (or R&B, as it
came to be known) into the popular music of black America in the years
after World War II.

In the case of soul, the gospel-charged derivative of rhythm and blues
that came to define the sound and ethos of black popular music during
the 1960s, there is much to be said for the state of Georgia as the seminal breeding ground. Of the four male recording artists who would exert
the greatest influence on the soul style—Ray Charles, Sam Cooke, James
Brown, and Otis Redding—all but Cooke were born or raised there. The
state was also the home of "Little" Richard Penniman, whose meteoric
manifestation in the 1950s brought a new kind of frenzy to R&B, which
then became a hallmark of the hybrid style known as rock 'n' roll. Another Georgian who exerted an incalculable, if unintended, influence on
the soul style was Thomas A. Dorsey, who in the late 1920s abandoned a

successful career as a bluesman called Georgia Tom to settle in Chicago and found the "gospel" movement, which revolutionized the music of the black church throughout America. And, for good measure, Georgia was also the birthplace of the parents of Berry Gordy Jr., the Detroit-based impresario whose genius at marketing music to young people on the basis of taste, rather than race, turned Motown Records into the most success-ful independent label in the history of the American recording industry.

Yet of all these native sons, none maintained as close and constant a connection with his home state as Otis Redding. Alone among his musi-cal contemporaries, Redding was not only born and raised in Georgia, but chose to continue living there well after his economic circumstances and his expanding professional horizons would have allowed him to move away. His loyalty to his roots and to his hometown of Macon has caused him to be more closely identified with Georgia than any of his peers, and it epitomized a devotional streak in Redding's personality and outlook that ran throughout his work and set him apart from nearly every other soul singer of his day.

As the most prominent and populous state in the Deep South, Geor-gia occupied a special place in America's musical imagination long before Ray Charles turned Hoagy Carmichael's Tin Pan Alley standard "Geor-gia on My Mind" into a #1 record in 1960. A century before, when Ste-phen Foster sought the name of a sonorous southern locale in which to set his nostalgic lament "Old Folks at Home," it was South Georgia's Suwan-nee River that caught his ear. "Old Folks at Home" went on to become the bestselling popular song of its era, the nineteenth-century equivalent of a triple-platinum record. Its success, along with that of other "plantation melodies" like "Oh! Susanna" and "My Old Kentucky Home," enabled Foster to become the first significant figure in the annals of American show business to earn his living as a popular songwriter. Uncoinciden-tally, he was also one of America's first great musical sentimentalists, a composer whose genius at sugarcoating reality extended beyond the mere vicissitudes of boy-girl romance into a realm of human relations that in-cluded the institution of slavery, which, despite his abolitionist sympa-thies and his total ignorance of the South, Foster portrayed as a kind of *family* romance, in which a benevolent Massa and Missus presided over a brood of guileless slave children whose fondest hope was that their innocence would never end. Foster was not alone in this portrayal, but by virtue of his success, he helped to institutionalize both the denial of social reality and the embrace of social fantasy as highly lucrative strains of American popular culture.

After serving as staples of chorus and campfire singing for more than a hundred years, the songs of Stephen Foster are now regarded as a form of innocuous Americana, heard mainly on the soundtracks of documentary films about the nineteenth century. To modern ears, they evoke a world that is far removed from musical milestones like Otis Redding's breakthrough performance at Monterey, the sound and staging of which, fifty years on, would not seem out of place at a contemporary music festival. Yet while the outcomes were drastically different, the ascendancy of African American popular music during the second half of the twentieth century, which provided the basis and backdrop of Redding's career, was characterized by many of the same patterns and paradoxes that applied to the mass popularity of Foster's "minstrel songs" during the second half of the nineteenth century—so much so that this could be seen as another example of history repeating itself, first as tragedy, but then, in an inspiring twist on Marx's dictum, as triumph rather than farce. To understand and appreciate the full import of the cultural breakthrough that propelled soul singers like Otis Redding to international prominence in the 1960s, it is necessary to start with an understanding of the cruel and seemingly unyielding constraints of the culture, musical and otherwise, that was being broken through. Like that of every other black American of his generation, Otis Redding's story begins with a long and bitter chapter of American social history that the great majority of Americans have always been determined to dismiss, forget, or ignore.

NEARLY ALL OF Stephen Foster's songs were introduced by a New York troupe called Christy's Minstrels, and the popularity of his music was synonymous with the popularity of the blackface minstrel shows that took root in the cities of the Northeast in the decades before the Civil War. On a commercial level, blackface minstrelsy—in which white performers impersonated African Americans and caricatured their music, dance, dialect, and humor for the amusement of white audiences—created the template of organized show business in America. At the same time, on an aesthetic level, minstrelsy represented the first systematic expression and exploitation of the fascination of white people with black people and their culture that has underlain America's singular tradition of popular music and dance at every step of the way. From the start, race was not merely a factor in the development of American popular entertainment; rather, race was the *defining* factor that set American popular entertainment apart from that of every other country in the world.

The practice of white performers blackening their faces with burnt cork as a form of theatrical makeup had existed since pre-Revolutionary times, but it was not until the 1830s, as plantation slavery spread across the South and the cities of the North absorbed the first wave of European immigration that would transform the face of the country in the decades ahead, that itinerant "Ethiopian delineators" became popular with the general public. Early blackface performers included Thomas D. Rice, whose rendition of an African American song-and-dance number called "Jump Jim Crow" created a sensation in 1832, inspiring one of the first "dance crazes" in American history. ("Never was there such an excitement in the musical or dramatic world," the *New York Herald* observed. "It was as if the entire population had been bit by the tarantula; in the parlor, in the kitchen, in the shop and in the street, 'Jim Crow' monopolized public attention.") Rice was soon joined by contemporaries like Joel Sweeney, a Virginian credited with adapting the African banjo to its modern form; when joined with the Celtic fiddle, this Afro-European synthesis endowed the young nation with its first indigenous style of popular music. Early blackface performers like Rice and Sweeney had traveled widely in the South, and their commercial ambitions were combined with a genuine appreciation for aspects of the African American slave culture they encountered there.

The appreciation turned sharply to ridicule in the 1840s, when blackface entertainment coalesced into the organized format of the "minstrel show," which originated in New York, spread to the cities of the Northeast, and eventually reached as far as the capitals of Europe, where troupes of "Yankee Nigger Minstrels" entertained the courts of kings and queens. Minstrel shows presented the same diffuse mixture of song and dance, satire and sentiment, found in other nineteenth-century forms of popular theater like the English music hall and the French cabaret. But again, only in America was this familiar elixir distilled through the filter of race. In the service of entertainment, minstrelsy created and promoted a pair of racist stereotypes that would define and drastically constrain the roles available to African American men in popular culture for more than a hundred years to come. Minstrel humor was centered on the interplay between a pompous straight man called the Interlocutor (who often wore whiteface) and a pair of verbal and physical contortionists called the End Men, who portrayed the savage caricature of Zip Coon, the shiftless northern dandy: joking, jiving, preening, and pontificating in a ludicrous attempt to ape the manners, speech, and dress of the Interlocutor—and, by extension, of other respectable whites. Minstrel sentimentality, on the other hand, was centered on the pathetic caricature of Sambo, the contented southern slave: a stoic, subordinate, and childishly dependent figure who lived to serve his master and longed for the day (given the northern locale) when he could return to his happy home. It was the Sambo character that Stephen Foster extolled in his plantation melodies, and that Harriet Beecher Stowe ennobled as a Christian martyr in *Uncle Tom's Cabin*, the bestselling novel of its time. Taken together, these two stereotypes of the comical coon and the sentimental sambo conveyed a re-assuring message to the white working-class men who formed the prime audience for minstrel entertainment. Minstrelsy affirmed that blacks *belonged* in the South, where their subordinate status made them docile and happy, and they did *not* belong in the North, where their pretentions to equality made them utterly ridiculous.

The enthusiasm for blackface minstrelsy was firmly rooted in the so-cial history of an era when large numbers of newly self-identified "white" people in the North were coming to terms for the first time with the very idea of African Americans, nearly all of whom lived as slaves in the South. For the freshly arrived Irish and German immigrants who flocked to the "Ethiopian opera houses" in New York, Boston, and Philadelphia, minstrel shows provided an opportunity to laugh at the antics—and to identify with the displacement and homesickness—of another group of people whose status was even lower, and whose grasp of American language, manners, and customs was portrayed as even more tenuous than their own. "Since the beginning of the nation," the author Ralph Ellison observed, "white Americans have suffered from a deep inner uncertainty as to who they really are. One of the ways that have been used to simplify the answer has been to seize upon the presence of black Americans and use them as a marker, a symbol of limits, a metaphor for the 'outsider.' Many whites could look at the social position of blacks and feel that color formed an easy and reliable gauge for determining to what extent one was or was not an American. Perhaps that is why one of the first epithets that many European immigrants learned when they got off the boat was 'nigger'—it made them feel instantly American."

The Civil War and its aftermath added bizarre new layers of irony to the original paradox of minstrelsy, which wrapped itself in the flag of Union patriotism even as it began to replace its overtly African American content (now that "longing for the old plantation" was an affront to the Union cause) with material pitched directly to its urban ethnic audiences. While retaining the theatrical convention of blackface, minstrel troupes began to broaden the range of their social satire, featuring jokes, songs, and skits lampooning and sentimentalizing the Irish, the Germans, and other immigrant groups. Flush with new commercial possibilities after the end of the war, the troupes also began to expand the scope of their operations, touring by rail in the Midwest and, for the first time, in the South. Yet the most astonishing development in the wake of the Civil War was the advent of *black* minstrel troupes composed of actual African Americans, most of them organized by white promoters, all of them extolling the "authentic" slave origins of their performers. Beginning with a group called the Georgia Minstrels in the late 1860s, black minstrelsy completely revitalized the form, providing a new generation of black entertainers, many of them recently emancipated, with the first professional outlet for their talents. Made up in their own version of blackface (often with a band of white around their lips), black minstrels were hailed by critics and audiences across the country as the "real thing," vastly superior to their white "imitators." Even as they conformed to the racist stereotypes of the genre, these troupes incorporated a great deal of authentic black folk culture into their repertoires. This included some of the first professional performances of the spirituals and "sorrow songs" of the African American church, which proved so popular with white audiences that black minstrel songwriters began composing their own imitations of spirituals and adapting their melodies to secular lyrics. Black minstrelsy brought the cultural contradictions of American popular entertainment to an early, dizzy height. But it also established the exorbitant price in human dignity that black performers would be required to pay in return for the opportunity to earn a living and display their talents in front of appreciative whites.

In the waning years of the nineteenth century, the popularity of minstrelsy finally yielded to the more modern pleasures of vaudeville, musical comedy, and burlesque. By 1900, the genre was extinct in every region of the country *except* the South, where touring troupes of black minstrels would remain exceedingly popular with both white and black audiences for decades to come. But the theatrical stereotypes of the comical coon and the sentimental sambo carried over into the newer forms of mass entertainment. Ragtime-based "coon songs" were all the rage in the 1890s, giving rise to a new generation of Tin Pan Alley composers led by Irving Berlin. As it had done for the mainly Irish performers of the mid–nineteenth century, the mask of blackface enabled a new cohort of mainly Jewish performers to obscure their own ethnicity by adopting the guise of a theatrical African American. The most famous exponent of blackface in the musical theater of the early twentieth century was the Russian-Jewish singer Al Jolson, whose wildly exaggerated performances of ragtime- and jazz-inflected coon songs brought these robust new styles of music to the attention of the general public, making him, in retrospect, the Elvis Presley of his day.

A dramatic demonstration of the power of Jolson's persona came in 1919, sixty years after Stephen Foster published "Old Folks at Home," when a pair of aspiring New York songwriters named George Gershwin and Irving Caesar wrote an overheated parody of Foster's song for a Broadway show called *Demitasse*, where it was performed by a company of dozens of dancers equipped with battery-powered lights in the soles of their shoes. Despite this electrifying production, the song, titled "Swanee," attracted little notice until Al Jolson happened to hear Gershwin play it one night in a Harlem bordello and liked it well enough to incorporate it into his current hit show, *Sinbad*. With Jolson's imprimatur, "Swanee" became George Gershwin's first and biggest hit. The song sold a million copies in sheet music and two million copies of Jolson's recording on the Columbia label, the proceeds from which underwrote Gershwin's brilliant career as a Broadway composer and an American musical icon.

IN THE SPRING of 1918, a year before Gershwin and Caesar composed their homage to "my dear old Swanee," a crowd of several hundred white men, women, and children in Brooks County, Georgia, a cotton-rich region near the headwaters of the actual Suwannee River, seized a twenty-year-old African American woman named Mary Turner, who was eight months pregnant at the time. Her abductors hogtied Turner, hung her by her ankles from a tree, doused her body with gasoline, and set her on fire. As she burned alive, members of the mob sliced open her abdomen with a butcher's knife, threw her fetus on the ground, and crushed it beneath their feet. Then hundreds of bullets were fired into the woman's body as it swayed over the trampled corpse of her unborn child. According to the Associated Press, Mary Turner met her fate for making "unwise" remarks about the death of her husband, Hayes, who along with three other black men had been lynched the day before for their alleged complicity in the murder of Hampton Smith, a wealthy white planter who was known throughout the county for his brutal mistreatment of his black farmworkers.

All told, thirteen blacks from Brooks County were lynched in retaliation for the murder of Hampton Smith. None of them, with the exception of a nineteen-year-old drifter named Sidney Johnson, had played any part in the crime. Smith had "hired" Johnson as a convict laborer after Johnson was arrested for gambling in public and could not pay his thirty-dollar fine. When the two men quarreled over whether or not Johnson had worked off his debt, Smith administered a beating to Johnson, who responded by stealing a revolver and shooting Smith dead. After eluding

capture for nearly a week, Johnson was killed during a standoff with police in the neighboring town of Valdosta that attracted a crowd of several
hundred onlookers. Denied the satisfaction of lynching Johnson, members of this crowd seized his body, cut off his genitals, and dragged his
mutilated remains behind an automobile through the black wards of the
town.

The past half-century of persistent and sometimes heroic progress in
the struggle for civil rights has gone a long way toward obscuring the
true nature of day-to-day existence for the many millions of African
Americans who lived in the South during the hundred years that followed the issuance of the Emancipation Proclamation in 1863. To the
extent that modern-day Americans choose to think of these things at all,
most whites, and a good many blacks as well, subscribe to an inspiring
historical narrative in which the status of black Southerners is seen as a
long hard climb from the antique evil of slavery, through the long inter-
regnum of the Jim Crow era, to a series of landmark events in the years
after World War II—the 1954 decision by the Supreme Court rejecting
the legal canard of "separate but equal," the 1955 Montgomery Bus Boycott, the 1957 confrontation at Little Rock High School—that marked
the start of the modern civil rights movement. What has been lost in this
aspirational "up from slavery" narrative is the extent to which, for much
of that hundred-year period, conditions only worsened for the 10 million
African Americans who lived in the states of the former Confederacy, as
the gains of the Reconstruction era—when blacks voted in large numbers,
served on juries, and held elective office, and when black schools flourished, literacy rates rose, and hundreds of thousands of black freedmen
owned their own farms—were brutally and systematically reversed.

Also lost in the narrative (despite the efforts of historians dating back
to C. Vann Woodward in the 1950s) is any awareness that the regime
of racial segregation that was imposed throughout the South around the
turn of the twentieth century had little precedent in southern law or cus-
tom. Instead, the tenets of what the white South came to embrace and
defend as its "way of life" were a set of self-serving ideological constructs
that were adopted and promoted by a relatively small group of southern
landowners, mill owners, railway barons, bankers, merchants, and media

magnates, together with the Democratic politicians and Protestant clergymen who served them and the northern capitalists who financed them. Their goal was pragmatic: to replace the ruined system of plantation slavery with a dynamic "New South" economy in which huge quantities of cotton would be grown by a rural peasantry of poor blacks and milled into textiles by an urban proletariat of poor whites. To realize this vision, it was essential that these two downtrodden groups, which together comprised the vast majority of Southerners, be divided against one another and made beholden, in their different ways, to a paternalistic white elite.

It was perversely fitting that the colloquial term for the South's system of racial oppression, *Jim Crow*, should be derived from a minstrel song, for it was the proliferating media of popular culture, including novels, plays, songs, films, newspapers, magazines, and commercial advertising, that played a leading role in generating and disseminating the ideology of southern racism and imprinting it upon the American mind. The basis of that ideology was a blend of revisionist history and crackpot social science that enjoyed the endorsement of some of the most eminent academics of the time. It began with a romantic characterization of the "Old South" as a model neo-feudal society led by men of culture and breeding, in which the benevolent institution of slavery exerted a civilizing influence on the African "savages" who were brought to this country in chains. In this revisionist view, the rise and fall of the Confederacy was recast, not as a ruinous act of treason, but as a gallant Lost Cause of southern self-defense, while Reconstruction was portrayed as a tyrannical attempt by radical Republicans to subjugate and mongrelize the white population of the South by subjecting them to the ravages of a generation of "New Negroes" whose emancipation had caused them to revert to a state of savagery. In due course, however, the outrages of Reconstruction were reversed by a heroic crusade called Redemption, in which the sons of the Confederacy, led by vigilante groups like the Ku Klux Klan, drove out the Yankee interlopers, struck mortal fear into the hearts of the rapacious freedmen, and restored the principles of agrarian gentility and white supremacy on which southern civilization was founded.

Many contemporary writers, scholars, politicians, and clergymen from all parts of the country contributed to this historical wish-fulfillment fantasy, which would be enshrined as a form of civic religion in the South and taught as fact to generations of schoolchildren. But its most effective popularizer was a now-forgotten novelist named Thomas Dixon, who had grown up during Reconstruction in North Carolina, where his father, a Baptist minister, was a member of the Ku Klux Klan. After pursuing a series of bright yet disillusioned careers as a graduate student at Johns Hopkins (where his classmates included Woodrow Wilson), a stage actor, a state legislator, a lawyer, and a minister, Dixon finally found his métier at the turn of the century as a pulp novelist and racist propagandist. His first book, *The Leopard's Spots*, was a mere bestseller in 1902, but its sequel *The Clansman* was a national sensation, selling more than a million copies in the four months following its publication in 1905 and inspiring a stage play of the same name that toured the country to packed houses for years to come.

Dixon's novels wove the revisionist mythology of Reconstruction and Redemption into a crude but compelling narrative haunted by the specter of a far more malignant racist stereotype than the minstrel caricatures of the comical coon and the sentimental sambo. Both of his books climaxed in lurid accounts of the attempted rape of virginal white women by bestial black men, who were then duly lynched for their crimes by white vigilantes. The stereotype of the black brute was the logical extension of the "scientific" theory that African Americans were regressing to a state of savagery under the influence of emancipation. According to this logic, black freedmen, frustrated by their genetic inferiority as they tried and failed to make their way in the world, would naturally seek revenge on that which white civilization held dearest: white womanhood. Never mind that actual instances of "black-on-white" rape were exceedingly rare. And never mind that, for generations, white southern men had been openly obsessed with the sexuality of black women, raping and exploiting them with an impunity that had populated the region with hundreds of thousands of mixed-race offspring. Sigmund Freud would not get around to articulating the psychological concept of "projection" until 1911, but the age-old phenomenon of repressing one's own guilty and aggressive impulses and attributing them instead to others reached a murderous apotheosis in the social psychology of the Jim Crow South.

The passion with which so many white Southerners embraced the dogma of white supremacy and black inferiority was itself a projection of the shame and inadequacy that was felt throughout the South in the aftermath of a catastrophic military defeat, an affront to the identity and economy of the region that was compounded in the 1890s by an economic depression that destroyed the livelihoods of hundreds of thousands of its small farmers. But the stereotype of the black brute took the psychology of southern racism to a new level of paranoid unreality. By explicitly sexualizing the threat posed by black men, this projection externalized the aggression, fear, lust, envy, and guilt that many white southern men felt—not only toward the black men and women who had borne the brunt of their oppression, but also toward the white women they had placed on such a lofty Victorian pedestal. The black brute tapped into the deepest and most primitive feelings of white male inadequacy, and it set the stage for a moral panic that swept the South around the turn of the century, as race-baiting politicians and a sensationalistic press conspired to convince their white constituents that the region was experiencing an "epidemic" of rape. By turning every black man into a potential dragon, and every white man into a potential knight in shining armor, this "rape complex" (as the southern writer W. J. Cash named it) provided the justification for one of the most barbarous forms of social control in American history.

The ultimate goal of Thomas Dixon and his fellow New South ideologues was to reunite the United States—North, South, East, and West— under the flag of "a white man's country." It was a prospect in keeping with the imperialistic spirit that prevailed in the wake of the Spanish-American War, which brought new dark-skinned populations in Cuba and the Philippines under US domination. And by 1913, when scores of aged Union and Confederate veterans fell tearfully into one another's arms at the fiftieth-anniversary reenactment of the Battle of Gettysburg, the work seemed all but done. The year before, Woodrow Wilson, whose own distinguished academic career had contributed to the myth of Redemption, became the first native Southerner to be elected president since the 1840s. The year after, the filmmaker D. W. Griffith, himself the son of a Confederate colonel, adapted *The Clansman* to the screen. Upon its release in 1915, Thomas Dixon arranged for the picture, pointedly retitled *The Birth of a Nation*, to be shown for his former college classmate in the White House. "It is like history written with lightning," President Wilson reportedly said, adding, "My only regret is that it is all so terribly true." Hailed as a cinematic masterpiece for its technical innovations, its unprecedented three-hour length, and its stirring orchestral score, *The Birth of a Nation* went on to become Hollywood's first "blockbuster," setting box office records that would endure for decades to come. Its success left no doubt that overtly racist entertainment was still big business in America. The film was also widely credited with inspiring a revival of the Ku Klux Klan, which reestablished itself in Georgia in 1915 and quickly spread throughout the South and the Midwest, enlisting a new generation of bigots by broadening the scope of its hatred to include Catholics, Jews, and foreigners of all description. By 1925, the Klan claimed nearly four million members.

In truth, of course, it was the white South—men and women, rich and poor—that had reverted to a state of savagery. Apart from the fact that the victims were a pregnant woman and her unborn child, there was nothing unusual about either the method or the madness of the bloodlust that seized the white residents of Brooks County, Georgia, in 1918. According to the most conservative estimates, well over 3,000 African Americans were conspicuously lynched in the South and its border states between 1892 and 1925—a nearly twice-weekly average that does not begin to include the untold numbers of blacks who were routinely murdered with impunity by whites in arguments, altercations, sexual assaults, or simply for exceeding the so-called "Dixie limit" of prosperity above which people of color were not permitted to rise. While Georgia led the nation in racial murder, the practice was endemic throughout the region known as the Black Belt: the great crescent of agricultural land that ran south through the Carolinas, across the middle of Georgia, and west through Alabama, Mississippi, Arkansas, and Louisiana to east Texas, where the demographics of the cotton culture ensured that blacks outnumbered whites, often by margins of four or five to one.

Though the threat of lynching cast a perpetual shadow over African American life in the South, the practice reached an early peak around the turn of the century, when the Jim Crow laws were being imposed, blacks were being disenfranchised and driven off their farms, and the "rape complex" first inflamed the paranoia of white Southerners. "What was strikingly new and different in the late nineteenth and early twentieth centuries was the sadism and exhibitionism that characterized white violence," the historian Leon Litwack has written. "The ordinary modes of execution and punishment were deemed insufficient; they no longer satisfied the emotional appetite of the crowd. To kill the victim was not enough; the execution needed to be turned into a public ritual, a collective experience, and the victim needed to be subjected to extraordinary torture and mutilation." As the name suggests, these so-called "spectacle lynchings" were themselves a variety of popular culture in the South: a form of execution-as-entertainment in the tradition of the Roman Coliseum and the French Revolution, for which spectators came from far and wide, factories and schools let out early, special trains were scheduled, newspapers published "extra" editions, and commemorative postcards were sold.

The Brooks County murders of Mary Turner and twelve others were part of a second wave of racial violence that peaked between 1917 and 1923, inspired, this time, by economic rather than moral panic. The outbreak of war in Europe in 1914 put an end to the floodtide of immigrants who had been pouring into the United States at the rate of a million a year. This caused a shortage of labor in the industrial cities of the Northeast and the Midwest that only became more acute as the country began to mobilize for its own entry into the war. To keep up with demand, northern factories turned to two types of workers they had previously shunned, blacks and women. Black Southerners had been migrating northward since the turn of the century; by 1915, there were 100,000 African Americans living in New York, half that many in Chicago. But these numbers could not begin to satisfy the growing demand for labor, and as news of abundant jobs at unheard-of wages spread throughout the South in letters from relatives and articles in nationally distributed black newspapers like the *Chicago Defender,* "Northern Fever" took hold. In Georgia alone, 10,000 blacks left in the fall of 1916, and 50,000 more the following year. They would be joined over the next three years by half a million African Americans from all parts of the South. Thus began the demographic phenomenon known as the Great Migration, the most sustained and influential social and cultural diaspora in the nation's history, in which a total of 4 million black Southerners would leave the region over the next forty years.

In the spring of 1917, as growing numbers of farmworkers deserted the fields and the threat to the New South economy grew, a clamor for official action arose. Black migrants were arrested on trains and railway platforms, jailed as vagrants, then hired out as convict laborers. Black newspapers were banned, and northern labor agents were harassed and fined. Inevitably, when official action proved insufficient, harsher measures were employed. Between the resurgence of the Ku Klux Klan and the efforts of planters and merchants to intimidate blacks from leaving, a vicious cycle developed, as the "pull" of economic opportunity in the North combined with the "push" of racist brutality in South. An added source of tension followed the Allied victory in 1918, when hundreds of thousands of African American troops returned to the States after serving in France, where they had been treated with greater respect than they had ever experienced at home. The mere sight of black soldiers in uniform unhinged many southern whites; five uniformed blacks were lynched in Georgia in 1919 alone.

But the real reckoning was still to come. For more than a decade, a hardy pest called the boll weevil had been working its way up the spine of the Black Belt, moving from west to east. Its progress was uneven, and its impact varied from place to place, depending on the weather conditions and the quality of the soil. In the early 1920s, the boll weevil finally reached the "old" cotton counties of Georgia and South Carolina, where the once-fertile soil had been depleted by nearly a century of single-crop agriculture. The result was pure devastation. Blinded by their greed and indifference, the Bourbon oligarchy of the New South had staked the region's entire economy on a single vulnerable commodity. Now, faced with the loss of their sole source of subsistence, a million more black Southerners would leave for the North in the 1920s. As one black migrant assessed the situation, "I suppose the worst place there is better than the best place here."

LAURA

It's the most important thing about me—my background.

—OTIS REDDING

A<small>MONG THE MULTITUDE OF</small> A<small>FRICAN</small> A<small>MERICANS WHOSE LIVES</small> were uprooted by the conditions that inspired the Great Migration and the backlash of racist terror it unleashed across the South was Laura Fambro Redding, a Georgia woman who had lived the first forty-five years of her life in the rolling countryside outside Forsyth, the seat of Monroe County, which straddled the tracks of the Central of Georgia railway as it ran between Macon and Atlanta in the heartland of the state. "Negroes born in Georgia had to be strong simply to survive," Malcolm X wrote in his autobiography. He was referring to his own father, a Baptist minister from Taylor County, thirty miles south of Monroe. But he might as easily have had Otis Redding's paternal grandmother in mind.

Born in 1877, Laura was the fourth child and eldest daughter of George and Carrie Fambro, a pair of ex-slaves who had adopted the surname of their former master at the end of the Civil War. Monroe County was suddenly filled with Fambros in 1865, thanks to a Virginia-born planter named Roberson Fambrough who had settled there in the 1830s and built up large holdings in land and slaves.

In 1891, at the age of fourteen, Laura Fambro "took up" with a sharecropper's son from the southern part of the county named Will Redding. Their first child, a daughter named Ella, was born that same year. The couple were married in 1893, and by 1900, they had added two more daughters to their family and were living on the cotton fields northeast of Forsyth, where Will Redding worked as a wage hand—the lowest-paid, most tenuous form of farm labor. Over the next decade, Laura gave birth to another daughter and two sons, the first of whom was named Willie after his father. In the 1910 Census, however, Laura Redding listed herself as the sole head of her household, and she described her marital status as "widowed." Laura supported her family by working for her older brother Charles Fambro, who sharecropped a parcel next door.

The fate of Will Redding remains a mystery. He may indeed have died young from illness or misfortune. But "widowed" was a relative term for an African American woman in Laura Redding's position. In slave times, under an economic system that valued women as producers of human "capital," marriage had barely existed as a social institution for blacks in the South. Despite the efforts of white northern missionaries to promote a model of monogamous domestic life, the roles of husband and father had little precedent for black men of Will Redding's generation, and fully a third of the African American households in the Black Belt of Georgia were headed by women whose husbands had abandoned their families. (Not for nothing does the theme of desertion and abandonment loom so large in blues lyrics.) Since divorce was virtually unknown, most of these women described themselves as widows. In Laura Redding's case, this status did not prevent her from continuing to bear children. A son, James, was born in 1912, and another, Otis, in 1913. The father of these children is unknown, although some evidence suggests that he may have been a sharecropper named Monroe Myrick, who lived in the area with his wife and family.

"How curious a land is this—how full of untold story, of tragedy and laughter, and the rich legacy of human life," W. E. B. Du Bois wrote of rural Georgia when he toured the region in 1902. What is not known about the lives that Laura Redding and her family lived in Monroe County during the early decades of the twentieth century could surely fill a book. Yet there is every reason to believe that their experience conformed to that of the hundreds of thousands of other impoverished black families who scraped out an existence as sharecroppers and farm laborers, not only in Georgia but across the length and breadth of the Black Belt during those years. Monroe was typical of the so-called "decadent" cotton counties of Middle Georgia, where the soil had been exhausted by generations of agricultural malpractice, and the plantation system had been fragmented by the predominance of absentee landlords. To survive in such a place, tenant families tended to move frequently from farmstead to farmstead in a quixotic search for "something better" in the way of fair treatment or productive land. Wherever they came to rest in a given year, however, the circumstances of their lives remained primitive and unchanging. They made their home in one of the dilapidated sharecropper's cabins that were ubiquitous throughout the South: a rickety one- or two-room structure, set up on blocks, roofed in tin, and sided with rough-hewn boards. Light and ample ventilation were provided by cracks in the walls and unglazed and unscreened windows, heat by a smoky hearth, water by a shallow well, "sanitation" by an uncovered hole in the ground, and shade by nothing at all, since every square yard of land surrounding the house was cleared and planted "up to the doorstep" with cotton.

In the eyes of southern society, the production of cotton was the only reason for people like the Reddings to exist. For eight months out of the year, Laura's entire family, including her children over the age of five, rose before dawn and labored in the fields until dusk: plowing, planting, and weeding in the spring and summer, harvesting the crop in the fall. Everything they needed for farm work, from their tools and their mule to their seed and fertilizer, was "furnished" by their landlord in return for half of their crop and absolute obedience to his every wish and whim. Sharecroppers like the Reddings lived in a state of enforced dependency; they enjoyed none of the autonomy that brought a sense of dignity and self-sufficiency to farming. In a climate ideal for agriculture, most Georgia landlords forbade their tenants from growing their own food, requiring them to subsist instead on a debilitating diet of cornbread, salt pork, and molasses—all of it furnished on credit, at rates up to 40 percent. To defy a landlord was to invite immediate eviction or violent reprisal, for sharecroppers had no contract or legal recourse, least of all at the end of the growing season, when the settlement time arrived, and the landlord, after taking his half of the crop, determined how much he owed his tenant for the remainder. More often than not, once the costs of seed, fertilizer, feed for the animals, and of food, clothing, and incidentals for the cropper and his family were deducted from the landlord's calculation of how much cotton was picked and the price it fetched at the gin, this exercise turned into a demonstration of how much the tenant owed him. The "settle" was the paradigm of the paternalistic exploitation that pervaded every form of economic exchange between whites and blacks in the South. If the landlord had a good year, and he considered his tenant worth keeping, he would see to it that the tenant came out slightly ahead. If not, he would take whatever he needed from his tenant to pick up the slack. The exact numbers didn't matter, since most sharecroppers could no more do the math than they could read a passage of Greek. Education, like marriage, had been forbidden to slaves by law, and in the countryside, most of the black schools that were established by northern missionaries during Reconstruction had deteriorated under the willful neglect of local government into destitute institutions that imparted little in the way of useful knowledge.

The rural isolation of Monroe County served to insulate its black residents from the labor agents and the promise of factory jobs that pulled so many of their contemporaries northward at the time of World War I. Monroe was all about cotton, and the price of cotton reached new heights during the war and its immediate aftermath, causing land values to spike as planters rushed to place new acres under cultivation. At the start of the 1920s, Laura Redding and her brother Charles were still living and sharecropping side by side in the cotton fields north of Forsyth. Laura's sons worked on the farm; her daughters Emma and Mary worked as servants for white families in the town; and her eldest daughter, Ella, lived nearby with her husband, a sharecropper named Lee Laster. Then, in the summer of 1921, after a series of earlier, milder visitations that had left the region with a false sense of security, the boll weevil descended on Middle Georgia like a biblical plague. By 1923, the yield from the infested fields amounted to less than a tenth of what it had been five years before. Faced with financial ruin, the heavily mortgaged landowners of Monroe County sold off their woodlots and abandoned their farms to foreclosure. Their dispossessed tenants now faced a stark choice between starvation and migration.

Whites in Middle Georgia responded to the collapse of King Cotton the way they did whenever they felt their "way of life" was at stake. The blight was accompanied by a sharp upturn in racial violence. For residents of Monroe, it began in 1921 when a prominent planter in neighboring

Jasper County named James Williams was charged with the murder of eleven black farmhands he had "hired" from the Macon city jail under the provisions of Georgia's illegal yet still thriving practice of convict labor. Fearing prosecution, Williams had disposed of the "evidence" by chaining his victims together and throwing them into a local river. On account of the sheer numbers involved, the "Georgia Death Farm Trial" attracted so much national attention that Governor Hugh Dorsey felt compelled to issue a public statement calling for justice to be done. This helped to earn James Williams the distinction of becoming the first white man to be convicted and imprisoned for the murder of a black man in Georgia since the end of Reconstruction.

A year later, the terror came closer to home when a black hoodlum named John "Cocky" Glover shot and killed a deputy sheriff during an altercation in a Macon poolroom. With Glover at large, the police shut down the black business district of the city and searched from house to house, while armed bands of vigilantes roamed the streets, taking potshots at any black residents they saw. Two days later, Glover was arrested on a train bound for Atlanta. When the police attempted to return him to Macon, they were met on the highway outside Forsyth by a mob of three hundred whites who lynched Glover and brought his corpse back to Macon, where they dragged it through the streets of the city before dumping his remains in the lobby of the black-owned Douglass Theatre. Five men, including the manager of the posh Dempsey Hotel, were charged and acquitted in the killing. Among those who witnessed the atrocity was a twenty-six-year-old Macon resident named Elijah Poole, who wrote that he had "seen enough of the white man's brutality to last me twenty-six *thousand* years." Soon after, Poole took his family to Detroit, where he would adopt the name Elijah Muhammad and head the Nation of Islam.

The murders in Jasper and Forsyth combined with the blight on the cotton fields to provide the 13,000 African American residents of Monroe County with all the "push" they could ever need. Between 1921 and 1924, more than half of them moved away. Joining this exodus were the families of Laura Redding, Charles Fambro, and Lee Laster. They most likely left in the winter of 1924, a few months after Charles's wife, Ada, died in childbirth. Much less likely was their destination. While most of their fellow migrants, including Laura's eldest son, Willie, moved to Macon or Atlanta or to cities in the North, the Reddings, Fambros, and Lasters journeyed a hundred miles in the opposite direction, to Terrell County, Georgia, in the southwest corner of the state.

It could be seen as a move from the frying pan into the fire. Not only was Terrell an even more remote and backward county than Monroe but, along with the rest of South Georgia, its reputation for racist brutality exceeded that of any other part of the state. (Later, during the civil rights era, it would earn the sobriquet "Terrible Terrell.") The county seat of Dawson was a typical "sundown" town, where a black person found on the streets after dark could expect, at the very least, to be arrested and jailed for vagrancy. For a family of sharecroppers who were not yet ready to give up their lives on the land, the one redeeming feature of Terrell County was that its soil was significantly more fertile (and resistant to the depredations of the boll weevil) than the farmed-out fields in the middle of the state. Southwest Georgia had been settled more recently, on the eve of the Civil War, and while the fixation on cotton had been as relentless as everywhere else, the isolation of the region had encouraged its inhabitants to grow more food, raise more livestock, and diversify their cash crops.

By 1930, Laura Redding was living with three sons, three daughters, and four grandchildren, all of them jammed into a three-room cabin on a stretch of unpaved highway in the unincorporated hamlet of Clarks Mill, seven miles south of Dawson, near the Calhoun county line. Living nearby were the Lasters, the Fambros, and Monroe Myrick, whose presence in Terrell, minus his wife and children, suggests either a remarkable coincidence or a more substantial link to Laura and her kin. With the Redding boys now in their late teens and twenties, the family had ample manpower to work their own plot of land, which they sharecropped for a pair of brothers named Will and Milton Laing.

The Laings had been farming in Terrell for three generations. Their 1,500-acre plantation—one of the largest in the county—resembled an autonomous village, centered on a complex of houses, barns, and shacks that included a commissary store, a gristmill, and a one-room schoolhouse, surrounded by more than two square miles of table-flat fields planted in cotton, peanuts, corn, and wheat. Contrary to Terrell's reputation, the Laings were known as fair-dealing landlords, which probably explains why the Reddings and most of their neighbors stayed put for the rest of the decade, in circumstances that resembled the model of the "old" plantation system far more than anything they had known in Monroe. Planters like the Laings exerted a form of sovereignty that afforded "*their* niggers" a measure of protection in their dealings with the rest of the world.

Even so, the Great Depression of the 1930s was more than another downturn in the cycle of boom and bust that had always characterized the cotton economy of the South. The policies of the New Deal would succeed in saving southern agriculture from itself, but they also spelled an end to the era of labor-intensive, single-crop farming that, even in the best of times, had provided little margin of error for the sharecroppers and wage hands who bore the brunt of the work. As the last of Laura Redding's children reached adulthood, members of her family began to gravitate back toward the middle of the state in search of gainful employment. Her son James (who went by the nickname Brown) was the first to go, taking a job with a WPA construction crew based in Macon. His sister Mattie followed him there, finding work as a cook for a white family. She was soon joined by two of her sister Mary's children, and then by Mary herself.

In 1936, Laura's youngest son, Otis, married Fannie Roseman, the daughter of an elderly sharecropper, John Roseman, and his wife, Lizzie, who had raised a family of ten children in Clark's Mill. According to family lore, Otis made a habit of driving his mule cart past Fannie's house on his weekly trips to Dawson on Saturday afternoons, when one day the mule just stopped of its own accord and the two of them struck up a conversation. Whatever the truth of this story (they had lived in close proximity to each other for many years), Otis and Fannie's first child, a daughter named Louise, was born that same year, followed by Christine in 1938 and Darlene in 1939.

As the parents of three young daughters, Otis and Fannie Redding had three good reasons to envision a different destiny for their family than the backbreaking routine of farm labor that had been their forebears' heritage since their arrival in the New World. Otis had received only four years of schooling as a sharecropper's son in Monroe, but Fannie had gone as far as a black child could go in the one-room schools of Terrell, through the seventh grade, and that was enough to fill both of them with a fervent belief in the power of education that was shared by countless African Americans of their generation. However overburdened and poorly paid, schoolteachers were often the only black professional women their students had ever known, and the Reddings dreamed of having their daughters grow up to finish high school, possibly go to college, and lead respectable lives. At the same time, they knew that such a future for their children was out of the question in Terrell County, Georgia, in 1939.

A similar spirit of restless, stifled aspiration was rising among African American families across the South as the 1930s came to a close, and the leading edge of modernity slowly penetrated the desolation of pastoral hellholes like Terrell. Radio sets had been unknown among blacks in the county at the start of the 1930s; by the end of the decade, despite the absence of electricity, one in five tenant families owned a battery-powered "farm radio," which offered a powerful antidote to the cultural isolation of rural life. An even higher percentage of black households owned phonographs, which had fallen out of favor as a form of home entertainment among middle-class Americans since the proliferation of radio in the 1920s.

Still another new source of entertainment was provided by the automatic phonograph, or "jukebox" as it came to be known, which first appeared in cafés, drugstores, dance halls, and country stores in the mid-1930s; by the end of the decade, there were 250,000 jukeboxes in operation, half of them located in the South. ("Two things which shaped me for the rest of my life," Ray Charles recalled of his Depression-era childhood. "Talkin' 'bout a piano and a jukebox.")

Even more pronounced than the impact of these new sources of news and entertainment were the new forms of physical mobility that were now within the reach of rural blacks. The mass production of automobiles during the 1910s and '20s had endowed Depression-era America with its first generation of cheap used cars, the acquisition of which enabled Black Belt families not only to expand their range of travel, but also to experience an unprecedented form of personal autonomy. "The feel of power, even in an old automobile, is most satisfying to a man who owns nothing," the sociologist Arthur Raper wrote in 1936. "Only in automobiles on public roads do landlords and tenants and white people and Negroes of the Black Belt meet on a basis of equality." For the first time, blacks in southwest Georgia could venture at will beyond their local county seats to regional centers like Albany and Columbus—cities with large enough populations to support their own black commercial districts, where families like the Reddings, the children and grandchildren of slaves, could experience firsthand the culture and commerce of the modern world.

GALLANTRY'S LAST BOW

> There was a Land of Cavaliers and Cotton Fields called
> the Old South,
> Here in this pretty world Gallantry took its last bow,
> Here was the last ever to be seen of Knights and their
> Ladies Fair
> Of Master and Slave.
>
> *—GONE WITH THE WIND*

I N DECEMBER 1939, THAT WORLD OF CULTURE AND COMMERCE CAME to Georgia on a scale that dazzled the state's inhabitants and seized the imagination of the entire country, as the city of Atlanta hosted the world premiere of *Gone with the Wind,* David O. Selznick's production of Margaret Mitchell's bestselling novel, starring Clark Gable, Leslie Howard, Olivia de Havilland, and Vivien Leigh. The debut of the film was accompanied by three days of parades, receptions, and gala events. More than a million visitors came to attend the festivities, and a crowd of 300,000 lined the route from the airport to witness the arrival of the stars. On hand to welcome them was the entire political establishment of Georgia, led by Governor Ed Rivers and Atlanta mayor William Hartsfield. They were joined by the governors of five neighboring states; a delegation of northern industrialists that included various Whitneys, Vanderbilts, and Rockefellers; an antique contingent of Confederate war veterans; and the woman of the hour, Atlanta's own Margaret Mitchell. In the judgment of Jimmy Carter, who was a teenager living in Plains, Georgia, at the time, it was "the biggest event to happen in the South in my lifetime."

The cultural symbolism of the moment was something to behold. Like *The Birth of a Nation* before it, *Gone with the Wind* would prove to be the most costly and commercially successful film that Hollywood had ever produced. A quarter century after D. W. Griffith turned Thomas Dixon's racist manifesto of the New South into the first blockbuster of the Silent Era, David O. Selznick turned Mitchell's turgid romance of the Old South into the first blockbuster of the Sound Era. In its rewriting of history, *Gone with the Wind* functioned as "prequel" to the earlier film. Where Griffith was a cinematic genius who sought to institutionalize the myth of Redemption, Selznick was a promotional genius who sought to conflate the hard times of Reconstruction with those of the Great Depression, thereby encouraging the whole country to identify with Scarlett O'Hara's defiant vow, "As God is my witness, I'll never be hungry again." This turned the premiere, in the words of W. J. Cash, into "a high ritual for the reassertion of the legend of the Old South."

In keeping with the spirit of the occasion, the two African American actresses with featured parts in the film, Hattie McDaniel (who won an Academy Award for her performance) and Butterfly McQueen, were banned from the festivities in Atlanta, and their names and faces were excised from all the publicity connected with the event. Indeed, apart from an army of servants, the only black faces to be seen in the course of the three-day pageant belonged to the fifty-odd members of a "slave chorus" drawn from the choirs of several black Baptist churches, who serenaded the stars with a selection of spirituals at a formal ball sponsored by the Junior League of Atlanta. Dressed as sambos, mammies, and pickaninnies and arrayed on a stage set of Tara, they were introduced by the publisher of the *Atlanta Constitution,* who set the scene: "Tonight, we want to give you a glimpse into the past, and visit an old plantation on a warm, fragrant June evening. Can you smell the wisteria? Can you hear those darkies singing? They're coming up to the Big House." Among the singing darkies was the son of a prominent Atlanta minister, a round-faced ten-year-old by the name of Martin Luther King Jr.

Apart from McDaniel and McQueen, the one other featured cast member who missed the premiere of *Gone with the Wind* was the English actor Leslie Howard, who had returned to Britain three months before following the outbreak of World War II. Howard's absence from the festivities in Atlanta had a symbolism all its own. World War I and its aftermath had applied the first seismic shocks to the Jim Crow regime, setting off waves of migration and violent reaction across the South. The war that began in Europe in September 1939 would have an incomparably greater impact, redoubling black migration and transforming the social, economic, and ideological nature of American society for generations to come. This war and its aftermath would initiate the process by which the malignant social and historical fantasies that reached their apotheosis in the Atlanta premiere of *Gone with the Wind* would begin to unravel at the seams. For more than a century, the stereotypes promoted by American popular culture had contributed on a day-to-day, year-to-year basis to the oppression and misery of black people in all walks of life. But in the years after World War II, a great effusion of African American talent and ambition would combine, slowly at first, to colonize the mass entertainment media of the country, beginning with professional sports and popular music. In less than a generation, black voices, black faces, and black bodies would become a permanent and growing presence in the mainstream of American cultural life, while ministers' sons from Georgia would throw off the burden of bigotry and white domination in order to stand up, speak out, and make their mark upon the world.

HAVING DECLARED ITSELF "the great arsenal of democracy," the United States began the massive mobilization of its armed forces and its defense industries well before the Japanese attack on Pearl Harbor brought the country into the war in December 1941. One of the architects of that mobilization was the Georgia congressman Carl Vinson, longtime chairman of the House Naval Affairs Committee and an ardent proponent of American military power. Vinson's Sixth Congressional District encompassed much of Middle Georgia, centering on the city of Macon, the seat of Bibb County, twenty-five miles southeast of the Reddings' old home in Monroe. Beginning in the spring of 1941 with the construction of a naval ordnance plant that brought 8,000 jobs to Macon, Vinson saw to it that his home district received a bonanza of federal defense dollars as the country prepared for war. That same year saw the reactivation of Camp Wheeler, a sprawling World War I–vintage infantry training base on the outskirts of Macon; the establishment of a flight school for British Royal

Air Force pilots at neighboring Cochran Field; and the start of construction on a huge army air force base in the whistle-stop town of Wellston, fourteen miles to the south. When it opened, in 1942, the Warner Robins Army Air Depot was one of the largest AAF maintenance, supply, and training facilities in the country. Over the course of the war, it would employ a workforce of more than 23,000 military and civilians and provide support and training for more than 100,000 air force personnel.

Otis and Fannie Redding had family living in Macon—Otis's mother, Laura, had recently gone to live with her daughters there—and news of the city's resurgent defense economy made its way back to Terrell. In the meantime, on September 9, 1941, the couple welcomed the birth of their fourth child and first son, christened Otis Ray Redding Jr. For Otis Sr., the birth of a son and namesake only intensified his desire to spare his children the poverty and uncertainty that he had known growing up in a fatherless home. In the fall of 1942, shortly after the Warner Robins airbase became operational, the Reddings summoned the hope and courage they needed to leave the only lives they had ever known, packed up their belongings, and made their move to Macon. Otis Sr. quickly found work as a laborer at Warner Robins. As an added benefit, his status as a defense worker qualified the Reddings for a place in a federal housing project that had recently opened on the west side of Macon, in the area known as Tindall Heights.

With its prewar population of 58,000 more than tripled by the influx of defense and military personnel, Macon was booming by the time the Reddings arrived there. Along with Augusta to the east and Columbus to the west, it was one of three small cities that owed their existence to a geologic formation called the fall line, which runs through the middle of the state, dividing the red clay of Georgia's rolling Piedmont from the sandy soil of its coastal plain. The fall line had once marked the limit of upstream navigation on Georgia's principal rivers, and it was here that Augusta, Macon, and Columbus were founded as frontier outposts. As the Cotton Kingdom spread from east to west during the first half of the nineteenth century, these towns became commercial centers, where cotton was collected and shipped downstream to the ports of Savannah and Mobile.

Spared the wrath of Sherman's army in the fall of 1864, Macon came into its own with the rapid expansion of the railroads after the Civil War. Strategically located at the conjunction of seven rail lines at the absolute center of the state, it served as the transportation hub for Georgia in the way that Atlanta served as the hub for the entire Southeast, handling more than a hundred freight and passenger trains a day. The town grew into a city during the early decades of the twentieth century as a proud expression of the New South economic model of cotton production and manufacturing. By 1920, it was home to eleven textile mills and two large clothing factories, along with the financial, commercial, and transportation services needed to support these enterprises. The city's manufacturing base cushioned the effects of the cotton blight that decimated other Middle Georgia communities in the 1920s, but the Depression hit the local economy very hard, causing bank failures, plummeting real estate values, and bitter labor unrest, as poor whites and poor blacks competed for diminishing jobs. In this sense, Adolf Hitler was the best thing to happen to Macon since the invention of the cotton gin.

The city's central business district was laid out on a grid, five blocks wide and seven blocks long, running parallel to the Ocmulgee River. Its wide streets were lined with municipal buildings, banks, department stores, theaters, hotels, restaurants, professional offices, and shops of every description. At the south end of Cherry Street, the main downtown thoroughfare, stood Terminal Station, surrounded by an industrial district of warehouses, workshops, brickyards, and processing plants; at the north end of the business district stood a cluster of imposing buildings that included the City Hall, a pair of towering Victorian-era churches, numerous antebellum mansions, and the neoclassical City Auditorium, built in 1925 and topped by what was reputed to be the widest copper-clad dome in the world. Macon's cultural resources included Mercer University, a Baptist-affiliated institution known for its law school, and Wesleyan College, founded in 1836 as the first accredited women's college in the United States.

Though it lay in the heart of Georgia's Black Belt, Macon's substantial middle class and its large population of white factory workers ensured that the racial balance in the city hovered around 45 percent African

American, which was still a higher proportion than that of any other city in Georgia besides Savannah. The original, racially integrated pattern of housing dated from slave times, when whites lived on the main streets and blacks lived on the alleys or "lanes" that ran behind them. During the early decades of the twentieth century, however, living conditions had become segregated by class as well as by race. By 1942, most of Macon's 26,000 African American residents lived on the outer fringe of the business district in poor black neighborhoods that abutted poor white neighborhoods. Beyond this ring of working-class housing was a growing expanse of white middle-class suburbs, built on former farmland whose development was accelerated during the 1910s and 1920s by the cotton blight and the extension of the city's bus and streetcar lines. The suburbs west of Macon were also home to two of the four textile mills owned by the combine-like Bibb Manufacturing Co., the largest employer in the county, which ran its facilities as semi-autonomous company towns. The relatively few black residents in these outlying districts lived in the sort of rural poverty that mirrored conditions throughout the Black Belt.

The Reddings' new neighborhood, Tindall Heights, occupied the crest of a gently rising slope on the far side of the Central of Georgia railroad tracks, a mile southwest of the business district. Parts of the neighborhood dated from the late nineteenth century and consisted of modest Queen Anne– and Craftsman-style bungalows, many of which had fallen into disrepair after their white owners moved to the suburbs and the properties were converted to rental use. The rest of Tindall Heights was a good deal less architecturally distinct, its unpaved streets lined with the sort of shotgun shacks and dilapidated cabins that were found in the "nigger town" sections of cities throughout the South. Well before the collapse of the real estate market during the Depression, low-cost housing in Macon was sorely deficient for blacks and whites alike; in 1930, nearly a third of the city's 16,000 rental units lacked indoor plumbing of any kind. A local housing authority was formed in 1938 to administer the funds that were appropriated for slum clearance and redevelopment under the economic recovery programs of the New Deal. Over the next few years, four federally funded housing projects were built on the west side of the city. In keeping with the Roosevelt administration's need to appease its southern

Democratic base, these projects were strictly segregated: two for whites and two for blacks. The main section of Tindall Heights Homes was built in 1940 on the freshly bulldozed site of a former shantytown that had overlooked the campus of Mercer University. A second adjoining section opened two years later. In its completed form, the project consisted of sixty-two rectangular, barracks-like, two-story brick buildings that provided shelter for approximately 450 families. The buildings were set in rows, separated by barren strips of grass and connected by concrete walkways. In the middle of the complex were a playground and recreation field.

Tindall Heights Homes, 1942

The design of the Tindall Heights project was based on the "garden apartment" model that was developed by architects and planners in the 1920s. It was perhaps an ironic term for such a spartan and regimented environment. Yet for families like the Reddings, who had never enjoyed the benefits of electricity, much less gas heat and indoor plumbing, the place was a dream come true. Their unit, 97-B, was a five-room duplex. On the ground floor was a living room and kitchen, with a gas range and a small refrigerator. Up a narrow flight of stairs were three small bedrooms and a bathroom. There was a window in every room, glass in every window, and a solid roof overhead. Otis and Fannie Redding hadn't just moved their family into a new home. They had moved their family into the twentieth century.

SONNY

As far back as I can remember he was always singing or beating on something.

—RODGERS REDDING

Though their move to Tindall Heights marked a significant improvement in the Reddings' living conditions, the social conditions they faced in their new surroundings were in some ways more challenging than ever. "Perhaps never in history has a more utterly unprepared folk wanted to go to the city," wrote the novelist Richard Wright in his 1941 Federal Writers' Project commentary, *12 Million Black Voices.* Having arrived in Macon as virtual strangers, the Reddings had to learn new ways of relating to the people around them, of engaging in work and leisure, and, not least, of navigating a much more complex and impersonal landscape of southern racial "etiquette."

In Terrell, their interactions with whites had been few and far between, involving their landlords, the handful of other white farmers who lived in their part of the county, and the few merchants they dealt with on their weekend trips into Dawson. In Macon, by contrast, their lives were governed by a powerful white political and economic establishment, and their day-to-day existence was regulated not merely by the premise that a white man's word was law but by a codified legal system that was designed to keep the city's black residents firmly in their "place."

Like most southern cities, Macon had dozens of Jim Crow laws on the books, specifying what black people could and could not do, where they could and could not go. And it had a police force of seventy-five officers—reinforced, during the war, by platoons of military police—who made it their business not only to enforce these laws, but also to educate the city's black residents in the proper attitude and behavior toward their white superiors. The African American novelist John Oliver Killens, who grew up in the Pleasant Hill section of Macon, recounted an incident from his youth in which a minor brawl between rival groups of white and black schoolboys ended with both sides going home "proud and happy." The next day, the police descended on the all-black Pleasant Hill school and arrested half a dozen students, whose mothers were then summoned to the police station, where they were required to flog their own sons in front of the police in order to teach them not to fight with white boys. Racial tensions in the city were heightened during the war by the influx of black and white migrants competing for defense jobs and by the presence of black recruits at Camp Wheeler, many of whom came from the North and lacked the habits of deference that southern whites expected of them. Little had changed since World War I, when the mere sight of a black man in uniform was more than many patriotic Georgians could bear.

For fresh arrivals like the Reddings, a disconcerting difference between their new surroundings and their old life in Terrell involved how much more there was to be excluded from in Macon. The only culture to speak of in Terrell had been agriculture. Macon by contrast had libraries, theaters, concert halls, and colleges, not to mention parks, stadiums, golf courses, and swimming pools—all expressly off-limits, or severely restricted, to blacks. At the same time, African Americans made up nearly half the population of the city and accounted for a major share of its economic base. Many of the downtown merchants were heavily dependent on black patronage, and in most cases, the city's lawyers, bankers, doctors, dentists, insurance brokers, and realtors were more than happy to sell their services to a black clientele. Macon's accommodation with its black consumers included such amenities as "colored" lunch counters at several downtown department stores, along with the usual Jim Crow complement of separate water fountains, restrooms, and waiting rooms. More important, the city had developed a sizable black business community, most of it concentrated along a pair of streets, Broadway and Cotton Avenue, that lay at opposite ends of the white business district. Black-owned businesses included approximately twenty retail stores, four hotels, two theaters, four mortuaries, three real estate offices, and several insurance agencies. There were two black lawyers in the city, four black dentists, and half a dozen physicians affiliated with the black-owned St. Luke's Hospital. The black business and professional community formed the basis of a small but dynamic middle class, a few of whom had managed to achieve real wealth. The most successful black businessman in the history of Macon, Charles Henry Douglass, had died in 1940, leaving behind a handsome block of buildings across from the railway station that included a theater, a hotel, and a restaurant, all bearing his name.

The Reddings were hardly alone in their need to adjust to these new surroundings; Macon in 1942 was filled with black families fresh from the Georgia countryside, including many of their neighbors in Tindall Heights. The controversial nature of the New Deal public housing initiatives—the claims by congressional Republicans that they were socialistic, and that they would sap the initiative of their residents—caused the local authorities charged with administering these programs to vet their tenants carefully, so as to ensure that the benefits of decent housing were made available only to the "deserving" poor. In the case of Tindall Heights, this meant that eligibility was restricted to families with children in which at least one of the parents was gainfully employed.

These requirements helped to give the project the feeling of a village, in which the daily routines of the residents were closely in synch. Nearly all of the men and many of the women left for work each morning, lining up for rides or buses that took them to their jobs in the city center, the white suburbs (where two-thirds of the working black women in Macon were employed as domestic servants), or out to the base at Warner Robins. All of the school-aged children in the project walked down the hill each morning to the B. S. Ingram School, which stood at the foot of Telfair Street, a few short blocks away. At the end of the day, this process was reversed, as the children returned from school and their parents returned from work, some of them stopping off at the small commercial strip that adjoined the project, which included a grocery store, a barbershop, a poolroom, and several cafés. Adding to this village atmosphere were the stern standards of propriety that applied when hundreds of young families were thrown together in a new environment, each of them anxious to preserve their good name. Adults in the project would not hesitate to admonish and even physically discipline another person's child, and most parents dealt harshly with children who did anything that could cause them to lose face with their neighbors.

The Reddings arrived in Tindall Heights in time for their eldest daughter, Louise, to enter first grade at the B. S. Ingram School, where she was joined over the next three years by her sisters, Christine and Darlene. Otis Sr.'s job at Warner Robins was secure as long as the war continued. While he was employed at the base as a common laborer, earning approximately forty cents an hour, the steady paycheck and the satisfaction of supporting his family without the servility of sharecropping were ample compensation for the work. Fannie became pregnant in the fall of 1943; the Reddings' second son, christened Luther Rodgers, was born the following year. But the joy of his arrival was dampened by the death of Fannie's mother, Lizzie, shortly after the baby's birth.

One of the main ways the Reddings went about assimilating themselves into their new surroundings was by joining a local church. Though both of their families had attended church in Terrell, the Rosemans were a good deal more devout than the Reddings. "My mother was very serious about her religion," Louise recalled. "She was what you call a natural woman. She didn't believe in makeup. She didn't drink. She didn't believe in dancing. She didn't believe in gossip. And my mother was very fiery." It was Fannie who took the lead in deciding where the family would worship after their arrival in Macon. She had a wide selection to choose from, for the city had more than 140 churches, one for every 400 residents. Half of those churches were Baptist, and two-thirds of them served black congregations. For Fannie, selecting from among the many options had more to do with affinity than proximity. Apart from its purely religious function, church was the social hub of African American life in the South. The great majority of black churchgoers were women, and they tended to harbor strong opinions about what they wanted in a pastor and a congregation. Most of all, the Reddings were looking for a church community whose style of worship and social makeup would make them feel "at home." The one Fannie eventually settled on, Vineville Baptist, stood on the far side of the Mercer campus, more than a mile from Tindall Heights. It was here that the Reddings attended Sunday services, Fannie joined the choir, and their children went to Sunday school.

The Allied victory in Europe in the spring of 1945 had an immediate effect on operations at Warner Robins; as the weight of the war effort shifted to the Pacific theater, the base began to scale back. Staffing was further reduced during the rapid demobilization that followed the Japanese surrender in August of that year, and by the spring of 1946, Otis Sr. was out of a job. But Macon's economic boom was only beginning, for the war had finally broken the last vestiges of Middle Georgia's dependence on cotton and textiles as its principal means of support. The number of industrial jobs in the city tripled during the second half of the 1940s as new plants opened and old ones expanded, geared to the manufacture of ceramics, paper products, and building materials. Menial jobs were plentiful as white workers found more lucrative forms of employment, and Otis Sr. had no trouble finding work as a porter for a parcel delivery service, Railway Express, whose offices stood on Broadway next to Terminal Station.

Though the circumstances are unknown, some sort of drama occurred in the Reddings' marriage around this time. As Rodgers recounted it, his mother told his father "he was going to have to change his life, or she was going to leave him." In Louise's view, "My father had no positive examples in his family. Most of them were drinkers. My mother was always afraid that those genes would be inherited." Now in his mid-thirties, Otis Sr. seems to have responded to his wife's ultimatum by devoting himself to the Vineville Baptist Church, singing with Fannie in the choir each Sunday, and taking on a set of roles and responsibilities that would lead, within a few years, to his election as a deacon. The change in him appears to have been sudden and profound, and while it would have important implications for his entire family, its impact would prove to be especially strong on the extroverted second-grader whom everyone, following his father's lead, had taken to calling Sonny.

In the only photograph of him that survives from his childhood, Otis Redding faces the camera squarely, his plaid shirt buttoned up to his neck, his oval face and strong jaw animated by arched eyebrows and full lips framing an enormous toothy grin. His winning expression has an openness, eagerness, and insouciance that can be seen in the faces of many well-loved and well-cared-for African American children, boys es-

Otis, age eight

pecially, before the weight of the world descends upon them. Otis's face would never lose that openness, which would be qualified but not erased by more guarded and calculated shades of expression over the next two decades of his life. He was outgoing, charming, and well aware of his charm, and there was nothing timid about him as a boy. "Our household was quiet until he arrived," his sister Louise recalled. "Whenever he came on the scene, he just took over. Whatever you were talking about—no longer. And when he went outside, you could hear him miles away. We knew where he was. His voice would carry." From his brother Rodgers's perspective, "He was always in the spotlight about something. I don't care whether we were kids shooting marbles, he would always win. When we would have what we called field day, he could always run faster." While this sounds like the sort of hero worship one might expect from a younger brother, Otis's attraction to the "spotlight" would soon be affirmed by something more than child's play.

Two doors down from the Reddings lived the family of Carter and Inez Jones, a devoutly Christian couple whose determination to be fruitful and multiply would lead them to raise a total of fifteen children in their three-bedroom duplex in Tindall Heights. The Jones family belonged to a Holiness church, and their home was pervaded by the exuberant musical spirit of their faith. According to Rodgers, "Everybody in that house could sing, from father on down to baby." A machinist by trade, C. J. Jones performed on weekends with a gospel group called the South Wind Quartet. Two of his many sons, Floyd and Bill, were close to Otis in age, and along with another neighbor, Eddie Ross, the four of them formed a gospel quartet of their own. Several days a week, they would meet after school to rehearse in the resonant space between two of the apartment blocks. Otis and Bill shared the leads, Floyd sang baritone, and Eddie, to the extent possible for a prepubescent boy, handled the bass. Around this same time, Otis also joined the junior choir at the Vineville Baptist Church. Without fanfare or formality, his musical education had begun.

GEORGIA TOM

Blues are songs of despair, but gospel songs are songs of hope. When you sing them, you are delivered of your burden. You have a feeling that here is a cure for what is wrong.

—MAHALIA JACKSON

AM NOW SATISFIED THAT THE FUTURE MUSIC OF THIS COUNTRY MUST be founded upon what are called Negro melodies," the celebrated Czech composer Antonín Dvořák told the *New York Herald* in 1893. "In the Negro melodies of America I discover all that is needed for a great and noble school of music." Dvořák had come to New York the year before to serve as director of the city's National Conservatory of Music, where his students included several young African American composers who introduced their famous teacher to the sacred folk songs, or "spirituals," they had learned from their parents and grandparents. Melodies from two of those songs, "Swing Low, Sweet Chariot" and "Go Down, Moses," would soon resound in Dvořák's acclaimed "New World" Symphony No. 9.

By the end of the nineteenth century, a good many people in the United States and Europe were in thrall to the expressive power and beauty of "Negro melodies," including some of the same people who chose to believe that the Negroes who created this music represented a subhuman form of life. But the spirituals Antonin Dvořák learned from his students sounded appreciably different from the music that was sung by slaves in the plantation "praise houses" and later, after Emancipation, in the free black churches of the South. African American religious practice had evolved over the course of the nineteenth century as a rapturous form of worship in which Protestant teaching and preaching were combined with vestiges of the animism and spirit possession the slaves had retained from their West African ancestry. The music of the black church was shaped by a similar synthesis, in which the words of Protestant hymns were animated by call-and-response singing, collective vocal improvisation, and forms of rhythmic interplay that had their roots in the indigenous folk music of West Africa.

A major shift came in the early 1870s, when a white choirmaster at one of the new black colleges in the South, Fisk University in Nashville, organized a glee club of four men and four women and taught them to sing "classical" arrangements of spirituals using European harmonies, strict intonation, and "proper" diction. The Fisk Jubilee Singers became a popular sensation in the North following a series of concerts in 1872. They performed for President Grant at the White House, toured in Europe, and raised substantial sums of money for their underfunded university. Their financial success prompted other black colleges to form harmony groups of their own, and their popularity encouraged black minstrel troupes to add less formalized renditions of folk spirituals and newly written "jubilee songs" to their repertoires.

The renown of these early jubilee groups and the racial pride they inspired helped to establish harmony singing as a popular form of recreational activity among African American men and boys in the South. Male quartets, some of them performing spirituals and hymns, others performing popular songs and ballads, still others mixing sacred and secular material, proliferated during the early decades of the twentieth century, as cities like Birmingham, Norfolk, and Memphis became known for their own distinctive styles of harmony singing. The phenomenon became ubiquitous: "Pick up four colored boys or young men anywhere and the chances are ninety out of a hundred that you will have a quartet," the African American writer and composer James Weldon Johnson observed in 1925. Professional groups like the Golden Gate Quartet and the Norfolk Jubilee Quartet (which doubled as the Norfolk Jazz Quartet, performing songs like "Big Fat Mama") thrived in the booming race record market of the 1920s.

The polished style of the Fisk Jubilee Singers and their fellow black collegians was no mere affectation; the refinement of these groups reflected the ambivalence and embarrassment felt by many newly emancipated and educated blacks toward the legacy of slave culture in general

and the ecstatic practices of slave religion in particular. The tension between restraint and demonstrativeness, "respectability" and "emotionalism," reflected a new set of social and geographic distinctions in African
American life, and it would pervade black religious practice throughout
the late nineteenth and early twentieth centuries.

In the "mainline" Baptist, African Methodist, and Episcopal churches
that served the growing black populations in the cities of the North and
the Upper South, a self-conscious standard of dignity and decorum prevailed. Services were led by ordained ministers, hymns were accompanied
by choirs and organs, and the requisite style of congregational singing was
stately and "by the book."

But for the great majority of blacks who lived in the rural counties and
small towns of the South, expressive worship remained the be-all and
end-all of their religious practice. Churchgoing for them was a cathartic
experience, in which the trials and tribulations of their daily lives were
transcended every Sunday by a corrective force of hellfire preaching and
collective singing. In a weekly ritual of improvised rapture, hymns were
"lined out" by a deacon and answered by a congregation whose individual
members were free, in this one place, to express themselves as the spirit
moved them, with shouts, moans, screams, cries, and spontaneous embellishments of every kind. This was the style of worship that Otis Redding's
parents and grandparents had grown up with in the rough-hewn Baptist
churches they attended in Monroe and Terrell.

The early twentieth century also saw the emergence of an urban black
folk church centered on the Holiness and Pentecostal sects, whose ad-
herents aspired to the rapture of the early Christian saints. The music of
these "sanctified" churches was relentlessly upbeat and celebratory, and
it became the practice for entire congregations not only to sing but to
dance, stomp, clap their hands, and work themselves into altered states of
consciousness in which worshippers talked in tongues or writhed ecstati-
cally when the Holy Spirit entered their bodies. Whereas black Baptists
and Methodists traditionally proscribed the use of musical instruments in
their services (apart from an occasional piano or organ), the new sanctified
churches encouraged the practice, finding biblical sanction in a passage
from the Book of Psalms that listed a full orchestra's worth of instruments

as being suitable for praising the Lord. Employing pianos, guitars, horns, and drums along with the ubiquitous tambourine, musicians in the sanctified churches played with the same spirit of abandon as the singing they accompanied, and they drew on many of the styles and techniques that were associated with the use of their instruments in popular music. The poet Langston Hughes compared the "stepped-up rhythms" of a Holiness service he attended as a boy in Chicago to the experience of seeing the blues singer Ma Rainey and her band at one of the city's vaudeville halls.

Inevitably, the first decade of the Great Migration brought the underlying social and geographic tensions in black religious life to a head. The hundreds of thousands of blacks who streamed north in the years after World War I instinctively sought comfort and community in the Baptist and Methodist churches that had stood at the center of their lives in the South. Yet nearly everything about these northern churches was disconcertingly different from what they were accustomed to. Most black Protestant churches in the North were large, affluent, impersonal institutions compared to their counterparts in the South. Their services were conducted with reserve and formality, and their congregations were dominated by proper middle- and working-class blacks who looked with dismay and disdain upon the rabble of ill-spoken, ill-groomed, and ill-mannered migrants who came to fill the pews. Feeling the chill, many of the newcomers sought refuge in the Holiness and Pentecostal churches, or in the many storefront Baptist and Methodist churches that were founded by southern "jackleg" preachers who had followed their parishioners north. But apart from its otherworldly concerns, Protestant religion was a big business in the black communities of the North, and it wasn't long before the entrepreneurial pastors who presided over the mainline churches responded to their loss of market share by seeking ways to entice the southern migrants back into their fold. In the early 1930s, they found their salvation in the person of a minister's son from Georgia named Thomas A. Dorsey.

Dorsey was born in Villa Rica, a farm town outside Atlanta, at the turn of the century. His father was a college-trained Baptist preacher, his mother a devout church lady who accompanied her husband's sermons on the pump organ. Early in Dorsey's childhood, his father served as the pastor of a country church near the Reddings' old home in Monroe County. But in 1908 his family moved to Atlanta, where his parents were reduced to working as domestic servants. Disillusioned with religion on account of his father's fall from grace, Dorsey left school at an early age and set his sights on becoming a piano player, specializing in a rough brand of gutbucket blues. In 1916, he rode the first wave of the Great Migration to Chicago, where he scraped out a living for several years playing for house parties and brothels. In 1920, after Mamie Smith's million-selling recording of "Crazy Blues" exposed the market for race records, Dorsey turned his attention to writing and arranging blues songs, first in the northern "vaudeville" style popularized by W. C. Handy, and later in the southern "down-home" style associated with Gertrude "Ma" Rainey, a fellow Georgian with whom Dorsey worked as a bandleader, a pianist, and an arranger.

In the midst of this otherwise promising career, however, Dorsey suffered from periodic bouts of depression and nervous collapse that led him to flirt with the idea of renouncing his life as an entertainer and devoting himself to the Lord. As early as 1921, inspired by the singing he heard at a Baptist convention in Chicago, he had tried his hand at writing sacred songs. When the market for race records evaporated at the start of the Great Depression, Dorsey was finally ready to renounce his (dwindling) secular success. He threw himself into his new calling with the same resourcefulness he had shown as a bluesman—catering, once again, to the sensibilities of southern migrants like himself. In 1930, he made his mark with a song called "If You See My Savior," which sold tens of thousands of copies in sheet music. The following year, an ambitious pastor at Chicago's Ebenezer Baptist church invited Dorsey to form a "gospel chorus" to supplement the church's highly regarded choir.

Singing like a well-tuned version of a southern congregation, Dorsey's chorus was an immediate sensation, and he was soon organizing similar groups at other mainline Chicago churches. He also founded a music publishing firm devoted to what he called "gospel blues." Building on the work of predecessors like C. A. Tindley, a Philadelphian whose best-known compositions included "Stand by Me" and "I'll Overcome Some Day" (which would become even better known as "We Shall Overcome"),

Dorsey's work as a composer combined the tonality of blues and the syncopated rhythms of jazz with lyrics that adapted the personalized outlook of popular songs to sacred themes. Whereas the slave spirituals and jubilee songs had been drawn mainly from third-person Old Testament parables, Dorsey's gospel blues mirrored the orientation of popular songs by addressing religious experience as a form of personal experience, writing, he said, "about hope and love." Black preachers had always employed the device of speaking about biblical characters with an air of familiarity, as if Old Jonah or Poor Job were members of their own congregation. Dorsey incorporated this air of familiarity into his songs, directing it not at characters from the Old Testament but at God himself. (His acknowledged masterpiece, "Take My Hand, Precious Lord," written in 1932 in response to the death of his wife and infant son in childbirth, set a standard of simple, searing eloquence that has rarely been equaled.) Perhaps most important, by addressing the experience of faith directly, with little regard for doctrinal distinctions, Dorsey's songs reached across denominational lines. In this sense, he was a classic popularizer. In the words of his great protégé Mahalia Jackson, "He was our Irving Berlin."

The result was a musical revolution that went all but unnoticed outside black religious circles, but whose influence on the sound of American music in the decades ahead would rival that of secular blues and jazz. During the 1930s, Dorsey's work as a chorusmaster, composer, song publisher, and promoter had a catalytic effect on black sacred music, combining the collective improvisation of the folk church, the harmony singing of the jubilee quartets, and the rhythmic intensity and band instrumentation of the sanctified sects. His hybrid genre of gospel blues became the common denominator of black worship across the United States, spreading from the urban centers of the North, where his music first fulfilled the longings of the new migrants, to the cities, towns, and rural churches of the South, where his music gave freshness, variety, and focus to familiar forms of self-expression.

By the early 1940s, the choir in most black churches was a gospel choir, and the music performed in those churches was a mixture of jubilee songs, spirituals, and gospel blues. The stage was set for a golden age of gospel, a decade when the innovations pioneered by Dorsey and his disciples in Chicago were taken up and refined by a new generation of soloists, groups, and composers, the most popular of which were the practitioners of what became known as gospel quartet. In the 1930s, the commercial success of the Mills Brothers and their secular pop- and jazz-influenced material helped bring the sound of black harmony singing into the popular mainstream. This opened the door for established jubilee groups like the Dixie Hummingbirds and the Golden Gate Quartet, both of which went on to record for major labels and perform regularly on national radio networks, where they were popular with black and white listeners alike. (Both "The Birds" and "The Gates" also appeared at New York's Café Society, the first openly integrated urban nightclub in America.)

With the lifting of travel restrictions after the end of the war, hundreds of professional and semiprofessional groups began performing on an ad hoc circuit of black churches, auditoriums, and storefront halls known as the gospel highway. Innovative new quartets like the Soul Stirrers from Chicago, the Sensational Nightingales from South Carolina, and the Five Blind Boys of Mississippi, each fronted by their own charismatic lead singer, developed large national followings and competed fiercely with one another, both stylistically and commercially. Some, like the Soul Stirrers, were known for their polished musicality; others, like the Nightingales, specialized in a "house-wrecking" style that evoked the hellfire preaching of the primitive Baptist and Holiness churches.

Macon, as the home of ninety black churches and a 4,500-seat municipal auditorium, became a prime stop on the Georgia leg of the gospel highway, attracting local, regional, and nationally known quartets and soloists on a regular basis. For a child especially, gospel music had a much stronger presence in the city during the 1940s than black popular music, which was performed in nightclubs and could not be heard on the radio during daytime hours. Given his family's growing involvement with the Vineville Baptist Church, it was all but inevitable that Otis Redding would chose to focus his early musical energies on gospel singing. Like generations of African American children before him, his musical education began in the church. But unlike the children of any generation before him, the version of black church music he was exposed to was far more diverse, professionalized, and accomplished than any that had come before.

Inspired and instructed by C. J. Jones and his entire singing family, Otis and his three partners saw their quartet as a way of standing out amid the thousands of other children who lived in Tindall Heights. In a city where black people and their culture had been rendered all but invisible to the public eye, it was the brightest spotlight they could find.

SISTER ROSETTA AND
THE JUKEBOX KING

I started singing spiritual songs in my father's church, from about seven on up until I was grown.

—OTIS REDDING

WHETHER OR NOT THEY CAN BRING THEMSELVES TO ADMIT IT, musical artists are the sum of their musical influences. Originality is by definition a rare thing, but it does not spring forth spontaneously. It results instead from an extended process of imitation and emulation in which young singers, musicians, and songwriters almost always begin by doing their best to sound like someone else. Often, it is only by ultimately failing in this initial effort that a truly gifted artist is able to discover his or her own distinctive sound. In the prime of his professional career, Otis Redding would be forthright in acknowledging a pair of celebrated role models, Little Richard and Sam Cooke, as the yin and yang of his mature singing style. But specific information about the music Otis was drawn to in his childhood is scanty at best. It is mainly through a process of inference and association that some sense of his early musical influences can be gained.

Family members recall that one of Otis's favorite songs to sing as a child was the spiritual "Didn't It Rain," an account of Noah and the flood that he knew from a pair of 1947 recordings: the one a dignified arrangement by the Roberta Martin Singers, the other a boisterous duet by "Sister" Rosetta Tharpe and her protégé Marie Knight. Martin and Tharpe were two of Thomas Dorsey's most talented and commercially successful disciples. Both women were born outside Memphis in rural Arkansas and came to Chicago in the first wave of the Great Migration, and both were skilled instrumentalists as well as singers. By the late 1940s, they had come to represent the opposite poles of gospel sensibility.

Though Roberta Martin had never played a note of gospel music before she applied for a job as the pianist for Dorsey's chorus at Ebenezer Baptist Church, the eponymous group she formed in the 1930s was known for its high musical standards and its novel combination of male and female leads. Their sound was the ultimate in refined, reverential emotionality, anchored by Martin's expert piano playing, which drew on her classical training and her ear for subtle chord voicings to set the style of gospel keyboard accompaniment for a generation to come. Martin was no stranger to commerce. She toured constantly, cofounded a gospel publishing house, and sold hundreds of thousands of her group's recordings. But she remained a devout and proper Baptist, resisting the pressures of overt commercialization and refusing all offers for her group to perform in secular settings.

If Roberta Martin's nuanced command of the keyboard made her the Count Basie of gospel piano, Rosetta Tharpe was more like the gospel version of Jimi Hendrix: a flamboyant guitar virtuoso whose singing and playing were steeped in the blues and whose outlandish and carefully crafted public persona pushed the limits of churchly propriety well past the breaking point. Raised by an evangelical mother who preached in a Holiness church, Tharpe and her family moved to Chicago in the late 1920s. Over the next decade, as a young prodigy on the guitar, she absorbed the strains of jazz and gospel that were pulsing through the city's dance halls and church halls. In 1938, at the age of twenty-three, she made her way to New York. There, in the span of three months, Tharpe performed with the Cab Calloway Orchestra at the swank, whites-only Cotton Club, appeared in the first of John Hammond's fabled Spirituals to Swing concerts at Carnegie Hall, and signed with Decca Records, which added the "Sister" to her name and recorded her singing an exuberant version of Thomas Dorsey's "Hide Me in Thy Bosom" that Decca's A&R chief Milt Gabler sagely retitled "Rock Me." She spent the next few years touring the country with Calloway's and Lucky Millinder's big bands, performing in nightclubs, ballrooms, and theaters. In 1945, Tharpe's boogie-woogie arrangement of the spiritual "Strange Things Happening Every Day" spent three months on the *Billboard* Race charts, peaking at #2. That same year, she performed with Millinder at the Macon City Auditorium, where she invited a star-struck local teenager named Richard Penniman to sing with her onstage. "It was the best thing that ever happened to me," recalled Penniman, who would shortly emulate Sister Rosetta by adding the appellation "Little" to his name.

By the late 1940s, Tharpe's live performances and record sales were earning her more than $100,000 a year, along with the distinction of being the first of the post-Dorsey gospel singers to attract the condemnation of pious Christians who believed that there was something blasphemous about performing sacred songs in secular venues where alcohol was served and dancing (not to mention half-naked chorus girls) was permitted. It was not so much the money she was making or the trappings of her success, for she was hardly the only gospel artist to earn a substantial living at her trade. But as the musical underpinnings of popular music and gospel converged, it was the trappings of the performance, not the performer, that took on greater significance. The unease of the churchgoing community turned on the essential paradox that stemmed from the efforts of the Holiness churches to revitalize black worship by adopting the styles of popular music and the instruments used to play them. In Tharpe's case, it surely did not help that she accompanied herself on the guitar, a traditional blues instrument that she had the temerity to play as well as any bluesman of her era.

The controversy over Rosetta Tharpe's propriety was entirely confined to the black community; as with other forms of potentially transgressive behavior, whites felt no qualms about a black performer crossing a line that might not have been tolerated if she were white. And by the late 1940s, Tharpe had developed a large following among white listeners, especially in the South. When she performed before 10,000 fans in Atlanta in 1945, the city's black newspaper estimated that 40 percent of the crowd was white. "O-o-h Sistuh! Rosetta 'n' Her Gitar Grab Bible Belt Moolah," read the headline in the trade paper *Billboard* on an account (written by a young staffer named Gerald Wexler) of Tharpe's 1949 southern tour. Later that year, when Tharpe returned to the Macon City Auditorium, in keeping with the usual practice when black artists performed there, a section of the balcony was roped off for the use of any whites who wished to attend the show. On this occasion, Tharpe worked the crowd into such a state that the walls of Jim Crow briefly came tumbling down. "The police were running around [yelling], 'The white folks are all over on the colored side!'" Tharpe's agent recalled of the scene.

THOUGH GOSPEL SINGING was by far the predominant musical influence on Otis Redding's early years, it was not the only form of music that he was exposed to as a child. The Reddings owned both a phonograph and a radio, and Macon had four local stations, three of which were affiliated with the national networks that dominated the airwaves prior to the advent of television. The music programming on network radio was geared to a mass audience and consisted mainly of white singers and dance bands performing live on nationally sponsored variety shows. (For the most part, the networks did not consider the sound quality of phonograph records to be suitable for broadcast until the late 1940s.) Locally produced music programs like the Grand Ole Opry (from NBC's Nashville affiliate WSM) were also broadcast nationally and, like most black Southerners of his generation, Otis was exposed to a great deal of "hillbilly" music while he was growing up. The Opry stars Hank Williams and Roy Acuff became particular favorites of his. Black popular music was harder to find on the radio in Macon, apart from the late-night broadcasts of WLAC, a Nashville station whose signal could be heard up and down the Eastern Seaboard. Instead, Otis heard black pop mainly on records and on the nickel-a-play jukeboxes that had become a ubiquitous feature of urban life. One of his earliest musical memories dated from an encounter with a jukebox at a recreational center called Sawyer's Lake in the summer of 1948. "There was a calypso song out then called 'Run, Joe,'" Otis recalled. "My mother and daddy used to play that for me all the time."

As a child of the 1940s, it was hardly surprising that Otis should remember "Run, Joe." The song was one of an unprecedented string of hit records by the singer, songwriter, bandleader, saxophonist, and comedian Louis Jordan, who dominated black popular music during that decade in a manner that has not been equaled by any artist since. Jordan was the first black recording star to reap the full harvest of the Great Migration, tapping a new mass market by appealing equally to the millions of blacks who had left the South and the millions who had stayed behind.

Louis Jordan was yet another Arkansan, having grown up in the farm town of Brinkley, seventy miles west of Memphis, as the son of a local music teacher and bandleader who toured with F. S. Walcott's Rabbit Foot Minstrel Show. The younger Jordan did a stint of his own with the Walcott troupe before making his way to New York in the 1930s, where he joined Chick Webb's legendary big band at Harlem's Savoy Ballroom. In addition to playing in Webb's sax section, Jordan shared the singing with the band's young female star, Ella Fitzgerald. He left Webb in 1938 to form his own group, the Tympany Five, and spent several years refining his sound before signing with Decca Records and hitting his stride in 1942 with a song called "What's the Use of Getting Sober (When You're Gonna Get Drunk Again)?" It was the first of the eighteen #1 (and forty-two Top 5) records he would release over the next eight years. This astonishing run of success would establish Jordan and his group as the foremost exponents of a musical style called "jump blues," which effectively laid the groundwork for the next revolution in American popular music.

World War II gave a new prominence to all forms of popular entertainment as a booster of national morale, but the military draft and wartime travel restrictions wreaked havoc with the operations of the big swing bands that had dominated mainstream popular music since the mid-1930s. Big-band jazz was an extravagant form of entertainment that first captured the imagination of the public during the hard times of the Depression, when young Americans thrilled to the musical spectacle and social fantasy provided by large groups of impeccably dressed musicians dutifully "playing their parts" in a cooperative enterprise held together by the seemingly effortless aesthetic of swing. The great black bands of the 1940s—Ellington, Basie, Lunceforth, and the rest—were not only an urban but an urbane phenomenon. Their musical sophistication and sartorial splendor were as unfamiliar and intimidating to the great tide of southern migrants pouring into the cities during the war as the restraint and propriety of the mainline Baptist and Methodist congregations had been to their predecessors in the 1920s. Like their forebears, these newcomers no sooner set foot outside the South than they began to pine for cultural reminders of home. Adding to their feelings of musical alienation was the turn that jazz had taken during the war, when the innovations of bebop first surfaced in New York. Bop was an even more sophisticated style than big-band jazz, and while the kinetics of swing had inspired a whole new genre of social dancing, bop was the first form of jazz that ordinary people, black and white, found it virtually impossible to dance to.

Louis Jordan was far from the only black musician of the 1940s to capitalize on the need for something new and hip that appealed to the sensibilities of America's migratory population of southern-born, inner-city blacks, but he did it in more ways, with vastly greater wit, confidence, and musicality, than any of his contemporaries. He began by stripping the big band down to its bare essentials: a four-piece rhythm section of piano, guitar, bass, and drums, to which he added an abbreviated horn section of two saxes and a trumpet. This leaner instrumentation was enough to suggest the interplay of brass and reeds that was the hallmark of big-band swing, while rebalancing the overall sound of the group so as to make the rhythm section more prominent. Jordan and his producer at Decca, the ubiquitous Milt Gabler, were among the first to pick up on the way recent improvements in recording technology had made it possible for a small group to sound as loud and full on a record as a big band, and this configuration, with or without the trumpet, became the standard instrumentation of the emerging genre of rhythm and blues. (It was also, unsurprisingly, the same instrumentation that Otis Redding would use on his recordings in the 1960s.)

In addition to these musical innovations, Jordan was an exceptionally prolific and witty songwriter who pitched his lyrics directly at his intended audience. Some of his hits, like "Don't Worry about That Mule" and "Ain't Nobody Here but Us Chickens," evoked aspects of southern life his listeners had left behind. Others, like "Is You Is or Is You Not My Baby" and "Deacon Jones," satirized black dialect and religion. In addition to the familiar blues themes of nightlife (his timeless "Let the Good Times Roll"), predatory women ("Beware Brother Beware"), infidelity ("Somebody Done Changed the Lock"), and temptation (his outrageous "That Chick's Too Young to Fry"), Jordan sang about migration ("Choo

Choo Ch'Boogie"), wartime austerity ("Ration Blues"), and postwar prosperity ("Penthouse in the Basement"). Nor did he neglect the less salutary aspects of the urban black experience. Otis's favorite, "Run, Joe," described the aftermath of a police raid on a liquor house, while Jordan's acknowledged masterpiece, "Saturday Night Fish Fry," was inspired by an actual incident involving a mass arrest at a house party in New Orleans in 1949. (The year before, Jordan became one of the first black stars to re-fuse to play segregated shows in the South, telling his fans, "If you really want to do something, y'all need to mix a little politics with your love of entertainment.")

However much his lyrics reflected the realities of contemporary black life, a wry and self-mocking humor remained the common denominator of nearly all of Louis Jordan's songs. As such, Jordan's records helped to establish one of the principles that would differentiate the postwar vari-ety of blues from its prewar antecedents. For all its bawdiness, the clas-sic blues of the 1920s and '30s presented a deeply pessimistic, not to say tragic, view of human relations, one in which the themes of loss and lone-liness, betrayal and alienation far outweighed the joys of sex and com-panionship. The rhythm and blues that came to dominate black popular music in the 1940s and '50s, by contrast, would be a fundamentally come-dic medium, a celebration of urban life and leisure in which the romantic and economic predicaments of ordinary people were treated with humor and irony far more often than despair. Jordan's recordings dominated the black jukebox trade throughout the 1940s, both "up north" and "down home." As such, he exerted a seminal influence on an entire generation of black musicians and songwriters and set a new standard of success as a black recording star in terms of sales, longevity, and visibility, thanks to his appearances in dozens of shorts and several feature films made for the African American market. Louis Jordan's jump blues stood in relation to the prewar country blues the way Rosetta Tharpe's gospel blues stood in relation to the pre-Dorsey spirituals and jubilee songs. By adding a spirit of fervent optimism and celebratory humor to forms of music that had previously served mainly to reflect the gravity of the black experience in America, their records contributed to the hope that a new day might be dawning for African Americans throughout the United States.

MACON MUSIC

Mr. Brantley is who I'd call the father of rock 'n' roll in Macon. Mr. Brantley had a reputation for being dependable so people flocked to anything he sponsored. He had a tremendous eye and ear for entertainers. He could spot those who were able.

—ALBERT DIMMONS

FORTUNATELY FOR THE RESIDENTS OF MACON AND THE REST OF the state of Georgia, Rep. Carl Vinson's influence over the purse strings of the federal government did not wane with the end of World War II. While the American public demanded a rapid demobilization of the 20 million men and women who had served in uniform, Vinson, newly installed as the chairman of the House Armed Services Committee, saw to it that the infrastructure of the war effort remained firmly in place: in the shipyards of Savannah, in the huge army bases at Fort Benning and Fort Gordon, and in Macon, in the continuing operations of the naval ordnance plant and the revival, after a brief postwar lull, of the air base at Warner Robins. In 1947, when Congress established the air force as an independent branch of the military, President Truman appointed a progressive Missouri Democrat, Stuart Symington, as its first secretary. The following year, after the Mississippi and Alabama delegations walked out of the Democratic convention in Philadelphia to protest the adoption of a civil rights plank, Truman responded to the "Dixiecrat" wing of his party by issuing an executive order banning racial discrimination in the armed forces. As the secretary of the newest and least-tradition-bound branch of the military, Symington took it upon himself to implement this order with a special enthusiasm. Black enlistment in the air force soared during the late 1940s, as the service gained a reputation for the fair treatment of its African American personnel. ("The Air Force Leads the Way," read a headline in the *Chicago Defender*.) Robins Air Force Base, renamed and reactivated in response to the operational demands of the Berlin Airlift and the start of the Korean War, became an island of federally mandated integration in the segregationist sea of Middle Georgia.

Within a few years, these machinations of domestic and cold war politics would result in Otis Redding finding himself in the right place at the right time, as the growing presence of black airmen at Robins and Macon's proximity to the army bases at Fort Benning and Fort Gordon transformed this sleepy city into a regional center of black entertainment during the late 1940s and early 1950s. Every weekend, furloughed black servicemen arrived by the bus- and trainload to patronize the clubs on Broadway and Cotton Avenue, attend shows at the City Auditorium, watch films at the Douglass Theatre, and generally partake of the city's burgeoning nightlife. "They had what they called 'party houses' down on Fifth Street—prostitutes and gambling and stuff," local musician Jessie Hancock recalled. "It was just like it was up in Memphis and Kansas City, right here in Macon. They had gambling houses down on Broadway and the police would be sitting up there gambling."

The sovereign figure of this demimonde was a tall, light-skinned black man in his late forties named Clint Brantley. Brantley had grown up in Sandersville, twenty-five miles east of Macon, where he trained as a barber and learned to play the drums. After a few years of scuffling as a musician, he came to Macon in 1922 and opened a barbershop on Fifth Street, just east of Terminal Station, in the heart of the city's "Nigger Block." For the next twenty years, Brantley presided over his barbershop and played occasional gigs around town with a dance band called the Sultans. When the war came to Macon in 1942, Brantley sensed an opportunity and opened a nightclub called the Two Spot. A year later, as the troops streamed through Camp Wheeler at a rate of 17,000 a month, he opened a second venue called the Cotton Club, and began promoting concerts by nationally known acts at the City Auditorium. In the process, Brantley made his accommodations with the cops, commissioners, and other local officials who ruled the roost in Macon, while sealing his connections with the handful of northern talent agencies that dominated the network of southern nightclubs, dance halls, auditoriums, and armories that was becoming known as the "chitlin' circuit." "I'd hire ten or fifteen policemen to do the shows," Brantley recalled, but the soldiers still "raised hell. I've seen it where the floor was so bloody that you couldn't walk on it." By the late forties, Brantley controlled the lion's share of the black entertainment scene in Middle Georgia. In Macon alone, he was supplying bands to a half dozen clubs, as well as several roadhouses that were strategically located in neighboring Jones County, where the Sunday blue laws were less strenuously enforced.

Macon's "Nigger Block," with Clint Brantley's Two Spot in the foreground

Macon's location and Clint Brantley's connections made the city an attractive base of operations for musicians who made their living on the chitlin' circuit. The blues singer John Lee Hooker was the best-known of Brantley's clients who settled in Macon in the late 1940s. Hooker had made his mark with the hit single "Boogie Chillen," which was recorded in Detroit and released on the Modern label out of Hollywood. But most of his work was in the roadhouses and dance halls of the South, and Macon became his staging ground. As his accompanist Eddie Kirkland recalled, "We toured with Clint Brantley out of Macon, Georgia, and they'd put a band with us. A lot of times the musicians didn't know how to play what we were doing or didn't want to play what we were doing. . . . A lot of bands out there with us didn't like us because John had that fame. He was John Lee Hooker, and he was popular, and you know how jealous some musicians are."

Kirkland's comment inadvertently affirms that the emergence of a black entertainment scene in Macon was something of a geographic and historical accident. The city had no distinction as a music center prior to World War II, and if anything, it suffered from a lack of trained musicians. Some of this had to do with the long-standing tendency of Maconites with serious artistic ambitions to follow the example of the city's most celebrated cultural figure, the nineteenth-century poet and musician Sidney Lanier, who left town at the first opportunity to pursue his career in Baltimore. On a more practical level, the shortage of competent musicians owed to the absence of the sort of high school band and music programs that had helped to train several generations of black musicians in larger, less provincial southern cities like Memphis and New Orleans. Prior to the 1950s, the only form of secondary education for blacks in Macon consisted of the fee-paying Ballard Normal School, which was beyond the reach of most black families, and the Hudson Industrial High School, whose band program was severely underfunded and indifferently run.

This meant that for a child like Otis, too young to go to nightclubs, the best form of music education that Macon had to offer was found in the pews of its black churches, in the shows Clint Brantley promoted at the City Auditorium, and most of all, on the radios, phonographs, and jukeboxes that had the capacity to turn any living room, soda shop, or automobile into an impromptu music conservatory.

It is impossible to overstate the impact that the proliferation of records and radio had on the practice of music-making during in the middle decades of the twentieth century. While phonograph records had existed as an established form of popular entertainment since the 1910s, and radio since the 1920s, the full influence of these new media on musicians and musicianship was delayed by a series of factors that included their expense, their limited availability, and, until the 1940s, their poor audio quality. Nobody could confuse the sound of a 1930 recording by Duke Ellington or Bessie Smith with the experience of hearing those artists live; in the days of wind-up phonographs, a recording was just that—an adequate but inferior "record" of an actual musical performance. By the late 1940s, however, advances in the technology of audio recording and reproduction had turned the sound of "Run, Joe" booming out of a Seeburg jukebox, an Altec Lansing theater speaker, or the resonant dashboard of a Buick sedan into a very plausible substitute for Louis Jordan live, rendered with great clarity, at a volume that allowed listeners to fully immerse themselves in the music.

The effect of this new fidelity on the popularity of records as a form of musical entertainment was matched by its effect on musical training and practice. For as long as music had existed as a geographically localized art form, the only way musicians could expand their range of experience was by traveling from place to place or by living in a place that other musicians traveled to. Records and radio changed all of that. They democratized the practice of music-making by bringing vernacular and regional styles of music to the attention of people who lived half a continent away, and allowing would-be singers and instrumentalists to listen closely and repeatedly to expert performances in a manner that had never been possible before. The generation of singers and instrumentalists who were born in the 1930s and '40s were the first generation of music-makers to grow up under the influence of these new technologies, and the results, as measured by the range and quality of the music they would go on to make during 1950s and '60s, speak for themselves.

THOUGH THE REDDINGS' move to Macon had spared their children the grinding poverty they had endured growing up in rural Georgia, the debilitating conditions of Otis Sr.'s own life caught up with him in 1950 when he was diagnosed with pulmonary tuberculosis. TB remained a leading cause of death at the time, especially among African Americans, whose rate of infection was three to four times that of whites. Antibiotic drug therapy for the disease was still in its infancy, and the prescribed course of treatment was isolation, bed rest, and good nutrition, none of which was readily available to a working-class black man in Macon. Instead, Otis Sr. was sent to Battey State Hospital in Rome, Georgia, in the northwest corner of the state, a three-hour drive away. Situated on a campus of two-story, barracks-like buildings reminiscent of Tindall Heights, Battey had been built as a military hospital during the war and later converted into a tuberculosis sanatorium capable of treating 2,000 patients at a time. (A portion of the facility also enclosed a juvenile reformatory, whose inmates in 1950 included an Augusta teenager named James Brown.)

In Otis Sr.'s absence, Fannie did her best to support the family, taking a job as a cleaning woman at the F. W. Woolworth store in downtown Macon. But it was mainly Otis Sr.'s siblings Mary, Mattie, and James who helped the family get by. "The Rosemans were very proud people," Louise Redding recalled. "Before they would ask for help or beg, they would go hungry. But my daddy's people would never go hungry. Because they were going to get food from somewhere, and they had no hang-ups about how they would do it. My mother would have her nose turned up sometimes about members of my father's family. But when my father had to go to the hospital, they made sure that we had food every morning. They were the sustaining force." Louise also remembered a white couple named the Asbells, who owned a grocery near Tindall Heights, coming by with boxes of food from time to time.

Otis Sr. returned home in 1951, but he was not yet strong enough to work, and his incapacity weighed on him. While he struggled to regain his health, he sought to bolster his self-esteem by standing for election as a deacon at the Vineville Baptist Church. It was a position that called on him to set an example of personal rectitude, or as the Bible said, to be a man "of honest report, full of faith and wisdom." Deacons were also expected to "rule their children and their own houses well." For a thirty-seven-year-old man who had never been in a position to exert any form of authority over anyone outside of his home, this was an empowering role, and Otis Sr. was well suited to it. According to Rodgers, "My father was more like a teacher than anything. He would always say, 'Son, come here. Son, sit down.' He expected us to take care of ourselves, but he talked to us a lot about what we should and should not do." "He was always planning, devising, and letting us know what was expected of us," Louise recalled. "He had already decided before we were teenagers what sort of jobs he wanted us to do. To him a teacher was the most outstanding and important profession. I could be nothing but a teacher."

One of the ways Otis Sr. fulfilled his role in the church was by encouraging Otis and his friends in their gospel group. The Reddings' neighbor Carter Jones was now singing with a quartet called the Spiritual Crusaders, which was attracting a considerable following on the church circuit of Middle Georgia. (In various incarnations, the group would continue for decades to come.) The members of Otis's quartet now began calling themselves the Junior Spiritual Crusaders. Carter Jones coached them, and Otis Sr. began taking them around to sing in local churches, where the pastors would take up a collection on their behalf.

These early gospel programs lit a spark in young Otis. They were his first real opportunity to stand out in a context that mattered, bask in the admiration of an audience, and make his parents proud. By not merely participating but performing in church at such an early age, he began to make a visceral connection between the gospel singing he heard on records and radio, and something he could actually do.

In Otis's case, the impact of this musical initiation was magnified by the harsh reality that African American children who grew up in the era of segregation tended to develop a sense of ambition early or not at all. Richard Wright, who as a young Mississippian "dreamed of going north and writing books," addressed the problem in his autobiography, *Black Boy*: "But where had I got this notion of doing something in the future, of going away from home and accomplishing something that would be recognized by others? . . . I was building up in me a dream which the entire educational system of the South had been rigged to stifle." For boys especially, the window of aspiration tended to close by the early teens, at precisely the point when a black boy began to be seen as a black male, and the white world felt a pressing need to remind him of his place. Not that this message was confined to the Jim Crow South. Twenty years after Richard Wright, the Harlem-born writer James Baldwin restated the problem in even more forceful terms: "You were born into a society which spelled out with brutal clarity, and in as many ways as possible, that you were a worthless human being. You were not expected to aspire to excellence; you were expected to make peace with mediocrity."

For budding writers like Wright and Baldwin, their ambition was sparked by their love of books. But for many black children, including the many boys who saw no future for themselves in school, it was the male-dominated world of the church rather than the female-dominated world of the classroom that fueled their desire to "be something" when they grew up. "The church was the main area of social life in which Negroes could aspire to become the leaders of men," the sociologist E. Franklin Frazier observed. "It was the area of social life where ambitious individuals could achieve distinction and the symbols of status. . . . This was especially important to Negro men who had never been able to assert themselves and assume the dominant male role, even in family relations." Women outnumbered men in most black congregations, often by margins of three or four to one. This meant that church life in the African American community generally consisted of a few strong men—pastors and deacons—commanding the attention and admiration of a mostly female congregation. Small wonder that so many young boys like Otis felt themselves drawn to this role. Not only did a high proportion of the black professional singers who grew up in the 1940s and '50s learn to sing in the gospel church, but a surprising number of them, including Nat King Cole, Clyde McPhatter, Nina Simone, Sam Cooke, Johnny Ace, Ruth Brown, Don Covay, James Carr, Marvin Gaye, and Aretha Franklin, were, like Otis Redding, the sons and daughters of preachers. "That was their Juilliard," explained Otis's future collaborator, the songwriter Jackie Avery. "To be around their parents who had to be public speakers, who had to be able to convince people, and who could really, really deliver. I guess it's part acting, but it's not really acting when you get into it. You just immerse yourself in the part, and that's what their fathers as preachers did."

Still another young Maconite with a church background who was having a hard time making his peace with mediocrity was the audacious young man who had convinced Sister Rosetta Tharpe to invite him onstage at the City Auditorium in 1945. Richard Penniman had grown up as the third of eleven children in Macon's oldest black neighborhood, Pleasant Hill. His father, Charles, son of a Methodist minister, worked as a mason and earned a comfortable living by selling moonshine whiskey on the side. Between his Methodist father, his Baptist mother, and an uncle who preached in a Holiness church, Richard was exposed to the full gamut of African American religion during his formative years. As a small child, he sang with two of his brothers in a gospel quartet called the

Tiny Tots that performed at churches around Macon. As his family grew larger, they formed a group called the Penniman Singers and competed in church-sponsored contests with other musical families and amateur gospel quartets.

Richard's own recollections of his childhood leaned heavily on his exploits as a practical joker, which may have been his way of diverting attention from his growing awareness that he was gay. Early in his adolescence, he adopted a strategy of exaggerating his effeminacy to the point of self-parody as a way of defusing its threat. This was a technique that worked better with some people than with others; one of the people it didn't work with was his father, whose disapproval eventually caused Richard to leave home and take refuge with a white couple who ran a nightclub called the Tick Tock, which catered to the thriving gay subculture that was yet another by-product of Macon's proximity to Georgia's military bases.

The following year, at the age of fourteen, Richard struck out on his own. He spent the late 1940s touring the South as a singer and female impersonator in several of the region's vestigial minstrel and medicine shows, acquiring the sobriquet "Little" along the way. In 1951, he was performing in Atlanta with a drag troupe called the Broadway Follies when an A&R man for RCA Records, on the recommendation of a local deejay, recorded him singing a nondescript "crying blues" called "Every Hour." The record sold poorly, but it did allow Richard to return to Macon with his head held high, as the city's first and, for the time being, only homegrown "recording star." There he began singing with a sometime bassist, sometime drummer named Melvin "Percy" Welch, who played in the bands Clint Brantley sent out with John Lee Hooker and other touring acts. In Richard's estimation, Welch "wasn't a great bass player—he was a clown more than a musician." But he was tight with Brantley, who began booking the group, grandly billed as Little Richard with the Percy Welch Orchestra, on a circuit that reached north to Chattanooga, west to Memphis, and south to New Orleans. It was around this time that Richard began accompanying himself on the piano, masking his rudimentary technique with a surfeit of campy, risqué showmanship that left many of his listeners in the roadhouses and USO clubs of the rural South grinning and shaking their heads.

BROWN V. BOARD

The South was now undergoing a new convulsion over whether black children had the same rights, or capacities, for education as the children of white people. This is a criminally frivolous dispute, absolutely unworthy of this nation; and it was being carried on, in complete bad faith, by completely uneducated people . . . But the dispute has actually nothing to do with education, as some among the eminently uneducated know. It has to do with political power, and it has to do with sex.

—JAMES BALDWIN

In February 1951, Otis's paternal grandmother, Laura Fambro Redding, died at the age of seventy-four. Her obituary notice in Macon's newspaper, the *Telegraph*, stated that she was survived by five of her nine children: Mary Taylor, Mattie Redding, Otis Redding Sr., Ellie Laster of Dawson, and James Redding. (It is unclear whether her other offspring were deceased or had simply lost contact with the family.) Laura was also survived by a brood of twenty-three grandchildren and thirty-five great-grandchildren, many of whom would grow up unaware of her existence, with no sense of the debt that they owed to this woman who sustained her family through decades of untold hardship and delivered them to a better life. Like many migrants, Laura chose to return to the place she had always thought of as home. She was laid to rest in the Rice Grove Cemetery in Forsyth.

The fortunes of the Redding family took a turn for the better in 1952, as Otis Sr.'s health improved to the point where he was able to secure a steady job on the night shift at Robins Air Force Base. With the Korean War in its third year, Robins was a very different place than it had been during his previous employment there. The air force had entered the jet age, and the base was now home to squadrons of silver-skinned Sabrejet fighters, Stratojet bombers, and massive Globemaster transports. Equally revolutionary was that the facilities, including the cafeterias, drinking fountains, and restrooms, were now officially integrated for military personnel. On a daily basis, Otis Sr. saw black officers and NCOs commanding white airmen and ground crew. And on a daily basis, he returned home to Macon, where nothing whatsoever had changed.

In addition to his night shift at Robins, Otis Sr. took every opportunity to supplement his income during daytime hours. "My father was always a worker," Louise recalled, "and did he work. He had three or four jobs. There were times when he didn't come home, and I had to take him his lunch." He worked part-time as a laborer at Mercer University and at the Procter & Gamble manufacturing plant in Macon. He and Fannie also sold Avon products door-to-door. "Poor is nothing but a state of mind," Otis Sr. liked to say.

With both parents now employed full-time, the Reddings had reached the point where they could afford an occasional indulgence for their children. Otis had spent his childhood banging away on anything he could find. Fannie now took it upon herself to buy him a set of drums, with which he set about endearing himself to their neighbors in Tindall Heights. Though Otis never developed much technique on the instrument, he did not lack for intensity. Rodgers recalled his brother's performance in an assembly at the B. S. Ingram School, when Otis got so carried away with his playing that he broke the top head of the snare, flipped the drum over, and continued to pound away, while everyone else in the production stopped what they were doing and gaped at him until his solo came to an end.

Otis's sisters had preceded him at B. S. Ingram, and all three of them were known as dutiful, diligent students. They had given their family a good reputation at the school, and when Otis came along, his teachers cut him considerable slack. But despite his parents' stress on education, Otis had trouble fitting his outsize, outspoken personality into the regime of a classroom. As Louise saw it, "He was onstage every day he went to school." Drumming on his desk, teasing his classmates incessantly, and speaking out of turn, he survived on the basis of his charm and his quick intelligence. "I always thought Otis was a kind of divine invention, because nobody ever taught him anything; he just knew everything," his sister recalled. From an early age, he had shown an ability to learn by observation that was masked by his tendency to dominate whatever situation he was in. Louise remembered an instance when, as a senior student at B. S. Ingram, she was assigned to monitor Otis's class while the teacher was out of the room. When one of the students started to struggle with a paragraph he was asked to read aloud, Otis snatched the book out of his hands and read the passage fluently. After assuring the class that it wasn't hard, he then turned the book upside down and "read" it verbatim again.

In the fall of 1953, Otis left B. S. Ingram and entered the eighth grade at Ballard-Hudson Junior High, which shared a campus with the Senior High on a stretch of unpaved road in West Macon, a twenty-minute walk from the projects in Tindall Heights. Built in 1949 at a cost of $2.5 million, the Ballard-Hudson complex included a gymnasium, a 2,000-seat auditorium, and modern science labs. It owed its existence to a sudden rash of spending on black education that swept the South in the late 1940s, as state and local governments began a belated effort to validate the principle of "separate but equal" schools for blacks at a time when multiple challenges to that principle had begun working their way through the federal courts.

As the name implied, Ballard-Hudson was a merger of two institutions. Ballard Normal had been founded during Reconstruction by white Congregationalist missionaries as a privately funded teacher-training school. By the 1920s, it was considered one of the best black secondary schools in Georgia, but by the 1940s, it was on the brink of insolvency. Hudson Industrial, founded in 1922 as Macon's first and only public high school for blacks, had a vocational curriculum in the Booker T. Washington mode. To some extent, the merger of the two had compromised both, since Ballard's conversion to public funding had forced it, by law, to shed the white members of its faculty, while Hudson's vocational programs languished in the new facility.

Though Macon's booster spirit had convinced many of the city's residents that its public schools, white and black, were among the best in the state, local spending on education was in fact below average even for

Georgia. Ballard-Hudson may have been built as a segregationist show-place, but the school was underfunded and overcrowded from the day it opened its doors. Students worked with old textbooks that had been dis-carded by the city's white high schools. Some of the classes had sixty or more pupils, seated two to a desk. One teacher compared the sound of the many course sections meeting simultaneously in the school gymnasium to the Tower of Babel.

Offsetting these conditions, the teachers at Ballard-Hudson were often better educated than their white counterparts in the Macon city schools; many of them held master's degrees, and they brought a sense of mission to their work. "It was a very close feeling of affection and respon-sibility that we all had," said Dolores Cook, a Smith College graduate who taught English. "Our whole thrust was to prove [the whites] wrong. They think that you're ignorant, so we need to prove them wrong." With a drop-out rate of more than 50 percent, the faculty was required to prac-tice a form of educational triage. Any student who showed a spark of interest or initiative was singled out, encouraged, and, if necessary, chal-lenged to achieve.

Otis was not one of those students. By the time he entered Ballard-Hudson, the prospect of educational advancement had lost its allure for him. School continued to serve Otis mainly as an outlet for his sociabil-ity and his talents as a class clown. ("Let me put it this way," his more studious brother recalled, "he liked to go to school, but he didn't like to buckle down.") The overworked teachers at Ballard-Hudson had no time or patience for his antics, and for the first time in his life, he was unable to get by on his charm.

In May of 1954, near the end of Otis's eighth-grade year, the United States Supreme Court repudiated more than half a century of judicial precedent and ruled that the principle of "separate but equal" that had provided the legal basis for segregation throughout the United States was "inherently unequal" and therefore in violation of the Fourteenth Amend-ment of the Constitution. The infamous 1896 case that established the precedent, *Plessy v. Ferguson,* had upheld the policy of segregated seat-ing on the streetcars of New Orleans. By focusing on the issue of public schools, the case that reversed the precedent, *Brown v. Board of Education,* involved something much dearer to the aspirations of black Americans. Yet the *Brown* ruling had little immediate impact on black activism in the South. The implications of the decision were on the one hand so monumental, and on the other hand so abstract, that groups like the Georgia NAACP proceeded with caution in its wake. (The first legal challenge to school segregation in Georgia was not filed until four years later.) Acutely aware that the states of the former Confederacy had a proud history of defying the Constitution and the authority of the federal government going back to 1861, black leaders and educators retained a sense of skepticism. "We didn't even talk about *Brown v. Board of Education*," Dolores Cook recalled. "We just said, 'Yeah, right.'" The Supreme Court had postponed its determination on how the decision should be implemented. Until that ruling came down, a feeling of uncertainty prevailed.

Whites in Georgia and throughout the South, on the other hand, saw the *Brown* decision as a ticking time bomb. They responded at first with rhetoric. The outgoing governor of Georgia, Herman Talmadge, declared that "non-segregation in our schools will never work so long as red blood runs in white men's veins." His successor, Marvin Griffin, proclaimed, "If we have to choose between integrated schools and no schools at all, we will have no schools at all." Toward that end, the Georgia legislature passed a law making it a crime punishable by two years in prison for a public official to allocate funds for a mixed-race school or for a public employee to teach in a mixed-race school.

What needed no explanation at the time was why the question of racial integration should center on the schools. When whites in Georgia and elsewhere in the South reacted to *Brown v. Board of Education*, they had in mind the scenario that President Dwight Eisenhower articulated three years later, at the height of the Little Rock school desegregation crisis, when he told Chief Justice Earl Warren, "These are not bad people. All they are concerned about is to see that their sweet little girls are not required to sit next to some big overgrown Negroes." The reaction to *Brown* only reaffirmed the extent to which, for whites in the South, the subject of race was inseparable from the subject of sex. "In the summer of 1954, a river of interracial sexual fantasies flowed through the South," wrote the historian Pete Daniel, who grew up in North Carolina during these years. "Although they wielded enormous power, white men still feared that illiterate, unskilled, impoverished black men could dominate them. They were uneasy with black males and magnified and coveted their sexual power . . . In a fair fight, white men feared, blacks would win. Every black baseball player who stepped to the plate, every black musician who performed in front of a white audience, every black actor projected on a silver screen, every NAACP lawyer who won a case," Daniel concluded, "challenged white domination. In a world of total white privilege, the figure of the aggressive and untamed black male assumed fantastic proportions."

BROTHER RAY

Now soul I find easy to define. It's a feeling you can acquire only from some sort of depression, from a hard life, hard times.

—RAY CHARLES

IN 1991, WHEN ATLANTIC RECORDS ISSUED A SET OF COMPACT DISKS documenting the recordings Ray Charles made during the seven years he was under contract to the label between 1952 and 1959, they named the collection *The Birth of Soul*. The title was apt. Though the origins of what came to be known in the 1960s as "soul music" were diverse and complex, its existence as a distinct musical style dates from the records that Ray Charles made during the second half of the 1950s, beginning with the release of a song called "I Got a Woman" in 1955. Every style and era of African American music has had its catalytic genius. In the twenties, it was Louis Armstrong; in the thirties, Duke Ellington; in the forties, Charlie Parker. And in the fifties it was Ray Charles: the artist, songwriter, and bandleader who showed an entire generation of young black singers *how* to combine the vocal practices they had learned in the musical church founded by Thomas Dorsey with the urbanized style of ribald rhythm and blues popularized by Louis Jordan. For Otis Redding and his contemporaries, "Brother" Ray was the seminal influence.

Prior to "I Got a Woman," Charles spent the first decade of his professional career as a singer in search of a style. Born in Albany, Georgia, in 1930 and raised in dire poverty by his single mother in the North Florida town of Greenville, Charles was blinded by disease in childhood and spent eight years in the Colored Department of the Florida School for the Deaf and Blind in St. Augustine, where he learned Braille and received a formal education in music that became his salvation after his mother died when he was fourteen. During the second half of the 1940s, Charles scuffled for work in Orlando, Tampa, and Seattle (a city he picked because it was as far from the South as he could get), honing his skills as a pianist, singer, and saxophonist. Like many precocious black musicians of his generation, he was enthralled by the virtuosity and sophistication of modern jazz but hard-pressed to make a living playing it.

After settling in Los Angeles in 1950, Charles released a number of recordings on the Swing Time label in the mellifluous "club blues" style associated with Nat King Cole, and he toured the country as a featured sideman with the R&B singer Lowell Fulson. Two years later, with Swing Time on the brink of bankruptcy, Charles's contract was purchased by Atlantic Records, an upstart New York–based label that was straddling the fence between jazz and R&B. His first sides for Atlantic were a grab bag of club blues, jump blues, and New Orleans piano blues, on which Charles's prodigious ability at the keyboard was compromised by his chameleon-like singing, which took on the coloration of whatever style he was performing.

In 1953, during a layover in New Orleans, Charles played piano and arranged the horns on a landmark recording by Eddie "Guitar Slim" Jones, whose testimonial, gospel-tinged performance of "The Things I Used to Do" became a huge hit, selling more than a million copies on the Specialty label. The commercial success of this record seemed to concentrate Ray Charles's mind. In 1954 he formed his own seven-piece band and summoned the owners of Atlantic to an impromptu recording session at a college radio station in Atlanta. There he unveiled a new batch of songs that included a sixteen-bar blues called "I Got a Woman" that was closely modeled on "It Must Be Jesus," a recent gospel record by a quartet called the Southern Tones. Charles had sped the song up, arranged it for his band, and equipped it with a new set of decidedly secular lyrics: "There's a man going round, taking names" became "I got a woman, way over town, that's good to me." He then sang this hybrid confection in an incomparably rougher voice than he had used on a record to date—a voice that incorporated the rasps, growls, whoops, and cries associated with "hard gospel" singers like Ira Tucker of the Dixie Hummingbirds. The result, for the first time in Ray Charles's career, was a record that sounded like no one else.

Released in January 1955, "I Got a Woman" gave Charles his first hit single and set the style for a series of recordings on which he adapted the rhythms, chord progressions, verse structures, and vocal conventions of gospel music to songs with overtly secular and often sexualized lyrics. Some, like "This Little Girl of Mine" and "Leave My Woman Alone," were taken virtually note for note from the gospel standards "This Little Light of Mine" and "Leave That Liar Alone." Others, including his 1956 hit "Hallelujah I Love Her So," were artful pastiches that drew on multiple sources.

The effect of these records was world-changing. Previously, the lively exchange between the sacred and secular forms of black music had centered on the vocal and instrumental style of the music itself. While Thomas Dorsey had drawn on his background as a popular songwriter to "personalize" the lyrics to his gospel songs, and Rosetta Tharpe had scandalized the faithful by referring to the Lord as "My Man," there had been little overt correspondence between the lyric content of these sacred and secular genres. Ray Charles changed that by retaining the emotional rhetoric and testimonial style of the sacred songs he adapted, applying the gospel themes of devotion, protection, companionship, and celebration to expressions of romantic and sexual desire. "Who is my friend, when all friends are gone? / Nobody but you, and I do mean *you*," Charles sang in "Talkin' About You." In "Ain't That Love," he asked, "Don't you need me by your side / To protect you and be your guide?" And in "Tell All the World About You," he proclaimed, "I want to walk about it, talk about it, tell all the world about it." By exalting profane emotions in a voice suffused with the ecstatic fervor of gospel singing, Ray Charles laid the groundwork not merely for a new musical style but for an entirely new school of pop romanticism, in which the desire for love and the satisfactions of sex were imbued with the ardor of salvation.

Adding to the impact and influence of these records was the sound of Charles's band, a tight, hard-swinging ensemble modeled on Louis Jordan's Tympany Five and staffed with jazz-trained musicians who could sight-read, meld styles, and generally fulfill their leader's perfectionist demands. Charles (along with his music director Hank Crawford) had serious ambitions as an arranger. His horn charts employed sophisticated voicings, and he helped to pioneer the use of Latin American rhythms in R&B. In 1956, he would introduce the final component of his signature sound by supplementing his band with a quartet of female singers, who were eventually dubbed the Raelettes. Previously, it had been unusual for women to sing behind a male lead in any genre of popular music. Not only did the Raelettes institutionalize the female "backup" chorus, but their presence turned Charles's songs into male-female dialogues, in which the male lead and female chorus variously teased, taunted, questioned, and answered one another. This call-and-response interaction was drawn directly from gospel quartet, but the sexual tension generated by the mixture of genders produced an entirely different effect.

It would take some time for the full impact of this remarkable synthesis of the sacred and secular strains of African American music to be felt. But the most immediate influence of Ray Charles's hits from the 1950s on his contemporaries came from the way the success of his records, first with an audience of black listeners, and later with growing numbers of whites as well, made Charles the most important African American singer since Louis Armstrong to enhance his popularity by deliberately playing up the roughness—or, as some would have it, the *blackness*—in his voice. Most black singers of the postwar years, whether in jazz or rhythm and blues, had tended in the opposite direction, toward clearer diction and a more modulated tone, in their efforts to broaden their appeal. In one fell swoop, Ray Charles reversed this assimilationist trend. Having perfected a convincing imitation of Nat King Cole's polished and race-neutral delivery, Charles went on to apply those same powers of musical mimicry to sounding as "black" as he could. This embrace of blackness—that is, the proud and forthright advertisement of an African American identity—would be a defining quality of soul music. "We all idolized him . . . all the cats who really knew music," recalled the soul singer Marvin Gaye. "Ray had crossed over by being his bad self, and that impressed us."

Perhaps the crowning irony of Ray Charles's reputation as the man who, more than any other, inverted the process that Thomas Dorsey began by using the expressive power of gospel to rejuvenate the blues, is that Charles spent less of his upbringing singing in church than the great majority of his contemporaries. While allowing that he "wasn't what you would call religious as a boy," he did attend Baptist services with his mother in Greenville, where he sang spirituals in the traditional manner, without musical accompaniment. But the eight years he spent at the Florida School for the Deaf and Blind took him far from those musical roots, and compared to the long list of black children, including Otis Redding, who grew up during the golden age of gospel in the 1940s and '50s and went on to adapt the vocal techniques they learned in church to their singing of popular songs, Ray Charles's upbringing hardly accounts for the iconic voice he unveiled on "I Got a Woman." Like the rest of Ray Charles's musical sensibility, that voice was the creation of a mature and gifted stylist, who synthesized the timbres and techniques he absorbed from listening to the great gospel singers of his day on records and radio. Far more than most sighted people, Ray Charles lived in a universe of sound, and the moans and cries and whoops and rasps that immortalized his singing were not so much a birthright as a cultural legacy that entered his voice by way of the most acutely developed organ in his body—his musical ear.

Our music makes the feet of the whole world dance, even the feet of the children of the poor white workers who live beyond the line that marks the boundary of our lives. Some of the white boys and girls, starved prisoners of urban homes, even forget the hatred of their parents when they hear our sensual, wailing blue melodies.

—RICHARD WRIGHT (1941)

In January 1955, as "I Got a Woman" began its ascent of the R&B charts, Little Richard Penniman was gigging out of Macon with a brash new band called the Upsetters, working part-time as a dishwasher at the Greyhound Bus Terminal on Broadway, and helping to support his family after his father was murdered at the liquor house he ran in Pleasant Hill. That same month, in his hometown of St. Louis, an unknown singer-songwriter named Chuck Berry was playing club dates and working five days a week framing houses with his father, a local building contractor. And at his home on Caffin Avenue in New Orleans's Ninth Ward, Antoine "Fats" Domino was nursing his voice back to health after undergoing a tonsillectomy the previous fall.

By the end of 1955, Little Richard, Chuck Berry, and Fats Domino would be well on their way to becoming household names throughout the United States, and *Billboard* magazine would be heralding the "mass acceptance of rhythm & blues" in a special report that cited the pervasive influence of black music not only on the magazine's record charts but on other forms of mainstream mass entertainment such as film and television. A prime example of this was the success of *Blackboard Jungle*, a "social problem" film released in the summer of 1955, which introduced American audiences to the twenty-seven-year-old Bahamian actor Sidney

Poitier, whose portrayal of a charismatic black teenager in an integrated inner-city high school was firmly in the mode of such disaffected fifties "antiheroes" as Marlon Brando and James Dean. Poitier would go on to become the first black leading man in the history of Hollywood, while a song from the film's soundtrack called "Rock Around the Clock," a Louis Jordan–style jump blues performed by a white group called Bill Haley and the Comets, became an international hit, turning the portly, spit-curled Haley into the world's first rock 'n' roll star. At the same time, in another field of mass entertainment, October 1955 would see the World Series triumph of the Brooklyn Dodgers, led by Jackie Robinson and a cohort of black stars, whose victory over the imperious (and nearly all-white) New York Yankees brought the former "bums" of Brooklyn their first championship and vindicated the integration of major league baseball that began with Robinson's 1947 debut.

In the realm of real-life race relations, Georgia's Governor Ernest Vandiver would soon cite *Blackboard Jungle* as an example of what would befall the high schools of the South if integration were imposed: "an environment of switchblade knives, marijuana, stabbings, rapes, [and] violence." Spurred by a second Supreme Court ruling that called for the implementation of desegregation in public schools across America with "all deliberate speed," 1955 was the year when the full import of the landmark decision in *Brown v. Board of Education* permeated the mind of the South. Whereas the first decision had been met with defiance and uncertainty, *Brown II* (as the ruling came to be known) unleashed a wave of hysteria and violence that would shock the conscience of the country and lead, by year's end, to the Montgomery Bus Boycott and the start of the modern civil rights movement. "Massive resistance" was the rallying cry sounded by Senator Harry Byrd of Virginia to describe the South's response to the court's rulings, as the white "Citizens Councils" that first formed in Mississippi in 1954 spread throughout the region, and state legislatures passed ever more stringent segregationist statutes. "We hold these truths to be self-evident," Senator James Eastland of Mississippi declared at a Citizens Council meeting in Montgomery, Alabama. "That all whites are created equal with certain rights. Among these are life, liberty, and the pursuit of dead niggers."

In August of 1955, a black woman from Chicago named Mamie Till Bradley put her fourteen-year-old son Emmett on a train to Mississippi, where he planned to spend the remaining weeks before the start of his freshman year in high school visiting with his cousins in Tallahatchie County. "A cocky, self-assured boy who loved to be the center of attention," Emmett Till had never been to the South before, and before he left, Mamie gave her son a stern lecture about the racial etiquette of the region.

On the third day of his visit, Till was one of a group of teenagers who stopped to buy soda and candy at a grocery store in the tiny hamlet of Money, Mississippi. There, in an effort to impress his country cousins with his urban savoir-faire, he either whistled or made a remark to the twenty-one-year-old white woman behind the counter, Carolyn Bryant, whose husband, Roy, owned the store. When the woman reacted indignantly, Till and his friends left in a hurry and drove away. Four days later, in the middle of the night, Roy Bryant and his half brother J. W. Milam came to the house where Till was staying with his great-uncle's family and abducted him at gunpoint. They spent the next few hours driving around the county, beating and torturing the boy at several locations before shooting him in the head and dumping his body in the Tallahatchie River, where his decomposed corpse was found three days later and identified by a ring he was wearing that had belonged to his late father.

According to the annual accounting by the Tuskegee Institute, 1952–54 had been the first years on record with no reported lynchings in the South. But the practice resumed with a vengeance in the wake of the *Brown* decision; Emmett Till was one of at least seven African Americans lynched in 1955, four of them in Mississippi. None of those other murders elicited much response outside of the communities that were terrorized by them. But the world, if not yet the South, was changing. Mamie Till Bradley had her son's body brought back to Chicago, where tens of thousands of mourners lined up to view his remains, which were displayed, at his mother's insistence, in an open casket. Local television stations covered the scenes of anguish around Till's funeral, and a ghastly photograph of his body was published in the African American press. Amid a national outcry, Bryant and Milam were arrested and indicted for Till's murder. White Mississippians, more incensed by the condemnation being heaped on the reputation of their great state than by the barbarity of the crime, rallied to their cause.

So it was that in September 1955, the national press descended on the sleepy county seat of Sumner, Mississippi, with an intensity that reminded seasoned reporters of the frenzy that had surrounded the Lindbergh kidnapping case. What transpired in the late-summer heat and humidity of the Tallahatchie County courthouse was a southern gothic novel come to life. The principal witness for the prosecution was the victim's great-uncle, an elderly sharecropper and jackleg preacher named Moses Wright, who did what few southern blacks had ever dared to do when he stood in open court and literally fingered the defendants from the witness stand. (Fully aware of the implications of his act, Wright left for Chicago the following day.) The principal witness for the defense was the sheriff of Tallahatchie County, Clarence Strider, a 280-pound monstrosity who cheerfully greeted the black reporters assigned to the trial with the words "Hello niggers!" and took the stand to expound his theory that the body found in the river was not that of Emmett Till but rather a cadaver that had been placed there by the NAACP. In the end, it was Strider the jury chose to believe, accepting the defendants' claim that they had indeed abducted Till but had released him unharmed. Six months later, shielded by the law against double jeopardy, Bryant and Milam sold their story to *Look* magazine, in which they freely admitted to killing "the Chicago nigger." "I just decided it was time a few people got put on notice," Milam was quoted as saying. "As long as I live and can do anything about it, niggers are going to stay in their place."

Barely fifteen years after the star-struck eyes of the nation had turned to Atlanta for the premiere of *Gone with the Wind*, the murder of Emmett Till drew back the curtain on the reality of race relations in the modern South. In place of a romantic tableau of Rhett and Scarlett and Tara, the American public was now confronted with the gleefully defiant faces of a small-town grocer and his half-witted half brother as they boasted about murdering a child for his rudeness. The circumstances of the Till lynching reduced to absurdity the myth of the rapacious black male on which the Jim Crow regime had been founded. In place of the black brute, a fourteen-year-old boy. In place of "the unpardonable crime," a wolf-whistle. In the glare of national media attention, the depravity and sadism of the "southern way of life" was exposed as never before.

"When people saw what had happened to my son," Mamie Till Bradley recalled, "men stood up who had never stood up before. People became vocal who had never vocalized before." Three months later, on December 1, 1955, while Rosa Parks quietly waited to be arrested for refusing to relinquish her seat on a city bus in Montgomery, Alabama, she steeled her nerves, she later said, by thinking of Emmett Till. By that time, the black residents of Tallahatchie County were well on their way to driving the Bryants out of business by refusing to shop at their store.

YET ANOTHER "COCKY, self-assured boy who loved to be the center of attention," Otis Redding also turned fourteen in 1955. That September, he entered the ninth grade at Ballard-Hudson High School. The year before, his sister Louise had become the first member of her family to graduate from high school, but Otis showed little sign of following in her footsteps. School by now was mainly a source of distraction for him, though he did toy with the idea of athletic glory by trying out for the Ballard-Hudson football team, the Maroon Tigers, only to withdraw after the first few times he was hit really hard in practice.

Otis, age thirteen

The Reddings' home life was in a state of flux around this time. Louise had left her cleaning job at the Chichester Pharmacy in order to enroll at Morris Brown College in Atlanta. (She would go on to complete her degree at Bethune-Cookman College in Florida.) Darlene had taken over for Louise at the pharmacy, while Christine was now working behind the lunch counter at a downtown store called H. L. Green's. But the biggest change in the family was the birth of baby Deborah, whose arrival in May prompted the Reddings to think about moving from Tindall Heights. Though the project's modern amenities had seemed like a dream back in 1942, the quality of life there had begun to deteriorate during the 1950s as the screening of applicants ended and the transience of the resident population increased. Informal gangs of adolescents who had grown up in the project were becoming more territorial and brazen in their defiance of adult authority, and the Reddings had every reason to fear that their sons would fall in with this crowd. Americans were buying homes in unprecedented numbers during the 1950s, and for Otis Sr. and Fannie, the purchase of a home was the next logical step on the gentle slope of upward mobility that had brought them to Macon in the first place. In November 1955, with the help of a loan from the previous owner, they bought a small house in a run-down neighborhood on the western outskirts of Macon called Bellevue.

The Bellevue district adjoined one of the big textile mills owned by Bibb Manufacturing; as a result, it was home to a large population of working-class whites. The black section, known as Log Cabin after the name of its main thoroughfare, lay outside the city limits of Macon, and its rutted streets, shotgun shacks, and scruffy yards had the look of rural Georgia. Among blacks and whites alike, Bellevue was regarded as an insular community whose residents kept to themselves. The Reddings' new home, located at the far end of a dirt road called Pike Street, was a drafty four-room structure that felt anything but new. Otis's parents and the baby occupied one of the bedrooms, his sisters took the other, while Otis and Rodgers slept in the living room. As winter approached, the house's kerosene heater proved to be insufficient, which forced them to rely on a wood stove as well. This was one of the many rustic features of their new surroundings, which included a yard large enough for a vegetable garden, a chicken coop, and a hog pen. Otis's parents could enjoy the sense of self-reliance that came from raising their own food. But Otis himself despised the household chores he was suddenly expected to perform, to the point of paying his brother to do his share of hauling the firewood and feeding the hogs. As he entered the fullness of adolescence, standing nearly six feet tall, Otis had plenty of strength but little appetite for physical labor. He was also becoming very particular about how he looked and dressed. In reaction to his new surroundings, he felt a special disdain for anything that smacked of "country," flatly refusing to wear the overalls his parents bought for him.

Though the Reddings remained as active as ever in the Vineville Baptist Church, their departure from Tindall Heights marked the end of Otis's involvement with the Junior Spiritual Crusaders. To his parents' chagrin, the focus of his musical interests and ambitions had been shifting in the direction of popular music for some time. Rhythm and blues had become much more available to the black youth of Macon in 1955, thanks to the introduction of black-oriented programming on the local radio station WBML. Like other network affiliates across the country, WBML had seen its mainstream audience dwindle in the early 1950s as television supplanted radio as America's favorite form of home entertainment. (Macon's first TV station, the CBS affiliate WMAZ, went on the air in the fall of 1953.) In February 1955, WBML hired Hamp Swain, a local insurance agent and part-time musician, as Macon's first black deejay. Swain was a familiar figure on the local music scene, having fronted a band called the Hamp Tones, whose members had included Little Richard from time to time. Styling himself as the King Bee, Swain was a natural on the radio, with a wide-ranging knowledge of music and a deeply resonant voice that exuded warmth and wit. The listener response to his initial two-hour R&B show was so strong that, by October, the station had expanded his on-air presence to five and a half hours a day.

Radio broadcasting was emerging as yet another new arena for black self-assertion in the mid-1950s. Seven years before, *Ebony* magazine had reported that exactly sixteen of the roughly 3,000 radio announcers in the country were African American (none of whom worked in the South). This made the conversion of WDIA in Memphis to a format of black programming in 1949 a watershed event in American broadcasting. After failing for several years to attract listeners with a schizophrenic mix of country and classical music, the station's white owners decided to target the huge black population in Memphis and the Delta by hiring a local luminary named Nat D. Williams to host a show called "Tan Town Jamboree." Williams was a pillar of the city's black bourgeoisie: a history teacher at Booker T. Washington High School, a syndicated newspaper columnist, and a fixture in the Beale Street entertainment scene. His on-air voice and rhyming banter were unmistakably African American, and his show proved to be such an immediate success with listeners and advertisers that the station wasted little time in converting its entire format to what became known as "black-appeal" programming. WDIA's rapid turnaround sent a powerful message through the broadcasting industry; within a few years, stations in every urban market were competing fiercely for black listeners. One of the most successful black-appeal stations was WLAC, a clear-channel behemoth in Nashville, which capitalized on WDIA's dawn-to-dusk hours by blanketing the eastern half of the country with a late-night mixture of rhythm and blues and gospel. In the tradition of the syndicated radio show *Amos 'n' Andy*, all of WLAC's deejays were white men who affected African American diction and dialect with enough expertise that few of their listeners ever suspected they were white.

In the long run, the unintended consequences of black radio would prove even more important than its commercial success. On the most obvious level, music radio in general and black radio in particular were a godsend to the independent record labels that specialized in rhythm and blues. Deprived of the nationally sponsored network programming that had once been their stock-in-trade, local stations had hours of airtime to fill, while the record business was churning out as many as a hundred new releases a week with which to fill it. The matchmaker of this marriage made in heaven was a new type of media celebrity, the disk jockey, who combined a feel for the music his audience wanted to hear with an on-air personality that was designed to capture their attention and loyalty. The "personalized" nature of radio—its ability to speak to people on an individual basis in the privacy of their own homes and automobiles—was the medium's saving grace, and the new emphasis on recorded music only amplified this effect, since the deejay was now the only "live" person on the air.

In addition to providing the record business with an incomparable marketing tool, music radio also helped to further what the jukebox had started by relaxing the long-standing ties between the consumption of music and the consumption of alcohol—a connection that had always barred teenagers from most of the venues where popular music was played. For people too young to drink in bars and nightclubs, the sound of records on the radio opened up new vistas of musical experience. For the radio stations and their sponsors, the growth of the teenage audience opened up yet another new market for their goods and services.

But the most revolutionary effect of the rise of black-appeal radio was something so obvious that it is hard to imagine in retrospect that anyone was surprised by it. Teenagers liked to listen to music, and teenagers liked to dance. Both of these activities figured heavily in the social lives of American adolescents regardless of color or creed. The segregation of black culture in the South and the ghettoization of black culture in the North had gone a long way toward insulating young whites from direct exposure to the sound of black music. This was especially true outside metropolitan centers like New York and Chicago, and it was a form of insulation that only promised to increase with the wholesale movement of middle-class whites to the suburbs in the postwar years. Black-appeal radio began subverting this trend from the day that Nat D. Williams first took to the air. White teenagers had access to the same radio frequencies as black teenagers, and they had the same musical needs. In the early 1950s, as the last echoes of the swing era faded, the rhythmic content of white popular music was reaching one of its periodic nadirs of over-refinement, as a generation of big-band musicians and arrangers settled into a complacent and nostalgic middle age in the studio orchestras that serviced the broadcasting and recording industries. Black popular music, on the other hand, was exploding with vitality and innovation. There was nothing subtle about the difference between white and black pop during this period, and when white teenagers found themselves confronted for the first time in their lives by the sound of undiluted rhythm and blues on the radio, they succumbed to its influence like an aboriginal population exposed to a new strain of flu.

Hamp Swain's "King Bee" program on WBML was the source of this infection in Macon. In addition to introducing his listeners to the latest in R&B, Swain's program provided another service that was particularly enlightening for the many whites in his audience. Most white people in Macon had little contact with blacks, and what contact they did have was entirely constrained by the modes of southern racial etiquette. This made listening to Hamp Swain's mellifluous voice and hip banter ("Have no fear. The King is here!" he announced at the start of each show) feel like an act of cultural eavesdropping for the city's white teenagers, most of whom had never heard a black man speak like Swain before, with such overt confidence, knowingness, and wit—the very qualities that southern blacks were careful to avoid in their interactions with whites, lest they be accused of being impertinent, uppity, or worse. Though they cloaked their messages in signifying and rhyming slang, deejays like Swain and stations like WBML functioned as mouthpieces and switchboards for the black communities they served. As WDIA's Martha Jean "The Queen" Steinberg recalled, "We were the 'mayors' back then. . . . You didn't have any so-called black leaders. So we were the ones who spoke out. . . . We were shaping the minds and hearts of the people, and we did a good job. We encouraged them to go to school, to get degrees, to be educated. Told them about racial pride. We kept our communities intact." For white Southerners in the mid-1950s, the sound of black music, speech, and humor on the radio was like nothing they had ever heard. And at teenage hang-outs like Macon's Pig 'n' Whistle Drive-in, they listened to little else.

Tutti Frutti, good booty . . .

—LITTLE RICHARD

Y ET ANOTHER SIDE EFFECT OF THE RISE OF BLACK-APPEAL RADIO
involved the fluid mixture of sacred and secular music that many of
these stations presented. Prior to the 1950s, gospel music had been much
more readily available on southern airwaves than rhythm and blues. Network stations like WBML in Macon, which at one time would never have
broadcast a "race record," were happy to present live Sunday morning gospel shows that were popular with black and white listeners alike. Gospel
programming expanded dramatically with the proliferation of stations
catering to a black listenership, and it was by no means confined to Sundays. Top black stations like WDIA in Memphis broadcast many hours of
gospel music a day on shows hosted by celebrity deejays like Theo "Bless
My Bones" Wade. Together with the trend toward the presentation of
gospel in commercial concerts (rather than church programs) that began
with Rosetta Tharpe, black radio blurred the line that Ray Charles had
begun to straddle with such aplomb. It also provided a powerful marketing tool for the half-dozen independent labels that by the early 1950s were
competing in the lucrative market for records by gospel quartets. Like
many of the artists they recorded, the owners of these labels—nearly all
of them (with the notable exception of Don Robey at Peacock Records in
Houston) white, and nearly all of them Jews—were engaged in their own
balancing act between sacred and profane realms of entertainment.

The rise of the indie labels, which underwrote the ascendancy of black
popular music in the 1950s and provided the model for soul labels like
Motown and Stax in the 1960s, was the outgrowth of a particular set
of social and historical circumstances. During the fifteen years it took

the record business to recover from its commercial collapse at the start of the Great Depression, a great transformation took place in the American entertainment industry, as the expansion of national radio networks, the proliferation of mass-circulation magazines, and the unbridled success of Hollywood combined to establish a unified market in popular culture that reached from coast to coast. The revival of the American economy during World War II was a boon for show business as a whole, but the rationing of raw materials and the restriction of electrical manufacturing to war production placed special constraints on record and phonograph sales, as did a two-year strike by the American Federation of Musicians, which in 1942 banned its members from playing on commercial recordings in an effort to reform the royalty structure of the record business. When the smoke finally cleared at the end of the war, the American record industry was dominated by a trio of New York–based labels, Columbia, Decca, and RCA, joined by a dynamic new Hollywood-based competitor, Capitol. All of these so-called "major" labels were subsidiaries of larger media corporations, and all of them focused on serving the mainstream of popular taste as it was defined by the New York–Hollywood nexus of mass entertainment.

The mass-market mentality of the major labels was further encouraged by the introduction in the late 1940s of a revolutionary new format: long-playing "microgroove" records made of lightweight vinyl plastic that offered much better durability and sound quality than the fragile 78 rpm shellac disks that had served as the industry standard for fifty years. These new "LPs" held more than twenty minutes of music on a side. They could be shipped and mailed without concern for breakage, and they had the added benefit of being packaged in foot-square cardboard sleeves that could be displayed on racks in a wide variety of stores, where their cover art and copy served as an advertisement for the product within. Microgroove technology was also applied to the manufacture of 78 rpm records, which were gradually superseded by seven-inch vinyl "singles" that turned at 45 rpm and held up to four minutes of music on a side. Initially, the confusion and competition between these new formats (which required record buyers to purchase new, multispeed phonographs) caused a sharp fall-off in record sales. But by the early 1950s, singles and albums were well established as the new standard of the recording industry: 45s for popular songs, LPs for everything else.

At a time when only one in five American households owned a phonograph, one of the qualities that made LPs especially attractive to the major labels was their appeal to the more affluent sectors of the record-buying public. LPs inspired a boom in the market for classical music, cast recordings of Broadway shows, film soundtracks, "easy listening" music, and modern jazz, as well as collections of songs by mainstream pop singers. Costing three to four dollars apiece (as opposed to less than a dollar for a 45), albums sold mainly to a growing audience of middle-class consumers who were incorporating record listening into their leisure lives, turning "hi-fi" audio systems into a standard amenity of the modern American home.

Though the sale of "race" records had enjoyed great popularity during the boom years of the 1920s, the major labels tended to ignore the new market in black popular music that arose in the urban centers after World War II. The majors were happy to record established black stars like Duke Ellington and Louis Armstrong and race-neutral pop crooners like the Ink Spots and Nat King Cole. But the more specialized varieties of black dance music that were grouped under the new rubric of rhythm and blues existed outside the corporate consciousness and beyond the pale of the distribution and promotional networks on which the major labels relied. (The exception was Decca, whose roster included Louis Jordan.) Some of this indifference was a function of musical geography. New York had always been a jazz town, not a blues town, and the sensibilities of its record executives, music publishers, managers, agents, songwriters, arrangers, and musicians had been shaped by the self-consciously sophisticated standards of Broadway and the swing era, when jazz bands became "orchestras" and musicians performed in evening dress. Many of these people looked down on the newer forms of black popular music as a crude throwback to a déclassé world of juke joints and rent parties. In addition to this institutionalized snobbery, there is no question that some degree of institutionalized racism also contributed to the major labels' disregard of rhythm and blues, as evidenced by the enthusiasm with which these same companies catered to the other burgeoning market that lay outside the mainstream:

that of "hillbilly" or "country and western" music, which by the early 1950s accounted for a nearly a third of all the popular singles sold.

The independent labels that sought to fill the vacuum created by the majors' indifference were based in the cities that absorbed the brunt of the 2.5 million African Americans who left the South during the second wave of the Great Migration. Most of them were founded by small-time entrepreneurs who got their start in the retail end of the music business, running nightclubs, record shops, or jukebox chains—men like Leonard Chess of Chess Records in Chicago, Syd Nathan of King Records in Cincinnati, and Lew Chudd of Imperial Records in Los Angeles. Though some of these budding moguls developed shrewd instincts about what would appeal to their customers, they were businessmen first and last, and their interest in music was confined to what would sell.

Specialty Records had been founded in Los Angeles in the mid-1940s by a methodically minded Pennsylvanian who called himself Art Rupe. Born Arthur Goldberg in 1917, Rupe moved to California in the late 1930s to study business at UCLA. While working in a shipyard during the war, he began looking for ways to involve himself in the entertainment industry. In 1944, he invested his savings in a small Los Angeles record label called Atlas, only to see the company's prime asset, Nat King Cole, lured away by the newly founded major label Capitol. The loss of his investment convinced Rupe that his best hope for success was to focus on types of music that the major labels ignored, and with this in mind, he conducted a thorough analysis of the market for race records, categorizing the current hits on the basis of style, tempo, and theme. This analysis became the business plan of a new record label that Rupe initially called Juke Box and then renamed Specialty. His first success came with the jump blues singer Roy Milton, whose "R. M. Blues" sold a million copies in 1947. But a year later, when the American Federation of Musicians announced a second round of punitive strikes against the recording industry, Rupe had the bright idea of finessing the union's ban on instrumental accompaniment by moving into the growing market for a capella gospel quartet.

His timing could not have been better, and by the early 1950s, having added the Soul Stirrers, the Pilgrim Travelers, and "Professor" Alex Bradford to his roster, Rupe had built Specialty into one of the top gospel labels in the country. But the commercial constraints of the religious market began to chafe on him. Impressed by the early hits his friend and rival Lew Chudd at Imperial Records was enjoying with the New Orleans singer-pianist Fats Domino, Rupe made a field trip to the Crescent City, where he signed a seventeen-year-old singer named Lloyd Price. Price's first release on Specialty, recorded in New Orleans in 1952 with the backing of Domino and his band, was a rollicking blues ballad called "Lawdy Miss Clawdy" that sold nearly a million copies and was named R&B "Record of the Year" by *Billboard* and *Cashbox*. The following year, Rupe's New Orleans connections yielded another hit with Guitar Slim's "The Things I Used to Do."

It's unclear whether Art Rupe was aware of the part that Ray Charles had played in "The Things I Used to Do." But there is no question that when "I Got a Woman" reached the top of the R&B charts in the winter of 1955, Rupe began looking for singers who could apply a gospel feeling to rhythm and blues. Around this time he received a demo tape from Little Richard Penniman, who had met Lloyd Price after a show at the Macon City Auditorium and was following up on Price's suggestion that he try his luck with Specialty. Rupe was impressed with the tape but disappointed to learn that Richard was already under contract to Don Robey at Peacock Records in Houston. Rupe's efforts to buy out Richard's contract took some time, and it was another six months before he was able to schedule a recording date in New Orleans. Rupe himself did not attend the session; instead he sent his A&R man, Robert "Bumps" Blackwell, with a detailed set of instructions on how to go about turning Little Richard into the next Ray Charles.

New Orleans in the mid-1950s was the center of an infectious brand of piano blues that was the legacy of several generations of indigenous keyboard stylists. The most recent and influential of these was an eccentric figure named Henry Roeland Byrd, who performed under the sobriquet Professor Longhair. In the late 1940s, Longhair had made a number of records on which he fused elements of boogie-woogie and gospel piano with a sinuous rumba rhythm that was popular with New Orleans Mardi Gras parade bands. Longhair's own prospects as a recording artist were limited by a warbling vocal style that was much too idiosyncratic for him to achieve anything more than a local celebrity. But that was not an issue for Fats Domino, whose genial Creole baritone, as winning as Longhair's voice was weird, would earn him fame and fortune as the great popularizer of New Orleans piano blues, beginning in the summer of 1955 with his million-selling single "Ain't That a Shame."

Domino's records were produced by the trumpeter Dave Bartholomew, who led the house band at the city's one recording studio, which occupied a back room at the J&M Music Shop on North Rampart Street. In their work behind Domino, Lloyd Price, and nearly every other singer who recorded in New Orleans during these years, Bartholomew's band, anchored by their drummer Earl Palmer, had perfected a distinctive rhythmic style that combined the rolling triplets associated with gospel pianists like Roberta Martin with a steady jolting accent on the second and fourth beats of the bar. For musicians schooled in the principles of swing and bebop, this insistent accent sounded like a throwback to the marchy two-beat feel of early New Orleans jazz. But its real genesis came from the long-standing practice of black church congregations to keep time by stomping their feet and clapping their hands. When this simple alternation was transposed to the drum set, the dull thud of the bass drum contrasted with the sharp smack of the snare to produce a so-called "backbeat." In and of itself, a backbeat was nothing new. But by transforming an effect that had once been reserved for the climactic "shout choruses" of big-band arrangements into a regularized rhythm, Dave Bartholomew's band was orchestrating a sea change in the sound and feel of American popular music.

Little Richard and Bumps Blackwell had never laid eyes on each other prior to their meeting at the J&M studio in September 1955. A dapper, light-skinned African American in his late thirties, Blackwell had gotten his start as a bandleader in his hometown of Seattle, where his sidemen had once included teenagers Ray Charles and Quincy Jones. Many of the musicians who worked with him on a regular basis chafed at his self-importance and regarded him as a poseur. ("He would just talk loud and boss everybody around and create the impression that he knew what he was doing," recalled the guitarist René Hall.) But Blackwell's true talent lay in his ability to bridge the cultural chasm between Art Rupe and the artists he recorded by translating his boss's half-baked ideas into terms that singers and musicians could actually understand.

As for Little Richard, the first impression he created was summed up by Earl Palmer, who greeted his arrival in the studio by announcing, "What the *fuck* is this?" His face aglow with pancake makeup and crowned by a marcelled pompadour that towered six inches over his head, Richard's gay flamboyance had increased by several orders of magnitude during his years as a journeyman singer on the chitlin' circuit. Yet there was little outlet for that flamboyance in the songs he sang that day, most of them plaintive "crying blues" from his Specialty audition tape. The second day of the session began no better than the first. Discouraged, Bumps Blackwell called a break for lunch, during which Richard insisted that they head across town to a popular musicians' hangout called the Dew Drop Inn. There, inspired by the coterie of drag queens who frequented the place, Richard sat down at the piano and pounded out a paean to the pleasures of anal sex that began with the soon-to-be-immortal lines "Awop-bop-a-loo-mop a-lop-bam-boom / Tutti *Frutti*, good *booty*." By the time he was done, the club was in an uproar, and Bumps Blackwell had forgotten all about his search for the next Ray Charles. After commissioning a quick rewrite of the lyrics by a local songwriter named Dorothy LaBostrie (who sagely substituted "all rooty" for "good booty"), he escorted Richard back to the studio. Shrieking the song in a lascivious tenor punctuated by random side trips into an exultant falsetto whoop, Richard accompanied himself on the piano with a steady stream of eighth notes that clashed subtlely, yet explosively, with the loping backbeat of the band.

No less than "I Got a Woman," Chuck Berry's "Maybelline," and Fats Domino's "Ain't That a Shame," the crazed energy and driving rhythm of "Tutti Frutti" marked another stylistic watershed in the miraculous musical year of 1955. While Ray Charles drew on the vocal embellishments, "preacher chords," and devotional lexicon of gospel music to bring new depths of emotion to the shopworn clichés of the blues, Little Richard was tapping into the fervent, unhinged frenzy of the storefront Holiness churches to lay the groundwork for a new style of music that was based less on emotion than on raw sensation. "Tutti Frutti" was as loud, flashy, freakish, and superficial as the wildly camp persona Richard had adopted as a mode of self-expression and self-defense. Both musically and attitudinally, it marked the moment when black popular music gave birth to its bastard child, whose biracial appeal would mandate a change in the nomenclature, from "rhythm and blues" to "rock 'n' roll."

Released in December 1955, the record rose to #2 on the R&B charts and entered the Pop Top 20 as well. It was the first of fourteen hit singles Little Richard would release over the next two years, as he refined the principles of musical chaos laid down by "Tutti Frutti" on such riotous records as "Long Tall Sally," "Good Golly Miss Molly," "Jenny Jenny," and "Lucille." (He based nearly all of his characters on drag queens he knew.) Nine of those hits would cross over into the Pop Top 40, earning Richard a large following among the millions of white teenagers whose enthusiasm for blues with a backbeat was catalyzed by the avatar-like emergence of Elvis Presley, who exploded into the national spotlight in the spring of 1956 to the strains of "Heartbreak Hotel." (It was no accident that Presley included covers of both "Tutti Frutti" and "I Got a Woman" on his first LP.) In the fall of 1956, Richard's wild-eyed, shamanistic performance was the acknowledged high point of the big-budget rock 'n' roll musical *The Girl Can't Help It*, whose international success made him a star in Britain, where his record sales rivaled Presley's for the next two years.

Little Richard's meteoric rise was by far the most spectacular case of local-boy-makes-good that the African American population of Macon had ever witnessed, and it had a galvanizing effect on the city's music scene. Richard himself was unable to partake of his status as a hometown hero, however, having been banned from Macon by a court order stemming from his arrest on a charge of "lewd conduct" in the summer of 1955. In fact, he had no desire to return home—he soon bought a house in Los Angeles and moved his whole family there—not least because that would have required him to settle his accounts with Clint Brantley, who had lent him a considerable amount of money and support over the years. But his physical presence in Macon was superfluous. It was the example of his success that mattered, and that was more than enough to spur the hopes of other aspiring young singers from the dead-end streets of neighborhoods like Pleasant Hill, Tindall Heights, and Bellevue.

Otis and his sister Deborah in Bellevue

My brother in his younger days was a very nice person. A real gentle person, who liked to have fun. He wouldn't get into fights until he got older, until we moved into the Bellevue area.

—RODGERS REDDING

No one in Macon would take the example of Little Richard closer to heart than Otis Redding. Richard's success came at a time when Otis was beginning to shake off his parents' influence by shifting his musical orientation from gospel to rhythm and blues, and it filled him with a palpable sense of possibility. (Though Richard's sexual orientation was well known in Macon, his absence from the city probably made it easier for a decidedly heterosexual teenage boy to adopt him as a musical role model.) Otis knew that Richard, like himself, had gotten his start in a children's gospel group, performing, like himself, on the local church circuit. Less than a year before, the man had been washing dishes at the Macon bus station. Now his crazed voice was booming out of radios and jukeboxes across the country. Learning to sing, like learning to talk, begins as an act of mimicry, and most good singers are excellent mimics. From the time of "Tutti Frutti," Otis began to apply all his powers of mimicry to sounding like Richard Penniman.

In the spring of 1956, not long after the Reddings moved into their new home, Otis's father suffered a relapse of tuberculosis and was forced to return to Battey State Hospital for another extended stay. His absence hit the family very hard. Fannie had left her cleaning job at Woolworth's during her pregnancy; now, with the baby less than a year old, she found work at the Log Cabin Laundry in Bellevue. This left her with little time to keep tabs on an adolescent son who was looking and acting more like a young man every day. Deprived of his father's quiet authority at home, with the rest of his household preoccupied by economic survival, Otis was on his own. Increasingly, his life was becoming centered on the two activities that would consume his attention for several years to come: hanging with his new friends from Bellevue, and looking for ways to act on his desire to be a singer someday.

Two activities that did not figure heavily in this picture were school and work. To his parents' despair, school had outlived its usefulness as far as Otis was concerned. Though he returned to Ballard-Hudson in the fall of 1956 for the start of his sophomore year, he didn't last long, withdrawing before the end of the fall semester. (Of her father's reaction to this, Louise recalled, "The only time he got really upset was when Otis dropped out.") Work was another matter. With Otis Sr. in the hospital, the family needed money. Menial jobs were plentiful in Macon in the 1950s, and from the moment he left high school, Otis had no trouble finding low-paying work at grocery stores, gas stations, and construction sites. Holding a job, on the other hand, was a constant challenge for him. Rodgers's recollection that his brother "never kept a job for more than five minutes" was an obvious exaggeration, but it gives some sense of Otis's blasé attitude toward any form of work that was not related to his musical ambitions.

Otis's outgoing nature had always made it easy for him to make friends, but his family's move to Bellevue in the middle of his freshman year in high school had thrust him into an alien social setting, and establishing himself in his new surroundings was a good deal more complicated than simply "making friends." His arrival in Bellevue in the fall of 1955 would have been noted by every other male adolescent in the neighborhood. While Otis may have known some of the local teenagers from Ballard-Hudson, he was identified with Tindall Heights, and any acceptance in Bellevue would have to be hard-earned. His early vetting took place on the long bus rides to and from school each day. (Denied the school bus service that was provided for white students, black students from Bellevue had to take the city bus into the center of Macon and then back out to the Ballard-Hudson campus on Anthony Road.) It was here that Otis first met the teenagers who would form his social circle in the years ahead. They included three pairs of brothers: William and Herbert Ellis, who lived next door to the Reddings on Pike Street; Charles and Bennie Davis, whose family had moved to Macon from Chicago; and Charles and Sylvester Huckabee (Ves to his family and Huck to his friends), who lived on the far side of Durr's Lake, a whites-only recreation center that lay at the foot of Pike Street. The Huckabees in turn were tight with a pair of "cousins" named Willie Howard, whom everyone called Bubba Howard, and Willie Sailor, whom everyone called Bubba Sailor. Like Otis, the Ellis and Davis brothers were relative newcomers to the neighborhood. But the Huckabees and both Bubbas were born and bred in Bellevue, and they considered it their home turf.

It is telling that, until recently, most of the writing about the street culture of African American teenagers and young adults has come from white sociologists rather than black authors. The reason for this is simple: historically, for most young blacks with the sort of literary or academic ambitions that might lead them to write about their lives, the pursuit of those ambitions was predicated on *escaping* from the world of their peer group and freeing themselves from a lifestyle that, then as now, existed mainly to compensate for the absence of viable opportunities. As Macon's John Oliver Killens recalled, "Most of the girls and boys I'd grown up with now looked upon me as a stranger. . . . By my very presence, I was an unspoken accusation, as if I were challenging each and every one of them: 'Why in hell haven't you had the gumption to leave this hell-hole like I did.'" In the Jim Crow South, outside the big cities, it was rare for young blacks with serious artistic or academic ambitions to stay in the place where they grew up. In Otis's case, the tensions between his musical ambitions and his loyalty to his friends in Bellevue would play out over the next decade of his life in ways that would sometimes help, sometimes hinder, and on at least one occasion, threaten to destroy the prospects of his career.

Beginning in the 1960s with pioneering work like Ulf Hannerz's *Soulside*, and continuing in the more contemporary writings of the black sociologist Elijah Anderson, social studies of African American communities have recognized a pervasive distinction between families and individuals who subscribe to the mainstream values enshrined in words like *respectability* and *decency* and those who subscribe, in Anderson's term, to an oppositional "code of the street." "These two orientations—decent and street—socially organize the community," Anderson notes, "and their coexistence has important consequences for residents, particularly children. Even youngsters whose home lives reflect mainstream values . . . must be able to handle themselves in a street-oriented environment." The fact that black Americans have historically been oppressed by the hypocrisies of "middle-class morality" has never resulted in a wholesale rejection of that morality; if anything, it has led many middle- and working-class black families to embrace the social values of respectability and decency with a special tenacity. As a hardworking, churchgoing, two-parent household, the Reddings epitomized this mainstream sense of propriety. They were "good people," as it was said in the South—all the more so now that Otis

Sr. had begun to study with a local minister, the Rev. Obie Orr, as the first step toward adding the title of Reverend to his own name. Schools and churches were the bastions of decency and respectability in the black community, and the Reddings had shown a strong commitment to both.

For many generations, the alternative to these mainstream values has been the Darwinian code of the street, which can apply to whole families, but which has found its fullest expression in the social lives of adolescents and young adults. People who grew up in postwar Macon are quick to point out that the street life in neighborhoods like Tindall Heights and Bellevue was, in Rodgers Redding's words, "nothing like it is today." But while the threat of gangs and guns and drugs was indeed much less dire in the 1950s, casual violence, petty criminality, and the trade in bootleg liquor were very much a part of the social setting in which Otis and his contemporaries were raised. Then as now, young black men had to navigate this street life on a daily basis from the moment they left their homes. Elijah Anderson has characterized this street culture as a relentlessly competitive social environment regulated by an aggressive "campaign for respect," in which young men seek to project personas of exaggerated physical toughness and verbal and sexual prowess, and where social standing is gained and maintained by getting the better of other people in verbal or physical interactions. While concerns with toughness and prowess loom large in the lives of male adolescents at all levels of American society, the difference in urban black neighborhoods, then as now, involved the high stakes that applied in an environment where the most elementary forms of human dignity were denied, and the opportunities to enhance one's self-esteem were so drastically limited. For many young black men, Anderson suggests, respect and credibility on the street are something "to be fought for and held and challenged as much as honor was in the age of chivalry."

On the most basic level, this meant that Otis had to literally fight his way into his new neighborhood as a way of demonstrating that, win or lose, he understood the need to stand up for himself and possessed enough "heart" and "nerve" to hold his own in a social setting where self-assertion was largely synonymous with physical aggression. As suggested by Rodgers's statement that his brother had been "a real gentle person" who didn't get in fights until their family moved to Bellevue, Otis exemplified what Anderson describes as "the dilemma of the decent kid." "For children from decent homes," he writes, "the immediate and present reality of the street situation can overcome the compunctions against tough behavior that their parents have taught them, [as] the child is confronted with the local hierarchy based on toughness and the premium placed on being a good fighter."

To navigate these competing value systems, kids from decent homes develop an ability to think, speak, and behave in one way with their parents, teachers, and employers and another way with their peers. The term for this is "code-switching," and it came as second nature to many blacks in the Jim Crow South, since it was a technique they were required to practice in virtually all their interactions with whites. For people of high intelligence, the constant need to read social signals and adjust one's behavior accordingly became the basis of an education in "street smarts" that served as an essential survival skill. Otis became sufficiently adept at this adaptation that different people retained dramatically different impressions of him during his teenage years. There were plenty of adults in Macon like the Rev. Moses Dumas, a friend of the Redding family, who saw Otis as the bane of his parents' existence, an unruly kid who ran with a rough crowd and lived on the edge of delinquency. And then there were people like Alice Bailey, a Tindall Heights resident who knew Otis as the sweet-natured friend of her brother Prate, and one of the few people her protective mother would trust to chaperone her to the record hops she hosted during her tenure as a teenage deejay on the Macon radio station WIBB.

Big as he was, Otis was by no means the dominant member of his peer group in Bellevue. Though he was approaching his full-grown height of six foot one, he was still a gangly kid compared to formidable figures like Bubba Howard and Sylvester Huckabee, both of whom were not only big but immensely strong. The fights he fought to gain credibility were ritualized rather than no-holds-barred affairs, and they usually lasted just long enough for one person to gain a clear advantage over the other. ("We would fight early in the morning and that afternoon we'd be back playing together," Rodgers Redding recalled.) By determining the hierarchy of dominance and deference in the group, these contests opened the door to a satisfying sense of belonging and camaraderie. Once Otis had proven his mettle, the older, stronger boys accorded him their respect, and advised him on how to build and maintain a reputation on the street. While self-esteem was an important consideration, the need for self-protection was paramount. Each of Macon's black neighborhoods was regarded by its teenaged guardians as sovereign territory, and the presence of outsiders was welcomed as a prime opportunity for the local boys to add to their store of "respect." Safe passage through the city for a black youth was dependent not only on his ability to advertise his own toughness but also on the reputations of his running buddies and their willingness to back him up.

On a daily basis, when Otis and his friends would meet up and hang out after school or work, their main activity was talk: a competitive repartee of bantering and teasing, shucking and jiving, critiquing each another's appearance, opinions, and behavior, boasting about real and imaginary sexual exploits, discussing and dissecting employers, parents, siblings, and girlfriends, retelling favorite stories about getting in and out of trouble, and cheerfully exchanging the sorts of obscene insults (including the formalized "dozens") that would only be tolerated among close friends. In this context, Otis was known as a big talker and a good talker, someone who could "run his mouth" and hold his own in the endless arguments and verbal contests that constituted a prime form of recreation among people who quite literally didn't have anything better to talk about.

As with all male adolescents, the unspoken subtext of their social discourse was manhood. Ulf Hannerz has characterized the "streetcorner sociability" common to urban black neighborhoods as a form of mutual mythmaking that is centered on the promotion of a shared ideal of masculinity that allows each male to see himself as "a bit of a hero, a bit of a villain, and a bit of a fool, but none of them all the way." One component of this masculine ideal is the posture of toughness and aggression that Elijah Anderson ascribes to the code of the street. But Hannerz emphasizes another aspect of this "ghetto-specific masculinity," which he relates to the "trickster" characters found in African American folklore going back to slave times: archetypal figures like Brer Rabbit who navigate the proverbial "jungle" of life by relying on brains rather than brawn, in a manner that mirrors the efforts of many black adolescents to mediate between the orientations of "decent" and "street."

While there is little to suggest that Otis engaged in any concerted criminal activity apart from occasional instances of petty theft, some of his friends in Bellevue certainly did. Herbert Ellis went on to sell bootleg liquor, which was the drug trade of its time, involving some of the same battles over turf and supply. Bubba Howard, who cultivated an aura of "craziness" that caused everyone to regard him as the most frightening and belligerent member of Otis's social circle, was never without a gun, which lent a whole other character to his reputation on the street. And Sylvester Huckabee turned into an exceedingly shrewd and intimidating young hoodlum who left Macon in 1957 to try his hand at professional boxing before embarking on a life of crime that began in earnest with his arrest and imprisonment for armed robbery in California in 1959. Still it remains that most of these teenagers came, like Otis, from "decent" homes, and apart from Huckabee, nearly all of them—including Herbert Ellis and Bubba Howard—would eventually settle into reasonably stable, respectable lives. (Herbert's younger brother C. Jack Ellis would return to Macon after a distinguished career in the army and win election as the city's first black mayor in 1999.) Otis was one of many decent kids from Bellevue who found it necessary to develop a tough, aggressive street persona as a means of assuring his physical safety and preserving his self-respect. But he was the only member of his peer group who would find a way to combine that aggressive posture with his gentler and more fun-loving nature in the creation of a *musical* persona that would provide him with a much more durable source of security, satisfaction, and self-esteem in the years ahead.

HILLVIEW SPRINGS

The guy who got the most applause won five dollars. A bunch of us would go down with Otis and pound the tables when he sang so he'd be sure and win. Then we'd split up the money.

—SYLVESTER HUCKABEE

CHARLES AND BENNY DAVIS WERE THE ONLY MEMBERS OF OTIS'S new circle of friends in Bellevue who shared his interest in playing music. Charles played drums, Benny played guitar and harmonica, and at some point toward the end of 1956 the three of them joined with a piano player named Charles Smith to form a pickup band. Smith did a creditable imitation of Little Richard's breakneck piano style, which gave Otis an opportunity to start rehearsing Richard's repertoire. Their group was sometimes joined by a sax player in his mid-twenties named Ishmael "Ish" Mosley, who had played with Little Richard back in the day. Mosley had grown up in Bellevue and trained as a bandsman during his service in the army. Following his discharge in 1949, he got married, found a steady job at Robins AFB, and began performing locally with the bands led by Percy Welch and "Jazzbo" Brown. It was during a stint with Welch that he had played behind Little Richard at the Tick Tock Club on Broadway.

The principal venue for live music in the Bellevue area was the Hillview Springs Social Club, which occupied a barren cinder-block building, set beside a lake in the woods off Mumford Road, a short walk from Pike Street. Hillview Springs was an adult, unlicensed drinking club, and teenagers were not welcome there except on Sunday nights, when the place featured a talent show hosted by the pianist and singer Gladys Williams, whose five-piece group was regarded as the most professional black dance band in Macon. Williams had grown up in the city, survived a bout of polio as a child, and graduated from the Hudson High School in

1925, at which point an "unknown white benefactor" (to quote the *Telegraph*) arranged for her to receive a music scholarship to the Hampton Institute, an all-black college in Hampton Roads, Virginia. She returned to Macon and spent the next twenty-five years teaching piano, playing for area churches, and fronting a group whose eclectic repertoire and polished presentation allowed them to work extensively in both black and white venues. Williams was a grand dame in her late forties, elaborately coiffed and powdered, whose affection for pancake makeup had made a lasting impression on Little Richard.

A great many Macon musicians had passed through her group, including Percy Welch, who claimed to be playing with her on the night Otis Redding, with the moral support of his buddies from Bellevue, first summoned the nerve to enter the Hillview Springs talent show. In Welch's account, Otis launched into a headlong rendition of Little Richard's "Long Tall Sally," only to lose his way a few bars into the song—a miscue that earned him some strong words of admonishment from Miss Gladys about the importance of singing in time and in tune. Otis persisted, however. That November, Richard's new single "Heebie Jeebies" came on the radio. The song was another piece of perfect nonsense with a chorus of "You gotta *jump* back, *jump* back, heebie jeebie" that could teach almost anyone to sing on the beat. Otis made a study of "Heebie Jeebies," and by the time he returned to Hillview Springs in the winter of 1957, he had the song down pat. "I won the talent show for fifteen Sunday nights straight with that song," Otis recalled. "And then they wouldn't let me sing anymore, wouldn't let me win that five dollars anymore. That inspired me." Rodgers Redding had the same impression: "When he won that first talent show, I kind of felt that he knew that he was going to make it, because he would win every week. He loved to perform. He loved being applauded."

While Otis was refining his impersonation of Little Richard for the patrons of Hillview Springs, Little Richard himself was storming through the zeitgeist of the Eisenhower fifties like a fey figment of Thomas Dixon's racist imagination. Under the rubric of "rock 'n' roll," growing numbers of rhythm and blues singers were escaping the orbit of the chitlin' circuit and touring coast-to-coast in well-organized "package shows" that played to predominantly white audiences in many parts of the country.

Though white Americans had a long history of using black performers for their amusement and entertainment, between the exhibitionist spirit of the music, the large numbers of teenage girls in the audiences, and the currents of racial and sexual hysteria that were roiling the red blood of the white South, these seminal black rock 'n' roll stars were walking a very fine line indeed. Wherever they went, they performed under the watchful eyes of local police who were eager to step in aggressively at the first sign of anyone, white or black, crossing the color line. In Little Richard's case, he played up his effeminacy as a form of self-protection. "That's the strategy Richard used," his drummer Chuck Conners recalled. "We put on pancake makeup and one earring if possible, and we wore grilled hair or a process. The reason we looked like a bunch of gay guys with loud-color pants and shirts and swishing on the stage was that we could play the white clubs and we wouldn't be a threat to the white girls." Fats Domino was somewhat insulated by his corpulence; Ray Charles (though he appealed more to adults than to teenagers) by his blindness. Chuck Berry was the one black rock 'n' roll star who made no effort to defuse the threat he posed to white racial sensibilities, and Berry was also the one black rock 'n' roll star who would end up being arrested, convicted, and imprisoned in his home state of Missouri on a trumped-up charge of sex trafficking involving an underage prostitute. Twenty-six states still had laws on their books forbidding interracial marriage in 1957, and 96 percent of the white Americans in a recent Gallup poll had expressed their disapproval of the practice. Yet no one looking at the situation could fail to see that the supreme taboo of segregation was under assault, if only in the hormonal imaginations of white teenagers. For the first time in the history of American popular entertainment, sexualized black men were openly taking their place alongside sexualized black women as objects of white fantasy and desire. This process would be accelerated in the fall of 1957 by the emergence of a twenty-seven-year-old black singer whose seductive mixture of looks, talent, and style would shortly bring new meaning to the concept of crossover success.

Two months prior to his first session with Little Richard in New Orleans, Bumps Blackwell had assisted Art Rupe in recording a concert at the Shrine Auditorium in Los Angeles that featured a bill of Specialty's gospel acts, headlined by the Soul Stirrers. At the time, Blackwell couldn't have cared less about gospel music, which he associated with a world of "superstition and ignorance." But the riotous response of the women in the audience to the handsome lead tenor of the Soul Stirrers made an immediate convert out of him. "He was like the black Billy Graham," Blackwell recalled, and he promptly informed Art Rupe that in his professional opinion, this young gospel singer had the makings of a pop star. It was not an original insight on his part.

When Rupe first signed the Soul Stirrers to Specialty in 1950, the group was synonymous with its lead singer, Rebert H. Harris, a minister's son from Texas who was renowned for his subtle phrasing and sublime falsetto. Since their founding in the late 1930s, the Stirrers had emerged as the most innovative and influential of all the post-Dorsey gospel quartets. In addition to Harris's artistry, the group had pioneered the use of rhythmic chanting, vocal interpolations, and the double-lead format that added a new excitement and complexity to quartet singing (turning it, in effect, into gospel *quintet*). Shortly after the Stirrers signed with Specialty, however, Harris announced that he was leaving the group, weary of the constant touring and, he said, unnerved by the response the Stirrers and their brethren were eliciting from the women they encountered on the gospel highway. "The moral aspects of the thing just fell out into the water," Harris told the gospel historian Anthony Heilbut. "The singers didn't care anything about it. They felt they could just do whatever they wanted."

Art Rupe was understandably incensed at the news of Harris's departure, but everyone connected with the group expressed complete confidence in his designated replacement. For all his commanding vocal presence, "Pops" Harris in 1951 was a balding, thick-set man in his mid-thirties with a fussy mustache and the demeanor of a deacon. His replacement Sam Cook was a fresh-faced, almost willowy twenty-year-old. Born in Clarksdale, Mississippi, Cook was still an infant when his father, a Holiness preacher, moved his pulpit and his family to the South Side of

Chicago. The fifth of seven siblings, Sam began performing at the age of six with a family group called the Singing Children. The Rev. Cook balanced his ministerial rectitude with his material aspirations and, unlike many Holiness preachers, took a tolerant attitude toward popular culture. Granted unfettered access to the movies and the radio, his son's musical tastes broadened to include mainstream pop singers like Bing Crosby and Nat King Cole. But Chicago's South Side was the center of the gospel universe, and in 1947, Cook and some high school classmates formed a quartet called the Highway QC's, who modeled themselves so faithfully on the Soul Stirrers that one of the Stirrers, R. B. Robinson, began to coach them. By the end of 1950, when the call came, Sam Cook was already a seasoned performer who had studied every nuance of the Soul Stirrers' repertoire.

Over the next few years, Cook's boyish features would mature into the face of a strikingly handsome young man, and his voice would mature from a thin-blooded imitation of R. H. Harris into one of the most supple and distinctive leads in the annals of gospel quartet. (Harris himself would later describe his protégé as "the greatest singer I ever heard.") Bucking the trend among hard-gospel stalwarts like Ira Tucker and Jules Cheeks toward greater and greater levels of sheer vocal ferocity, Cook's style, epitomized by the lilting, melismatic "whoa-oh o-o-oh"s with which he embellished his melodies, was seductive rather than aggressive. He was a crooner, not a shouter, who rarely betrayed a sense of exertion when he sang (although a brief tenure by Cheeks as the Soul Stirrers' second lead did inspire him to add a hard rasp to his battery of vocal effects). He extended this sense of ease into his performing style, confining his movements to conversational hand gestures and a gentle swaying in place. Set against the more animated choreography of the rest of the group and the frenzy his singing and stage presence produced among the women in his audience, Cook invariably came across as the calmest man in the room; combined with his good looks, this quality made him the absolute embodiment of R. H. Harris's worst fears about the eroticization of the gospel highway.

By the time Bumps Blackwell saw Sam Cook perform at the Shrine Auditorium, it was no secret that he was seriously considering the possibility of crossing over in the manner of the many gospel-trained singers, such as Clyde McPhatter and Ruth Brown, who had gone on to enjoy successful careers in popular music. Yet from Art Rupe's perspective, Cook's prospects were complicated by the fact that, unlike McPhatter and Brown, he was not merely a gospel-trained singer but a reigning gospel star. Rupe feared that Cook's departure from the Soul Stirrers would prompt a backlash from gospel fans that would compromise the future of one of his most lucrative acts. Nevertheless, in 1956, Rupe authorized Blackwell to set up a solo recording date for Cook in New Orleans. Among the songs they recorded was "Loveable," a thinly disguised rewrite of a gospel standard, "He's So Wonderful," that Cook had sung with the Stirrers the year before. Specialty released it in January 1957 and promoted it as the debut of a new artist named Dale Cook. While the record sold poorly, its very existence brought the larger question of Cook's future with the Soul Stirrers to a head. In May of 1957, he relocated from Chicago to Los Angeles, leaving behind not only the group that had made him famous but his wife and family as well. As if to mark his passage to a new life, he added an *e* to his name.

Bumps Blackwell scheduled a recording date for Cooke as soon as he arrived in L.A. The selection of material for this session, which included the Gershwin standard "Summertime" and a dreamily repetitive ballad that Cooke had written called "You Send Me," reflected the shift in Blackwell's ambitions in the two years since he had first heard Cooke sing. Inspired by the successes of Harry Belafonte and Johnny Mathis, both of them "conventionally" handsome, light-skinned black men who recorded for major labels, Blackwell now believed Cooke's mellifluous voice and matinee idol good looks made him capable of crossing over not only from gospel to rhythm and blues but from gospel to mainstream adult pop. This vision was not shared by Art Rupe, who insisted that Cooke retain the backing of a gospel-style quartet in his transition to secular music. Their different viewpoints collided at Cooke's first West Coast recording date when Rupe arrived unexpectedly halfway through the session, noted the presence of a *white* harmony group called the Lee Gotsch Singers that Blackwell had hired to lend an unequivocally pop flavor to the proceedings, and promptly hit the roof, openly berating his producer for defying his instructions. Fueled by years of mutual resentment over Rupe's patronizing manner and Blackwell's success with Little Richard, the argument escalated to the point where Rupe offered to release both Blackwell and Cooke from their contracts with Specialty. In return for a $10,000 bonus he owed Blackwell for his work with Richard, Rupe also gave them the rights to the material they had just recorded.

In a matter of days, Sam Cooke and Bumps Blackwell had signed with an upstart Los Angeles label called Keen Records, which released the tracks from the ill-fated session—"Summertime" backed with "You Send Me"—in September 1957. From the start, deejays favored the B-side of the single. By the end of November, they had favored it so enthusiastically that "You Send Me" stood at #1 on the R&B charts. It then went on to dislodge Elvis Presley's latest hit, "Jailhouse Rock," from its seven-week residency at the top of the *Billboard* Hot 100. This made Sam Cooke the first black solo artist since Nat King Cole in 1950 to place a record at #1 on the Pop charts, and it qualified "You Send Me" as one of the most spectacular pop debuts in a decade of spectacular pop debuts. The song seemed to come out of nowhere, and its success was all the more impressive for the fact that it was such a slight musical confection, utterly lacking in narrative, drama, or intensity. Instead, it consisted simply of Cooke singing the song title in triplicate, three times a verse for the nine verses it took to cycle through the standard AABA format. This turned the whole production, by default, into a showcase for the sheer beauty and nuance of Sam Cooke's voice. In line with the ambitions that Cooke and Blackwell had come to share, nothing about the record—not the conventional thirty-two-bar structure or the backing of demure guitar and wispy drums, and certainly not the Caucasian mewing of the Lee Gotsch Singers—bore much resemblance to rhythm and blues.

On the strength of this stunning initial success, Sam Cooke embarked on what he and Bumps Blackwell hoped would unfold as a mainstream pop career. In keeping with the standard script for a new singing sensation, Cooke appeared on the *Ed Sullivan Show,* only to have his debut cut short when the live broadcast ran over its time limit—an indignity that earned him a good deal of sympathetic publicity and a well-advertised return to the program a month later. In the winter of 1958, Cooke released his second single, a cover of Nat King Cole's 1946 hit "(I Love You) For Sentimental Reasons," followed by an album of show tunes and standards like "Ole Man River" and "Danny Boy." Sales of the single were respectable. Sales of the album were negligible, and Cooke's recording career went into a tailspin during the first half of 1958, after his fourth single on Keen failed to make the charts. That spring, following the example of his role model Harry Belafonte, Cooke played a three-week engagement at the Copacabana, the famous mob-owned nightclub that served as one of New York's premier showcases for mainstream talent. Booked as an opening act to the Borscht Belt comic Myron Cohen, Cooke was completely out of his element, and his stilted performance earned him a raft of bad reviews.

The Copa engagement was a fiasco, but by deflating his mainstream ambitions, it may have saved Sam Cooke's career. When the time came to make his next record, Cooke took over from Blackwell in the studio. Selecting a self-written song (his first since "You Send Me") called "Win Your Love for Me," he dispensed with the white backup singers and oversaw the creation of a punchy Latin groove that allowed him to sing with a freedom and flair he had not shown since his days as a gospel star. Though the lyric content remained conventionally romantic, the melody had a lilt of sadness that hinted, for the first time, at emotional depth. Not only did "Win Your Love" reverse the downward spiral of Cooke's recording career; it also emboldened him as a songwriter and pointed him in the direction of rhythm and blues.

As for Art Rupe, his decision to banish Sam Cooke from his label marked the start of a very bad year. Having lost his biggest gospel star to pop, Rupe was about to lose his biggest pop star to gospel. In October 1957, just as "You Send Me" began its ascent of the charts, Little Richard was performing outdoors at a sports stadium in Sidney, Australia, when he glanced up at the sky and saw a proverbial "great ball of fire" hovering overhead. Richard, who would later attribute this apparition to the launch of the Soviet satellite *Sputnik,* had read his Book of Revelation and took this as a sign. Convinced that some aspect of the world as he knew it was coming to an end, he canceled the remainder of his Australian tour and announced that he was retiring from show business in order to devote his life to the service of the Lord. After returning to the United States for a final recording session in Los Angeles and a farewell performance at the Apollo Theater in New York, Richard made good on his promise. By the summer of 1958, he had shed his pompadour, removed his pancake makeup, and enrolled as a divinity student at a Seventh Day Adventist Bible College in Huntsville, Alabama.

Week in and week out, Otis stole the show.

—HAMP SWAIN

I t would take some time for Sam Cooke to rise to the top of Otis Redding's musical pantheon as a singer, a songwriter, and, in due course, a role model for how to pursue a professional career. "You Send Me" was a huge hit, but it lacked the sort of rhythmic intensity that would appeal to a sixteen-year-old boy, and in the absence of a strong follow-up single, Cooke's voice seemed to evaporate from the airwaves and juke-boxes of Macon once the record had run its course. Otis was familiar with the Soul Stirrers' records, and he may even have seen Cooke perform with the group during one of their regular appearances at church programs in the Macon area. But the nuance of Cooke's singing was well beyond Otis's capacity at this point in his musical development. In the mean-time, Clint Brantley had conjured yet another young comet to bedazzle the local music scene.

Brantley was not a man to be trifled with, but he had taken Little Richard's abdication from Macon in stride. After filing a claim against his former protégé to recoup what he was owed (which earned Richard the beating of his life after he resisted the efforts of a deputy sheriff in Augusta, Georgia, to repossess his Cadillac), Brantley shifted his atten-tion to a young vocal group from the north Georgia town of Toccoa called the Flames, whose lead singer, a diminutive twenty-two-year-old by the name of James Brown, he used to fulfill some of the bookings that Rich-ard had left behind. At first, banking on the visual anonymity of most R&B recording stars, Brantley sent Brown out pretending to *be* Little Richard. But the need for that soon faded as Brown's own talent came to the fore. In the fall of 1955, Brantley gathered the "Famous Flames" (as he had renamed them) in the studio of radio station WIBB in Macon to record a demo tape. The song they sang, "Please, Please, Please," was a drastic abridgment of a classic blues called "Baby Please Don't Go," which had been recorded by various artists over the years, most recently by the Orioles, who had a minor hit with it in 1952. The Flames' version turned the song's title into a droning background chant, over which James Brown, singing in a high, throaty, piercing voice suggestive of Little Richard, impersonated a man rendered all but speechless in the face of romantic loss. For two and a half minutes, Brown repeated a series of monosyllables, beginning with the word *please* and culminating with the pronoun *I.* By investing each repetition with a different inflection, his singing commanded attention—if only to determine when and how the next repetition would sound.

With the help of Hamp Swain, who played the tape religiously on WBML, Clint Brantley threw his weight behind the Famous Flames, shopping their demo around to several independent labels before finally signing the group to a talent scout from King Records, whose cantankerous owner Syd Nathan hated the song so much that he released it on a bet that it would fail. "Please, Please, Please" was a pure novelty, the sort of record people refer to by asking, "Have you heard the one . . ." But this did not prevent "the begging song" from spending nineteen weeks on the R&B charts over the second half of 1956. Resentment over James Brown's star billing on the record led to the extinction of the original Flames, and his subsequent attempts to repeat the single's success were unavailing. With the exception of Brown himself, no one could have imagined that this quirky, gimmicky record marked the start of a monumental musical career. But, if nothing else, "Please, Please, Please" demonstrated that Little Richard's success and Macon's status as a seedbed of R&B talent were something more than a fluke.

Richard's sudden retirement in the fall of 1957 had left his backup band the Upsetters at loose ends. "We were not really too surprised," his drummer Chuck Connors recalled. "We were not too worried either. We knew the band was hot, we knew we were good, [and] we were sure that someone else would grab us." As Connors predicted, the Upsetters were eventually hired by Little Willie John, who was at the peak of his popularity following his top-selling R&B hit "Fever" and could therefore afford to carry a seven-piece band on the road. In the meantime, Clint Brantley tided the group over by finding them work on his circuit of clubs in Georgia and North Florida. Though the details are sketchy, they were fronted at some of these gigs by sixteen-year-old Otis Redding, whose impersonation of Little Richard at the Hillview Springs Social Club had come to the attention of Henry Nash, a Macon resident who served as the Upsetters' road manager. "His impressions of Richard were word perfect and he had all of his moves down pat," Nash recalled. Otis's sojourn with the group lasted no more than a few weeks, and by some accounts it ended badly, with Otis getting stranded in Florida and having to prevail on his parents to wire him the money to come home. But the opportunity to perform with such a topflight band gave a substantial boost to Otis's self-confidence, even as it deepened his fixation on Little Richard.

That same fall, WIBB succeeded in hiring Hamp Swain away from his position at WBML. Founded in 1947 as Macon's first independent station, WIBB had struggled to attract a listenership with a format of country music for many years. On the advice of a consultant, it began to introduce black-appeal programming in 1955, in the person of a deejay named Charles "Big Saul" Greene, whose show proved so popular that the station converted to an all-black format two years later with the addition of Swain and another deejay named Ray Brown, a local blues singer who adopted the on-air moniker "Satellite Papa" after the launch of Russia's *Sputnik*. Big Saul, Satellite Papa, and King Bee now became known in Middle Georgia as the Three Horsemen of WIBB. Shortly after Swain was hired, the station's owner Thomas Maxwell decided to sponsor a Saturday-morning talent show geared to Macon's black teenagers.

The first live radio broadcast of *Teenage Party* took place in February 1958. It was hosted by Swain and held at the smaller of the city's two black theaters, the Roxy, which was housed in a World War II–vintage Quonset hut on Hazel Street, down the hill from Tindall Heights, on the edge of a tough black neighborhood called Tybee. The show was such an immediate success that in May, the station arranged to move it to the larger, grander, more centrally located Douglass Theatre on Broadway in downtown Macon. Every Saturday morning, hundreds of festive

The *Teenage Party* at the Roxy

teenagers gathered outside the theater in a line that stretched the length of the block. In addition to Hamp Swain, who emceed and doubled on saxophone, the show had a house band led by the keyboard player Roye Mathis, along with a regular appearance by "Satellite Papa" Brown, who kicked things off on a high note by donning a silver "spacesuit" and descending from the rafters on a rope to the delighted screams of the crowd. The program itself was carefully planned. Auditions were held on the preceding Thursday night, which gave the participants a chance to rehearse their numbers with the band. At the end of the Saturday-morning performance, all the contestants were brought out onstage, and the winners were chosen on the basis of who got the most applause.

It's not known precisely when Otis made his first appearance on *Teenage Party*. He had a roofing job at the time that required him to work on Saturday mornings; at some point, he began paying Rodgers to substitute for him so that he could take part in the talent show. He did not sing with the house band at first, preferring to play with members of his pickup group from Bellevue. But he was soon approached by the guitarist in Roye Mathis's band, a flashy kid from Tindall Heights named Johnny Jenkins. "The group behind him just wasn't making it," Jenkins recalled. "So I went up to him, and I said, 'Do you mind if I play behind you? And he looked at me like, 'Who are you?' 'Cause he didn't know me. And I said, 'I can make you sound good.'" Jenkins was true to his word. With his help, Otis began winning the talent show on a weekly basis during the summer of 1958, cycling through his repertoire of Little Richard and Chuck Berry songs.

Johnny Jenkins was nineteen years old at the time he introduced himself to Otis in the spring of 1958. Though he now lived with one of his sisters in Tindall Heights, Jenkins had grown up in Swift Creek, a rural area on the eastern outskirts of Macon. The son of a disabled railroad worker, he left school at an early age, ostensibly to help his mother care for a family that grew to include eleven children. Like many black musicians of his generation in the South, Jenkins grew up listening mainly to country music on the radio. By the age of nine he was singing songs by Hank Williams and Hank Snow and soliciting tips from passing motorists at the gas station in Swift Creek, accompanying himself on a guitar he had fashioned out of a cigar box, a stick, and some rubber bands. This makeshift contraption eventually gave way to a secondhand Gibson electric that was given to him by one of his sisters' boyfriends. Finding it more comfortable to play left-handed, Johnny flipped the instrument upside down in the manner later made famous by Albert King, inverting the usual configuration so that the treble strings were on top. (Most left-handed guitar players, such as B. B. King, simply learned to play the instrument right-handed; others, like Jimi Hendrix, inverted the guitar but restrung it in the standard manner.) When WBML began broadcasting rhythm and blues in Macon in the mid-fifties, Johnny devoted himself to learning songs from the radio, copying the guitar styles of Muddy Waters, Jimmy Reed, and Freddie King. The guitar became his constant companion. He once recalled in an interview how the birds would accompany him when he walked through the woods near his home in Swift Creek. "I'd go through there playing and singing. . . . They'd be in the tops of the pine trees, singing along and following me through the woods."

Or so he said. As Johnny Jenkins grew older, his precocity as a guitarist was matched by his flair for self-dramatization, both on and off the stage, a characteristic that makes it hard to ignore the similarity between his account of his childhood in Swift Creek and that of another poor country boy from "back up in the woods among the evergreens"—the one that Chuck Berry immortalized in his 1958 masterpiece, "Johnny B. Goode," who "never ever learned to read or write so well, but could play a guitar just like a-ringing a bell." There is no question that in his creation of a musical persona, Johnny "Guitar" Jenkins modeled himself closely on Berry and his most famous character. Like Berry, Jenkins was a lithe young black man with an impishly handsome face and a marcelled pomp of processed hair. ("Hollywood handsome" was the way people in Macon described him.) And, like Berry, Jenkins augmented his guitar playing with an acrobatic stage presence derived from the pioneering electric guitarist Aaron "T-Bone" Walker, who was among the first performers to grasp the way this brash new instrument lent itself to a new kind of showmanship. Playing behind his back, between his legs, and over his head, Walker treated the guitar as if it were a dancing partner, laying the groundwork for generations of suggestive stagecraft. Chuck Berry was one of Walker's most ardent disciples, and it was from Berry that Johnny Jenkins learned the moves that would soon earn him a reputation as the most exciting and indeed electrifying guitarist in Macon.

At the time he met Otis Redding, Jenkins was a proudly untutored musician who thought of himself as a budding master of the guitar. In addition to playing with Roye Mathis, he was a featured performer with Pat Teacake and the Mighty Panthers, a band led by Mathis's drummer, whose real name was Charles Abrams. The singer in this group was Bill Jones, Otis's former quartet partner from Tindall Heights, now billing himself as Little Willie Jones in homage to the R&B star Little Willie John. Booked by Clint Brantley, Pat Teacake and the Mighty Panthers were regulars at the Jones County roadhouses Club Manhattan and Club Fifteen, as well as Macon venues like the Hillview Springs and the VFW post on Poplar Street. In July 1958, they appeared as a supporting act at the first Homecoming Dance and Show Brantley put on for James Brown and the Famous Flames at City Auditorium. A week later, on August 1, Brantley presented Hank Ballard and the Midnighters and the Five Royales at the auditorium; after the show, Pat Teacake played a dance "in honor of" the headliners at Sawyer's Lake.

That same night, the band Ish Mosley played with, Jazzbo Brown and His House Wreckers, performed at the Disabled American Veterans (DAV) Club on Poplar Street. According to the notice in the *Telegraph*, their featured vocalist was Otis Redding. As near as can be determined, this appearance, coming two months shy of Otis's seventeenth birthday, was his first "professional" engagement in Macon. Over the next few months, Johnny Jenkins gradually drew Otis into the orbit of Pat Teacake and his band. In the middle of November, Otis made his debut with the group at a club called the Showbar on Cotton Avenue, where he was billed as "Macon's newest rock 'n' roll vocalist." As "Rocking Otis Redding," he continued to perform with Pat Teacake and His Mighty Panthers during the winter of 1959. Among the better-paid engagements they played was a fraternity party that was booked by a Mercer University student named Phil Walden, a Macon resident who had hired the group for a dance sponsored by his high school fraternity the previous year.

On a cold night in the middle of that winter, the kerosene heater at the Reddings' home on Pike Street malfunctioned, sending streams of burning oil across the pinewood floor. The family got out safely, but the tinder-dry house and most of its contents were a total loss. (In addition to their furniture and personal possessions, nearly all of the family's written records and photographs were destroyed.) In the immediate aftermath of this disaster, the Reddings moved in with their daughter Christine, who was living in South Macon. Later that year, they would move back to the familiar confines of Tindall Heights. This was even more of a dislocation for Otis than for the rest of his family. While he retained some ties to his old friends in Tindall Heights, he was now completely identified with Bellevue, and reestablishing his street credibility in the projects would take some time. For the most part, he continued to hang out with his buddies from Bellevue, especially Bubba Howard, who was able to get Otis a job with the well-drilling company he worked for.

In the spring of 1959, Johnny Jenkins split with Pat Teacake to form his own band, taking Otis with him as his featured vocalist. Johnny had worked from time to time harvesting pulpwood for a logging company in Jones County; between this and his yarn about playing for the birds in the trees in Swift Creek, he decided to call his group the Pinetoppers. The musicians he recruited included Otis's friends from Bellevue—Charles

Davis on drums and Ish Mosley on sax—along with Sam Davis (no relation to Charles) on second guitar. Sam Davis—or Poor Sam as he was known—had a steady job at a car dealership in Macon; by itself, the old Cadillac he drove was enough to qualify him as the group's manager.

For all his good looks and flamboyant demeanor, Johnny Jenkins would prove to be an oddly ambivalent performer—beginning with the fact that, unlike nearly all the artists he modeled himself on, he showed little interest in singing or writing songs. He may have simply lacked confidence in his voice, or found that singing crimped his style as a guitar player. But his desire to front a band as a lead guitarist was fairly unusual in the field of rhythm and blues. Piano and horn players occasionally made their mark as bandleaders and featured instrumentalists, but the persona of a blues guitarist had always been inseparable from that of a blues singer.

The lasting mystery about Jenkins involves the question of how good a guitarist he really was. His reputation in Georgia's clubs and frat houses was that of a sensational performer, but the few examples of his playing from this period that survive on record are unimpressive on both technical and expressive grounds. The electric guitar was coming into its own in popular music in the late 1950s. Rhythm players like Chuck Berry and Jimmy Reed had developed muscular styles of accompaniment; soloists like T-Bone Walker and B. B. King had adapted the swinging, single-note style of the jazz master Charlie Christian to the vocal cadences of blues; colorists like Bo Diddley and Hubert Sumlin had expanded the palette of the instrument using distortion and a range of tonal effects. Johnny Jenkins played with a piercing, piquant tone that owed something to the inverted stringing of his guitar. But he was not an especially fluid or versatile player, nor was he in any sense an improviser. What he lacked in technique he made up for with flash and showmanship.

(Jenkins's left-handed theatrics would eventually give rise to a local legend that a Seattle teenager named Jimmy James had seen him perform while visiting with relatives in Macon during the 1950s, only to emerge years later as Jimi Hendrix. This story, with its implication that Hendrix modeled himself on Jenkins, was a myth. There is nothing to suggest that Hendrix ever visited Macon as a teenager, and in any case, Jimmy James was a stage name he briefly assumed in the 1960s. Hendrix first met Jenkins while he was playing behind Little Richard in 1964, by which time Hendrix's virtuosity and theatricality were well established.)

"I was never interested in being no musician," Jenkins would later say. "I never was interested in being no star." As a young man on the scene in Macon in the late 1950s, however, he did everything he could think of to call attention to himself, affecting the manner of a small-town celebrity. "He talked very fast, very un-southern, and un-black," Phil Walden recalled. "He talked in rhymes and everyday life was a show for him. At fraternity parties, he would approach these young kids with their cigarettes in their oxford cloth shirts and madras jackets and say, 'May I be so bold as to ask you for a ready-roll?'" Onstage and off, Johnny's egotism and flamboyance were heavily fueled by alcohol, and stories abounded of his taste for moonshine, his violent temper, and the pair of switchblade knives he would brandish at the slightest sign of an affront to his fragile self-esteem.

Like every local band in Macon, the Pinetoppers functioned as an animated jukebox, mixing R&B favorites from the recent past with the latest hits off the radio. Johnny Jenkins rehearsed them often to keep their repertoire up-to-date. Among the songs Otis sang with the group in that first year (in addition to his Little Richard and Chuck Berry numbers) were such current top-sellers as Clyde McPhatter's "A Lover's Question," Jackie Wilson's "Lonely Teardrops," Bobby Day's "Rockin Robin," Wilbert Harrison's "Kansas City," "Try Me" by Macon's own James Brown, and a trio of crossover hits from the summer of 1959, all of them released on the Atlantic label: "There Goes My Baby" by the Drifters, "Charlie Brown" by the Coasters, and Ray Charles's next big breakthrough, a six-minute extravaganza called "What'd I Say."

We were making black records, with black musicians and black singers for black buyers. It never occurred to us in the beginning that there were crossover possibilities. Because if there were we probably would not have gone into that business. The only reason we could survive was because we were specialists.

—JERRY WEXLER

RAY CHARLES'S TALENT AS A SINGER, SONGWRITER, PIANIST, bandleader, and arranger loomed so large that his success, in retrospect, could seem all but preordained. But Charles's career was significantly enhanced by his affiliation with Atlantic Records, the independent label that would play a pivotal role in the careers of Otis Redding and a half dozen other outstanding soul singers in the decade ahead. Atlantic Records and Ray Charles came of age together. Not only did the label show an unusual degree of respect for Charles's talent, but it also promoted his music with a mixture of shrewdness and imagination that went well beyond the capabilities of its rivals in the record business. From its inception, Atlantic was a breed apart from the other upstart labels that helped to transform the landscape of American popular music in the years after World War II.

Ahmet Ertegun and his older brother, Nesuhi, first came to America as teenagers, when their father, a distinguished Turkish diplomat, was appointed as their country's ambassador to the United States in 1934. Consigned to the cultural backwater of Washington, D.C., the boys became ardent jazz fans. Together they assembled a large record collection and sponsored recitals at the Turkish Embassy in segregated Washington that featured an integrated guest list and artists such as Duke Ellington and Ella Fitzgerald. After their father's death and their family's return to

Turkey at the end of World War II, both of the Ertegun brothers chose to remain in the United States. Nesuhi settled in Los Angeles, where he started a small record label dedicated to the revival of classic New Orleans jazz. Ahmet headed for New York, where he became friendly with Herb Abramson, a fellow jazz and blues aficionado. A Brooklyn native, Abramson had been trained as a dentist by the army during the war; after his discharge, he began producing records for a New York label called National and an even smaller, self-owned label called Jubilee, which released an unaccountable mixture of gospel music and Yiddish comedy. In 1947, Abramson sold his stake in Jubilee and joined with Ertegun to found Atlantic Records. "We wanted to make the kind of records we wanted to buy," Ertegun recalled, underscoring Atlantic's distinction as the only independent label of the postwar era that was owned and operated by record *fans.*

Their first taste of success came in 1949 with a Louis Jordan–style jump blues by Stick McGee called "Drinkin' Wine Spo-dee-o-Dee." The strong sales of the record in the South prompted Ertegun and Abramson to take a trip to New Orleans, where they got their first direct exposure to southern music and developed their first clear idea of what they wanted to do with their company. Despite their New York base of operations, they decided to concentrate their efforts on what Ertegun described (with typical obliqueness) as "the southern market, and the extension of the southern market in all the big cities where there was a large population of people who had migrated from the South." Over the next few years, Atlantic managed to capture nearly a third of that market with hit records by the blues shouter Big Joe Turner, the pop singer Ruth Brown, and a roster of vocal groups headed by the Clovers and the Drifters, whose lead singer Clyde McPhatter became a solo star. From the beginning, Ertegun and Abramson relied heavily on the expertise of two key employees: their music director Jesse Stone and their chief engineer Tom Dowd. Jesse Stone was a consummate professional who had worked as an arranger for Chick Webb and Jimmy Lunceford and written hit songs for Benny Goodman and Louis Jordan. He brought an exceptionally high standard of musicianship to Atlantic's recordings, hiring top-notch sidemen and rehearsing the singers for days and even weeks in advance of their sessions—an unheard-of practice at the time. He also wrote some of the label's biggest hits, including "Money Honey" for the Drifters, "Shake, Rattle and Roll" for Big Joe Turner, and "Sh'Boom" for the Chords. Tom Dowd was a native New Yorker who came from a musical family and had served as an army technician on the Manhattan Project during the war— only to learn when he sought to earn a graduate degree at Columbia that his working knowledge of nuclear physics had not yet been declassified. On a whim, Dowd took a job at a recording studio, surmising that audio engineering would seem like "child's play" after his military experience. In addition to his technical background, Dowd possessed a sensitive musical ear, and when Atlantic hired him as their staff engineer in the early 1950s, he brought an exceptional clarity, depth, and creativity to the recordings he made in the label's makeshift studio.

In 1953, shortly after Atlantic purchased Ray Charles's contract, Herb Abramson was recalled to active duty as an army dentist and posted to West Germany. Seeking someone to assume his senior partner's role, Ahmet Ertegun turned to a music journalist and fellow record fan named Jerry Wexler. Thirty-six years old at the time, Wexler had grown up in a working-class Jewish family in New York's Washington Heights. After graduating from high school at the age of fifteen, he enrolled at City College, where he developed a dual passion for the jazz and marijuana he discovered in the neighboring clubs of Harlem. The following year, his parents shipped him off to Kansas State in an effort to straighten him out, but proximity to the jazz mecca of Kansas City proved a fatal distraction and he was forced to withdraw from school. Wexler married in 1941 and served an uneventful hitch as a clerk in the army during the war. After his discharge, he re-enrolled at Kansas State on the G.I. Bill and earned a degree in journalism. Returning to New York, he was hired as a reporter by Paul Ackerman, the erudite music editor of *Billboard*, who became Wexler's mentor. In 1949, when Ackerman decided that the designation "race records" had outlived its usefulness, it was Wexler who coined the term that *Billboard* (and with it, the entire music business) would henceforth apply to black pop: rhythm and blues. In the early 1950s, Wexler left *Billboard* and took a job with a big music publishing firm, where he showed an eclectic talent for matching artists with songs. (Among his unlikely successes was Tony Bennett's hit recording of Hank Williams's "Cold Cold Heart.") But what Wexler really wanted was the chance to make records, and the offer to become a partner in Atlantic turned his life around. Anxious, ambitious, hotheaded, hyperarticulate, and even more of a true believer in the power and glory of African American music than his Turkish partner, Jerry Wexler was the perfect Hebraic complement to Ahmet Ertegun's Byzantine brand of cool. Where Ertegun was the consummate "outside" man, hanging with musicians in nightclubs, speaking in a patois that commuted fluently between Harlem and the Hamptons, Wexler commanded the office and worked the phones, badgering distributors, publishers, managers, deejays, and his own promotion men.

In the second half of the 1950s, Atlantic catered to the expanding teenage market for rock 'n' roll by promoting the pop idol Bobby Darin and importing the Los Angeles songwriting and production team of Jerry Leiber and Mike Stoller to work with a pair of vocal groups, the Coasters and the Drifters. The Coasters were hip novelty singers whose records satirized the emerging biracial youth culture with an appreciative and subversive wit. The Drifters were a reconstituted version of Clyde McPhatter's old group, now fronted by Ben E. King, for whom Leiber and Stoller concocted a distinctly "uptown" production style that applied gospel-tinged vocals, Latin American rhythms, and swirling strings to the well-crafted pop songs of a coterie of young Jewish composers who were turning New York's Brill Building into the latest outpost of Tin Pan Alley.

Around this same time, Nesuhi Ertegun moved back east, bought out Herb Abramson's share in the company, and began building a distinguished roster of jazz artists that included John Coltrane, Charles Mingus, and the Modern Jazz Quartet. Nesuhi brought a refined sense of aesthetics to the marketing of the label's jazz albums, hiring first-rate graphic designers and photographers to work on their cover art. Atlantic's involvement with jazz, and with the LP market in general, was another attribute that set it apart from its competitors in the field of R&B, and it created some interesting collaborative opportunities for the artists on their roster. Ray Charles's formidable chops on piano, the hipness of his arrangements, and above all the grit, depth, and nuance of his singing had earned him the admiration of many jazz musicians. This was especially true of the younger East Coast players who in the mid-1950s began to shy away from the harmonic preoccupations and broken rhythms of bebop in favor of a more overtly blues- and groove-based style that was initially labeled "hard bop."

"It was Horace Silver as musical director of Art Blakey's Jazz Messengers who first announced it," Martin Williams wrote in the jazz journal *Downbeat.* "He and the rest had turned to church and gospel music and the blues as sources of renewed inspiration. If these men were reluctant to listen to King Oliver and Bessie Smith, they heard Ray Charles and Mahalia Jackson with a kind of reverence." The marketing term for this new genre became "soul jazz," and the style reached its height in the work of bandleaders like Silver ("The Preacher"), Blakey ("Moanin'"), and Mingus, whose 1959 Atlantic album *Blues and Roots* included evocatively titled tracks like "Wednesday Night Prayer Meeting" and "Jelly Roll Soul." The "soul jazz" trend found another outlet in the proliferation of small groups built around the "churchy" sound of the electronic Hammond organ. Invented in the 1930s, the Hammond first made its way into jazz as a novelty in the hands of pianists like Count Basie and Fats Waller. In the 1950s, it became the centerpiece of the popular "organ trio" format pioneered by Jimmy Smith, whose 1958 album *The Sermon* affirmed the link to the church.

Under the direction of Nesuhi Ertegun, Atlantic did a brilliant job of promoting the affinities between this popular trend in jazz and the music of Ray Charles. In the spring of 1958, the label released an album called *Soul Brothers* that featured Charles on piano in collaboration with the vibraphonist Milt Jackson of the Modern Jazz Quartet. This was followed by an LP called *The Genius of Ray Charles* ("genius" was a benediction bestowed on the singer by none other than Frank Sinatra). The first side of the album presented Charles and his band augmented by members of the Count Basie and Duke Ellington orchestras; the second side had Charles singing pop standards against a background of woodwinds and strings. The critical and commercial success of these albums (both of which, unlike R&B singles, were reviewed in the mainstream press) enhanced Charles's popularity with a white, affluent, jazz- and pop-oriented listenership that otherwise would not have been inclined to pay attention to a rhythm and blues singer.

As if to flaunt the range of his talent, Charles followed the release of the *Genius* album with the single that would become his musical signature and reward him with the crossover hit he had sought for several years. "What'd I Say" began as a hypnotic twelve-bar riff that Charles liked to play on piano. While vamping on this figure at a gig one night, he began to improvise a wailing vocal that strung together a bunch of hoary blues catchphrases like "Hey mama don't you treat me wrong" and "See the girl with the red dress on." The band fell in behind him over a skittering mambo beat, and the result, after Charles was done embellishing, arranging, and recording it, was a two-part, six-and-a-half-minute concerto of carnality that filled both sides of a single, interrupted by a false ending in which everyone in the studio can be heard to take a break, laughing and chatting, until Ray calls them back to their places for a series of stop choruses in which he and the Raelettes exchange a colloquy of moans and groans, ooohs and aahhs, gasps, wails, and wall-shaking screams that, despite the song's rhetorical question of "what'd I say?" sounds exactly like what it is: a male singer having exuberant musical sex with his entire female backup chorus. "What'd I Say" brought R&B's celebration of physical pleasure to a new level of artistry, and it propelled Charles into the Pop Top 10 for the first time in his career.

Ultimately, Atlantic Records did too good a job of promoting Ray Charles. In the fall of 1959, with "What'd I Say" blaring out of radios across the country and *The Genius* climbing the LP charts, Charles stunned Ahmet Ertegun and Jerry Wexler by signing a three-year contract with one of Hollywood's new major labels, ABC-Paramount. The terms of the deal were unprecedented for any recording artist of the time: a $50,000-a-year guarantee and a 75 percent share of the net profit on every record sold. (Frank Sinatra had recently left Capitol over their refusal to pay him more than a 5 percent royalty.) In due course, Atlantic would lose two more of its bestselling artists, who were lured away by two other major Hollywood labels, Capitol and MGM, also with the promise of a yearly guarantee.

Though Ertegun and Wexler felt betrayed by these defections, the poaching of R&B stars by major labels as their original contracts expired was an industry-wide phenomenon at the time: a migration of proven talent that was facilitated by the paternalistic business practices the independent labels employed. (Spared the chronic cash-flow problems that plagued the independents, the well-capitalized major labels could more easily afford to pay their artists on time and in full.) Atlantic was not exempt from the creative accounting of the record business, although the esteem in which its owners held many of their artists, along with a modicum of actual morality, saved them from the worst excesses. But for Jerry Wexler especially, the departure of Ray Charles was a humbling experience. Charles's willingness to act in his own best interests taught Wexler a new respect for the African American talent he worked with—beginning with the realization that he wasn't doing anyone a favor by putting their records out.

PHIL

The pragmatic philosophy of some Negroes, particularly in the
smaller Southern towns, used to be: "The way for a black man
to get along is to attach himself to some well-to-do *good* white
folks. Just one big white folks is all you need."

—JOHN OLIVER KILLENS

A T ONE OF THE PINETOPPERS' EARLIEST GIGS AT THE LAKESIDE
Park recreational center in the summer of 1959, Otis Redding was
introduced to the white college boy who had been hiring Pat Teacake and
the Mighty Panthers to play at high school and college fraternity parties
over the course of the previous year. Phil Walden was nineteen years old
at the time, and he had just completed his freshman year at Mercer University,
whose stately campus of redbrick buildings and lofty Victorian
spires provided residents of Tindall Heights and the surrounding black
neighborhoods of West Macon with a daily reminder of how the children
of the other half lived.

Though Phil Walden was born in the textile town of Greenville, South
Carolina, in January 1940, his parents were native Georgians. His father,
C. B. (whose given name was Clemiel Barto), had been raised on a farm
in DeKalb County, the youngest of eight children. Phil's mother, Carolyn,
was descended on her mother's side from Col. William W. Clark,
a prominent lawyer, planter, slave owner, and railway magnate who had
lent his name to the town of Clarkston, a suburb of Atlanta. She too had
grown up on a farm but, unlike her husband, who failed to finish high
school, Carolyn had attended college, graduating from LaGrange with a
degree in art before settling into the role of a wife and mother with such
a steadfast dependence on the men in her life that she never learned to
drive a car.

The Waldens moved back to Georgia the year after Phil's birth so that C. B. could take a job as a salesman at Gay Clothing, a downtown Macon haberdashery that had recently been purchased by his older brother Roy. Sociable, hard-drinking, and unambitious, C. B. struggled to supplement his meager income at Gay Clothing with various second jobs, the most consistent of which was a morning and afternoon paper route for the *Telegraph* that covered a large swath of the expanding northern and western suburbs of the city. After living at first in a cramped house on Madden Avenue, the Waldens moved in 1947 to the outskirts of Macon, where they bought a converted barn on an abandoned twenty-five-acre farmstead off Ayers Road, about six miles west of the downtown. Close by was the campus of Wesleyan College and the lush fairways of the Idle Hour Country Club, a pillar of Macon society that would refuse Phil Walden membership until the day he died.

Phil was the second of three sons. His brother Clark was seven years older, his brother Alan three years younger. As might be expected in such a male-dominated household, a competitive atmosphere prevailed. Clark, who went by the nickname Blue, was short, stocky, stolid, and pragmatic. After graduating from high school in 1951, he attended a technical college in Atlanta before moving to Fort Wayne, Indiana, to work for an electronics firm. (Some years later he returned to Macon and took a civilian job at Robins AFB.) Alan, nicknamed Red for his strawberry-blond hair, was the baby of the family—an affable, asthmatic, yet physically active boy who liked to fish and hunt on the land around their home. Where Alan took after his father, Phil was the acknowledged favorite of his mother. Alone among his brothers, he shared her interest in art and literature and an appreciation of the finer things in life. She in turn encouraged him from an early age to draw and write and cultivate his creative sensibilities. Phil also seems to have shared his mother's classically southern sense of the lost grandeur of her family. Starting in elementary school, he developed a lifelong fascination with a millionaires' enclave off the Georgia coast called the Jekyll Island Club, a famous watering hole of the New South elite whose social cachet and fanciful "cottage" architecture had rivaled that of Newport during the early decades of the twentieth century. The bond between Carolyn and Phil did not sit well with C. B., who teased his son about his sissified interest in the arts. All three of the Walden boys felt protective of their mother and resentful of their father for the overbearing way he sometimes treated his wife. C. B.'s own shortcomings as a provider did not prevent him from instilling a strong work ethic in his sons, beginning with the requirement, in Phil's case, that he get up before dawn each morning to do his part for the family paper route. But the constant money worries and C. B.'s heavy drinking lent a strong undercurrent of tension to their home. Both Clark and Phil emerged from their childhoods with explosive tempers—a trait they would later compound by inheriting their father's affection for alcohol.

For Phil Walden, the self-described "epiphany" that would change the course of his life came in junior high school, when Clark returned from Indiana for the 1954 Christmas holiday bearing a phonograph and a stack of records by R&B groups like Hank Ballard and the Midnighters and the Five Royales. Years later, Phil described the impact of this music as akin to "a slap in the face." "It had a rawness and a realness that was unlike anything I had ever heard. I was just infatuated by it." He soon became a regular listener to Hamp Swain's "King Bee" program on WBML, and he began to follow the local black entertainment scene by scanning the ads in the *Telegraph*'s supplement, "Social and Personal Notes of Our Colored Community." Then, in the spring of 1955, Phil found the nerve to attend his first R&B concert at the City Auditorium, a Clint Brantley production that featured the blues pianist Amos Milburn, with Little Richard Penniman as the opening act. Though Richard was little known outside Macon at the time, from the perspective of an enraptured fifteen-year-old, "hanging over the edge" of the deserted whites-only section of the balcony, he stole the show. Later in life, Phil Walden would recount this experience as a true rite of passage, describing how, having "secretly" purchased a ticket, he accompanied a group of friends to a youth club meeting at the Macon YMCA before taking a literal "left turn" to cross the street to the Auditorium. "I had never been around that many black people in my life," he recalled. "I had no idea what I was going to see, or what would be done to me. I was just this naïve young kid." Eight months later, when "Tutti Frutti" came on the radio, Phil experienced his first thrill of connoisseurship as a music fan. That C. B. Walden derided his son's interest in "nigger music" added a satisfying note of adolescent defiance to his new enthusiasm.

By the time of "Tutti Frutti," Phil was coming into his own as a sophomore at Macon's Sidney Lanier High School. Named after the poet and musician who predated Little Richard as Macon's most famous native son, Lanier and its sister school, A. L. Miller, were the city's all-white counterparts of Ballard-Hudson High. Since the 1920s, secondary education for whites in the Macon public schools had been segregated by gender as well as by race. (While local lore extolled this unusual policy as a visionary hedge against the miscegenational threat of integration, it was more likely an expression of the social fundamentalism with which many Bible Belt communities greeted the specter of encroaching modernity in the years after World War I.) By the mid-1950s, Lanier had evolved into a typically hidebound southern high school with an atypically paramilitary bent. The entire thousand-member student body was enrolled in a compulsory Junior ROTC program that required them to report to school in uniform three days a week and submit to daily instruction in close-order drill and military science. "Lanier was never intended to produce aggressive, intellectually daring individuals," the journalist Peter Schrag wrote in a contemporary survey of American high schools. "For forty years it has functioned to develop soft-spoken, well-mannered young men who knew their responsibilities in a rather slow-moving, polite, and well-structured society." The cadet corps and team sports (the Lanier "Poets") were the organizing principles of the school, while a robust network of fraternities and A. L. Miller sororities governed the students' social life. Notable Lanier alumni included several generations of all-state Georgia football and basketball stars along with John Birch, Class of '39, whose service as a Baptist missionary and American intelligence officer in China during World War II led to his death at the hands of Maoist insurgents and his martyrdom by a group of right-wing fanatics who in 1958 founded the "society" that bears his name.

Tall and thin, with wide cheekbones, a jutting chin, and a wry squint that earned him the nickname "Tokyo," Phil Walden's good looks, quick tongue, and brashly confident manner made him a ringleader of his social circle in high school. A bright but indifferent student, Phil joined

Phil

a fraternity, Lambda Tau Beta; contributed a record column called "Platter Chatter" to the school newspaper; and ran with a crowd that was considered somewhat arty and offbeat by the standards of Lanier High. Many of his friends came from families that were distinctly better off than his own; they were the sons of lawyers, businessmen, and corporate executives, and to judge by their subsequent careers, a number of them had artistic leanings. Jimm Roberts became a successful commercial photographer; Seaborn Jones became a published poet; Stephen Chanin became a jazz drummer. As a group, they shared an interest in voguish writers such as Henry Miller and Tennessee Williams (who had briefly lived in Macon during the summer of 1942), vied with one another to see who could look more like the doom-struck Hollywood icon James Dean, and prided themselves on their prowess at smoking and drinking and raising hell. Phil's role was that of an organizer and an arbiter. It was he who bestowed nicknames on his friends and teased them with a zest that could verge on cruelty at times; he who voiced his opinions on music and art and film and fashion with an avid certainty that was easily interpreted as arrogance. On a more practical level, with a steady girlfriend and a full complement of part-time jobs, Phil exuded a certain maturity and worldliness. By his senior year at Lanier, in the words of his classmate Bobby Wallace, he was literally "too cool for school."

Still, behind his brash demeanor, Phil Walden was carrying a considerable chip on his shoulder during his years at Lanier High. Race was only the most obvious social division in Macon. Like most southern communities of any appreciable size, the city had a sharply stratified class structure based not only on income, occupation, and place of residence but also on heritage, reputation, and extended family ties. By these standards, the Waldens were first-generation Maconites, with shallow roots in the community. While C. B.'s white-collar job as a salesman and Carolyn's obvious refinement made them nominally middle class, their family was lacking in the trappings of conspicuous consumption that affirmed a middle-class lifestyle in the booming suburban milieu of the time. Nor did it necessarily enhance the self-esteem of a young man who considered himself to be a good deal smarter and more sophisticated than most of his peers to be known to hundreds of local residents as their "paperboy." The Waldens' tenuous economic status ensured that as Phil grew older, he became increasingly obsessed with keeping up appearances in both the social and sartorial senses of the word. While some of his high school classmates sought to rise through the ranks of the cadet corps, or distinguish themselves on the playing field, Phil set out at an early age to earn money and the respect it could command.

Atlantic Records' Jerry Wexler once described Walden as the "archetype" of the young white Southerners who were enthralled by their exposure to black music on records and radio during the 1950s. Just as many children who came of age during the postwar era would later insist that *theirs* was the first family on their street to acquire a television set, many white teenagers of the period remember their discovery of black music as a uniquely personal experience. But as Wexler's statement affirms, the phenomenon was widespread. Phil Walden was hardly the only white teenager in Macon who tuned in to Hamp Swain's "King Bee" show on WMBL and thrilled to the musical provocations of Little Richard and Hank Ballard; as his schoolmate Seaborn Jones recalled, "I think that vicarious attitude was in a lot of us white boys." What made Phil different was not so much his enthusiasm for black music as the ways he found to act on that enthusiasm.

In the fall of 1957, at the start of his senior year, Walden was elected president of his high school fraternity. He wasted no time in combining his new executive powers with his passion for popular music by hiring Hamp Swain to host a rush party, where the brothers of Lambda Tau Beta entertained the pledges by lip-synching to a selection of current hit records. Later in the school year, most likely on Swain's recommendation, Walden hired Percy Welch to perform at an LTB dance. As far as anyone can remember, they were the first black band to play for a fraternity party at Lanier. "Up until then our high schools used white bands, very clean cut, in white dinner jackets, playing very middle-of-the-road–type music," Phil's brother Alan recalled. Welch's appearance was such a rousing success that other fraternities and sororities contacted Phil and asked him to provide them with bands. One of the groups he hired was Pat Teacake and the Mighty Panthers, with Bill Jones singing lead.

Walden's next step was to enlist a group of black teenagers—one was a carhop at the Pig 'n' Whistle Drive-In, another was a porter at the Greyhound bus terminal—who sang in a doo-wop quartet called the Heartbreakers. After rehearsing the group for several weeks in his girlfriend Violet Neblet's living room, he encouraged them to enter the *Teenage Party* talent show at the Douglass Theatre. Though barred from attending the show by the Jim Crow laws, Phil would sit in his car on the street outside, listening to the live broadcasts on WIBB while the Heartbreakers lost, week after week, to Otis Redding.

PHIL WALDEN GRADUATED from Lanier High School in June of 1958. In September, he enrolled at Mercer, thereby becoming the first male in his family to attend a four-year college. His choice of Mercer seems to have been based on pure proximity: it allowed him to stay close to home and close to his circle of friends, many of whom joined him at the school. To defray the cost of his tuition, he took a part-time job as a salesman at Ben Jones, an upscale clothing store that specialized in the latest fashions. Ben Jones was a cut above his uncle Roy's store, and Phil's job there put him in contact with some of Macon's most affluent residents. It also allowed him to indulge his growing obsession with dressing well.

Like the city of Macon itself, Mercer University in the fall of 1958 remained all but untouched by the social turmoil that was spreading across the South in the wake of the *Brown* decision and its immediate aftershocks in Montgomery and Little Rock. Founded in Penfield, Georgia, in 1837 and relocated to Macon shortly after the Civil War, Mercer was an all-white, Baptist-affiliated institution with an enrollment of eleven hundred undergraduates, 90 percent of whom came from within the state, 50 percent from Macon itself. Many of the buildings on its campus were named after prominent members of Middle Georgia's bygone planter aristocracy, who had relied on the college and its law school to educate their sons and, from 1923 onward, daughters. The political and legal establishment of Georgia had been heavily populated by Mercer alumni, whose ranks included numerous governors, senators, congressmen, judges, and state legislators. In 1939, however, the tensions between Mercer's Southern Baptist orthodoxy and its status as a modern university came to a head when a group of undergraduates led by Lanier's own John Birch filed formal charges of "heresy" against five of their professors, alleging offenses that ranged from teaching evolution to denying the existence of "demons." Though the professors were subsequently acquitted after a day-long trial by a special committee of trustees, the controversy caused an uproar on the campus, led to the resignations of several senior faculty, and made a laughingstock of the school.

In the years after World War II, under the leadership of a new president, Mercer set out to restore its standing by recruiting a nucleus of southern-born, northern-educated faculty, centered in the Christianity Department, whose teaching reflected the progressive precepts of the social gospel. The most charismatic of these newcomers, a theologian educated at the Yale Divinity School named G. McLeod Bryan, served as a mentor to a group of students who became known on the campus as Bryanites. In 1950, one of Bryan's students caused a stir when he and his wife joined the congregation of a local black Baptist church. A few years later, another of Bryan's students was arrested and briefly jailed by Bibb County sheriffs' deputies for the nonexistent offense of entertaining a black friend in his home. In 1956, when Governor Marvin Griffin attempted to ban the Georgia Tech football team from competing against an integrated opponent in the Sugar Bowl, the Bryanites organized a protest march. By that time, however, Professor Bryan's outspoken support of Dr. Martin Luther King Jr. and the Montgomery Bus Boycott was proving too much for the Mercer administration, whose efforts to curtail his teaching responsibilities led to his resignation from the school. "I left because I said there is no way you can breathe in Georgia," Bryan wrote. "You can't go to the drugstore, you can't take a bus ride, you can't go to a ballgame, you can't go to church, you can't go anywhere, without race. . . . Who wants to spend your life in a place in which every single moment of your existence has to do with race?" His departure came as a reminder that the progressive views of the Christianity Department, while influential, were by no means shared by a majority of the Mercer community. A poll conducted by the student newspaper shortly before Phil Walden's enrollment showed that 60 percent of the undergraduates favored continuing the university's whites-only policy. That same year, the Mercer debate team attracted national attention when it toured northern colleges defending the proposition that racial segregation should be maintained throughout the South.

Notwithstanding his growing involvement with the local black music scene, Phil Walden showed little interest in social activism during his four-year career at Mercer. After briefly entertaining the possibility of majoring in art, Phil settled on economics as a more practical course of study. His extracurricular activities consisted of enlisting in Mercer's Reserve Officers Training Corps and joining a popular fraternity, Phi Delta Theta (the national chapter of which, to its credit, had recently abolished a covenant restricting its membership to "white persons of full Aryan blood"). Both of these affiliations reflected Phil's belief that attending college was more an avenue for social advancement—or as he put it, "a social obligation"—than an intellectual pursuit. Any additional time and energy he had to spare was channeled into entrepreneurship rather than altruism. This included his paper route, his job at Ben Jones, and his fledgling career as a booking agent.

Throughout his freshman year, Walden continued to provide bands for fraternity and sorority dances at Lanier and Miller as well as Mercer and Wesleyan, the venerable women's college that helped to offset the two-to-one male-to-female ratio among Mercer undergraduates. In addition to these local dates, Phil found that he could use the so-called "Greek network" to expand the reach of his booking operation to nearby universities like Emory, Auburn, and the University of Georgia. With college enrollments at an all-time high, fraternities and sororities were a dominant feature of student life on many campuses in the 1950s, especially at the big universities, and especially in the South, where they provided a respite from the social conservatism of the prevailing culture. Many southern fraternities and sororities spent lavishly on entertainment, hosting dances, pledge parties, and mixers, often at off-campus clubs and restaurants where alcohol could be served. Rather than operate on a commission basis, Walden would pay his bands a set amount (generally much more than they could earn by playing at a black club), strike his own deal with the fraternity, and pocket the difference. While he was by no means the only person booking black bands at white colleges in the South, it does appear that he was one of the first, apart from Clint Brantley, to do so in Middle Georgia. Still, the logistics of the operation could be dicey. Bandleaders like Pat Teacake and Percy Welch presided over loose agglomerations of musicians who often lacked reliable transportation and left a lot to be desired in the way of a professional attitude. (Walden recalled that the first time he booked Welch's band, they showed up an hour late and neglected to bring a sound system.) To compensate for this, Phil took to borrowing his family's car and chaperoning his bands to their gigs. He also prevailed upon some of his friends to play this role, among them Seaborn Jones, who not only served as a designated driver for Pat Teacake and the Panthers, but also invited the group to rehearse in his family's home when his parents were away. For Phil as well, there was a clandestine aspect to his involvement. "When I initially started booking bands," he later said, "I didn't even tell my father I was doing it. My mother knew that I was doing it . . . but my father didn't have a clue."

It is unclear if Phil Walden had any influence on Johnny Jenkins's decision to split with Pat Teacake in the spring of 1959 and form his own band. What is certain is that, by the summer of that year, Phil's aspirations as an agent-manager were firmly focused on Jenkins, who epitomized the flamboyant Little Richard style of performance that had attracted him to black music in the first place. "I thought my entire world revolved around Johnny Jenkins's guitar," he later said. "I was convinced he could have been the greatest thing in rock 'n' roll. He had all the earmarks of stardom. He looked the part, he played the part, he acted the part." By the time Phil met Otis Redding at Lakeside Park in the summer of 1959, he had heard Otis sing on the *Teenage Party* radio broadcasts and most likely had seen him perform with Pat Teacake over the previous year. But up until the moment when Jenkins introduced them, from Phil's perspective, Otis was just a singer in Johnny Jenkins's band.

OTIS AND PHIL

I do not want you to see so much of the physical as of the spiritual town, and first you must see the color line. It stands at the depot with "waiting room for white people" and "waiting room for colored people," and then the uninitiated might lose sight of it; but it is there, there and curiously wandering, but continuous and never ending. And in that little town, as in a thousand others, they have an eleventh commandment, and it reads "Thou shalt not Cross the Line." . . . And yet you must not think the town inhabited by anything inhuman. Simple, good hearted folks are there—generosity and hospitality, politeness and charity, dim strivings and hard efforts—a human world, aye, even lovable at times; and one cannot argue about that strange line—it is simply so.

—W. E. B. DU BOIS

IN HIS COMING-OF-AGE NOVEL *YOUNGBLOOD*, SET IN MACON IN THE late 1930s, John Oliver Killens describes an encounter between his main character, a precocious black teenager named Rob Youngblood, and an older white man named Oscar Jefferson, who works with Rob at the Oglethorpe, a thinly fictionalized version of Macon's Dempsey Hotel. One night after work, Oscar takes Rob aside to warn him that his talk of unionizing his fellow workers has come to the attention of the hotel manager, jeopardizing Rob's job and possibly even his safety. As the estranged son of a murderous plantation overseer, Oscar lives in a state of quiet rebellion against his racist upbringing; earlier in the story, seated in the whites-only section of a jubilee concert at the City Auditorium, he is moved to tears by the singing of a chorus of black schoolchildren. For his part, Rob doesn't know what to make of Oscar's warning: "He wanted desperately to trust this white man with the friendly face and the eyes that were crying out loud to be trusted, but how could he trust him in Crossroads, Georgia?" Instead, standing on the corner of Cherry Street, Rob limply shakes Oscar's extended hand, cursing himself for his timidity while reminding himself, "He was still a white man in Georgia. He was still a cracker and couldn't be trusted. He wanted to trust him, this plain-faced friendly-looking white man, but something wouldn't let him."

In Phil Walden's recollection, he and Otis "really hit it off instantly." Otis himself never had a chance to comment on their first encounter, but Phil's sense of an immediate connection is best taken as an expression of his admitted "naïveté," for the notion that a nineteen-year-old white college student and a seventeen-year-old black high school dropout could "hit it off instantly"—at least in the sense that Phil meant—was as implausible in Macon, Georgia, in the summer of 1959 as it was in "Crossroads, Georgia" twenty years before. What Phil meant was that he liked Otis right away, and that Otis seemed to like him as well. At the time, what Phil could not understand was something that generations of white people in the Jim Crow South had failed to understand, which was how adept black Southerners were at giving white Southerners the impression that they "liked" them. For blacks in the South, the ability to ingratiate themselves with whites was an essential social skill, especially in the case of whites who were in a position to do them significant harm or good.

As a fan of Johnny Jenkins and a potential source of bookings for his band, Phil Walden was in a position to do Otis Redding some good, and Otis responded accordingly, with a mixture of charm, curiosity, calculation, and caution, for as Richard Wright described it: "Even when a white man asked us an innocent question, some unconscious part of us would listen closely, not only to the obvious words, but also to the intonations of voice that indicated what kind of answer he wanted; and automatically, we would determine whether an affirmative or negative reply was expected, and we would answer, not in terms of objective truth, but in terms of what the white man wished to hear." It takes nothing away from the bond that these two young men would form in the years ahead to acknowledge that, in the early stages of their relationship, Phil had no idea what he was dealing with, and it was mainly up to Otis to navigate the gulf of incomprehensibility and mistrust that lay between them. As Phil would later recognize, "You didn't trust a white man if you were a black man in the late fifties. . . . I was part of this white group that had created these laws to restrict their lives. 'Keep them in their place' was the common expression at the time."

Of the many social fantasies that pervaded the Jim Crow South, none inspired more contempt among blacks than the belief of many whites that they enjoyed a special familiarity and intimacy with blacks by virtue of living in proximity to them. In small rural communities outside the Black Belt where poor whites and poor blacks sharecropped side by side, there may have been some truth to this. But it wasn't white sharecroppers who touted this notion of a special bond. Rather, it was middle- and upper-class whites who based this belief on their contacts with the blacks who worked for them as domestic servants and manual laborers. Phil Walden's comment about his first Little Richard concert—that he had never been around so many black people in his life—speaks volumes about the social invisibility of African Americans and their culture to the white residents of Macon, at a time when blacks made up nearly half the population of the city. During the years when Otis and Phil were growing up there, black cooks, maids, and "yard boys" worked in the homes of white people, black laborers worked under the supervision of white bosses and foremen, black waitstaff served white customers at local restaurants, and black customers patronized shops and businesses that were owned and operated by whites. Apart from these economically structured forms of contact, there was little social interaction between blacks and whites in Macon—a condition that only deepened over the course of the 1950s, as growing numbers of whites moved into the new suburban subdivisions on the outskirts of town. Under these circumstances, it was beyond presumptuous for whites to believe that they possessed a privileged form of insight into black people and their lives. Instead, in their ignorance, southern whites were free to see southern blacks precisely as they needed to see them in order to preserve their sense of how the world should be.

For blacks, however, the level of social knowledge was very different.

Black servants spent long hours in the homes of white people, observing their domestic lives on an intimate level. Black laborers monitored the behavior and expectations of their employers with an eye toward staying in their good graces and keeping their jobs. In the daily interactions of life in cities like Macon, whether walking on the street, entering a shop, or delivering a bag of groceries, it was largely up to blacks to navigate public and private space in a manner that made whites feel comfortable. To do this successfully, black people paid close attention to the ways of white people. As the social historian Leon Litwack noted, "For black men and women to know white folks—their whims, expectations, moods, and moves—was more than a matter of curiosity; their very survival depended on such knowledge, and they had every opportunity to acquire it."

THE CANON OF southern literature includes a small but searing subgenre of memoirs and autobiographical essays by white authors recounting their struggles to free themselves from the doctrines and dogmas of white supremacy into which they were born and bred. The literary critic Fred Hobson has applied the term *racial conversion narratives* to these accounts, which first appeared in the late 1940s in the work of two Georgia-born authors, Lillian Smith and Katherine Lumpkin, followed a decade later by a Virginian named Sarah Patton Boyle and a growing number of other writers whose racial attitudes were transformed by their involvement in the civil rights movement.

It was surely no accident that the first of these books were written not only by women but by women of remarkably similar backgrounds. Lillian Smith, Katherine Lumpkin, and Sarah Boyle were all born around the turn of the century into the first generation of Southerners who grew up with segregation as an established fact of life. All were raised in "fine old families" whose forebears owned large slave plantations, by genteel parents who epitomized the spirit of noblesse oblige, and who exposed their daughters to the full force of high-church southern Christianity. In the case of Smith and Lumpkin, the similarity went even further, since both of them lived their adult lives as closeted lesbians, an orientation that led

Smith in particular to write about the links between sexual repression and racial oppression ("the sex-race-sin cycle," as she put it) in psychologically trenchant terms.

Finally, all three women traced the dawn of their awakening to the reality of racism in the South to an epiphany that made them aware of their own racial identity and challenged some basic precept of the Christian values with which they were raised. For Lillian Smith, it involved her parents' adoption of an indigent girl who appeared to be white but was later found out to be mulatto, at which point she was immediately cast out of their home. For Katherine Lumpkin, it involved the sight of her beloved, gentlemanly father viciously thrashing their family cook for "talking back" to his wife. Sarah Boyle's epiphany came later in life, as a result of conversations with a black newspaper editor in Charlottesville who agreed to her request that he speak frankly with her about race.

These experiences caused each of these writers to come at their subject from a slightly different angle. Lillian Smith focused on the utter artificiality of racial distinctions, the commitment to unreality that was necessary to sustain them, and the moral cowardice of the many white Southerners who recognized the evils of the Jim Crow regime but did nothing to challenge or change it. A Freudian, Smith also dared to write about the strong homoerotic attraction that many white men felt for black men in the South, the mixture of admiration and jealousy they felt for black male sexuality, and the toxic consequences of their efforts to keep these feelings hidden. Katherine Lumpkin's domineering father had been a well-known southern patriot and proselytizer for the Lost Cause ("how the plaster walls of our parlor rang with tales of the South's sufferings," she wrote). The revelation of his brutishness caused her to concentrate on debunking the historical myth of the South as a land of gentility, honor, and virtue that reached its fullest expression in *Gone with the Wind*. And for her part, Sarah Boyle wrote with devastating honesty about the sanctimony and paternalism of genteel whites like herself, whose racism took the form of benevolence rather than antipathy: "It was proper—indeed, it was Southern—to be friendly and chatty with all Negroes, provided you watched the emotional balance and instantly withdrew into a more formal attitude if a note of equality crept in. . . . My paternalistic relationship to

Negroes gave me the release of unobstructed, uncostly love, and provided me with easily found ways of proving myself gentle, high-principled, and kind. I thought my relationship with Negroes altogether beautiful."

In their different ways, Smith, Lumpkin, and Boyle all arrived at the same unpopular if self-evident conclusion that the sociologist Gunnar Myrdal reached in his groundbreaking 1944 study, *An American Dilemma*: that the "Negro problem" in the South and throughout America lay with whites, not blacks. And all three were inspired by their Christian beliefs to seek a form of "redemption" very different from the meaning most Southerners applied to that word: the redemption of a society that was corrupted and stunted by its fictions and fantasies of white supremacy and black inferiority. Referring to the cultural impoverishment of the white South, Lillian Smith wrote, "It is one of the many paradoxes of our way of life that among the dominant free, talent was so bound by anxiety that it could not be released, while among the slaves and the segregated, talent burst forth spontaneously. . . . The creative activities of Negroes were for a long time limited to what could be done with their bodies, for that was all they had to do with. Their songs and dance, their spirituals and their jazz, were welcomed by all the people of the Western world as hungrily as an undernourished child eats candy. For these creations, this poignancy of song, this access to sorrow and abandon to instinctual rhythms, met a deeper need than most realized, reuniting us with a part of ourselves so long hidden away in shame."

The personal journeys that Smith, Lumpkin, and Boyle recounted would be joined in the late 1950s and early 1960s by a growing number of white Southerners that included Phil Walden and most of his immediate family. That said, there was nothing obvious in Phil's upbringing or education that might have accounted for the sort of "conversion" experience these writers described. The closest thing to an epiphany in Phil's racial narrative was the Little Richard concert he attended at the Macon City Auditorium in 1955. (Family members liked to joke that Phil's sympathies may have been enlisted by an African American nursemaid he had in Greenville, but the Jim Crow South would have been a very different place if the experience of being suckled by a black woman in infancy caused whites to renounce their racist views.) Nor was there anything in the education Phil received in the Macon schools that would have encouraged him to question the South's racial orthodoxy. Like most high schools of the 1950s in the North and the South alike, Lanier taught its students a carefully hedged version of American history in which slavery was a southern "tradition," the Civil War was a conflict between "brothers," Reconstruction was a "troubled" period in the nation's past, and the subject of race in the modern era was scrupulously ignored. Phil's experience at Mercer, on the other hand, may have had a moderating effect, since the school, like many private colleges in the South, was inching toward integration during his tenure there. A 1961 poll showed that the student body had reversed itself on the subject of admitting blacks, which they now favored by a two-thirds margin. But the actual admission of a black student would not take place until a year after Phil's graduation.

As for his family, Phil was forthright in describing his father as "an out-and-out racist" who routinely referred to "niggers" and sharply disapproved—at first—of his son's infatuation and involvement with black music. As a salesman at Gay Clothing, C. B. Walden dealt with a sizable black clientele, and he was skilled in the art of solicitous patronization with which white merchants treated their black customers. (Phil would recall with a mixture of amusement and embarrassment his father's ability to persuade bereaved relatives to purchase a new hat along with the burial suit for their loved one, sealing the deal with the cheerful assurance that "Size doesn't matter!") Phil's mother, on the other hand, was regarded by virtually everyone who knew her, white and black, as the very model of a gracious southern lady. Like the racial conversion writers, Carolyn Walden was descended from a fine old family of former slaveholders, and the gentility of her background, together with her devout Methodism, imbued her with a set of racial attitudes similar to the ones that Sarah Boyle described. Phil identified strongly with his mother's "aristocratic" heritage; as her favorite son, he seems to have absorbed some of her racial orientation as well. Indeed, for Phil and his brother Alan, their struggle with racism would not center on learning to "like" black people; rather, it would center on moderating the reflexive paternalism that would pervade their relationships with Otis Redding, Johnny Jenkins, and the many other black artists they would deal with in the years ahead.

Those attitudes would shortly be tested, for 1960 was the year that the civil rights movement came to Georgia. To be sure, there had been skirmishes up to that point. In January 1957 a group of black clergymen in Atlanta had sought to emulate their colleagues in Montgomery by challenging their city's policy of segregated seating on buses. But it had taken two full years for their case to inch through the courts and for a federal judge to void the statute and desegregate the city's bus lines.

Starting in 1960, however, the pace of change quickened beyond all expectation. In February of that year, the Rev. Dr. Martin Luther King Jr. left his congregation in Montgomery and returned home to Atlanta, joining his father at the pulpit of the Ebenezer Baptist Church. King's return to Georgia was greeted by a statement from Governor Ernest Vandiver: "Wherever M. L. King Jr. has been there has followed in his wake a wave of crimes including stabbings, bombings, and inciting of riots, battery, destruction of property, and many others. For these reasons, he is not welcome in Georgia. Until now, we have had good relations between the races."

In the same week that Dr. King came home, four freshmen at North Carolina's all-black Agricultural and Technical College entered a Woolworth's in Greensboro and sat down at the lunch counter there. Refused service, they remained in their seats for the rest of the afternoon. The next day, their "sit-in" was joined by nineteen of their fellow students; the day after that, by sixty-two more. By the weekend, their number had grown to more than four hundred. The following week, sit-ins took place in Raleigh, Durham, and Winston-Salem. By the end of February, demonstrations like these were occurring on a daily basis in more than thirty cities across the South. In March, the sit-in movement reached Savannah, while in May, on the sixth anniversary of *Brown v. Board of Education*, 1,500 students from Atlanta University marched quietly through the streets of the city. "I didn't know there were that many niggers *in* college," one white bystander told a reporter at the scene.

ZELMA

She not only loved him, she worshipped him.

—LOUISE REDDING

As the kid brother of three older sisters, Otis Redding grew up surrounded by enough female attention to make him feel comfortable and confident around the opposite sex from an early age. ("For some reason, girls used to love him, always," his brother Rodgers said.) Throughout his teenage years in Bellevue and Tindall Heights, Otis did not lack for female company, but he had avoided any steady relationships, preferring to play the field. ("He would fall in love with someone one week, and then fall in love with someone else the next week," Charles Huckabee recalled.) In the summer of 1959, however, right around the time he first met Phil Walden, Otis's eye was caught by the looks and style of a petite seventeen-year-old by the name of Zelma Atwood, who lived with her parents on Jackson Street Lane, a short walk down Telfair Street from the projects in Tindall Heights.

Zelma's father, James, had worked for many years as a clerk at the Timberlake Wholesale Grocery on Plum Street; her mother, Essie, better known as Bee Bee, took in laundry and kept a spotless house. Zelma was a rarity among African American families in Macon—an only child. (Her parents had lost a son in infancy before she was born.) A year younger than Otis, she had followed him through B. S. Ingram and on to Ballard-Hudson, though the two of them had no contact with each other at either school. After dropping out of high school in the spring of 1958 at the end of her sophomore year, Zelma found work at a restaurant in downtown Macon. She first became aware of Otis later that year, when she saw him perform at one of the *Teenage Party* talent shows, after which Otis approached her on the street ("Hey baby!") and Zelma brushed him off ("You don't know me, and I'm not your *baby*").

Following a number of subsequent chance encounters that served mainly to reinforce the impression that Zelma did not suffer fools lightly, she and Otis finally had a civil conversation outside the Grand Dukes Club on Poplar Street at one of the Pinetoppers' many engagements there, and they began seeing one another regularly in the fall of 1959. He was her first real boyfriend. Physically, they were an odd couple. Zelma stood just over five feet tall and wore a size 3 dress, which made her look tiny next to Otis's gangly height. Otis's friends professed to be mystified by his interest in her, for while Zelma was pert and pretty and well turned out, neither her face nor her figure conformed to the prevailing adolescent ideal. ("I'm a plain Jane," she would later say. "I'm not a hot fashion woman. I'm *me*.") But whatever she lacked in size and shape she made up for in personality, and there was nothing superficial about Otis and Zelma's mutual attraction. They had been dating for only a few months when Zelma learned she was pregnant, in February 1960. (Birth control was a taboo subject among most southern blacks at this time.) There was never any doubt that Zelma would have the baby or that her mother, Bee Bee, would help her care for it. The only real question was how her eighteen-year-old boyfriend would respond to the prospect of fatherhood.

Otis's initial response did not inspire confidence. Shortly after learning that Zelma was pregnant, he announced plans to spend some time with his relatives in Los Angeles, ostensibly in an effort to get something happening with his singing career. He assured Zelma and her parents that he loved her and that, one way or another, he would return to Macon before the baby was due. The Atwoods responded with the skepticism that any sane people would feel under the circumstances.

Otis arrived in Los Angeles by bus in February 1960. He moved in with his mother's brother Willie Roseman, who got him a job at a car wash, and began looking for ways to involve himself in the local music scene. Though this was Otis's first experience outside of the South, little about it was different apart from the vastly greater scale of his surroundings. Los Angeles in 1960 was one of the largest and most rigidly segregated cities in America, ruled by an avowedly white-supremacist police chief, William J. Parker, whose department, with the full blessing of the city's administration, had virtually declared war on the 400,000 residents of the sprawling black ghetto that spread west from Central Avenue and south from the downtown. ("The police of Los Angeles fall just a stone's throw short of being as Jim Crow as if the department were situated in the heart of Georgia," a local black newspaper declared.) More than a quarter of the city's black families lived below the poverty line, while the rate of black unemployment ranged above 13 percent. For the 300,000 African Americans who had arrived there since 1940, Southern California had proved to be a very dour vision of the Promised Land.

Within a few weeks, at a barbershop on Central Avenue, Otis met a twenty-three-year-old singer and songwriter from Gulfport, Mississippi, named Jackie Avery. Avery had come to Los Angeles the year before at the invitation of Don Henry, a high school friend from Gulfport, who was working for the post office and playing the saxophone on weekends with an R&B revue called Don Henry and the Senders. Most nights, Henry's group was fronted by Bobby Day, a paradigmatic "one-hit wonder" whose irresistibly catchy recording of "Rockin' Robin" had risen to #2 on the Pop charts in 1958. They played at military bases up and down the California coast and were booked into obscure clubs in the hinterlands of Southern California and western Arizona by a part-time promoter and bail bondsman named Lawrence Wells.

Like Clint Brantley, Wells capitalized on the isolation of the local R&B scene by having his acts impersonate East Coast recording stars. (One of his singers billed himself as James Brown Jr., with the *Jr.* in tiny print.) Otis's talent for musical mimicry made him a natural for Wells's scam. "He could imitate anybody," Avery recalled—and he was soon going out on weekends with Henry's group pretending to be Barrett Strong, whose hit single "Money (That's What I Want)" spent twenty-one weeks on the R&B charts in 1960 but whose face was virtually unknown west of the Mississippi. On one such occasion, returning from a gig in Tijuana, the entire group was detained at the border when a customs agent noticed that Otis's identification didn't jibe with the name beneath his photograph on the poster affixed to their car.

As advertised by the eponymous architecture of the newly built Capitol Records Tower, looming over the fabled intersection of Hollywood and Vine, the music business in Los Angeles was in a rapid ascent at the time of Otis's arrival. The glamour and money of Hollywood had been luring successful singers and songwriters to the city since the 1920s, but the actual music business had remained firmly rooted "back east" until the 1950s, when the aggressive expansion of film studios like Paramount and Warner Brothers into the recording industry combined with the growth of Capitol Records and the rise of the indie labels to turn Los Angeles into a recording center that by 1960 had begun to rival, and would soon surpass, New York.

Prior to that, a massive influx of migrants from the Gulf Coast states of Louisiana, Mississippi, and Texas during and after the war had transformed Southern California into the largest market for black entertainment west of Chicago, and it was the allure of this market that first prompted labels like Specialty and Imperial to enter the field of rhythm and blues. Yet it was indicative of the lingering parochialism of the Los Angeles music scene that both these labels achieved their greatest success by signing southern artists like Fats Domino and Little Richard and recording them back in New Orleans. In the late 1950s, however, a contingent of New Orleans's best session men joined the westward trek. Led by the drummer Earl Palmer and the sax player Plas Johnson, this cadre of Crescent City émigrés would play a major role in the emergence of the Los Angeles studio scene. Stylistically at home in every genre, equally adept at sight-reading or improvising arrangements, they finished what Atlantic Records and Ray Charles had started by bringing a standard of hip professionalism to a style of popular music that had previously been derided as child's play by many mainstream musicians and record executives. Though they performed on countless sessions for countless labels, Palmer and Johnson, together with guitarist René Hall, keyboard player Ernie Freeman, and bassist Red Callender, became colloquially known as the house band for Rendezvous Records, for whom they recorded a series of hit instrumentals, beginning with a rock 'n' roll arrangement of Glenn Miller's "In the Mood" that sold a million copies in 1959.

By the start of the 1960s, the major black recording stars who had made Los Angeles their home included all three of the singers who exerted a primary influence on Otis Redding: Little Richard, Ray Charles, and Sam Cooke. Richard was still ostensibly retired from show business and living in relative seclusion in the upscale black neighborhood of Lafayette Square. Charles had wasted no time in capitalizing on the crossover success of "What'd I Say" and his extraordinary deal with ABC-Paramount by recording an album of geographically themed songs called *Genius Hits the Road*. One of its tracks, his incomparable rendition of Hoagy Carmichael's "Georgia on My Mind," would shortly earn him his first #1 record on the Pop charts.

Sam Cooke, meanwhile, was consolidating his grip on a similar form of crossover success. When his contract with Keen Records expired in 1959, Cooke had severed his ties with Bumps Blackwell and continued his emulation of Harry Belafonte by signing with RCA. In typical major label fashion, RCA assigned its new black star to a pair of mainline producers, Hugo Peretti and Luigi Creatore, who were best known for their work with the crooner Perry Como. Their first effort together was a string-heavy debacle called "Teenage Sonata" that barely made the charts. Yet the failure of the record was a blessing in disguise, for it forced Cooke to repeat his earlier experience at Keen by once again asserting control over his material. He began by writing and recording a brilliant pop single, inspired by a recent road trip through Georgia. Titled "Chain Gang," the song combined a quartet-style backing of earthy grunts and mellow bass with a lyric that verged on social commentary in the nicest possible way. It was easily the best nongospel record that Cooke had ever made, and only the simultaneous release of Elvis Presley's operatic aria "It's Now or Never" confined it to #2 on the Pop charts during the summer of 1960.

It was during his stay in Los Angeles that Otis fell firmly under the spell of Sam Cooke. It would have been hard not to, given the recent surge in Cooke's success and his prominence in L.A.'s nascent black celebrity culture. In Macon, apart from the package shows that Clint Brantley brought to the City Auditorium, it was easy to live in the past, and to imagine that a singer like Little Richard retained some currency. The chitlin' circuit existed in a time warp; it was filled with artists milking the success of an old hit that gave them enough name recognition to pretend they were still in the game. But one could not hide from the present in music capitals like New York and Los Angeles. A recording artist was as popular as his last hit record, and in 1960, Sam Cooke, between his chart success and his sex appeal, was beginning to look like the black equivalent of Elvis Presley, his new stablemate at RCA. As Otis strived to assume some of the urban style of his new surroundings—among other things, he had his hair done in a "process"—Cooke's star was rising in his firmament.

THERE WAS LITTLE distinction on the "street" level between the music business and the film business in Los Angeles in 1960. The city was teeming with aspiring performers, producers, and pretenders of all description, looking for a break in any medium they could find. One such figure was James McEachin, a decorated Korean War veteran from North Carolina who was trying to make it as a record producer under the stage name Jimmy Mack. (Under his real name, McEachin would go on to enjoy a successful career as an actor, appearing with Clint Eastwood in *Play Misty for Me* and starring as a street-smart detective in the television series *Tenafly*.) McEachin had already met up with Jackie Avery, and after hearing Otis Redding sing, he decided to take the two of them on, inviting them to his home in Gardena to work on their songs and make some demo tapes. One of the tunes they rehearsed was a Little Richard–style rocker called "Gamma Lama," cowritten by Otis and Jackie with some help from Otis's cousin Benny Roseman; another was a plaintive ballad called "These Arms of Mine" that Avery had written and demoed at Chess Records in Chicago the year before.

Within a few weeks, McEachin began shopping the tapes of these rehearsal sessions around to the dozens of indie labels that dotted the musical landscape of Los Angeles. After failing to garner any interest from the big independents like Specialty, McEachin turned to Al Kavelin, a former society bandleader, music publisher, and practicing Jehovah's Witness who was in the process of starting a label called Lute. Kavelin had no affinity whatsoever for rhythm and blues, but he was about to experience an enormous stroke of luck. Around the time that McEachin approached him, a pair of Hollywood hustlers named Gary Paxton and Kim Fowley presented him with a song based on the popular comic-strip character Alley Oop. The tune had been written and recorded without success by a country singer named Dallas Frazier a few years before, but Paxton and Fowley proposed to recast it in the sardonic style of the Coasters. This inspiration prompted Al Kavelin to bankroll a riotous recording session where a drunken Paxton and an indeterminate cast of backup singers imbued the song with enough slurry swagger to propel it to the top of the Pop charts in the summer of 1960. Having inaugurated his record label with a million-selling single, Kavelin was suddenly in a position to throw some money at "Jimmy Mack" McEachin, who booked time for his two young protégés at Gold Star Studios in Hollywood and hired the house band from Rendezvous Records to back them up.

So it was that Otis Redding found himself standing in a recording studio for the first time in his life, surrounded by a band that included Earl Palmer and René Hall, musicians who had played on hits by his idols Little Richard and Sam Cooke. (Hall had been the arranger on the fateful "You Send Me" session that launched Cooke's secular career.) Working with their usual efficiency, the band arranged, rehearsed, and recorded four songs in three hours' time. Otis sang lead on three of the tracks: "Gamma Lama," "She's All Right," and "Gettin' Hip." Jackie and Otis shared the singing on the fourth, a song by James McEachin called "Tuff Enuff." The Blossoms, a female vocal group led by Darlene Love, sang backup on two of the numbers.

These Gold Star recordings are the first known examples of Otis Redding's voice on record. As recording debuts go, this one is remarkable for the extraordinarily high quality of the accompaniment and production; two months shy of his nineteenth birthday, Otis is supported, not by the usual collection of bar band amateurs, but by one of the most accomplished studio bands in the world. Earl Palmer provides all four of these uptempo tracks with a steady, surging backbeat and a battery of propulsive fills. Ernie Freeman's swirling organ lends a maniacal energy to the otherwise straightforward shuffle "Gettin' Hip," which is further enhanced by Plas Johnson's eloquent sax solo. Johnson also plays the piping flute on "She's All Right," a call-and-response number performed in the style of the great New Orleans novelty group Huey "Piano" Smith and the Clowns.

The surprise of the Lute recordings is the extent to which Otis manages to hold his own in the midst of this seasoned talent. Given the critique of his rhythmic feel by Gladys Williams, perhaps the most impressive feature of his performance is the sureness of his phrasing; on his three lead vocals, working within the context of tightly arranged backup singing, he never misses a beat. The overall sound and style of his delivery on "Gamma Lama" and "Gettin' Hip" confirm his reputation as a die-hard Little Richard imitator; though he avoids the outlandish falsetto mannerisms, there is no mistaking his debt to Richard's throaty timbre, convulsive delivery, and down-home diction. In his lyrics as well, Otis borrowed freely from Richard's songs. "She's All Right" echoes "The Girl Can't Help It" in extolling a girl with a "fig'guh that's made to squeeze"; "Gettin' Hip" reprises the "done got hip to your jive" sentiment of "Slippin' and Slidin'"; "Gamma Lama" trades on Richard's fondness for nonsense rhymes. (Otis had been singing some version of this song since his childhood, having taken the title from a one-eyed Macon street musician who sang the refrain "Bamalama, you shall be free / In the morning, you shall be free.")

The one song on which Otis did not sound at all like Little Richard was "Tuff Enuff," which was performed as a duet with Jackie Avery's voice predominating. In a straightforward attempt to mine the vein of "Alley-Oop," the song was done in the style of the Coasters, with a stuttery sax reminiscent of "Yakety Yak" and a lyric decrying the Soviet Union's recent success in sending a rocket to the moon: "Well I woke up this morning and I heard the news / They were shootin' at the moon, they're trying to blow out the fuse."

Of the four tracks they recorded, Al Kavelin and James McEachin selected "Tuff Enuff" and "She's All Right" for the single. Having decided to call the group The Shooters (a name derived from the "just a'shootin'" refrain of "Tuff Enuff"), they credited one side of the record to "The Shooters with Jackie," the other to "The Shooters with Otis."

Shortly after the Gold Star session, Al Kavelin signed his two new artists to a contract and presented each of them with a $100 advance. A few days later, as Jackie Avery recalled it, he and Otis had plans to meet at a clothing store in downtown Los Angeles to buy some new stage outfits. Otis never showed. The store was located a block from the Greyhound bus terminal and, unbeknownst to Avery, Otis had a promise to keep. Since his arrival in L.A., he had been writing Zelma on a regular basis, calling her from time to time, and sending her small amounts of cash. Don Henry was under the impression that Otis had received a phone call from someone back in Macon saying that if he didn't return of his own accord, they were going to come get him. But one way or another, Otis had taken his $100 and bought a bus ticket home.

A two-toned Cadillac purred to a stop on a sleazy block of Manhattan's West 45th Street. Out climbed a distinguished-looking, gray-haired man . . . For a moment, he stared dubiously at a hole-in-the-wall honky-tonk called the Peppermint Lounge, then rushed back to the waiting limousine burbling, "This is the place!"

—*TIME* magazine

OTIS ARRIVED BACK IN MACON AT THE END OF AUGUST AND IMmediately picked up where he had left off with the Pinetoppers, playing regular weekly gigs at the D.A.V. club on Poplar Street and the Royal Palm on Broadway. "Just Back from L.A. California: Otis 'Rockin'' Redding," read the ad in the *Telegraph*. Apart from his processed hair and his newly acquired taste for marijuana, Otis had left Los Angeles with little to show for his stay there, and there's no telling what his family and friends in Macon thought when he told them about making a record with the members of Sam Cooke's studio band. ("When he first came back and was telling people about it, they didn't believe him," Rodgers recalled.) Until Al Kavelin released the single, it was nothing but talk.

In September, Phil Walden sealed his status as a big man on the Mercer campus by winning election as the president of his Phi Delta Theta fraternity at the start of his junior year. He assumed the position with his usual energy and enthusiasm, organizing the fall rush season and instituting a community service program that was intended to give the house a more public profile. Phil was now dating Katherine Kennedy, a Wesleyan College sophomore who had been chosen as Phi Delt's official "sweetheart." The daughter of a local businessman, Kathy was an attractive, high-spirited young woman who rode horses and drove a white Chevy convertible that had once belonged to the pop crooner Pat Boone. Her family lived on Rivoli Drive in West Macon, directly across from the Wesleyan campus, in an expansive new house whose basement recreation room, equipped with the latest in consumer electronics, became a home away from home for the brothers of Phi Delta Theta. Dating Kathy Kennedy was a substantial step up the social ladder for Phil. Yet despite their affluent lifestyle, her parents were considered nouveau riche by the FOFs (fine old families) who ruled the social roost in Macon, and Kathy shared with Phil a certain sense of resentment toward the local grandees.

That same September, Phil took a big step toward formalizing his sideline as a booking agent by borrowing a few hundred dollars from the father of his close friend Lee Martin and joining with his fraternity brother Bobby Wallace, who contributed an equal amount of seed money, to rent an office for Phil Walden Artists and Promotions in the Professional Building on Mulberry Street, a few blocks north of the central business district. (As suggested by the name of the agency, Bobby Wallace was content to serve as a relatively silent partner in this fledgling enterprise.) With help from Otis and Sam Davis, Phil and Bobby painted the office, furnished it with a couple of army-surplus desks, and settled down to wait for the phone to ring. Phil had letterhead printed and sent out hundreds of inquiries and flyers to college fraternities throughout the Southeast. His description of their early operations sounds like a vaudeville routine: "I'd answer the phone in one voice, then lay the receiver down and make them wait, as if I'm too busy to talk. Then I'd come back on in my best New York voice, short and clipped." In addition to his duties as the road manager for the Pinetoppers, Sam Davis provided the agency with a liaison to the black clubs around Macon, while Phil and Bobby handled the bookings for the high school and college fraternities.

Along with various medical, legal, and insurance agency offices, the Professional Building was also the home of the studios of WIBB, a happy coincidence that afforded Phil and Otis a certain amount of casual contact with Hamp Swain, Satellite Papa, and the other deejays at the station. This proved helpful in October, when Al Kavelin released the two tracks from the Gold Star session, "Tuff Enuff" and "She's All Right." The single came out on the Trans World label, a subsidiary of Lute. Though neither track was designated the A-side, the listing in *Billboard*'s New

Releases featured "Tuff Enuff." "The side is done in Coasters style," the entry read. "Good sound and a lot of excitement. Merits a hearing." The write-up of "She's All Right" noted the presence of a "fem group" singing backup and advised, "Watch this one, too."

"Alley Oop" notwithstanding, Al Kavelin was an old-school song publisher who knew little about promoting a pop single, and the listing in *Billboard* marked the highpoint of the Shooters' recording career. (Kavelin would go on to release an unbroken string of flops in the early 1960s, including a cover of "She's All Right" by an openly gay country singer named Troy Walker.) Though its sales and airplay were negligible, the existence of the single did enable Phil Walden to start promoting Otis as a "recording artist" on the club and college circuit during the fall of 1960. An early mimeographed flyer advertised "Otis Redding and His Shooters Singing Their Trans-World Recordings" as the Walden agency's "special attraction." The flyer went on to list a roster of nearly a dozen acts, ranging from Johnny Jenkins and the Pinetoppers ("The South's Most Exciting Combo") to Sonny Cole, a corpulent Macon rockabilly singer who was locally known for his 1957 single "I Dreamed I Was Elvis."

The same month that the Trans World single was released, Zelma Atwood gave birth to a boy, christened Dexter. Zelma was so petite that she had to have a cesarian, which left Otis with a sizable hospital bill. Nevertheless, he celebrated the birth of his son by presenting Zelma with an engagement ring, borrowing the money for the down payment from his brother Rodgers, who had a steady after-school job. For the time being, Zelma and the baby continued to live with her parents at their home on Jackson Street Lane, while Otis continued to live mainly with his parents at their home in Tindall Heights. Bee Bee Atwood welcomed the arrival of Dexter as the son she never had, and Zelma was grateful for her mother's devotion to the child, for she was eager to return to work and get on with her life. Most days, Otis came by the Atwoods' house and spent several hours with his son. His concern for Dexter was encouraging, but from Zelma's perspective, this was a stormy period in their relationship. "We went through changes of him being out in the streets and stuff. We used to really go at it, 'cause all the girls liked him. He was popular. They liked him and I said I ain't gonna worry about these women. I'm gonna play my role because that's gonna be my man. The singing part, it didn't matter to me. He could have been a garbageman, he could have been anything. I loved him."

Though fraternity gigs remained the backbone of the Pinetoppers' tenuous livelihood, tensions were rising on some of the college campuses they relied on for steady work. In January 1961, on the eve of John F. Kennedy's inauguration, a federal judge named William Bootle ordered the University of Georgia to admit its first two black students, Charlayne Hunter and Hamilton Holmes. (A Macon resident and Mercer alumnus, Judge Bootle was promptly hung in effigy on both the Mercer and Athens campuses.) Undergraduate life at the University of Georgia was completely dominated by fraternities and sororities, many of which were in the forefront of opposition to the admission of blacks to the school. This meant that the Pinetoppers were now playing for the entertainment of some of the same fraternity brothers and sorority sisters who rioted outside the university's women's dormitory on Charlayne Hunter's second night there, throwing bricks through the windows of her room and chanting "One-two-three-four! We don't want no nigger whore!" As the mob of students grew to over a thousand, the state police referred all calls for help to the governor's office, which issued a statement saying, "The students at the university have demonstrated that Georgia youth are possessed with the character and courage not to submit to dictatorship and tyranny." The university itself responded with a more passive form of aggression, suspending Hunter and Holmes "in the interests of their own safety." Later, when the two students were reinstated by a court order, the administration forbade their families and friends from visiting them on the campus.

Because it involved one of white Georgia's most beloved institutions, Judge Bootle's ruling set off waves of reaction throughout the state. In Macon, the local chapter of the Ku Klux Klan held a cross-burning rally, and followed that up by burning crosses on the lawns of the cochairmen of the city's Council on Human Relations—one a white Mercer college professor (and former Bryanite), the other a black minister who had recently sent an open letter to Mayor Edgar Wilson and other city, county, and state officials urging them to use "sense and realism" in complying with recent federal court rulings. Mayor Wilson was himself a Mercer law pro-

fessor and a racial moderate who had formed a working relationship with
the president of the local branch of the NAACP, a wealthy black building
contractor named William Randall. With the support of W. T. Anderson, the longtime editor of the *Telegraph,* Wilson and Randall were laying
the groundwork for a series of initiatives that would lead in the months
ahead to the desegregation of Macon's municipal golf course, its public
library, and, following a peaceful campaign of sit-ins, the lunch counters
in the city's downtown department stores.

That same January, an incident occurred that Phil Walden would later
recount as a turning point in his relationship with Otis. As Phil described
it, he had "overspent" his resources ("on myself and others") during the
holiday season, and found himself with insufficient funds to pay the
two-hundred-dollar tuition he owed for his upcoming quarter at Mercer.
When he asked his father to loan him the difference, C. B. turned him
down. Sitting in his office with Otis one day, Phil looked so morose that
Otis asked him what was wrong. Phil explained the situation, describing
how humiliating it would be for him, as the president of his fraternity, to
have to withdraw from college for lack of funds. It was a "social disaster,"
he said. Otis listened and left, only to return few hours later with a paper
bag full of coins and crumpled bills, having solicited everyone he knew for
a contribution to the Phil Walden College Fund. Phil was "stunned" by
the gesture. "Up to that point it had always been me giving him or band
members money. Nobody had ever said, 'I care about you.' And he said,
'You know, if we're going to make it, it's really important you get that
education.'"

If nothing else, this anecdote illustrates the shifting mixture of ambition, calculation, and affection that underlay the bond forming between
Otis and Phil. Previously, the two of them had been playing out a familiar script of white paternalism and black dependence. Phil had been
drawing on his rudimentary business sense, his connections as a Mercer
student, and above all his status as a white man in Georgia to provide
Otis, Johnny Jenkins, and the other musicians he represented with a set
of rather meager opportunities they might not otherwise have had. And
Otis, in the time-tested manner of ambitious blacks in South, had been
ingratiating himself with a young white man who was in a position to

help him earn some money, further his musical ambitions, and afford him some degree of protection in his dealings with the white world. It was Phil who first deviated from this script, by revealing to Otis not only his financial predicament, but the loss of face it would cause him as well. And Otis responded, not with the nominal expressions of sympathy that would have sufficed, but with an act of empathy and generosity that utterly defied Phil's expectations. In *The Mind of the South*, W. J. Cash wrote of "the ancient Southern love of the splendid gesture." Otis's splendid gesture toward Phil was the first of many steps that would gradually level the ground between them.

For the time being, however, it was Johnny Jenkins, not Otis, who remained the apple of Phil's managerial eye. The Pinetoppers had settled into a routine of steady work on weekends, playing fraternity parties at Mercer, Georgia, Emory, Georgia Tech, Auburn, and Alabama on Friday and Saturday nights. On Sundays, they would start by playing a late-afternoon "music hour" at the Gay Knights Social Club on Anthony Road, then move on to a dance at the Middle Georgia Veterans Club on Cotton Avenue from 8:00 to 11:30, and then drive out to Club Fifteen in time to start their show at a minute past midnight on Monday morning, when liquor could again be sold legally in Jones County. A publicity photograph of the group from this period paints a clear picture of the nature of their appeal. It shows the five of them arrayed on a low stage dressed in dark blazers, bow ties, and scuffed-up jeans. Johnny Jenkins stands front and center, facing the camera directly, his guitar slung low, his legs splayed wide, his hair piled high on his head. He takes up more space than all the other band members combined as they crouch on either side of him like saints in a Renaissance painting. The only other upright figure is Otis, who stands way in the back, a head taller than Johnny but dressed in neutral tones that make him all but invisible against the backdrop of the stage.

Phil Walden's most immediate concern was to get Johnny Jenkins some kind of recording deal, which would increase the price the Pinetoppers could command on the college circuit. One Sunday in March of 1961, Phil stopped by the Lanier Hotel in Macon for a regular afternoon jam session that drew jazz-starved musicians and fans from all over Middle Georgia. One of the participants was a piano player in his early

Johnny Jenkins and the Pinetoppers, 1961

thirties named James Newton, who ran a real estate business in Tifton, a small town in the southern part of the state. Upon learning that this amiable Mercer alumnus was also the co-owner of a small record label called Tifco, Phil began singing the praises of Johnny Jenkins and the Pinetoppers.

James Newton was a part-time musician, not a record producer, but his partner was a transplanted Northerner named Gus Statiris, who had run a New York–based jazz label called Progressive before marrying a woman from Tifton, moving to Georgia, and opening a record shop in his wife's hometown. After determining that "selling jazz in Georgia is about as easy as selling ice to Eskimos," Statiris teamed up with Newton to record a local doo-wop group called the Tifanos, whose first and only offering on the Tifco label came out in 1960. Like many jazz fans, Newton and Statiris had little regard for rhythm and blues. But their main concern at this point lay with building enough of a catalog to lend them some credibility with their distributors, and given the available talent in South Georgia, they were in no position to be choosy. James Newton agreed to record Johnny Jenkins and the Pinetoppers without ever hearing them play. The contract he signed with Phil Walden in the spring of 1961 called for the two of them to split the expense of recording and pressing the first 1,000 copies of a single, with the cost of any additional pressing and promotion to be paid by Tifco. If and when Phil recouped his initial investment, he would receive a royalty of 15 percent on any additional copies of the record that sold. To describe this arrangement as paternalistic would be putting it mildly. Unlike standard recording contracts between an artist and a label, Johnny Jenkins's name, much less his signature, did not appear on the agreement Phil Walden signed with James Newton. In the event the record made money, any royalties that Jenkins received would come at his manager's discretion.

From Phil Walden's perspective, the point of the Tifco deal was to showcase Johnny Jenkins's skills as an instrumentalist, and there was never any question about having Otis Redding sing on the record. Otis, in any case, had other things on his mind. In July, Zelma learned that she was pregnant with their second child. Otis greeted the news by suggesting to Zelma that the time had come for the two of them to formalize their relationship. On August 17, with the Reverend C. J. Andrews of the Vineville Baptist Church presiding, Otis and Zelma were married at the Atwood home—though not before Otis had tried the patience of his bride and her parents by arriving more than an hour late for the ceremony. The newlyweds moved in with Zelma's widowed grandmother in her apartment in the Fort Hawkins district of East Macon. Their son, Dexter, remained with Zelma's parents on Jackson Street Lane.

Zelma recalled the intensity of Otis's belief in himself during this period—his conviction that he would succeed. "He was saying, 'I'm gonna be a star and I'm gonna make all this money and we're gonna have this, don't you worry.' And I'd say, 'Well, whatever. You gotta get a *job*, you know. I'm pregnant. How we gonna survive? I was determined to take a job and work, and he was determined to just go out and mess around with musicians all day. But everything he told me, I just believed him, because he believed in himself to the fullest." The money Otis made playing with the Pinetoppers on the weekends did not amount to much, ten dollars here, twenty dollars there, but he found a way to sabotage every day job he could find. After working for several weeks as an orderly at the Macon Hospital, Otis was singing to himself on the elevator one day when a doctor told him to keep his voice down. "So one word led to another," Zelma recalled, "and he *slaps* the doctor on the elevator. He didn't really want to be rolling those people around."

Otis continued to spend his abundant free time with his running buddies from Bellevue, including Sylvester Huckabee, who had returned to Macon after his release from Soledad Prison in California at the end of 1960. Prison had served as a kind of finishing school for Huck. Like many convicts, he had done a great deal of reading during his incarceration, absorbing a range of miscellaneous knowledge that he was fond of quoting to his friends. He also developed a bisexual orientation, which served mainly to add another option to his already formidable repertoire of physical domination. Having made his mark in the outside world, Huck had come home looking to apply the lessons he had learned on the street and in prison to establishing himself as the criminal kingpin of Bellevue. On one occasion, when Otis was badly beaten up after getting into a fight with a half dozen adversaries at a crap game in Pleasant Hill, Huck took great pleasure in organizing an appropriate response, which consisted of him and Otis and Bubba Howard cornering each of the assailants and beating them, individually, to a pulp. Otis's friendship with Huck did wonders for his reputation on the street, but the fierce loyalty they felt for one another transcended mere utility. In their different ways, Otis and Huck were the two most intelligent and charismatic members of their circle in Bellevue. Now that Huck had irrevocably "gone for bad," he seemed to feel a need to look out for Otis, even though his presence would prove a constant source of trouble in Otis's life.

Although James Newton and Gus Statiris ran Tifco Records on a shoestring, they did not stint when it came time to record the Pinetoppers. Late in the summer of 1961, they booked a three-hour session for the group at the NRC studios in Atlanta. (NRC was owned by Bill Lowery, a prominent music publisher whose ownership of the copyrights to Gene Vincent's "Be-Bop-A-Lula" and Sonny James's "Young Love" had helped him sign a bevy of rising country stars.) In Phil Walden's view, the recording date was "absolute chaos" on account of the difficulty he had rounding up the musicians and haggling with them over whether they would be paid for the session. Nevertheless, over the course of an afternoon, the Pinetoppers recorded a pair of instrumental tracks, both of them credited to Johnny Jenkins. "Pinetop" was a raucous shuffle dominated by Ish Mosley's honking sax. "Miss Thing" was a medium-tempo blues with a scampering rumba beat that served as a showcase for Jenkins's plaintive, piercing guitar.

The early 1960s were the swan song of the pop instrumental as a viable commercial form, with dozens of instrumental records placing high on the *Billboard* charts. Instrumentals had been the norm up through the 1940s, when the primary function of popular music was to provide accompaniment for dancers, and their resurgence in the early 1960s owed to the popularity of a new crop of R&B-oriented dances that were geared to the demographics of the youth market. The first of these dances to achieve a crazelike popularity was the Twist, which took its name from a 1959 single by Hank Ballard and the Midnighters, its form from the black teenagers who matched Ballard's record with a suggestive, swiveling dance step, and its fame from the promotional acumen of the pop impresario Dick Clark, who commissioned a more palatable version of the record after seeing a more palatable version of the dance performed by the white teenagers on his nationally syndicated *American Bandstand* television show. (The problem was not so much with the record itself as with the Midnighters' reputation as one of the bawdiest acts on the R&B circuit.) The beneficiary of Dick Clark's promotional largesse was a part-time singer and full-time poultry worker from Philadelphia named Earnest Evans, who had sought to follow in the portly footsteps of Fats Domino by calling himself Chubby Checker. Checker's note-for-note remake of Ballard's song was released in May of 1960. It entered the charts in August (sweeping aside a re-release of Ballard's original version), rose to #1 in September, and remained in the Top 10 for another two months.

As practiced by Chubby Checker and the model teenagers on "American Bandstand," the Twist was a mechanical, toned-down version of the sort of suggestive pelvic movement that first gained widespread popularity in the 1920s with jazz-inspired dances like the Charleston and the

Lindy Hop. (It also owed something to the Hula Hoop craze of the late 1950s.) But the salient feature of the Twist had less to do with the hips than the hands, for it extended the choreography of what dance instructors called "open position" to the point where the partners *never actually touched one another*. The crossing of this seemingly innocuous threshold would prove to have profound consequences, for it freed the very idea of social dancing from its traditional role as a courtship ritual and turned it into a form of individualized self-expression in which it wasn't always clear, or even particularly relevant, who was dancing with whom.

By the spring of 1961, the Twist had run its course as a teenage dance craze, and Chubby Checker had gone on to apply his slender talent to other lucrative song-and-dance combinations with names like the Pony and the Fly. But in the fall of that year, the Twist and the record that inspired it enjoyed an unprecedented resurgence when a clique of fashionable New York socialites, infatuated by the Parisian fad for *discothèque,* began to patronize a seedy, mob-run Times Square dance club called The Peppermint Lounge. In a matter of weeks, the New York fashion and society press picked up on this déclassé taste, which seemed to resonate with the new confluence of wealth, style, youth, and vigor epitomized by the Kennedys. National magazines and television networks quickly followed suit, sending Chubby Checker's entire oeuvre rocketing back up the charts.

News of this impending Twist revival reached Georgia in October, right around the time that Tifco was preparing to release the Pinetoppers' single. James Newton had already placed an initial order for a thousand copies with Nashville's RCA pressing plant. Surmising that "Miss Thing" was the more "twistable" side of the single, he now contacted RCA with instructions to change the title of the song to "Love Twist." Tifco released the renamed single in November. By the end of the month, the label had shipped enough copies to radio stations and distributors that Newton ordered a second thousand, followed, in late December, by a third. With any luck, Johnny Jenkins and the Pinetoppers would ride the wave of "America's newest adult dance craze" onto the national record charts. With Jackie Kennedy reportedly dancing the Twist at the White House, anything was possible.

He changed my life. I was really his son, and we became very, very close.

—PHIL WALDEN

I N February 1962, three months after the release of "Love Twist," Phil Walden was sitting in his office in the Macon Professional Building when he received a phone call from an unlikely-sounding character who introduced himself as Joe Galkin. Hemming and hawing in a pugnacious New York accent that must have caused Walden to question the caller's description of himself as an Atlanta-based record promotion man, Galkin announced that he had just purchased the rights to "Love Twist" from James Newton and needed to obtain Walden's signature on some paperwork related to the sale. The two men agreed that Galkin would stop by Walden's office the following day.

In person, Joe Galkin was even more of an anomaly in the milieu of Middle Georgia than he was on the telephone. A short, balding, pear-shaped man in his late fifties with a huge gut, a slight stammer, and an air of street-smart aggression, he came across like a refugee from a touring company of *Guys and Dolls*. His sharkskin suit and urban-ethnic demeanor only made Phil Walden more surprised to learn that Galkin had actually grown up on Forsyth Street in Macon, where his father, a Jewish tailor, had settled with his family after emigrating from Russia when Joe was two. Befitting a man who dealt in hyperbole for a living, the particulars of Galkin's past were hard to pin down. But at some point in the 1930s, after dropping out of Lanier High School and taking up the trumpet, he left Macon and made his way to New York, where he established himself first as a sideman, then as the manager of a genteel white dance band called the Tommy Tucker Orchestra, and eventually as the co-owner of a Queens nightclub called the Melody Lounge.

By 1950, Galkin was an established figure in the Broadway demimonde of agents, managers, song publishers, and record men who formed the human infrastructure of the music business in New York. Within a few years, however, the Melody Lounge went bankrupt, and Galkin, like many of his contemporaries, felt his livelihood threatened by the changing demographics of the music scene. (Notably, he had passed on the opportunity to manage the pop singer Johnny Ray, who became a teen sensation in 1952.) Unlike many of his contemporaries, however, Galkin read the writing on the wall. In the mid-1950s, flat broke, he moved to Atlanta and reinvented himself as the world's first freelance record promotion man. His self-assigned territory encompassed the Deep South from the Atlantic Ocean to the Mississippi River, and he covered this region the way he had once made the rounds of his show business haunts in New York, driving from town to town, radio station to station, a one-man exercise in culture shock. He courted the deejays, station owners, and record distributors of the South with bottles of bourbon, suitable applications of payola, and a relentless style of New York shtick that most of his clients knew mainly from television variety shows. (People often compared him to the comedian Buddy Hackett.) Stories abounded of Galkin marching into broadcast booths, lifting the needle off the current selection, and replacing it with an offering of his own. "It's a goddamn smash!" he'd say of any record he was promoting at a given moment.

Phil Walden's taste for the outlandish made him an easy mark for Joe Galkin's uncouth brand of charm. At their first meeting, Galkin explained how, having paid James Newton a thousand dollars for the rights to "Love Twist," he planned to re-release the record on his own label and see if he could generate enough regional interest to entice a larger label, most likely Atlantic, to distribute the record nationally. Though Galkin worked on a freelance basis for a number of record companies, his relationship with Atlantic was especially strong. Galkin and Atlantic's vice president Jerry Wexler shared a sense of kinship as classic Jewish types. (Many years later, Wexler would affectionately describe Galkin in his memoirs as an "obnoxious Hebe.") In the summer of 1961, Galkin had been instrumental in helping Atlantic promote a record by the R&B singer Solomon Burke, the success of which, coming on the heels of Ray Charles's departure, had restored Wexler's faith in the future of gospel-based rhythm and blues. From that point on, Wexler considered Galkin to be his roving ambassador to the Southland.

Record men like Joe Galkin were not to be confused with music fans. Regardless of their personal tastes, they acted on the basis of their own informed sense what the public would like, and they relied on a network of personal contacts to keep them abreast of what was happening—and more important, what was about to happen—in the record business. Joe Galkin was an unusually pure example of the species. Unlike the salaried sales representatives who worked for individual labels, Galkin's freelance status allowed him to pick and choose; whenever he heard a record he thought had potential, or when his contacts told him a new release was starting to generate airplay or sales, he would approach the label and offer his services. Once hired, he treated the success of the record as a point of honor. Like many consummate professionals, Galkin took his business personally.

A man of comical unattractiveness, Joe Galkin never married (though not for lack of trying, and stories of his amorous misadventures rivaled those of his professional acumen). Instead, he made the music business his home, cultivating long-standing friendships with clients, colleagues, and a series of young protégés who drove him around, did his bidding, and provided an audience for his profane wisdom. A key to his success was his relationship with Southland Records in Atlanta, the largest wholesale distributor in the Southeast. Southland's owner, Jake Friedman, and sales manager, Gwen Kesler, were like family to Galkin, who relied on them for inside information. It was Kesler, a striking redhead whose good looks and shrewd business sense would make her a legend in the Georgia music business, who brought "Love Twist" to Galkin's attention.

At their first meeting, Joe Galkin saw something in Phil Walden that he liked, and "Love Twist" marked his first step in taking Phil under his wing. It is hard to know how much he really believed in the potential of Johnny Jenkins and the Pinetoppers as a commercial recording act. As a product of the swing era, Galkin was partial to instrumentals, but the most likely explanation for his interest in "Love Twist" had to do with the fact that the record had a danceable beat and contained the magic word *twist* in its title. By the winter of 1962, Chubby Checker's recording of "The Twist" had become the first hit single in history to *return* to #1 after falling off the charts; it was succeeded by the "Peppermint Twist," performed by the Lounge's house band Joey Dee and the Starliters, freshly elevated from playing mob weddings in New Jersey to performing for the likes of Greta Garbo and the Crown Prince of Monaco. Dozens of records were being issued and reissued in an effort to capitalize on this resurgence, ranging from the sublime satire of Sam Cooke's "Twistin' the Night Away" to the sheer silliness of the Marvelettes' "Twistin' Postman," a sequel to their earlier hit "Please Mr. Postman."

Up to a point, things played out with "Love Twist" much as Joe Galkin planned. Having purchased the rights, Galkin re-released it a month later as the first offering on his own label, Gerald Records, which he nepotistically named after the son of Southland's owner. Over the next two months, he pushed the single hard enough in the southeast radio market to persuade Atlantic to pick it up for national distribution. In the summer of 1962, however, as the second wave of the Twist Craze receded, "Love Twist" went out with the tide.

For Phil Walden, the advent of Joe Galkin was a godsend. Phil was due to graduate from Mercer in the spring. He and Katherine Kennedy had plans to marry and start a family. Though his talent agency had proved to be a lucrative sideline—his most recent brochure listed forty local acts—Phil was still hedging his bets, considering the possibility of law school or of going into some conventional form of business. Instead, he recalled, meeting Joe Galkin "really changed my life. He basically became my rabbi, my Jewish godfather. He helped me break the regional bondage. He helped me move to the big playing field."

For Otis Redding, on the other hand, Phil's sudden involvement with Joe Galkin was more of a mixed blessing. The re-release of "Love Twist" by a national label could only help to boost the reputation and asking price of Johnny Jenkins and the Pinetoppers. At the same time, if the record went on to achieve any significant success, it would virtually seal the group's identity as an instrumental band. Otis and Zelma were awaiting the arrival of their second child in March of 1962—their daughter Karla was born that month—and the pressure was mounting on Otis to make something happen with his so-called career.

His response was to turn to Bobby Smith, a former car salesman and would-be record producer whose office, conveniently enough, was located on the floor above Phil Walden's in the Macon Professional Building. At the age of twenty-nine, Smith was another babe in the woods of the Georgia music business. Two years before, after barely surviving an automobile accident that left him legally blind, he began to manage a white rockabilly singer from Thomaston, Georgia, named Wayne Cochran. In the fall of 1961, at Smith's suggestion, Cochran wrote a maudlin teen death ballad called "Last Kiss," which was modeled on the recent Top 10 hits "Teen Angel" and "Tell Laura I Love Her." Smith arranged to have the song recorded and released by Gala Records, a tiny country and western label based in Vidalia, Georgia. Though its sales were negligible, "Last Kiss" established Bobby Smith as the only person in Macon who could plausibly claim to be involved in the record business. At the time Otis approached him, he had recently started a label of his own, which he proudly named Confederate Records.

Though they would end up as bitter rivals, Phil Walden and Bobby Smith were on amicable terms in the spring of 1962, and Phil had no reason to discourage Otis from making a record of his own. When Smith asked Otis what sort of material he wanted to sing, Otis showed him a rewritten version of "Gamma Lama," the song he had recorded in Los Angeles two years before. Now called "Shout Bamalama," the new title affirmed the song's debt to Macon's one-eyed street singer. Otis also showed Smith a Little Richard–inspired knock-off called "Fat Gal," and Jackie Avery's ballad "These Arms of Mine," which he presented in a way that led Smith to believe that Otis was still in the process of writing the song.

Bobby Smith was sufficiently taken with "Shout Bamalama" to set up a recording date. Because Macon lacked a commercial studio of its own, Smith relied on the facilities at WGTV in Athens, a public television station affiliated with the University of Georgia. This was where he arranged to record Otis, backed by the Pinetoppers, on a Sunday afternoon in late March, when the station was off the air. On the day of the session, however, Johnny Jenkins and most of the other Pinetoppers were nowhere to be found. Given Jenkins's reputation for unreliability, it's entirely possible that he simply failed to show. But it is equally possible that Joe Galkin, having recently purchased the rights to "Love Twist," may have discouraged Jenkins and his band from playing on a record that was being released by another label. Either way, in their place, Bobby Smith recruited Wayne Cochran and members of his group, the Rocking Capris, to play behind Otis that day.

It was not a promising situation. By his own admission, Bobby Smith knew next to nothing about how to make a record at this point in his career, while the Rocking Capris were a bunch of white high school kids who were just learning how to play their instruments. The recording of "Shout Bamalama," starts off with a staged "house party" ambience based on the interlude Ray Charles orchestrated in the middle of "What'd I Say." After a full ten seconds of shouting, high-fiving, and general revelry, Otis steps in ("OK, hold it, hold it right there"), counts off the tempo, and launches into what may be the strangest, most discursive set of lyrics he would ever sing. In its original form, "Gamma Lama" told the tale of a pistol-packing gambler from "down in Louisiana" who managed to talk or shoot his way out of every losing hand. The revised version retained the "down home" geography of the original while recasting the song's protagonist as a chicken thief. Over a muted rumba rhythm and a toxic dose of blaring saxophone, Otis sings in his best Little Richard voice, "Lord have mercy on my soul / How many chickens have I stole?" The verses that follow sketch a series of vignettes drawn from common themes of African American folklore. These include a trash-talking exchange between a lion and a signifying monkey (strongly reminiscent of the pair in Chuck Berry's "Jo Jo Gunne") and an irreverent encounter between a preacher, a deacon, and a passing bear that ends with the punch line "Lord, a prayer won't kill this bear." The result is a pastiche of Little Richard that makes "Long Tall Sally" sound like a model of narrative coherence. The coup de grâce of weirdness is provided by a chorus of male backup singers who repeat the catchphrase of the real-life Bamalama, "You shall be free," behind each of Otis's lines.

The second song Otis recorded, "Fat Gal," was somewhat more concise, consisting of a two-verse homage to the fleshly delights of a girl with an arresting "wiggle in her walk." Taken at a headlong tempo over a New Orleans–style groove of piano and sax, "Fat Gal" manages to generate a frantic edge of carnal excitement, though the sketchy lyric doesn't give Otis much to work with.

Coming more than a year and a half after his session for Lute in Los Angeles, "Shout Bamalama" can safely be described as the low point of Otis Redding's recording career. On the Lute recordings, Otis was backed by one of the best studio bands in the world; the playing was impeccable, the arrangements crisp, the technology state-of-the-art, and the songs, however mediocre, were coherent and well-rehearsed. On the Confederate sides, by comparison, Otis was working with a bunch of amateurs on the far fringes of the record business. Virtually the only redeeming feature of these tracks lies in the strength and assurance of his singing, which is still compromised by his stubborn dependence on the impersonation of Little Richard with which he had made his name.

Upon their return to Macon, "in consideration of the sum of one dollar, paid in hand to Otis Redding," Bobby Smith signed Otis to a one-year recording contract, with a one-year option to renew. In April, the single was duly pressed and sent out to radio stations and record distributors, its label emblazoned with the iconic "stars and bars" of the Confederate battle flag.

Bobby Smith would later insist that the name and motif he chose for his record label "meant nothing." If so, he may be regarded as one of the more naive Southerners of his generation. For many decades after the Civil War, the Confederate flag had served as a sacred symbol of southern heritage, its display carefully regulated by the veterans' groups and memorial societies that upheld the civic religion of the Lost Cause. Beginning with its adoption by the States Rights Party in 1948, however, the flag took on new meaning as a symbol of segregationist defiance. In 1956, the Georgia legislature added the stars and bars to the official state flag as an expression of massive resistance to the *Brown* decision. (As Macon's state representative Denmark Groover declared, the new flag "will show that we in Georgia intend to uphold what we stood for, will stand for, and will fight for.") By the fall of 1961, when Bobby Smith started his record label, the Confederate flag was universally recognized as a banner of white supremacy. To take Smith at his word, it also could be said to stand, if not for his racial insensitivity, then surely for his utter cluelessness as an R&B record producer.

In the larger world, the fate of "Shout Bamalama" was ably explained by Bobby Robinson, the owner of Harlem's best-known record store, and himself the producer of more than a dozen Top 10 hits: "It didn't sound too good to me from the start, having a label name like that, with the Confederate flag on it and all. But I put the record on, and it was an imitation of Little Richard. That sound was as dead as could be, so I didn't follow up on it." Much the same verdict was delivered when Bobby Smith and Otis Redding drove to Columbia, South Carolina, to meet with "Big Saul" Greene. The former WIBB deejay had taken a radio job there after being fired from WIBB for refusing to apologize for a letter he had written to the *Telegraph* complaining about the discriminatory treatment his wife had received from a white doctor in Macon. After Big Saul made it clear to Bobby Smith that he would play "Shout Bamalama" only if the name of his label was changed, Smith decided to re-release the record with a neutral yellow label bearing the legend Orbit Records. (The new name was presumably chosen in honor of John Glenn's recent space flight.) But the damage was already done. As Bobby Robinson noted, Smith's promotional ineptitude was matched by the anachronistic sound of the record itself.

Never one to mince words, Joe Galkin would later characterize "Shout Bamalama" as "the worst record I ever heard." At the time, however, this did not prevent him from contacting Bobby Smith and offering to promote the single for a healthy five-cent royalty on every copy sold. Galkin's willingness to plug the record may have owed something to the amicable relationship that still existed between Bobby Smith and Phil Walden. But it also coincided with a shift in his attitude toward Otis Redding. By the spring of 1962, Galkin had grown familiar enough with the Macon music scene to recognize that Otis, far more than Johnny Jenkins, possessed the combination of talent, ambition, and determination that might take him beyond the roadhouses and frat houses of Middle Georgia. By all accounts, it was Galkin who impressed this on Phil Walden, whose world was still revolving around Johnny Jenkins's guitar.

Together, Galkin and Walden came up with a scheme designed to further the interests of both Jenkins and Redding. Galkin knew that Atlantic Records had formed an affiliation with an upstart Memphis label called Stax, whose principal success to date had come with an instrumental called "Last Night," which Atlantic's promotional network had helped to parlay into a Top 10 hit in the Twist-crazed summer of 1961. Now, a year later, Stax was looking to repeat that success with another instrumental, "Green Onions," which featured the impeccably spare stylizations of Booker T. and the MGs, the label's studio band. Though the record had just been released, Galkin's instincts told him that "Green Onions" was a "goddamn smash" if ever there was one. So he proposed to capitalize on its impending success by having Johnny Jenkins make his next record in Memphis with the backing of the Stax band. Toward this end, Galkin contacted Jerry Wexler in New York and solicited an advance to offset the recording costs. (Galkin had recently helped Atlantic break a #1 record by the eccentric British clarinetist Acker Bilk, leaving Wexler eager to repay the favor.) Since Johnny Jenkins didn't like to drive, the plan called for Otis Redding to chauffeur him to Memphis. The plan also called for Joe Galkin to attend the session and persuade Jim Stewart, the owner of Stax, to give Otis a chance to sing.

SATELLITE

I can't place too much importance on the fact that Otis was signed by Stax . . . The Stax sound was impossible to separate from Otis's sound, and in reality they became one.

—PHIL WALDEN

I N THE SUMMER OF 1962, WHEN OTIS REDDING FIRST SET FOOT IN the studio on McLemore Avenue in Memphis that would serve over the next five years as the crucible of his professional career, Stax Records had been doing business under one name or another for a little over three years. The company's origins dated from 1958, when Jim Stewart, a part-time country fiddler and full-time bank officer, convinced his sister Estelle Axton to loan him fifteen hundred dollars toward the purchase of some professional recording equipment. Jim and Estelle had grown up on a farm in Middleton, Tennessee, sixty miles east of Memphis. Estelle was born in 1918, Jim in 1930. Estelle moved to Memphis in 1941 and married a factory worker named Everett Axton. Jim followed her there in 1950. After serving two years in the army, he earned a degree in business administration at Memphis State and secured a job in the mortgage department at the First Tennessee Bank.

He could have been hired on the basis of his looks alone. Jim Stewart was the very model of a bank clerk: a small, gaunt man with a receding chin, horn-rimmed glasses, and a nervous, finicky air. Beneath his milquetoast exterior, however, Stewart longed to be involved in something more exciting than the banking business. He had played the fiddle in country and western bands since his teens, and had minored in music at Memphis State. After college, he continued to perform in local honky-tonks, eventually landing a gig with the house band at a Memphis club called the Eagle's Nest, where a teenager named Elvis Presley began per-forming as an intermission act during the summer of 1954, shortly before his first recording session at Sun Records. Over the next few years, Jim Stewart watched as Elvis became an international sensation and Mem-phis, on the strength of Sam Phillips's Sun label, became a regional re-cording center. At a time when millions of young American males were identifying with Presley, Stewart identified with Phillips. In 1957, he ac-quired some makeshift recording equipment. A year later, with the money he borrowed from his sister, he bought a professional Ampex tape deck and set up shop in a vacant storeroom in Brunswick, a town on the out-skirts of Memphis. Echoing the celestial motif of Sun, Stewart, with no apparent irony, named his label Satellite.

By virtue of the money she loaned him, Estelle Axton became Jim's partner in the record business. A feisty redhead in her early forties, Estelle also held a bank job, as a bookkeeper at the Union Planters Bank, but she was temperamentally the opposite of her brother. Where Jim was shy, Estelle was outgoing. Where Jim was a worrier, Estelle was an optimist. Where Jim's voice was reedy, Estelle's voice was brassy. In addition to pro-viding Satellite Records with its seed money, she also gave the company a much-needed dose of warmth and personality.

For the first few years of its existence, Satellite was essentially a hobby. Unlike Sam Phillips, who liked to describe his career in the record busi-ness in messianic terms, Jim Stewart had no particular vision for the com-pany. "I just wanted music, anything to be involved with music," he later said. His focus began to narrow in 1959, when he met a young white gui-tarist from Lagrange, Georgia, named Lincoln "Chips" Moman, who had recently returned to the South after working for several years as a session musician in Los Angeles. At loose ends, Moman began to hang around the makeshift studio in Brunswick. In addition to his skills as a guitar player, he was one of the first people Jim Stewart had ever met who knew something about rhythm and blues.

"I had scarcely seen a black person till I was grown," Stewart recalled of his youth in rural Tennessee. "I never heard black music and never even had an inkling of what it was about." Given this background, Chips Moman can be credited with introducing the founder of one of the premier R&B labels of the 1960s to the existence of R&B. He began by encouraging Stewart to record a local doo-wop group called the Veltones, for whom Moman cowrote a song called "Fool in Love." Released in the summer of 1959, this utterly generic record generated enough airplay in Memphis to induce Mercury Records, an established label, to purchase the master for the sum of five hundred dollars. Nothing much happened after that, but Satellite had made its first money in the record business.

Even before Chips Moman arrived on the scene, Jim Stewart had determined that Brunswick was too far removed from the center of Memphis to serve as a viable location for a commercial recording studio. Now, with Stewart's blessing, Moman began to look for a venue closer to the center of town. Aware that another local label, Hi Records, had recently built a studio in an abandoned theater, Moman set his sights on a run-down movie house called the Capitol, on East McLemore Avenue in South Memphis. A casualty of the television age, the Capitol had lain dormant for several years, leaving its owner ready to rent the place for a hundred dollars a month. During the spring of 1960, Stewart and Moman supervised the conversion of the theater into their idea of a recording studio. Having removed the seats, they erected a partition down the middle of the auditorium, built a control room on the elevated stage, and installed carpeting and drapes to dampen the acoustics of the space. In a cost-cutting move that lent a faintly surreal quality to the entire setup, they left the sloping floor of orchestra section intact.

Also left intact were the marquee and the lobby—complete with its concession stand—an amenity that led Estelle Axton to decide that if she and her brother were going to make records, they might as well sell them as well. While Jim focused on the studio, Estelle supervised the conversion of the lobby into the Satellite Record Shop, an inspiration that not only promised to generate some income but also gave the whole enterprise a public presence on East McLemore Avenue.

The founding of what would become Stax Records might have been guided by some elusive principle of southern Zen. With the notable exception of Estelle's record shop, almost nothing that furthered the interests of the company seems to have occurred by intelligent design. Instead, after laboring for two years in obscurity on the outskirts of Memphis, Jim

Stewart's most significant achievement was to suddenly find himself in the right place at the right time.

McLemore Avenue was a main east-west thoroughfare in a residential section of Memphis that lay to the south of the central business district. In the years since World War II, this area, known as Southside, had been subjected to an intensive campaign of urban renewal, in the course of which many blocks of substandard housing were condemned and torn down and thousands of units of federally funded public housing were built in their place. This initiative disrupted the patchwork of intermingled white and black residential blocks that distinguished the racial geography of Memphis, and replaced it with what, by 1960, was on its way to becoming a uniformly black community. Yet the atmosphere of transition and displacement was still relatively recent, and the neighborhood retained a definite vitality. A few blocks north of the Capitol Theater lay the campus of Le Moyne College, the city's principal black institution of higher learning. A few blocks to the east lay Le Moyne Gardens, a 500-unit public housing project teeming with families.

For the first year or so, the public face of Satellite Records was Estelle Axton's record shop, which quickly became a magnet for local music fans. Located on a main avenue, directly across from a supermarket and a liquor store, the shop attracted the curiosity and patronage of Southside residents, who then spread the word about the record label. One of the first people who simply walked into the place in the summer of 1960 was Rufus Thomas.

Thomas was a fixture of the black entertainment scene in Memphis. In the 1930s, as a student at Booker T. Washington High School, he caught the attention of Nat D. Williams, the history teacher who went on to pioneer black radio at WDIA. After spending several years refining his skills as a singer, dancer, and comedian with the venerable F. S. Wolcott's Rabbit Foot Minstrels, Thomas took a day job at a Memphis textile mill and began performing regularly in the clubs on Beale Street, where he succeeded Williams as the emcee of the popular weekly talent shows at the Palace Theater. In 1951, he replaced the blues singer B. B. King as an afternoon disk jockey on WDIA. Two years later, Thomas made his recording debut on Sam Phillips's Sun label with a gruff-voiced effort called

"Bear Cat," which was promoted as an "answer record" to "Big Mama" Thornton's top-selling single "Hound Dog." "Bear Cat" was itself a hit, reaching #3 on the R&B charts. By 1960, Thomas had added an evening show called "Hoot 'N' Holler" to his afternoon hour of "Sepia Swing" on WDIA, and he had begun grooming his teenage daughter Carla for a career in show business.

Jim Stewart had met Rufus Thomas a few months before while visiting WDIA to promote the Veltones' "Fool in Love." At their second encounter, Thomas played him a demo of a song called "'Cause I Love You," which he had written as a duet for his daughter and himself. Intrigued by Rufus's radio connections, Stewart agreed to let the Thomas family inaugurate his new recording studio. Produced by Chips Moman and accompanied by Thomas's son Marvell on piano, the record consisted of Rufus and Carla trading professions of love over an arrangement of strutting rhythm and blaring horns that was heavily beholden to the contemporary style of New Orleans R&B associated with the young producer Allen Toussaint. The instrumental hook of the track was a honking baritone sax part played by a sixteen-year-old musical prodigy named Booker T. Jones.

Booker Jones was a kid from the neighborhood who began to frequent the Satellite Record Shop as soon as it opened its doors. A quiet young man with luminous, watchful eyes, he dated his musical awakening from the age of eleven, when he first heard Ray Charles's recording of "Drown in My Own Tears." As a student at Booker T. Washington High School, where his father taught science and math, Jones directed the school's concert band from his freshman year on; he also joined with two of his classmates, guitarist David Porter and drummer Maurice White (who would later found the band Earth, Wind & Fire), to perform at dances and proms. Whereas most musicians start out by developing a relationship with a particular instrument, the precocious Jones could play almost anything he put his hands on. After familiarizing himself with the piano, he moved on to guitar, trombone, oboe, saxophone, and bass. It was as a bass player that he began to sit in, at the age of fourteen, with a pair of topflight club bands led by trumpeters Willie Mitchell and "Bowlegs" Miller, playing at venues like the Rainbow Room on Beale Street and the Plantation Inn in West Memphis, Arkansas. After attending a club date by the soul-jazz organist Jack McDuff, Jones was in the process of adding the Hammond organ to his instrumental repertoire.

Released in September 1960, "'Cause I Love You" sold well enough in Memphis that a local record distributor called Buster Williams took it upon himself to contact Jerry Wexler at Atlantic Records in New York and suggest that it might be worth his while to buy the rights to the single and distribute it nationally. Wexler did just that, and though sales were slow outside the Memphis market, he concluded a deal with Jim Stewart that, in return for a $5,000 advance, gave Atlantic an option on anything Satellite recorded by Rufus and Carla Thomas. If Atlantic exercised its option, it would cover the full cost of manufacturing, distribution, and promotion, paying Satellite a substantial royalty on the records as they sold. In one fell swoop, Jim Stewart had inaugurated his new studio, made his first R&B record, earned his first serious money, and formed the business relationship that would underwrite his label's commercial success in the years to come.

Having never had a hit record, it's unlikely that Stewart understood how important the deal with Atlantic would prove for the future of his company. Though the start-up costs were minimal, the economics of the record business were daunting for a small label like Satellite. The distinction between the majors that dominated the mainstream market and the independents that fostered the success of rhythm and blues was more than a matter of size. The majors were well-capitalized, vertically integrated companies that owned their own pressing plants, distribution facilities, and promotional networks. The independents, by contrast, had to pay up front for the cost of manufacturing, distribution, and promotion and then wait, often for months on end, before they recouped any money for the records that actually sold. While this didn't mean much with an initial release of a few thousand singles, in the rare and happy event that a record began to sell in significant numbers, the label was suddenly required to pay out thousands of dollars to pressing plants in order to keep up with demand. (This was the situation that made the independents vulnerable to "cover" versions of their records that were hastily recorded and mass released by major labels. It was also the situation that opened the doors of the record business to organized crime, since banks refused to underwrite this sort of speculation, while loan sharks were happy to oblige.) The deal with Atlantic, which by 1960 had attained something close to major status in the world of R&B, absolved Satellite of these up-front expenses, allowing the label to focus all of its limited resources on making records, not marketing them.

The pros and cons of the arrangement with Atlantic were demonstrated in the fall of 1960, when Rufus Thomas played Jim Stewart a tape of a dreamy ballad called "Gee Whiz" that his daughter Carla had written as a kind of high school love poem. Stewart had felt from the beginning that Carla was a more commercially viable artist than her father, whose strained shout lent an air of raucous comedy to everything he sang. Stewart saw "Gee Whiz" as the ideal vehicle for her. It was a conventionally sentimental pop ballad ("Gee whiz, look at his eyes / Gee whiz, how they hypnotize"), sung with the sort of pining, palpably adolescent affect that was being promoted with great success in 1960 by a new breed of New York–based "girl groups" like the Shirelles. Flush with his advance from Atlantic, Jim Stewart decided to make a big production of "Gee Whiz" by hiring a string section from the Memphis Symphony to accompany the track. He released the song in November 1960. A few weeks later, Stewart received a phone call from Jerry Wexler. "I hear my record's doing good," Wexler offered. When Stewart responded, "What record?," Wexler reminded him that Atlantic's option applied to anything Satellite recorded with Rufus *or* Carla Thomas, together or apart. This was news to Stewart, but it led to the re-release of "Gee Whiz" on Atlantic in February 1961. Over the next eight weeks, the single peaked at #5 in R&B, #10 in Pop, selling close to half a million copies in the process. Though "Gee Whiz" was a far cry from anything that could be described as rhythm and blues, Satellite had produced its first hit. In the spring of 1961, when Jerry Wexler flew down to Memphis to meet Jim Stewart and Estelle Axton, they agreed to extend Atlantic's option deal to anything Satellite recorded.

Another key figure who entered the orbit of Satellite around this time was a lanky, poker-faced guitarist from the white suburbs of east Memphis named Steve Cropper. Like Jim Stewart, Cropper began as a country boy, born on a farm in the Ozark Mountains of southern Missouri in the fall of 1941. An only child, he was ten years old when his parents moved to Memphis. The Croppers belonged to the Church of Christ, which forbade the use of musical instruments in its services, but Steve's exposure to country music whetted his appetite for the guitar, and the sound of gospel on the radio in Memphis, he said, "literally blew me away." In 1957, as a student at the all-white Messick High School, he joined with two of his classmates, guitarist Charlie Freeman and bassist Donald "Duck" Dunn, to form a band called the Royal Spades. Another of their classmates was Charles "Packy" Axton, Estelle's son, who took up the saxophone in order to join the group. Since Packy could barely blow a note, his main qualification was that his family owned a record label, and it wasn't long before his bandmates began hanging around the Satellite studio in Brunswick. By the time they all graduated from high school in 1959, the Royal Spades had acquired a lead singer, a horn section, and a reputation as one of the better white club bands in Memphis. Playing a mixture of rock 'n' roll, rhythm and blues, and jazz standards, they performed at high school and college dances and an assortment of local dives.

You didn't think of it. It's like if you've got a wart on your hand, you grow up with it . . . It might be an ugly thing, but it's always been there.

—BUDGIE LINDER, Plantation Inn patron

THAT A GROUP OF WHITE HIGH SCHOOL STUDENTS COULD BLITHELY advertise their enthusiasm for black music by calling their band the Royal Spades says a lot about the racial psychology of Memphis at the time. With approximately 200,000 African American residents—two-fifths of the total population—Memphis in the early 1960s was proportionally one of the blackest major cities in the country. It was also one of the most rigidly segregated. The interspersed pattern of white and black housing that had marked its growth during the first half of the twentieth century was not a reflection of racial harmony; if anything, it was a testament to the absolute nature of the color line in a place where it was common for white and black residents to live on adjoining blocks, enjoy neighborly relations with members of their own race, and virtually ignore the existence of the "other" in their midst. While these blinders were worn by whites and blacks alike, the balance of social power, as elsewhere in the South, was entirely one-sided. In Memphis, a black person who overstepped the boundaries of racial etiquette could expect to be challenged by any white person who felt threatened in any way. Whites, by contrast, could move with relative impunity through the black locales of the city. While their presence might not be appreciated, it was nearly always tolerated. This was true even on Beale Street, the famous shopping and entertainment district that occupied a four-block stretch in the heart of downtown Memphis and advertised itself as the Main Street of Negro America.

In the decades before World War II, Beale Street had grown into a freewheeling hub of commerce and vice that catered to the needs of black Memphians and the tens of thousands of rural blacks who flooded into the city every weekend from the surrounding countryside. By day the street was home to myriad shops and businesses, most of them owned by Greek or Jewish immigrants: clothing stores, drugstores, department stores, pawnshops, barbershops, beauty parlors, restaurants, and roominghouses, along with the offices of the city's tiny black professional class. By night the life of the street was given over to a concentration of bars, nightclubs, theaters, dance halls, pool halls, gambling houses, and brothels—a wide-open pleasure district whose praises were sung throughout the South. Two big theaters, the Palace and the New Daisy, provided a showcase for national acts. The clubs, dance halls, and brothels provided employment for local jazz bands, jug bands, and barrelhouse piano players. And the public parks at either end of the street—the only parks in the city that were open to blacks—served as the main venue for the itinerant Delta-born singers and guitarists who afforded Memphis its reputation as the proverbial Home of the Blues.

All this was made possible by an accommodation that existed between the civic and religious leaders of the black community and the Democratic political machine of E. H. Crump, a local power broker who ruled Memphis as a personal fiefdom during the first half of the twentieth century. Unlike their disenfranchised contemporaries throughout the South, blacks in Memphis voted in large numbers—provided that they voted for the candidates chosen by Boss Crump. In return for this support, the city government tolerated both the legitimate and illegitimate expressions of black enterprise, and spent a small but significant portion of the revenue it collected in taxes, federal aid, and graft for the benefit of the black community.

On the eve of World War II, however, following the belated repeal of Prohibition in Tennessee (which eliminated a major source of graft), the Crump machine abruptly ended the rapprochement. Under the familiar rallying cry "This is a white man's country," the city's commissioner of public safety unleashed a campaign of intimidation that culminated in a wholesale effort to "clean up" Beale Street. The big saloons, gambling houses, and bordellos were shut down and their proprietors were exiled from the city. Much of the hard-core vice simply decamped across the Mississippi River to West Memphis, Arkansas, which became renowned as a regional den of iniquity in its own right. Beale Street continued to function as the main shopping district for black Memphians, and its nightlife underwent a revival in the early 1950s, thanks to the waning of Crump's power (he died in 1954) and the popularity of a new crop of electrified Delta blues singers that included Howlin' Wolf, Sonny Boy Williamson, and the brilliant young guitarist Riley "B. B." King.

For most white Memphis residents in the 1950s, a desire to commune with the black subculture of Beale Street was the last thing on their minds. White Memphis responded to the *Brown* decision with a defiance that served only to sharpen the city's formidable racial divide. (In 1959, for example, an unprecedented turnout by black voters was offset by an even more unprecedented turnout by white voters, who elected Henry Loeb, a fierce segregationist, as mayor.) During these same years, however, the massive postwar influx of white and black migrants from the failing farms of the mid-South had begun to blur some of the lines of race and class. The city's notoriously brutal police force saw to it that the children of the black migrants were as rudely educated in the exigencies of Jim Crow as ever before. But the children of the white migrants had a different experience. Some, like Jim Stewart and Steve Cropper, came from rural areas where they'd had little or no contact with blacks. While they accepted the presence of strict segregation as a fact of life, they had not necessarily been conditioned by the social attitudes that underlay those strictures. Instead, many of the white teenagers who came of age in the high schools of Memphis during the 1950s were drawn to the local varieties of black music, fashion, and dance as a source of fascination in their leisure lives.

Without a doubt, the single most spectacular exponent of this fascination was Elvis Aaron Presley, who had arrived in Memphis with his parents at the age of thirteen, lived in the all-white Lauderdale Courts housing project, and attended all-white Humes High School, but whose taste in music and fashion was shaped by his exposure to Beale Street and the blues and gospel he heard on the local jukeboxes and radio stations. From 1955 onward, Presley's success had a powerful effect on the white youth of his adopted city, providing them with the same lodestar of possibility that Little Richard and James Brown had provided for the black youth of Macon. Before Elvis, there was little reason for a white boy in Memphis to contemplate the prospect of a career in the music business. Nashville, not Memphis, was emerging as the recording capital of the South, home to the Grand Ole Opry and the studios of several major labels. The music scene in Memphis, by contrast, was completely dominated by blacks, and for young whites, access to the world of black clubs, theaters, and dance halls was proscribed by law in a city that policed the racial purity of its popular culture as aggressively as it policed the purity of its schools and public accommodations.

This meant that for Elvis and the generation of culturally displaced "hillbilly cats" he represented, radio was the determining influence, since radio was the one medium of mass communication that lay beyond the control of the white supremacists. As the home of WDIA and the neighbor of WLAC in Nashville, Memphis stood at the epicenter of black-appeal radio in the South. (In the mid-1950s, WDIA was joined by a second all-black station, WLOK.) Day and night, black music was a ubiquitous presence on the airwaves, where deejays like Nat D. Williams and Martha Jean "The Queen" Steinberg played a role akin to that of Hamp Swain in Macon, presenting their white listeners with on-air personalities whose eloquence, wit, and self-confidence defied racist stereotypes.

When these influences were combined with the local-hero status of Elvis Presley and the rest of the Sun Records stable, it was hardly surprising that some of the city's white teenagers took their fascination with black music beyond the pleasures of listening and dancing and began to entertain the idea of learning to play it as well. Something similar was happening all across America in the late 1950s; the difference in Memphis was that the wellsprings of the music were so near and yet so far. Strict segregation lent an added allure to those few venues where white acolytes like the Royal Spades could listen and learn from black bands. Sympathetic owners at clubs like the Handy on Beale Street or the Flamingo in North Memphis would sometimes allow Steve Cropper and his friends to loiter outside, within earshot of the bands on stage. But the great shrine of white enchantment with black music was a sprawling roadhouse in West Memphis, Arkansas, called the Plantation Inn.

Owned by a dapper impresario named Morris Berger and advertised by a garish neon sign that flashed the words *Having Fun with Morris* into the Delta night, the PI, as it was known, boasted a sunken dance floor and a supper club ambience that set it apart from the other West Memphis dives. Patrons came from far and wide: teenagers from area high schools, eager to dance the "bop"; college students from as far afield as Jonesboro and Little Rock; middle-class couples out for a night on the town; blue-bloods from the country club suburbs of East Memphis looking to let down their hair. The audience was entirely white, the musicians and wait-staff were entirely black, and the main attraction was the quality of the music and dancing. Morris Berger made a point of hiring the best black bands in Memphis. In the late 1950s, that meant Willie Mitchell and the Four Kings, with a five-piece horn section anchored by Lewie Steinberg on bass and Al Jackson Jr. on drums. In the early 1960s, Ben Branch and the Largos took over as the house band, supplemented by vocal groups like the Veltones and the Del Rios. The personnel of these groups was drawn from a common pool of musicians playing a common repertoire that ran the gamut from current pop and R&B hits to ballroom standards like "Tennessee Waltz." Their musical style was strongly influenced by the jazz-tinged synthesis of blues guitar and riffing horns associated with the bands of B. B. King and his protégé, Bobby "Blue" Bland. The high level of musicianship was matched by a high level of showmanship, with the uniformed sidemen animating their performances with synchronized steps, dips, and turns. For the young white musicians in the audience, it was an education in both playing and stagecraft. In the words of the trumpeter Wayne Jackson, who joined the Royal Spades in 1960, "We learned what you had to do to make people dance."

Back in the 1950s, a white Memphis saxophonist named Bill Justis had scored a Top 10 hit with an instrumental called "Raunchy," which was one of the first successful records to capitalize on the twangy, deep-throated tones of the solid-body electric guitar. The guitar-and-sax sound of "Raunchy" was adopted by a number of instrumental groups, includ-ing the Bill Black Combo, whose 1960 hit "White Silver Sands" added the tinny sound of an electronic organ to the mix. Bill Black was Elvis Presley's former bassist and a fixture in the Memphis clubs, where Chips

Moman often sat in with his band. In the spring of 1961, Moman, Packy Axton, and keyboard player Jerry Smith decided to honor this local tradition by coming up with an organ and horn riff of their own. Packy had been nagging his mother for months to record the Royal Spades; now, with Estelle's blessing, Moman brought the group into the studio to work out an arrangement for the tune, which they called "Last Night." It took any number of sessions to get a usable take, in the course of which Moman wound up replacing all of the Royal Spades besides Axton and Wayne Jackson with a contingent of black musicians he recruited from the local club scene. The finished version of "Last Night" had a gritty dance-floor groove, with stuttery downbeats from the horns, a stuttery backbeat from the drums, and a profusion of stops, starts, and pregnant pauses that set the stage for the song's hook: a spoken-word interjection of "Oh! . . . last night," intoned in a salacious African American baritone.

Jim Stewart felt no enthusiasm for "Last Night," but after auditioning the track on the Memphis station WLOK and receiving a positive response, Estelle Axton basically demanded that he release it. Estelle's hopes for the record also led her to suggest that it was time for the Royal Spades to change their name to something more palatable to a prospective R&B audience. After toying with calling themselves the Marquees, in honor of the Capitol Theater's architectural landmark on McLemore Avenue, the group deferred to the unpretentious spirit of Memphis by changing the spelling to *Mar-Keys*. (As Steve Cropper dryly noted, "None of us spoke French.")

Released in the summer of 1961, "Last Night" was perfectly timed to ride the resurgence of the Twist craze to the top of the national record charts. The single sold nearly a million copies and earned the seven Mar-Keys—only two of whom had actually played on the record—an appearance on Dick Clark's *American Bandstand* and a spot on a package tour that featured such current pop sensations as Bobby Vinton and Bobby Vee. Although Atlantic handled the distribution, Jerry Wexler agreed to give Jim Stewart's fledgling company some national recognition by releasing the single on the Satellite label. This prompted a small West Coast label with a competing claim to the name *Satellite* to contact Stewart and offer to sell him the rights. Instead, the parsimonious Stewart chose to rename his company Stax, an acronym based on the first two letters of his and his sister's last names.

Beginning with the name of the band and the name of the label, "Last Night" changed everything. Previously, there had been little at stake among the small group of people who had more or less fallen together on McLemore Avenue. Now, with a hit record on the charts, tensions and rivalries flared. After a few weeks on the road together, Steve Cropper and Packy Axton had a dispute over the leadership of the Mar-Keys that resulted in Cropper's leaving the band, returning to Memphis, and taking a job as a clerk in the Satellite Record Shop. An even more serious source of strain centered on the status of Chips Moman. "Last Night" only reaffirmed the extent to which Moman had served as the creative force behind the label. It was Moman who ran the studio while Jim Stewart worked at the bank; Moman who groomed the talent and developed the material they recorded; Moman who produced and engineered most of the sessions. As a working musician, Moman also served as the label's principal liaison to the Memphis club scene, which enabled him to attract the cohort of first-rate instrumentalists who would prove essential to the future of Stax.

The bass player on "Last Night" was Lewie Steinberg, who came from a well-known musical family in Memphis (his sister was Jean "The Queen"). In the fall of 1961, Chips Moman put together a club band that included Steinberg on bass and Booker Jones on organ. He named the group the Triumphs, after the brand of British sports car he drove. With Moman on guitar, the Triumphs were one of the first openly integrated bands to perform in Memphis clubs. (Whites were barred from patronizing black clubs but not explicitly from performing in them.) Moman wrote and produced an instrumental for the group, a rumba-inflected blues called "Burnt Biscuits," and he also used the Triumphs on a session with William Bell, another Satellite Record Shop walk-in whose Stax debut was a self-written ballad called "You Don't Miss Your Water." Bell had previously sung doo-wop with the Del Rios, but "You Don't Miss Your Water" was a complete departure for him, thanks to an arrangement in which the 12/8 feel of New Orleans piano blues was given a new poignancy by Booker Jones's churchy organ, which lent an unmistakable gospel flavor to the track. With "Last Night," "Burnt Biscuits," and "You Don't Miss Your Water," Chips Moman had effectively drawn the musical blueprint for what would become known as the Stax sound.

At the same time, Moman's heavy drinking and domineering personality were getting on everyone's nerves, particularly those of Jim Stewart and Estelle Axton. Early in 1962, when Moman approached Stewart about formalizing his role at Stax by giving him a share in the company, the discussion turned into a shouting match that led to a bitter parting of the ways. Incensed by what he saw as Stewart's betrayal, Moman wound up moving to Nashville and hiring a lawyer, who eventually negotiated a small settlement on his behalf. (Several years later he would return to Memphis, open a rival studio, and produce a string of hits.)

Moman's departure presented a prime opportunity for Steve Cropper, who assumed his former mentor's role as studio manager and house guitarist. Cropper's sober, stable manner was a welcome change from Moman's hard-drinking bluster, and Jim Stewart felt far more comfortable relying on him. Yet Cropper was not nearly as adept at recruiting or cultivating talent as Moman had been. As a result, the first half of 1962 was a fallow period at Stax. Repeated attempts by the Mar-Keys to follow up on the success of "Last Night" proved unavailing. Records by the Del Rios and the Tonettes sounded as anachronistic as their names, and a nadir of sorts was reached when Stax recorded a white deejay named Nick Charles singing "The Three Dogwoods," an insipid allegory (co-written by Cropper) about the crucifixion of Jesus Christ.

By the summer of 1962, Jim Stewart was reduced to booking jingle sessions, including one with Billy Lee Riley, a rockabilly singer whose career at Sun Records had fizzled a few years back. The band for this session consisted of the usual lineup of Cropper, Jones, and Steinberg, accompanied for the first time by the drummer Al Jackson Jr. Jackson, like Steinberg, came from a musical family, having gotten his start by playing in his father Al Sr.'s big band. Now, at the age of twenty-seven, he was widely regarded as the best club drummer in Memphis. Jones and Cropper had been trying to recruit him for Stax, and a jingle session, which paid union scale, seemed like a good way to begin.

Accounts differ as to whether Billy Lee Riley got drunk and left early or simply failed to show. Either way, with time on their hands, the musicians entertained themselves by jamming on a slow, contemplative blues that showcased Booker Jones's quicksilver chops on organ. Jim Stewart liked the sound of the tune well enough to record it. When he asked the group to come up with another track that could serve as the B-side of a single, Jones brought out a medium-tempo minor-key blues he liked to play. The band worked out a simple arrangement, with Jones and Cropper trading jagged, laconic solos over a relentless shuffle rhythm that seemed to gain momentum with each repetition of the verse. Next, having created a record out of thin air, they had to come up with some song titles. They called the slow blues "Behave Yourself." They called the shuffle "Green Onions." When it became clear that Jim Stewart was serious about releasing the tracks, they also had to decide on a name for their group. Booker Jones's organ was the signature sound of the music; in recognition of his and Steinberg's previous service with the Triumphs, they settled on another brand of British sportscar and christened themselves Booker T. and the MGs.

Booker T. and the MGs (left to right): Duck Dunn, Booker Jones, Steve Cropper, Al Jackson Jr.

No one would ever accuse Jim Stewart of thinking outside the box. "Behave Yourself" was the tune that originally caught his ear, so "Behave Yourself" was the track he planned to release as the A-side of the single. Steve Cropper disagreed, and after test-marketing "Green Onions" on WLOK, he was able to convince Stewart that the shuffle, not the slow blues, was the more commercial track. The trajectory of the single would prove to be almost identical to that of "Last Night." Released in July and optioned by Atlantic, it would take about a month and a half to complete its ascent of the charts, passing the flotsam and jetsam of early-sixties pop—the Beach Boys' "Surfin' Safari," Little Eva's "Loco-motion," Peter Paul and Mary's "If I Had a Hammer"—along the way.

In the summer of 1962, then, the Stax record company had been in business for about three years, during which time it had produced an unspectacular total of two hit singles by two different artists, with a third hit on the way. That two of those singles were instrumentals reflected the company's principal asset, its capable studio band. Yet despite the popularity of Carla Thomas's "Gee Whiz," Stax had been notably unsuccessful at recruiting and developing talented singers. That was where things stood on the August afternoon when Joe Galkin arranged for Johnny Jenkins and Otis Redding to walk in the door.

THESE ARMS OF MINE

It was different, but I don't think anyone jumped up and down.

—JIM STEWART

THE USUAL PRACTICE AT STAX WAS TO SCHEDULE SESSIONS ON SATurdays, when Jim Stewart wasn't working at his bank job. Having rented a station wagon from Bobby Smith and driven nearly five hundred miles from Macon to Memphis, sleeping in the car along the way, Otis and Johnny Jenkins arrived around midday at the converted theater on McLemore Avenue. They were met on the street by Stewart, Joe Galkin, and the four members of Booker T. and the MGs, whose first impression of Otis Redding was that he was Johnny Jenkins's valet. Otis started unloading amplifiers and microphone stands from the back of the car. "That's OK," Steve Cropper told him. "We're a recording studio. We have our own microphones."

The session began with Johnny Jenkins running through his repertoire of instrumental set pieces for Jim Stewart and the band, none of whom were particularly impressed by what they heard. The tepid reception had a predictable effect on Jenkins's fragile ego, and things went downhill from there. Eventually it was decided to record a remake of "Love Twist" with a new arrangement and a new title ("Spunky" was the eventual choice). The resulting track was a significant improvement over the original, thanks to the solid rhythm section and a burbling organ part played by Booker Jones. But after several more hours of rehearsal and taping, during which they also recorded a slow blues called "Bashful Guitar," Jim Stewart announced to Joe Galkin that he simply couldn't make a record with Johnny Jenkins, and suggested that they call it a day. As the MGs began eagerly packing up their instruments, Galkin reminded Stewart that Atlantic Records was paying for the session and that time was left on the clock.

He then explained to Stewart that Otis Redding was not only Johnny Jenkins's driver but also the singer in his band, and he proposed that they use the remaining studio time to see what Otis could do. (Several of the musicians present recalled that Otis had been lobbying all afternoon for a chance to sing.) While Galkin and Stewart were busy sorting things out between them, however, Booker Jones went home.

The first track they attempted was the latest of Otis's Little Richard impersonations, an uptempo rant called "Hey Hey Baby." With Steve Cropper playing rhythm and Johnny Jenkins on lead, the band struck an uneasy balance between rockabilly and stomping blues that only exaggerated the outdated sound of the material. After Jim Stewart muttered something about how the world wasn't waiting for another Little Richard, Joe Galkin volunteered that Otis had a ballad he'd like to sing.

In Booker Jones's absence, Steve Cropper sat down at the piano, an instrument he could barely play. When he asked Otis what key he wanted to sing in, Otis said it didn't matter. "Just play me those church things," he told Cropper, who correctly took that to mean a sixteen-bar gospel progression in 12/8 time. Otis led them into the song with a vocal pickup that began, "These . . . arms . . . of . . . *mi—ine.*"

The Discovery Myth is one of the most appealing stories that pop culture has to tell. Sixteen-year-old Lana Turner is spotted by a casting agent while sitting at the soda fountain of a Hollywood drugstore. Eighteen-year-old Elvis Presley breaks the tension during an aimless recording test by clowning his way through a blues he's heard on the radio. . . . And the rest is pop history. ("We're not going to do the one about the record being put on the turntable by mistake," the Beatles assured the press about the premise of their first film.) Stories like these carry a subtext of vindication and suggest an almost Dickensian drama of innate beauty, talent, or virtue finally getting its due. But in the self-reflexive world of the recording studio (in the bygone era before home recording equipment became commonplace), where prospective young singers were given a rare opportunity to monitor, repeat, and refine their performances, the real drama has often been one of *self*-discovery. Time and again since the advent of recording, the experience of hearing one's voice on playback has enabled a gifted but unformed singer to realize a vocal personality that had previously been obscured—most often by the nightly struggle to be heard over the clamor of a live band. "I never sang like that in my whole life before I made that record," Elvis Presley said of his first Sun single.

In the case of "These Arms of Mine," there is no record of how many takes it took to obtain the finished track. The bare, generic accompaniment of piano, bass, and drums, broken only by the mandolin-like tremors of Johnny Jenkins's guitar, imbues Otis's singing with a naked presence that completely dominates the recording. Forced by the exceptionally slow tempo to abandon all his patented Little Richard mannerisms (for this was precisely the sort of material that Richard had failed to sing convincingly early in his career), Otis responds by pouring himself into this mere slip of a song, with its two formulaic verses and ad-libbed coda, filling all the available space left by the instruments. The slow tempo also serves to afford his performance with an element of suspense, for his voice seems to be hanging on every note as he lavishes attention on the lyric's courtly expressions of desire (his arms are *"yearning . . . burning . . .* from wanting you"), drawing the words out over three or four syllables. For the first time on a recording, Otis is singing, not shouting, without a trace of aggression in his voice. That changes in the song's coda, where he adopts a more colloquial tone, pleading, "Mama! Come on, baby! I need me somebody, somebody to treat me right," while the music, faint to begin with, slowly fades away. The utter simplicity of "These Arms of Mine" recalls such minimalist debuts as James Brown's "Please, Please, Please" and Sam Cooke's "You Send Me," both of which served to highlight the distinctiveness of the singer's voice by giving him nothing but a feeling to work with. The result in this case, rough and halting as it is at times, was the first recording on which Otis Redding sounded like the singer the world would come to know—a singer, like Ray Charles on "I Got a Woman" or Little Richard on "Tutti Frutti," who suddenly sounded like nobody else.

In keeping with the mythic nature of this session, accounts differ as to the response in the studio that day. In Steve Cropper's recollection, his hair stood on end the moment Otis began to sing, and Jim Stewart emerged from the control room at the end of the first run-through declaring that they needed to get the song down on tape. Stewart himself recalled no such enthusiasm. "No one was particularly impressed," he later said. "It was different, but I don't think anyone jumped up and down."

What no one disputes is that both Jim Stewart and Joe Galkin considered "These Arms of Mine" a much more promising recording than anything they had cut on Johnny Jenkins that day. (Jenkins's recording of "Spunky" would languish in Stax's vault for nearly two years.) Acting as Otis's self-appointed manager, Galkin proposed that Stewart sign his client to a recording contract. In return for brokering the deal, Galkin asked Stewart for a half share, after expenses, of "any and all monies" Stax made on Redding's record sales and publishing royalties. That Galkin felt free to represent Otis in this manner suggests how thoroughly he enjoyed Phil Walden's trust. It also suggests the level of sheer chutzpah he brought to his work, considering that the session had been bankrolled by Atlantic Records, which under normal circumstances would have owned the rights to any of the music recorded there. But when Atlantic's Jerry Wexler finally figured out what Galkin had done with his advance, he decided to let it ride. Wexler prided himself on his hard-nosed business sense, but he had a genuine soft spot for both Joe Galkin and Jim Stewart. More important, his standing deal with Stewart gave Atlantic the option to distribute anything Stax recorded. One way or another, Wexler knew that his label would share in any success that Otis Redding achieved.

Over time, Johnny Jenkins would perfect his own account of what happened at Stax that day, claiming it was he, not Joe Galkin, who suggested that Otis be given the opportunity to record. "I had a lot of time left over, and I asked if it would be OK if my friend could sing in the spare time I had left." When the people at Stax balked at the idea, Jenkins dug in his heels. "I said if you can't use him, then I won't cut any more. And they talked about it and they said OK." Jenkins's account was a complete fabrication—by that point in the session, Jim Stewart would have been happy to see him go—but it does give some sense of the awkwardness that would creep into his relationship with Otis in the aftermath of their trip to Memphis. Otis had seized the moment; Johnny had fallen apart.

Within a week of their return to Macon, at Joe Galkin's direction, Phil Walden presented Otis with a management contract. The language of this agreement was standard show business boilerplate, which in 1962 meant that its terms were skewed entirely in favor of management. The contract ran for three years, with a three-year option to renew; it covered Otis's work as a "singer, orchestra leader, instrumentalist, comedian, and composer" in every conceivable medium of entertainment up to and including "vaudeville." It granted his managers the exclusive right to represent and advise him, irrevocable power of attorney, and total creative control ("artist will follow managers' directions and instructions during all rehearsals, performances, and recording sessions"). In return for acquiescing to this modern form of indentured servitude, Otis agreed to pay his managers 30 percent of his gross income from all engagements, compositions, performances, and contracts—in addition to any promotional expenses they incurred along the way. They in turn agreed to make "all reasonable efforts to promote, develop, and advance" his professional career.

Though this typewritten agreement contained its share of spelling and punctuation errors, the use of the plural *managers* was not one of them. The contract was signed by both Phil Walden and Sam Davis, who were jointly listed as managers, with the stipulation that their 30 percent commission should be "divided equally." Since it is inconceivable that Phil Walden would have accepted Sam Davis as his partner if he had any choice in the matter, this contract affirms the role that Davis continued to play as a liaison with the black-owned clubs in Georgia—and, it seems, as a liaison between Otis and Phil.

The contract also contained a standard exclusivity clause in which Otis allowed that he had "made no other arrangements, oral or written, which shall in any manner interfere or prevent him from carrying out the terms and conditions of this contract." This would have come as news to Bobby Smith, who was under the impression that he had signed Otis Redding to a one-year recording contract less than five months earlier. Smith first heard about the impending release of "These Arms of Mine" from John Richbourg, a deejay at WLAC, who contacted Smith after Joe Galkin played him a test pressing of the record at a radio convention in St. Louis. Smith's response was to walk downstairs from his office in the Professional Building and confront Otis and Phil, both of whom initially denied any knowledge of the recording. Soon afterward, however, Smith received a call from Galkin, who began by informing him that Redding's contract with Confederate/Orbit was invalid because Otis was underage, and ended by suggesting that Stax was nevertheless willing to buy out Smith's interest. Given a choice between a lawsuit, a buyout, or a fractional royalty on Redding's future record sales, Smith opted for a cash payment, and for seven hundred dollars, granted Otis his release.

Otis's first publicity photo, 1962

If you want to be a singer, you've got to concentrate on it twenty-four hours a day. You can't have anything else on your mind but the music business. You can't be a well-driller too. You've got to concentrate on the business of entertaining and writing songs.

—OTIS REDDING

B Y ANY MEASURE, IT WAS A FORTUITOUS TIME FOR A YOUNG BLACK
singer to be launching a recording career, for the sales of R&B singles
were booming in the summer of 1962, and the mainstreams of black and
white popular music were edging closer together than ever before. Of the
sixteen songs that placed at #1 on *Billboard*'s R&B charts that year, all but
one (the King Curtis instrumental "Soul Twist") were Top 10 hits on the
magazine's Pop charts as well, and of the year's ten bestselling Pop singles, four were recorded by black artists. Some of this convergence owed
to the continued success of established crossover stars like Ray Charles
and Sam Cooke, some to the arrival of gifted newcomers like Solomon
Burke, Mary Wells, and Marvin Gaye, and some to the ever-increasing
popularity of R&B-based dance music among black and white teenagers
alike.

That August, while Otis Redding was finally shaking the monkey of
Little Richard off his back in a Memphis recording studio, Little Richard himself was meeting with an English promoter named Don Arden
to arrange a tour of Britain that would mark his first appearances in five
years as a secular singer. Arden's success at promoting package tours of
Britain with fading American rockers like Gene Vincent and Jerry Lee
Lewis had alerted him to a musical subculture that had taken root among
working-class teenagers in the depressed industrial cities of Northern
England, where nostalgia for 1950s rock 'n' roll had merged with enthusiasm for contemporary American rhythm and blues to produce a hybrid
style, locally known as "beat music," and a host of native imitators, locally known as "beat groups." Arden knew that Little Richard's place in
the pantheon of beat music rivaled that of Elvis Presley himself, and he
surmised that the singer's first appearance in Britain would be hailed as a
Second Coming.

As a way of hedging his bets on Richard and catering to the more
contemporary tastes of his teenage clientele, Arden booked Sam Cooke to
costar on the tour. It was an astute move, for Cooke was nearing another
peak of popularity in the fall of 1962. Now in the third year of his contract
with RCA, he had achieved something close to complete creative control
over his music, having relegated his producers to a largely administrative
role. Cooke had begun the year with the immaculate pop production of

"Twistin' the Night Away," his bestselling single since "Chain Gang." He followed this hit with a stunning single that combined "Having a Party" with "Bring It on Home to Me." The first was a wistful social vignette in the uptown style of the Drifters; the second, even more powerful, track was derived from a 1959 recording of "I Want to Go Home" by the West Coast bluesmen Charles Brown and Amos Milburn, which Cooke had rearranged in the call-and-response, dual-lead style of the Soul Stirrers. (The uncredited second lead was sung by his protégé Lou Rawls.) Both sides of the single placed near the top of the R&B charts and breached the Pop Top 20 as well. RCA owned its own subsidiary label in Britain, and Cooke's records had sold well there since he signed with the company in 1960. But the tour with Little Richard would be his first visit to the country, and as a budding Anglophile, he was eager to make a favorable impression.

Little Richard was no less determined to make an impression, favorable or not. On the first night of the tour, at a shabby provincial cinema in the coal-mining town of Doncaster, he walked onstage wearing ecclesiastical robes and regaled his dumbfounded teenage audience with a full program of gospel songs. Backstage, when an apoplectic Don Arden began citing the terms of his contract, Richard denounced him as a Jewish devil, and it fell to Sam Cooke to cajole his costar into fulfilling the expectations of his fans. To Arden's relief, it didn't take much. Night after night, Cooke's own electrifying performances goaded Richard to greater and greater heights of secular theatricality (including a simulated heart attack in the middle of "Lucille"). The tour ended in late October at the Empire Theatre in Liverpool with an encounter worthy of Richard's self-proclaimed status as the king *and* queen of rock 'n' roll. Second on the bill at the Empire were the paragons of the beat music craze in Britain, a local quartet called the Beatles, who had just released their debut single, "Love Me Do." Their backstage audience with Richard was a dream come true for the group, which had idolized him since their formation in the late 1950s. After witnessing the frenzy they inspired in their teenage fans, Richard returned to the United States raving about these four English boys who, he said, could "imitate anyone."

For Sam Cooke, the experience of being upstaged on a nightly basis by a singer who hadn't had a record on the charts in five years served as both a challenge and an inspiration. Returning to New York for a week at the Apollo Theater, Cooke downplayed his usual urbanity and sang instead with a raw intensity that harkened back to his days as a gospel star. The response he received from the Apollo's famously demanding audiences emboldened him, and he next set out on a tour of the South on which he was backed by the saxophonist King Curtis and his hard-edged R&B band. A live recording they made at the Harlem Square Club in Miami captured the flavor of Cooke's more aggressive, earthy style. As if to confirm his new identity, he was introduced at the start of the show as Mr. Soul.

RCA elected not to release the live recording of Sam Cooke at the Harlem Square Club. (The record was issued posthumously in 1984.) Though the success of Cooke's singles qualified him as a crossover star second only to Ray Charles, the Miami performance was unequivocally rhythm and blues, and it was an article of faith in the record business that black people didn't buy LPs. Ray Charles was the only R&B singer who consistently sold large numbers of albums, and Charles's unprecedented versatility—his early-1960s output included jazz albums, live albums, greatest-hits albums, and, most successfully, country and western albums—qualified him as the exception that proved the rule. James Brown came up against this same commercial taboo in the fall of 1962, when he proposed to capture the extraordinary dynamism of his stage show by making a live recording at the Apollo in New York. Syd Nathan, the owner of King Records, was so adamantly opposed to the idea that Brown wound up financing and producing the record himself. The result was a revelation—for James Brown, Syd Nathan, and the record business as a whole.

Up through 1962, James Brown's career had been something of a throwback to the era before record sales began to compete with box office receipts as the measure of success in the music business. "Please, Please, Please" had put Brown's name before the public in 1956, but it wasn't until 1961 that he became a consistent presence on the record charts. In the meantime, he earned his living and built his reputation by performing live three hundred nights a year, perfecting a sweat-drenched persona that lived up to his billing as the Hardest Working Man in Show Business. (The contrast with Sam Cooke's aura of effortless grace could not have been more pronounced.) During most of his long, hard climb, Brown had maintained his own band, and it was as a front man, dancer, and bandleader, more than as a singer per se, that he had made his mark. *Live at the Apollo* (as the record came to be known) was a seamless, breathless thirty-minute race through a half dozen of Brown's best-known numbers. All were elaborations on the basic principle of "Please, Please, Please," in which Brown took simple catchphrases ("try me . . . I don't mind . . . I'll go crazy") and repeated them with innumerable shades of emphasis and inflection over the droning refrains of his backup singers and the tightly wound vamps, stops, and starts of his band. Like no popular singer before him, Brown was a screamer, and on *Live at the Apollo,* his screams were answered by the screams of the women in the audience, so much so that in some of the numbers (especially the ten-minute tour de force "Lost Someone"), the sound of the crowd was an integral part of the performance. This made the album a kind of audio documentary, and for white listeners especially, most of whom had no prior exposure to this type of ritualized call and response, it orchestrated an experience not unlike the one that Phil Walden recounted, sitting in the balcony at the City Auditorium while Little Richard and the black citizens of Macon had the time of their lives down below.

Following its release in the spring of 1963, *Live at the Apollo* (or *The James Brown Show,* as the record was officially titled) exploded onto the *Billboard* LP charts with the force of a hit single, leaping to #5 in the second week of its release, peaking at #2 in August, and remaining on the magazine's list of top-selling albums for well over a year. In response to listener demand, many black radio stations overrode their usual format and played the album in its entirety. *Live at the Apollo* was a commercial sensation, a personal vindication for James Brown, and a harbinger of things to come: an unadulterated dose of R&B whose success revealed the extent to which whites and blacks alike were prepared to respond to contemporary black music in its rawest, most undiluted form.

————————

BACK HOME IN Macon, Otis Redding waited anxiously, week after week, for Joe Galkin and Jim Stewart to settle their business with Bobby Smith and put out "These Arms of Mine." Finally, in late October, Stax released the single as its first offering on a new subsidiary label called Volt Records. "The side features a strong, soulful, blues-touched ballad vocal from Redding against strong combo work," *Billboard* noted in its review. The record caused a stir on the radio in Macon, where Hamp Swain and his colleagues at WIBB played it enthusiastically. But in the early going, it attracted little attention outside the hometown market. Stax was totally lacking in promotional know-how, which meant that any help in that regard would have to come from Atlantic, and Atlantic was relying on Joe Galkin to push "These Arms of Mine." In an effort to prime the pump, Galkin convinced Jim Stewart to offer Stax's share of the song publishing to WLAC's John Richbourg in return for his professional consideration, thereby ensuring that the record became a fixture on John R's playlist throughout the fall and into the winter of 1963. (Stewart would later insist that the single was originally released with "Hey Hey Baby" on the A-side, and that Richbourg was responsible for turning it over. But beginning with the review in *Billboard*, every mention of the record in the trade press focused on "These Arms of Mine.")

Atlanta was one of the few places where the single was selling in any volume, thanks to an authoritative push from Gwen Kesler at Southland Records. In December, Phil Walden and Sam Davis managed to book Otis as an opening act at the city's premier black nightclub, the Royal Peacock, an Auburn Avenue landmark run by Henry Wynn, an enterprising black businessman whose company Supersonic Attractions was a major promoter of R&B package tours. Located up the street from Dr. King's pulpit at Ebenezer Baptist Church, the Royal Peacock had become popular with white college students, who were provided with their own segregated seating area. Otis was paid $150 for three nights' work, two-thirds of which he spent on a new suit. In January, he was invited back to the club, this time to appear on a bill headed by Bettye LaVette, a spirited Detroit teenager whose debut single on Atlantic Records stood at #7 on the R&B charts. The Royal Peacock was by far the most prestigious venue that Otis had ever played, and his appearances there helped him to land a spot on a Henry Wynn package tour of Atlantic-affiliated artists that included the Drifters (currently riding the success of their hit single "Up on the Roof") and their former lead singer, Ben E. King. This step up the ladder of black show business took Otis as far as the Howard Theatre in Washington, D.C. From there, the headliners went on to play the Apollo in New York, while Otis caught a bus back to Macon. According to Phil Walden, when Otis asked the girl in the seat beside him if she had heard "These Arms of Mine," she said she liked the record. "I made it," he told her. "Then what are you doing on this *bus*?" she replied.

This brief tour marked the beginning of the end of Otis's career as a Pinetopper. Though Phil Walden continued to book Otis and Johnny Jenkins together at local club and college dates, Jenkins was resistant to any form of extended travel, and he was reluctant to yield the spotlight to his former protégé. In his place, Otis turned to the journeyman singer and guitarist Eddie Kirkland to serve as his bandleader. Kirkland, who performed variously as Eddie Clark and Eddie Kirk, was a grizzled, thirty-nine-year-old bluesman who had stayed on in Macon after serving for more than a decade as the second guitarist and road manager for John Lee Hooker. He supplemented his musical skills with a wealth of practical knowledge about how to survive on the road. With his help, Otis put together an R&B revue that included the singers Bobby Marchan and Oscar Mack. Mack was a Maconite who had occasionally sung with the Pinetoppers and was best known for his dancing and showmanship. Bobby Marchan was a bona fide recording star who had recently moved to Macon after serving for years as lead singer and road manager for New Orleans's answer to the Coasters, Huey "Piano" Smith and the Clowns. A habitué of the same Dew Drop Inn demimonde that inspired Little Richard, Marchan's cherubic features and piercing falsetto had earned him a reputation as one of the most popular female impersonators on the R&B circuit. In 1961, after leaving the Clowns, he recorded a gender-bending version of Jay McFeely's recent hit "There Is Something on Your Mind," to which he added a spoken-word soliloquy advocating a murderous solution to the song's adulterous theme. Marchan's comic cover far outsold the original, rising to the top of the R&B charts. (It also inspired a rash of lawsuits, since Marchan was simultaneously under contract to three different record labels—a situation that may have influenced his decision to take refuge in Macon at the time.)

Toward the end of March, nearly five months after its release, "These Arms of Mine" made a sudden, chimeric appearance at #20 on the *Billboard* R&B charts, only to vanish the following week. Normally, this would have marked the end of the line for a single, but Joe Galkin parlayed this flicker of hope into a major initiative. Citing sketchy reports of strong airplay in Washington, Cincinnati, and New Orleans, Galkin persuaded Atlantic to "reservice" the record—a procedure that involved sending out fresh copies and promotional material to radio stations and placing new ads in the trade papers. This effort paid off six weeks later, when "These Arms of Mine" enjoyed a brief resurgence, this time on the *Billboard* Pop charts, where it "peaked" at #85 before fading away for good. Still, by the middle of May, after nearly seven months in circulation, the single had sold more than 100,000 copies. This was enough to persuade Jim Stewart to invite Otis back to Memphis for a recording date. For good measure, Stewart extended the invitation to the other three singers in Otis's revue, Eddie Kirk, Bobby Marchan, and Oscar Mack. Whether out of guilt or loyalty, Otis asked Johnny Jenkins to accompany them to Memphis as well.

Stax Records had spent the preceding eight months trying and, for the most part, failing to follow up on the success of "Green Onions"—an effort that was compromised from the start by the departure of Booker Jones, who in September 1962, at the height of the single's popularity, enrolled as a freshman music student at Indiana University. "I knew it was best not to count on just making it as a popular musician," Jones would later say. "There was no guarantee that popularity would last." Jones had remained in Memphis long enough for the MGs to record a passable album of R&B cover tunes. But the newly formed group had barely begun to gel, and neither of their follow-up singles, "Jelly Bread" and "Home Grown," made a dent on the charts. With Jones seven hours away in Bloomington, Indiana, available only on occasional weekends and school vacations, Stax's already meager output slowed to a crawl over the first half of 1963. Apart from instrumentals by the MGs and the Mar-Keys, the only records the label released during this period were singles by

Carla and Rufus Thomas and a pair of tracks by William Bell. Of these, only the Thomases' contributions—a weepy ballad by Carla called "What a Fool I've Been" and a howling, growling dance-floor workout by Rufus called "The Dog"—enjoyed any measure of success.

Yet while Stax continued to struggle, a creative nucleus was forming on McLemore Avenue. The success of "Green Onions" had been a boost to everyone's confidence. In Steve Cropper's case, it inspired him to fully embrace the multifaceted role of guitarist, songwriter, and studio manager that Chips Moman had formerly played. Cropper earned a songwriting credit on five of the eight singles Stax released during the first half of 1963, and he had begun to work with the Mar-Keys' horn players on adapting the group's punchy, riffing style to the support of vocalists. Working with singers also helped Cropper come into his own as an accompanist. In a musical milieu that had been dominated by keyboards and horns, his work with the MGs was the first prominent guitar playing to be heard on a Stax recording. The fact that Cropper rarely played outside the studio at this point allowed him to focus on the subtleties of vocal accompaniment in a way that most working guitarists, performing in clubs for dancers, could not afford to do.

Perhaps the most important repercussion of "Green Onions" was the way its success underwrote the presence of Al Jackson Jr. at Stax, laying the cornerstone for one of the great R&B rhythm sections of the 1960s. At twenty-eight, Jackson had spent a decade in the bands of Willie Mitchell, Ben Branch, and Bowlegs Miller, performing at venues like the Plantation Inn. His playing combined a fluid technique with a seasoned musical sensibility. Like most urban black musicians of his generation, Jackson had come up listening to jazz—big-band swing in the 1940s, hard bop in the 1950s. His personal idols were Sonny Payne and Art Blakey, a pair of powerhouse drummers whose names were synonymous with a pair of jazz institutions. Payne had joined the Count Basie Orchestra in 1955, filling the shoes of two of the greatest drummers in jazz history, Jo Jones and Shadow Wilson. Basie's band was universally regarded as the epitome of vibrant, bluesy swing, and Jackson's emulation of Payne contributed to his mastery of tempo, phrasing, and dynamics. Art Blakey, by contrast, was a hard-driving modernist whose group, the Jazz Messengers, had served as the seedbed of the soul-jazz movement in the 1950s. Blakey's trademarks included an unyielding backbeat on the hi-hat and a preference for playing with the butt end of the stick on the snare; these became traits of Jackson's playing as well. Jackson was preceded by his reputation at Stax, and everyone at the label deferred to his quiet musical authority.

The growing capability of the Stax studio band was the common denominator on the tracks recorded in May with the Otis Redding Revue. Eddie Kirk's "The Hawg" was a porcine variation of Rufus Thomas's "The Dog": a prospective dance craze record on which Kirk's ludicrous instructions ("C'mon girl, root! root!") were offset by the more convincing sound of his blues harmonica, wailing over a booming bed of bass and drums. Oscar Mack's "Don't Be Afraid of Love," co-written with Phil Walden and sung with the help of a backup chorus (which may have included Otis), was similarly held together by a tight groove of horns, bass, and drums. Bobby Marchan's revival of Donny Elbert's 1957 hit "What Can I Do?" featured Marchan in full femme mode, chatting his way through the song's verses in a duet with Wayne Jackson's muted trumpet, which sounded like a trombone next to his campy falsetto.

Otis's main contribution to the May session was an ostensibly self-written ballad called "That's What My Heart Needs." The song took its melody, chords, and opening line directly from "Let's Go Steady Again," the B-side to Sam Cooke's 1959 hit "Sweet Sixteen," to which Otis added a courtly lyric ("I'm down on bended knee") and an extended, ad-libbed coda modeled on "These Arms of Mine." The track is distinguished from its predecessor by Otis's more confident delivery and a proper arrangement that features a chorus of background horns and an instrumental hook in which Al Jackson's bright cymbal splashes and Steve Cropper's ascending three-note guitar lick frame the title line. The coda as well is altogether more forceful, with Otis compressing his voice into a raspy screech in which he seems to be channeling Ray Charles in "Ain't That Love," imploring his lover, "I need you right here by my side / To protect me and be my guide."

For the B-side, Otis reached back to a facetious version of "Mary Had a Little Lamb" that he had been singing for the amusement of his family and friends since childhood. Recasting the nursery rhyme as a tale of girl meets lamb, girl loses lamb, and girl gets lamb again, Otis plays the part of a sympathetic classmate, scoffing at the "silly rule" that banished Mary's lamb from school. Johnny Jenkins plays guitar on the track (recycling, yet again, the riff from "Love Twist"), while a male backup chorus chants "*Mary* had a *lit-tle* lamb" as Otis milks the joke, reminding Mary, "When you go home today / You and your lamb can play / You can even do the Twist / And it goes a-something like this."

Jenkins also played behind Otis on a mawkish ballad called "Come to Me" and a swinging blues called "Don't Leave Me This Way," both co-written with Phil Walden and set aside by Jim Stewart for possible future release. This session would be Jenkins's last encounter with a recording studio for many years to come, and it figured heavily in the narrative of victimization and betrayal with which he would nurse his pride. "They stopped supporting me and threw all the attention on [Otis]," he later said. "They kept me hid. They took my music and gave my licks to a white boy, but he couldn't play like me. If you notice the first two or three Redding records with Cropper, you'll see he's copying what I used to play behind Otis. But he just couldn't follow through."

Stax issued the new singles by Eddie Kirk, Oscar Mack, Bobby Marchan, and Otis Redding late in the spring of 1963. In keeping with the label's recent run of luck, only Otis's "That's What My Heart Needs" enjoyed even a glimmer of success. This time around, it was Joe Galkin's turn to award his share of the publishing to John Richbourg, who returned the favor by playing the record throughout the summer despite weak sales and a general lack of interest in the rest of the southern radio market—an inauspicious follow-up to a promising debut.

THE HOT SUMMER REVUE

It was my first time out on the road, so I booked the dates, rented a bus, and lost my fanny. The only white people on the bus were me and the driver.

—PHIL WALDEN

DURING THE FIRST HALF OF 1963, PHIL WALDEN HAD BEEN NURS-ing an open secret. Having spent his four years at Mercer as a cadet in the university's Reserve Officers Training Corps, Phil had graduated in the spring of 1962 with a degree in economics and a commission as a second lieutenant in the United States Army. The latter came with a deferred commitment to serve two years of active duty, beginning in the summer of 1963. Lt. Walden's orders, when they finally came, instructed him to report in July for a six-week course at the army's Adjutant General School in Indianapolis, for training as a personnel officer. (Among other things, the AG Corps was responsible for providing entertainment on army bases.) Upon completion of this course, Phil could expect to be posted overseas. His exact assignment was yet to be determined, but in 1963, the most likely destination for an army lieutenant with a wife and a baby—Phil and Kathy's son, Philip Jr., had been born the previous November—was West Germany.

Unaccountably, Phil seems to have dealt with this looming commitment by barely mentioning it to his associates. (In March 1963, the Kennedy administration issued an executive order exempting married men with children from the military draft; despite the fact that he was already a commissioned officer, he may have been hoping against hope that this would somehow earn him a reprieve.) In May, however, Phil took it upon himself to sign Otis to a second management contract, supplanting the three-year agreement they had signed the summer before. Joe Galkin had been quite correct in telling Bobby Smith that Redding's contract with Confederate Records was invalid because Otis was underage, but the same applied to the contract Otis had signed with Phil Walden and Sam Davis the previous August, a month before his twenty-first birthday. The revised contract eliminated Sam Davis's role as comanager and reduced the commission on Otis's gross earnings from 30 to 20 percent. (With Davis out of the picture, this represented a 5 percent increase in Walden's share.) Phil would later claim that the original contract was voided under the terms of its "mutual consent" clause, but it is hard to imagine that Davis would voluntarily relinquish his interest in Otis at the very moment when Otis's career was starting to take off. The more likely explanation was that Phil and Otis had decided that Poor Sam had become super-fluous and cut him out of the deal. (Davis would wait nearly four years before hiring a lawyer and filing a breach-of-contract suit that was settled out of court.)

In place of Sam Davis, the new contract was cosigned by Phil's father, C. B., whose professed distaste for "nigger music" had gradually succumbed to the warmth of Otis's personality and C. B.'s growing sense that his son's talent agency might involve some genuine prospect of economic gain for the Walden family. In March, Phil had had to prevail on his father to bail Otis out of the Bibb County Jail after he was arrested on a misdemeanor charge for selling a car with a lien on its title to a local garage. C. B. posted a bond; later in the summer, he would draw on his courthouse connections to get Otis off with a small fine. In the course of these interactions, C. B. was sufficiently charmed by Otis—who had taken to calling him "Pops"—that he and Phil began to discuss the possibility of C. B.'s running the talent agency while Phil fulfilled his commitment to Uncle Sam. Toward that end, Phil hired a young assistant named Bill Hall to help out around the office.

In anticipation of his departure for Indianapolis, Phil went into a whirlwind of activity in the spring of 1963. Previously, he had confined himself to booking college and club gigs on a piecemeal basis. Now, drawing on his growing list of contacts, he put Otis, Bobby Marchan, and Eddie Kirk together with a pair of established R&B acts, Joe Tex and the Fiestas, on a tour of clubs, colleges, ballrooms, and armory dances that he called the Hot Summer Revue. Joe Tex had recorded for a number of different labels without much chart success, but he was an exciting live performer whose dancing and stagecraft had influenced better-known artists such as James Brown and Jackie Wilson. The Fiestas were a vocal group from New Jersey, best known for their 1959 single "So Fine," which was just enough of a hit to consign them to a lifetime of one-nighters on the chitlin' circuit.

Though Phil had spent long hours driving his bands to and from their gigs, the Hot Summer Revue was a much more involving experience: traveling on a rented bus with more than a dozen black singers and musicians for days on end, sleeping on the bus or staying in colored motels and boardinghouses, and eating, when they could find them, in colored restaurants. They played dates in Georgia, the Carolinas, and Virginia, and Phil remembered it as "a wonderful experience. The first step in my new education. It was unbelievable to have this opportunity to be part of another culture, and to eventually be considered part of it, and accepted to a large degree—though I don't know that I was ever *completely* accepted."

What Phil Walden described as his "new education" was exactly that: an immersion in the culture of the black musicians he had been working with that was unlike anything the vast majority of white Americans of his generation had experienced, least of all in the South. In his seminal work *The Nature of Prejudice,* providentially published in the same year as *Brown v. Board of Education,* the psychologist Gordon Allport drew on a substantial body of research that had been accumulating since the 1930s to cast new light on the ancient phenomenon of social antipathy based on racial, ethnic, or religious difference. Among the many virtues of Allport's work was his willingness to address not only the processes by which prejudiced beliefs and attitudes are formed and sustained, but also the processes by which such beliefs and attitudes have been known to yield to positive feelings of tolerance, empathy, and identification. Unsurprisingly, Allport concluded that social contact between individuals is a prerequisite for any moderation of bias. But he also determined that contact alone is not enough. Casual contact, he found, has the effect of strengthening prejudice by creating the illusion of social knowledge, as does the sort of unequal, hierarchical interactions that characterized most workplace relations between whites and blacks in the United States. Instead, Allport wrote, it is "only the type of contact that leads people to *do* things together," on terms of roughly "equal status . . . in pursuit of common goals," that is likely to result in any significant moderation of the negative stereotypes that support prejudice. The most dramatic study he cited to substantiate this view was a US Army survey from World War II assessing the attitudes of white soldiers toward the idea of serving with blacks in combat. In all-white units that had no contact with all-black units, two-thirds of the soldiers expressed strong opposition to the idea of fighting alongside blacks. Among whites who served in regiments and companies that included all-black platoons, however, two-thirds of the soldiers expressed a strong willingness to fight alongside blacks, while only a very small minority opposed the idea. Lest combat seem too extreme a test, Allport also cited the more recent phenomenon of integrated professional team sports to support his contention that sustained contact, equal status, and common goals were all essential to breaking down racial and ethnic stereotypes.

While Phil Walden's position as the promoter of the Hot Summer Revue afforded him a different status than that of the musicians on the tour, there was a limit to Phil's ability or desire to maintain the illusion that he was in charge of anything—especially since, in his dealings with the local promoters and club owners, he had to rely on the help of the savvier artists such as Joe Tex and Eddie Kirk to ensure that they even got paid. For the most part, Phil's experience met the criteria of equal status and common purpose that Allport's work prescribed, and there is no question that his exposure to a world he had previously glimpsed from the comfort and safety of his position as a young white man in a Jim Crow city had a profound effect on him. In turn, Phil's willingness to forgo that comfort and safety had an effect on the black musicians he was traveling with, and with Otis to vouch for him, there is no reason to doubt his impression that that "they were as curious about *me* as I was about them." (At one black club, Phil recalled, he was accosted by an angry patron who cursed and spat at him, whereupon Sylvester Huckabee, who had been hired as Otis's valet and bodyguard, knocked the man unconscious with a single punch.) One aspect of Phil's curiosity centered on the age-old subtext of white-black relations in the South, his attraction to black women. "You know, that was forbidden fruit, so of course I couldn't wait to do it," he recalled of his initiation by a waitress at a club in Richmond. Phil had a much more puritanical response to another revelation that awaited him on the tour, involving the taste for marijuana that Otis and his fellow musicians shared. ("I was terrified of it," he later said.)

Though their itinerary steered clear of the civil rights cauldron of Mississippi and Alabama, the late spring and summer of 1963 was an anxious time for a busload of black musicians to be traveling the roads of the South. That May, amid concerns that the momentum of their move- ment was flagging, the Southern Christian Leadership Council organized a series of demonstrations in Birmingham, Alabama, with the express in- tent of provoking an overreaction from the city's arch-segregationist com- missioner of public safety, Eugene "Bull" Connor. The SCLC's high-risk strategy succeeded beyond its leaders' wildest dreams, resulting in televi- sion footage and news photographs of Connor's men attacking throngs of black schoolchildren with police dogs and fire hoses. The images drama- tized the brutality of the racial confrontation that was occurring in the Deep South, and the press and public responded with a sense of outrage that was duly noted in Washington. Several weeks later, in the middle of June, Alabama's newly elected segregationist governor George Wallace threatened to defy a federal court order by blocking the admission of the first black students to the University of Alabama. (After posturing bravely for the cameras, Wallace meekly yielded to the rule of law.) That same night, just hours after President Kennedy delivered a nationally televised speech calling for civil rights legislation to redress "a moral issue . . . as old as the Scriptures and as clear as the American Constitution," Medgar Evers, the fearless NAACP field secretary who had been instrumental in enrolling James Meredith at the University of Mississippi the previous fall, was assassinated in the driveway of his home in Jackson by a Klans- man named Byron de la Beckwith. Evers's last words, spoken to police and neighbors as they attempted to rush him to a hospital, were "Turn me loose."

When the Hot Summer Revue tour ended in the middle of July, Phil Walden took a page from Clint Brantley's book and rented the Macon

City Auditorium the week before Brantley's annual James Brown Homecoming show for an Otis Redding Homecoming Dance and Concert. This was Phil's first venture into concert promotion, and he prevailed on Jim Stewart to send him several Stax artists to perform. In addition to Otis and two of his opening acts, Eddie Kirk and Oscar Mack, the bill included Rufus and Carla Thomas and Booker T. and the MGs. In keeping with the mores of Macon, the concert took place before a segregated audience, with blacks on the dance floor and an advertised Special Section for White Spectators in the balcony.

PAIN IN MY HEART

We were never the same once we met Tom Dowd.

—BOOKER JONES

J ERRY WEXLER WAS A CHRONICALLY ANXIOUS MAN, AND HIS ANXI-
ety was reaching one of its periodic heights during the summer of
1963. On the surface of things, Atlantic Records was doing remarkably
well. At a time when most of its independent competitors (whom Wexler
would one day compare to "the Lost Tribes of the Sinai") were falling
by the wayside, the label had weathered the loss of Ray Charles, Clyde
McPhatter, and Bobby Darin and seemed to be holding its own with
a mixture of uptown rhythm and blues and progressive jazz in a record
market that was increasingly dominated by major corporate labels with
deep pockets and a shallow understanding of the music they released.

And still, according to Wexler, "I had this feeling that a puff of smoke
could come along and blow us all away, instantly. All you had to do was
make a succession of flop records." As the summer wore on, Wexler began
to worry that the flops were adding up. The latest releases by Atlantic's
rising star Solomon Burke and its old standby the Drifters seemed to be
falling flat, as were the new singles by Carla Thomas and Otis Redding
on Stax. Ben E. King's recording career had been in remission for more
than a year, and his most recent single, a melodramatic ballad called "I
(Who Have Nothing)," was stalled in the lower reaches of the charts. In
addition, Wexler and his partners were feeling an acute sense of competition from the Detroit-based Motown label, which was starting to oc-
cupy a position in the world of black popular music analogous to that of
Atlantic in the 1950s, with its own distinctive sound and its own ideas of
how records should be made and marketed. In the summer of 1963 alone,
Motown had broken Top 10 hits by Martha and the Vandellas ("Heat

Wave"), Marvin Gaye ("Pride and Joy"), the Miracles ("Mickey's Monkey"), and "Little" Stevie Wonder, a blind, twelve-year-old singer and harmonica prodigy whose precocious talent elicited comparisons with Ray Charles and whose live recording of "Fingertips" was the #1 single in America. "Motown scared the shit out of me," Ahmet Ertegun later admitted. "We didn't understand how to write it, we didn't understand how to play it, and we didn't understand how to sing it. It was newer and hipper than what we were doing and it got to the public in a very heavy way."

Though he could not have known it at the time, Jerry Wexler's intimations of disaster may also have owed to the fact that he had recently made the biggest blunder of his professional career. Atlantic's legal business was handled by the New York attorney Paul Marshall, who also provided US representation for the British recording conglomerate EMI. EMI was the parent company of Capitol Records in America, with which it enjoyed a reciprocal licensing deal. In February 1963, EMI contacted Marshall and asked him to find alternative licensing in the States for an album by a British group that Capitol's A&R department had declined. Marshall's first move was to forward a copy of the record to his client and good friend Jerry Wexler, who took one listen and dismissed it out of hand as "too derivative." The record was *Please Please Me,* the Beatles' first LP.

Wexler's way of managing his stress was to work the phones, badgering his personal network of label heads, distributors, deejays, and promo men. Early in August, he telephoned Jim Stewart to ask when Atlantic might expect to see some fresh product from its Memphis affiliate. In the course of their conversation, Stewart mentioned that the studio's Ampex tape deck had broken down. A week later, when Wexler called again, Stewart told him that the deck was still broken, and that the parts needed to repair it were back-ordered. Incredulous at Stewart's nonchalance, Wexler blew a fuse of his own. He ordered Atlantic's chief engineer, Tom Dowd, to get on the next flight to Memphis and fix the goddamn deck.

When Dowd arrived at the Stax studio the following day, he found that the unit had *never* been properly serviced; its brake bands had simply worn out. Dowd called his assistant in New York and had him buy the necessary parts, which were delivered to Memphis the next morning by an obliging Eastern Airlines stewardess. While Jim Stewart and his staff looked on in wonder, Dowd rebuilt the Ampex deck before their very eyes. He was in the process of testing its operation when Rufus Thomas walked in, having deduced from the number of cars in the parking lot that the studio must be up and running again. In a matter of minutes, with Dowd behind the board, Thomas recorded a sequel to his previous single, "The Dog." The new track, titled "Walkin' the Dog," was a great improvement on the original, and Dowd was astonished at how quickly the improvised arrangement, which featured a seamless interplay of horns and guitar, came together in the studio. He returned to New York the next day with a master tape of the track and a newfound respect for the way they made records at Stax. "Walkin' the Dog" was the most fully realized vocal recording that Stax had made to date, and it went on to become a Top 10 hit in the fall of 1963. Its success, combined with Tom Dowd's account of the manner it which it was made, helped to focus Jerry Wexler's attention on Memphis as a way of easing his troubled mind.

On August 27, 1963, W. E. B. Du Bois died in Ghana, where he was living and working, at the age of ninety-five, on an encyclopedia of the African diaspora. The following day, at what would prove to be the first mass demonstration of the 1960s, Dr. Martin Luther King Jr. delivered his epic "I Have a Dream" speech in front of 250,000 people who had gathered at the Lincoln Memorial in Washington. "We must rise to the majestic heights of meeting physical force with *soul* force," King declared. The greatest black intellectual of his era, Du Bois had lived long enough to see the rise of a social movement in America that represented the realization, if not yet the triumph, of a social vision he had first articulated more than sixty years before. He had also lived long enough to see the attribute he was the first to ascribe to his race, "soul," become a catchphrase for black identity. Though he was influenced like most thinkers of his time by pseudoscientific theories of race and blood, soul in Du Bois's view was not so much a genetic quality as the sum of the black experience in America. As he wrote with characteristic eloquence in a famous passage from his 1897 *Atlantic Monthly* article "The Strivings of the Negro People," "One ever feels his twoness—an American, a Negro: two thoughts, two unreconciled strivings, two warring ideals in one dark body, whose dogged strength alone keeps it from being torn asunder. The history of the American Negro is the history of this strife—this longing to attain self-conscious manhood, to merge his double self into a better, truer self. In this merging he wishes neither of the older selves to be lost. He would not Africanize America, for America has too much to teach the world and Africa. He would not bleach his Negro soul in a flood of white American-ism, for he knows that his Negro blood has a message for the world."

Two weeks after Du Bois's death and King's speech in Washington, back in the land where gallantry took its last bow, a dynamite bomb planted by members of the Birmingham Ku Klux Klan exploded at the Sixteenth Street Baptist Church, extinguishing the lives of four black teenage girls who had been attending Sunday school, and testing anew the strength of Dr. King's recently expressed hope that "one day, down in Alabama, with its vicious racists . . . one day right there in Alabama, little black boys and black girls will be able to join hands with little white boys and white girls as brothers and sisters. I have a dream today!" Though the identities of the terrorists were known to both the Birmingham police and the local office of the FBI, the only charges brought were for illegal possession of dynamite, for which one of the murderers, Robert Cham-bliss, was convicted and assessed a small fine. It would be another four-teen years before Chambliss was tried, convicted, and sentenced to life in prison for his part in this atrocity, and nearly forty years before two of his three aging accomplices were finally brought to justice for their crimes.

That same September, Jim Stewart invited Otis Redding back to Stax. "That's What My Heart Needs" had been in release for four months and had sold less than 40,000 copies, but everyone felt that Otis could do better, and Stewart wanted to schedule a session with him before Booker Jones returned to Indiana for the fall semester.

Accompanying Otis on this trip to Memphis was his brother, Rod-gers, who had graduated from Ballard-Hudson High School in the spring with the apparent intention of fulfilling his parents' hopes by enrolling at an all-black college in neighboring Fort Valley in the fall. Over the summer, however, the excitement of his brother's musical career began to outweigh the allure of higher education. An honors student, Rodgers had a head for math, and in the heyday of the Pinetoppers, Otis and Sam Davis had called on him from time to time to help them haggle with club owners over the percentages they were due. With Davis now out of the picture, Otis needed someone he could rely on to act as his road manager, and the two brothers managed to convince their parents to let Rodgers take the job (though not before Fannie hit the roof after receiving a call from the principal at Ballard-Hudson informing her that her son, contrary to the impression he had given her, had never actually applied to Fort Valley State).

The major issue facing Otis at this point in his recording career centered on the fundamental question of what he was going to sing. Most of his musical role models, including Ray Charles, Little Richard, and Sam Cooke, were songwriters as well as singers. Their ability to write their own songs had enabled them to craft material suited to their own voices and vocal personalities, and it also significantly increased their financial return from their recordings. Song publishing was the great underground revenue stream in the music business, a penny-ante enterprise that added up to many millions of dollars in income for writers and publishers each year.

In Otis's case, the virtues of recording his own material were affirmed by the royalty checks he received for his songwriting credit on "These Arms of Mine." Like most independent labels, Stax owned its own publishing company, East Memphis Music, which held the copyrights on all the original songs they recorded. Unlike most independent labels, however, Stax was run by a bank officer, and Jim Stewart took an almost perverse pride, by the standards of the recording industry, in paying his artists in full and on time. By the summer of 1963, "These Arms of Mine" had sold nearly 130,000 copies, which had earned Otis about $3,600 in record royalties (equivalent to roughly $28,000 in 2017 dollars). But his writer's share of the publishing on the two-sided single came to another $2,600, and this was all the incentive he needed to focus his attention on the economic merits of writing the songs he sang.

The rub for Otis, of course, was that he hadn't actually written "These Arms of Mine." Nor, to judge by such mediocre and derivative efforts as "Hey Hey Baby" and "That's What My Heart Needs," had he written anything remotely as good as the simple tune Jackie Avery had unwittingly bequeathed to him two years before. (When he and Avery met again in Gulfport, Mississippi, in 1963, Otis promised he would "make it up" to Jackie for his theft of the song.) Songwriting had been little more than a hobby for Otis during his semiprofessional career as a singer in a cover band, and his skill at conveying a musical emotion was far more developed than his skill at composing one. Like many artists who start off as singers and then try their hand at songwriting, Otis was hampered by his lack of facility on an instrument. He could bang out chords on the piano and the guitar, but only well enough to sketch the most basic harmonies, and not nearly well enough to explore the rhythmic patterns and harmonic relationships that bring nuance and originality to songwriting. Otis's guitar technique was especially confining, for he relied on an open E tuning (favored by slide guitarists) that effectively limited his playing to major chords.

His approach to songwriting was like that of most neophyte composers, which was to take a piece of a song that he liked—a melodic line, a lyric phrase, a rhythmic feel—and literally *play* with it, repeating and recombining the words, melody, or rhythm, twisting it this way and that, until it started to sound like something he could plausibly call his own. Another common method he tried was to think of a phrase that sounded like a song title, and then use both the sense and the sound of the words as a guide to composing a lyric and a melody.

Still another constraint on Otis's efforts at songwriting was his insecurity about language. Though he had grown up in the rich oral culture of the African American South, exposed to the King James eloquence of the black church and the native wit of many ordinary people who had an extraordinary way with words, Otis's self-consciousness about his diction and his vocabulary was a major source of inhibition when it came to the quasi-poetic formality of writing song lyrics. He knew his speech was "country," and unlike many blues artists who turned this colloquiality to their advantage, he was reluctant to play it up. The most elaborate lyric he had written to date, "Shout Bamalama," had been artfully assembled from snatches of African American folklore—the Preacher and the Bear, the Lion and the Monkey—but once he began making records, Otis did not return to these themes. Instead, he enlisted Phil Walden as his collaborator, presumably drawing on Phil's college education and undeniable gift of gab. Yet the results, which included the ballad "Come to Me" and a more upbeat number called "Something Is Worrying Me" ("I can tell by the look in your eye / That you've been loving some other guy"), were no improvement on the lyrics Otis had written on his own.

In the normal course of things, it would have been up to Otis's record label to provide him with suitable songs. Before the term *producer* came into vogue in the late 1950s, recording sessions were run by "artist and repertoire" (A&R) men, whose job it was to sign singers, procure songs, and put the two together in commercially successful ways. As Solomon Burke recounted his experience at Atlantic, "My beginning of learning what the record business meant was hearing Jerry Wexler say, 'I am your producer and we pick the songs. Now if you think you'd like to sing a song, you let us know, but we're gonna have the final decision on the song because we know what's best for you, we know what the market can stand, and we know where we can play a record and how it can be played and when it can be played and who's going to play it.'"

Atlantic's rival Motown was taking this approach even further, organizing its entire operation around songwriting producers who competed openly with one another to work with the label's top acts. At Motown, it was not uncommon for a producer like Smokey Robinson or William Stevenson to write and record a finished arrangement of a song before deciding which of the label's artists would sing it. Both Atlantic and Motown subscribed to the conventional wisdom in the music business that a good song, far more than a good singer, was the key to a hit record, and they put a great deal of time and effort into obtaining suitable material for their artists to sing.

Stax Records, unfortunately, was in no position to offer its singers much help in this regard. Memphis was far removed from the centers of music publishing, and neither Jim Stewart nor anyone else connected with the label had any professional contacts they could draw on in New York, Nashville, New Orleans, or Los Angeles. As with the artists he recorded, Stewart was content to sit and wait for songs to walk in the door. Eventually, they would do just that, in the person of Booker Jones's former high school bandmate David Porter, who in 1965 would form a successful songwriting partnership with Isaac Hayes, a keyboard player Stax was using to fill in for Jones during the academic year. But that was well in the future, and for the time being, Stax left the matter of repertoire up to the artists themselves.

Otis's technique of elaborating on existing material reached an early height of audacity with the song he brought to Stax in September 1963. On the strength of Top 10 hits by Ernie K-Doe ("Mother-in-Law"), Chris Kenner ("I Like It Like That"), and Lee Dorsey ("Ya-Ya")—all written and recorded by the brilliant young producer Allen Toussaint— New Orleans had retained its cachet as a recording center during the early 1960s. Toussaint had been less successful with Irma Thomas, an inexperienced singer with whom he recorded a number of atmospheric ballads. These included the future New Orleans standard "It's Raining," followed in the spring of 1963 by a single called "Ruler of My Heart," which featured a haunting introduction of piano and background vocals, a punchy lyric ("Ruler of my heart / Robber of my soul / Where can you be? / I wait patiently") and a strong hook that turned on the line "*Come* back! *Come* back! *Come* back / I've had enough." Irma Thomas would soon mature into a singer of considerable power and presence, but her voice was swallowed by the production on "Ruler of My Heart," and the record never broke out of the Gulf Coast radio market. This relative obscurity made the song ripe for poaching, and when Otis came to Memphis in September, he showed Jim Stewart and the Stax band a thinly disguised rewrite he had concocted with Phil Walden called "Pain in My Heart." "Pain in my heart / Treating me cold / Where can my baby be?" it began, mirroring the melody and phrasing of Thomas's record. Though Stewart himself was unaware of the song's provenance, the musicians at Stax were avid students of New Orleans R&B and had recently recorded an album with Rufus Thomas that included covers of several of Toussaint's songs. By replacing the background vocals with a moaning chorus of horns, they generated an arrangement whose stately power transformed the song into a perfect vehicle for Otis, who sang it with a finely tuned sense of dynamics, turning the vowel sounds in *heart* and *cold* into quick-flaring bursts of emotion. Steve Cropper's guitar stood front and center in the mix, alternating between high-pitched filigrees and low, bending runs in the verse, before joining with the horns to drive home the rhythm in the bridge, where Otis dispensed with all pretense of originality as the band shuddered to a stop behind his plea of "Come back! Come back! Come back, *baby*—I've had enough."

"Pain in My Heart" was the record that convinced Jim Stewart of Otis's talent once and for all. "After about probably the third single, I really began to understand what Otis was about, how special he was," Stewart recalled. Released in late October, the record had a much stronger impact than either of its predecessors; it would go on to sell more than 200,000 copies and rise to #61 on the *Billboard* Pop charts. Given the meager sales of the Irma Thomas version, Allen Toussaint had every reason to welcome its success. But when Stax first issued the record, the songwriting credit on the label read "Redding - Walden" and the publisher was listed as East-Time Music. (Time was the firm that handled Joe Galkin's share of Otis's publishing.) This prompted a strongly worded response from Toussaint's New Orleans–based publisher, Jarb Music, which demanded its full share of both the writing and publishing royalties on every copy sold. Jim Stewart was in no position to contest the matter, and all subsequently pressed copies credited the song to Jarb. On his third try, Otis had produced something close to a hit single, but not yet with a song of his own.

I knew absolutely nothing about the business, but Otis worked with me. I guess it was the first time an entertainer trained the manager.

—ALAN WALDEN

A FEW WEEKS BEFORE OTIS WENT TO MEMPHIS TO RECORD "PAIN in My Heart," Phil Walden completed his training at the Adjutant General's School in Indianapolis and returned to Macon, where he and his wife, Kathy, began packing up their belongings in anticipation of his assignment overseas. They were in the midst of these preparations when Phil's father suffered a strokelike seizure that put him in the hospital in critical condition, fighting for his life. Though C. B. survived, it would take him months to regain his ability to talk and walk, and his left arm was permanently disabled. This family crisis qualified Phil to apply for a monthlong emergency leave. When his furlough ended in October and he received no further orders, he began to hope that he had somehow fallen through the cracks of the army bureaucracy. But at the beginning of November, a telegram came directing him to report immediately for assignment to the Special Services branch of the Third Infantry Division in Würzburg, West Germany.

C. B.'s infirmity precluded any possibility that he would be able to take over the operation of Phil Walden Artists and Promotions as Phil and his father had planned. Phil's older brother, Clark, had a full-time job at Robins AFB and a family to support. That left his younger brother, Alan, who had recently enrolled as a freshman at Mercer, as the only available candidate. According to Alan, Phil called him into the office, informed him of his imminent departure, and spent the next twelve hours showing him how to run the talent agency in his absence. Phil told Alan that "they" had six thousand dollars in the bank, neglecting to mention that "they" owed over ten thousand dollars in outstanding debts. Prudent fiscal management would never be Phil's forte.

One can well imagine how Otis Redding felt upon learning that his manager was leaving on short notice for a sixteen-month tour of duty overseas, to be replaced, not by his father, but by his younger brother, who was not yet old enough to sign a legal contract. Coming just as his career was starting to gain some momentum, this turn of events must have caused Otis to question the wisdom of placing his trust in the Waldens, and he would have been well within his rights—such as they were in Georgia—to seek alternative management. The fact that he didn't do so is hardly explained by the prospect of Alan Walden's stepping into his brother's shoes. Though the two of them would eventually become fast friends, Otis and Alan barely knew each other at this point. Alan looked up to Phil, but few people would say that he resembled him, having shown little of his brother's intellect, ambition, or artistic sensibility. After graduating from Lanier with mediocre grades, he had attended a year of community college before enrolling at Mercer in September 1963. Alan could talk a blue streak like his brother, but he lacked the staccato brusqueness and the air of self-importance that Phil had cultivated. Instead, having modeled himself on his father's sociable nature, Alan at the age of nineteen was well on his way to becoming a prime specimen of the southern good old boy.

For the moment, the main thing Alan had going for him was the fact that "managing" Otis Redding—notwithstanding the Waldens' hefty 20 percent commission—consisted of little more than booking his gigs. Phil liked to talk and think about managerial strategy, and throughout his stay in Germany, he sent back "long letters detailing everything from how I wanted Otis to dress to which songs he should sing"—while Alan humored his brother by pretending to heed his advice. In fact, Phil's knowledge of artist management began and ended with whatever he had learned from Joe Galkin in the preceding year and a half, and from Otis's perspective, the saving grace of the whole situation was the role that Galkin continued to play in the management of his career. Jim Stewart was already dealing with Galkin as if he were Otis's manager; Phil Walden's existence, much less his departure, had barely registered at Stax. However little Alan knew about the music business, it was no less than Phil had known in the winter of 1962 when Galkin took him under his wing.

Two weeks after Phil's departure for Germany, Otis, Rodgers, and Sylvester Huckabee drove to New York, where Otis, through the good graces of Atlantic Records, was set to make his debut at the Apollo Theater. The commercial success of James Brown's *Live at the Apollo* had not been lost on Syd Nathan's competitors. Atlantic Records considered New York its home turf, so Jerry Wexler arranged with Bobby Schiffman, the owner of the Apollo, to have a half dozen Atlantic-affiliated artists make a live recording at the theater in the third week of November. Billed as "The Atlantic Caravan of Stars," the show was headlined by Ben E. King and the Coasters and supported by Doris Troy, Rufus Thomas, Otis Redding, and the Falcons, a Detroit-based group whose formidable lead singer, Wilson Pickett, had recently left to embark on a solo career. Backing for all six of the acts was to be provided by King Curtis and his band. An announcement in the *Amsterdam News* promised "the greatest array of recording stars to appear on one stage at the same time." In truth, the Coasters hadn't had a record on the charts in more than two years, and Ben E. King's career was on the verge of a precipitous decline. Rufus Thomas and Doris Troy, on the other hand, were riding the success of their Top 10 hits "Walkin' the Dog" and "Just One Look." They too were making their Apollo debut.

After arriving in New York, Otis and his two-man entourage checked in at the Hotel Theresa, a storied Harlem landmark that had long since gone to seed. He then presented himself at the Apollo, where he learned to his dismay that he was expected to provide King Curtis and his band with written charts of the arrangements to his songs. Since no such charts had ever existed—such was the difference in the music culture of Memphis and New York—Otis had to pay to have them made, which put a sizable dent in the $400 fee he was receiving for his week's work. The Atlantic recording was slated to be produced by Jerry Wexler and engineered by Tom Dowd; both were meeting Otis for the first time. "We liked him immediately," Wexler recalled. "He was a very ingratiating person. Relaxed, no put-on, and shy." Dowd knew Harlem from his days at Columbia, and he took it upon himself to shepherd Otis around the neighborhood and show him the sights.

An Apollo debut was an intimidating experience for any aspiring black entertainer, especially one as green as Otis Redding. Audiences at the theater had the same steely self-regard as all their fellow New Yorkers, and they could be vociferous in their disapproval of performers who didn't meet their standards. (As Rufus Thomas said, "They would boo their mama off the stage.") According to Ben E. King, "Otis told me he was up from home, and he was terrified. He was worried because he was country. 'You really think they're gonna go for what I do, what *we* do down home?'"

Adding to his apprehension was his growing awareness that his performing style was indeed completely unrefined. His years of service as a Pinetopper, singing in the shadow of Johnny Jenkins's theatrics, had absolved him of the need to develop a stage presence of his own. In Jerry Wexler's view, "He was inept on stage. He simply stood in front of the microphone, arms outstretched, body motionless." And yet, Wexler added, "Despite his inertia, the women at the Apollo loved him." (Rufus Thomas had advised Otis to single out one woman in the audience and address his performance to her.) If nothing else, the relentless routine at the Apollo gave Otis ample opportunity to work on his stagecraft, for the schedule consisted of five shows a day, beginning at 11:00 in the morning and ending after midnight. Otis's spot in the program put him fifth on the bill, following the Falcons, who opened the show. His segment was confined to his best-known song, "These Arms of Mine," and his new single, "Pain in My Heart." In the card file he kept on every artist he presented, Bobby Schiffman characterized Otis's Apollo debut with a single word: "Adequate."

Released in the spring of 1964, *Saturday Night at the Apollo* was a pale reflection of the James Brown extravaganza it was modeled on. Brown's show had been a sustained crescendo, thematically unified from start to finish by the voice and domineering presence of James Brown. The Atlantic compilation, by comparison, was a hodgepodge of uneven performances. Nevertheless, the album contains the first recording of Otis Redding singing live, and it betrays little of the nervousness that Ben E.

King recalled. Preceded by a frantic fanfare from the band and a word of encouragement ("This fellow can really sing") from the emcee, Otis starts off with "Pain in My Heart," and before he opens his mouth, a woman in the front row implores him, "Sing it pretty now!" (Later in the song, when he asks, "Where can my baby be?" another woman shouts, "Right here!") "These Arms of Mine" is more of the same—too much so, under the circumstances, since the sameness of the material reinforces the impression that Otis is nothing *but* a ballad singer. Though his performance retains the suspenseful phrasing that marked the studio recording, the song is saddled with a jazzed-up arrangement, and it doesn't come across as well.

The grueling performance schedule at the Apollo left Otis with little free time in New York, but he did cross paths with some celebrated figures during his stay, including his fellow guest at the Hotel Theresa, Cassius Clay, who was three months away from winning the world heavyweight championship in a stunning upset against Sonny Liston—a victory he would celebrate by announcing his conversion to the Nation of Islam and becoming Muhammad Ali. At this point, Clay was best known for the boastful public persona ("I Am the Greatest") he assumed in his contacts with the sporting press, whose jaded members found him to be an endless source of amusement and good copy on the way to what most of them assumed would be a humiliating defeat. As luck would have it, one of the inspirations for Clay's self-aggrandizing style, Little Richard Penniman, was also in New York, holding court at the Americana Hotel, where he invited Otis to visit him during his stay. Richard's version of hometown hospitality had its kinky edge. According to Sylvester Huckabee, who stayed on after Otis left, Richard prevailed on him to recount some of Otis's sexual exploits while Richard lay on the sofa in his hotel suite and pleasured himself.

Otis's weeklong engagement at the Apollo ran through Thursday, November 21. The following day, President John F. Kennedy was assassinated in Dallas. Kennedy's murder occurred in a southern city and resulted in Lyndon B. Johnson's becoming the first Southerner to hold the presidency since Woodrow Wilson. In its immediate aftermath, this led many Americans to associate the tragedy in Dallas with the same crescendo of political violence that had claimed the lives of Medgar Evers

and the Birmingham schoolgirls earlier in 1963. Few people could antici-
pate that as president, Lyndon Johnson would use his extraordinary political skills to end legalized segregation throughout the United States, or
that his administration would show a level of commitment to improving
the lives of disenfranchised Americans of *all* races that had no precedent
in the nation's history.

During his week in New York, acting on Joe Galkin's advice, Otis
signed a letter of intent with the veteran agent Frank Sands, who worked
for the Shaw Artists Corporation (SAC), one of the three big talent agencies that specialized in booking African American artists on a national
basis. SAC had been founded in 1949 by Billy Shaw, a beloved figure
whose high musical standards (his early clients included Charlie Parker
and Dizzy Gillespie, who wrote the song "Shaw 'Nuff" in his honor) and
reputation for fair dealing enabled him to attract a deep roster of jazz
and R&B talent. Billy Shaw died suddenly in 1956 and was succeeded
by his son Milton. By 1963, the agency had more than a hundred artists
under contract, led by Fats Domino, Ray Charles, Miles Davis, John Coltrane, the Drifters, and B. B. King. They also handled bookings for the
Miracles, the Marvelettes, and several other Motown acts. With offices
in New York, Chicago, and Hollywood, SAC knew the world of black entertainment inside out. Otis's decision to sign with the agency was a wise
move, and the fact that he didn't even mention it to Alan Walden when
he first returned to Macon suggests that he was grasping the need, with
Joe Galkin's help, to take matters into his own hands.

SECURITY

The black brothers are the mainstay of our pop music today. Artists like John Lee Hooker, Otis Redding, and others are heavy on soul—one thing our English friends can't imitate.

—NATHANIEL "MAGNIFICENT" MONTAGUE, WWRL deejay

T HAT NOVEMBER, SHORTLY AFTER THE RELEASE OF "PAIN IN MY Heart," the editors of *Billboard* responded to the growing correlation between the top-selling singles on the Pop and R&B charts by quietly suspending their magazine's long-standing practice of categorizing popular records according to the race of the listeners for whom they were ostensibly intended. In reality, of course, large numbers of black people had been buying and listening to white pop all along, and large numbers of white people had been buying and listening to black R&B. But in keeping with the rising integrationist spirit in the country, *Billboard*'s progressively minded music editor, Paul Ackerman, decided that the time had come to do away with these vestigial distinctions. Henceforth, records would compete in the pop marketplace on the content of their musical character, not the color of their musical skin.

Billboard's new policy was nothing if not well intended, and except for one unforeseen development, it might have been an idea whose time had come. But the first issue of the magazine in which the charts were merged carried a small story about a recent visit to New York by Brian Epstein, manager of the Beatles, whose ebullient songs, irreverent public personalities, and hysterical teenaged fans had turned them into a national preoccupation in Britain during the fall of 1963. Epstein, *Billboard* reported, had made arrangements for the group to appear on Ed Sullivan's top-rated CBS variety show in the year ahead. At a time when the Beatles were still completely unknown in the States—their first album had disappeared without a trace following its rejection by Capitol and Atlantic and its release by Vee Jay, a black-owned label in Chicago—this was a coup for Epstein. But Ed Sullivan prided himself on introducing his viewers to exotic forms of entertainment from around the world, and few things were more exotic to Americans in the fall of 1963 than the idea of a British rock 'n' roll band.

Over the next three months, in the grim aftermath of the Kennedy assassination, the Beatles would explode into the consciousness of the American public with a media-magnified intensity that dwarfed such earlier pop sensations as Frank Sinatra and Elvis Presley. Their appearance on the *Ed Sullivan Show* in February drew 73 million viewers, the largest prime-time audience in the history of American television, and their records so dominated the airwaves that at one point in the spring, they held the first five positions in the *Billboard* Top 100, having accounted for nearly 60 percent of *all* the singles sold in the US during the first three months of the year. Their success would have a catalytic effect on music, fashion, and popular culture around the world, but their impact on the entertainment industry was most dramatic in the United States, where they turned the record business upside down and opened the door to a host of other British bands, beginning with the Dave Clark Five, Gerry and the Pacemakers, Billy J. Kramer and the Dakotas, the Kinks, and Manfred Mann, whose sudden popularity among American teenagers prompted talk of a "British Invasion" of the American music scene.

Though many adult Americans were initially as deaf to the Beatles' artistic virtues as Jerry Wexler had been, the band was a musical phenomenon as well as a commercial sensation. Alone among the rock 'n' roll revivalists who had given rise to the "beat music" craze in the North of England, the Beatles wrote their own songs, and by the time of their success in America, they were beginning to demonstrate the precocious compositional talent that would eventually earn John Lennon and Paul McCartney recognition as two of the greatest popular songwriters of all time. Initially, their music was a synthesis of two successive strains of American rhythm and blues. They grafted the blunt rhythmic force of 1950s rockers like Little Richard and Chuck Berry—and their white acolytes Buddy Holly and Carl Perkins—onto the plaintive harmonies and call-and-response singing associated with 1960s vocal groups like the Drifters, the Miracles, and the Shirelles. Emboldened by their success, they would soon begin to incorporate a diversity of stylistic elements into their songs, drawing on folk, country, classical, and a wide range of contemporary and historical pop. In addition to their influence as singers, songwriters, and instrumentalists, the Beatles, with the help of their producer George Martin, would also have a revolutionary impact on the way in which popular records were made. By avoiding the use of session musicians and choosing instead to accompany themselves on record, they institutionalized the concept of a "rock group" as an autonomous musical unit, capable of writing, singing, playing, and arranging its own songs. This same self-sufficiency would cause them to rely heavily on the newly developed techniques of multitrack recording, which they would take to unheard-of creative extremes.

All of this lay in the future at the start of 1964, when Beatlemania (as the British press dubbed the phenomenon) was first greeted in America by well-publicized scenes of adolescent frenzy and skyrocketing record sales. Over the course of the year, the preoccupation with the Beatles and their fellow British bands on the part of American teenagers, media outlets, and the record labels that relied on the youth market for a major share of their business would have a depressing effect on the sales and chart success of many established black and white recording artists. Together with the suspension of the separate listings in *Billboard*, this would relegate many top-selling R&B records to the lower reaches of the Pop charts.

But the overall impact of the British Invasion on the commercial prospects of R&B singers and groups was by no means clear-cut. Though the percentage of Top 10 hits by black artists declined by more than half from its peak in 1963, the number of R&B records that placed in the *Billboard* Top 40 (thereby ensuring airplay on the many radio stations that based their playlists on the Pop charts) remained essentially unchanged. Motown charted more than twenty Top 40 singles in 1964, Sam Cooke four, Ray Charles three, and James Brown two. And while the initial effect of the Beatles was to monopolize the attention of American teenagers, the excitement they generated also worked to expand the size of the popular record market, as large numbers of college students and young adults were drawn back into the pop scene by the songs, style, and poise of a group that defied the adult stereotypes of "teen idols" as narcissists, louts, or dupes. In addition, the Beatles were outspoken in their admiration for the black recording stars of the fifties and early sixties from whom they had learned their craft, and their early albums (like those of Elvis Presley) included numerous R&B cover tunes. Thanks in part to their influence, Chuck Berry would celebrate his release from prison at the end of 1963 with a trio of Top 40 hits in the year ahead.

For Otis Redding, 1964 would unfold as a year of professional apprenticeship, when his modest success as a recording artist would earn him the opportunity to rub shoulders with some of the most accomplished performers in rhythm and blues. In the process, Otis would acquire a wealth of knowledge about how to present himself onstage, how to promote his records, how to build a fan base, how to run a band, and how to live on the road. Uncoincidentally, 1964 was also the year when the tensions between Otis's ambitions as a professional entertainer and his loyalties to old friends in Macon would abruptly come to a head.

By the start of the year, "Pain in My Heart" had already sold more than 100,000 copies and broken into the *Billboard* Top 100, where it would remain for eleven weeks and rise as high as #61. (The record would eventually peak at #11 on the still-extant *Cashbox* R&B chart.) This was more than enough in the eyes of the people who ran Atlantic Records to warrant the release of an Otis Redding LP. Though the singles charts remained a closely watched index of artist popularity, the sale of 45s accounted for barely 20 percent of the American record market; the remainder came from LPs. Much of Atlantic's resilience in the early 1960s owed to the fact that the label was significantly more involved in the LP market than most of its independent competitors. Sales of albums by R&B artists still lagged far behind those for pop, but it was apparent to everyone in the record business that albums were the future of the industry, and at the start of 1964, Atlantic announced a major campaign to increase its LP sales by offering discounts and incentives to its distributors. Otis Redding's debut album was a small part of this initiative.

It was a forgone conclusion that the album would feature the tracks from Otis's first three Stax singles, though the lamest of the B-sides, "Mary's Little Lamb," was mercifully set aside. With the exception of one new original, the record was filled out with a half dozen cover tunes on which Otis paid homage to some of his musical heroes. All six of these tracks were recorded in a hurried session at Stax in January 1964. They included serviceable if uninspired versions of Little Richard's "Lucille" and Ben E. King's "Stand by Me," a stilted rendition of Sam Cooke's "You Send Me," and slapdash covers of Rufus Thomas's "The Dog" and the Kingsmen's recent hit revival of Richard Berry's "Louie, Louie," both of which were marred by uneven playing and poor engineering, with Otis's voice all but buried in the mix.

The best new tracks on the album were a pair of uptempo songs. One was a raucous cover of "I Need Your Loving," a gospel-flavored hit by Don Gardner and Dee Dee Ford that spent thirteen weeks on the Pop charts in 1962. Revitalized with a hard-swinging arrangement in the riffing, horn-band style of the Memphis favorite Bobby "Blue" Bland, the track gave Otis a chance to cut loose in the studio in a way he had never attempted before, and he threw himself into the wordless refrain of *w'whoa w'whoa whoa whoa* with a zeal that lifted the song to new heights of loony intensity. Even better was "Security," whose words and music, set to a loose-jointed mid-tempo groove, marked a breakthrough for Otis and the Stax band. The lyrics to "Security" were written by Sylvester Hucka-bee and a girlfriend from Tindall Heights, and they represented the first plausible variation on the theme of begging and pleading that Otis had sounded since his Stax debut. Neither Huck nor his friend was credited on the song, but Otis's performance is mostly an improvisation, in which he starts each verse with the declaration "I want *security,* yeah" and takes it from there, renouncing the usual trappings of success ("don't want no money . . . don't want no fame") in favor of "those sweet tender lips that tells me *that* . . . you're the one for me." The shapely, upturned horn lines, hammering drum fills, and chirping notes on guitar that surround his singing sound more like a commentary than an accompaniment, and the different sections of the song can be heard as a set of duets—between Otis and the horns in the verse, Otis and the guitar in the chorus, and the guitar and the horns in the break—until the whole ensemble combines to pound out a series of staggered half-time triplets near the end. "Don't it sound pretty good right now, chil'ren?" Otis asks, clearly pleased with the result.

"Security" was Otis's first original dance tune, and its strong rhythmic undertow was enhanced by the playing of Donald "Duck" Dunn, formerly of the Mar-Keys, who at Steve Cropper's instigation was on his way to replacing Lewis Steinberg in the Stax band. A purely electric bassist, Dunn took a more aggressive and inventive approach to the instrument than Steinberg, whose playing reflected his old-school background on the string bass, and whose brooding, hard-drinking temperament had begun to clash with the sober work ethic at Stax. Duck Dunn, by contrast, was a puckish young man in his early twenties with a goofball personality that lifted the spirits of everyone around him. His day job at a Memphis record distributorship gave him a comprehensive knowledge of contemporary rhythm and blues, and he was also an accomplished dancer, whose physicality pervaded his playing. Musically and otherwise, Dunn was the perfect foil to his close friend Steve Cropper, and his eventual replacement of Steinberg in Booker T. and and the MGs (which became final toward the end of 1964) evened the racial balance in the group, turning its mixture of black and white musicians from an anomaly into more of a social statement.

Titled *Pain in My Heart*, Otis Redding's first album was released in March on Atlantic's subsidiary label Atco. Its cover featured a black-and-white photograph of Otis onstage at the Apollo, shot from below and lit from above, just as Jerry Wexler described him: standing stock-still at the microphone, his right arm outstretched stiffly in a vaguely ministerial gesture. Between his gray suit and the deep gray shadows on his face, he looks more like a man in his mid-thirties than a twenty-two-year-old upstart making his Apollo debut. The back cover of the album sleeve contained seven hundred words of copy written by an Atlantic promo man named Bob Altshuler, who provided a compressed account of Otis's origins in Dawson and Macon, his service with Johnny Jenkins, and his discovery at Stax. *Pain in My Heart* was reviewed that month in *Billboard*, which praised the record's "strong blues feel" and singled out "I Need Your

Loving" as "a first-class track." But sales of the album were disappointing, totaling less than 10,000 copies in the first six months of its release.

Otis at the Apollo, 1963

"Security" may have been a stylistic breakthrough, but Jim Stewart's cautious nature made him unwilling to deviate from the steady diet of ballads that Otis had released to date. (The level of marketing imagination at Stax during this period is suggested by the titles of two recent releases, "Mo' Onions" by Booker T. and the MGs and "Can Your Monkey Do the Dog?" by Rufus Thomas.) Stewart waited until the single of "Pain in My Heart" fell off the charts in March before releasing the outtake ballad "Come to Me" as Otis's first single of 1964. The record was a concerted attempt to recapture the minimalist magic of "These Arms of Mine," right down to the absence of horns and the presence of Johnny Jenkins on guitar. In an effort to breathe some life into the hackneyed lyric, Otis adds a catch in his voice as he murmurs *"Come* to me" at the start of every line, singing with a dreamy insistence that makes the sentiments that follow ("for I'm lonely . . . for I'm begging . . . for I love you") sound like afterthoughts. In the inevitable coda, he invokes the titles of his earlier songs: "You know that *these arms of mine,* they have been lonely so long, but I know, I know *what my heart needs.*" What Otis really needed at this point was a decent song to sing.

"Come to Me" had a lukewarm reception, spending eight weeks in the lower reaches of the *Billboard* Top 100 but barely making a dent on the *Cashbox* R&B charts, and its sales lagged far behind those of "Pain in My Heart." It also had the dubious distinction of earning Otis his first bad reviews, albeit in another country. Atlantic had been selling records in Britain since the mid-1950s under the terms of a licensing deal with Decca, a major British label. In recent years, Atlantic's jazz and R&B releases had gained a cult following among the metropolitan dandies of British youth culture, working-class kids from London and its suburbs who referred to themselves as Mods (short for "modernists") and drew their fashion sense from the sleek "Continental" styles they associated with the black musicians pictured on the covers of American LPs. The Mods' enthusiasm for R&B was well represented in the half-dozen weekly music papers that competed fiercely for the attention of the country's teenagers.

"Pain in My Heart" was the first Otis Redding recording that Decca released in Britain, and it established him as a promising newcomer in the eyes of the country's R&B subculture. As the follow-up, "Come to Me" was widely reviewed in the British music press, whose writers prided themselves on their strong critical opinions. The pulpy sentiment of "Come to Me" did not sit well with them. "Slow, drawling, bluesy material from Otis," noted the reviewer for *Disc,* who went on to deride the single as "a hearse-drawn vehicle that gets nowhere." *New Musical Express* was similarly unimpressed, citing the record's "stodgy, uninspired backing." Yet the seriousness with which these British writers were prepared to take the work of a relatively obscure American R&B singer boded well for things to come.

BERRY, BROWN, AND BURKE

Otis was like a sponge. He wanted to learn about everything and anything that had to do with the entertainment business.

—PHIL WALDEN

IN MARCH, OTIS'S NEW AFFILIATION WITH THE SHAW AGENCY BEGAN to bear fruit when he returned to the Howard Theatre in Washington as an opening act for the Motortown Revue, the road show sponsored by Motown Records to promote its growing stable of stars. Unlike Stax, Atlantic, or any other label at the time, Motown signed its artists to management as well as recording contracts. This enabled the company to involve itself in every aspect of its singers' careers, from their wardrobes, grooming, and stagecraft to their tour schedules, transportation, and comportment on the road. Acting on a vision that was years ahead of its time, Motown's founder, Berry Gordy, was engaged in the creation not merely of a record label but of a national "brand." He would have been the first to say that he was basing his approach on the success of Atlantic, which had been the first R&B label to cultivate a distinctive "sound." But Motown was in a position to exert a much more comprehensive form of control than the owners of Atlantic, whose passion for black music caused them to revere many of the artists they recorded. Gordy paid lip service to the talent on his label, but with the exception of his alter ego, Smokey Robinson, and his brother-in-law, Marvin Gaye, he treated everyone who worked for his company as servants of his will.

Motown's official mythology held that Gordy's corporate vision came from the (unquestionably brief and possibly apocryphal) time he spent working on a Ford assembly line in the early 1950s. Aspects of Motown's operation did resemble the methods of mass production, like the label's extraordinary "quality control department," or its preference for overdubbing its singers onto prerecorded rhythm tracks like so many different car bodies being mounted on the same chassis and drive train. But as time would tell, Gordy's vision had more to do with David O. Selznick than Henry Ford. The real model for Motown was the "star system" as it functioned during the heyday of Hollywood, when the big studios set out to industrialize the production of movies and the talent it needed to make them by recruiting young actors, teaching them their craft, creating personas for them to inhabit on the screen, and—in return for their obedience to the studio's every directive—rewarding them with the trappings of success. Along these lines, Motown sent its singers and groups to an in-house "charm school" where they were taught how to walk, talk, dance, dress, and behave with proper decorum on and off the stage. And in a manner that carried more than an echo of the world his parents had fled in Georgia, Berry Gordy "furnished" his artists with their clothes, cars, and living expenses, and then deducted the cost of these items (along with the cost of their studio time and their studio musicians) from their record royalties and performance fees. As a result, many of the label's artists existed in a state of perpetual debt to the company.

Still, the success of these methods was unprecedented on both a commercial and a creative level, and Otis's dates at the Howard with two of Motown's most choreographed acts, the Miracles and the Temptations, were an education in self-presentation and stagecraft. Show after show, he got to observe how these groups dressed and moved onstage, how they engaged with the audience, and how they paced their short sets. Otis also got to perform at the Howard with the support of a crack R&B band, for Detroit was one of the country's great jazz centers, and the level of musicianship Motown drew on was second to none.

Three months before, Otis had felt a need to ask Ben E. King whether the audiences at the Apollo would accept a down-home performer like himself. Now he was appearing with some of the slickest "uptown" acts in the world of R&B, and the audiences at the Howard were responding enthusiastically to him as well—despite his awkwardness and lack of polish. Otis was engaged in his own campaign to refine the way he dressed and spoke and presented himself onstage. But his ability to hold his own at big-city theaters like the Apollo and the Howard steeled him in his determination to be his own man.

That determination was about to be sorely tested when Alan Walden called him during his week at the Howard to say that the finances of the Walden agency were in such a state of disarray that he felt he had no choice but to shut the business down. As Alan explained it, on top of the debts he had inherited from his brother, clients like the Fiestas and Bobby Marchan had been asking him constantly to advance them money against future bookings. A soft touch, Alan had been unable to refuse them. This had forced him to borrow from his relatives, including his cousin Robert and his brother Blue, to make up the difference between what these artists took out and what they brought in. Those debts were coming due.

Otis reacted to this news by flying back to Macon and informing Alan in no uncertain terms that he hadn't been paying Phil Walden Artists and Promotions twenty cents out of every dollar he earned in order to stand by and watch Phil's kid brother run the agency into the ground. (Alan remembered thinking that he had never heard a black man speak to him this way before.) When Otis finally calmed down, they agreed that Alan would shed the agency's other clients and concentrate on Otis's bookings in the months ahead. They also agreed that Alan needed some help in running the business. When Otis asked him whom he had in mind, Alan told him that the only person he trusted was his father. So Otis and Alan paid a visit to C. B. Walden at home, where he had been convalescing since leaving the hospital a few months before. He was still in terrible shape, looking wan and withered and confined to a chair. But according to Alan, his father lit up when Otis told him simply, "Pops, we need you." The next morning, C. B. got up, got dressed for the first time in six months, and accompanied his son to the office.

In April, Otis joined a thirty-city Supersonic Attractions tour headlined by James Brown and costarring Solomon Burke, with Dionne Warwick and Garnett Mimms as the other supporting acts. Warwick was coming off the first of her many Top 10 hits, "Anyone Who Had a Heart." Mimms was an understudy of Burke, best known for "Cry Baby," a topselling R&B single in 1963.

"His emphasis on ego breaks all bounds," the dance historian Mura

Dehn once wrote of James Brown. By 1964, Brown's unbridled egotism had made him one of the most widely disliked figures in the world of black entertainment. But like many grandiose personalities, he was also capable of behaving magnanimously toward younger performers whose talent he respected—provided they gave him his due. Otis knew precisely how to deal with Brown, massaging his ego by calling him "Bossman" and treating him like all the other petty tyrants he had grown up with in the Jim Crow South. In return, Brown enjoyed playing the role of mentor to his fellow Maconite. The year before, Sam Cooke had arranged for his protégés, a group called the Valentinos, to tour with Brown as a way of refining their act. "Something was always wrong, and when you came off, he was right there telling you," said the Valentinos' leader, Bobby Womack, who likened the experience to "boot camp." Night after night, Otis was given the benefit of a similar critique.

To say the least, the diminutive James Brown and the monumental Solomon Burke were a study in contrasts. Burke was now established as Atlantic's top R&B star, signed by Jerry Wexler to make up for the loss of Ray Charles. Wexler's final stroke of inspiration as Charles's producer had been to record him singing a version of Hank Snow's country classic "I'm Movin' On." The record had sold well, and a year later, when Burke came to Atlantic, Wexler assigned him a weepy country ballad called "Just Out of Reach (of My Two Open Arms)." Burke, who grew up in Philadelphia as a boy preacher in his family's storefront church, Solomon's Temple, had no idea what Wexler was getting at, but he could sing virtually anything, and "Just Out of Reach" became a crossover hit in the fall of 1961. His next record, "Cry to Me," was done in the uptown style of the Drifters, and it showcased Burke as a singer of great nuance, capable of shifting from a hard gospel rasp to a mellifluous croon in the space of a single bar. ("Of all the attributes of soul singing, I consider sweetness the most important," Wexler once said. "Sam Cooke was the great prophet of this school and Solomon Burke its next great proponent.") Beginning with his 1963 hit "If You Need Me," Burke adopted the habit of delivering romantic homilies in the middle of his songs, using a voice that mimicked the heartfelt testimony of Christian worship. Live, he expanded on this practice by extolling his prowess as a lover, assuring the men in his audience that he could take any of their women away from them merely by stepping down off the stage. Burke was an even bigger man than Otis; by 1964, he was approaching his fighting weight of 280 pounds, which he encased in skintight gold lamé suits. The clothes aside, his corpulent figure made him look more like a prosperous preacher than a pop singer, but women loved the aura of sheer formidability he projected onstage. Watching him perform on a nightly basis, Otis could not help but be impressed by the way that Burke relied simply on his voice, his warmth, and his powerful masculine presence to put himself across.

James Brown, on the other hand, epitomized the sort of performer who would walk through fire to win the love of a crowd. Like his great rival Jackie Wilson, Brown practiced a histrionic, self-delighted brand of showmanship that harkened back to entertainers such as Al Jolson. Otis knew that he couldn't begin to compete with Brown on this level, for Brown had an athletic grace and a radioactive vanity that Otis simply lacked. (Brown had his bouffant hairdo washed and set three times a day. "Hair and teeth. A man's got those two things, he's got it all," he liked to say.) Instead, it was Brown's style as a bandleader and businessman that Otis sought to emulate. In the spring of 1964, Brown was touring with a trio of male backup singers, a quartet of female dancers, and a thirteen-piece band composed of a rhythm section, four trumpets, four saxes, and a trombone. He had been assembling and fine-tuning this ensemble for years, having recently added a new music director, Nat Jones, and the brothers Maceo and Melvin Parker on sax and drums. As affirmed by Brown's next record, a bubbling blues vamp called "Out of Sight," they were coming into their own as one of the most tightly disciplined and distinctive R&B bands of all time. Like many great popular musicians, James Brown did not read music, but he had a remarkable ability to know what he wanted and to get his ideas across. In the midst of their grueling tour schedule, he rehearsed his band constantly, before and even after their shows. This gave Otis an opportunity to watch the hands-on manner in which Brown would create an arrangement out of thin air: sidling up to his sidemen as they ran through the harmonic changes of the song, singing in their ears and gesturing with his body to show them the parts he wanted them to play. Once he had what he wanted, his music director would write up charts, which the band members would memorize, so that they could move and play onstage without the encumbrance of music stands. James Brown ran his band the way Berry Gordy ran his record label, as an extension of his will—to the point, famously, of fining his sidemen for musical and sartorial infractions. In the midst of a performance, if Brown detected an errant note or a scuffed shoe, he would hold up any number of fingers, each of them worth five dollars, to indicate the severity of the violation and the penalty it required.

Otis with James Brown: "hair and teeth"

During the period when Otis toured with him, Brown was beginning to assert this same sense of fierce proprietorship over his business affairs. Early in 1964, flush with the success of his *Live at the Apollo* album, he walked away from his contract with King Records, formed his own label (which he pointedly named Fair Deal), and signed a distribution agreement with Mercury. The ensuing litigation between King and Mercury would drag on for more than a year, during which Brown was constrained from releasing any more records under his own name. But the lifeblood of Brown's operation had always been his nonstop schedule of live shows, which was overseen with a kind of military precision by his manager, Ben

Bart. Like Otis, Brown had a white manager with whom he was very close, although Bart was more of a Joe Galkin than a Phil Walden: a hard-nosed Jew from Brooklyn who had founded Universal Attractions in the 1940s and built it into one of the top black talent agencies in the country. Universal had many clients, but Bart's relationship with "Jimmy" (as he alone called Brown) was unique—so much so that in 1962 he turned the agency over to his son and began working full-time as Brown's manager. Together, they perfected an innovative system by which Brown co-promoted his own shows, usually in collaboration with local black disk jockeys, who repaid Brown for their piece of the action by playing his records and advertising his appearances on the air. From his seat on the tour bus, Otis got to observe the nuts and bolts of this operation, beginning with the way Brown "took care of" the deejays, program directors, record distributors, and anyone else who was in a position to do him some good. Brown's business sense, his grasp of what he called "big-city thinking," and his ability to command respect were a special source of inspiration for Otis, who recognized that, under the cosmetic gloss, Brown was even more "country" than he was, and as lacking in personal charm as a man could possibly be.

By the middle of May, the weak sales of "Come to Me" had run their course. Otis had been singing "Security" on tour with James Brown (who liked the song so much that he recorded his own version of it called "Out of the Blue"), so Jim Stewart relented and released the track as a single. It would go on to sell around 100,000 copies over the next four months, but the record failed to get much airplay outside of the South. Along with the rest of the American music business, Atlantic Records was still reeling from the shock wave of Beatlemania, and the label's executives and promo men had more pressing matters to deal with than Otis Redding's latest single.

Inspired by the experience of performing on a nightly basis with the backing of a first-rate band, Otis returned to Macon determined to form a group of his own. Most of the work he had done since the Hot Summer Revue tour of 1963 had been as a "single" in venues where the local promoter was required to provide him with a band. Some of these groups were better than others, but from Otis's perspective, the best was a collection of black college students called the Rocking Cabanas, who had backed him frequently at his gigs in the Tidewater region of Virginia and North Carolina. They were led by their bass player, McEvoy Robinson, with whom Otis got on well, and fronted by the singers Roy Hines and Gloria Stevenson. That June, Otis hired the Cabanas, Hines, and Stevenson and renamed them the Otis Redding Blues Band and Revue. They left almost immediately on a Henry Wynn tour called the Summer Shower of Stars, headlined by Solomon Burke, with Otis, Garnett Mimms, Joe Tex, Rufus Thomas, and the diminutive Filipino-American singer Sugar Pie DeSanto, as the supporting acts. Over the next two months, this tour ranged up and down the East Coast from New England to the Deep South.

Otis and Solomon Burke had taken a real liking to each other by now, and they often rode together in Burke's capacious Cadillac limousine, a gift from his manager, who ran a car dealership in Philadelphia. Black entertainers driving the roads of the South in late-model cars routinely attracted the attention of sheriffs and state police, and the sight of Burke's limo with its Pennsylvania plates was more than any self-respecting southern lawman could resist during the "Freedom Summer" of 1964, when the entire region was consumed with the primal southern fear of "outside agitators." On one occasion, Burke, Otis, and Joe Tex were driving from Atlanta to a gig in Birmingham with Rodgers Redding at the wheel when Burke decided to stop at a roadside army-surplus store to buy a box of whistles to give away as souvenirs to his fans. In addition to the whistles, he wound up buying several rifles and shotguns, as well as some dummy hand grenades that caught his eye. A short time later, as they neared the outskirts of Birmingham, they were stopped by a flotilla of Alabama state police, who had been alerted by the store owner. Burke grabbed his Bible, pulled an enormous cross out from under his shirt, lumbered out of the limousine, and introduced himself as the Reverend Solomon Burke, en route to a prayer meeting in Birmingham. After the troopers opened the truck of the car and discovered Burke's arsenal there, the headliners of the Summer Shower of Stars found themselves unceremoniously spread-eagled on the blacktop. It took them some time to convince an Alabama judge to release them with a warning and a fine.

ROY STREET

Part of what protects a person is both how many people can be counted on to avenge his honor if he is rolled and who these defenders are. . . . Many inner-city young men in particular crave respect to such a degree that they will risk their lives to attain and maintain it.

—ELIJAH ANDERSON, *The Code of the Street*

ON JUNE 10, 1964, THE UNITED STATES SENATE VOTED TO END A filibuster by a bloc of southern senators that had paralyzed the work of the Congress for nearly two months. Ten days later, the Senate passed the civil rights bill that John Kennedy had proposed on the night of Medgar Evers's murder and that Lyndon Johnson had made the centerpiece of his legislative agenda in 1964. Two weeks after that, with Dr. Martin Luther King Jr. and Rosa Parks in attendance at the White House, President Johnson signed the bill into law. The Civil Rights Act of 1964 banned racial discrimination in employment and "public accommodations," including hotels, motels, restaurants, bars, theaters, stadiums, auditoriums, and public facilities of all kinds, throughout the United States. After more than six decades, the day-to-day exclusions and humiliations of legalized segregation were coming to an end. Apart from the outspoken opposition of demagogues such as George Wallace and Lester Maddox, the Atlanta restaurant owner who used his defiance of this law to launch his political career, there was widespread compliance in the cities and larger towns. The commercial sector of the South's economy had recognized for years that segregation was bad for business. The passage of a federal statute abolishing the Jim Crow regime allowed many white merchants and businessmen who lacked the moral courage to defy the racist ideologues to gratefully accept the "coercion" of the federal government and open their doors and their cash registers to black customers.

The impact of the Civil Rights Act on the world of black entertainment in the South was both mundane and profound. In theaters, auditoriums, stadiums, and armories across the region—some of which had already begun to desegregate of their own accord—the ropes and signs designating "colored" and "whites only" seating, concession stands, and restrooms came down. Though they were still subject to frequent harassment, touring black entertainers were suddenly able to eat at many roadside restaurants and stay at their choice of hotels. "I've waited forty-one years for this," Medgar Evers's brother Charles told a *New York Times* reporter after receiving his key to a room in a Holiday Inn in Laurel, Mississippi.

The same week that the act was signed into law, Otis Redding took advantage of a break in the Summer Shower of Stars tour and returned home to Macon for the July Fourth holiday. Looking back over the first half of 1964, Otis could take considerable satisfaction in the progress of his career. His appearances with the Miracles, James Brown, and Solomon Burke had shown that he could hold the stage with some of the most popular performers on the R&B circuit. Though his records were far from national hits, several of them had sold well in a number of major markets. Working together, Otis, Alan, and C. B. Walden had straightened out the financial mess that Phil had left behind, and Otis's affiliations with Shaw Artists and Supersonic Attractions were providing him with steady work in bigger and better venues. On the domestic front, Zelma had recently learned that she was pregnant with their third child, due in December, and the couple had just purchased their first home, a two-bedroom, $15,000 bungalow on a street of identical houses in an East Macon subdivision called Charlton. Its amenities included a carport, a backyard, and—wonder of wonders for Georgia in 1964—central air-conditioning. Otis had also been able to move his parents into an apartment of their own in the Unionville section of Macon, roughly equidistant from Bellevue and Tindall Heights.

As usual when Otis returned to Macon, he sought out his buddies from Bellevue, only to find them embroiled in a crisis of sorts. A few days before, Herbert Ellis had gotten into a fight over a girlfriend with a young man named David McGee, whose family ran a rival liquor house in West Macon. McGee and several of his friends had pistol-whipped Ellis and beaten him up badly. After deciding that nothing short of full-scale retribution was required, Ellis prevailed on Sylvester Huckabee and Bubba Howard to help him settle the score. As Huck explained it, "We wanted to show them that we wasn't afraid of them, 'cause they had jumped on one of our boys, and that's what we went over there to do." Since Otis was in town, he felt obligated to take part. On the Fourth of July, a Saturday, this posse from Bellevue armed themselves with pistols and shotguns, piled into Otis's inconspicuous white Cadillac, and drove to the McGee residence on Roy Street at around 6:30 in the evening. "They were waiting on us," Huck recalled. A gunfight erupted, in the course of which Bubba Howard, David McGee, and his father Willie McGee were wounded. Otis himself was grazed in the leg by buckshot after one of his friends dropped a shotgun and it accidentally discharged.

The shoot-out on Roy Street could have ended Otis Redding's career. The police arrived at the scene and took the McGees to the hospital, where they found Bubba Howard being treated in the emergency room. Everyone involved, including Otis, was subsequently arrested on a preliminary charge of "disorderly conduct with a pistol." David McGee was seriously wounded, underwent surgery, and spent the rest of the summer in the hospital.

For the next eight months, as the case slowly wound its way through the Bibb County courts, Otis would live under the cloud of a possible indictment for attempted murder. Eventually, thanks to C. B. Walden, who vouched for him the way that any white employer in Georgia might vouch for one of "his niggers" who had run afoul of the law, Otis managed to avoid criminal prosecution. Even so, it would take a considerable sum of money and all of C. B.'s powers of persuasion, honed over many long evenings drinking with cops, judges, and city officials at local watering holes, to get the charges against Otis dropped in February 1965.

By that time, the lesson of this whole sorry episode had been learned. Since his teens, Otis had been living a double life, navigating between the respectable values of his family, his own responsibilities as a husband and a father, and the delinquent code of the street he shared with his friends from Bellevue. Now, at the age of twenty-two, two years into a promising musical career, he had reached the point where these competing loyalties could no longer be finessed. The threat of losing everything focused Otis's mind. "It taught him a very good lesson," Zelma recalled. Until then, Otis had always been a bit "wild"—intemperate, impulsive, and irresponsible in the way that many parents and spouses expected a young black man to be. But from then on, in Zelma's view, "He changed completely. He settled down and concentrated on his business, his music, and his family."

Two weeks after the gunfight with the McGees, the Summer Shower of Stars tour came through Macon for Otis's second annual Homecoming Dance and Concert at the City Auditorium. Alan and C. B. Walden enlisted their entire extended family to help in staging this show, which sold out the auditorium and contributed some welcome cash flow to the Walden agency. On the evening of the concert, tension from the Roy Street shooting was still high, and the auditorium was swarming with police. (Solomon Burke recalled hearing a deputy sheriff tell Otis that bomb threats had been received.) In his capacity as Otis's bodyguard, Sylvester Huckabee came to the concert armed to the teeth, but the show went off without incident.

Early in August, Shaw Artists booked Otis and his band on a ten-day tour of the Caribbean, with stops in Jamaica, Nassau, St. Thomas, and St. Croix. "The Islands" had become a popular destination for American R&B acts, beginning with Sam Cooke's tour of the region in 1960 and Fats Domino's visit the following year. English-speaking Jamaica and the Bahamas were well within range of black radio stations in Miami and New Orleans, and thousands of Jamaicans, mostly young men, were admitted into the States as migrant workers each year, providing a conduit for American records purchased during their stay. The headliners on Otis's tour were the Drifters, who had just released their latest (and, as it turned out, last) big record, "Under the Boardwalk." But the real attraction was Millie Small, an eighteen-year-old Jamaican singer, whose pixie-voiced, "bluebeat" recording of "My Boy Lollipop" was a huge hit that summer in Britain and America. As Jamaica's first international pop star, Small was received as a national hero in her homeland. When the tour played the Carib Theater in Kingston during the country's second annual Independence Week celebration, Prime Minister Alexander Bustamante attended the show.

The following month, in anticipation of Booker Jones's departure for the fall semester, Otis returned to Stax to record his third single of 1964. It was now more than two years since he had recorded "These Arms of Mine," and while the character of his voice remained substantially unchanged since that artistic breakthrough in August 1962, the emotional range of his singing had grown by leaps and bounds. By rehearsing and performing with his own band on a regular basis, Otis was learning how to exert much greater control over the sound of his music. His bass player Mack Robinson had begun to function as his music director, helping him translate his ideas to the other musicians in the band, and a newly hired trumpet player from Macon, Sammy Coleman, had begun to work with Otis on his horn arranging. At the same time, Otis's exposure to Solomon Burke's amiably assertive style had encouraged him to look for ways to broaden the scope of his songwriting beyond the narrow theme of romantic longing he had relied on thus far.

Evidence of this new musicality and assertiveness could be heard on both of the tracks he recorded at Stax in September 1964. Written with help from Alan Walden, the ballad "Chained and Bound" featured the most accomplished lyric Otis had composed to date. The playful irony of the title belies a song of celebration, sung by a man who's "so glad, so glad, so glad" to be bound to a woman whose love is "sweeter than a grape on the vine." Patterned on the chords and thirty-two-bar structure of "Pain in My Heart," "Chained and Bound" was also the first song Otis had written that had a proper bridge. "I feel like standing up and telling the world," he proclaims in this eight-bar interlude, which echoes the evangelical spirit of Solomon Burke's recent hit "Everybody Needs Somebody to Love." The uptempo B-side of the single sounded a similar note of confident assertion. "These are the words that I have to say / Live by them and love me . . . each and every day," Otis sings in "Your One and Only Man." Over the next three months, the single would sell more than 140,000 copies and rise to #6—by far Otis's best showing to date—on the *Cashbox* R&B chart.

Otis marked the release of "Chained and Bound" with a weeklong engagement at the Regal Theater in Chicago on a Shaw Artists bill headlined by the Miracles, with the Four Tops and the comedian Flip Wilson as the other supporting acts. Like their labelmates the Temptations, the Four Tops were a Detroit vocal group that had been rescued from years of professional purgatory by Berry Gordy, who turned them over to the songwriting and production team of Brian and Eddie Holland and Lamont Dozier, with instructions to accentuate the overtly masculine, gospel-trained voices of the group and its lead singer, Levi Stubbs. Their first hit record, "Baby I Need Your Lovin'," stood at #11 on the *Billboard* Pop charts.

Otis's schedule of live performances during the remainder of 1964 reflected the growing dichotomy between his career in the North, where he was booked by Shaw at urban theaters and nightclubs that drew an almost exclusively black clientele, and his career in the South, where he was booked by the Walden agency at a mixture of all-white colleges and all-black clubs and dance halls. One week he would be performing at the Royal in Baltimore or the Howard in Washington on a bill with established stars like Jerry Butler and Dionne Warwick. The next week he would be alternating sets with a band called The Brown Beatles at a University of Georgia fraternity party, or sharing the spotlight at a black ballroom in Portsmouth, Virginia, with a singer named Flip Flop Stevens and a shake dancer named Tiawana.

Otis's band at this point had grown to include five horn players, several of whom, including Sammy Coleman and a tall, thin saxophonist named Harold "Shangalang" Smith, were recruited from the Macon music scene after several of the former Rocking Cabanas returned to college in the fall. Roy Hines left around this time as well, to be replaced by Earl "Speedo" Sims, a singer from Macon. In addition to Rodgers, Sylvester Huckabee was still traveling regularly with Otis as his bodyguard and enforcer, his vast bulk and fierce glare providing ample deterrence to tightfisted promoters and jealous boyfriends.

In December, buoyed by the success of "Chained and Bound," Otis returned to Memphis, where Steve Cropper presented him with a ballad that had recently fallen through the cracks in a manner reminiscent of

Irma Thomas's "Ruler of My Heart." "That's How Strong My Love Is" had been composed in a fit of adulterous passion by a Memphis medical technician named Roosevelt Jamison, who moonlighted as a songwriter and talent scout. Earlier in the year, Jamison had walked into the Stax studios and auditioned the song for Cropper, who liked it well enough to record a demo but expressed no further interest.

Undeterred, Jamison made another tape of the song with a local gospel singer named Overton Vertis ("O. V.") Wright and shopped it to an upstart Memphis label called Goldwax. Wright's recording for Goldwax was affectingly sung but fatally compromised by the song's verbose lyrics and overblown arrangement. Released in the summer of 1964, it spent a few weeks "bubbling under" the *Billboard* Top 100 before defaulting to the status of a local hit. When Otis came to town in December, Cropper suggested that he try recording "That's How Strong My Love Is" with a more succinct arrangement. Otis did that and more. While the Stax band replaced the churchy organ and strident backup singing of the original with Cropper's ringing guitar fills and a beer-hall chorus of horns, Otis completely revamped the phrasing of Wright's vocal, halving the number of bars he took to sing the verse. (He also dispensed with the worst of Jamison's rhetorical excesses, including the line "If I were a fish that had been cast upon the land / I would stay there if you would let me hold your hand.") The new arrangement brought out the lilt of the melody and gave the song a more direct emotional impact that qualified it, in Jim Stewart's mind, as the obvious choice for Otis's next single.

Steve Cropper had earned a cowriting credit on nearly half the records Stax released over the course of 1964, so it was probably only a matter of time before he began writing with Otis as well. The intended B-side of "That's How Strong My Love Is" marked the start of their collaboration, and it set the pattern for the dozen or so songs they would produce in the years ahead. Although he and Otis were born within a few weeks of each other in 1941, it had never occurred to Cropper that they were the same age. Instead, he had come to think of Otis as a streetwise "big brother" with an outsize personality and a singular talent. Of all the people at Stax, Cropper was the one most taken with Otis from the moment he heard him sing, and the episodic nature of their relationship lent a special quality to their developing friendship. Every time Otis came back to town, Cropper could hear the improvement in his singing and sense the growth in his musicianship. "Otis Redding did more to change my sound than anybody," Cropper later said. "He made me think and play a lot simpler, so that the notes would really count dynamically. The stuff I did with Otis [had] a distinctive tone and style that I didn't play with anyone else."

"Mr. Pitiful" was a nickname that had been bestowed upon Otis by A. C. "Moohah" Williams, a deejay at WDIA, in recognition of his reputation as a singer who was not too proud to beg. But it was Cropper who had the inspiration to turn the sobriquet into a song. He and Otis hashed out the opening verse in the time it took them to drive to Stax on the morning of the session, with Otis ad-libbing the rest of the lyrics (such as they are) as the arrangement came together in the studio. "They call me Mr. Pitiful," he declares over a surging groove of heaving bass and popping snare, "that's how I got my fame." Any pretensions to seriousness are preempted by the perfect pratfall of a drum fill with which Al Jackson sets up the verse, and further dispelled by a breezy two-note trill from the horns that flutters through the middle of the song like a cartoon of unconcern. "Mr. Pitiful" marks the point where Otis, after spending two years of his recording career wearing his heart on his sleeve, first steps across the threshold of romantic comedy in a song—beginning with the implication that his heartbroken persona might have been a subterfuge all along. "Can I explain to you?" he asks in the coda. "I've lost everything I ever had, and I have to sing these sad songs to get back to her, and I want *you*, and I want *you*, and I want *you*," he sings, squealing with delight, as if picking girls out of the crowd.

SOUL BALLADS

I want to fill the silent vacuum that was left when Sam Cooke died.

—OTIS REDDING

On the eve of the "Mr. Pitiful" session, in the early-morning hours of December 11, 1964, Sam Cooke was shot to death by the night manager of a seedy motel in South Los Angeles. Earlier in the evening, Cooke had picked up a prostitute named Lisa Boyer at a Hollywood nightclub and driven with her to the motel. Shortly after they checked into their room, Cooke, wearing only his sport jacket, knocked on the door of the manager's office looking for Boyer, who had fled with his wallet and his clothes. Told that she wasn't there, Cooke became enraged, broke down the door, and got into a physical altercation with the manager, a fifty-three-year-old African American woman named Bertha Franklin, who grabbed a revolver she owned and shot Cooke once in the chest. He died almost immediately, though not before Franklin broke a broomstick over his head.

The investigation into Cooke's death by the Los Angeles police was perfunctory, as was the coroner's inquest, which returned a finding of justifiable homicide without ever considering Boyer's known occupation or questioning her claim that she had been "kidnapped" by Cooke. The consensus among Cooke's friends and fans was that the official story was a whitewash. People found it hard to believe that Sam Cooke "needed" to consort with prostitutes, or that a man of his means and taste would patronize a fleabag motel, or that he could come out on the wrong end of a fight with a middle-aged woman (albeit one who outweighed him by thirty pounds). Rumors abounded that he had been shot by Boyer's pimp or set up by his protégé Bobby Womack (who married Cooke's widow less than two months after his death) or murdered by the Mafia as a result of some issue stemming from his New York appearance at the Copacabana the summer before. Cooke's business manager, Allen Klein, hired a private investigator who uncovered numerous inconsistencies in the official account of his death. But the investigation also determined that little about Cooke's behavior, including his choice of a companion and his choice of a destination, was out of character for him. Fearful that damaging information about Cooke's private life and his troubled marriage would come to light, Klein abandoned his independent inquiry.

Sam Cooke's death hit Otis hard. Like many of his contemporaries, Otis had idolized Cooke since the 1950s as the epitome of a church-raised, gospel-bred singer like himself who had successfully crossed over into *both* pop and R&B. "He talked about him a lot," Steve Cropper recalled, "how Sam worked for a white company but was a black man to the end, that he was in total control of himself with his publishing and [his management of] young singers." Earlier in 1964, Cooke and Otis had met while passing through the airport in Washington, D.C. Cooke had greeted Otis warmly, and spent some time talking to him about his career, emphasizing the importance of song publishing and suggesting that he buy stock in progressive southern companies like Coca-Cola and Holiday Inn. As one of the first prominent black entertainers to adopt the "natural" hairstyle that became ubiquitous in the 1960s, Cooke also urged Otis to stop wearing his hair in a "process." Or, as Rodgers Redding remembered him saying, "Get that thing off your head."

At the time of his death, Cooke was about to release the record that would serve as his epitaph, a single that combined the best of his many good dance tunes, simply titled "Shake," with his greatest ballad, an album track he had recorded a year before but hesitated to put out as a single on account of its "political" content. Inspired by Bob Dylan's "Blowin' in the Wind," a masterpiece of "protest" music that had become a civil rights anthem and a million-selling hit for the folk group Peter Paul and Mary, "A Change Is Gonna Come" was nothing less than a secular hymn, and it attained a depth of personalized emotion that Cooke had not approached since his days with the Soul Stirrers. It also contained an eerie premonition in the lines "It's been too hard living, but I'm afraid to die / Cause

I don't know what's up there, beyond the sky." Coming from a minister's son who had once been the foremost male gospel singer of his time, this poignant play on "Old Man River" was a remarkably forthright expression of mortal doubt.

Otis would honor Cooke's memory by recording both sides of this posthumous single in the year ahead, but the record that had the greatest effect on him was the live album of Cooke's triumphant return to the Copacabana, which RCA had released in the fall. Recorded in July 1964, *Sam Cooke at the Copa* was a last testament to the breadth of Cooke's ambition. Having spent the preceding eighteen months burnishing his credentials as a soul singer, he had returned to the scene of his greatest professional disappointment, determined to gain the acceptance of the most mainstream white audience of them all. The supper club ambience of the Copa was a world apart from the swooning woman at the Harlem Square Club in Miami. But by choosing his material carefully (mixing standards with folk-pop hits like "Blowin' in the Wind"), hewing closely to the rhythmic conventions of big-band swing, and affecting an air of self-amused nonchalance modeled on his friend Sammy Davis Jr., the Copa regular who introduced the show, Cooke won over the high-rollers, out-of-towners, and expense-account types who patronized the club. For Otis Redding, *Sam Cooke at the Copa* became his own personal version of charm school. Otis wore out his copy of the album memorizing every song, every bit of banter, every ad lib. From standards like "Try a Little Tenderness" and "Nobody Knows You When You're Down and Out" to verbal quips and catchphrases, much of this material would reappear on Otis's records and in his live performances in the months and years ahead.

Sam Cooke's sudden, senseless death was not the only major loss the world of black popular music suffered in 1964. In October, while returning from a concert in Toronto, Ray Charles was arrested by customs agents at Logan Airport in Boston for possession of marijuana and heroin. Charles had been busted for drugs twice before, and had avoided prosecution both times, but this was a federal charge that could not be so easily quashed. He responded by returning home to Los Angeles and canceling all public appearances in the year ahead. In the summer of 1965, at his lawyers' urging, Charles would check himself into a clinic in Santa Monica and kick the heroin habit that had been the organizing principle of his life for more than fifteen years. His recovery would enable his lawyers to negotiate a plea bargain that kept him out of jail, but that was yet to come. In the fall of 1964, at a time when black popular music was exerting a more direct influence over white popular music than perhaps ever before, its two most accomplished and distinctive singers, Sam Cooke and Ray Charles, had suddenly fallen silent, leaving, as Otis recognized, a vacuum that begged to be filled.

IN JANUARY 1965, a year to the week since the sessions for *Pain in My Heart,* Otis returned to Memphis at Jim Stewart's invitation to record the tracks for his second LP. "That's How Strong My Love Is" was about to be shipped to stores, and Atlantic Records, encouraged by the sustained sales of "Chained and Bound," was anxious to capitalize on any success the single achieved by releasing an album in its wake.

Anxious was putting it mildly. The success of the Beatles, Motown, and the British Invasion bands had combined with the growing demand for stereo LPs to make 1964 a banner year for the American record industry, with sales up nearly 9 percent over 1963. At Atlantic, however, 1964 had been the year when Jerry Wexler's intimations of disaster had threatened to come to pass. After holding its own in the market for pop and R&B throughout the early 1960s, Atlantic had managed to place exactly one of its records, the Drifters' swan song "Under the Boardwalk," on *Billboard*'s list of the hundred top-selling singles of 1964. Otherwise, the label had limped through the year on the sales of Solomon Burke, Rufus Thomas, Otis Redding, and its catalog of jazz LPs. At a time when the reissue of "oldies" in album form was becoming a major industry trend, the owners of Atlantic had been forced to raise cash by selling their lucrative song-publishing firm, Progressive Music, which owned the copyrights to dozens of hits from the fifties and early sixties. And in a move that smacked of desperation, they had also explored the possibility of a merger with Red Bird Records, a hot new label owned by Jerry Leiber and Mike Stoller, in a badly mishandled initiative that caused an unspoken but permanent rift between Ahmet Ertegun and Jerry Wexler. This year of turmoil would have important consequences not only for Atlantic, but also for labels like Stax and artists like Otis Redding, whose fortunes were hitched to Atlantic's star. Though it all but ended their personal friendship, the rift between Wexler and Ertegun would prove to be a blessing, for it freed each of these shrewd, dynamic record men to act on his own initiative in turning Atlantic around.

To a certain extent, the two of them had been drifting apart for years, as their shared passion for music yielded to the differences in their backgrounds and personalities. Since their marriage in 1961, Ahmet Ertegun and his aristocratic Romanian-born wife, Mica, had established themselves as prominent figures in a stratum of New York society where new money and old wealth communed with movers and shakers from the worlds of media, fashion, and the arts. Ertegun's love of nightlife kept him in constant contact with musicians, but he often seemed more intent on socializing with them than in producing or promoting their records. "Eclectic, Reminiscent, Amused, Fickle, and Perverse" (as George Trow would characterize him in a celebrated *New Yorker* profile), Ertegun had always been a dilettante in the classic old-world sense, and by the early 1960s, contemporary black music was losing its ability to fascinate and amuse him. His involvement with Bobby Darin had introduced him to the entertainment scene in Hollywood, and it was there that he now turned in his efforts to revitalize Atlantic. With a lavish lifestyle to support and a coterie of wealthy friends to impress, Ertegun was not about to let his standards of musical taste get in his way. His first important signing was a pair of "folk-rock" poseurs from Los Angeles who had languished as a duo called Caesar and Cleo; renamed Sonny and Cher, they would go on to sell several million records for Atlantic, beginning with a song called "I Got You Babe" in the summer of 1965.

While Ertegun breezed through Atlantic's offices on his way to the next soiree, Jerry Wexler was commuting each day from his house in the suburbs, overseeing the nuts and bolts of the label's operations, and fighting his own sense of exhaustion and ennui. "The arrangers were out of ideas, the songwriters out of material, the session players out of licks, and I was out of inspiration," Wexler later wrote. Over the course of 1964, the full import of his decision to pass on the Beatles had come to weigh on him like a stone. The group sold 25 million records in the United States that year, and while music business insiders had initially viewed them as a passing Twist-like craze, no one was prepared for the astonishing impact their songs, their looks, their wit, and their exuberant personalities would have, not only on popular music but on popular culture as a whole. Like the rise of rhythm and blues and rock 'n' roll in the 1950s, the Beatles and their fellow British bands represented an insurgency in the eyes of the music business establishment. They came as yet another reminder that the wellsprings of innovation in popular music have always arisen on the social and geographical margins of society, not in its metropolitan centers. Atlantic Records' success in the 1950s had rested on this realization, and on the readiness of the label's founders to seek out the provincial locales and backwaters where great vernacular music was being made.

Jerry Wexler had missed out on those early talent hunts, but this was precisely the approach he adopted in his own campaign to restore Atlantic to its former glory. Nicknamed the Purist by the editorial staff at *Cashbox,* Wexler was not about to abandon his devotion to black music in favor of what he liked to call the "pop compromise." Instead he set out to affiliate himself and his label with every talented, uncompromising, and underachieving R&B singer he could find. In the summer of 1964, Wexler acquired the distribution rights to Don Covay's "Mercy, Mercy," which promptly rose to #1 on the *Cashbox* R&B charts. (The record featured twenty-one-year-old Jimi Hendrix on lead guitar.) Wexler next signed a distribution deal with Dial Records, a Nashville-based label whose principal artist was Joe Tex. "Hold What You've Got," Tex's first release under the aegis of Atlantic, went to #1 on *Billboard*'s revived R&B chart—which had recently been reinstated in response to pressure from R&B labels and black-appeal radio stations—in January 1965. But the main thrust of Wexler's revival strategy centered on his relationship with Stax. By the end of 1964, he had developed a clear sense of both the strengths and deficiencies of Atlantic's Memphis affiliate, along with a clear idea of how he might use the label as an antidote for the creative exhaustion and hidebound thinking that was rapidly draining the life out of the record business in New York.

Otis Redding spent the winter of 1965 shuttling back and forth between the grinding southern circuit of clubs and colleges that paid his bills and a series of northern theater dates, booked through Shaw, that were intended to expand his audience in the Northeast and Midwest. Though his record sales had nearly doubled over the course of the previous year, Otis was still widely perceived as a "southern artist" by promoters and deejays in the rest of the country. ("A lot of artists, they had a record that was real good in four cities," the agent Dick Alen recalled. "And you booked them in those four cities, but no one had heard of them in the fifth city.")

The theater dates functioned as weeklong residencies that gave Otis an opportunity to build his fan base and cultivate the disk jockeys who controlled access to the airwaves in the major black radio markets of New York, Chicago, Philadelphia, Baltimore, and D.C. Despite the celebrated "payola scandal" in 1960, which had compromised the careers of several prominent white deejays and helped to institutionalize the chart-based Top 40 format, payola in the form of cash, gifts, sex, and drugs was ubiquitous in the field of black-oriented radio, whose pay structure was based on the assumption that deejays would have access to supplementary sources of income. Otis had been schooled in the art of commercial bribery by a pair of masters in Joe Galkin and James Brown, and while he was not yet in a position to offer the sort of lucrative copromotion deals that Brown specialized in, his gregarious, streetwise personality made him a natural at the fifty-dollar handshake and the unspoken quid pro quo. Some indication of his success in this regard was his fourth-place finish behind Marvin Gaye, Jerry Butler, and James Brown as Top Male Vocalist in *Billboard*'s March 1965 poll of black deejays.

Back in Macon, spurred by Joe Galkin's constant prodding, Alan and C. B. Walden were now presiding efficiently over Otis's booking operation. "Galkin would call three or four times a day," Alan recalled. "He talked all the time. He would not let up. We called him 'Squawkin' Galkin.'" Alan was also in the process of setting up an official Otis Redding Fan Club, having hired his first employee, Carolyn Brown, an attractive African American secretary, to answer the fan mail forwarded from Stax and Atlantic. He had even managed to get a story about Otis published in the *Telegraph*, written by the paper's "Tween Teens" editor Bob Lamb. "Music people all over the country are hailing 1965 as THE year for Macon's dynamic Otis Redding," the piece began. It went on to list a series of impressive if inflated achievements, including the "countless hundreds of thousands" of records Redding had sold in the previous year, along with his upcoming tours of "California, South America, the Bahamas, England, and the whole of Europe." That same month, Otis received his first coverage in a national publication when *Jet* magazine pictured him in a vignette of black achievement, presenting his beaming parents with the keys to a brand-new car.

Otis with Dexter, Otis Sr., Fannie, and Deborah

And still, the unresolved legal situation stemming from the shootings on Roy Street cast a shadow over his affairs. In February, a preliminary court hearing ended with the dismissal of the misdemeanor charges against David and Willie McGee and a ruling that Otis Redding, Sylvester Huckabee, Herbert Ellis, and Willie Joe Howard should be bound over to the Bibb County Superior Court on two counts of attempted murder. It was at this point that C. B. Walden stepped in, drawing on his contacts in city and county government to suppress the felony indictment against Otis and expunge the record of his arrest. Once the requisite bribes had been paid to the responsible parties in the county solicitor's office, a second hearing was held at which Sylvester Huckabee graciously took the rap, testifying that he alone was the gunman who had shot the two McGees. (When questioned on the witness stand about the quality of his marksmanship, Huck assured the prosecutor that he could shoot off the spots on his tie.) For Otis, however, the matter did not end with the criminal charges against him being dismissed, for the McGees had retained a prominent Macon attorney (and former Confederate-flag-waving state representative), Denmark Groover, who filed an $80,000 civil damage suit against Otis on their behalf. Within a few weeks of its filing, this suit was settled for a payment of approximately $30,000, which Otis obtained as an advance against his royalties from Stax. Later in the year, by prearrangement with the court, Sylvester Huckabee would plead guilty to a misdemeanor charge of "shooting at another person" and was released on probation with a two-year suspended sentence and a $150 fine.

Immediately after the February hearing at which he was charged with attempted murder, Otis returned to the Apollo Theater after an absence of fourteen months, appearing on a bill headlined by the Miracles and Etta James. Bobby Schiffman paid him $2,500 for the week, a significant improvement on the $400 fee he had received for his first appearance there. Though he was booked as a single, Otis insisted on performing with his own band, taking a significant financial loss in order to sound his best at such an important venue. In keeping with his rising status, he shunned the convenience of Harlem's Hotel Theresa and chose instead to stay, like Little Richard, at the ultramodern Americana in Times Square. In the midst of his weeklong stay in the city, on the afternoon of February 21, Malcolm X was assassinated at the Audubon Ballroom in upper Manhattan by a trio of Black Muslim hitmen. It had been a year since Malcolm's break with the coercive orthodoxy of Elijah Muhammad's Nation of Islam; eight months since he returned from a pilgrimage to Mecca with a renewed faith in Islam and a new hope for the possibility of racial reconciliation in the United States.

Otis's return to the Apollo coincided with the release of "That's How Strong My Love Is." The record sold strongly, rising to #18 on the *Billboard* R&B charts before being surpassed by its even more popular B-side, "Mr. Pitiful," which went on to peak at #10 in *Billboard*, #2 in *Cashbox*. (Danceable numbers tended to thrive on the *Cashbox* charts, which were strongly influenced by jukebox plays.) By the end of March, despite the confusion on the part of radio stations as to which of the sides to feature, the single had sold more than 160,000 copies, making it the closest thing to a self-written hit that Otis had ever achieved. More important, by establishing Otis as something more than just a ballad singer, the success of "Mr. Pitiful" worked to broaden his appeal.

Atlantic released Otis's second album on its Atco label just as "Mr. Pitiful" reached its high point on the charts. Titled *The Great Otis Redding Sings Soul Ballads,* the record was packaged in an elegant sleeve designed by Loring Eutemey, one of the cadre of New York graphic artists and photographers that Nesuhi Ertegun had recruited to provide the "modernist" look of Atlantic's jazz LPs. Eutemey's cover featured a more flattering and youthful photograph of Otis than the almost spectral image that was used for *Pain in My Heart*; it shows him poised and smiling, his looks transformed by the "natural" hairstyle he had recently adopted on Sam Cooke's recommendation. Tinted in alternating pastel shades of orange, pink, and blue, the stamp-sized image was reproduced some two dozen times in a grid pattern suggestive of Andy Warhol's recent silkscreen portraits of Marilyn Monroe. (Warhol, after all, was a recent addition to Ahmet Ertegun's social circle.) At Jerry Wexler's request, the album's liner notes were written by Paul Ackerman of *Billboard,* whose opinion carried great weight in the record business, though his wooden prose—a far cry from his magazine's trade talk of "orks" and "jocks"— read in places like a parody of white discourse about black music. "This makes a wonderful tapestry indeed," Ackerman wrote of the album's synthesis of gospel, blues, and pop, "for the resultant performance contains the excitement of the so-called 'church sound.' Also implicit in the Redding technique is the soulful blues quality."

In the growing market for R&B LPs, sales of *Soul Ballads* were much stronger than those of *Pain in My Heart,* totaling more than 40,000 copies during the spring and summer of 1965. The record rose as high as #3 on *Billboard*'s new R&B album chart, which was otherwise dominated by Motown's Miracles, Temptations, and Supremes. The format of the album was virtually identical to that of its predecessor, combining the sides from Otis's last three singles with a half-dozen cover tunes, mostly well-known ballads from the late fifties and early sixties that Otis had sung with the Pinetoppers. These included Sam Cooke's "Nothing Can Change This Love," Jackie Wilson's "A Woman, a Lover, a Friend," Jerry Butler's "For Your Precious Love," and Chuck Willis's "It's Too Late." Otis's ability to make his mark on these R&B "oldies" (most of which, notwithstanding the album title, predated the soul era) was a showcase of the way his talent had matured over the course of 1964. Equally apparent was the improvement in the playing of the Stax band, its horn section bolstered by the addition of trumpeter Sammy Coleman, which produced sleek, modernized arrangements that rescued these familiar songs from the period clichés of the original recordings. "A Woman, a Lover, a Friend" is given new life by Packy Axton's shapely sax solos and Steve Cropper's bluesy licks. On "For Your Precious Love," Otis replaces Jerry Butler's orotund vocal with a delicately restrained performance that draws the pretension out of the song, while the band falls in behind him, instrument by instrument, and builds to a solemn end. Even better is his version of "It's Too Late," sung to the bare accompaniment of a plinking piano that is far better suited to the song's mood of solitude than the moaning New Orleans–style horns and backup chorus of the original.

The least successful of the covers was Otis's version of one of Sam Cooke's personal favorites, "Nothing Can Change This Love," a half-great ballad whose heartfelt verses were marred by a throwaway release in which Cooke served up a medley of saccharine clichés—"You're the apple of my eye . . . cherry pie . . . cake and ice cream . . . sugar and spice"—in a misguided attempt at a Cole Porter–style "list" lyric. Otis does his best to imitate Cooke's insouciance by chuckling to himself before he recites this dessert menu, but his performance is marked by the same self-conscious diction and awkward phrasing that subverted his attempt at "You Send Me" on *Pain in My Heart*. Sam Cooke's effortless grace still eluded him.

With the exception of "For Your Precious Love" at its start and "Mr.

Pitiful" at its end, the second side of the *Soul Ballads* album did not amount to much. It included "Come to Me" and its flip side, "I Want to Thank You," both sounding thoroughly archaic by the spring of 1965; "Keep Your Arms Around Me," a mediocre song by a Satellite Record Shop walk-in named O. B. McClinton that Estelle Axton somehow convinced Otis to sing; and Solomon Burke's "Home in Your Heart," which Otis turned into a spirited tribute to the singer from whom he had learned so much, bringing a special zest to Burke's chortling interjections of "*gotta got-ta* find a home"—a mannerism that Otis would soon appropriate and make his own.

I'VE BEEN LOVING YOU TOO LONG

I'd never really worked with a singer who could reach down so deep and bring out that warmth and feeling. . . . [Otis] was an arranger, he was a producer, he was an artist, he was a performer. He was a total package.

—JIM STEWART

O TIS HAD GOTTEN TO KNOW JERRY BUTLER DURING THE FALL OF 1964, when they performed together often as fellow clients of the Shaw agency. The child of Mississippi sharecroppers, Butler had moved with his family to Chicago in 1942 and grown up listening to the cream of the city's gospel talent. (Mahalia Jackson was a frequent guest soloist at his church.) As a teenager, he sang in a gospel quartet with his close friend Curtis Mayfield, with whom he formed the Impressions in 1957. Following the success of "For Your Precious Love," Butler left the group to begin a solo career as a baritone singing in the dramatic, choked-voice style of tenors like Clyde McPhatter and Jackie Wilson, scoring a #1 hit with "He Will Break Your Heart" in 1960. In March 1965, while they were performing together in Buffalo, Butler showed Otis an unfinished song called "I've Been Loving You Too Long." As soon as Otis heard it, he wanted to record it. A few weeks later, after adding a second verse and roughing out a horn arrangement with the help of Sammy Coleman, he returned to Stax on short notice and cut the track. Butler was delighted with the results—although his publisher had to prevail on Jim Stewart to add his name to the writing credits after the record was released listing Otis Redding as the sole author of the song.

"I've Been Loving You Too Long" was the culmination of a long line of impassioned 12/8 ballads that Otis had recorded since "These Arms of Mine." For two and a half years, his blossoming talent as a singer had been constrained by the mediocrity of his own compositions and the inability of his record label to provide him with first-rate songs. Otis had worked wonders with one-dimensional ballads like "These Arms of Mine" and "Chained and Bound," drawing every ounce of emotion from their pedestrian melodies and formulaic lyrics. "I've Been Loving You Too Long" was something less than a masterpiece, but its words and melody had a dramatic flair that those earlier songs had lacked. As Jerry Butler remarked, "There's not a lot to it, but the way Otis interpreted it, he really found the meat to what was there." Otis did not so much finish Butler's half-written song as *inhabit* the world of heartache evoked by its title and haiku-like verse:

> *I've been loving you too long to stop now . . .*
> *You are tired, and you want to be free*
> *My love is growing stronger,*
> *As you become a habit to me . . .*

"I've Been Loving You Too Long" was also the first romantic ballad Otis ever recorded in which the object of his desire gets to have her say, and its impact hinges on the melodic climax in the middle of the verse where his romantic reverie collides with her emotional reality. Otis begins, as ever, by professing his love, stretching out the title line in gentle starts and stops across six bars of dreamily arpeggiated chords on the piano. Phrasing behind both the beat and the chord changes, he's clearly in no hurry to get to the matter at hand. Then a snare accent brings him up short, and he rides a chorus of horns as they crescendo up the scale an octave and more, to end on a high A at the top of his range. "You are *ti-i-i-i'ed,*" he cries, dropping the *r* and holding the note with an anguished emphasis till his breath gives way and he lowers his voice to add, "And you want to be free." In the face of her discontent, he then describes his love as a "habit" he can't break, betraying the trap of routine and dependence his lover is wanting to flee. "I've Been Loving You Too Long" was the first song Otis ever sang that allows for the possibility that one can love too much, or that simple devotion might not be enough. At the end of the second and final verse, where the song changes key as it enters its coda, the horns set up a dirge-like refrain, the dreamy piano gives way to a storm of pounding chords, and Al Jackson's slow-motion rolls and doubled downbeats add a thudding, visceral emphasis to Otis's plea of "I'm down on my knees." "I love you with all my heart," he cries as the song fades, but no one within the sound of his voice can doubt how this will end.

Coupled with an upbeat but forgettable B-side called "I'm Depending On You," "I've Been Loving You Too Long" came out in May and took about a month to rise to #2 on the R&B charts, where it was shut out of the top position by the immutable presence of the Four Tops' million-seller "I Can't Help Myself," which remained at #1 for nine weeks during the spring and summer of 1965. With sales approaching a half-million copies during its first three months of release, Otis's eighth single on Stax was the unequivocal R&B hit he had been seeking for three long years. Its success was a testament not only to the strength of the song and its performance but also to the amount of time and effort Otis had put into cultivating black deejays. Whereas "Mr. Pitiful" had rated a single Pick of the Week selection on *Billboard*'s survey of black radio stations, "I've Been Loving You Too Long" was named by deejays at stations in Nashville, New Orleans, and Columbus, Ohio, in its first week of release; Memphis, Miami, and Buffalo the second week; Washington, Boston, Newark, Albany, Charlotte, Louisville, and Port Arthur, Texas, in the weeks after that. It was no coincidence that all of these cities had been stops on Otis's itinerary the winter before.

THAT SPRING, AFTER serving as his brother's keeper for a year and a half, Rodgers Redding was forced to step down as Otis's road manager after receiving an induction letter from the Macon draft board. In the six months since Congress had approved the Gulf of Tonkin resolution authorizing the use of American forces in Southeast Asia in August 1964, the Selective Service System had been quietly increasing the size of its draft calls as the military situation in South Vietnam deteriorated and the Johnson administration prepared for the direct commitment of US ground troops to the war. As a healthy high school graduate with no dependents, Rodgers was a prime candidate. His induction letter ordered him to report for assignment and basic training in three weeks' time.

Rodgers's place was taken by Earl "Speedo" Sims, who had earned Otis's friendship and trust since joining his revue as an opening act in the fall of 1964. A twenty-nine-year-old native of Baltimore, Sims first came to Macon in the mid-1950s as an airman at Robins AFB. Attracted by the local music scene, he stayed on in the city after his discharge, eventually marrying a local woman and forming a group called the Premiers. Sims first met Otis as a fellow contestant at the *Teenage Party* talent shows, by which time he had taken his stage name from the 1956 hit by the Cadillacs ("Now they often call me Speedoo / But my real name is Mr. Earl"). Sims and his group soon fell into the orbit of Clint Brantley, who booked them as a backup band for national acts when they toured as singles in the Southeast. Along the way, Brantley taught his willing young student how business was done on the chitlin' circuit.

As Rodgers Redding was entering the service, Phil Walden was coming out. Phil completed his overseas tour of duty in May 1965 and returned from West Germany on the first available flight. Alan and his parents met him at the airport in Atlanta and drove him back to Macon, stopping at a gas station along the way so that Phil could telephone Otis, who was somewhere out on the road. It was the first time they had spoken in sixteen months, and Phil remembered it as "a very emotional experience." In his excitement, he began talking during the car ride home about the plans he had made and the many things he meant to tell Otis to do now that he was back. Alan recalled interrupting his brother and explaining that things had changed since Phil had left, beginning with the fact that no one "told" Otis to do anything anymore; instead, Alan and his father made suggestions, which Otis often took.

It was not an easy transition. Phil was returning to a situation that bore little resemblance to the small-time college talent agency he had left in 1963. Otis's national bookings were now being handled by Frank Sands and his colleague Larry Myers at Shaw Artists in New York. (Myers was a diminutive Brooklyn native who had engineered Ray Charles's signing with ABC-Paramount in 1959.) The supervision of Otis's recording career was firmly in the hands of Jim Stewart, Joe Galkin, and Jerry Wexler.

Otis's touring operation—his road band, his supporting acts, his transportation and lodging—was entirely run by Otis himself and his new road manager, Speedo Sims. And then there was the matter of Alan. From Phil's perspective, his brother had been minding the store. From Alan's perspective, he had spent the past sixteen months *running* the store. Phil came home vaguely assuming that Alan would want to resume his studies at Mercer and otherwise get on with his life. Instead, with C. B.'s full support, Alan made it clear that he expected to participate as an equal partner in what had become, in effect, the Walden family business.

Phil Walden sometimes referred to the fact that Otis had a white manager as if it were an anomaly of some kind. While it may have been unusual by the standards of Macon, Georgia, Otis was well aware by now that most successful black entertainers relied on white managers to represent their interests, given the realities of American show business at the time. Louis Armstrong had Joe Glaser. Clyde McPhatter had Irvin Feld. James Brown had Ben Bart. The anomaly in Otis's relationship with Phil and Alan Walden had more to do with the closeness in their ages and with the Waldens' southern Methodist background than it did with the color of their skin. Glaser, Feld, and Bart were all northern Jews who served as managers, mentors, and father figures to their southern-born clients, who took the paternalism of the relationship for granted. Otis's relationship with the Walden brothers, by contrast, was decidedly fraternal, and by the spring of 1965, having effectively run his own operation for the past eighteen months, Otis knew more about the music business than Phil and Alan combined. It was left to Joe Galkin, Jerry Wexler, Jim Stewart, Frank Sands, and C. B. Walden, in their different ways, to provide him with the benefit of their wisdom and experience. The question facing Phil Walden upon his return to Macon was where he fit into this cast of characters, some of whom he had never even met.

Characteristically, Phil was not shy about reasserting himself. In the course of his military service, he, too, had gained experience, promoting shows at army bases and USO clubs, and he was brimming with pent-up energy and ideas. Leaving the oversight of Otis's bookings to Alan, Phil began, for the first time, to function as a manager, focusing his attention on the direction and promotion of Otis's career.

His first step was to reestablish his relationship with Joe Galkin, whose advice he sought at every turn. "Joe promoted Otis day and night," Jim Stewart recalled. "Joe was the one who kept pushing and pushing. He was the motivating force behind me and Jerry Wexler and Phil Walden, kicking us in the butt, saying let's do this, let's do that. Otis Redding was his life." Phil began spending a considerable amount of his time with Galkin in Atlanta and accompanying him to the record and radio conventions where much of the business of the music industry was done. Through Joe, he would get to know Jerry Wexler and Ahmet Ertegun, who both took a liking to this earnest young Southerner and considered him, in Wexler's words, "more Redding's soul brother than his manager."

IN THE WINTER of 1965 Jerry Wexler had contacted Jim Stewart about Sam Moore and Dave Prater, a pair of singers he had recently signed to Atlantic. Moore was a former pimp and street hustler from Miami; Prater had grown up on a farm outside Ocilla, Georgia, in the southern part of the state. Billed as Sam and Dave, the duo had been together since 1961, when they began performing at a Miami nightclub called the King of Hearts. Over the next three years, they cut a half dozen uninspiring singles on the Roulette label and perfected an incendiary live act based on their dynamic stagecraft and their adaptation of the double-lead format of gospel quartet to R&B. Wexler and Ertegun first heard them while attending a record convention in Miami in the summer of 1964 and signed them as soon as their contract with Roulette expired at the end of the year.

Rather than record the pair in New York, Wexler thought their churchy style might be right for Stax, so he offered to "loan" them to Jim Stewart, with the understanding that while Stax would produce them and Atlantic would distribute their records under the terms of their usual deal, Atlantic would retain the ownership of their contract and a share of their song publishing. Though Stewart agreed to the arrangement, he was unenthusiastic about it, so he put the pair together with David Porter, Booker Jones's old high school bandmate, who had been hanging around

the Satellite Record Shop, dabbling in singing and songwriting and waiting for someone to give him a break.

Sam and Dave's first single for Stax consisted of a ballad by Porter
and Steve Cropper called "Goodnight Baby" and an uptempo number by
Porter alone called "A Place That's Hard to Find." Like much of Stax's
self-generated output during this period, the record was an unabashed
imitation of Motown that failed to make the charts. But Jerry Wexler
had opened up a new collaborative chapter in the relationship between
Stax and Atlantic, and he soon contacted Jim Stewart about another artist he had recently signed and didn't quite know what to do with. Born
in Alabama in 1941, Wilson Pickett had moved to Detroit as a teenager.
After singing with a gospel quartet called the Violinaires (with whom
he perfected a fearsome imitation of June Cheeks), he crossed over into
popular music with the Falcons, whose 1962 Atlantic-distributed hit "I
Found a Love" featured Pickett singing lead. After leaving the Falcons at
the first opportunity to pursue a solo career, he signed with a small label
called Double L and recorded a James Brown–influenced number called
"It's Too Late." His next release on Double L was a self-written ballad,
"If You Need Me," to which Jerry Wexler, who knew a hit song when he
heard one, had recently purchased the publishing rights. Wexler wasted
no time in cutting "If You Need Me" with Solomon Burke, and the two
versions, both first-rate, went head-to-head during the summer of 1963,
with Burke coming out on top thanks to Atlantic's relentless promotion.

A year later, having agreed to let bygones be bygones, Wexler purchased Pickett's contract from Double L. But his initial sessions for Atlantic yielded nothing of value, owing, in Wexler's view, to the singer's
"obstreperous" personality. Handsome, headstrong, and profoundly ego-
tistical, "Wicked" Wilson Pickett was the living embodiment of Stagolee,
the original "outlaw nigger" of African American folklore, giving full
vent to his bad self with little regard for the consequences. In the spring
of 1965, convinced of Pickett's talent but at a loss as to how to record him,
Wexler decided to personally escort his temperamental artist to Memphis,
in the hope that a change of scenery would do them both some good.

In anticipation of their visit, Wexler dispatched Tom Dowd to equip the Stax studio with a Scully tape deck that had the capacity to record in stereo, which was fast becoming the requisite format on popular LPs. Since Jim Stewart did not know how to mix in stereo and showed no desire to learn, Dowd configured the system so that it still effectively functioned in mono, with the playback booming out of a single enormous speaker that Stewart had salvaged from the Capitol Theater's sound system and crammed into the studio's control room. When mixing mono singles, Stewart could keep on doing what he had always done. On album cuts, the four-track tapes would be sent to Atlantic in New York for mixing and mastering in stereo. While he was at it, Dowd also attenuated the system so that it was impossible for Stewart to overload the microphone inputs on the studio's mixing board. (Stewart had developed a bad habit of boosting the volume excessively in a quixotic effort to achieve the bright sound heard on Motown's records, unaware that Motown achieved its distinctive high end through the use of tone controls.) At a time when the technology of recording was improving by leaps and bounds, Stewart was superstitious about employing new techniques, fearful that they would rob his studio of its distinctive sound. As a result, the setup at Stax remained so static, said Steve Cropper, that "the microphones never moved from day to day."

On one point, however, Jim Stewart's Luddite tendencies paid off. The advent of multitrack recording was leading many studios (Motown most of all) to adopt the efficient practice of cutting vocal and instrumental tracks separately. This allowed singers to refine their parts by repeating them over a prerecorded backing, and it allowed producers to add additional voices or instruments on top of the original rhythm track. The creative use of "overdubbing," as the technique came to be known, was turning recording studios into compositional laboratories, but for as long as Jim Stewart remained behind the board, this practice had been avoided at Stax. All recording on McLemore Avenue was done live, with the singers and instrumentalists performing simultaneously, and this old-school approach contributed significantly to the chemistry and spontaneity of the records that were made there.

Jerry Wexler and Wilson Pickett arrived in Memphis in the middle of May. Aware that no one from outside the label had ever produced a session at Stax, Wexler took pains not to step on anyone's toes. He began by putting Pickett and Steve Cropper together in a hotel room with a directive to write some songs. They emerged the next day with several numbers, the best of which was based on a phrase from the standard gospel litany—"early in the morning, late in the evening, *in the midnight hour*"—that Pickett had sung as an interjection in the coda of "I Found a Love." Like Tom Dowd before him, Wexler watched in amazement as the Stax band improvised an arrangement for "In the Midnight Hour," falling in behind Pickett and Cropper as they ran through the changes of the song, coming together on a stirring horn introduction and a solid mid-tempo groove. Up to this point, Wexler's career as a record producer had been based on careful preparation: picking the songs, commissioning the arrangements, rehearsing the artist, selecting the sidemen, cutting the tracks. The approach at Stax was a revelation for him. "Watching the way they made records organically, inductively, from the bottom up, taught me what the components of a piece of music are," he later said. "There was such an interaction between me and the musicians, and there was never anything like that in New York."

As the arrangement of "Midnight Hour" took shape, Wexler had an inspiration of his own—one that propelled him out of the control room and onto the studio floor. There he began to enact his version of the Jerk, a trendy teenage dance whose hallmark was an emphatic thrusting motion with the shoulders, chest, and arms. Wexler's pantomime was meant to convey a subtle sense of delay on the second and fourth beats of the bar. Suppressing their amazement at the sight of Atlantic's forty-eight-year-old executive vice president boogying around the room, the MGs picked up on Wexler's idea immediately, for he was urging them to accentuate a tendency that already existed in their playing, a precise but flexible approach to rhythm that gave full value to the space between the notes.

"In the Midnight Hour" marked the dawn of a new era at Stax. "I think it was the first time we had a chance to work with somebody that was up on the music scene from a different part of the country," Steve Cropper recalled. "We had been doing our own kind of thing, the way we wanted to do it." In Tom Dowd's view, "They'd be the first to say that they learned as much from Jerry as he learned from them. Jerry would be

demanding; he made them less laid back. They taught him musical relaxation, he schooled them on concentration and intensity." Wexler spoke
a different musical language than the Memphis musicians were used to.
"He was from such a different culture, and even the words he used were
funny," said the bassist David Hood, who later worked with Wexler at
the Fame Studio in Muscle Shoals, Alabama. "But he had great intuition
and depth of knowledge. He knew that when something is in the pocket,
it can be one click faster or slower and it won't work. He could tell when
it was *there*." By pushing the MGs to exceed themselves, Wexler finished
what Otis Redding had started at Stax, breathing new life into a creative environment that was high on musical integrity but low on musical
imagination. Wilson Pickett was so pleased with the results that he sent
the band members a bonus even before the single came out. And Wexler's
judgment was quickly affirmed by commercial success. Released in the
summer of 1965, "In the Midnight Hour" was hailed as an instant classic,
the best-sounding, bestselling record that Stax had ever produced. In July,
it would finally dislodge the Four Tops' "I Can't Help Myself" at #1 on
the R&B charts.

The success of "Midnight Hour" was not lost on Otis Redding. Working in the same studio, with the same musicians, drawing on the same
principles of rhythm and horn arranging that Otis had helped to develop,
Wilson Pickett, Steve Cropper, Jerry Wexler, and Tom Dowd had pooled
their talents to produce the first #1 record ever made at Stax. Otis was
the label's premier artist, and the fact that he was not the beneficiary of
this collective triumph did not sit well with him. But it did serve to whet
his competitive instincts, and it introduced him to the possibility that the
men who ran Atlantic Records might have creative resources to offer that
reached beyond the limited horizons of Memphis.

OTIS BLUE

[Otis] would come in the door with the whole recording in his mind, and be able to tell all of us what he wanted. He was the greatest horn arranger I ever knew. He'd get down there and sing horn parts to us until you would think you were going to come out of your shoes.

—WAYNE JACKSON

In the course of Jerry Wexler's visit to Memphis, he and Jim Stewart agreed that the time had come to formalize the handshake deal that had been such a boon to both their labels over the preceding five years. Both men would later insist that they never bothered to read the letter of agreement that Atlantic's attorney Paul Marshall drew up, the implication being that it was indeed a formality to them. But a good deal of discussion went into the terms of this contract. Among other things, Stewart requested that Wexler be named as a "key man" in the deal, and a stipulation was added stating that Stax could withdraw from the accord if Wexler ceased to work for Atlantic or if the company itself should be sold. Wexler's biggest concern was that Stax re-sign Otis Redding, whose original three-year contract with the label was due to expire in the months ahead. Wexler knew that RCA's aggressive head of A&R, Joe D'Imperio, was interested in signing Otis as a replacement for Sam Cooke, and that RCA was prepared to sweeten the deal with a large cash bonus. But in Wexler's view, Otis *was* Stax. He recognized that Rufus Thomas, Carla Thomas, or Booker T. and the MGs might turn out a hit record from time to time. But he was also aware that Jim Stewart had failed to sign a single successful new singer in the three years since Otis had shown up on McLemore Avenue in the summer of 1962.

Joe Galkin was equally intent on Otis re-signing with Stax, since his half share of the earnings from Otis's record sales and song publishing was dependent on his agreement with Jim Stewart. But Galkin wasn't concerned; he knew that Otis had no intention of going to another label. Otis was well aware that Galkin had been the driving force behind his recording career, ably abetted by Wexler, Stewart, and the musicians at Stax, whom he regarded as colleagues and friends. He was not about to abandon these relationships for the chance to make records with unfamiliar producers, engineers, and session musicians in New York, Nashville, or Los Angeles. The negotiation of Otis's new recording contract was the first significant piece of business that Phil Walden took part in since his return, but Walden was happy to let Galkin take the lead, and the terms of the new contract they worked out with Jim Stewart were fair by the standards of the time. Effective immediately, Otis's royalty rate was increased from 3 to 4 percent, with a further raise to 5 percent by the end of 1965. In addition, Otis would henceforth receive a one-third interest in the publisher's share of his song publishing, thereby making him a co-owner of the copyrights to his original songs.

Otis's new contract with Stax led to the establishment of several new business ventures. These included Redwal Music, a partnership between Otis and the Waldens that was set up to administer his publishing, and a boutique record label called Jotis, jointly owned by Otis and Joe Galkin, which, along with a company called Big O Productions, was founded to help Otis follow Sam Cooke's example by producing other artists. The first release on Jotis was a record by Billy Young, an amateur singer from California whom Phil Walden had met in the army and invited to Macon after his discharge. Young soon found himself signed by Walden, working as an opening act for the Otis Redding Revue, and inaugurating Jotis with a pair of songs, both credited to Otis, titled "Same Thing All Over" and "The Sloopy." The first was a morose ballad that *Billboard* vainly predicted "should spiral up the chart rapidly"; the second was a prospective dance craze ("Keep on *sloopin'* baby"), inspired by the McCoys' hit single "Hang On Sloopy," that never got off the ground.

Jotis's second signing was a more promising acquisition. During one of Otis's dates in Baltimore during the spring, a local impresario named Rufus Mitchell had given him a copy of a single called "I'm a Lonely

Stranger," sung by a nineteen-year-old Atlanta native named Arthur Conley, that Mitchell had released on his own Ru-Jac label. Otis was taken with the performance, though not the production, and without ever meeting Conley, he signed him to Jotis and arranged for him to re-record the song at Stax. The remake—to which Otis added his name as a co-writer—was a hauntingly beautiful ballad that somehow fell through the cracks when Jotis released it later in the summer of 1965.

In June, Jerry Wexler sent Jim Stewart another newly signed Atlantic artist, the singer-songwriter Don Covay, whose collaboration with Steve Cropper would yield an R&B hit called "See Saw." But the full flowering of the Stax-Atlantic partnership came in the middle of July, shortly after Wexler and Stewart signed the new contract between the two labels, when Tom Dowd was dispatched to Memphis to work with Otis Redding on his second LP of the year. *Soul Ballads* had sold a respectable total of 20,000 copies in three months' time, and Atlantic wanted to capitalize on the Top 40 success of "I've Been Loving You Too Long" by releasing a follow-up single and a stereo album. Though Dowd was ostensibly sent to Stax to handle the stereo production, the ulterior motive for his presence, given the ongoing concerns about Jim Stewart's engineering, was to ensure that Otis's next record was mixed to Atlantic's specifications. Dowd was well suited to this task, for in addition to his musical ear and technical expertise, he possessed an exceptionally congenial and diplomatic personality. "He's probably the most positive person you'll ever meet," said his colleague Phil Ramone.

The LP that emerged from Dowd's visit, titled *Otis Blue,* has earned a reputation over the years as a landmark in Otis Redding's career. (An elaborate CD reissue in 2008, complete with "bonus tracks," stereo and mono mixes, and effusive liner notes, helped to reaffirm this status.) Though *Otis Blue* was indeed a more accomplished, consistent, and commercially successful album than anything Otis had yet produced, the circumstances under which it was made were even more constrained than usual. All eleven tracks (including a stereo remake of "I've Been Loving You Too Long") were recorded during a two-day gap in Otis's tour schedule, in a single marathon session that began on a Friday morning, broke off around eight in the evening so that the members of the Stax band could play their usual Friday-night club dates, resumed at two in the morning, and continued well into the next day. This absurdly tight schedule ensured that little thought or preparation went into the selection of the material, and it left little time to refine the arrangements and performances during the recording process itself. Nevertheless, what sets *Otis Blue* apart from its predecessors is the confidence, intensity, and joyful spirit that Otis and the band were able to bring to their work, as well as the wonderfully clear, well-balanced sound that Tom Dowd achieved on many of the tracks. Fresh from their fine-tuning at the hands of Jerry Wexler, the Stax band was on a collective high, and there was a strong sense of anticipation in the air. "You could feel the excitement when he was coming," recalled the trumpeter Wayne Jackson. "The Stax studio would light up when Otis came in," added Duck Dunn. "He got performances out of us like no one else. He was an incredible creative spark."

Out on the road, Otis had continued to struggle with his songwriting, and he came to Memphis with only a pair of unfinished songs, both of which had their origins among members of his entourage. The lyrics to the ballad "Ole Man Trouble" had been written by Sylvester Huckabee, while the title and verse of "Respect" came from Speedo Sims. At Otis's suggestion, Sims had recently tried to record "Respect" at Bobby Smith's studio in Macon, for possible release on Jotis. Having never sung in a studio before, Speedo froze in front of the microphone, and he was pleased when Otis asked if he could make something of the song.

On the eve of the recording session, Otis got together with Steve Cropper to rough out the arrangements for the two original songs and discuss some possible cover tunes. Otis was intent on paying tribute to Sam Cooke on the new LP. Musical memorials to Cooke had been pouring forth during the first half of 1965, led by Motown's Supremes, whose appallingly slapdash collection *We Remember Sam Cooke* contained three songs that found their way onto *Otis Blue*: both sides of Cooke's posthumous single, "Shake," and "A Change Is Gonna Come," along with his 1960 recording of "Wonderful World," which had recently been revived as a Top 10 hit by the British band Herman's Hermits. In addition, Cropper and Booker Jones felt that Otis should cover another hit single by another British group. Stax had just learned through its publishing company that the Rolling Stones had recorded a version of "I've Been Loving You Too Long" for possible inclusion on their next album. (The track wound up being released a year later, doctored with crowd noise, on the group's first live LP.) This counted as the third of Otis's records that the Stones had covered to date. On the reasonable assumption that Stones fans might share their heroes' enthusiasm for Otis, Cropper suggested that he repay the compliment by covering their single "(I Can't Get No) Satisfaction," which currently stood at #1 on the *Billboard* charts.

The first order of business when Otis and the band convened at Stax on the first morning of the *Otis Blue* session was to record the tracks for a new single. Since the advent of pop LPs, the usual practice in the record business had been to time the release of an album to follow the release of a hit single by several months, on the theory that consumers would be less inclined to buy a single if they could purchase the same song, at the same time, on an LP. It was the Beatles who turned this conventional wisdom on its head. The group's popularity in the States was such that sales of their singles were not appreciably compromised by the simultaneous release of the same songs on their LPs. If anything, their singles seemed to drive the sales of their albums, so much so that by 1965, a new marketing strategy was taking hold, as labels began to encourage their artists to endow each new album with a prospective hit single. In the case of Otis's third LP, "Respect" was the obvious candidate to play this role.

Though the lyric was originally written by Speedo Sims as a retort to his flagrantly unfaithful wife, "Respect" addressed a situation that Otis dealt with in his own life on a regular basis. An associate of James Brown once speculated that Brown never spent a night alone on the road, and there is no reason to think that things were appreciably different for Otis, such were the sexual opportunities available to a touring R&B star. Away from home for weeks at a time, Otis had countless casual liaisons with the women who flocked to his shows. (In a memoir written some twenty years after the fact, Phil Walden compared the after-hours scene in Otis's hotel suite to a "doctor's office," with any number of women patiently waiting their turn.)

By all accounts, Otis managed this aspect of his life with considerable care, seeing to it that no word or sign of his extramarital affairs ever got

Otis and Zelma, 1965

back to Zelma, and that none of his liaisons ever assumed any emotional importance for him. His discretion was helped by the fact that the activities of black entertainers on the club and theater circuit received little press coverage of any kind during this period, making it highly unlikely that he would be photographed or otherwise documented in the company of another woman. In addition, since many of Otis's associates had an interest in hiding their own behavior from their wives and girlfriends, a conspiracy of silence prevailed.

Even so, like many guilty spouses, Otis was prone to intense jealousy, and he constantly harbored suspicions that Zelma was unfaithful to *him* during his absences. He would sometimes call her three or four times a day, at all hours, to make sure that she was home. For her part, Zelma professed to be philosophical about this aspect of their relationship. "I happened to think my husband was a very handsome man," she later said, "and it didn't come as a surprise to me that other women felt that way about him too." On a pragmatic level, she believed that no man was going to resist the temptations that Otis was presented with. The important question for her was how he handled it, and how he made her feel when they were together. "I told him, don't bring nothing home and respect me," she recalled, adding, "I never, ever, runned around on him. Never thought of it. Goodness. Living better than I ever lived in my life, and I'm just not letting nobody talk *me* out the door. I might be a fool, but I'm not that big a fool!"

According to Speedo, the version of "Respect" he tried and failed to record in Macon bore little musical resemblance to the finished track. The arrangement that Otis and Steve Cropper showed the band had a pounding quarter-note pulse, an empirically derived six-bar verse, and a boisterous, syncopated horn riff in its intro and chorus. Having worked with some of the most accomplished musicians in jazz and R&B, from John Coltrane to Ray Charles, Tom Dowd was taken aback on this first track by Otis's command of the session and his ability to get his ideas across: "Otis was a very strong individual. He did not have the acumen or the experience musically to be able to say, 'More like this or more like that.' He'd just say, 'That ain't right,' and he'd sing a part to you." Duck Dunn recalled the bewilderment on the faces of the horn players when Otis first showed them what he wanted to play. "When he came in there and did 'Respect' and he started that intro, they looked at him. They'd never heard anything like that before. I didn't believe it was going to work."

Coming from a singer who had based his career on his skill at conveying a sense of single-minded devotion, the lyrics to "Respect" paint a starkly unromantic picture of domestic relations. The song turns on an interchange between a "little girl" who's "sweeter than honey" and a man who's about to reward her with "all my money." The money-for-honey dynamic is driven home by the celebratory blaring of the horns, which seem to be heralding a carnal reunion of epic proportions, and the almost comical insistence of Duck Dunn's loopy, pulsating bass line and Al Jackson's sputtering rolls. With help from Tom Dowd, Otis's voice explodes across the track, phrasing in staccato bursts. "What you want / Honey you got it" he barks in the opening verse. "You can do me wrong honey / While I'm gone," he allows in the second. Either way, he assures her, "All I'm asking is for a little *respect* when I come home" (to which a Greek chorus of male voices adds the tagline "Hey, hey hey!"). What's surprising about the song is the apparent modesty of its expectations: the way it takes a word that commonly refers to personal esteem and scales it down to serve as a euphemism for sexual reward. This is the "street" meaning of "respect," bound up with issues of deference and power. But only up to a point. In the coda that follows the final verse, Otis goes to work, wresting the word free of this narrow meaning, asserting his prerogative with an insistent determination that turns the song in its final moments into a plea for simple human dignity—"Respect is what I want! / Respect is what I need! / I got-ta got-ta have it! / Just give me some respect!"—that doesn't stop at mere discretion.

With "Respect" as the leading candidate for the A-side of a single, the session next turned to "Ole Man Trouble," one of the few ballads Otis ever sang that was *not* in triplet time, unfolding instead in a steely 4/4 meter set by Steve Cropper's mesmerizing rhythm guitar. Cropper and Redding would wind up sharing the writing credits on nearly a dozen songs, but it's hard to say why "Ole Man Trouble" wasn't considered one of them, so thoroughly does Cropper's playing determine the character of the track. The year before, while passing through Memphis as a sideman with an R&B revue, Jimi Hendrix spent several hours hanging around the Stax studio waiting to meet Cropper, whose influence he had been absorbing for several years. With its shifting mixture of thickly voiced chords, sliding sixths, muted clicks, and driving bass-note runs, Cropper's playing on "Ole Man Trouble" is a premonition of the hybrid style of rhythm guitar that Hendrix would shortly spring upon an unsuspecting world.

In contrast to this artful accompaniment, Sylvester Huckabee's lyric has the unself-conscious eloquence of a folk song. Though nothing is known about how Huck came to write it, the lyric sounds like a dance with the devil from a preacher's sermon, and Otis plays up the personification by turning each line into a form of direct address: "*Ole* man trouble leave me along / *Go* find yourself someone else to pick on / *I* live my life in doubt you see / *Ole* man trouble stay away from me." Not since the jokey verses of "Shout Bamalama" and "Mary's Little Lamb" had Otis sung about something other than romantic love. Designated as the opening track of the album, "Ole Man Trouble," while technically not a blues, substantiates the title *Otis Blue* in spirit if not in fact.

Once the tracks for the single were completed, Tom Dowd suggested that they record an updated, stereo version of "I've Been Loving You Too Long" for inclusion on the LP. Otis had been singing the song on the road for several months, and his performance on this slower, surer, subtler remake was a great improvement on the original, especially in the coda, which now culminated in a gospel oath of "Good God Almighty, I love you!"

"Old Man Trouble," "Respect," and "I've Been Loving You Too Long" gave *Otis Blue* a smaller but much stronger core of original songs than Otis's previous LPs. All three were placed on the first side of the album, together with Sam Cooke's "A Change Is Gonna Come" and Solomon Burke's "Down in the Valley." The six tracks on the second side were all covers. They included the two other songs by Cooke, "Shake" and "Wonderful World"; Smokey Robinson's exquisite ballad "My Girl," a #1 record for the Temptations earlier in 1965; "Rock Me Baby," an unprecedented Top 40 hit for B. B. King in 1964; and "(I Can't Get No) Satisfaction" by the Stones. The final track was a reprise of "You Don't Miss Your Water," William Bell's all-but-forgotten ballad from Stax's formative years.

With one notable exception, the covers on *Otis Blue* are marked by an almost casual mastery. Otis has his usual fun with Solomon Burke and his oddball take on the traditional folk song "Down in the Valley," cackling and chortling in the verses, chattering through the horn breaks, and ad-libbing in the fade ("So low! So low! Can't go no further! *Down!*"). On "Wonderful World," he sounds a lot more convincing than Sam Cooke ever did as an academically challenged high school student striving to impress his girlfriend; Otis's down-home diction brings the ring of truth to lines like "Don't know much about the al-*gee*-bra." Cooke's version of "Shake" was a debonair dance lesson set to the magisterial rhythms of Earl Palmer's cascading tom-toms. Otis sings the song faster and hotter than Cooke, with more of a gospel feeling, but the track really belongs to Al Jackson Jr., who twists, bends, and upends the beat in a series of explosive solo breaks. (Thanks to Tom Dowd, Jackson's drums are heard as never before on *Otis Blue*.)

Constrained by the lumbering blues shuffle of B. B. King's "Rock Me Baby," Otis happily turns the song over to Steve Cropper, who pays his respects to King with a stinging twelve-bar solo that might contain more notes than Cropper had otherwise played in the course of the previous year. On "My Girl," one of the breezy masterpieces that would qualify Smokey Robinson as the Cole Porter of 1960s pop, Otis lets the song do the work. He sings the pentatonic melody with perfect intonation and an understated tenderness while his accompanists draw an explicit contrast with their counterparts in Detroit, replacing Motown's frilly symphonic strings with the sonorous warmth of Memphis horns.

A similar simplicity pervades William Bell's "You Don't Miss Your Water," the record on which Chips Moman laid the groundwork for Stax's

distinctive, churchy approach to the ubiquitous 12/8 ballad, thereby setting the stage for Otis Redding's whole career. Otis repays this debt by
turning in a definitive version of the song, updating Bell's plodding vocals by reshaping each line of the verse into a fluent, well-formed musical
phrase that rises and falls on the offbeats with the lilt of conversation, not
declamation. Instead of the clunky, full-stop ending of the original, Otis
contrived a coda in which he extended the metaphor of the song, repeating the lines "I miss my water / I want my water / I *need* my water / I *love*
my water / And I'm a little thirsty now . . ."

Considering the haste with which these eleven tracks were recorded,
the quality of the singing and playing on *Otis Blue* was remarkable
throughout. The sole misstep was Otis's rendition of "A Change Is Gonna
Come," which was clearly intended as a tour de force, given its pride of
place as the third track on the LP. Otis had struggled with Sam Cooke's
ballads in the past, sounding reticent and unsure. Here he throws himself into the song's opening lines with complete abandon, tethered by a
restrained arrangement that substitutes Booker Jones's gospel piano and
Steve Cropper's limpid guitar for the strings, brass, and tympani of the
original recording. It's a brave beginning, and Otis sustains it until the
end of the second verse, where he loses his grip on the lyrics and starts
groping for the sense of the song.

Under normal circumstances, someone—whether Jim Stewart, Tom
Dowd, or Otis himself—would have stopped the take so that Otis could
get his bearings, refresh his memory, and re-record the track. But with
time of the essence, Otis forges ahead, faking it as he goes, mangling
the song's parable of a man who's shunned by his biblical "brother" to
include his "little mother" as well, and discarding the ethereal ending of
the original (a rapturous swell on the line "Oh yes it is") in favor of an
unconvincing coda that ends with some bantering wordplay ("You know,
and I know, that you know, that I know") lifted from another song on
Cooke's *Live at the Copa* LP.

On a practical level, "A Change Is Gonna Come" suffered from the
extent to which Otis was beginning to function as his own producer at
Stax, leaving no one in the studio who was in a position to tell him, unequivocally, when he needed to sing a song again. It also highlighted the

cavalier attitude toward lyrics and their meaning that remained his principal shortcoming as a singer and a songwriter. Yet this same tendency to take liberties with language yielded a very different result on Otis's version of the Rolling Stones' "Satisfaction," which began as a throwaway and wound up as one of the album's most notable tracks. Otis claimed that he had never heard the song, before Steve Cropper and Booker Jones played him the record and suggested that he sing it on *Otis Blue*. "They asked me if I'd heard the new Rolling Stones song, but I hadn't," he explained. "If you notice, I use a lot of words different from the Stones' version. That's because I made it up."

His ignorance of the record says something about his radio listening habits at the time, since the song was an inescapable presence on Top 40 stations across America during the summer of 1965. "Satisfaction" was a commercial and creative breakthrough for the Stones—their first #1 single in the United States and their first great original song. After making their name as a cover band in the London R&B scene of the early 1960s, the group had turned to songwriting under the spell of the Beatles, whose popularity among British teenagers they began to rival in 1964. But fans in America had been slower to respond to the Stones' deliberately surly image and their hard-edged, bluesy sound. Recorded in Los Angeles in the spring of 1965, "(I Can't Get No) Satisfaction" was a pastiche of contemporary pop trends. The four-to-the-bar "stomp" rhythm was derived from current Motown hits like "Nowhere to Run" and "I Can't Help Myself." Mick Jagger's leering lyric was an anti-establishment manifesto that drew on the themes of social and sexual alienation that Bob Dylan had brought to the popular lexicon with the songs on his first "electric" album, *Bringing It All Back Home*. And Keith Richards's soon-to-be-iconic eight-note guitar hook—*dum dum*, dum-dum-*dum,* dum-*dum* dum—echoed the ostinato motifs of recent Beatles hits like "I Feel Fine" and "Ticket to Ride." (Richards had originally conceived of the riff as a soul-style horn part but wound up playing it on a guitar equipped with a saxlike distortion effect called a fuzz tone.)

Otis's version embraced Richards's conception of the song and made mincemeat of Jagger's. While the bass and guitar, trumpets and saxes bandy the hook back and forth like the theme from Beethoven's Fifth,

Otis sings the opening chorus and verse more or less as written, adding a flat nasality to his voice that verges on a parody of Jagger's drawling impersonation of black American dialect. (Whether this was merely the mimic in Otis or a more deliberate send-up is anybody's guess.) But in the later verses, where the song goes on to present a critique of consumer culture and pop celebrity, Otis wants none of that, so he shifts the focus of his singing from the satisfaction he lacks to the satisfaction he wants. "We gotta have it!" he proclaims, and after exhorting the band to "keep on grooving" behind him, he sets off in search of "somebody to love me and give me some reaction," stringing together a series of semicoherent words, phrases, grunts, groans, and scat syllables in a stream-of-consciousness monologue that pushes the fashionable 1960s concept of "alienation" to the verge of derangement. The result was a cultural inversion that could scarcely have occurred in popular music prior to 1965. Stripped of all nuance, Otis's version of "(I Can't Get No) Satisfaction" is a caricature of the song's original intent. Historically, it had always been the province of white musicians to appropriate and oversimplify black musical styles in pursuit of commercial gain. But here, for a change, was a black artist soliciting the attention of white listeners by riding roughshod over one of the great pop songs of the day.

MY GIRL

Interviewer: I have a question for all the Beatles here. If you were sitting at home listening to record albums of other recording artists, who are some of the American recording artists you prefer?

John Lennon: Otis Redding is one.

ONE WEEK AFTER THE *OTIS BLUE* SESSION, OTIS RETURNED TO Macon for his annual Homecoming show at City Auditorium. His costar was once again Joe Tex, topping a bill of ten acts that included Atlanta's Gladys Knight and the Pips, balladeer Billy Stewart, and Stax's William Bell, who had just completed a two-year stint in the army and was looking to resume his career. The following night, Otis and Joe Tex performed for the largest audience of their young lives when they opened for James Brown in front of 25,000 people at Atlanta's newly built Fulton County Stadium. ("A woman of about 65, dressed in black suit and hat, drink in hand, her fingers snapping, rocked, wiggled and frugged her way down the aisle," the *Atlanta Constitution* reported.) In a backhanded compliment to Otis's growing stature, James Brown's magnanimity toward him had expired. As Joe Tex was coming off the stage and Otis was about to go on, Brown had his manager, Ben Bart, tell Otis to cut his set in half. "We'll cut it to even less than that," Phil Walden told Bart, rising to the challenge. "How about if we cut it to *zero*? He's gonna do his whole show or we're not gonna do a show at all." In the event, Otis performed his set as planned.

The 1965 Homecoming concert was Phil's first promotion since his return, and he followed it by booking Otis and his revue on a six-week Summer Parade of Stars tour that took them through Georgia and the Carolinas, around the Gulf Coast, and down the length of Florida. In the course of this tour, Otis hired a singer from Mobile named Loretta Williams as one of his opening acts. He also reunited with Don Henry, his former bandmate from Los Angeles, who joined Otis's band on tenor saxophone, bringing a trumpet player from Gulfport named John Farris with him. But the most important new addition to Otis's band was an exceptional drummer from Washington, D.C., Elbert "Woody" Woodson. Woodson had previously toured with Marvin Gaye and a number of other Motown acts. He was the first drummer Otis had ever worked with on the road who played with the same power and facility as Al Jackson Jr., and for the next year and a half, he would serve as the musical anchor of the Otis Redding Show.

"Respect" came on the radio around the middle of August, followed two weeks later by the release of *Otis Blue,* to which Atlantic added the subtitle *Otis Redding Sings Soul.* (No one has ever claimed credit for the album's evocative title, which may have been suggested by the jazz standard "Afro Blue.") Eager to reaffirm the partnership between Atlantic and Stax, Jerry Wexler authorized a major promotion for the album that began with full-page ads in *Billboard* and *Cashbox.* Wexler also went out of his way to give Jim Stewart his due by listing him in those ads as the "producer" of the LP. (Previously, Stewart had been credited with the "supervision" of Stax recordings.) The album cover was the work of Haig Adishian, one of Nesuhi Ertegun's stable of graphic artists. It featured a grainy half-tone photograph, softly lit from the side, of a beautiful, blond, unmistakably white woman, her delicate features wearing a dreamy expression. Atlantic had placed a photograph of a white model on a record by a black artist once before, in 1962, on an album called *Lonely Woman* by the Modern Jazz Quartet. But no freelance designer would have taken it upon himself to suggest such a bold move in 1965, and the concept for the *Otis Blue* cover could only have originated with Atlantic's department of sales and promotion. As such, it could be seen either as a calculated effort to obscure Otis's racial identity or as a forthright acknowledgment of his growing appeal to white listeners. Either way, it was an effective marketing ploy that unquestionably increased the number of retail outlets across the country that would not only stock the album but also display it for sale.

The same week the record was released, Otis opened at the Apollo Theater for the first time as a headliner, topping a bill that included Motown's Marvelettes, Dionne Warwick's sister Dee Dee, and Atlantic's Sam and Dave, who were still looking for a record that would jump-start their career. "Respect" had begun its ascent of the charts, where it would peak in the middle of October at #4 in R&B and #35 in Pop, thereby becoming the second of Otis's singles in a row to breach the programming threshold of Top 40 radio. The success of the single had its intended effect on sales of *Otis Blue*, which reached #1 on the R&B album charts in the last week of October. Far more telling was the record's performance on *Billboard*'s listing of top-selling Pop LPs, where it debuted at #100 and remained for the next six months, rising as high as #75, and selling more than 70,000 copies in that time.

Phil Walden accompanied Otis on this trip to New York, where Joe Galkin introduced him to Jerry Wexler and Ahmet Ertegun and took him around to his old music business haunts. ("What can I tell ya? I'm fucking rich!" Galkin crowed to his cronies.) As part of his ongoing "education" in African American culture, Phil marveled at the backstage scene at the Apollo. "It was like a shopping center. Slick-looking black guys would pull in clothes racks with merchandise from the best shops in New York. They hired junkies to steal the goods. If you didn't like what they had on the racks, you could place an order, 'I want a pair of such and such alligator shoes in a size 9.' Two hours later you'd have them."

Mainly, though, Phil marveled at the transformation he had seen in Otis since his return from Germany. "You could see his confidence grow in the way he tilted his head. He knew he was a star and he carried that pride in his walk. And as his confidence grew, so did his sophistication and his understanding of his vocation. It was written all over him, in everything from the way he walked to the way he talked to the way he dressed." Phil had always recognized the discerning intelligence that operated behind Otis's extroverted personality, but he had a new appreciation of it now. Like Louise Redding recalling the way her brother, as a child, had seemed to master tasks without any apparent preparation, Phil was impressed by Otis's "ability to learn something from a one-time explanation. He had a real yearning to know, and he did not hesitate to confess ignorance about something. He always said, 'If I say something wrong, tell me what I said.'" The sixteen months they had spent apart had given Phil a new appreciation of Otis: "He may have been the most original, most intelligent person I ever met in my life."

In the course of this New York visit, Phil, Joe Galkin, Jerry Wexler, and Ahmet Ertegun began to talk in earnest about how to capitalize on the recent surge in Otis's record sales. The American record market was expanding and diversifying at a dizzying rate in 1965. While a number of the original British Invasion bands had begun to fall by the wayside, they were being superseded by harder, bluesier groups like the Rolling Stones, the Yardbirds, and the Kinks. Bestselling R&B singles by the Four Tops ("I Can't Help Myself"), Marvin Gaye ("I'll Be Doggone"), Joe Tex ("Hold What You've Got"), and James Brown ("Papa's Got a Brand New Bag") were once again placing in the Pop Top 10. And a new contingent of "folk-rock" groups such as the Byrds, the Lovin' Spoonful, Sonny and Cher, and the Mamas and the Papas, most of them based in Los Angeles and all of them inspired by Bob Dylan's recent "conversion" from acoustic folk to electric blues, were coming onto the scene. Otis's last two singles had gained him his first airplay on the Top 40 stations that dominated the mainstream radio market, exposing him for the first time to casual white listeners who weren't actively tuning their radios to rhythm and blues. Finding ways to expand his presence with this new and growing audience for pop and rock was the obvious agenda for Otis's career in the year ahead.

Since his departure for West Germany in 1963, Phil Walden had been content to have his agency collect its 20 percent commission, plus expenses, on everything Otis made; since his return, Phil had been content to travel around the country, at Otis's expense, as Joe Galkin's understudy. It was only now, in the fall of 1965, that he began to pull his weight as a member of Otis's management team. Compared to his older colleagues like Galkin and Jerry Wexler, Phil had a personalized understanding of something the others were only beginning to grasp, which was the nature of Otis's appeal to other young whites like himself. This had been his singular vision all along, the awareness that people like him *wanted* something from people like Otis Redding. ("Black people teach you how to live," he once said.) Phil knew better than anyone that Otis had been performing in front of white college students since the start of his career. He knew how those fraternity boys and sorority sisters had responded to the sight and sound of this big, good-looking, self-assured yet reassuring black man, and he had seen Otis's ability, as a black Southerner of uncommon intelligence, to read white people, gauge their responses, and put himself across. The United States in the mid-1960s had the largest population of college students of any country in the history of the world. (Nearly half of the 20 million college-age Americans were pursuing some form of higher education during these years.) As the Beatlemaniacs of 1964 grew older and the college kids, folk bohemians, and other young adults were drawn into the vortex of popular music that the Beatles had set in motion, the constituency for what soul singers like Otis Redding had to offer promised to explode. This was something that Phil Walden, at the age of twenty-four, could feel in his very bones.

By September 1965, on the strength of #1 records by Sonny and Cher ("I Got You Babe") and the McCoys ("Hang On Sloopy"), together with a sudden effusion of top-selling R&B singles by Joe Tex, Wilson Pick-

Otis performing for an integrated audience, 1965

ett, Solomon Burke, Otis Redding, Barbara Lewis, and Don Covay, Jerry
Wexler and Ahmet Ertegun were well on their way to turning the fortunes
of Atlantic Records around. Having already doubled their sales totals from
1964, the label announced a raft of new signings, including the saxophonist King Curtis, the girl group Patti Labelle and the Blue Belles, and the
Young Rascals, a "blue-eyed soul" band that Ahmet Ertegun had discovered during his summertime rambles in the Hamptons.

That same month, Jerry Wexler and Jim Stewart agreed to share the
cost of hiring a black disk jockey from Washington, D.C., to serve as
Stax's first director of sales and promotion. Alvertis Isbell hailed from
Little Rock, Arkansas. As Al Bell, he began working at the city's first
black station, KOKY, during his senior year in high school. From that
point on, the particulars of Bell's résumé were inflated by the same talent for overstatement that would make this six-foot-five-inch dynamo
a natural promo man. After high school, Bell studied political science
at Philander Smith College in Little Rock (but dropped out after his
sophomore year). He then prepared for the ministry by enrolling at the
same Alabama Bible college that Little Richard had once attended (but
failed to complete his degree). He next worked as a field organizer for
the Southern Christian Leadership Council in Georgia, in the course of
which, he said, he became convinced that African Americans could use
music to empower themselves economically, "the way the Irish used whiskey and the South Africans used diamonds." Like his tenure as a "political
scientist" and an "ordained minister," Bell's career as a "civil rights activist" was short-lived, and he next signed on as a deejay at WLOK in Memphis, where he got to know Jim Stewart and Estelle Axton. In 1963, Bell
moved to WUST, the number-two black station in Washington, where he
championed Stax and other varieties of southern soul despite (he claimed)
the objections of his program director and the indifference of his listeners. Bell also started a small record label called Safice, in partnership with
Eddie Floyd, a Detroit native who had sung with Wilson Pickett in the
Falcons. Atlantic Records distributed Floyd's singles on Safice, which is
how Bell met Jerry Wexler, whom he adopted as a mentor ("Jerry Wexler
taught me all I know about the record business"). His veracity notwithstanding, Al Bell's opportunistic brand of flimflam was precisely what

had been lacking at Stax, and from the moment of his arrival in the fall of 1965, he was lionized by Jim Stewart and much of his staff. "He was our Otis for promotion," Booker Jones recalled. "It was the same type of energy and charisma."

With their cash flow and confidence restored, the owners of Atlantic Records next turned their attention overseas. Ahmet Ertegun was the Atlantic partner who would eventually make London his second home, turning the British pop scene into the label's most lucrative source of talent in the years ahead. But it was Jerry Wexler who flew to Britain that fall to meet with Sir Edward Lewis, the patrician president of Decca, the UK's second-largest record company. The purpose of Wexler's trip was to negotiate a renewal of the decade-old licensing deal between Atlantic and Decca on terms that would bring a new reciprocity to the relationship. That the exchange of talent between the two labels had been entirely one-sided had mattered little so long as the idea of a "British pop star" remained an oxymoron in the American mind. But now that British bands were colonizing the American record charts, Wexler wanted Decca to start licensing its British acts to Atlantic for distribution in the States. In addition, Wexler wanted Decca to put more effort into promoting Atlantic's releases in Britain. With the help of EMI's stateside subsidiary, Motown had breached the British market in 1965 with hit singles by its two top girl groups, the Vandellas and the Supremes, who had toured the country in the spring with a transatlantic version of the Motortown Revue. "In the past three or four years established R&B artists have broken through to become regular Top 40 sellers in the U.S.," Wexler told the British music press. "We've done it in America and I am sure we can do it here." As if to prove his point, at the time of his visit, "In the Midnight Hour" stood at #12 on the British Pop charts.

In one of many myopic decisions that would eventually marginalize Decca in the world of British pop, Sir Edward Lewis declined Jerry Wexler's request for a reciprocal licensing deal. But Wexler found an ally in Tony Hall, Decca's thirty-seven-year-old head of promotion. A popular deejay and music journalist, Hall was a die-hard fan of American R&B. He had served as a mentor to Andrew Oldham, the manager of Decca's top group, the Rolling Stones, and he shared the Stones' enthusiasm for

Otis Redding. Decca's handling of Otis had become a particular sore spot earlier in 1965, when the label had simply declined to distribute "I've Been Loving You Too Long." (It was later released as the B-side of "Respect.") Together, Wexler and Hall hatched a plan. If it was Motown British fans wanted, it was Motown they would get. In November, at Hall's direction, Decca took a mono mix of "My Girl" from *Otis Blue* and released it as a single in the UK. The result was a masterstroke.

"My Girl" entered the British Top 30 at the end of November, rose to #11 in January, and spent a total of sixteen weeks on the charts, thereby becoming the bestselling R&B single that Atlantic had released in Britain since the Drifters' 1960 recording of "Save the Last Dance for Me." Even more impressive was its effect on the sales of *Otis Blue*, which rose to #5 on the British LP charts in February 1966, rubbing shoulders with the latest releases by the Beatles and the Beach Boys. Otis's arrival on the Pop charts prompted a flurry of attention from the British music press. The *Record Mirror* ran a long article by staff writer Norman Jopling heralding Otis's transition from cult favorite to commercial success. Noting that "The Beatles and the Rolling Stones are two of the top pop groups who have been raving about him for months," the *New Musical Express* hired a stringer to interview Otis in the States. "I've had eleven hits altogether," Otis told the paper (give or take a few). "They all broke first in the South. I'm a pretty big star down there."

THAT HE WAS. By the end of 1965, Otis was earning a substantial living from his live performances, record royalties, and song publishing. He had traveled all over the country, spent time in New York, Chicago, and Los Angeles, and gained a sense of how life was lived outside of the South. Atlanta and Memphis, with their aspiring middle-class black populations, were even more familiar to him. Almost without exception, the southern-born singers Otis had grown up admiring and emulating—Ray Charles, Clyde McPhatter, Little Richard, and James Brown—had left the South as soon as they could afford to do so, preferring to live in cities where they were treated with a modicum of respect. In Otis's case, it was not as if leaving home was an alien concept; by 1965, two of his sisters,

Louise and Christine, had both moved to Los Angeles. But there was something fundamental about his attachment to Macon, and he does not seem to have seriously considered living anywhere else. His loyalty to his hometown was of a piece with his loyalty to Zelma and their children, to Phil and Alan Walden, and to his old friends from Bellevue and Tindall Heights. It was the sentiment of a proud young Southerner who felt a desire not only to remain close to his roots but to stake a claim to those roots by owning a piece of the place where he grew up. In this spirit, Otis prevailed on C. B. Walden in the fall of 1965 to help him find a new home.

Of the unlikely combination of blacks, whites, Northerners, Southerners, Protestants, Catholics, and Jews that Otis had come to rely on to manage his affairs, "Pops" Walden was the most unlikely figure of them all. In the eyes of his family and friends, C. B. had undergone a startling transformation in the eighteen months since he first started working with Alan on Otis's behalf. "There may be a little jealousy on my part," Phil Walden admitted. "My father was born and bred and raised as a racist, as all of his contemporaries were. To see that evolve [to where] he considered Otis Redding as close to himself as Alan and myself . . . I confess there were times when he cared more about Otis than he cared about us." Phil attributed the change in his father (which was all more striking to him since he had been out of the country while it was taking place) to the power of Otis's personality. "Otis really taught Daddy a lot about being human," Phil later said. C. B.'s racial conversion conformed to the process Gordon Allport described, in which prejudice yields to sustained, personal contact in pursuit of a common goal. Thrust into a world of agents, promoters, and performers of which he knew nothing, C. B. was able to see with fresh eyes how tirelessly Otis worked at his career. He was also able to appreciate how generous Otis had been with Alan, helping him learn the booking business with a solicitous concern that Phil, certainly, had never shown for his younger brother.

As they all began to succeed together, feelings of empathy, solidarity, and mutual affection took hold. Over time, C. B. did more than change his racial views. In a manner that was all too rare for a white man of his generation in the South, he began to act with the courage of his new convictions. Phil recounted a time when the sales manager of a local car dealership in Macon stopped by their office to deliver one of the many station wagons that the Waldens leased to move their artists around. The man thanked them for their business, but added that, for the life of him, he couldn't understand how they managed to "get along with all these niggers." To Phil's astonishment, his father slapped this prominent Macon businessman across the face and threw him out of their office. "We don't use that word around here," he said.

C. B.'s most tangible contribution involved keeping a tight rein on the agency's expenditures and helping Otis manage his personal finances, steering him away from the many supplicants and scammers who saw him as an easy mark. "Pops" was also available to provide Otis, Phil, and Alan with the sort of authority that was his by right as a grown white man in the South. Along with his brother Roy, C. B. had belonged to the Macon business community for more than twenty years, and this made him well qualified to handle the tricky business of finding Otis Redding a new home. Complicating matters was that Otis, to the surprise of his family and friends, had decided that he wanted a place in the country, on a piece of land large enough and far enough away from Macon to afford him complete privacy. As Phil recalled it, "Otis told Daddy, 'I want a farm, but I don't want to be there on the first night and have some son-of-a-bitch burning a cross in front of my house.'"

The Civil Rights Act of 1964 set out to right many wrongs, but it did nothing to redress the numerous forms of race-based housing discrimination that were rampant in communities throughout the United States. What Arthur Raper wrote in his 1936 study of Georgia remained true thirty years hence: "The Negro buys land only when some white man will sell it to him. Just because a white man has land for sale does not mean that a Negro can buy it, even if he has the money. He must be acceptable. Being acceptable here is no empty phrase. It means that he and his family are industrious and that his credit is good. It means that he is considered safe by local white people—he knows his 'place' and stays in it." This was the situation that Otis confronted after C. B. found a house for sale on a 270-acre parcel in the rural hamlet of Round Oak, deep in the heart of Jones County, twenty miles north of Macon, and twenty miles east of the section of Monroe County where Otis's grandparents Will and Laura Redding had met and started their family some seventy years before.

Like much of rural Georgia, Jones County had been drastically depopulated by the cotton blight and the Great Depression, and a large swath of its abandoned farmland had since been acquired by the federal government and incorporated into the 35,000-acre Piedmont National Wildlife Refuge. The parcel that Otis wanted to buy lay just to the east of this preserve, where the neighbors were few and far between. Taking the bull by the horns, C. B. Walden set up a meeting with the local white residents. "He told them that Otis Redding was considering buying this property and what did they think," Phil Walden recounted. "He told them that Otis didn't want to move out there if people were going to come round bothering him, either to seek him out as a friend or an enemy, and that he wanted to live in this place in peace and privacy." In the absence of any objections, the sale went ahead as planned. Otis and his family continued to live in Macon while the house underwent extensive renovations. That gave Zelma some much-needed time to acclimate herself to her husband's surprising new ambition to live the life of a country squire.

I CAN'T TURN YOU LOOSE

If you can't march to it, it ain't no good.

—OTIS REDDING

WHILE C. B. WALDEN ATTENDED TO THE BUSINESS OF FINDING Otis and his family a new home, Otis was spending the last months of 1965 perpetually away from home. A recording date at Stax in early November was followed by weeklong residences at the Royal in Baltimore and the Uptown in Philadelphia, a string of one-nighters in the Midwest, a quick trip to California to tape some television appearances, a swing through Louisiana, and a ten-day stand at the Howard Theatre in Washington from Christmas through New Year's Day. After three years of intensive effort, Otis was now in sufficient demand on the theater, club, and auditorium circuit that he could work as often as he wanted. And Otis wanted to work as often as time and distance allowed. Though his gross income from record and song-publishing royalties came to well over $50,000 in 1965 (the modern equivalent of $375,000, minus the Waldens' 20 percent), live performances remained the lifeblood of his operation. His guarantee stood in the range of twelve to fifteen hundred dollars a night. This was still a good deal less than top-tier R&B acts like Ray Charles or James Brown, but his contracts typically awarded him 50 percent of the receipts in excess of twice his guarantee, and in the larger clubs and auditoriums, this could more than double his nightly take. At this rate, Otis was consistently earning between eight and ten thousand dollars a week. Commissions, band salaries, and travel expenses took a large bite out of this total, but his personal income from live performances was now well over $100,000 a year. That was a lot of money in 1965, and Otis reveled in his identity as an earner. "Got to go make that dollar" became his catchphrase around this time.

Otis arrived in Memphis in November with his usual grab bag of fragments and unfinished songs. (As Jackie Avery once put it, "Otis wouldn't have a *song*; what he had basically was an *idea* for a song.") The most promising of these was "Just One More Day," a tune that his bandleader, Mack Robinson, had helped to compose; Steve Cropper contributed enough to the final version to earn a writing credit as well. As the first romantic ballad Otis had recorded since "I've Been Loving You Too Long," "Just One More Day" picks up where its predecessor left off—"I've been missing you for so many days"—though it lacks the melodic drama of Jerry Butler's song. The lyrics tell of a love gone wrong, with Otis pining for "the sweet things you used to do" as he promises to "do anything . . . say anything . . . *be* anything, if you just let me have one more day." The pathos of his performance rests on his conviction that another twenty-four hours would somehow be enough to change this woman's mind, and the precariousness of his hopes is achingly mirrored in the interplay between Steve Cropper's quivery arpeggios and Isaac Hayes's quavery organ, which sounds in the background of the track like the strains of a long-lost love.

The flip side of the single called for an uptempo song, and with little to go on, Otis and Steve Cropper conjured one out of thin air. "Otis worked it up with the horns in about ten minutes," Cropper recalled, "just a riff and one verse that he sings over and over. That's all it is." From this utter simplicity came one of the most powerful grooves in the annals of rhythm and blues. It begins with a variation on the bass line of the Four Tops' "I Can't Help Myself," an undulating seven-note riff that burns like a short fuse, ignited, two bars in, by an earsplitting drumroll, a stomping beat, and a transcendent flourish of horns, sounding in octaves (*DAH!* dat-da *dah!*) as they reach for a high C at the top of the melody. A series of spiky, syncopated, stop-time accents throws the music back on its heels, setting up Otis's entrance. "I can't turn you loose now / If I do I'm gonna lose my pride," he sings, phrasing evenly on the upbeats, splitting the difference between *loose* and *lose,* repeating the title line twice until he bears down hard on the downbeat to add, "Hip shaking mama I told you (honey) / I'm in love with only you." The horns return in force, sounding the opening fanfare in response to Otis's interjection of "I gotta-gotta-got," and then they do it all again, and again after that. The effect of all this repetition is nothing short of hypnotic, as the unyielding groove lends an exaggerated emphasis to the smallest variations in Otis's singing.

Lording it over the whole production is Al Jackson Jr., who drives the music forward with a thundering intensity that challenges Otis to keep up. ("It was more the conviction he played with, rather than the strength," the studio drummer Jim Keltner once observed.) Jackson's relationship with Otis was much less deferential than that of the other musicians at Stax. Some of this had to do with his age—he was six years older than Otis and most of his bandmates—and some had to do with his commanding musical presence. "Otis never tried to tell Al Jackson anything," Alan Walden recalled. "He just said, 'Stay with me, Al, just stay with me.'" On "I Can't Turn You Loose," Jackson stays so close that he's breathing down Otis's neck, and Otis responds to the pressure by shifting the focus of his singing from "I can't" to "I must" in the long vamp on which the song fades. "*Got* to," he shouts, "Hold on . . . *Got* to . . . Hold on . . ."

Defying one of the most cherished stereotypes of black physical prowess, Otis was by all accounts a notably inept dancer. (He shared this professional handicap with two of his most illustrious contemporaries, Sam Cooke and Marvin Gaye, both of whom went to great lengths to learn how to move onstage.) As a singer and arranger, Otis's sense of rhythm was acute; it was rather that his sense of rhythm didn't translate easily to his oversize frame. Now in the fullness of manhood, he stood at six foot one and weighed over two hundred pounds, but his physical presence was such that people were constantly overestimating his height, an effect that was further amplified onstage. He was well built, with a broad chest and shoulders, thick hips and thighs, and he carried himself with the blunt force of an athlete rather than the grace of a dancer. His physical awkwardness was less of an issue during his early years as a ballad singer, and by performing night after night as the star of his own show, Otis had gradually gained enough confidence to adopt his own way of moving to uptempo numbers onstage. This consisted mainly of *marching* in place, keeping the beat by shifting his weight from foot to foot, bending at the waist, pumping his elbows and swinging his hips while holding the microphone in one hand and stirring the air (and maintaining his balance) with the other. "Otis always said, 'If you can't march to it, it ain't no good,'" his trumpeter Wayne Jackson recalled. With its smooth, driving, unbroken rhythm, "I Can't Turn You Loose" qualified as the ultimate of Otis's "marching" songs.

In addition to refining his movements onstage, Otis had also begun to dress with a more assured sense of style over the course of 1965, replacing his simple black "preacher suits" with open-collared shirts, closely fitted vests and slacks, and custom-made suits in a range of deep reds and greens that showed off his body to advantage. Perhaps the most significant change in his overall appearance, onstage and off, came from the "natural" hairstyle he had adopted at Sam Cooke's suggestion, which not only made him look younger and more cosmopolitan but also put the features of his face—his broad nose, thick lips, strong jaw, and wide grin—in a much more flattering perspective.

First popularized by the Jamaican black nationalist Marcus Garvey in the 1920s, the "Black Is Beautiful" slogan was revived in 1962 in connection with a fashion show at the Harlem-based African Jazz-Art Society. It soon became the catchphrase of a cultural movement, an unapologetic celebration of black identity, sexuality, and physical beauty that was closely allied with the concept of "soul." In this new cultural context, dark-skinned entertainers with overtly "negroid" features were seen to embody a new aesthetic of attractiveness, countervailing the long-standing tendency for aspiring African Americans in all walks of life to cultivate and accentuate physical traits associated with whites—beginning with light skin and straight hair—and for whites to feel more comfortable with blacks who exhibited those characteristics.

Charismatic performers defy conventional taste as a matter of course, and they have the capacity to change the public perception of what is physically attractive or appealing in a popular entertainer. At one time, a singer who looked like Frank Sinatra or Mick Jagger would not have been considered attractive by the general public—until they made it so. The same applied to many black entertainers of the 1960s, and in the pantheon of soul music, few singers benefited from this aesthetic shift more than Otis, whose strong features and robust physical presence combined with his lack of pretension and artifice onstage to embody the African American ideal of a "natural" man.

As LONG AS R&B revues toured almost exclusively by road, California could seem like a world apart for acts that were based in the East. The chitlin' circuit reached as far west as Dallas, and the R&B venues between there and Los Angeles were few and far between. In the summer of 1965, Estelle Axton had set out to raise Stax's profile in the L.A. radio market by arranging a brief promotional tour for Booker T. and the MGs, Rufus and Carla Thomas, and a pair of newly signed vocal groups, the Astors and the Mad Lads. Coproduced by the KGFJ deejay Nathaniel "Magnificent" Montague, this trip included television appearances, radio spots, and a performance at the 5-4 Ballroom, the city's top R&B showcase—all taking place just days before the weeklong outbreak of looting, arson, and mayhem that convulsed the Watts district of South Central Los Angeles in August of that year.

Though Otis did not take part in this California trip, his Top 40 success in the summer and fall of 1965 had earned him invitations to appear on several of the syndicated music television shows that originated from Los Angeles. The presentation of popular music on television was changing in the mid-1960s as a result of the British Invasion and the antic style of the Beatles' films *A Hard Day's Night* and *Help!* The stilted dance party format of Dick Clark's *American Bandstand* was giving way to quirkier weekday programs like *The Lloyd Thaxton Show* and prime-time network productions modeled on the kinetic British series *Ready Steady Go!,* whose American equivalent *Shindig!* premiered on ABC in the fall of 1964.

Otis had flown to Los Angeles without his band during the summer of 1965 to lip-synch "I've Been Loving You Too Long" on Thaxton's show. In December he returned to L.A. to pantomime performances of "Respect" on Thaxton, "Pain in My Heart" on Dick Clark's *Where the Action Is,* and "Just One More Day" on NBC's prime-time series *Hollywood a Go Go.* To defray the cost of this trip, Shaw Artists arranged for him to appear as a single, costarring with B. B. King and his band at the 5-4 Ballroom in Watts and the Fillmore Auditorium in San Francisco.

That same December, Wilson Pickett returned to Stax, unchaperoned by Jerry Wexler this time. Pickett spent his first few days in Memphis cloistered at the Lorraine Motel with Steve Cropper and Eddie Floyd, his old bandmate from the Falcons, who had recently been hired as a song-writer at Stax on the recommendation of his partner Al Bell. The fruit of their collaboration included a pair of songs with numerological and par-enthetical titles: "634-5789 (Soulsville U.S.A.)" and "Ninety-Nine and a Half (Just Won't Do)." The first was an homage of sorts to a 1962 single called "Beechwood 4-5789" by Motown's Marvelettes; the second took its title and theme from a 1956 gospel recording by June Cheeks's fiery female counterpart, Dorothy Love Coates. The Stax band outdid itself on both tracks, applying the synthesis of power and restraint they had perfected on "In the Midnight Hour" to a driving shuffle on "634-5789" and an imposing, almost sinister, eighth-note groove on "Ninety-Nine and a Half."

Released in January, "634-5789" surpassed the success of "Midnight Hour" by spending seven weeks at #1 R&B and placing high in the Pop Top 40. For Steve Cropper, it was the fifth top-selling single he had co-written in the previous year. But even before the record came out, Jim Stewart informed Jerry Wexler that, with the notable exception of Sam and Dave, Stax was no longer interested in producing records for artists under contract to Atlantic. Stewart offered a number of reasons for this sudden change of heart. Now that Stax was devoting more of its time to album sessions, he maintained that the studio was simply too busy to ac-commodate "outside" work. Stewart also made no secret of the fact that he disliked working with headstrong artists like Wilson Pickett and Don Covay (who lacked the habits of deference that he was used to in South-ern blacks). Despite the fact that Cropper, in particular, was earning a bonanza of songwriting royalties from collaborations with these singers, Stewart insisted that the musicians at Stax felt the same way. "It got to the point where the guys felt they were being used," he later said. "So I put a stop to it." For Cropper, however, Stax's new policy was "a big pill to swallow."

Stewart's decision was the first of many changes he would institute at Stax over the course of 1966 under the influence of Al Bell. Like everyone else at the label, Stewart was captivated by Bell's personality, energy, and knowledge of the radio business. For his part, Bell was determined to dispel the laissez-faire, build-it-and-they-will-come atmosphere that had always prevailed on McLemore Avenue. He understood that promoting Stax's records involved promoting Stax itself, and to do that, he needed to cultivate a greater sense of the label's musical identity. Though Bell named Jerry Wexler as his mentor in the record business, his personal hero and role model was Berry Gordy, who had merged the principles of production and promotion developed by Atlantic with the spirit of black enterprise and empowerment that Bell embraced. Following Gordy's example, Bell set out to "brand" Stax, in effect, as Pepsi to Motown's Coke—with the significant difference that he meant to characterize the gritty, churchy sound of Stax as the Real Thing. Taking his lead from the *Hitsville U.S.A.* sign that advertised Motown's headquarters in Detroit, Bell christened the Stax studio *Soulsville U.S.A.* and had the slogan posted on the Capitol Theater's marquee. *Soul* became the watchword of Bell's promotional strategy. He extolled the rawness and authenticity of Stax's music, contrasting it with the artifice of Motown's densely layered productions and carefully choreographed groups. Though Bell had once considered the regional flavor of Stax's music a stigma during his days as a deejay in Washington, he now trumpeted the label's southern identity, referring to it at every opportunity as the Memphis Sound. As he worked tirelessly to generate a Motown-like mystique around Stax, Bell impressed on Jim Stewart the need to protect the label's brand. Hence the ban on outside production. "We had that policy to preserve the sound that we had developed," Bell explained. "That was our identity, our trademark, our secret, and we preserved it in that fashion."

The only problem with Stax's attempt to preserve its unique musical identity was that by 1966, its identity was no longer unique. In February, shortly after Jim Stewart informed him that Stax would no longer accept outside work, Jerry Wexler received a phone call from Rick Hall, a white producer who ran a recording studio in Muscle Shoals, Alabama, two and a half hours east of Memphis. Wexler had first heard about Hall's studio from Joe Galkin, and he had duly added the young producer to his professional network with the usual invitation to give him a call whenever he heard something good. What Hall had heard was a song called "When a Man Loves a Woman," sung with operatic intensity by a local black hospital orderly with the incomparable name of Percy Sledge. Wexler agreed with Hall that the song was a sure-fire hit—"I called Ahmet in Europe and told him that I'd found a single that was going to pay for our whole summer"—and signed a distribution deal. With its soaring melody and its heartfelt, gospel-tinged lyric ("When a man loves a woman / He'll trade the world for the good thing he's found"), Sledge's single went on to become the first record by a southern soul singer other than Ray Charles to reach #1 on the *Billboard* Pop charts.

For Jerry Wexler, Rick Hall provided the ideal solution to Jim Stewart's sudden inhospitality. In the spring of 1966, exactly one year after the "Midnight Hour" session at Stax, Wexler and Wilson Pickett descended on Muscle Shoals to sample the local brand of musicianship for themselves. Though Pickett was mortified by the sight of the neighboring cotton fields, his fears were quickly assuaged by a rhythm section, composed entirely of young white Alabamians, that was every bit the equal of the studio band at Stax. In an unsubtle dig at his Memphis affiliate, Wexler had arranged with Rick Hall to hire the entire Stax horn section for the session, along with Jim Stewart's old nemesis Chips Moman on guitar. Together they recorded a furious remake of Chris Kenner's 1963 single "Land of 1000 Dances" that would extend Pickett's streak of #1 records, dent the mystique of Stax, and establish the sleepy backwater of Muscle Shoals as a viable rival to Memphis as the R&B recording capital of the South.

THE SOUL ALBUM

I can tell you that from the musicians' standpoint . . . everybody
that I ever talked to could not wait for Otis Redding to return.
His enthusiasm, and his energy level. He made you play things
that you never thought you could play, or that you would never
have thought to have played. He was comfortable in the studio.
It was like he had been there all of his life.

—STEVE CROPPER

OTIS MOVED HIS FAMILY INTO THEIR NEWLY RENOVATED HOME IN
Round Oak during the winter of 1966. Understandably unnerved at
finding herself in the wilds of Jones County, a half-hour drive on country roads from the familiar confines of Macon, Zelma insisted that her
mother, Bee Bee, stay with her whenever Otis was away. Otis had already
decided to build a house for his own parents at the mouth of the gated
driveway to his home. His intention was to turn the Big O Ranch (as he
named the place) into a working farm, complete with horses, cattle, and
hogs, which would give his father the opportunity to *dabble* in farming for
the first time in his life. The Rev. Redding had recently been named pastor of one of Macon's oldest black congregations, the Lundy Chapel Baptist Church, founded in 1868. The church was in the process of moving
into a new building in North Macon, for which Otis donated the funds
to erect a steeple.

With his family suitably (if reluctantly) ensconced, Otis spent the winter and spring constantly on tour. He began in early January with a week at
the Apollo, topping a bill that included Patti La Belle and Fontella Bass,
a big-voiced singer in the Martha Reeves mold who was riding the success of her top-selling single "Rescue Me." Though the *Amsterdam News*
reported that Otis had been the third-best draw at the Apollo in 1965,

behind James Brown and Jackie Wilson, Bobby Schiffman's typically taciturn notation read, "Real stomper and shouter. Just fair reception— got a little loud." From New York, the Otis Redding Show headed west, playing one-nighters in Kentucky, Ohio, and Wisconsin before settling in for a week at the Regal in Chicago alongside Jerry Butler's old group the Impressions, now led by Curtis Mayfield, whose Top 40 hits "Keep On Pushing" and the neospiritual "People Get Ready" had become R&B anthems of the civil rights movement in 1965. From Chicago, the revue crisscrossed the Midwest, playing dates in Indiana, Michigan, and Ohio before swinging south through Maryland, Virginia, and the Carolinas. On an off day early in February, Otis flew to Memphis for a quick recording date.

After a strong debut in December, airplay and sales of "Just One More Day" and its flip side, "I Can't Turn You Loose," had faltered during the winter as R&B stations wavered between which side of the record to play. (The two songs peaked at #15 and #11 respectively on the R&B listings, and began to fade after a run of only seven weeks.) Stax had repeated the mistake it had made the year before with "That's How Strong My Love Is" and "Mr. Pitiful," initially pushing the ballad side of the single, only to reverse itself when the rhythm side proved to be the more popular track. To some extent, this reflected Jim Stewart's personal preference for ballads, especially where Otis was concerned. But it also reflected Stewart's chronic inability to assess the commercial potential of the records he released. At established labels like Motown and Atlantic, there was rarely if ever an instance in which the designated A-side of a single was inadvertently surpassed by its B-side. At Stax, beginning with "Green Onions," it happened all the time. "Anything that Jim Stewart said wouldn't sell, put it out," Rufus Thomas insisted. "Anything that Jim liked, forget it. What he disliked sold. What he liked did nothing."

The disappointing sales of the new Otis Redding single marked an inauspicious start to Al Bell's tenure as Stax's promo man, but it emboldened Bell to take a more forceful role in the selection of the label's releases. Inspired by the success of "My Girl" in Britain, he persuaded Jim Stewart to release another of Otis's album tracks, his cover of "(I Can't Get No) Satisfaction," as a single in the States. Otis returned to Stax in

February to record "Any Ole Way," an original song cowritten with Steve Cropper, to serve as the B-side (thereby providing himself with a share of the record's publishing royalties). An amiable shuffle with a sentiment firmly rooted in the pre-Internet era of romance ("I don't do the things that you do / I don't go the places that you go / But I love you any ole way"), the track was endowed with an infectious sax riff that would resurface nine months later in the melody of Cannonball Adderley's soul-jazz hit "Mercy, Mercy, Mercy."

It had been a bold move for Otis to cover "Satisfaction" in the first place; releasing it as a single was bolder still, and the record went on to match the showing of "Respect" by rising to #4 R&B in *Billboard*, #1 in *Cashbox*, breaching the Pop Top 40, and spending a total of three months on the charts. Together with the release of Stax's first successful effort to harness the talents of Sam and Dave, a Top 10 R&B single called "You Don't Know Like I Know," Al Bell, after six months on the job, was beginning to deliver the sort of results he had been hired to produce.

In March, courtesy of Jerry Wexler, Jim Stewart and Estelle Axton played host to Brian Epstein, the urbane manager of the Beatles, who came to Memphis to explore the possibility of his group recording tracks for their next album at Stax. Having cut their musical teeth on American R&B, the Beatles had been fans of Otis Redding, Rufus Thomas, and Booker T. and the MGs since their records first became available in Britain in 1963. The title of their recent album *Rubber Soul* had been meant as a dig at the very notion of English soul singing, but the music on the record was no joke, with tracks like "Drive My Car" and "The Word" showing the band's affinity for Memphis-style R&B. ("Drive My Car" had a bass line inspired by "Respect" and a lyric derived from Memphis Minnie's 1941 recording of "Chauffeur Blues.") While the Beatles had thus far made all of their records at EMI's Abbey Road studios in London, other British bands, led by the Rolling Stones, had had great success recording at well-known American studios like Chess in Chicago and RCA in Hollywood. The Beatles had dispatched their manager to Memphis to arrange for them to participate in this new form of musical tourism. Given the climate of hysteria that still existed among many of their younger fans, Epstein emphasized the need for total secrecy surrounding the Beatles' intentions. But news of their impending visit quickly found its way onto the front page of *The Commercial Appeal*—"Beatles to Record Here"—thereby forcing the group to scuttle its plan. Four months later, when the Beatles performed at the Memphis Mid-South Coliseum during their last American tour, their concert was picketed by hundreds of Christian fundamentalists and menaced by a klavern of Klansmen incensed at John Lennon's offhand remark that the group was now "bigger than Jesus."

By the spring of 1966, artistically ambitious rock groups such as the Beatles, the Stones, and the Beach Boys had begun to seek refuge from the frenzy of their public lives by sequestering themselves in recording studios, spending unprecedented amounts of time refining their songs, overdubbing vocal and instrumental parts, and generally devoting the sort of attention to album tracks that had once been reserved for singles. The results of this practice, beginning with the albums *Rubber Soul, Aftermath*, and *Pet Sounds*, would revolutionize both the aesthetics and the economics of the popular record business. In years to come, albums, not singles, would be the coin of the realm in rock. In a medium that had long been dominated by producers, publishers, and arrangers, recording artists themselves would henceforth exert a new auteur-like autonomy over their work. And the combination of recording and publishing royalties generated by million-selling albums composed entirely of original songs would allow bands like the Beatles and the Stones to curtail their live appearances in order to expend even more time and effort in the studio.

In some ways, the approach that was being pursued by these groups was an extension of the informal process that had prevailed at Stax all along, of writing and recording songs from the ground up, without prepared arrangements or preconceived ideas. But in 1966, the idea of devoting weeks (much less months) at a time to making an album was an indulgence that no successful R&B artist believed he or she could afford. Performers like Otis Redding and James Brown had large touring operations to support. The relatively modest returns they stood to gain from the sale of their albums could not begin to justify the lost income from live shows that such a period of idleness would entail. And the idea that album sales could be dramatically increased by improving the quality, consistency, and range of one's music had not yet taken hold in a branch of the record business that was still preoccupied by the prospect of hit singles. For the time being, the great majority of R&B albums remained simple, workmanlike affairs that were recorded as quickly as possible and filled with cover tunes.

The speed with which songwriting, arranging, and recording were done at Stax lent a palpable sense of immediacy and spontaneity to the best of the music made there. But the pressure to do things quickly also encouraged a conservatism that militated against experimentation and innovation. Commercial success in the record business has often been fickle and fleeting, and there has always been an incentive for artists and producers to replicate the sound of a record that sells in hopes of replicating its success. (The Motown team of Holland-Dozier-Holland made a lucrative joke out of this imperative when they followed the Four Tops' smash hit "I Can't Help Myself" with an almost identical Top 10 single called "It's the Same Old Song.") Jim Stewart's cautious temperament only amplified this tendency; as a result, innovation at Stax tended to occur either by accident or under the influence of "outsiders," like Jerry Wexler and Tom Dowd. In Otis's case, this conservatism was apparent in the way that Stax had single-mindedly promoted him as a ballad singer for two full years following the gradual success of "These Arms of Mine." It could also be heard in the unvarying consistency of the instrumentation and arrangements on his records, beginning with the fact that virtually every track he recorded, whether on a single or an album, ended with a coda and a fade.

All these factors combined with the strong sales of *Otis Blue* in the United States and Britain to ensure that Otis's next album, recorded in March 1966, would hew closely to the format of its predecessor. Titled simply *The Soul Album,* the record was once again built around a core of three original songs: "Just One More Day," "Any Ole Way," and a newly recorded ballad called "Good to Me." Once again, there were Sam Cooke covers, the 1960 hit "Chain Gang" and the blues standard "Nobody Knows You When You're Down and Out," which Otis knew from Cooke's *Live at the Copa* LP. Once again, there was a Temptations hit, "It's Growing," written by Smokey Robinson, and a down-home blues, Slim Harpo's

"Scratch My Back," which had crossed over, like "Rock Me Baby" on *Otis Blue,* into the Pop Top 40. The album was rounded out by an obscure ballad from 1961 called "Cigarettes and Coffee," cowritten by Jerry Butler; "Treat Her Right," a recent Top 10 hit by the blue-eyed soul singer Roy Head; a cover of Wilson Pickett's "634-5789"; and a song called "Everybody Makes a Mistake," written by Al Bell and Eddie Floyd.

These eleven tracks added up to an unpromising collection of songs. None of the three originals was nearly as distinctive as the three on *Otis Blue.* "It's Growing" had been an unmemorable sequel to "My Girl." Both "Scratch My Back" and "Treat Her Right" were novelty hits that owed their popularity to their vaguely risqué lyrics, while the inclusion of "Everybody Makes a Mistake" and "634-5789" (which falls completely flat) had more to do with the office politics at Stax than with their suitability as vehicles for Otis. Yet the mediocrity of the material only served to showcase the extent to which Otis had come into his own as a singer and arranger, for he found ways to make something special happen on nearly every track. The horn parts on the album are a particular source of delight. As written, "Everybody Makes a Mistake" is a tuneless lament about a man who plays around on his woman, only to come home to an empty house and a letter by the door; as performed, the song is transformed by a somber horn chorus that sets the scene and a series of poignant countermelodies that bring the pedestrian lyric to life. On "Scratch My Back," the horns pick up on the "chicken-scratch" guitar of Slim Harpo's original and expand the barnyard metaphor into a whole menagerie of clucking and crowing. And on "Treat Her Right," the Stax band completely revamped the song, revisiting the swinging horn groove of "I Need Your Loving'" on *Pain in My Heart.*

With the exception of the fine new ballad "Good to Me," the strongest performances were collected on the first side of the album, which began with "Just One More Day" followed by "It's Growing," "Cigarettes and Coffee," and the two Sam Cooke covers. Otis was in great voice on "It's Growing," bringing out the wit of Smokey Robinson's lyric ("Like a snowball rolling down the side of that snow-covered *hiill* / Like the size of the fish that the man claims broke his *reel*") in a way the Temptations' version did not. The Stax band once again drew an explicit contrast with their counterparts in Detroit, renovating Motown's fussy arrangement of strings, brass, and somersaulting drum fills with a simpler and tighter groove of seamless backbeat and sassy horns. On "Cigarettes and Coffee," Otis replaced the tinkling cocktail piano that made a late-night cliché of the original with deep swelling chords from the horns as he shapes the song's caffeine- and nicotine-fueled table talk ("I don't want no cream and sugar cause I've got *you* now, darling") into a torrent of romantic appreciation.

Otis's earlier struggles with Sam Cooke's material made his rendition of "Chain Gang" one of *The Soul Album*'s high points. Cooke's song was a triumph of empathetic observation, inspired by the sight of a prison road gang he encountered while touring in Georgia. The original recording was a polished pop production whose grim vignette of the convicts "moaning their lives away" was softened by the lilting beauty of the melody and a wry bass-voiced pickup of "Well don't you know . . ." As a native Georgian, Otis was in a position to bring a more personal form of identification to this modern manifestation of the slave era (especially since he could easily have *been* one of those convicts if things had worked out differently in 1964). Whereas Cooke sang in the third person to evoke "the sound of the men working on a chain gang," Otis gradually inserts himself into the song, bemoaning the "sound of *us* men, when *we're* working." His every other word is seconded by the hammer blows of Al Jackson's snare, and his voice is answered in the later choruses by a heartrending upturn from the horns (da-da-dat *DAH* da) that seems to rise out of the music like a fleeting glimpse of freedom.

Otis was equally bold in making his mark on "Nobody Knows You When You're Down and Out," a classic blues about a fallen millionaire that was immortalized by Bessie Smith's prophetic hit record, released a month before the stock market crash in 1929. Sam Cooke's rendition was sung in a Copa-friendly style of genteel big-band swing that gradually worked itself up to a blaring, Sinatraesque finale. With considerable help from Steve Cropper's biting, echoing, looping fills on guitar, Otis restored the song to its roots in down-home blues, singing in a voice so choked with regret and rejection that he sounds almost comical at times.

The new ballad "Good to Me" was by far the strongest cut on the album's second side. The song was jointly credited to Otis and Julius Green, a member of Stax's Mad Lads, whose main contribution had been to suggest to Otis as he walked into the studio that he should write a song called "Good to Me." Otis proceeded to do just that, improvising a romantic reverie that begins, "I don't know what you've got baby, but you're so *go-o-o-od* to me" and culminates with the lines "I've been loving you, woman, twenty long years / I'll love you twenty more, 'cause I've got that will to *try.*" This was an improbably mature sentiment to come from the mouth of a twenty-four-year-old singer—not that anyone would think to question it, such was the timeless quality of Otis's voice, which seemed to draw on depths of experience far beyond his years. The exceptionally slow tempo and Isaac Hayes's sepulchral organ lent an almost meditative quality to the track.

The Soul Album was released in April of 1966. Its alluring cover, designed by Atlantic's Loring Eutemey, drew a stark contrast with the racial obfuscation of *Otis Blue* by presenting a full-color portrait of a strikingly beautiful African American model wearing a head scarf and a coy half-smile, her warm brown eyes staring directly into the lens. From a marketing perspective, the album suffered from the absence of a hit single on the order of "Respect." Yet sales of *The Soul Album* outpaced those of *Otis Blue,* totaling more than 80,000 copies in the six months following its release. The record entered the *Billboard* LP charts in April, peaked at #54 in July, and remained among the hundred bestselling albums until the fall. It also stimulated sales of Otis's back catalog, prompting *Otis Blue* to reappear on the *Billboard* charts throughout the month of July, and pushing the sales totals for that album well past the 100,000 mark. Across the board, Otis's albums were selling at twice the rate of 1965.

THE WHISKY

Otis at the Whisky a Go Go

Ladies and gentlemens, holler as loud as you wanna. You ain't home!

—OTIS REDDING

I N THE WINTER OF 1966, AFTER RUNNING THE TALENT AGENCY HIS
father had founded for nearly ten years, Milt Shaw sold the Shaw Artists Corporation to a New York–based attorney and real estate developer
named Don Soviero. (A longtime heroin addict, Milt Shaw died of an
overdose a few months later, at the age of forty-one.) Soviero had made
his money building ski resorts in the Berkshires during the 1950s, in the
course of which he bought into the music business by purchasing a well-
known jazz and folk venue in Lenox, Massachusetts, called the Music
Inn. No sooner did he acquire Shaw Artists than he announced plans to
restructure the agency by cutting its roster of artists and firing a number
of its long-term employees, including Larry Myers, the veteran agent who
had worked most closely with Otis in recent years. Myers was quickly
hired by Shaw's rival, Universal Attractions.

Phil Walden took an instant dislike to Soviero, and he saw the change
of ownership at SAC as an opportunity to get Otis out of the three-year
contract he had signed with the agency in 1964. Though the affiliation
with Shaw had been crucial to Otis's success in the early years, Phil had
played no part in it, and he was eager to start booking Otis on a national
basis by himself. At a time when the Waldens were seeking to expand
their roster of artists, this would enhance their agency's reach and influence and enable them to strike their own deals with promoters and club
owners on behalf of Otis and their other acts. Accordingly, in April 1966,
Phil sent a letter to the American Guild of Variety Artists requesting
Otis's release from his contract with Shaw, citing the change in ownership
and the departure of Larry Myers. Even before the letter went out, Phil
began working with Myers and his colleague Dick Alen at Universal Attractions to plan a summer package tour for Otis and two of the Walden
agency's newly signed acts, Sam and Dave and Percy Sledge.

It was almost undoubtedly Ahmet Ertegun who first suggested that
Otis should perform at the Whisky a Go Go nightclub in Los Angeles
as a way of showcasing his talent with the burgeoning white audience for
rock. Ertegun's involvement with Sonny and Cher and Bobby Darin (who
had re-signed with Atlantic after his contract with Capitol ran out in
1965) was causing him to spend more of his time in Los Angeles, where
he held court at the Whisky on a regular basis. The club was owned and

managed by Elmer Valentine, a former Chicago policeman with admitted mob connections who had moved to Los Angeles in 1960 after he was indicted for extortion and forced to relinquish his badge. In 1963, Valentine took a trip to France, where he happened to visit a nightclub in Paris called the Whisky Au Go Go. The Paris Whisky had begun as a jazz club in the late 1940s, deriving its name from the Gallic infatuation with American pop culture that followed the end of the war. ("Whisky" was presumed to be the American beverage of choice, while "go go" was a nod to the "go-getter" spirit of the American national character.) In the 1950s, the Paris Whisky became the model for a new type of dance club, presided over by a live deejay, which the French called a *discothèque*, and which soon began to attract an international celebrity clientele. When the Twist craze had its resurgence in 1962, it was the cachet of Parisian discotheque that inspired New York's café society to flock to the Peppermint Lounge. Among the people who saw commercial potential in the prospect of affluent adults dancing to rock 'n' roll was Valentine, who opened his version of the Whisky a Go Go on West Hollywood's Sunset Strip in January 1964, just in time for the advent of Beatlemania. He hired a white rock 'n' roll singer, Johnny Rivers, to provide live entertainment, and he hired a troupe of female dancers clad in fringed dresses and vinyl boots to provide visual stimulation, enhancing their impact by having them perform in metal cages suspended from the ceiling of the club. A live album called *Johnny Rivers at the Whisky a Go Go* spent six months on the charts and gave the place an instant reputation, while the image of caged "go-go girls" in their "go-go boots" captured the erotic imagination of mainstream America, leading Valentine and his partners to open a chain of Whisky franchises in Chicago, Denver, and Atlanta.

By the spring of 1966, the Whisky was the hottest and hippest club on the Sunset Strip. Atlantic Records had already used the place to showcase the Young Rascals on the West Coast in January 1966, and Elmer Valentine was a fan of rhythm and blues, so he was happy to book Otis and his revue for four nights in the middle of April. Envisioning a live album, Atlantic hired Wally Heider, a West Coast engineer who specialized in remote recording, to tape the last two nights of the engagement. In addition to Otis's own supporting acts, Valentine booked a local blues band called the Rising Sons to open the show. Its members included a young white guitarist from Santa Monica named Ry Cooder and a young black singer from Massachusetts who called himself Taj Mahal. "Word got out that this was a super hot show," Cooder recalled. "Nothing like anyone had seen in Los Angeles unless you went to the 5-4 Ballroom. Black musicians didn't come to Sunset; it was a white scene."

After playing their way westward with a series of dates in Texas, Otis and his band arrived in Los Angeles the weekend before the Whisky gig, in time to perform at a benefit concert at the Hollywood Bowl that was sponsored by the pop radio station KHJ and headlined by Atlantic's stars Sonny and Cher. He opened at the Whisky the following Thursday night. According to Rodgers Redding, who was granted a furlough from his army unit in California in order to attend the show, the scene on Sunset Strip looked like something out of a Hollywood awards ceremony, with movie stars like Clint Eastwood and Julie Christie arriving in limousines. Dressed for the occasion in a tuxedo, crammed with his band onto the club's narrow stage, and flanked by a pair of blond go-go girls in sequined turquoise outfits, Otis performed several sets a night for the next four nights, replicating essentially the same revue-type show he had been presenting in clubs and dance halls over the course of the previous year.

All four nights began with an instrumental warm-up by the band and a perfunctory number by each of his current opening acts. Then Al "Brisco" Clark, a sax player who had previously played with James Brown, stepped to the microphone to introduce Otis in a grandiloquent manner modeled closely on Brown's *Live at the Apollo* LP, reciting a list of song titles punctuated by blaring chords from the band. "Are you ready for Star Time?" Clark asked as he announced "the young man who sings such songs as 'Pain in My Heart' [*blaaah!*], 'I'm Depending on You' [*blaaah!*], I've *got* to have some 'Respect' [*blaaah!*]." With that, Otis took the stage and launched into a forty-minute set that alternated between big ballads like "I've Been Loving You Too Long" and "Just One More Day" and back-to-back versions of his latest uptempo hits, "I Can't Turn You Loose" and "(I Can't Get No) Satisfaction." With the exception of "Chained and Bound," which was transformed into a long testimonial reminiscent of James Brown's epic version of "Need Someone" on *Live at the Apollo*, the ballads hewed closely to the recorded arrangements, with the ostensibly ad-libbed codas reproduced word for word. But the uptempo numbers were played at breakneck tempos and extended for the benefit of the dancers into hypnotically repetitive rhythmic vamps overlaid with Otis's percussive scat singing and horn solos from the band.

For an audience accustomed to the laid-back informality of Los Angeles folk-rock groups, the explosive energy of Otis's performances, in Ry Cooder's estimation, "was unbelievable. . . . He'd get up, stomp his foot, wave his arm, grab a microphone, and sing with such searing intensity, I thought, this man's going to have a heart attack. This was a real traveling R&B show, the likes of which I had never seen." "Picture a calliope, spouting blasts of sound, and imagine a steam generator in the innards of the calliope, frantically driving the whole mechanism," the critic Pete Johnson wrote in his *Los Angeles Times* review.

Wally Heider's live recording faithfully captured the domineering quality of Otis's singing and stage presence. But the tapes also revealed that the sound and fury of the performance masked some serious deficiencies on the part of Otis's band. The most glaring of these was a trumpet player—most likely a stringer hired especially for the show—who was so jarringly out of tune that Atlantic Records deemed the tapes unsuitable for release. (With careful editing, a live album was eventually issued in 1968.) The personnel in Otis's band had been in flux for several months. Several of the horn players had left as a result of personality conflicts and salary disputes, including a trombonist, Norman Sellers, whose mistreatment of Speedo Sims made Otis so angry that, according to one account, he wrapped Sellers's trombone around his head. Otis had also had a major falling-out with his bass player and bandleader Mack Robinson over Robinson's compensation as a cowriter of "Just One More Day"—a grievance that caused him not only to quit but to abscond with a briefcase containing the band's payroll on his way out the door. The saxophonist Bobby Holloway had ably assumed Robinson's role as Otis's music director, but the Whisky recordings suggest that the band was still in a state of disarray. The saving grace was the rock-solid playing of drummer Woody Woodson and the new bassist, Ralph Stewart, who brought their own distinctive embellishments to the grooves laid down in the studio by Al

Jackson and Duck Dunn, with Woodson's pounding cymbals adding a deliciously lewd emphasis to Otis's "hip-shaking mama" in "I Can't Turn You Loose."

No one who worked for Otis Redding ever accused him of undue generosity. Having grown up in a place where black labor was so cheap and expendable that giving a man a job was often construed as doing him a favor, Otis seems to have incorporated some of this attitude into his own employment practices. "He wasn't the best paymaster in the world. He was pretty selfish about the money," his saxophonist Don Henry recalled. By the mid-1960s, there was no shortage of journeyman musicians willing to tour with an R&B revue. (Thanks to the peacetime draft and the proliferation of military bands, horn players were especially plentiful.) Road work could be debilitating and demeaning, but compared to the alternative, which for the average black man in his twenties consisted of some form of manual labor, it was glamorous and well paid. Most touring musicians earned between $100 and $200 a week, minus their room and board.

Otis took pride in the size and splendor of his band, which served as a tangible symbol of his success—to the point of hiring additional horn players when he played in big-city theaters and other important venues like the Whisky. But most of it was for show. The horn arrangements for his songs duplicated the three- or four-part lines heard on his recordings, which meant that the extra horns simply doubled the existing parts. And, unlike the great bands of James Brown and B. B. King, who performed on their leaders' recordings, Otis's sidemen played no part in creating the arrangements to his songs, only in reproducing them. This put them in the position of living up to someone else's standard of playing, rather than establishing their own. It also meant that they had little opportunity to hear how they actually sounded, given the primitive public address systems in most clubs and auditoriums. Otis rehearsed them regularly, but he was neither a musical taskmaster on the level of James Brown nor a master musician on the level of B. B. King.

Nevertheless, if the live recording suggests that Otis's dates at the Whisky were something less than an artistic peak, they were unquestionably a promotional triumph. By 1966, a new spirit of communion was taking hold among the younger members of the entertainment industry in Los Angeles. Much of this was fueled by the almost sacramental popularity of recreational drugs, the enthusiasm for which marked a divide between the Old Hollywood and the New. Its name aside, the Whisky was a bellwether of this generational shift—a place where pot-smoking film, television, and music stars, like Steve McQueen, the Smothers Brothers, and John Phillips of the Mamas and the Papas, could gather knowingly under one roof. The rapturous reception Otis received there established him, overnight, as Soul Brother Number One in the precincts of this new, hip Hollywood. Two years before, Sam Cooke had set his sights on the Copacabana as the pinnacle of mainstream success. But the mainstream itself was shifting by the spring of 1966. In the churning wake of the Beatles' success, the American music business had slipped its moorings in the conventional showbiz world of hotel ballrooms, glitzy Las Vegas casinos, and supper clubs like the Copa, with their arriviste aura of "class" and their Prohibition-era ambience of alcoholic bonhomie. But where it all was heading was still anybody's guess.

Nothing attested to this sea change in the music business more than the emergence of Bob Dylan as a rock star over the course of 1965, and nothing attested to Otis's growing cachet with the new rock audience more than Dylan's presence at three of his four Whisky shows. After honing his skills as a blues and folk revivalist in the Greenwich Village coffeehouse scene of the early 1960s, Dylan had burst to national attention as the enfant terrible of the "folk protest" movement after Peter Paul and Mary turned his civil rights anthem "Blowing in the Wind" into a million-selling Top 10 hit in 1963. In the soul-searching aftermath of the Kennedy assassination, Dylan's own album of biblically prophetic protest songs called *The Times They Are a-Changin'* led to his anointment by the mainstream press as America's troubadour. A year later, however, inspired by the success of the Beatles and the imperatives of his own restless genius, Dylan had shocked the sensibilities of his fans, first by shifting his attention from social to sexual politics with a series of scathingly unromantic love songs, and then by releasing a pair of albums, *Bringing It All Back Home* and *Highway 61 Revisited,* along with a hit single, "Like a Rolling Stone," on which he was backed by an electric band. The influence of these records on the lyric content of popular songwriting in the 1960s would prove to be as revolutionary as that of the Beatles on the musical content of pop.

Dylan was in Los Angeles in April 1966, preparing to leave for concerts in Hawaii and Australia on a world tour with his new electric band, the Hawks, several of whom played a part in putting him together with Otis. Dylan's drummer, Mickey Jones, had introduced himself to Otis at a taping of *The Lloyd Thaxton Show* on the eve of the Whisky shows, and when Otis mentioned that he'd like to meet Dylan, Jones arranged with Elmer Valentine for Dylan and his entourage to attend on opening night. Dylan's guitarist, Robbie Robertson, had already suggested that Otis would be an ideal singer to cover the ballad "Just Like a Woman" off Dylan's forthcoming album *Blonde on Blonde*. This prompted Dylan to play an advance pressing of the track for Otis when he visited with him backstage. According to Phil Walden, Otis remarked that he loved the song but complained that it had "too many damn words" for him to sing. (As Dylan's work goes, it's a model of economy, consisting of three verses, a chorus, and a bridge.) Robertson was under the impression that Otis did eventually try to record the song but balked at singing the bridge. Either way, it was a missed opportunity, for Otis could have worked wonders with "Just Like a Woman." His failure to do so reflected his one remaining blind spot as a musical artist: his stubborn insistence that lyrics didn't matter. It was an attitude that set him apart from nearly all great popular singers and songwriters, including such personal favorites as Sam Cooke, Chuck Berry, and Ray Charles. It was also an attitude that ran counter to the prevailing trend of popular music in 1966, at a time when dozens of precocious young songwriters were following the lead of Dylan and the Beatles by applying vernacular language to a growing range of subjects that reached beyond the age-old preoccupations of pop romance. Given Otis's ambition and his musical awareness, it is hard to see his professed disregard of lyric content as anything but the defensiveness of an artist who feared that he was simply not up to the task.

Not since the great days of Sun Records and such Sun artists as Elvis Presley, Johnny Cash, and Charlie Rich has the Memphis sound been as important in the world of pop music as it is today. Today's Memphis sound is largely the product of Memphis-based Stax-Volt Records and its president Jim Stewart. Jerry Wexler, Atlantic Records executive, calls Stewart "the greatest independent producer in the record business today."

—*BILLBOARD,* August 1966

AT THE URGING OF JERRY WEXLER, PHIL WALDEN BEGAN EXPLOR-ing the prospect of Otis performing in Britain soon after the release of "My Girl." After rejecting an attempt by Shaw Artists to connect him with a British agent named Roy Tempest, Phil turned to Larry Myers, newly installed at Universal Attractions, and Myers put him in touch with the French promoter Henri Goldgran, who had long experience booking American artists in Europe, including Ray Charles's tours in 1961 and 1964. In April, Walden and Goldgran signed a letter of agreement committing Otis and his band to seven dates in Britain and France in September, with the specific venues to be determined later. This contract was later amended to include a total of ten dates, consisting of three nights at the Olympia in Paris, an appearance on the British television program *Ready Steady Go!,* and six shows at theaters and clubs in England. In keeping with the promotional nature of the tour, Otis and his nine-piece band would be paid a relatively modest fee of a thousand dollars a night.

In the meantime, having lost patience with Decca's Sir Edward Lewis, Ahmet Ertegun had negotiated a new licensing deal for Atlantic with Polydor, the pop music division of the German conglomerate Deutsche Grammophon, which was aggressively colonizing the British market by signing production and distribution agreements with several of the country's newly formed independent labels. The deal contained a reciprocity clause that gave Atlantic the option to release Polydor's artists in the States—a provision that would soon grant them the rights to such up-and-coming British groups as the Bee Gees and Cream. For the time being, however, both labels were happy to celebrate their new affiliation with Percy Sledge's "When a Man Loves a Woman," which went to #4 in Britain and spent seventeen weeks on the charts.

Otis followed his dates at the Whisky with shows at the 5-4 Ballroom in Watts and the Continental Club in Oakland. He then worked his way back east on a route that took him through Phoenix, Denver, and Baton Rouge before heading north to his first extended appearance in Detroit, at Phelps Lounge, where a delegation from Motown led by Berry Gordy and Marvin Gaye turned out for his shows. Along the way, Otis stopped in Memphis to record a wordy new ballad that he was openly excited about. Otis thought of "My Lover's Prayer" as his answer to "When a Man Loves a Woman," and he hoped it would earn him a similar kind of crossover success. With its tumbling melody and declamatory lyrics, the song extended the theme of romantic abandonment that began with "I've Been Loving You Too Long" and continued with "Just One More Day." "This is my lover's prayer / I hope it will reach out to you, my love," Otis sings in the opening verse, describing his life of "wanting, waiting, and wishing" as "such a weary thing." "What you gonna do tonight," he asks, "when you need some loving arms to hold you tight?"

For the uptempo side of the single, Steve Cropper and Eddie Floyd had recently collaborated on a hard-driving number called "Knock on Wood" that was written with Otis in mind. But Jim Stewart disliked the song, insisting that it sounded too much like "In the Midnight Hour" (which for some reason he regarded as a detriment). In its place, Otis and the Stax band concocted a bubbly groove behind another Cropper-Floyd composition (written with help from Stax publicist Deanie Parker) called "Don't Mess with Cupid," whose inane refrain of "Cupid he's not stupid" ensured that, if nothing else, no deejay in America would ever think about pushing the B-side of the single.

"My Lover's Prayer" was an appealing, well-made record, and Otis sang his heart out on it. But, like "Just One More Day," the song lacked any sense of drama, originality, or musical surprise. Sales and airplay were respectable, but nothing more than that. The record peaked at #10 R&B, failed to make the Pop Top 40, and sold in the neighborhood of 150,000 copies. At Stax, its release was completely overshadowed by the triumphant success of Sam and Dave's new single, "Hold On! I'm Coming," a Dave Porter–Isaac Hayes production that went on to displace "When a Man Loves a Woman" at #1 in the course of its twenty-week run on the R&B charts. The record was a breakthrough for Porter and Hayes, who had modeled their songwriting and production partnership on Motown's Holland-Dozier-Holland, with Porter as a classic "word man" and Hayes as a classic "music man." Hayes had come a long way from his early sessions with Otis, from whom he had absorbed a wealth of knowledge about head arranging and working with horns. As for "Knock on Wood," Eddie Floyd wound up recording his own version of the song, with production help from Hayes, but it took another two months for Floyd, Hayes, Steve Cropper, and Estelle Axton to convince Jim Stewart to release it as a single. When he finally relented, the record confirmed Rufus Thomas's assessment of Stewart's commercial obtuseness by selling three-quarters of a million copies and providing Stax with its second #1 single of 1966. Eddie Floyd was a journeyman singer of little distinction, and it is hard to imagine that Otis would have done any less well with the song.

In June, Otis returned to the Apollo as the headliner of The Soul Show, a joint presentation of Atlantic and Stax that included Sam and Dave, Carla and Rufus Thomas, the Mad Lads, and Johnny Taylor, a newly signed Stax artist who was best known for having replaced Sam Cooke in the Soul Stirrers in 1957. Their week at the Apollo was the prelude to a grueling summer package tour consisting of forty-two dates in forty-five days on which Otis shared the bill with Sam and Dave, Percy Sledge, and a half dozen supporting acts, most of them represented by the Walden agency. The tour was booked by Larry Myers and his colleague Dick Alen at Universal Attractions, and it marked a major step in Phil Walden's efforts to extricate Otis from his contract with Shaw. In anticipation of this long string of dates, Otis made some major improvements to his band, poaching three of Joe Tex's most accomplished sidemen, guitarist Leroy Hadley, bassist J. Alfred Cook, and trumpeter Leroy Monroe. To conserve the talents of Woody Woodson, he also hired J. Johnny Johnson (a future member of the Allman Brothers Band) as a backup drummer to accompany the supporting acts.

Playing in sold-out auditoriums, civic centers, and urban theaters, this tour grossed nearly half a million dollars and provided a financial wind-fall for Otis, the Waldens, and Universal Attractions. But it was also a humbling experience for Otis, who, for the first time since he became a headliner in 1965, was forced to share the spotlight with a pair of artists, Percy Sledge and Sam and Dave, whose records were outselling his own. Having gone from total obscurity to star billing in the space of a couple of months, Percy Sledge was still a rank amateur: an ungainly, unlovely performer who merely had to open his mouth and emit the title line of his chart-topping hit to satisfy his fans. Sledge remembered Otis as un-failingly supportive: "You can't describe the feeling that artists like me had for the Big O. He was the type of guy who always loved to see you did good, then stand back and laugh with you, 'Told you so!' That was the way he talked. He made you feel like you were a part of him." Sam and Dave were another matter. They had been grooming themselves for this moment for five long years, channeling all their ambition and frus-tration into the creation of an extraordinarily dynamic act that merged the double-lead call-and-response of gospel quartet with the visual grace and kineticism of great black dance teams like the Nicholas Brothers and Coles and Atkins. "Hold On, I'm Coming" was peaking at #1 just as the tour began, and from Otis's perspective, they were blowing him off the stage.

As Phil Walden remembered it, the trouble began in New York with a frantic phone call from Speedo Sims, summoning him to Otis's dressing room at the Apollo. "What are you trying to do to me?" Otis yelled at Phil when he arrived backstage. "You put my black ass on the show with those two bastards? Those guys are killing me." Phil's response was to tell Otis to pull himself together and act like the star he was. Over the next six weeks, working with the uptempo grooves of "Respect," "Satisfaction," and "I Can't Turn You Loose," Otis began to move onstage as never be-fore, adding twists and turns and side steps, striding back and forth in front of the band with a long-legged gait that seemed to parody his down-home style, dropping to his knees like James Brown in the middle of "I've Been Loving You Too Long," and doubling up on his marching to the point where he was actually running in place.

In the middle of July, twenty-four days out, the tour came to the Macon City Auditorium for Otis's fourth annual Homecoming show. Halfway through the evening, an off-duty policeman on the security detail tried to arrest a man for selling moonshine in the basement of the auditorium. After he handcuffed his suspect, the officer was attacked by several of the man's friends, one of whom grabbed the cop's revolver and threatened him with it before fleeing the scene. The Macon police stopped the show, blocked the exits, and fanned out through the crowd of nearly 7,000 patrons. Fights broke out on the dance floor and at one point several shots were fired in the balcony, causing a mad rush for the stairs. Though there were no serious injuries, it took more than half an hour and fifty arrests before order was restored and the show could resume. According to the *Telegraph,* neither the handcuffed suspect nor his accomplices were ever apprehended.

The tour ended in the middle of August with a concert at a Dallas wrestling arena called the Sportatorium and the taping of a syndicated television show called *The Beat* at the studios of the local ABC affiliate. (*The Beat* was hosted by WLAC deejay "Hoss" Allen, who got so drunk before the taping that Otis had to take over as the emcee.) A week later, Otis returned to New York to perform at the Rheingold Music Festival, a summer-long series of outdoor concerts sponsored by a local brewery and held at the Wollman Skating Rink in Central Park. The demand for tickets was so great that a second show was added. As had been the case at many of the dates on the summer tour, a large percentage of the audience was composed of young white fans. Otis's performance earned a glowing notice in the *New York Times*. "Otis Redding, one of the more volcanic rhythm-and-blues stars, erupted in two concerts last night," critic Robert Shelton wrote. He went on to describe Otis as "a gyrating, strutting dynamist, a pelvis-shaking showman unafraid of uninhibited sexuality."

At the end of August, Otis played a week at the Regal Theater in Chicago on a bill that included the twenty-four-year-old Columbia Records artist Aretha Franklin. Born in Memphis and raised in Detroit, Aretha was the daughter of the Rev. C. L. Franklin, whose fervent sermonizing and bestselling recordings had made him the most popular black preacher of his era. Like Otis, Aretha had first attracted attention as a child singing gospel in her father's church. But at the age of eighteen, with her father's blessing, she was signed to Columbia by John Hammond, the legendary promoter and producer who had played a pivotal role in the careers of Benny Goodman, Count Basie, Billie Holiday, and Bob Dylan. At the time, Hammond described Franklin as "the most dynamic voice I'd encountered since Billie." Though Otis and Aretha had never performed together before, they had known each other casually and admired one another from afar. Among other things, they shared a deep musical— and, in Aretha's case, romantic—infatuation with Sam Cooke, who had been sufficiently impressed with Franklin's 1962 recording of the Tin Pan Alley standard "Try a Little Tenderness" to sing an abbreviated version of the song on his *Live at the Copa* LP. At the Regal, Otis told Aretha that he planned to record his own version of "Tenderness" on his next album. She responded by telling him that she was working on her own arrangement of "Respect." In fact, Aretha had been performing the song as part of her live act for several months, but in deference to Otis, she did not sing it at the Regal.

OTIS AND PHIL REDUX

We were completely above board. We felt we had been charged with this responsibility, because this particular aspect of the music business had an awful reputation for cheating and swindling the artist. And we really established a code of ethics, or conduct, or whatever, early on.

—PHIL WALDEN

L ATE IN THE SPRING OF 1966, JAMES MEREDITH, THE AIR FORCE veteran who braved student riots and constant harassment to become, in 1962, the first African American to enroll at the University of Mississippi, set out to walk the length of Highway 51 from Memphis to Jackson, Mississippi, on a one-man March Against Fear. A year after the passage of the 1965 Voting Rights Act, many localities in the South continued to intimidate black residents from registering to vote, and Meredith hoped to embolden his fellow black Mississippians to stand up for their hard-won rights. Two days into his march, having just crossed into Mississippi, Meredith was hit by three blasts from a shotgun fired by a forty-year-old white man named Aubrey Norvell. Meredith survived the shooting and was visited in the hospital in Memphis by a contingent of civil rights leaders led by Dr. Martin Luther King Jr., who vowed to continue the march in his stead. In a matter of days, hundreds of demonstrators filled the road to Jackson. The Meredith March, as it came to be known, marked the end of an era for the civil rights movement in the South. On account of its improvised nature, the march was poorly organized and largely un-protected by the federal government. Over the course of two weeks, its participants were subjected to the unremitting hostility of Mississippi's white residents and the wanton brutality of its Klan-infested state and local police. Under the weight of this daily oppression, the intergenerational coalition of civil rights groups that King and his lieutenants in the SCLC had spent six years holding together under the ethos of nonviolent protest flew apart at the seams.

The pivotal moment came on June 16 in the Delta town of Greenwood, a crucible of the voting rights struggle in Mississippi, where the local newspaper welcomed Dr. King as a "hatemonger" comparable to Josef Stalin and Mao Zedong, and where Stokely Carmichael, a twenty-four-year-old firebrand from New York who had recently deposed King's disciple John Lewis as head of the Student Non-Violent Coordinating Committee, was arrested for failing to obtain a permit for the marchers to camp on the grounds of a local black school. That night, out on bail, Carmichael told a crowd of supporters that this was his twenty-seventh arrest and that he had had enough. "We've been saying 'freedom' for six years and we ain't got nothing. What we're gonna start saying now is Black Power," he proclaimed, unveiling a slogan he had been preparing for several weeks. "It's time we stand up and take over. Every courthouse in Mississippi ought to be burned down tomorrow to get rid of the dirt and the mess. From now on, when they ask you what you want, you know what to tell them. What do you want?" "Black Power!" the crowd replied.

The surprising thing, in retrospect, was that two words could mean so much. Though the civil rights movement had often assumed the tenor of a moral crusade, it was also a grassroots political campaign that had led to the passage of landmark legislation at the highest levels of government. The notion that there was something controversial, much less incendiary, about ascribing the term *power* to its ends might seem far-fetched. Yet leaders like King had gone to extraordinary lengths to avoid offending the sensibilities of sympathetic whites by shunning any hint of threat or coercion in their appeal to conscience, fairness, and decency. "While believing firmly that power is necessary, it would be difficult for me to use the phrase Black Power because of the connotative meaning that it has for many people," King explained. A great many other African Americans, frustrated with the slow pace of social and economic progress and the growing realization that civil rights legislation was only a start in reversing the legacy of racist oppression, did not share King's reticence. As if to dramatize the situation, a few days after Carmichael's speech, King and his entourage were attacked by a mob of white thugs when they stopped in the absurdly named town of Philadelphia, Mississippi, to honor the three civil rights workers who were lynched there by police and Klansmen in 1964. King would later describe it as the most fearful moment of his life.

Over the second half of 1966, intoxicated by his own rhetoric and his sudden status as a national media celebrity, Stokely Carmichael would preside over the expulsion of all white members from the Student Non-Violent Coordinating Committee (SNCC), renounce the commitment to nonviolence upon which the organization was founded, and emerge as the principal spokesman across the country for a belligerent new spirit of black separatism and militancy. Charismatic, eloquent, and utterly irresponsible, Carmichael was a wild-eyed demagogue out of central casting, and his all-purpose, ill-defined creed of Black Power provided the press with the perfect narrative complement to the phenomenon it had already dubbed White Backlash: a resurgence of "massive resistance," this time on a national level, in the form of an organized and increasingly violent response on the part of working- and middle-class whites to the prospect of racial integration in housing and public education in the cities of the North and the West.

As time would tell, Stokely Carmichael's sudden rise to national prominence was a sign of desperation on the part of many younger blacks, who recognized that the tide of public opinion was turning against the civil rights movement all across America during the summer of 1966. In Chicago, where Dr. King and the SCLC mounted their first major initiative against de facto segregation in the North, orderly protests against housing discrimination in the white, working-class Catholic neighborhoods on the city's South Side were met, despite a massive police presence, by mobs of rock-throwing residents brandishing Confederate flags and swastikas, screaming "Kill the niggers!" and "Burn them like Jews!" In Washington that summer, yet another Senate filibuster by southern Democrats was joined by midwestern Republicans in a successful effort to defeat the Johnson administration's third major civil rights bill, this one containing key provisions designed to outlaw discrimination in housing and education. In California, the former B-movie actor Ronald Reagan was campaigning for governor on a crypto-racist law-and-order platform that played on the fears fanned by the Watts riots of 1965 and the antiwar protests on the campuses of the state university system. And in Georgia, the arch-segregationist Lester Maddox was running for governor against a crowded field of more moderate Democratic rivals, including Jimmy Carter, then a young state senator. Following his nomination by 4,000 cheering delegates in the Macon City Auditorium in September, Maddox was awarded the governorship by the Democratic-controlled state legislature after failing to gain a majority in a three-way general election. "The seal of the great state of Georgia lies tarnished," said Atlanta's progressive mayor, Ivan Allen Jr. "Georgia is a sick state," added Dr. King.

A GREAT MANY Americans in all walks of life were affected by the polarization in racial attitudes that gripped the country over the course of 1966, but it was striking the extent to which this darkening of the national mood affected the personal and professional relationship that Otis Redding and Phil Walden had nurtured over the preceding seven years. During the first half of the year, Phil had drawn on his reputation as Otis's manager and his connections with Stax and Atlantic to sign management and booking contracts with a growing roster of black artists, thereby turning his talent agency into a major player in the world of R&B. In the spring, the Waldens moved their business into a converted chicken warehouse on Cotton Avenue in the heart of Macon's black commercial district. Renamed the Redwal Building, it now housed the offices of Walden Artists and Promotions, Redwal Music, and Otis Redding Enterprises. With a mixture of efficiency and bluster, Phil and Alan had mastered the essential skill of doing business on the R&B circuit. As Phil put it, "The way we made our reputation was, we got our people paid." Top Walden clients, like Otis Redding and Sam and Dave, had reached the point where they nearly always earned more than their guarantee, and in a cash business based on ticket receipts, it was essential for artists and their road managers to keep their own count of the box office. Accordingly, in the summer of 1966, C. B. Walden began accompanying Otis on tour to help ensure that the numbers came out right at the end of the night. But in the long run, the most persuasive form of leverage available to an agent was the power to deny a promoter access to his bestselling acts. "We wouldn't sell any of our artists to a promoter that shorted any one of them," Phil explained.

As their agency grew in size and stature, both the Walden brothers took a definite pleasure in throwing their weight around. Phil especially became known for a belligerent style of doing business that verged on caricature at times. On any given day, he could be heard throughout the office, ranting and raving on the phone, issuing threats and ultimatums to uncooperative artists and recalcitrant promoters.

Otis and Phil, 1966

When dealing with people he liked and admired, Phil could be disarmingly charming and polite, the very model of a progressive young southern businessman. But he could be dismissive and downright abusive with anyone he regarded as his social, professional, or intellectual inferior, and there was no shortage of people in the music business who fell into those categories. This did not sit well with Otis, who prided himself on the humility with which he wore his success.

It was probably inevitable that the expansion of the Walden agency and Phil's growing involvement with other successful acts would introduce a new set of stresses into his relationship with Otis. Apart from attending marquee gigs like the Apollo or the Whisky a Go Go, Phil rarely accompanied Otis on tour, and while Joe Galkin continued to attend nearly all of his recording dates, Phil had little personal involvement with Stax. ("I didn't pay him a damn bit of mind," he later said of Jim Stewart.) When Otis was home in Macon, he would spend at least part of the day in his office at the Redwal Building on Cotton Avenue. But his constant touring left little time and opportunity for Otis and Phil to renew and sustain the tight bond they had enjoyed in their earlier years. Outside the office, Alan Walden remained on much closer terms with Otis than Phil, especially after Alan moved into a cabin up the road from the Reddings' home in Round Oak, where he took it upon himself to introduce Otis to the rural pleasures of hunting, fishing, and horseback riding.

Most successful entertainers reach a point in their careers where their managerial relationships come due for reappraisal. For Otis and Phil, that point came in the summer of 1966. From Phil's perspective, "Otis got real distant all of a sudden. I'd call him on the road, and he was like, 'Uh-huh. Yeah.' Very un-Otis. No animation, no enthusiasm, no caring. I'd tell him about some great complicated deal we had just worked out, and he'd say, 'Well, don't sign that yet. We need to get together and talk.' So he came home and he was real moody." Phil attributed Otis's "moodiness" to the sudden intrusion of racial politics into their lives. "He went through about a three-month deal with a Black Muslim group that strained the relationship greatly. . . . There was even an interview in a Black Muslim magazine that Otis was going to announce his intentions to become a Muslim." In Phil's view, Otis had fallen prey to the separatist seductions of Black Power: "They wanted a piece of the action. They convinced him that I was a thief. They stirred up his anger at undeniable mistreatment by whites which made him distrust our relationship."

Like other worldly African Americans, Otis was familiar with the Nation of Islam. He had a subscription to *Muhammad Speaks,* and there is some indication that he may have visited Nation of Islam temples in New York and Washington during the early years of his career. Following their successful recruitment of Muhammad Ali in 1964, the group had tried, with limited success, to enlist other black celebrities, including

Otis's friend Joe Tex, who quietly joined the Nation of Islam in 1966. But none of Otis's close associates besides Phil Walden recalled any direct involvement on his part with the group. In all likelihood, Phil was using "Black Muslim" as a synonym for "black militant." But if so, he was still overstating the case.

From Otis's perspective, something else was going on. Despite Phil Walden's insistence that his agency's operations were "completely above board," the truth was more complex, beginning with the fact that the Waldens' practice of both managing and booking many of their artists served to blur the lines of the compensation they were due. Otis's management contract entitled Phil to 20 percent of his gross income from all sources. It also required him to reimburse the Walden agency for all "promotional" expenses, including the costs of publicity, travel, and telephone. That the terms of this contract were fairly standard for the music business at the time did not diminish the fact that it was completely one-sided and inherently exploitative. Though the Waldens liked to describe Otis as their "partner," he never shared in the profits of their agency. Rather, Phil and Alan had made themselves Otis's partners in Redwal Music, which ensured that they not only received their 20 percent commission on the writer's share of Otis's song publishing but also owned an interest in his publisher's share. Added to these built-in inequities was the fact that, as the agency acquired additional top-selling artists and combined them on package tours, it was by no means clear which promotional expenses were Otis's alone. Still another concern was the cavalier attitude toward money that Phil affected, almost as a point of pride. "I was never interested in how much we were making," he later said. "The money part of it was just not terribly important at the time." To say the least, this was not an attitude that many artists would welcome in a manager.

As the most prominent and glamorous form of black enterprise in America, the entertainment business was a magnet for opportunists of all sorts looking to ingratiate themselves with sports and music stars. One such figure was a young African American attorney named George Grogan Jr., who first befriended Otis at a gig in Tampa in the spring of 1966. Grogan's father, a respected high school teacher, businessman, and promoter, ran a club called the Manhattan Casino in St. Petersburg and had served since the 1950s as Universal Attractions' main operative in central Florida. But Otis's band member Don Henry described the younger Grogan as a member of the "black mafia," a loose term that referred to the small-time hustlers and gangsters who preyed on the black community by running numbers and protection rackets. At some point in the summer of 1966, Grogan Jr. approached Otis with an offer to use his legal knowledge and his father's connections with Universal Attractions to get him out of his contract with the Waldens, whom he characterized as exploitative whites living off the success of their black artists. Grogan's initiative ultimately went nowhere, but he does appear to have planted some seeds of doubt in Otis's mind.

From Phil Walden's perspective, a more formidable threat was posed by Leroy Johnson, an Atlanta attorney who in 1962, after the Supreme Court outlawed Georgia's corrupt county-based system of apportionment, became the first African American elected to the state legislature in half a century. Profiled by the *New York Times* as "a fascinating black Machiavelli . . . the single most powerful black politician in Dixie," Johnson was a consummate fixer and statehouse dealmaker who was subjected to some of the same double standards for behavior that were used to discredit black politicians during the Reconstruction era. Otis first approached him in the summer of 1966, when Sylvester Huckabee was arrested for assault and battery in Macon and sent to prison for violating the terms of the suspended sentence he had received for his part in the shoot-out on Roy Street. Johnson wasted little time in securing Huck's release, and from that point on, he began to provide Otis with legal representation.

Though it has since become routine for successful entertainers to hire their own attorneys to monitor their business affairs, Phil Walden took Otis's involvement with George Grogan Jr. and Leroy Johnson as a personal affront. "I had worked so hard on this career," Phil wrote in an overwrought passage in his unpublished memoir. "I had given part of my life, part of my father, my brother even. We had put our reputations on the line, representing this man as best we could. We'd offended people, kicked people, fought, clawed, to get everything in the world for this man, every fair deal. Then, to have somebody turn him around, even for a moment, for their own greedy and self-serving purposes that could ultimately have destroyed his career, was a challenge to our very dignity and integrity."

Phil's words conveyed a sense of the price his family had paid for their involvement with black musicians in the racist milieu of Macon. Most white managers, agents, and record executives who worked with black artists were based in cities of sufficient size and social complexity that few people paid them any mind. But the Waldens were highly visible in the fishbowl of Macon society, where they were resented and even ostracized by people in the community who saw them as unconscionable "nigger-lovers," in the parlance of the time. The growing success of their business, as advertised by the familiar spectacle of Phil and Alan and Otis careening around the streets of downtown Macon in the late-model Cadillacs they all drove, added a strong dose of envy to the feeling among many whites in the city that the Waldens were nothing less than traitors to their race.

At the same time, Phil's sense of self-sacrifice and self-congratulation needs to be put in some perspective. Prior to Otis Redding's entrance into their lives, the Waldens had been a lower-middle-class family struggling to make ends meet in the booming economy of postwar Macon. While Phil's intelligence, education, and ambition may well have prepared him for a more conventional career in business or the law, the fact remained that he and his family owed *all* of their newfound affluence and prominence to Otis's success. Phil's own role in that success had been qualified by his absence during the year and a half when Otis came into his own as a performing and recording artist—a year and a half when Otis had been personally responsible for the very survival of the Walden agency. By any meaningful standard, Otis Redding was the principal author of his own success. Yet such was the psychology of race relations in the South that Phil was quite capable of seeing the whole situation in terms of what he and his family had done *for* Otis—to the point, even, of attributing their own bad behavior ("we'd offended people, kicked people") to their selfless devotion to his cause.

In *The Mind of the South,* W. J. Cash referred to "the Southerner's native tendency to render all his impulses in terms of the highest purposes." Sarah Boyle touched on something similar when she described her own benevolent feelings toward blacks as a way of providing herself with "easily found ways of proving myself gentle, high-principled, and kind." In Phil's case, this native tendency allowed him to see everything that Otis had achieved as something that Phil, in the role of a benevolent white man, had made possible. To his credit, however, he recognized the stubborn nature of this paternalistic view. "Those traditions were so ingrained into every fiber of [Otis's] body and every fiber of my body," he later said. "Those were difficult things to break out of." In the Black Power summer of 1966, those traditions were under assault as never before.

READY STEADY GO!

I loved England from head to toe. I was there in the summer and it was nice. The people are so groovy. They treated me like I was somebody. I loved Paris, too.

—OTIS REDDING

Tensions between Otis and Phil came to a head in the weeks leading up to Otis's promotional tour of Britain and France in September 1966. The week before his departure, Otis spent several days in Memphis recording tracks for his next LP. He then flew to New York to meet up with Phil and his band, which was reduced to nine pieces for the purposes of the tour. Though they were staying at the same hotel, Phil was unable to get through to Otis on the phone, and at one point, he was told by George Grogan Jr. that Otis had decided to back out of the tour. Phil and the band members arrived at the airport unsure whether Otis would show. The two of them wound up having an emotional reconciliation on the flight to London, professing their love and loyalty to each other. But the balance of power in their relationship would continue to shift in the year ahead.

Over the summer, Nesuhi Ertegun had spent a month in Europe consolidating Atlantic's operations there, in the course of which he hired a thirty-year-old white South African named Frank Fenter to run the label's London office. A gregarious former actor with a passion for R&B, Fenter quickly established himself as Atlantic's eyes and ears in Britain, providing the label with an astute hands-on presence in the booming London pop scene. Otis's tour was Fenter's first important assignment, and he did everything he could think of to generate publicity, hiring a London public relations firm to set up a press conference at the airport that was attended by representatives of all the British music papers. The most established of those papers, *Melody Maker,* had recently listed Otis as the tenth most popular male singer in its annual readers' poll; he was the only black artist cited among such major stars as Elvis Presley (the perennial winner since 1957), Bob Dylan, Mick Jagger, and John Lennon. Asked by a reporter from the paper to name his own favorite singers, Otis went out of his way to express his enthusiasm for Dylan and the Rolling Stones. "Bobby is the greatest," he declared. "He gave me 'Just Like a Woman' to make as a record, but I didn't do it because I just couldn't feel it. Mind you, I dig his work like mad." Asked about his approach to recording at Stax, Otis explained, "I'll tell you what happens. All the songwriting is done in the studio. We don't get it prepared outside beforehand, no. We all get up and down to the studios at twelve, midday, and work through until nine in the evening. Then we quit. Go home and relax and sleep. Everybody has a good think about the things they've been doing and then we come back the next day at twelve—always at twelve—fresh and with a lot of new ideas." It was the first time that a reporter from any publication had ever thought to ask Otis Redding a question about his work.

After a brief layover in London, Otis and the band flew to Paris for their three shows at the Olympia Music Hall, a 2,000-seat theater on the Boulevard des Capucines that had served since the 1950s as the city's prime venue for popular music. In addition to French stars such as Édith Piaf and Jacques Brel, both of whom made celebrated live recordings there, the Olympia had showcased numerous American jazz and R&B artists, including Duke Ellington and Ray Charles, as well as major British bands like the Beatles and the Rolling Stones. The opening night at the Olympia coincided with Otis's twenty-fifth birthday, and the show was taped for broadcast on French television, documenting the remarkable change in Otis's performing style since his tour with Sam and Dave.

After Paris, the troupe returned to London, where their first order of business was a taping of the television show *Ready Steady Go!* for broadcast on the following Friday. Otis's British tour dates had been booked by Harold Davison, one of the country's top talent agents, whose clients included Eric Burdon, the lead singer of the recently disbanded Animals, and Chris Farlowe, whose cover of the Rolling Stones' "Out of Time," produced by Mick Jagger, had recently topped the British charts. Along with Jagger himself, Burdon and Farlowe were regarded as two of Britain's foremost exponents of "blue-eyed soul," and Davison had arranged for them to appear with Otis on *Ready Steady Go!* Though the program was nearing the end of its three-year run on British television, it was still recognized as the premier pop music show of its time, acclaimed for its stylish studio audience, its Pop Art set designs, and its unpatronizing attitude toward guests and viewers alike. Airing at 6:00 on Friday evenings and advertising itself with the slogan "Your Weekend Begins Here," it functioned as a weekly television magazine, apprising its teenaged audience of the latest trends in music, fashion, and dance as they headed out the door at the end of their working week. (Most English teenagers had left school and gone to work by the age of sixteen.)

Otis's half-hour appearance on *Ready Steady Go!* was by far his most polished presentation in live performance that had been filmed to date, and it provided a close look at the more confident and energetic stage presence he had developed over the course of 1966. After a beaming introduction by the show's host, Cathy McGowan, he sauntered onto the set wearing a light-colored jacket over a dark shirt and slacks (the broadcast was in black-and-white) and delivered high-energy versions of "(I Can't Get No) Satisfaction," "My Girl," and "Respect," joined halfway through by a multiracial trio of ponytailed, bell-bottomed go-go dancers. He then yielded the stage, first to Eric Burdon singing "Hold On! I'm Coming" with the help of cue cards, and then to Chris Farlowe, singing James Brown's "This Is a Man's World," both of them ably supported by Otis's band. Otis returned to sing a ten-minute medley that began with "Pain in My Heart," erupted into "I Can't Turn You Loose," and segued into "Shake," on which he was re-joined by Farlowe and the diminutive Burdon, who looked like an actual schoolboy standing next to Otis, and made no effort to conceal his delight at the chance to share the stage with one of his full-grown idols. "Feel all right, Eric? Feel all right, Chris?" Otis shouted as the go-go dancers and the studio audience flooded in around them and they ended the show with the "nah . . . nah-nah-nah-nah" refrain of Wilson Pickett's "Land of 1000 Dances."

The *RSG* taping was followed by a weeklong bus tour of England that began with a concert in Bristol (at Colston Hall, named after a prominent

Otis on *Ready Steady Go!*

seventeenth-century slave trader) and ended with shows in London at the massive Orchid Ballroom and a pair of hot new clubs, Tiles in Oxford Street and the Ram Jam in Brixton. All three of the London shows were held at venues associated with the city's Mod subculture, whose influence on music and fashion was a major component of the much-touted "swinging London" phenomenon of 1966—a wholesale embrace by the mainstream media in Britain, America, and Europe of the appealing irony that the august seat of the British Empire had reinvented itself as a world capital of pop culture.

Located in the heart of the city, Tiles epitomized this supercharged merger of youth, music, and fashion. Its performance space adjoined an underground arcade of shops, boutiques, and coffee bars that allowed the club's patrons to indulge their habits of conspicuous consumption throughout the night. The Ram Jam, by contrast, was more a social than a commercial phenomenon. Located in Brixton, the center of London's growing West Indian population, the club had a racially mixed clientele that reflected the uneasy sense of communion between the children of the country's first wave of black immigrants and the white Mod teenagers who had thrown off the legacy of working-class xenophobia to embrace black styles in music and fashion as fascinating exceptions to the homogeneity of English life. Among the fans Otis made a lasting impression on at the Ram Jam was sixteen-year-old Peter Gabriel, who went on to found the rock group Genesis with four classmates from Charterhouse, a prominent boarding school. "You just felt your heart being opened when you were in his presence," Gabriel recalled. "When he was on, it was like a factory of energy, love, and passion."

Though the reception Otis received in Britain was overwhelmingly positive, his appearances in London exposed him to the scrutiny of the country's purist music press, whose ideas about African American music mirrored their contemporaries in the American folk revival movement by extolling "authenticity" at the expense of "commerciality." After championing Otis's music in 1965, the *Record Mirror*'s Norman Jopling had already taken him to task for covering "(I Can't Get No) Satisfaction" ("one could almost believe the stories that he recorded it as a joke"). Now, writing in the first edition of a magazine called *Soul Music Monthly*, the critic Bill Millar began his review of Otis's appearance at Tiles by commenting, with evident distaste, on the "phenomenal" attendance at the club, wildly overestimating the size of the crowd and suggesting that "Otis should receive a mention in the *Financial Times* this year." Turning to the music, he complimented Otis on his "fantastic sense of rhythm" but complained about the loudness of the band, the sameness of the material, and the "hectic" pace of the uptempo numbers. "I feel compelled to say that Otis is overrated," Millar concluded in his review.

In the course of this visit to Britain, Phil Walden and Frank Fenter began a professional friendship that would serve them well in years to come. (Fenter would move to Macon and become Walden's business partner in 1969.) Like Phil, Frank was a dynamic young striver who saw himself as a breed apart from the many hacks and "suits" he dealt with in his work. Having grown up in South Africa, he shared Phil's fascination with black culture and his scorn for the racist ideology of his homeland. As Atlantic's man in London, Fenter was in a position to provide Phil with a crash course in the British pop scene, which, unlike its counterpart in the States, was increasingly dominated by imperious young managers like Brian Epstein of the Beatles, Andrew Oldham of the Stones, and Robert Stigwood of Cream. Fenter was convinced that the enthusiasm for American soul music was ready to explode in Britain, and he encouraged Phil in an ambitious plan to bring Otis back to Europe in 1967 as the headliner on a package tour of Atlantic-affiliated acts.

Phil began laying the groundwork for this tour as soon as he returned to the States, working with Fenter in London, who had introduced him to Arthur Howes, a veteran British talent agent and package tour promoter whose clients included the Beatles, the Kinks, and the Beach Boys. During the fall of 1966, Phil lined up a Stax-dominated bill of Atlantic artists to travel to Britain in the middle of March: Otis, Percy Sledge, Sam and Dave, Carla Thomas, and Eddie Floyd. Jerry Wexler suggested that, instead of their usual road bands, all the acts should be backed by Booker T. and the MGs and the Mar-Keys horns, whose records had earned them an underground reputation of their own in Britain. At the urging of Frank Fenter and the French agent Henri Goldgran, Phil expanded the scope of the tour to include a series of European dates in Paris, Oslo, Stockholm, Copenhagen, and The Hague.

DICTIONARY OF SOUL

I don't know of another man now who has a better sense of communication than Otis Redding. He seems to get over to the people what he's talking about, and he does it in so few words and little phrases that if you read them on paper they might not make any sense. But when you hear them with the music and the way he sings them, you know exactly what he's talking about.

—STEVE CROPPER

Stax released Otis's third single of 1966 the week he returned from Europe. Prefaced by a wistful, singsong horn line that seesaws through the notes of its opening chords, "Fa-Fa-Fa-Fa-Fa (Sad Song)" was cowritten with Steve Cropper, who revived the premise of his first collaboration with Otis, "Mr. Pitiful," by once again making light of his partner's penchant for lovelorn ballads. "I keep singing these sad, sad songs, y'all," Otis declares in the opening verse over a fastidiously restrained backing of piano, bass, and drums: "Sad songs is all I know." He goes on to extol the power of music to "capture your heart [and] put you in a groove," but the essence of the track is a chorus in which Otis and the horns trade a narrow sliver of melody back and forth in wordless call-and-response: two bars of Otis scatting "*Fah* fa-fa-fa-fa *fa-fah* fa-fa," answered by the same figure, voiced in sixths, by two saxes and a trumpet. The effect is richly soothing rather than sad, and the track comes across as an expression of Otis's own musical love affair with the sonorous sound of the Stax horns. The result was a respectable if unspectacular hit. Over the next three months, "Fa-Fa-Fa-Fa-Fa" went on to sell 275,000 copies, rising to #29 in Pop, #12 in R&B.

In the fall of 1966, Jim Stewart and Al Bell took another step in asserting their autonomy from Atlantic Records by deciding that Stax would henceforth handle the art direction, publicity, and promotion for its albums in-house. Previously, Atlantic had supervised all aspects of the packaging and promotion of the label's LPs, in keeping with its reputation as an industry leader in cover art and design. Now the responsibility for designing the covers of Stax albums was placed in the hands of Ronnie Stoots, an amateur artist and part-time singer who as "Ronnie Angel" played club dates around Memphis with members of the Stax band. The task of writing the jacket copy was assigned to Stax's publicity director, Deanie Parker. Parker, too, had started at Stax as a singer, recording a couple of nondescript sides for the label while she was still in high school, then working as a clerk in the Satellite Record Shop. She was a smart and personable young woman, and the fact that she knew nothing about public relations had not deterred Jim Stewart from hiring her as the label's publicist in 1964. In her press releases, fan club newsletters, and promotional handouts, Parker favored a florid style of prose that could sometimes read as if it had been translated into English from another language:

> For a long time now, the public has been thrilled by the essence of this famous man, Otis Redding. His original contribution to the world of music has conquered the nation like a restless hurricane, with only one difference, Otis and what he has to say is undoubtedly here to stay. . . . "These Arms of Mine" was the song that left the nation unrestrained in delight at the style of Otis so much that his name could no longer be chanted only within the walls of this country. His name, his songs, and his contribution to "The Memphis Sound" spread abroad and Otis was awarded, through public demand, another jewel for his crown as the king of rhythm and blues.

The first victims of Stax's new policy were its two premier acts, Otis Redding and Sam and Dave. The single "Fa-Fa-Fa-Fa-Fa (Sad Song)" was followed a month later by the release of an album cumbersomely titled *Complete & Unbelievable: The Otis Redding Dictionary of Soul,* faced with a cover that verged on the grotesque. In keeping with the "dictionary" motif, Ronnie Stoots had contrived a collaged image that shows Otis dressed in a red jacket and white pants, with a professorial mortarboard pasted on his head. Leaning against a crudely drawn book imprinted with the title of the album, he stands atop a row of giant red letters that read, "MY-MY-MY." The mortarboard served as an inadvertent clue, since the graphic resembled the sort of artwork typically found in a high school yearbook. Compounding this visual misadventure, Deanie Parker filled the back of the album jacket with a list of "definitions," complete with pronunciation guides. These included such entries as "Ou we ni (ū' wē nī) . . . getting gooder by the minute," and "Give it (gĭv' ĭt) . . . absitively posilutely not." Apart from serving as a caricature of black dialect that would have done *Amos 'n' Andy* proud, most of the terms (with the inevitable exception of "Gotta-Gotta") had nothing whatsoever to do with Otis's own list of personal catchphrases.

In the larger scheme of things, the ineptitude of Ronnie Stoots and Deanie Parker was almost beside the point. Since its inception, Stax had thrived on its affiliation with Atlantic, which maintained the highest standards for the presentation and promotion of African American music of any record label in the world. Jim Stewart, Estelle Axton, and, more recently, Al Bell had a golden opportunity to learn the record business from acknowledged masters like Jerry Wexler, Ahmet Ertegun, and Tom Dowd. Yet, in their sudden zeal to assert their independence, Stewart, Axton, and Bell appeared to have gained little from this experience. Bell's background in radio had given him an understanding of how to promote R&B singles, and he had done brilliantly at this in his first year on the job. But the radio business was not the same as the record business, especially now that the real money in the record business was coming from the sale of LPs. Bell, who should have been focused on how Stax products would look on display in chain and department stores, was clueless in this regard.

As for Jim Stewart, he exemplified the old-school breed of Southerners who took pride in their provincialism. Just as he had shown little interest in mastering the technology that was transforming the way records were made, Stewart showed little interest in learning the marketing and promotional strategies that were transforming the way records were sold. The difference between a good album cover and a bad album cover meant nothing to him. The sharp increase in Otis's LP sales, from 100,000 copies in 1965 to 250,000 copies over the course of 1966, attested to his growing popularity with the album-oriented audience for rock. But, along with Estelle Axton, Jim Stewart's contact with the record-buying public began and ended at the door of the Satellite Record Shop.

Dictionary of Soul would have been an apt title for either of Otis's previous two LPs, both of which drew extensively on recent R&B hits. The new album, by contrast, contained no contemporary R&B covers. It consisted instead of seven Otis Redding originals, including the singles "Fa-Fa-Fa-Fa-Fa (Sad Song)" and "My Lover's Prayer"; a blistering rendition of the Beatles' hit "Day Tripper"; an antique Chuck Willis ballad, "You're Still My Baby," from 1954; a Porter-Hayes throwaway called "Love Have Mercy"; and a pair of popular standards, "Tennessee Waltz" and "Try a Little Tenderness," both of which Otis knew from *Sam Cooke at the Copa.*

The unprecedented number of new originals did not represent some sort of compositional breakthrough on Otis's part. On the contrary, nearly all were made up extemporaneously in the studio, in the manner he described in his *Melody Maker* interview; along with "Fa-Fa-Fa-Fa-Fa," they were his most adamant expression to date of his conviction that song lyrics didn't matter. On each of them he took the title line—"I've been sick y'all," "She put the hurt on me," "My baby's nothing but a ton of joy"—and expanded it into a monologue of free association, picking up on whatever phrases the title brought to mind. Yet the almost willful sketchiness of the original material was substantially offset by Otis's brilliant take on three of the covers—"Tennessee Waltz," "Try a Little Tenderness," and "Day Tripper"—and by the power of the playing and the originality of the arranging on many of the eleven tracks. The result was a tour de force of collaborative music-making that ranked with his best work to date.

The creative spirit of the *Dictionary of Soul* sessions was enhanced by the presence of Booker Jones, who had returned to full-time service at Stax after completing his college degree in the spring of 1966. With Jones reinstalled at the piano, Isaac Hayes played organ on many of the tracks, and the interplay between their keyboards added a bold new dimension to the sound of the Stax band, which had previously tended to use piano or organ, but not both at the same time. (The combination of the two instruments had come into gospel music in the years after World War II, but it was rare in popular music until Bob Dylan, of all people, used it on his early electric albums and began to tour with a band that included both keyboards.) Isaac Hayes also contributed freely to the horn and rhythm arrangements on *Dictionary of Soul,* drawing on the lessons he had learned from working with Otis and Sam and Dave.

Once upon a time in the era of LPs, listening to albums was a two-part experience, determined by the need to turn the record over at the end of each side. Though long-playing records could hold up to twenty-two minutes per side, popular music in the 1960s remained wedded to the three-minute song, and the usual practice was to put eleven or twelve tracks on an album and then configure each half of the record as a semi-autonomous musical set with a beginning, a middle, and an end. From this perspective, the first side of *Dictionary of Soul,* which starts with the single "Fa-Fa-Fa-Fa-Fa (Sad Song)" and ends with "Day Tripper"—with "Tennessee Waltz," "Try a Little Tenderness," and a pair of originals, "I'm Sick Y'All" and "Sweet Lorene," in between—stands as one of the strongest album sides that Otis had yet produced.

Unlike its closest competitor, the first side of *Otis Blue,* the cover tunes are the high points on side one of *Dictionary of Soul,* while the original songs serve mainly as rhythmic interludes. "I'm Sick Y'All" is a driving monologue on which Otis flogs the familiar blues conceit of trouble in love as a case of romantic flu. "No doctor's medicine will do me no good," he announces, his voice buried deep in the mix, as he lists his symptoms ("pain in my heart . . . hands are tied . . . feels like a headache . . . burning in my side") over a sensuous, bass-heavy groove pierced on the third beat of every bar by a barbed trill from the organ and guitar that functions as more of a *spike* than as an instrumental hook.

This theme of heartache carries over into "Tennessee Waltz," a #1 hit for Patti Page in 1950 that was known to the members of the Stax studio band as a perennial favorite at the Plantation Inn. Sam Cooke had performed it as a swinging "jazz waltz" at the Copacabana, but Otis returned the song to its roots in Tennessee—beginning with a four-bar introduction of wistful guitar and spiraling horns that evokes an air of southern languor akin to the feeling that the publisher of the *Atlanta Constitution* had in mind when he asked the audience at the *Gone with the Wind* gala to "smell the wisteria" on a warm plantation night. In this case, however, the strains of that lyrical introduction were composed by the son of a former sharecropper, who recounts his betrayal by the friend "who stole my sweetheart away" while the Stax horns rise up behind him, making their mark on this familiar standard by quoting their own ascending line from "I've Been Loving You Too Long." It's a startling musical allusion, and it sets up Otis's sardonic revenge on the cracker sentimentality of the song, as he describes how he stood by helplessly while the band kept playing "that beautiful, that wonderful, that marv*u*lous, glorious, that *cotton-picking* Tennessee Waltz."

Cowritten by Otis, Isaac Hayes, and Al Bell, "Sweet Lorene" has the feel of committee work and functions as pure filler on the first side of the album. With more verses than it knows what to do with, assorted stops, starts, horn breaks, drum breaks, and turnarounds, the song seems to be pulling in all directions at once. Al Jackson does his best to pound some sense into the muddle, and Otis gets off a few good lines ("You got my mind messed up and shattered / I'm at the point where nothin' matters"). But the track serves mainly to set the stage for the masterpiece that follows it.

"If I had to pick the best record that Stax ever made," Jim Stewart once said, "it would be 'Try a Little Tenderness.' It has everything that Stax is or was about." Stewart's opinion was all the more compelling in light of his professed dislike of minor chords, since "Try a Little Tenderness" was the most harmonically complex song that Otis would ever record, chock-full of minor second and sixth chords, as well as patches of outright chromaticism. But the track is indeed a musical microcosm of the Stax sound, a seamless synthesis of the pleading ballads and pounding grooves that the artists and musicians who recorded for the label played better than anyone else.

There's nothing to suggest that Otis was familiar with the many recorded versions that established "Try a Little Tenderness" as a pop standard on the strength of its shapely melody and its genteel lyric extolling the sensitivities of men—and the diminished expectations of the women who love them. First popularized by Bing Crosby in the 1930s, it had been covered over the years by Frank Sinatra, Mel Tormé, Chris Connor,

Sammy Davis Jr., the Platters, Perry Como, and Little Miss Cornshucks, to name just a few. Otis knew it from *Live at the Copa*, where Sam Cooke folded it into a medley with "(I Love You) For Sentimental Reasons" and "You Send Me." Since Cooke sang only two of the song's three verses and didn't make it to the bridge, Otis probably learned the rest from the version Aretha Franklin recorded in 1962 on one of her Columbia albums, for his grasp of the lyrics is, just this once, acute. As for the shift in meter that distinguishes his arrangement from all other renditions of the song, it appears to have occurred spontaneously in the studio; if so, the track takes the concept of head arranging to a new level of sophistication.

Like most of Otis's recent ballads, this one starts with an elegiac horn introduction, courtesy of Isaac Hayes, who composed a somber four-bar line that carries an echo of the nursery rhyme "It's Raining, It's Pouring." Against a minimalist backdrop of muted guitar and furtive piano, Otis sings the first verse more or less as written, substituting "young girls" for the "women" of the original, conceding, "Young girls, they do get weary / Wearing that same old shaggy dress." Hayes embroiders the dress with a soap-opera swell of organ, and Andrew Love's saxophone answers Otis's first appeal to "try a little tenderness" with a bluesy trill. Cued by the line "You know she's waiting, just anticipating" at the start of the second verse, Al Jackson begins to tap lightly on the rim of his snare in a convincing simulation of a ticking clock (or perhaps the sound of the girl tapping her nails on a tabletop), quietly shifting the meter of the song into 4/4. Nudged by Duck Dunn's bass and Booker Jones's broken chords, the music starts to stir in the bridge, where Otis prescribes "soft words spoke so gentle" to soothe "her grief and care." He then sings the final verse to the bossa nova lilt of Steve Cropper's rhythm guitar. "But it's all so easy," he assures his listeners, "all you gotta do is try, try a li . . ." as the snap and pop of Jackson's snare splits the title line and brings the full band surging into the music. After taking a moment to collect himself, Otis goes from telling to showing what he's been talking about in this song. "Hold her where you want her!" he cries over the stamping quarter-note rhythm. "Squeeze her! Don't tease her! Never leave her!" Beneath him the harmony rises, marching in whole and then half steps up the scale, cresting on the tonic chord, then dropping back down to start its rise again. "You've got to rub her gentle, man," he advises on the second ascent, repeating his litany of "squeeze . . . tease . . . leave" and his pleas for "tenderness!" until the band lays out entirely and Otis, at a sudden loss for words, fills the space by gasping "gotta try . . . *mah nah nah*" over the leaden thud of the bass drum, before resuming his tutorial—"You gotta know what to do, man, take this advice"—as the music slowly fades.

When Sam Cooke performed "Try a Little Tenderness" for the affluent white patrons of the Copacabana in 1964, he did so as a way of demonstrating his prowess as an all-around entertainer. Cooke's rendition of the song hewed closely to the romantic conventions of "sincerity" and "sensitivity" associated with mainstream pop singers like Bing Crosby and Frank Sinatra, who had successfully merged a bel canto style of crooning with the principles of jazz phrasing and intonation they had learned from mentors like Louis Armstrong and Billie Holiday. The celebrated "sweetness" in Cooke's voice had been well suited to this act of cultural accommodation.

Otis's rendition was incomparably more ambitious, not least because he sang the opening verses in his own, surprisingly creditable version of pop bel canto, enunciating the lyric with a clarity and understatement that would have done Sinatra proud. But his well-heeled prologue gave way to a radical deconstruction and reinterpretation of the song, as Otis went on to subject the genteel sentimentality of "Try a Little Tenderness" to his own standards of emotional expression, in which "soft words," however well wrought, were simply insufficient to the depth of the feelings he meant to convey. The result was an act of cultural appropriation, not accommodation, analogous to the techniques of improvisation that jazz soloists of the swing and bebop eras used to breathe new life into the chords and melodies of the Tin Pan Alley standards that formed a substantial portion of their repertoires.

"Day Tripper," at the end of side one, involved a similar form of appropriation—this one directed at the work of the most popular musical act in the world. The song was first suggested to Otis by Duck Dunn, who loved the bass playing on this Beatles hit, which heralded a new style of guitar-heavy "hard rock" that was being championed by British bands like the Yardbirds and the Who. Otis's version of "Day Tripper" was an even more radical simplification than his version of "(I Can't Get No) Satisfaction." He dispensed with the Beatles' growling guitar riff and their atmospheric vocal harmonies, streamlined the rhythm into an unyielding uptempo stomp, and chopped up the song's three verses into a word salad of phrases—"one-way ticket," "got a good reason," "I found out"—that he repeated over and over in whatever order they occurred to him. While the Beatles brought a certain ironic distance to this portrait of a weekend femme fatale, Otis sounds indignant from the start, ready at the first opportunity to "take the easy way out." In this sense, the track is not so much a cover as a commentary on a song that was already familiar to millions of pop fans at the time. *What is it with you white boys,* he seems to be saying, *that you put up with this crap?*

With the exception of "My Lover's Prayer," which sounded even better as an album track than it did as a single on the radio, the original songs on the second side of *Dictionary of Soul* exposed an earthier, bluesier aspect of Otis's musical personality than he had revealed on record before. "She Put the Hurt on Me" is a sex song, pure and simple, consisting of a countdown to ecstasy—"She give me twenty minutes, I had to think about it / She give me forty minutes, I had to talk about it / She give me sixty minutes, I couldn't do without it"—set to a rollicking backbeat and a chorus of game-show horns. The dreamy mid-tempo ballad "Ton of Joy" takes a similarly quantitative approach to pleasure ("My baby's nothing but a ton of joy") by drawing on the lexicon of the blues: "She gives a blind man eyes to see / She knocks a preacher man straight on his knees." "Hawg for You" (which echoes Eddie Kirk's 1963 Stax single "The Hawg") was the most conventional country blues that Otis would ever record, much less compose, with a stiff shuffle rhythm and a formulaic lyric ("I'm a hawg for you, baby, I'm gonna root all around your door / I'm gonna keep on rooting, baby, till I can't root no more") that gives him a chance to show off some of the hog-calling skills he had acquired on his farm in Round Oak.

Though it took some time to do so, *Dictionary of Soul* was the first of Otis's albums to attract the attention of America's first generation of rock critics, many of whom got their start by writing for the journal *Crawdaddy,* which was founded by a Swarthmore undergrad named Paul

Williams in February 1966. One of those early critics was Ed Ward (or "Edmund O. Ward," as his byline read), who wrote a brief review of the album for the magazine's March 1967 issue. After working his way past the "garish and hideous cover" and admitting that "this is the first of Otis Redding that I have ever heard," Ward characterized *Dictionary* as a "superlative album" and singled out a pair of unlikely tracks, "Day Tripper" ("Redding turns it into an entirely different beast") and "Hawg for You" ("which harkens back to Muddy Waters in its deeply moving earthiness") for his highest praise. A few months later, another *Crawdaddy* regular, Jon Landau, published a piece about Otis that centered on *Dictionary of Soul*. "I have become convinced that Otis Redding's performances constitute, as a whole, the highest level of expression rock 'n' roll has yet achieved," Landau declared. Drawing an explicit contrast with West Coast groups like the Doors, he explained that "I would rather hear someone do something simple perfectly than hear someone do something complex terribly." Landau went on to praise the "clearness of purpose" in Otis's music, its "unambivalent development of a single thought," and he nominated "Try a Little Tenderness" as "the greatest of all [his] recordings."

Over in England, Otis's former champion Norman Jopling was having none of that. Sounding like a jilted lover, Jopling reviewed *Dictionary of Soul* in the *Record Mirror* as a "cleverly produced album, with Otis continually stuttering and out-of-breath and ever-so-soulful, but somehow it all seems to be a parody of 'Pain in My Heart.'" In Jopling's view, "no one could have done a worse job on a lovely song like 'Try a Little Tenderness.'"

Stax, of course, thought differently, releasing "Try a Little Tenderness" in November as the follow-up single for *Dictionary of Soul*. It went on to become Otis's bestselling ballad since "I've Been Loving You Too Long," rising to #4 in R&B, #25 in Pop, and selling 300,000 copies during the winter of 1967. The Top 40 success of the single helped to spur the sales of the album, which picked up strongly after a sluggish start in the fall.

THE FILLMORE

It was the best gig I ever put on in my entire life. I knew it then.
Otis for three nights at the Fillmore. That was as good as it got.

—BILL GRAHAM (1992)

THE INCENTIVE FOR OTIS TO APPEAR AT BILL GRAHAM'S FILL-more Auditorium in San Francisco came from Bill Graham himself, at a time when Graham and his famous venue were all but unknown to most professionals in the music business. Otis had already performed at the Fillmore during his trip to California with B. B. King in the fall of 1965, when it was still being run as an R&B dance hall in the heart of San Francisco's black entertainment district. Since then, the second-floor auditorium had been taken over by Graham, a failed actor from New York who first rented it in his capacity as business manager of a radical theater company called the San Francisco Mime Troupe. In the fall of 1965, several members of the Mime Troupe were arrested and charged with public obscenity during a performance in a San Francisco park. In response, Graham organized a series of benefits to raise money for their legal defense. The second of these was held at the Fillmore and featured a half dozen local bands, led by the recently formed Jefferson Airplane. Along with similar dance concerts at other venues around town, the Mime Troupe benefits served as coming-out parties for the city's emerging underground arts scene. Soon afterward, Graham began presenting weekend rock shows at the Fillmore on a regular basis (during the week, it still functioned as a black dance hall). By the fall of 1966, Graham's Fillmore was one of three "rock ballrooms" catering to the enthusiasms of a Bay Area music scene that had exploded in the previous year to include scores of local bands.

Bill Graham's personal taste in music tended toward Latin and jazz rather than blues or rock, but he was an aggressive and conscientious promoter, and despite the constant refrain from his more laid-back competitors that he was selling out to commercial interests, he kept his eyes and ears open for acts his patrons would like. "He was always asking us and other musicians, 'Who should I get in here?'" Bob Weir of the Grateful Dead recalled. The early shows at the Fillmore were confined to local bands, but over the course of 1966, Graham began booking groups from outside the Bay Area, including the Velvet Underground from New York and the Paul Butterfield Blues Band from Chicago.

Butterfield's numerous appearances at the Fillmore were a musical awakening for the entire San Francisco scene. Most of the bands that first came to prominence in the Bay Area were composed of former acoustic folk musicians whose world had been rocked by the Beatles and who had then followed the example of Bob Dylan and the Byrds by taking up electric guitars. The Butterfield Blues Band was represented by Dylan's manager, and they had backed Dylan during his electrified debut at the Newport Folk Festival in 1965. But the group itself was more like Chicago's equivalent of Booker T. and the MGs. Paul Butterfield and his guitarists Mike Bloomfield and Elvin Bishop were a trio of well-to-do white boys who had met in and around the University of Chicago and immersed themselves in the blues scene on the city's South Side, acquiring a black rhythm section and a level of proficiency that earned them the respect of local eminences like Muddy Waters and Junior Wells. Bloomfield and Bishop were both superlative guitarists whose dual-lead playing was unprecedented at the time and whose virtuosity moved the group beyond the parameters of standard electric blues. By the time they played the Fillmore, the Butterfield band had added a number of extended, jazzlike improvisations to their repertoire. One of these, a mesmerizing modal vamp called "East-West," provided the instrumental template for an entire genre of acid rock.

In addition to presenting the Butterfield Blues Band at every opportunity, Graham also prevailed on the members of the group for musical advice. "My earliest education I got about the scene came when Paul Butterfield first played for me," he later said, adding, "There was an ultimate musician that everyone wanted to see. Everybody said, '*This* is the guy.'

Otis Redding. He was *it* for everybody that talked to me." On the basis
of these assurances, Graham took the extraordinary step of flying to Atlanta and driving to Macon in order to make his pitch personally to Otis
and Phil Walden. After assuaging Phil's concerns about the mores of his
hippie clientele ("They thought it was, like, voodoo rites out there"), Graham was able to book Otis for three nights in late December. Though it
came out of the blue, this offer was a godsend to Phil, who correctly saw
it as the next logical step for Otis after his breakthrough at the Whisky a
Go Go.

With many local bands lobbying fiercely to open Otis's shows, Graham awarded the first night to the Grateful Dead, the last night to Country Joe and the Fish, and the middle night, hedging his bets, to a black
group from Oakland, Johnny Talbot and De Thangs. He was counting
on drawing a mixture of hippies from the Haight-Ashbury and blacks
from the Fillmore neighborhood. With this in mind, he had two posters
printed. One was designed by the artist Wes Wilson in the neo–Art Nouveau style of psychedelic lettering that was a trademark of the Fillmore;
the other was a conventional placard with a head shot of Otis and red
letters on a baby-blue background advertising The Otis Redding Show.

All three nights were well attended (though not sold out), with a substantial portion of the audience coming, as Graham anticipated, from the
Fillmore district itself. The Haight-Ashbury music community was also
there in force. "To this day," Graham recalled, "no musician ever got *everybody* out to see him the way [Otis] did. Every musician came." These
local luminaries included Janis Joplin, the new lead singer of Big Brother
and the Holding Company, who arrived hours early every night in order
to secure a spot in front of the stage. A former folkie who had set her
sights on becoming a blues singer in the style of Bessie Smith, Joplin idolized Otis and studied his every move, crediting him with showing her
how "to push a song rather than just sliding over it." "Janis wanted to *be*
Otis Redding," her then boyfriend, "Country Joe" MacDonald, recalled.

As for Bill Graham, his enthusiasm knew no bounds. In a memoir
published posthumously in 1992, Graham added two inches to Otis's
height and six additional horn players to his band, describing him as "a
black Adonis" who moved onstage "like a serpent [or] a panther stalking

its prey . . . beautiful and shining, black, sweaty, sensuous, and passionate." Accustomed to presenting hippie bands whose members hunched over their instruments, focusing all their attention on the effort required to play, Graham was particularly impressed by Otis's ability to interact with the crowd:

> There was this woman leaning against the front of the stage. A gorgeous young black lady in a low-cut dress. She started sighing like she just could not hold on. "Otis! Oh! Ah! Ooh!" He saw her. He was going back and forth and he walked across the stage, leaned down and looked at her, and he was a big, good-looking guy, and she was going "Oh! Oh!" And he said, "I'm gonna s-s-*sock* it to you, baby. One, two . . ." And the whole place went *"Hah!"* All together.

"With every passing year," Graham concluded, "those shows get better and better in terms of all the other people I've seen on stage since then . . . [Otis] hasn't been equaled. There's nothing close."

Ralph J. Gleason, the erudite jazz critic who had turned his weekly column in the *San Francisco Chronicle* into a house organ for the Haight-Ashbury music scene, was similarly struck by the sheer eroticism of Otis's performance, if more measured with his praise. "He has created a style of heavily emotional, overtly sexual singing that makes his slow ballads almost orgiastic in performance. . . . Redding is a handsome, athletic-looking guy who strikes me as a descendant of the Ray Charles 'What'd I Say' school with some touches of Harry Belafonte and James Brown," Gleason wrote in his review of the Fillmore shows. "He is a highly successful performer, oozing sex and swinging like mad and shouting the current call-to-arms 'sock it to me baby' with a certain lack of variation. His band is adequate but not outstanding."

Graham's and Gleason's descriptions of Otis's physical presence and sexual allure reflect how novel the sight and sound of an "overtly" eroticized black male singer was to most white audiences in 1966. Black female singers and dancers, of course, had been performing in an eroticized manner in front of white audiences since the birth of the blues (if not the birth of the nation). But black male singers had historically been subject to the same taboos and sanctions against expressing themselves sexually in the presence of whites that applied to all black men. Black rock 'n' roll stars of the 1950s like Chuck Berry and Little Richard had performed on-stage in a suggestive manner—and, in Berry's case, had paid a heavy price for doing so. But guitarists and piano players have a different sort of stage presence than lead singers, whose only prop is a microphone. Of the black male singers who achieved significant crossover success in the early 1960s, Sam Cooke was the soul of willowy nonchalance, the Motown groups were scrupulously regimented in their movements, and the triumvirate of Jackie Wilson, James Brown, and Joe Tex were all virtuosic dancers who channeled their sexuality into stylized movement and acrobatic exertion. Otis was another story. His lack of physical grace combined with his size, his good looks, and his obvious pleasure at being onstage to lend a more natural, unscripted, and unrefined sexual charge to his performances that amplified the intense emotionality of his ballad singing and the playful-ness of his uptempo songs.

Like his dates at the Whisky in the spring, Otis's appearances at the Fillmore exposed him to a world apart from his contemporaries in R&B. While top black stars like James Brown and Ray Charles continued to climb the ladder of conventional show business success—in Brown's case, by graduating to arena-sized venues like Madison Square Garden and prime-time outlets like the *Ed Sullivan Show*; in Charles's case, by staging a well-orchestrated comeback from his drug bust that included a major feature in *Life* magazine and a seventeen-page tribute in *Billboard* titled "A Touch of Genius"—Otis was generating the sort of word-of-mouth publicity, amplified by a growing network of alternative newspapers and FM radio stations, that fueled the underground music scenes forming across the country.

In particular, the rapid expansion of FM radio during the second half of the 1960s would have a revolutionary impact on the listening and record-buying habits of young Americans. Spurred by a 1965 FCC ruling that required jointly owned AM and FM stations to differentiate their programming, the free-form FM format took root in the Bay Area in 1966 and spread quickly to major markets across the county. Staffed, in many cases, by nonprofessional music fans, these new FM stations broadcast an eclectic mix of rock, pop, folk, blues, and R&B, much of it in album form, all of it enhanced by a much clearer audio signal than was possible on the AM band. They encouraged a resurgence of the pre–Top 40, deejay-programmed format that had spawned the rise of rhythm and blues and rock 'n' roll in the first place, and they played a role in promoting a sense of community and commonality among their listeners that was analogous, in many ways, to the advent of black-appeal radio in the 1950s. Though the great majority of underground FM deejays were white, many of them exhibited a palpable reverence for black music, and they defined their distance from the Top 40 mainstream by featuring black artists like Otis, whose recorded output (unlike that of the Motown groups) fit with the medium's album-oriented format.

KING & QUEEN

I had never experienced so much feeling coming out of one
human being.

—ROGER HAWKINS on Aretha Franklin

N JANUARY 1967, OTIS SPENT A WEEK IN NEW YORK, WHERE HE AND
Phil Walden attended Jerry Wexler's fiftieth-birthday party at the St.
Regis Hotel and met with Wexler and Ahmet Ertegun to discuss the
direction of his recording career. (Otis had taken to calling Ertegun
"Omelet"—a nickname that Wexler insisted was facetious and Ertegun
insisted was not.) "Otis was never cocky about his material," Wexler recalled of this meeting. "He was always reevaluating and reassessing himself, and he was always concerned about his material and his recorded
sound. He wanted to know if it was contemporaneous, whether it was
changing fast enough, whether it was a happening sound, whether his
songs were good." It was not lost on Otis that most of the big crossover
hits of the previous year, from the Four Tops' "Reach Out, I'll Be There"
to Percy Sledge's "When a Man Loves a Woman" to Aaron Neville's recent smash "Tell It Like It Is," had stronger lyric content than anything
he had written on his own. At long last, his insistence that words didn't
matter was yielding to his frustration at seeing the work of other, less
dynamic R&B singers high on the *Billboard* Pop charts. In addition to
encouraging Otis to focus more on his lyric writing, Wexler and Ertegun
suggested that he think about varying the instrumentation on his records,
supplementing the tried-and-true Stax formula of guitar, keyboards, and
horns.

Another topic of conversation in the meeting at Atlantic was Otis's
ambition to follow in Sam Cooke's footsteps by producing other artists.
Jotis, the independent label he had founded with Joe Galkin, had lain

fallow after its first spate of releases in 1965, but Otis and Galkin still had the young singer Arthur Conley under contract. In 1966, they had turned Conley over to Rick Hall in Muscle Shoals, where he recorded a ballad called "Take Me (Just As I Am)" and a Motown imitation called "I Can't Stop (No No No)." Both records were released on Hall's Atlantic-distributed Fame label, and both of them had gotten lost in the excitement surrounding the overnight success of Percy Sledge. At their meeting in New York, Wexler and Ertegun offered to purchase Conley's contract, sign him to Atlantic, and bankroll a session, with Otis producing, at Fame in Muscle Shoals. Having heard from Tom Dowd about Otis's commanding presence in the studio, they had few doubts about his ability to produce. In addition, Wexler thought it might broaden Otis's own musical horizons if he were to gain some experience working in a first-rate studio other than Stax.

A few weeks later, Arthur Conley returned to Fame, accompanied by Otis and his touring band. Like Otis in his early days, Conley was a singer who could imitate anyone, and one of the things he shared with Otis was a love of Sam Cooke. This led them to revive an album track that Cooke had recorded in 1964 called "Yeah Man." Begging the rhetorical question "Do you like good music?," Cooke's song cataloged a series of contemporary dance crazes—the Monkey, the Watusi, and the Swim—against an insistent refrain of "yeah man, yeah man." Otis and Conley retitled the song "Sweet Soul Music"—"Do you like good music? *(Yeah, man)* That sweet *soul* music"—and rewrote the verses to pay homage to an honor roll of contemporary soul stars that included Lou Rawls, Sam and Dave, Wilson Pickett, Otis himself, and James Brown (duly lauded as "the king of them all, y'all"). Working with the horn section from his band, Otis embellished the arrangement of Cooke's original with a booming riff taken from the theme of the 1960 Hollywood western *The Magnificent Seven,* which had since been adopted by Marlboro cigarettes for a national advertising campaign. For the flip side of the single, Otis and Conley chose "Let's Go Steady Again," the Sam Cooke B-side that Otis had appropriated for "That's What My Heart Needs." Delighted with the way the record turned out, Otis personally delivered the tapes of "Sweet Soul Music" to Atlantic in New York. While he was there, he sat in with

Booker T. and the MGs at a benefit concert at Hunter College. It was the first time he had performed with the MGs outside of the studio, and it only whetted his appetite for their upcoming European tour.

WITH JERRY WEXLER, every story seemed to start with a phone call. In the fall of 1966, Wexler was producing a late-night recording session with Wilson Pickett at Fame, where Pickett, the story goes, was picking a fight with Percy Sledge, who had inadvertently offended him by suggesting that he sounded like a combination of Otis Redding (whom Pickett admired) and James Brown (whom he despised). In the midst of the altercation, the phone rang. It was Wexler's wife, relaying a message from Louise Bishop, a deejay at WDAS in Philadelphia. Despite the late hour, Wexler called Bishop back immediately. "Aretha's ready for you," she said.

As a connoisseur of great voices, Wexler had been following Aretha Franklin's career since she signed with Columbia Records in 1960 at the tender age of eighteen. The Rev. C. L. Franklin had personally chosen Columbia for his daughter's secular debut on account of the label's mainstream orientation. With John Hammond producing, the early recordings Aretha made there had been cast in the soul-jazz mold, and they retained enough gospel grit to yield a number of R&B hits. But Columbia wasn't interested in R&B hits, and from 1962 onward, the label assigned Aretha to a succession of staff producers who sought to remodel her into an uncertain mixture of Dinah Washington and Barbra Streisand. Some of her recordings of pop standards and show tunes showed flashes of brilliance—the gospel historian Anthony Heilbut credits her with being "the first gospel star to switch fields without switching styles"—but Aretha was no chanteuse, and as time went on, the record-buying public didn't know what to make of her. Her album sales languished, and when the option year on her contract expired in 1966, Columbia had had enough.

A patrician WASP from New York with an ecumenical passion for gospel, jazz, and blues, John Hammond was one of Jerry Wexler's heroes in the record business, and Wexler jumped at the chance to succeed where Hammond had failed. But after signing Aretha to Atlantic in December 1966 on the basis of a $25,000 advance, his first impulse was not to produce her himself. Instead, aware that Aretha had been born in Memphis, where her father began his career, Wexler's first impulse was to offer her to Jim Stewart under the same terms that applied to Sam and Dave. The only difference, in light of the windfall Stax was reaping on its recent bounty of hits by Sam and Dave, Carla Thomas, and Eddie Floyd, was that Wexler wanted Stax to assume the cost of Aretha's advance. It did not take long for the parsimonious Stewart to make up his mind. "She's great," he told Wexler. "I just don't see her recording in this environment." In his memoir, Wexler's comment on Stewart's decision was "Thank you, Jesus." "Looking back," he added, "I can see that turning her over to Stewart would have been a colossal mistake."

It would be easy to see Jim Stewart's decision to pass on Aretha Franklin as yet another example of his chronic inability to think outside the tight little box he had built on McLemore Avenue. And the prospect of Otis Redding and Aretha Franklin recording for the same label would have been something to behold. But Stewart was probably right that Stax was the wrong "environment" for Aretha. Wexler's plan for succeeding where Columbia had failed was based on his conviction that Aretha was not only a great singer but also an exceptional pianist and head arranger whose musical talent was in many ways comparable to that of Ray Charles. Convinced that she had been fatally overproduced at Columbia, he wanted to grant her the sort of autonomy in the studio that Atlantic had afforded Charles. Whether Stax could have accommodated Aretha in this way was an open question, but it was exactly the sort of approach that Jim Stewart and his musicians had bristled at with artists like Wilson Pickett and Don Covay. Added to this was the fact that, apart from Carla Thomas, who was practically a mascot there, Stax had a dearth of experience in working with female singers, much less in deferring to them in the way Wexler had in mind.

Once he resolved, by default, to produce Aretha himself, Wexler, with Tom Dowd in tow, wasted little time in bringing her to Rick Hall's Fame Studio in Muscle Shoals. Aretha arrived there in January 1967, accompanied by her husband and manager, Ted White. Her one and only session at Fame began with Aretha and the band struggling to find a groove, reached a rapturous peak of inspiration on a song called "I Never Loved a

Man (The Way I Love You)," and ended in disaster when Ted White got into a pair of racially charged confrontations, first with one of the white trumpet players on the session, and later with a drunken Rick Hall. (In an inadvertent demonstration of just how ingrained the "traditions" of southern racism could be, Dan Penn, who went on to write several songs for Aretha, said of the trumpet player, "I always heard that he patted her on the butt or something. And what would have been wrong with that, anyway?") Aretha left in a hurry the following day. Wexler also left, furious with Rick Hall, embarrassed and appalled at the way things had turned out.

Back in New York, listening to the tape of "I Never Loved a Man," Wexler confirmed his initial impression that the song was a sure-fire hit, but he lacked the B-side he needed to release it as a single. On the pretext of hiring them to play on an album date with King Curtis, he managed to lure the Muscle Shoals rhythm section to New York, where he reunited them with Aretha and recorded enough material to fill both sides of an LP. Among the songs they cut were a Chips Moman–Dan Penn composition called "Do Right Woman, Do Right Man," Ray Charles's classic "Drown in My Own Tears," a divinely gospelized rendition of Sam Cooke's "A Change Is Gonna Come," and the version of Otis's "Respect" that Aretha had been refining in her live performances over the course of the previous year.

Though Aretha Franklin had made ten albums during her six years at Columbia, the release of the single "I Never Loved a Man (The Way I Love You)" in February 1967 marked one of the great debuts in the history of American popular music. Over the halting, two-steps-forward-and-one-step-back cadence of an electric piano, the song began, "You're no good, heartbreaker / You're a liar, and a cheat," delivered with a chilling conviction by the greatest African American singer of her generation. As had been the case with Ray Charles, Elvis Presley, Sam Cooke, and the Beatles before her, the record-buying public knew exactly what it was hearing, and purchased 250,000 copies of the single during its first two weeks in release. In the time it took for the record to rise to the top of the R&B charts (where it remained for the next two months), Atlantic received an additional 200,000 advance orders for the album it was scrambling to press and ship to stores.

In addition to the $25,000 advance, another factor that influenced Jim Stewart's decision to deny Stax the services of Aretha Franklin was Stewart's almost fatherly affection for Carla Thomas. Thomas's recording of "Gee Whiz" had put Satellite Records on the map in 1961, and she had practically grown up at Stax under Stewart's admiring eye. Like Booker Jones, Thomas had resisted the allure of a full-time professional career in order to pursue her education, first at Tennessee State in Nashville, and then at Howard University in Washington, where she would earn a master's in drama in 1966. Returning to Memphis on school breaks and summer vacations, she had recorded more than a dozen singles during her college years. Some were solo ballads, others were duets with her father, Rufus, that pitted his raucous shout against her girlish croon. But with the exception of a 1962 cover of Sam Cooke's "Bring It On Home to Me," none of her subsequent records sold in any great numbers until she began working with the team of Isaac Hayes and Dave Porter, whose production of "B-A-B-Y" yielded a solid crossover hit in the summer of 1966.

Eager to build on this success, Jim Stewart came up with the idea of recording another duet with Carla, this time with Otis in place of her father. Motown had been successful at pairing Marvin Gaye with several of its female stars, beginning with Mary Wells in 1964 and more recently with Kim Weston on an album whose exhilarating title track, "It Takes Two," was crossing over onto the Pop Top 20 in January 1967. Yet when Stewart first broached the idea of a duet with Otis and Carla, neither of them showed much enthusiasm until someone, possibly Stewart, possibly Otis, suggested that they try covering a current hit by the bluesman Lowell Fulson, who had just ended a ten-year hiatus from the record charts with a novelty single called "Tramp."

The combination of Otis, Carla, and "Tramp" may have been Jim Stewart's greatest stroke of inspiration. Fulson's record was a chip-on-the-shoulder monologue ("You can call me tramp . . . you can call me country") whose spoken-word verses extolled his down-home roots. By playing up their established musical personalities of Lover Man and Daddy's Girl,

Otis and Carla brought an odd-couple flavor of romantic comedy to the song. They begin their bickering over the naked thump and thwack of Al Jackson's backbeat, with Carla's accusation (*"Tramp!"*) and Otis's indignant response (*"What'd you call me?"*). The band comes in around them as Otis reveals the root of his self-esteem: "There's one doggone thing that I know, one thing that makes me feel good: I'm a lover!" "Matter of opinion," Carla mutters, before taking direct aim at his social origins. "You know what, Otis? (*What?*) / You're country (*That's all right*) / You're straight from the Georgia woods (*That's good!*)" The effect is both endearing and revealing as they wrestle over the fine distinctions of social class and style, with Otis deflecting Carla's carping about his lack of ready cash ("I got six Cadillacs, five Lincolns, fo' Fords") and his inability to provide her with all the "meats and seafood" she likes. "I can buy you meats, rats, frogs, squirrels, rabbits—anything you want, woman," he assures her. "You need a *haircut*," she replies.

The comic timing on "Tramp" was such a delight that Jim Stewart suggested Otis and Carla record a "concept" album of duets, to be titled *King & Queen*. The flaw in this concept, it turned out, was that all the romantic chemistry between them on "Tramp" had been spoken, not sung. When the two of them tried to sing together, the results were much less delightful. Though Carla had been recording professionally since 1961, she was a small-voiced singer in the Diana Ross mold who struggled with her intonation and often required repeated takes before a good performance could be coaxed out of her. Otis was just the opposite, and his singing suffered as he grew impatient with the need to repeat each song time and time again. ("That's the most non-singing bitch I ever worked with," he complained to Alan Walden.) After they had struggled their way through a handful of tracks, it was decided to have Otis record his vocals on the rest and have Carla overdub her parts afterward, taking the time she needed to get it right. This made *King & Queen* the first album ever recorded at Stax that relied extensively on the four-track capacity that Tom Dowd had installed in the studio eighteen months before.

A few days after he completed the sessions for *King & Queen*, Otis sat down with Jim Delehant, the young editor of the venerable fan magazine *Hit Parader*, for the first substantial interview of his career. Years before the advent of a viable rock press, Delehant had turned *Hit Parader* into one of the very few print journals in America that covered the world of R&B with any range and depth, publishing interviews with prominent black artists such as T-Bone Walker, Muddy Waters, Joe Tex, and many others. Otis began by telling Delehant how much he had enjoyed his tour of Britain and France and how pleased he was with *King & Queen*, though he did complain that his voice was hoarse from working on the album. He went on to talk about his musical upbringing in Macon and his eventual discovery at Stax. Asked why he thought white blues performers were so much more successful than their black counterparts, Otis answered matter-of-factly, "Because the white population is much larger than the colored." He then went out of his way to express his admiration for rock groups like the Beatles and the Stones. "I like what these white rock 'n' roll kids are doing. Sometimes they take things from us, but I take things from them, too—the things that are beautiful, and they do a lot of beautiful things."

Elaborating on the difference between rock 'n' roll and rhythm and blues, he offered the readers of *Hit Parader* a music lesson. "Everybody thinks that all songs by colored people are rhythm & blues but that's not true," he said. "Johnny Taylor, Muddy Waters, and B. B. King are blues singers. James Brown is not a blues singer. He has a rock 'n' roll beat and he can sing slow pop songs. My own songs 'Respect' and 'Mr. Pitiful' aren't blues songs. I'm speaking in terms of the beat and structure of the music. A blues is a song that goes twelve bars all the way through. Most of my songs are soul songs.

"If you want to be a singer," he continued, "you've got to concentrate on it twenty-four hours a day. Always think different from the next person. Don't ever do a song as you heard somebody else do it." Asked about his future in the music business, Otis predicted, "Five years from now, I know the kids are going to be tired of my singing. If I can keep a good mind with the help of the good Lord, I'm gonna keep producing records."

Otis was back on tour by the end of January, playing twenty-one dates in twenty-five days on a package that included the Marvelettes, James and Bobby Purify, and Aaron Neville. The bill was a big draw, for in addition to Otis's current success with "Try a Little Tenderness," all three of his costars were coming off major crossover hits. After making their name as Motown's original girl group with "Please Mr. Postman" in 1961, the Marvelettes had returned to the Pop Top 10 in 1966 with Smokey Robinson's "Don't Mess with Bill." James and Bobby Purify were a pair of flash-in-the-pan singers whose "I'm Your Puppet" became a #1 R&B hit for Rick Hall's Fame label in the fall of 1966. And Aaron Neville's tremulous ballad "Tell It Like It Is" was a million-selling single that inaugurated his long and varied career as a fixture in the world of New Orleans R&B.

Otis's winter tour was booked by the Associated Booking Corporation (ABC), a talent agency founded and run by Joe Glaser, the former Chicago mobster whose relentless management of Louis Armstrong had served since the 1930s as a paradigm for the paternalistic relationship between blacks and Jews in the music business. "Be sure and get yourself a white man that will put his hand on your shoulder and say, 'This is my nigger,'" Armstrong was advised when he first left New Orleans for Chicago in 1922 to join King Oliver's band. Glaser turned out to be that man, and he went on to parlay his underworld connections and his reputation as Armstrong's manager into the creation of one of the largest talent agencies in the country. Now in his late sixties, a figure of epic vulgarity, Glaser was a contemporary and crony of Joe Galkin, who had prevailed on him in 1963 for help in getting the Walden agency accredited by the American Guild of Variety Artists (AGVA)—a matter that Glaser resolved with a quick phone call. With Galkin's encouragement, the Waldens were turning to him now in the hope that Glaser's fearsome reputation would scare off Don Soviero in their ongoing dispute with Shaw Artists, whose contact with Otis was due to expire in February 1967. Unimpressed by the lurid rumors of what befell people who got in Glaser's way, Soviero responded by filing a half-million-dollar lawsuit against Associated Booking and a formal complaint with AGVA "for interfering with SAC's exclusive representation of Otis Redding."

In the middle of February, during a two-day break in the tour, Otis returned to Stax to record a haunting new ballad called "I Love You More than Words Can Say" for release as his next single. The song was written by Eddie Floyd and Booker Jones, and while Floyd's lyric was as simplistic as anything Otis had ever recorded, Jones's chromatic changes gave the song an unexpected twist. In keeping with Jerry Wexler's suggestion that he expand his instrumental palette, Otis had Jones write and overdub a string arrangement that blended seamlessly with Steve Cropper's prominent guitar arpeggios. Otis sang the song beautifully, his voice wavering with perfectly controlled emotion in long, melismatic passages that added new shades of meaning to the things that words can't say.

The flip side of the single was a collaboration between Otis and Booker Jones called "Let Me Come on Home," whose rolling backbeat and contrapuntal horns echoed the sound that Allen Toussaint achieved on Lee Dorsey's 1966 hit "Get Out of My Life, Woman." But the instrumental highlights of "Let Me Come on Home" are Duck Dunn's furrowing bass line and Steve Cropper's stinging, sawing fills. The MGs had just recorded an album with blues guitarist Albert King, a new Stax signing whose barbed tone and quirky bent-note style (like Johnny Jenkins, he played the guitar left-handed and upside down) seem to have rubbed off on Cropper.

Otis also recorded a half dozen cover tunes in the course of this February session, all of them drawn from the not-so-recent past, including relics such as Little Richard's "Slippin' and Slidin'," Ray Charles's "Tell the Truth," Paul Williams's "The Hucklebuck," and a pair of Tin Pan Alley standards—Irving Berlin's "White Christmas" and a ballad version of Billy Hart's "The Glory of Love," a top-selling record for the Benny Goodman Band in 1936 that was arranged in a manner similar to that of "Try a Little Tenderness."

In addition, at the request of Al Bell, Otis recorded a public service announcement for the US Department of Labor's Stay in School campaign, an outreach program directed at inner-city youth. The campaign had begun the year before, when Vice President Hubert Humphrey rewarded James Brown for his hit single "Don't Be a Dropout" by naming him as the honorary chairman of the initiative. Not to be outdone, Al Bell had committed Stax to producing an entire album of songs and testimonials by a half dozen of its top artists for distribution to radio stations across the country. (Bell also replaced the *Soulsville USA* sign on McLemore Avenue with the slogan *Stay in School,* which had to be taken down when kids from the neighborhood began throwing rocks at the marquee.) Otis's contribution to the campaign was written for him by Deanie Parker as a play on the theme of "Tramp." "Hi, this is the Big O, Otis Redding," he announced at the start of an awkward ditty that advised, "If you didn't go back to school this year / You're really not groovin' / Maybe you feel that school is a drag / But did you ever think how about square you'd look / Standing in an employment line because school didn't interest you? / You really ought to think about it / Without an education you could only be a tramp—brogan shoes, no haircut, just plain old country . . ."

HIT THE ROAD, STAX

I guess you could call me the father-figure of the show.

—OTIS REDDING

Otis's winter tour ended in late February, leaving him with several weeks before he was due to fly to Europe with the Stax-Volt Revue. In preparation, he dissolved the road band he had maintained for the past three years. Of the twenty-man entourage of musicians and supporting acts, only his road manager, Speedo Sims, and his valet, Wee Coates, remained on Otis's payroll, assigned to do yard work on his ranch. Several of his best sidemen, including Woody Woodson and Bobby Holloway, quickly signed on with Wilson Pickett's band.

In the meantime, Otis and Phil Walden had decided to replace Percy Sledge on the European tour with Arthur Conley, whose single of "Sweet Soul Music" had just been released by Atlantic. "When a Man Loves a Woman" had been an enormous hit in Britain, but Sledge's last single, "It Tears Me Up," had failed to make the charts there despite a strong US showing, and Otis wanted to promote his protégé, who was in any case a much more dynamic stage performer than Sledge. The official reason given for Sledge's withdrawal was that he had scheduling conflicts in the States, but considering that he was managed and booked by the Waldens, this scarcely made any sense.

Otis and Phil flew to London the week before the rest of the tour to make final preparations with Frank Fenter and Arthur Howes and to do some advance publicity, in the course of which Otis sang, backed by a straight-laced studio band, on a popular Sunday-night talk show hosted by Eamonn Andrews. The next morning, Otis went out to Heathrow Airport to greet the arrival of the tour. After clearing immigration, the entire Stax troupe was thrilled to be met by a fleet of Bentley limousines that Brian Epstein had dispatched as a gesture of hospitality on behalf of the Beatles. It was the beginning of a reception that none of them, with the exception of Otis, could possibly have anticipated.

The first two days in London were devoted to press events and intensive rehearsals. Though the MGs and the Mar-Keys had played on nearly every Stax recording, they had performed very little of this material live, and in many cases, they had long since forgotten the parts they played on the records. This was particularly true of the horn men, who had never worked from charts and had to reconstruct their lines from memory and intuition. Booker Jones had played piano on most of the Stax recordings, but he was confined to the Hammond organ on the tour, which required him to work out suitable variations for his original keyboard parts.

In addition to the thirteen performers—Otis, Sam and Dave, Arthur Conley, Eddie Floyd, the four MGs, the three Mar-Keys, and Carla Thomas for the first few shows—a whole coterie of people from Atlantic and Stax made the trip as well. Phil Walden was there in his capacity as Otis's manager and the promoter of the tour. Jerry Wexler and Jim Stewart were there to officiate. Tom Dowd was there to make live recordings of the opening concerts in London and Paris for rapid release in Britain and France. Al Bell was there to consult with Frank Fenter about promoting Stax in Europe; Bell also emceed at some of the shows. Joe Galkin was there, as always, to keep tabs on his investment in Otis Redding. Most of these auxiliaries were present along with the performers for a press reception at the Speakeasy, a popular London nightclub, where Otis once again found himself in the unfamiliar position of being taken seriously by members of the mainstream media. "Do you think rhythm and blues is drifting more and more toward rock 'n' roll, so to say?" asked a reporter from the BBC. "I think rock 'n' roll is drifting toward the blues," Otis replied. "People don't want to admit it, but a lot of the pop songs today are nothing but blues songs. Rhythm and blues has been here for a hundred years."

Officially billed as the Stax-Volt Revue, promoted in Britain as "Hit the Road Stax" (Frank Fenter's play on Ray Charles's "Hit the Road Jack"), and mistakenly advertised in some venues as The Otis Redding Show, the tour opened on a Friday night with two shows at the Finsbury

The Stax/Volt tour of Europe *(left to right)*: Tom Dowd, Otis, Sam Moore, Jim Stewart, Dave Prater, Jerry Wexler

Park Astoria, a 3,000-seat, Moorish-themed, Depression-era picture palace in North London, best known in pop circles as the site of a two-week Christmas show by the Beatles that sold 100,000 tickets at the height of Beatlemania in 1963. The concerts were emceed by Emperor Rosko, a popular deejay on Britain's offshore "pirate" station Radio Caroline. A native of Los Angeles, Rosko's introductions, delivered in a Mid-Atlantic accent suggestive of Austin Powers, relied heavily on the American cheerleading practice of spelling out the names of one's heroes ("Gimme an O, gimme a T . . ."). Booker T. and the MGs opened the show with a trio of instrumentals that culminated in "Green Onions"; they were then joined by the Mar-Keys for "Last Night" and their new single "Philly Dog." Next came Arthur Conley, a diminutive beanpole of a man, who elaborated on the principle of "Sweet Soul Music" by accompanying soul standards like "In the Midnight Hour" with his dead-on impersonations of the stars who sang them. Then Carla Thomas emerged in a gold-lamé gown to close the first half of the show with a set that included "B-A-B-Y" and her rendition of the Beatles' hit "Yesterday." After a brief intermission, the second part of the program began with a tiresome performance from Eddie Floyd that provided the perfect foil for Sam and Dave, who held the stage with an unbridled intensity that left the audience stunned. Despite their recent ascendancy as Stax's top-selling singles act, the pair were largely unknown in Britain, where their records had failed to make the charts, and they were by far the biggest and best surprise of the tour.

It was during Sam and Dave's sweat-drenched set that the singular nature of the Stax-Volt Revue first became apparent. Until now, the sound of Stax, like that of Motown, had been a product of the recording studio. The music had been made on record by artists like Otis Redding and Sam and Dave, who then reproduced it with their road bands in the live performances that formed the lifeblood of their careers. This was something quite different from the creative process of artists like Ray Charles and James Brown, who wrote, rehearsed, and recorded their songs with their own bands, often reproducing on record what they had already been performing live. The Stax-Volt Revue was the first time the label's top-tier artists had ever performed their songs outside of the studio with the backing of the musicians who played on their records. And the effect was overwhelming, because in live performance, this sleek, seven-piece ensemble showed itself to be nothing less than the best soul band in the world, exuding a power and majesty the likes of which had never been heard in public before.

Otis followed Sam and Dave at the Finsbury Park Astoria, as he would on every night of the tour, bolting onto the stage as the band launched into the stately stomp of "Respect," the horns sounding their fanfare behind his assurance, *"What* you want / Honey you *got* it!" His seven-song, thirty-minute set was designed with his British listeners in mind. It featured an affecting version of his UK hit "My Girl" that cascaded seamlessly into "Shake," with Al Jackson's drums exploding like firecrackers, the brass blaring on the offbeats, and the crowd bellowing the song title in response to Otis's command. This was followed by the Beatles' "Day Tripper," a sing-along on "Fa-Fa-Fa-Fa-Fa (Sad Song)," which took on a whole new character as an audience-participation number, and a scorch-

ing version of the Stones' "(I Can't Get No) Satisfaction" that Otis dedicated to Mick Jagger, who attended the show. The set ended with "Try
a Little Tenderness," to which Otis amended a series of false endings,
walking offstage as Emperor Rosko shouted his name, returning to sing
another chorus, repeating his exit and entry, until he was joined for one
last gasp of "Tenderness" by the other members of the revue.

To judge by the accounts in the music press, the response of the London audience was ecstatic—too much so for many British soul aficiona-
dos, whose sense of connoisseurship was threatened by the specter of mass
acceptance. Reviewing the concert for the *Record Mirror,* Norman Jopling
once again took Otis to task for the commercialization of his repertoire.
"To anyone who isn't a Redding fanatic the whole thing must have exploded the soul myth," he wrote. "I would rather have seen him sit at a
piano and sing 'I've Been Loving You Too Long' than attempt any number
of Rolling Stones, Temptations, or Frank Sinatra numbers." In the pious
pages of *Soul Music Monthly,* Bill Millar criticized the crowd for their
undiscerning enthusiasm and praised Sam and Dave to the skies ("God
bless Sam and Dave for reminding us what soul music is really about").
Where Otis was concerned, Millar repeated verbatim several paragraphs
from his review of the Tiles show in September, once again praising Otis
for his "remarkable sense of rhythm" and once again concluding, "I feel
compelled to say that Otis is overrated. His reputation puts him amongst
the top bracket of rhythm and blues artists, but, strictly as a performer, he
does not come within sight of Solomon Burke or James Brown, and any
exciting Little Richard influence he might once have had has long since
vanished."

In typical Stax fashion, the decision to record the show at the Finsbury
Park Astoria was barely thought out in advance. Given the limited time
for rehearsal and the pressure of opening night, there was every reason to
think that the performances would get markedly better as the tour progressed. As it was, Tom Dowd had to scramble to find suitable remote
recording equipment in London; he wound up patching together a pair
of borrowed three-track tape decks and setting up a makeshift mixing
board in the wings of the theater. The rush to record was prompted by
Stax's unrealistic desire to release a live album in Britain before the end

of the tour, and by Jim Stewart's insistence that Carla Thomas be repre-
sented on it. As a favor to his friend Jesse Jackson, Al Bell had committed
Thomas to perform at a benefit for Jackson's Operation Breadbasket in
Chicago in the third week of March. This meant that she was available
only for the concerts in London and Paris. As a consolation, Frank Fenter
had arranged for Thomas to perform a showcase with Booker T. and the
MGs at a private club in Soho called the Bag O'Nails, where Paul Mc-
Cartney stopped by to pay his respects. McCartney and his fellow Beatles
had been sequestered at EMI's Abbey Road Studios since the middle of
January, recording tracks for their upcoming album, *Sgt. Pepper's Lonely
Hearts Club Band*.

With opening night behind them, the revue went on to perform at a
London club called Billy Walker's Upper Cut, owned by a playboy boxer,
where the more intimate surroundings helped the band and the singers
to gel. The next day, the troupe flew to Paris for two nights at the Olympia Theatre. Tom Dowd found the recording facilities at the Olympia a
great improvement over those of the London Astoria, and the recordings he made there captured the performers hitting their stride. In Paris,
Otis expanded his set to include enough material for a live album of his
own, adding "I Can't Turn You Loose" and "I've Been Loving You Too
Long." The substitution of Booker Jones's organ helped to transform both
of these songs, lending a "can-can" flavor to the groove of "I Can't Turn
You Loose" and a sense of cathedral space to "I've Been Loving You Too
Long."

Having never backed Otis live (apart from the impromptu Hunter
College gig in January), the Stax band was unfamiliar with the practice
he had employed since his dates at the Whisky a Go Go of accelerat-
ing his uptempo songs. Drummer Al Jackson had a metronomic sense
of time, and in the studio he specialized in setting tempos that were
slightly slower than expected. Otis made it clear what he wanted. "We're
not going to let those songs just lie there onstage," he told the band. But
on the opening night of the tour, Jim Stewart objected to this and spoke
with Jackson about it, prevailing on him to hold the tempos down. This
back-channel communication infuriated Otis, who had angry words with
Jackson at several of the early shows. As far as he was concerned, the

MGs were *his* band when they played behind him, and he didn't want Jim Stewart meddling with his music in any way. At the Olympia, Stewart burst into Otis's dressing room after the first show complaining about the way he was speeding up the songs. "We're trying to make a recording here," he told Otis. Otis responded by showing a side of his personality that Stewart had never seen before, picking him up by his shirt collar and telling him in as many words to go fuck himself. "These people are fans of mine and I'm going to entertain them," he said.

From Paris the troupe returned to Britain for a string of one-night stands. Traveling by bus, they began in the North of England with shows in Leeds, Manchester, Leicester, and Liverpool. In Leicester the fans rushed the stage; in Liverpool they pulled Otis into the crowd. Next came dates in Croyden and Bristol, followed by a long drive to Glasgow and a return flight to London for a concert at the Roundhouse, a cavernous Victorian-era railroad shed that had been converted into a showcase of the city's psychedelic "underground" ("clearly an imperfect term for a phenomenon nine-tenths above ground and acutely publicity-conscious," noted the journalist Peter Fryer). After another swing through Lancashire and Wales, the troupe flew to Copenhagen for the first of three dates in Scandinavia.

"You don't know what it's like for a bunch of kids from a small southern city who have never done anything or been anywhere and someone says you're going to get to go to Europe, all over Europe," the trumpeter Wayne Jackson recalled. For the Memphis musicians especially, the Stax-Volt Tour was like a chapter out of *The Innocents Abroad*. None of the performers apart from Otis had ever been overseas, and they did their best to live up to the prevailing stereotype of the American tourist in Europe. They reveled in their lack of cultural sophistication and photographed everything they saw ("I was taking pictures of *clouds*," recalled the sax player Andrew Love). Wherever they went, they complained about the food and the lack of central heating. They gawked at forms of architecture they had seen only in pictures, and on the Continent, they shook their heads in wonder at the sound of people speaking strange languages. (Having determined that a cabdriver in Stockholm couldn't understand a word they said, Sam Moore and Dave Prater spent the ride telling the man he was the dumbest motherfucker they'd ever seen. When they reached their destination, the cabbie calmly informed them to "walk down this alley here and into the second door on your right.") Through it all, Tom Dowd served as their personable tour guide, advising them on the fine points of local culture and cuisine.

Most of all, as Dowd recalled, "They were amazed by the intensity of some of the crowds, overwhelmed." The fans in Britain especially had revered R&B with a cultlike intensity from afar, and they were informed about it in a way that fans in America, black or white, were not. Memphis to them was a city steeped in musical romance: the legendary Home of the Blues. Their enjoyment of the records that came from there was imbued with a sense of personal discovery, and they had read up on the musicians themselves. In addition to the headliners, Steve Cropper was singled out for special attention by the British music press. Lanky and impassive on stage, Cropper had a Marlboro Man demeanor that fit the English notion of how an American from the heartland should look, and British pop stars like Keith Richards of the Stones and Pete Townshend of the Who had made no secret of their admiration for his spare, exceptionally artful guitar playing. At many of the shows, the billing for Booker T. and the MGs included the tagline *Featuring the Fantastic Guitar of Steve Cropper.*

Befitting a company founded by a pair of siblings, people at Stax often spoke of themselves as a "family." And, as with many families when they leave home and go on vacation in an unfamiliar place, it didn't take long for the underlying strains to show. By this time, Al Bell's success as a promo man had dazzled his colleagues at the label, no one more than Jim Stewart, who had been ceding increasing amounts of control and responsibility to Bell. Over the preceding year, Bell had gradually marginalized Estelle Axton's role in the company by playing on Stewart's long-standing resentment of his sister's popularity. Now, in Britain, he set his sights on Steve Cropper, who had served for years as Jim Stewart's right-hand man. Summoning the Stax contingent (minus the headliners) to a meeting in his hotel room, Bell seized on the inordinate attention being paid to Cropper, accusing the MGs' guitarist of getting a big head, dressing him down in front of his band mates, and threatening to quit his job unless he was given authority over Cropper in his role as director of A&R. It was a stunning coup that permanently altered the balance of power at Stax. "Some things were said," Cropper recalled. "There were bad feelings that I never, ever got over. All of a sudden, I wasn't A&R director anymore."

In Cropper's view, the whole psychology of the tour marked the beginning of the end at the label. "Everybody came back with a totally different attitude about themselves, about music, about the future. We all left equally as guys that wanted to play and we go over to England and the fans all make us superstars. We came back with this attitude that we are greater than thou." Duck Dunn added, "I think we maybe took for granted the music we were making until we went to Europe. I guess we thought we were making regional Southern hit music in the U.S., but in Europe we found out it was worldwide."

The tour ended in the first week of April with the concerts in Copenhagen, Stockholm, and Oslo, followed by a sold-out finale in London at the Hammersmith Odeon that was added to the schedule after disappointing ticket sales led to the cancellation of a concert in The Hague. In Stockholm, the performers were completely unnerved when the audience withheld all response during the show, only to burst into prolonged cheering and applause at the end. The Oslo date, while poorly attended, may have been the best of all, and most of it was captured on film by the Norwegian state television network in an hourlong segment that survives as a remarkable documentary of Otis and Sam and Dave at the absolute height of their powers.

Everywhere the Stax-Volt Revue played, the crowds were enthusiastic, and in Britain, with the exception of one or two shows in the provinces, the crowds were very large. Still, by their own admission, the Memphis musicians had been starved for recognition, and it didn't take much to make them feel like "superstars." In the long run, this led almost everyone to overestimate the commercial impact of the tour. Whereas Steve Cropper and others have characterized their triumphant reception in Britain as something akin to the Beatles in reverse, it did not have a dramatic effect on Stax's international record sales. The live albums that were released in Britain and France failed to make the charts in either country, though a previously issued Atlantic compilation called *Midnight Soul* with tracks by Otis, Wilson Pickett, Percy Sledge, and Rufus Thomas gained a second wind. Otis's latest UK single, "Day Tripper," stalled at #43 in the British Top 50, and his live recording of "Shake" from the Finsbury Park Astoria would peak at a merely respectable #26 in the months ahead. The biggest boon to Otis came from Atlantic's sage decision to reissue *Otis Blue,* which became the touchstone of the Stax sound in Britain over the course of 1967, rising to #7 and remaining on the British album charts for a full year. Of the other Stax artists, Eddie Floyd got a boost when his 1966 single "Knock on Wood" reentered the British charts and rose to #19. But the biggest beneficiary was the one non-Stax artist on the tour, Arthur Conley, whose "Sweet Soul Music" entered the British Top 10 in April and continued to sell strongly for the next two months.

R-E-S-P-E-C-T

This is a song that a girl took away from me.

—OTIS REDDING

S WEET SOUL MUSIC" PROVED TO BE AN EVEN GREATER SUCCESS AT home, where it chased Aretha Franklin's "I Never Loved a Man (The Way I Love You)" up the *Billboard* charts in April to become the #2 single in America in both Pop and R&B. The record went on to sell a million copies by June, making it a commercial breakthrough for both Conley and his producer, Otis Redding. Indeed, the only cloud on the horizon of Conley's overnight success consisted of J. W. Alexander, Sam Cooke's longtime manager and publishing partner in Kags Music, who could not help but notice that the writing credit on the label of this smash hit read "Redding/Conley" without a trace of "Cooke." It's unclear whether Alexander's professional indignation ever reached the level of an actual lawsuit, for "Sweet Soul Music" was so blatantly based on "Yeah Man" that no one was prepared to pretend otherwise. (It seems likely that Otis had placed Alexander's own composition "Let's Go Steady Again" on the B-side of the single in the hope that he would be satisfied with the royalties from that.) Phil Walden quickly reached an agreement with Alexander whereby Redwal gave Kags a publishing credit, a share of the royalties, and a promise that Conley would record additional Kags material in the months ahead.

The production and publishing royalties Otis stood to earn from Conley's hit came as some consolation for the fact that his own single, "I Love You More than Words Can Say," was shaping up as one of the weakest-selling records of his career. Released in March, the song rose only as high as #30 before exiting the R&B charts after only three weeks. Given the inarguable quality of the song and its performance, the obvious con-

clusion to be derived from its commercial failure was that the onetime
staple of Otis's recording career—the slow, pleading 12/8 ballad—had
finally run its course.

Further commercial consolation came from the success of *King &
Queen*. Released in March, the album cover was graced with one of Ronnie Stoots's better efforts, a drawing of a pair of royal face cards with
the likenesses of Otis and Carla, surrounded by an abundance of Gothic
lettering. The back of the album jacket was given over to Al Bell's latest
effort to curry favor with politicians, consisting in this case of a letter
of "endorsement" written on United States Senate stationery and signed
by the newly elected Senator Howard Baker, the first Republican to represent Tennessee in the upper house since Reconstruction. Baker's two-
page, single-spaced letter was the liner note equivalent of a filibuster. He
began by reviewing his state's proud musical heritage and the contribution
of Tennesseans to the fields of opera ("Mignon Dunn and Marguerite
Piazza immediately come to mind"), pop (Pat Boone, Dinah Shore), and
country (Roy Acuff, Ernie Ford). He then turned his attention to Memphis and its storied past as the "birthplace of the blues." W. C. Handy
and Elvis Presley were both singled out for congressional approval,
along with the "ministrel [*sic*] tunes" of Stephen Foster and his fellow
non-Tennessean Jerome Kern, who, "legend has it," composed "the ever-
popular 'Old Man River'" after seeing the ever-popular cotton barges on
the Memphis riverfront. At long last, at the bottom of page 2, Baker paid
tribute to Stax-Volt, Otis Redding, Carla Thomas, and the other "leading
exponents of this new 'Memphis Sound.' . . . Their music has penetrated
the Iron Curtain and serves as a message of goodwill in our efforts to ease
the tensions of the Cold War," the senator declared.

Stoots's regal cover and Baker's proclamation heralded a collection of
eleven duets that served, too often, to bring out the worst in both the King
and the Queen. Apart from "Tramp," the album's best tracks were a Motown pastiche by Isaac Hayes and David Porter called "Let Me Be Good
to You," with Carla turning in a fine impersonation of Diana Ross; a ranting rendition of Ahmet Ertegun's R&B standard "Lovey Dovey"; and a
heartfelt number called "New Year's Resolution," on which Otis and Carla
actually sounded as if they were singing to each other. Otherwise, on the

Otis with Carla Thomas and Sen. Howard Baker

ballads especially, their voices did not blend and their phrasing did not agree. Otis's singing on Aaron Neville's "Tell It Like It Is" and Sam and Dave's just-released "If Something Is Wrong with My Baby" sounded as tortured as Carla's; both tracks rank among his worst performances on record. The uptempo numbers were marginally better, beginning with the opening cut, a credible if overeager reprise of "Knock on Wood," and ending with a string of banalities called "Ooh Carla, Ooh Otis," on which Otis and Al Bell contrived to claim a writing credit. But the pair's rendition of "It Takes Two" was an outright embarrassment compared to the hit single by Marvin Gaye and Kim Weston, and the overall sound of the album suffered from Jim Stewart's egregious engineering, which was all the more perplexing considering that Otis and Carla were isolated on separate tracks. On Sam Cooke's "Bring It On Home to Me," a song that Carla had a hit with in 1962, their voices are so imbalanced that Carla sounds as if she's phoning in her performance through an actual telephone line.

The uneven quality of *King & Queen* did not prevent the album from selling strongly in the months ahead, when it would spend a total of fifteen weeks in the R&B Top 10. In May, Stax wisely pulled "Tramp" off the record and released it as a single that rose to #2 in R&B and #26 in Pop, Otis's best showing since "I've Been Loving You Too Long." Apart from his cowriting credit on "Ooh Carla, Ooh Otis," Otis did not receive any publishing royalties on the single or the LP. But here, too, ample compensation was about to come his way from another source.

The same month that Stax released *King & Queen,* Atlantic released Aretha Franklin's new album, which took its name from her hit single. *I Never Loved a Man the Way I Love You* showed conclusively that the single was no fluke, and it instantly relegated Carla Thomas to the status of pretender to the throne of soul. "It was the greatest rhythm and blues music ever made," Ahmet Ertegun would later say of Aretha's Atlantic debut— this from the man who had "discovered" Ray Charles. As he had done for Otis and Wilson Pickett, Tom Dowd made Aretha's voice explode off the record with a force and a depth and a soaring presence that filled all available space. As for the Muscle Shoals band that Jerry Wexler had purloined from Rick Hall, the bassist David Hood spoke for many of his contemporaries when he said, "I thought that all of a sudden, music had jumped up another level. It was such a great rhythm section—so young and exuberant. I'd always measured stuff against Sam and Dave or Otis Redding. This was above it."

In addition to its eponymous hit single, the album contained a half dozen memorable tracks, including Aretha's own "Dr. Feelgood" and Dan Penn and Chips Moman's "Do Right Woman, Do Right Man." But the pièce de résistance was the opening cut, Aretha's rendition of Otis's "Respect," recast in a manner that neither Otis nor any other man on earth could possibly have imagined. Aretha had been refining her arrangement of the tune for many months, working with her sisters, Erma and Carolyn, who sang backup on the track, and by the time she was ready to record it, she had bent the song to her will. She began by dispensing with the stamping rhythm and celebratory horns of the original, replacing them with a jauntier groove and a more quizzical lick on guitar. Having adjusted the balance of the instruments, Aretha then changed, with one pronoun, the sexual politics of the song. Where Otis sang, "What you want, honey you got it," Aretha began, "What you want, baby *I* got it." In the second verse, where Otis sang, "Do me wrong, honey, if you want to," Aretha sang, "Ain't gonna do you wrong, if *I* don't want to." Her every word and inflection was amplified by the singing of her real and figurative soul sisters, who began with simple *ooh*s on the downbeats and expanded to chants of "justa little bit" and "re-re-re-re-spect" as the song progressed. ("Re," it so happened, was the family's nickname for Aretha.)

But the real twist came in the third verse, where Aretha changed everything by leaving the pronouns alone, promising, just as Otis did, "I'm about to give you all my money," before adding, "And all I'm asking in return, honey / Is to give me my *propers* when I get home." Those lines had a very different meaning coming from the mouth of an African American woman than they did from the mouth of a man. They evoked the experience of generations of African American women who had been required to support their men as a matter of course. And who had then been required, too often, to endure the abuse that some of those men visited on their wives and girlfriends to compensate for their emasculation at the hands of a system that denied them their worth. In Aretha's hands, "Respect" touched on a fundamental juncture of emotional, sexual, and economic reality in many black American lives. And she went on to drive the message home, following King Curtis's four-bar sax break and Roger Hawkins's cannonball roll with a final verse that had her spelling it out, one letter at a time: "R-E-S-P-*E*-C-T / Find out what it means to me!" Then the sisters set up a deliciously lewd chant of "sock-it-to-me-sock-it-to-me" as Aretha ended the song by demanding, "All the time, keep on trying / I'm running out of fools, and I ain't lying."

Atlantic released "Respect" as the follow-up single to her album in late April. It peaked at #1 R&B in the middle of May and remained there for the next two months. It reached the top of the *Billboard* Pop charts at the beginning of June for another two-week stay. Writing in the October 1967 edition of *Ebony,* Phyl Garland would refer to "Respect" as "the new Negro national anthem." Garland was among the first of many writers who would create a body of sociological literature around Aretha's version of the song, centering on its role not only as an expression of racial pride but, more tellingly, as a statement of black feminism at a time when the civil rights leader Stokely Carmichael could still get a laugh out of his listeners by remarking, "The only position for women in SNCC is prone." (With rare exceptions, like Rosa Parks and Fannie Lou Hamer, black women had been as conspicuously absent in the leadership of the civil rights movement as they had been in the leadership of the black church.)

While some members of Aretha's pop audience may have been unfamiliar with Otis's version of the song (despite its Top 40 success), members of her R&B audience knew full well that "Respect" had been previously recorded not only by a man, but by a man who epitomized the male prerogative of a soul singer. For Aretha to assume that prerogative was a statement in itself, but for her to exceed Otis's performance in the way that she did came as a revelation to her female listeners. "Thanks to her example," wrote Anthony Heilbut, "woman vocalists of all races were allowed a freedom, a chance at uninhibited transcendence, that never would have been the option of middle-class Brits or working-class Mexicans or Catholic girls from Newark. [But] her greatest power of example was within her own community. She introduced forms of self-representation that profoundly changed the way that black women lived in the world." In a tribute to the record's enduring influence, a joint panel of the Recording Industry Association of America and the National Endowment for the Arts would place Aretha's version of "Respect" fourth among the Top 365 Songs of the Twentieth Century in a 2001 retrospective. Ten years later, *Rolling Stone* would place the record at #5 on its list of the 500 Greatest Songs of All Time.

No ONE WAS more gratified by the success of "Respect" than Otis, for whom the song was a publishing bonanza. Whether or not he was aware that Jim Stewart had rejected Jerry Wexler's offer to sign Aretha to Stax, Otis saw her as a far more suitable singing partner than Carla Thomas, and he discussed with Phil Walden the idea of recording with her someday. For the moment, however, he had a more practical matter to deal with. Otis had returned from Europe thrilled by the experience of performing on a nightly basis with the backing of the Stax band, and he was determined to convince the group to tour with him full-time. To his great displeasure, the MGs made it clear that this was out of the question. All four of them were now salaried employees and staff producers at Stax. In addition, with Booker Jones returned to full-time service, the MGs had revived their own career as recording artists. Their recent single, "Hip Hug-Her," was a Top 10 R&B hit and their bestselling record since "Green Onions." Otis could not possibly pay them enough to make it worth their while to give up their careers at Stax. Still, hearing how good his music sounded without the encumbrance (not to mention the expense) of a large horn section had been a revelation to him, and he now resolved to tour with a smaller, tighter, more economical group. He and Carla Thomas were booked to perform for ten days at the Apollo in New York in early June, followed later that month by the start of a marathon Supersonic Attractions tour with Arthur Conley and Percy Sledge. One way or another, Otis was going to have to put together a band before the Apollo shows.

The answer to his dilemma was waiting in the wings at Stax. Among the budding musicians who made it their business to hang around Estelle Axton's Satellite Record Shop was a group of teenagers who played in a club band called the Bar-Kays. With the exception of their organist, Ronnie Caldwell, who was white, and their bassist, James Alexander, who was a grade behind, the Bar-Kays were all in their senior year at Booker T. Washington High School, where they were veterans of the school's celebrated music program and its Warriors marching band. Their trumpeter, Ben Cauley, had already played on a number of sessions at Stax, and the whole group had auditioned on several occasions for Steve Cropper, who had been unimpressed by their original material. In March, shortly before the Stax troupe left for Europe, Estelle Axton prevailed on Jim Stewart to give them a recording test, in the course of which they showed him a horn riff that sounded like something out of the Warriors' songbook. Stewart went on to record the track, enlisting the production assistance of David Porter and Isaac Hayes, who came up with the title "Soul Finger." (A play on the James Bond film *Goldfinger*, the name had already been used on an album by Art Blakey in 1965.) Porter and Hayes also had the inspiration to invite a gaggle of local schoolchildren into the studio to shriek the song title at regular intervals during the track. Ben Cauley added a Rufus Thomas–style introduction that quoted "Mary Had a Little Lamb" as a prelude to the song's bleating, whooping horn lines, and between guitarist Jimmy King's twangy breaks and drummer Carl Cunningham's relentless single-stroke rolls, the whole production sounded precisely like a junior-varsity version of the Stax studio band.

Stax released "Soul Finger" as a single at the end of April. The following week, Otis brought Arthur Conley back to Fame to record a revival of Big Joe Turner's classic "Shake, Rattle and Roll." With Conley sounding like the reincarnation of Sam Cooke, Otis crafted an arrangement that featured a soaring countermelody from the horns. The week after that, with Otis looking on, Conley performed with Wilson Pickett, Johnnie Taylor, and Solomon Burke at the Mid-South Coliseum in Memphis. After the show, the performers all gathered at the Hippodrome, a Beale Street club, where the Bar-Kays were the house band. Otis sat in with the group that night and promptly announced that he wanted to hire them as his new touring band. Upon learning that they were all still in high school, he came up with the absurd proposal that he would hire a "tutor" to accompany them on the road. The boys' parents would have none of that, but most of them were due to graduate at the beginning of June. On the day they received their diplomas, the whole group flew to New York to open at the Apollo the following night. Otis had previously told them to learn his songs off the records, and according to James Alexander, he rehearsed them "for about half an hour" in the basement of the theater before they went onstage. That same week, "Soul Finger" entered the R&B charts at #44.

The Apollo engagement went very well. The Bar-Kays did a fine job backing Otis and Carla Thomas, and Bobby Schiffman, for once, was entirely pleased with the results. ("Good. Loved by audiences. Duet with Carla Thomas very cute," Schiffman noted to himself.) James Brown caught Otis's show, and in his usual manner, invited himself onstage, where he and Otis performed a version of Brown's signature "Papa's Got a Brand New Bag" that earned the Bar-Kays a compliment from the Bossman himself. James Alexander also recalled that Brown's constant ragging of Otis backstage nearly caused the two of them to come to blows.

It was power, but not raw power. It was music, not just theater.

—JERRY WEXLER

A FEW WEEKS BEFORE HE OPENED WITH THE BAR-KAYS AT THE Apollo, Otis and Phil Walden flew to Detroit to meet with Aretha Franklin's manager-husband, Ted White, to discuss the possibility of Otis and Aretha touring together in the year ahead. At the airport in Atlanta, they found themselves boarding the same connecting flight as Dr. Martin Luther King Jr., who was en route to Louisville to lead an initiative against housing discrimination there. As fellow Georgia celebrities, Otis and Dr. King had a passing familiarity, and King playfully invited Otis to accompany him to Louisville. "I'd sure like to go with you, but I gotta go to Detroit and make that dollar," Otis replied. It was not the first time he had declined an invitation to take a more active role in the civil rights struggle in the South, and it reflected his self-protective belief that entertainers should confine their public activities to the business of entertaining. One of the ironies of Phil Walden's impression that Otis had been seduced by the ideology of Black Power was his notable lack of involvement in racial politics when compared to other R&B stars like Curtis Mayfield, Jerry Butler, and James Brown, not to mention Aretha Franklin, who had performed at many SCLC benefits and functions over the years. Otis was a member of the Macon chapter of the NAACP, but he felt much too exposed, living in the middle of nowhere in Round Oak, Georgia, to call attention to his political views.

Throughout the month of May, Phil Walden had been busy finalizing the arrangements for Otis, the MGs, and the Mar-Keys to perform at the Monterey Pop Festival in the middle of June. A few weeks after he returned from Europe, Phil received a phone call from Andrew Oldham, the twenty-three-year-old manager of the Rolling Stones, whom he had met in London when Otis first performed there in 1966. Oldham was calling from Los Angeles, where he had taken refuge from a world of trouble in Britain that included the arrests of three of the Stones on drug charges and the efforts of Sam Cooke's former business manager, Allen Klein (whom Oldham himself had hired), to usurp the management of the group. Oldham was staying with his friend Lou Adler, the owner of Dunhill Records and the producer of the Mamas and the Papas, who had released a string of Top 10 hits over the course of 1966.

In April, Adler and John Phillips, the leader of the group, had played host to Paul McCartney and his former press agent Derek Taylor during a visit to Los Angeles, in the course of which they all commiserated about the need for contemporary rock to be taken more seriously as an art form, in the manner of modern jazz. Soon after that, Adler and Phillips were approached by Alan Pariser, initiating the process by which Adler, Phillips, Oldham, Taylor, and Pariser would join in promoting an event they billed as the First International Pop Festival in the coastal resort of Monterey in the middle of June. Since Monterey was the site of a major annual jazz festival, it was hoped that the setting itself would confer a sense of artistic legitimacy, while the promoters' decision to produce the event on a nonprofit basis, with the proceeds going to charity and the performers waiving their fees, was in keeping with the utopian pretensions of the San Francisco bands whose participation was essential to the festival's aura of hip credibility. Andrew Oldham's role was to serve as a liaison to the London pop scene, and it was on his advice, seconded by McCartney, that the Who and the Jimi Hendrix Experience were included on the bill. As an acquaintance of Phil Walden, Oldham was also asked to invite Otis Redding, whose performances at the Whisky and the Fillmore in 1966 had made him an obvious choice.

Though the festival was heavily weighted toward West Coast acts, the promoters wanted to present a convincing cross section of the best in current popular music, and in addition to Otis, they sought to secure commitments from a number of other top black artists. (Prior to his success as a pop producer, Lou Adler had worked for Sam Cooke's original label, SAR Records, in the course of which he became friendly with

Cooke and familiar with the world of R&B.) Unfortunately, given the last-minute planning of the festival and the lack of compensation, most of the established black stars they contacted were unwilling to cancel existing bookings in order to fly to California to play for free. In addition to Jimi Hendrix, who was unknown in the States (and was not in any case recognized as an R&B artist), the only black acts besides Otis who accepted the invitation to perform were Dionne Warwick and Lou Rawls, both of whom specialized in a genteel brand of "supper club soul"; the South African trumpeter Hugh Masekela; and Curtis Mayfield's group, the Impressions. Warwick was already planning to be in San Francisco, performing at a local hotel (which subsequently refused to release her from her contract). Rawls was a former protégé of Sam Cooke and a personal friend of Lou Adler from his days at SAR. Masekela had gained a cult following in Los Angeles, having recently played on a recording by the Byrds. As for the Impressions, they never showed.

Lou Adler would later insist that "Phil Walden knew immediately that Otis was right for Monterey and Monterey would be right for Otis." Phil's initial response, however, was noncommittal. It was not lost on him that the promoters, for all their celebrity, had little experience at staging live concerts, and there was every reason to wonder, given the scope of the production and the last-minute, "Let's do the show right here!" spirit of the event, whether the festival would even come off. In addition, while Otis had performed at benefits in the past for this or that worthy cause, the idea of playing for free in front of a stadium-size audience of paying customers ran counter to his creed of "Gotta go make that dollar." Otis himself was unenthusiastic when Phil first raised the idea.

"I was wary," Phil recalled, "so I called Jerry Wexler and asked what he thought about it." Though Wexler wasn't personally familiar with the West Coast music scene, his partner Ahmet Ertegun knew it inside out by now, and Ertegun offered his assurance that Adler and Phillips were major players who knew what they were doing. (An L.A. group that Ertegun had signed to Atlantic, Buffalo Springfield, had already agreed to perform.) "I think it's going to work," Wexler told Phil. "But it could backfire. You need to consider how well you think he'll do. It could be the most brilliant move you'll ever make." Aware that Otis was still in the process of putting together a new band, Wexler urged Phil to insist that he be backed at the festival, as in Europe, by the MGs and the Mar-Keys. After clearing their participation with Jim Stewart, it was on that basis that Phil agreed to Otis's performing.

Monterey was the moment when Phil Walden came into his own as a manager. Previously, for all his brashness and bluster, he had played the earnest understudy, taking the good advice he was given by people like Joe Galkin and Jerry Wexler and following it faithfully. Now, emboldened by the success of the Stax-Volt tour, firm in his belief that Otis had something that other young whites like himself would find irresistible, Phil was dealing with a realm of the music business that was changing in ways that would eventually make people like Joe Galkin and even Jerry Wexler obsolete. Monterey would teach him to trust own instincts from this point on.

Initially, Otis was slated to perform on the second night of the festival on a bill headed by the Beach Boys, with the Byrds, Hugh Masekela, and a pair of San Francisco groups, the Jefferson Airplane and Moby Grape, as the other supporting acts. At the end of May, not long after the schedule was announced, the Beach Boys abruptly withdrew. California's seminal pop group had been living an oddly bipolar existence since 1965. While their leader, Brian Wilson, repaired to the womb of the recording studio to produce dreamily orchestrated, ever more intricate pop songs with an army of session men, the Beach Boys had continued to tour without him, dressed in their matching candy-striped shirts, reprising their greatest hits about surfing and sailing and girl-watching with the fervor of a high school pep squad. With good reason, Wilson feared that his group would be perceived as an anachronism in the new world of California acid rock.

It was by no means clear to the promoters how to deal with the Beach Boys' withdrawal. The staging of the festival called for each night to be headlined by a major pop act: Simon and Garfunkel on Friday night, the Beach Boys on Saturday night, the Mamas and the Papas on Sunday night. From a commercial perspective, there were no other artists of this stature on the bill at Monterey. The Byrds had released a number of top-selling records in 1965, when they were briefly touted as America's answer to the Beatles. But their career had been in decline for more than a year, and they had earned a reputation as a lackluster live band whose stoned-out members could barely rouse themselves to play. The Jefferson Airplane, on the other hand, were in their ascendancy, having acquired a charismatic new singer, Grace Slick, and an experienced drummer, Spencer Dryden. These additions had transformed the group from a slack-sounding folk-rock ensemble into a much more potent attraction whose single "Somebody to Love" had made them the first San Francisco band to receive extensive airplay on Top 40 radio. As a live act, though, the Jefferson Airplane was still an unknown quantity outside of the Bay Area in the spring of 1967. Lou Adler and John Phillips had both seen Otis at the Whisky and the Hollywood Bowl. They knew what a dynamic performer he was, which made him the best choice to replace the Beach Boys as the headliner on Saturday night.

Otis, Phil, and Joe Galkin flew out from Atlanta; the MGs and the Mar-Keys flew out from Memphis; Jerry Wexler flew out from New York. The musicians spent the first day holed up at their motel. It had been two months since they last played together in London, but in lieu of a full rehearsal, they simply discussed what they would do. Booker T. and the MGs were listed on the bill for Saturday night; with a current hit record to their credit, they planned to play a set of their own before Otis joined them onstage. It was a foregone conclusion that Otis would replicate his set list from the Stax-Volt tour; the only change he made was to start with "Shake," the live version of which had just been released as a single. Lest there be any doubt, Otis made it clear that he wanted to keep the tempos at the level of the European tour.

Otis had played the Fillmore six months before, but for the Memphis musicians, Monterey was their introduction to the California counterculture of music, love, and flowers that was blooming with a radiant intensity at the start of the Summer of Love. The band members spent the afternoon before their evening performance roaming the festival grounds, taking in the spectacle of thousands of long-haired young men and miniskirted young women parading their finery and openly smoking marijuana while the local police, some of them festooned with orchid blossoms, looked on. (An odd conceit of the drug culture at the time was that while several of the Stax musicians routinely used amphetamine-based "diet pills" as a stimulant, they professed to be shocked at the thought of pot and LSD.) The backstage facilities at the festival were luxurious by the standards of the day, and the Memphis musicians were thrilled to be introduced to real-life television stars like the Smothers Brothers. For some of them, most notably Booker Jones, the whole scene at Monterey—the freedom of the crowd, the communal spirit, the veneration of the music—had a profound effect. "It changed my life," Jones recalled. "It was our first announcement that something new was happening in the United States. I had never seen people dress like that. For the first time I saw restaurants giving food for free. People were sharing hotel rooms and disregarding money. Coming out of Memphis, it was a shock. History was changing at that moment, and we knew it."

At the same time, the culture shock they were experiencing only increased their uncertainty at how they would be received. Everyone agrees that Otis was nervous before his performance in a way that went well beyond his usual restlessness. A candid photograph that was taken of him sitting in the audience next to Jerry Wexler during the Saturday afternoon performances shows him looking visibly perturbed. It didn't help that Wexler, as he once said, "considered the musical tastes of the Flower Children to be infantile and retarded." The Saturday afternoon program consisted almost entirely of white blues bands. It included a breakthrough performance by Janis Joplin, the phenomenal lead singer of an otherwise lugubrious San Francisco group, Big Brother and the Holding Company. And it featured solid sets by the Paul Butterfield Blues Band and Mike Bloomfield's new cohort, the Electric Flag, both groups bolstered by the recent addition of Stax-style horn sections, and both of them featuring racially integrated personnel. But the cumulative effect was numbing, as one group after another paid homage to their heroes in the world of R&B.

The staging of the festival had gone smoothly, with exceptional lighting and sound, but a certain overconfidence had set in by Saturday night, as members of the crew, beginning with the stage manager Chip Monck, succumbed to the spirit of the occasion by indulging in psychedelic drugs. The result was a slackness that led to growing delays as the evening wore on. Moby Grape began the show with a short, taut set. They were followed by Hugh Masekela, whose rambling improvisations on pop hits by the Beatles and Janis Ian went well over his allotted time, and whose large ensemble took forever to set up and take down. Next came the Byrds, with a predictably lackadaisical performance ("Our set was a disaster," their bassist Chris Hillman recalled) that also ran past its time limit. Laura Nyro had originally been scheduled to play on Friday night, but she was added to the Saturday program after the Beach Boys withdrew. A fragile, brooding performer, Nyro was out of her element at Monterey, and the crowd responded with indifference. By the time the Jefferson Airplane went on, the official midnight curfew was minutes away. Accompanied by a light show that pulsated with a crazy intensity on a screen behind the stage, the Airplane played a powerful forty-minute set—powerful enough to push Jerry Wexler's Hebraic pessimism past its breaking point. "This really frightens me," he confessed to Phil Walden. "I'm afraid Otis is out of context here. This could be terrible."

Suitably shaken, Phil returned to the backstage area in time to take part in a discussion with John Phillips and Lou Adler about the fact that the program was running late. The Airplane finished well after midnight and it would take some time to break down their gear and set up for Booker T. and the MGs. Phillips and Adler wanted the group to forgo their solo spot so that Otis could perform a full set, but Booker Jones and Steve Cropper were insistent that the MGs and the Mar-Keys be allowed to play at least a sampling of their own material. It was decided that they would do a short instrumental set, followed by Otis, who agreed to reduce his performance to five songs, beginning with "Shake," ending with "Try a Little Tenderness," with "Respect," "I've Been Loving You Too Long," and "Satisfaction" in between.

The sight of the MGs and the Mar-Keys in their matching suits— lime green for the MGs, electric blue for the Mar-Keys, the colors magnified to an eye-popping intensity by the powerful stage lighting—was a curiosity to the crowd, as was the tight interplay of their performance. Betraying their own nervousness, the MGs actually rushed the beat in their opening number, "Booker-Loo," building to a chaotic climax before restoring order with their recent hit "Hip Hug-Her." Jerry Wexler's fears abated as the band settled down and the crowd responded enthusiastically, dancing in their seats as the Mar-Keys' rendition of "Philly Dog" filled the California night with the spirit of Memphis hotspots like Hernando's Hideaway and the Plantation Inn.

At the end of "Philly Dog," Tommy Smothers came out to introduce Otis, who was fidgeting and pacing beside Phil Walden at the side of the stage. Phil watched as Otis took a "huge hit" on a joint he was offered by a sympathetic bystander. The MGs and the Mar-Keys all turned, as always, toward Al Jackson, whose eyes twinkled as he nodded his head to count off the tune. Then Jackson stomped on the downbeat, the band came in around him, the crowd of 7,500 felt the first seismic shock of "Shake," and Otis took it from there, seizing the moment, dispelling all doubt, and delivering what may have been, song for song and note for note, the greatest performance of his career.

THE NEXT DAY, Otis, Phil Walden, and Joe Galkin rented a car and drove down the Pacific Coast Highway to Los Angeles. They arrived at night and checked into their hotel on the Sunset Strip. At breakfast the following morning, Phil regaled them with Pete Johnson's article about the festival in the Los Angeles *Times*. "Otis stirred the crowd to its greatest excitement of the first two days," Phil read aloud. "The paths between the rows of chairs were jammed with bobbing spectators, some of whom leaped onto the flanks of the stage, clapping and shouting along." ("Ecstasy, madness, loss, total, screaming, fantastic," read the notes that Michael Lydon of *Newsweek* scribbled during Otis's set.) A few days later, when Otis returned to Macon, he told Zelma that the festival had added five years to his career. The week after that, Richard Goldstein would provide a more vivid description of his triumph in New York's *Village Voice*: "He had the audience tied and spinning like a chicken on a spit. The grandstand was a turmoil of swaying, boogalooing faces. Countless hands were raised, palms out toward the stage, in a pentecostal salute. Otis took one look at all that flowery frenzy, and loved it."

BUSES TO PLANES

Phil Walden was in heaven. He knew he had just graduated from
buses to planes.

—ANDREW OLDHAM

A CTUALLY, IT WAS OTIS WHO GRADUATED TO PLANES IN THE
wake of Monterey. The logistics of touring were such that he had
often flown to Memphis for recording dates or back to Macon to see his
family and work in his office at Redwal during his off-days on the road.
If commercial flights weren't readily available, he would sometimes rely
on Jim Lowe, who ran the aircraft charter and maintenance service at
the Macon airport, to pick him up and take him where he wanted to go.
When Otis played the Regal Theater in Chicago in the summer of 1966,
he befriended a local funeral director who owned his own small plane
and offered to fly him whenever he could. Otis was well aware that Ray
Charles had been touring by air since 1962, when he purchased a Convair
turboprop airliner that could carry his entire troupe. More recently, James
Brown had acquired an eight-seat, $700,000 Learjet for his personal use.
("He is looking for a 'soul pilot,'" Brown's publicist told the press.) Just
before he went on tour in the summer of 1967, Otis leased a twin-engine,
six-seat Cessna and had it painted with the logo *Otis Redding Enterprises.*
In addition to running his charter service, Jim Lowe was also a senior
flight instructor, and one of the pilots he had trained was a twenty-five-
year-old Warner Robins resident named Dick Fraser, who had just been
discharged from the air force and was looking to start a career as a commercial pilot. Fraser (who had not flown in the air force) was instrument-
rated and qualified to operate multiengine aircraft, though Lowe was
concerned that he did not have much experience in that regard. Still, Otis

met him, liked him, and hired him. The Cessna was no Learjet, but Otis loved the prestige and flexibility it afforded him.

With Arthur Conley and Percy Sledge as his costars, Otis's summer tour began in Boston the week after Monterey and ran until the middle of August, consisting of forty-eight dates in fifty-three days. Having survived their trial by fire at the Apollo, the Bar-Kays backed up all the acts, while the success of "Soul Finger," which peaked at #3 on the R&B charts in July, earned them their own featured spot on the bill. The tour began in the Northeast, spent a week in Maryland and Virginia, detoured to Montreal for two shows at the Expo '67 World's Fair, and then headed south for dates in Texas, Florida, Georgia, and the Carolinas. On July 22, Otis played his fifth annual Homecoming concert in Macon, prompting an article in the *Telegraph* that listed his achievements of the previous year. The paper reported that "Otis's manager has contacted Sen. Richard Russell of Georgia and expressed Redding's desire to take his show to Vietnam to perform for our servicemen." Leaving Macon, the tour crisscrossed the South before returning to the Northeast early in August for shows in Newark, Brooklyn, Baltimore, and Trenton.

For Otis, a high point of the summer was the barbecue he held at his ranch in Round Oak on the eve of the annual convention of the National Association of Television and Radio Announcers (NATRA), which took place in Atlanta during the second week of August. NATRA had been formed during the early years of black radio as a trade association representing the interests of black deejays and announcers. Though it was originally opposed by the white owners and managers who controlled the great majority of black-appeal stations, the organization gained the support of the independent record labels, who viewed it as an indispensable promotional tool. As a result, NATRA's conventions became bacchanals of partying and payola. Following the national payola scandal in 1960 and the concurrent rise of the civil rights movement, the association elected a slate of activist leaders, headed by the New York deejay Del Shields, who promised to give it a new seriousness of purpose. In addition to chiding the membership for their "playboy" mentality and their lack of racial pride, Shields and his supporters began to press for greater black ownership of stations and greater black representation in management positions.

The organization's decision to hold its 1967 convention in Atlanta reflected that city's prominence in the civil rights movement, and Dr. Martin Luther King Jr. accepted the invitation to serve as the keynote speaker. Jesse Jackson and Sen. Leroy Johnson also addressed the delegates.

Al Bell had been active in NATRA for several years, and he viewed the 1967 convention as a prime promotional opportunity for Stax. Shortly before the Atlanta gathering, Stax announced Bell's appointment as the executive vice president of the label, making him, in the words of the *Chicago Defender,* "the highest ranking Negro recording executive south of the Mason-Dixon line." (One can only imagine what Don Robey, the notoriously foulmouthed owner of Peacock Records in Houston, had to say about this.) Bell arranged for Stax to have a major presence at the Atlanta convention, beginning with a concert by the label's entire roster of artists, headed by Otis and Carla Thomas, who would be joined onstage by Atlantic's new stars, Aretha Franklin and Arthur Conley.

On the day before the convention opened, Otis hosted a lavish barbecue for the NATRA members and their guests at his home in Round Oak. Five hundred people were invited; twice that number showed up. A fleet of buses was hired to transport the guests from Atlanta. The party began in the afternoon and ran throughout the night. Eight hogs, four cows, and fifty cases of whiskey were consumed. The Bar-Kays performed a brief set, but Otis was too tired and preoccupied to join them. The hoarseness he had complained about earlier in the year had grown worse over the course of the tour, and with another week of dates ahead of him, he welcomed any opportunity to rest his voice. Mainly, he was delighted to be able to show off his farm, his home, and his family to a group of people he was used to encountering on their own professional turf, some of whom never ceased to wonder why he continued to live in Georgia, much less Macon, when he could easily afford to leave. With its herd of Black Angus cattle, stable of riding horses, and acres of fields and streams, the appeal of the Big O Ranch spoke for itself as far as Otis was concerned. His only regret was that a massive O-shaped swimming pool he had hoped to have finished in time for the party proved too large to fill with water in the dry Georgia heat.

Jerry Wexler remembered the barbecue as "a big ball, with good feel-

ing. But there was also some edginess. The Black Power thing was starting to build. I remember some deejays that were running around, talking
a lot of trash. You know: What is whitey doing here?" Wayne Jackson of
the Mar-Keys was so unnerved by the hostility he encountered from some
of his fellow passengers on the bus ride from Atlanta that he sought refuge
with Phil and Alan Walden when he first arrived at Otis's ranch. For the
great majority of the participants, the barbecue was unaffected by these
tensions, but the following day in Atlanta, the opening of the NATRA
convention was graced by the uninvited presence of H. Rap Brown, the
gun-toting demagogue who had recently replaced Stokely Carmichael
as the chairman of SNCC. Brown was one of a new cadre of political
gangsters who were coopting the moral authority of the civil rights movement under the banner of Black Power, and he was not alone in seeing
the white-owned infrastructure of the black music business as a prime
target for extortion. At one point, when Otis and Nina Simone—who unlike Otis had been heavily involved with the movement, despite her own
ambivalence about its nonviolent philosophy—were being interviewed by
a reporter from *Life* magazine, Brown inserted himself in the conversation
and began expounding his views ("If America don't come around, we're
gonna burn it down"), effectively sabotaging the interview. Otis and Phil
Walden were furious with Brown, since any mention of Otis in *Life* would
have been a major coup. That same day, talking with Claude Hill, the
radio and television editor of *Billboard*, Otis predicted that there would
be "a gathering of twenty-five major black artists behind closed doors
and that some line of action on the racial situation would be forthcoming
within two to four weeks."

James Brown wrote in his autobiography that Otis contacted him
in the summer of 1967 to propose "a union of all black entertainers" to
exert leverage over promoters and record companies, a prospect Brown
dismissed as a form of "separatism." Though Brown was overstating it,
what Otis was referring to was an idea that had been floating around for
more than a year, ever since Solomon Burke and Don Covay saw themselves referred to in an English music paper as members of an invading
"Soul Clan." Seizing on the name (whose irony was surely lost on the
English editor who coined it), Burke and Covay suggested to their fel-

low Atlantic-affiliated artists Otis Redding, Wilson Pickett, Joe Tex, and Ben E. King that they form a fraternity of sorts, half social club, half lobbying group, to represent their interests with the label. The concept had never moved beyond the talk stage when Otis mentioned it to Claude Hill at the NATRA convention, and it would go no further in the immediate future, for Otis would shortly have a more pressing matter on his mind.

After spending two days at the convention, schmoozing with the deejays and program directors while Jerry Wexler, Al Bell, Joe Galkin, and Phil Walden plied them with payola on his behalf, Otis closed out the last week of his summer tour with dates in Charlotte, Chicago, Nashville, and St. Louis. Carla Thomas joined him in Chicago, where the two of them were the guests of honor at the city's Bud Billiken Parade and Picnic. Sponsored since its founding in 1929 by the *Chicago Defender,* the Billiken Day festivities comprised the largest annual African American gathering in the country, attended by upward of 700,000 Chicagoans each year. Otis and Carla began the day at an official breakfast with Mayor Richard Daley and Illinois governor Otto Kerner, who had just been named to head the Commission on Civil Disorders, which President Johnson formed in response to the riots that had devastated Newark and Detroit earlier in the summer. Enacting their roles as the King and the Queen, they then rode in the parade and performed at the picnic. Their appearance was especially welcome at Stax, since Chicago, despite Otis's many performances at the Regal, had remained the least-receptive major market in the country to the label's releases. Asked by a reporter from the *Defender* to describe his current goals, Otis named two: "First, I want to become an international recording and performing star. Then, I would like to fill the silent vacuum that was created when Sam Cooke died."

Otis returned home to Macon for a few days of much-needed rest before heading to California in late August for a week of shows at Basin Street West, a venerable jazz club in San Francisco's North Beach that had recently expanded its music policy to include rock, blues, and soul. Two months of one-nighters had taken a heavy toll on his voice, but *Billboard* would shortly report that his summer tour had grossed more than $600,000, which was $100,000 more than the year before. On the recording front, his ballad version of "The Glory of Love," released in July, had reaffirmed the lesson of "I Love You More than Words Can Say" by stalling at #19 before falling off the R&B charts after only four weeks. Stax responded by pulling "Knock on Wood" off *King & Queen* and releasing it as a single. In a demonstration of the enduring power of a good song, this single would fare much better, rising into the R&B Top 10 toward the end of the summer amid an epic array of hits that included Aretha Franklin's "Baby I Love You," Stevie Wonder's "I Was Made to Love Her," Wilson Pickett's "Funky Broadway," James Brown's "Cold Sweat," Jackie Wilson's "(Your Love Keeps Lifting Me) Higher and Higher," and Sam and Dave's tour de force "Soul Man," a masterful single that helped to finish what "Sweet Soul Music" had started in institutionalizing the word *soul* as the popular designation for contemporary R&B.

Before he left for California, Otis played host to a BBC film crew, which came to Macon to produce a pair of promotional shorts for broadcast on British television. Top British groups like the Beatles and the Stones had been making such films for several years as a way of maintaining a presence with their fans during the increasingly long gaps between their tours, and the production values of these early British "music videos" had grown quite refined. In one sequence, the BBC crew filmed Otis sitting on a rock beside a pond on his ranch, lip-synching "The Glory of Love." His salmon-colored suit contrasts nicely with the verdant background, and his pantomimed performance is remarkably convincing compared to his earlier, stilted efforts on American TV. A second film sequence was set to the soundtrack of "Tramp." It begins with shots of the "country" Otis decked out in a straw hat and overalls, sauntering around the barns and fields on his ranch as he preens with a pitchfork and makes himself at home on the back of a mule. The action then switches to the "city" Otis, dressed in an immaculate olive-green suit as he surveys his row of Cadillacs, poses next to his private plane, and stands in front of the Redwal Building on Cotton Avenue, stuffing his pockets with cash. In its flippant portrayal, the film satirized a dimension of Otis that Jerry Wexler later described: "It's not the cliché of the raw country boy—it wasn't like that. Otis was a highly evolved man. He knew who he was and what he was. He had good ideas about his own inner self and his direction."

Though Bill Graham had no affiliation with Basin Street West, he had arranged as a favor for Otis to stay on a houseboat in Sausalito that the Fillmore sometimes used to accommodate its out-of-town acts. The week that Otis spent in this picturesque setting, performing at night and spending his days looking out over the panorama of San Francisco Bay, was conducive to a form of reflection that he rarely allowed himself. (In the course of this visit, Speedo Sims was dosed by some hippie fans with a powerful psychedelic whose aftereffects plagued him for months to come.) The shows themselves went smoothly, though Otis's voice continued to trouble him. Like many singers of his day, he smoked regularly, menthol cigarettes as well as marijuana, without giving much thought to the strain this placed on his vocal cords.

In keeping with the increased press coverage of popular music that had been one of the aims of the Monterey Pop Festival, Otis's appearances at Basin Street West inspired a pair of sharply divergent reviews. "His show is too polished to achieve any deep musical expression," declared a stringer for the jazz journal *Downbeat,* which had recently expanded its scope to include rock and R&B. "Redding frequently displayed excellent projection and rhythmic timing and was indisputably adept at commanding the attention of his listeners. But his lyrics were trite and meaningless, and the more he sang the more predictable he became." Writing in the *San Francisco Examiner,* Ralph J. Gleason came to a very different conclusion. Gleason characterized Otis's performance as a "total emotional explosion." "It has been apparent for some time that part of white America needs the ecstatic release that has long been provided minorities by highly emotional church services," he wrote. "Redding can work his listeners into a frenzy more quickly than any nightclub performer of his time. . . . [He] has humor, too, and sophistication. But his basic use of deeply driving rhythms, vocal sounds of emphasis and ejaculated phrases couples the audience and the performer in a rhythmic trance."

WHAT MAKES THESE GUYS SO SPECIAL

I think it tended to sadden him, to chasten him a great deal, the fact that he couldn't get the kind of hit that James Brown and Wilson Pickett were getting out there.

—JERRY WEXLER

T HE WEEK THAT OTIS SPENT ON THE HOUSEBOAT IN SAUSALITO had given him a chance to reflect on the whirlwind of the preceding six months: his triumphant performances in Europe and at Monterey, his production and authorship of million-selling singles by Arthur Conley and Aretha Franklin, the financial windfall of his summer tour, the lucrative royalties he stood to gain from the hits by Conley and Franklin, *King & Queen,* and its spin-off singles "Tramp" and "Knock on Wood." Contrasting with these successes was Otis's awareness that his own solo recording career had seemed to plateau over the previous year. Though his album sales had doubled during 1966 and "Try a Little Tenderness" had rivaled the success of all but his biggest hit, "I've Been Loving You Too Long," "Tenderness" was a cover, and the weaker sales of his original ballads "My Lover's Prayer" and "I Love You More than Words Can Say" had been a major disappointment to him. In fact, Otis was the only contemporary black singer of his stature who had not yet had a #1 R&B hit. It had been five years to the month since he had recorded "These Arms of Mine," and during that time the world of popular music had undergone a revolution. As Otis told Jim Delehant, "I'd like to say something to the R&B singers who were around ten years ago. They've got to get out of that old bag. Listen to the beat of today and use it on records." He was referring to artists like Little Richard, Clyde McPhatter, and Fats Domino. But his advice was just as relevant to his own career.

Unlike Jerry Wexler, Otis was not inclined to dismiss the musical tastes of the counterculture out of hand. At the conclusion of the Jefferson Airplane's set at Monterey, he had thrilled the group's lead singer, Marty Balin, by telling him, "It would be an honor to play on the same stage with you anytime, man." The focal point of Otis's listening during the second half of 1967 was the Beatles' ubiquitous masterpiece *Sgt. Pepper's Lonely Hearts Club Band,* which monopolized his attention in the same way that *Sam Cooke at the Copa* had in 1965. "Otis came in one night and he had that *Sgt. Pepper* album and he said you got to listen to this," Zelma recalled. "Listen to it," he told her. "This is *bad.*"

Never before had a record album turned the world of popular music so conclusively on its ear. "The summer of 1967 was spent listening to *Sgt. Pepper,*" Paul Williams wrote in *Mademoiselle.* "It was unavoidable, inevitable, more constant and universal than the climate or any other aspect of the season." At a time when young people in America, Britain, and much of Western Europe were trying on flamboyant new identities, the members of the most popular and recognizable musical group in the world had adopted the persona of an old-fashioned, crowd-pleasing music hall band as a way of reinventing themselves anew. Far more than the ripple effect of the Monterey Pop Festival, *Sgt. Pepper* was the catalyst for the widespread acceptance of rock music as a legitimate popular art form by the mainstream media and the public at large. Hailed by classical composers and highbrow literary critics as a cultural watershed on the level of Gershwin's "Rhapsody in Blue" or Rodgers and Hammerstein's *Oklahoma!,* it was played from start to finish like an opera or a symphony on FM radio stations nationwide. In addition to its enormous commercial success, *Sgt. Pepper* inspired an effusion of reviews, articles, and commentaries in newspapers and magazines that had previously covered the world of rock 'n' roll as an exclusively economic or sociological phenomenon. Particular attention was paid to the production techniques on the album: its sophisticated use of multitrack recording, its eclectic instrumentation, its mixing of musical genres, and the pivotal role played by the proverbial "fifth Beatle," their producer, George Martin. The most celebrated track of all was the finale, a languorous, contemplative ballad called "A Day in the Life," which combined avant-garde production (including a forty-piece orchestra) with a folklike simplicity.

"I'm trying to figure out what they're doing here—what makes these guys so special," Otis told Phil Walden on one of the nights they spent listening to the album over and over again. "You know what they're doing?" Otis decided. "They're *manufacturing* a record. They put a rhythm track on, they put a vocal track on . . ." Up to this point, Otis's approach to making records had been like southern cooking: a few basic ingredients, expertly prepared. Now, his own production work with Arthur Conley and his appreciation of the densely layered arrangements on the Beatles' album were pushing him into the realm of musical cuisine. The multi-track recording on *King & Queen* had been done as a matter of expediency, but it had introduced him, however tangentially, to the creative possibilities of overdubbing. Tom Dowd had been using an eight-track system in Atlantic's New York studio since 1958, years ahead of the rest of the recording industry. This had allowed not only for the addition—and, in some cases, subtraction—of vocal and instrumental parts after the fact, but also for much more precise balancing and blending of the individual tracks, resulting in the sort of carefully crafted production heard on Aretha Franklin's new LP. For the first time, Otis began to think about applying these state-of-the-art techniques of recording and arranging to his own work.

Another concern that weighed on Otis during his stay in Sausalito was the weariness he felt after two long months on tour. For five years, he had devoted himself with a single-minded intensity to the business of "making that dollar" night after night on the road. But the Whisky, the Fillmore, Europe, and Monterey had exposed him to a domain of show business that lay beyond the civic auditoriums and ghetto theaters in which he had spent his career. He now began to think about shifting his priorities away from the constant grind of one-nighters and devoting more of his time to songwriting, recording, and producing. Over the course of the year, the Walden agency had succeeded in raising Otis's guarantee to a minimum of $3,000 a night, while the reduction in the size of his road band from ten or more pieces to the six-man Bar-Kays had made his touring operation much more economical. Since he had started using the Cessna on a regular basis, it had added a new flexibility to his schedule. Going forward, Otis envisioned restricting his performance schedule to two or three shows on weekends, flying to and from his dates and spending his weekdays working in Macon and Memphis. As it was, James Alexander of the Bar-Kays was about to start his senior year in high school, and other members of the group had enrolled in Memphis-area junior colleges. An abbreviated tour schedule would allow them to perform on the weekends and return to their classes in Memphis during the week.

Otis's first practical step in implementing this new approach was to speak with Jim Lowe and Dick Fraser about acquiring an airplane that could carry his entire band. After hearing how much he was willing to spend, Lowe felt the obvious choice was the Beechcraft Model 18—more popularly known as the Beech 18—a twin-engine workhorse that was introduced in the late 1930s as a small airliner, saw extensive military service as a transport and trainer during World War II, and remained in production throughout the 1950s and '60s as a popular corporate aircraft. The Beech 18 could carry up to eleven passengers and crew. It had a range of 900 miles and a cruising speed of 190 mph. Though it sold new for around $250,000, by 1967 it could be purchased used for less than a third of that, thanks to the recent introduction of a more refined and comfortable turboprop replacement called the Beech King Air. Though the Beech 18 was ideal for Otis's budget and needs, Jim Lowe had reservations about recommending it, owing to the fact that Dick Fraser had less than a hundred hours of flight time in twin-engine aircraft, all of it in the much less powerful Cessna 310. The Beech was a different class of airplane. Lowe had trained Fraser and respected his ability, but there was no substitute for experience when it came to flying planes.

Otis, however, was not one to hesitate once he had seized upon an idea. He asked Lowe and Fraser to find him a Beech 18. Within a few weeks, they located a well-equipped model, built in 1962, previously owned by a construction company in Pennsylvania that had traded it in on a Beech King Air. The cost was $78,000, and the seller was offering financing; Otis could acquire it with a $28,000 down payment. The cabin was configured to accommodate seven passengers in addition to the two seats in the cockpit, but there was room in the back to add another seat or two. Among its amenities was Beech's New-Matic autopilot, which Jim Lowe believed would help Dick Fraser handle the airplane more smoothly.

Otis and his Beech 18

EVERY SEPTEMBER, *Melody Maker* announced the results of its annual readers poll. In a remarkable testament to Otis's popularity in Britain, the 1967 poll placed him at #1 on the magazine's list of Top Male Singers, displacing Elvis Presley in a pop pantheon that included Lennon, McCartney, Dylan, and perennial British favorites Scott Walker and Tom Jones. This international tribute was proudly reported in the African American press, and the Los Angeles–based fan magazine *Soul* marked the occasion by publishing an "interview" with Otis that was actually written by Phil Walden on Otis's behalf. "Basically, I like any music that remains simple," Phil had Otis say. "There is beauty in simplicity whether you are talking about architecture, art, or music." The question "Why do you still live in Georgia?" gave Phil an opportunity to present his own views on race relations in the South: "I believe a great deal of the communication between [the] so-called white and black community of the South is lost by the very fact that the educated or talented Negroes of the South desert their home states for Northern communities. This leaves a large number of uneducated or unemployed to represent the Southern Negro." "Otis" went on to say that he wanted to start a summer camp for underprivileged children that would include "programs to teach civic and economic activities and the democratic processes of this country."

Later that month, the real-life Otis Redding returned to Muscle Shoals to produce the tracks for Arthur Conley's next Atlantic album, this time working with members of the rhythm section that had played behind Aretha Franklin and a horn section that included some of the many Memphis musicians, including Wayne Jackson and Andrew Love, who had been supplementing their incomes with work at Fame. Otis was still feeling his way as a producer, and he gave Conley a lot of free rein in the selection of material. The results were mixed. Conley lacked the emotional gravitas to bring off Otis's "I've Been Loving You Too Long," though he turned in a subtle, subdued version of "A Change Is Gonna Come" and gave a strong performance on Jimmy Reed's classic "Baby What You Want Me to Do." Otis added lyrical horn lines to a pair of Conley originals, "Love Got Me" and the Marvin Gaye–influenced "Hand in Glove." He also awarded himself a writing credit on a track called "Ha! Ha! Ha!" that was a brazen steal of "Don't You Just Know It," the 1958 hit by Huey "Piano" Smith and the Clowns, faintly disguised by the addition of a female backup chorus.

Otis went directly from his production work with Conley to a session at Stax, where he recorded three new ballads, all of them collaborations with lyricists Phil Walden had recruited to help him to upgrade the "content" of his songs. The naturalistic imagery in "Gone Again" ("Picture a winter, without any snow / Picture a river, with nowhere to flow") was the work of a Philadelphia talent scout named Gene Lawson. "Free Me" was a collaboration with Joe Rock, a Pittsburgh booking agent whose claim to fame was "I Don't Have You," a smarmy doo-wop hit by the Skyliners in 1959. Rock also contributed to the best of the new ballads, "I've Got Dreams to Remember," but Otis's main collaborator on this tune was his wife, Zelma, who had written it as a love poem while Otis was away in Europe in the spring of 1967 and presented it to him when he returned. His initial reaction, Zelma recalled, was rather dismissive, but Otis had filed the lyric away, and without mentioning it to her, rewrote it with Joe Rock's help. With the addition of these three new tracks, Otis had recorded more than enough material over the course of 1967 to fill both sides of an LP. But he wasn't satisfied with the work, and instead of a new album, Stax released a collection of his greatest hits, titled *History of Otis Redding,* in the fall of 1967. The cover was another marketing mishap, consisting of an amateurish, almost unrecognizable sketch of Otis by an unknown artist named Dot Ogden. The gatefold jacket opened to reveal several photographs from the Olympia in Paris and a long essay by Ralph J. Gleason that drew on his previous reviews of Otis at the Fillmore and Basin Street West. The first side of the album was all ballads, from "These Arms of Mine" through to "Try a Little Tenderness." The second side was all dance tunes, from "Security" through "Satisfaction."

At the start of October, Otis and the Bar-Kays flew to New York to play a week at the Apollo. Since the new plane had not yet been delivered, they took commercial flights. By the time they arrived, the hoarseness that had been plaguing Otis all summer had turned into a full-blown case of laryngitis that made it hard for him to talk, much less sing. Joe Galkin's frantic call to Atlantic Records turned up the name of a noted New York throat specialist, Dr. Leon Arnold, who practiced at Mount Sinai Hospital and whose list of celebrity patients included Harry Belafonte and Sammy Davis Jr. Arnold examined Otis and found that he had developed polyps on his vocal cords, a common ailment among professional singers in all genres, caused by chronic overuse of the voice. (Singing too much or too loudly causes swelling of the vocal cords, which can thicken and harden into polyps if the swelling is not allowed to heal.) Dr. Arnold recommended that Otis cancel his dates at the Apollo, rest his voice entirely, and return a week later for further evaluation and possible surgery. On exceptionally short notice, Chubby Checker filled in for him at the Apollo.

The following week, when Otis returned, Dr. Arnold found that his vocal cords were still badly inflamed and recommended surgery to remove the polyps. The procedure was done at the hospital under general anesthesia. Otis was discharged that same day with strict instructions not to speak at all for two weeks and not to try singing for at least a month. After the operation, Otis and Joe Galkin returned to their hotel suite, where Otis dolefully handed Phil Walden a note that read, "I'll *never* sing again." "You told me everything was going to be alright with this fucking celebrity doctor!" Phil screamed before the two of them burst out laughing at his response. Joking aside, the procedure had gone well, but the concern about how the surgery might affect his voice was very real.

Otis flew back to Macon while the Walden agency sent out telegrams canceling his upcoming bookings. The requirement that he not utter a word for two weeks would have been difficult for most people, but for someone as voluble as Otis, it was a torment—as was his constant presence at home for Zelma, who was accustomed to Otis's comings and goings. "I really got to realize what having a husband was all about," she later said. "I had to cook every day. I had to wait on him. I said, if this man doesn't leave, he's just driving me crazy. 'Cause we hadn't spent *that* much time together." Still, Zelma decided, "[i]t was like the Lord intended for us to spend some time together and let him see what his kids were doing during the day." For the first two weeks, Otis moped around the house, ringing a bell whenever he needed something, communicating with his family by means of written notes, mutely strumming his guitar into a tape recorder and scribbling song lyrics on scraps of paper. When at last he was allowed to whisper and then talk, his speaking voice sounded fine, and what he had to say surprised Zelma. Otis had let his beard grow during his convalescence. "I said Otis, you're not going to live with that beard," Zelma recalled. "He said, 'When I go back out it's going to be the new Otis Redding. I've got to change my style now. People are tired of hearing me plead and beg. I've got to be different. I'm gonna be new.'"

Encouraged by the way his voice felt, Otis made plans to ease his way back into singing by doing some recording at Stax during the second half of November and resuming a limited schedule of live shows the following month. Phil Walden lined up a series of weekend dates for him in December, culminating in a trip to the West Coast at the end of the month to perform for six nights at Winterland, an ice-skating rink in San Francisco that Bill Graham was using to present larger shows than the Fillmore could accommodate. In the meantime, Dick Fraser began familiarizing himself with the Beech 18, which was delivered toward the end of October, freshly repainted, like the Cessna, with the logo *Otis Redding Enterprises*. Otis also applied to the FAA to have the airplane's identification number changed to include his initials: 39OR.

THE DOCK OF THE BAY

When I heard some of the songs he was writing, I said, "You're
right. You are going to be new. You're not begging anymore."

—ZELMA REDDING

IN THE FALL OF 1967, THE AMERICAN RECORD BUSINESS PASSED THE
milestone of a billion dollars in annual sales, having grown by more than
50 percent over the preceding five years. Much of this rapid expansion
owed to the tightening grip of major corporate labels on the pop market,
a trend that began with RCA's acquisition of Elvis Presley in 1956, picked
up steam with Capitol's acquisition of the Beatles in 1963, and reached
a new level of audacity when Columbia plunged into the realm of "underground" rock by signing a half dozen acts at Monterey. The defiant
exceptions to this rule of major label domination were Motown, which
had brought black music into the popular mainstream as never before, and
Atlantic, whose incomparable roster of R&B singers combined with its
promotion of white pop groups like Sonny and Cher, the Young Rascals,
and the Bee Gees to generate what *Billboard* described as "a virtually unprecedented blitz" of the Pop charts during the summer of 1967, when the
label and its affiliates held eighteen positions in the Hot 100, including
the top two spots.

Celebrated by *Time* magazine as the Turkish Tycoon of Soul, Ahmet
Ertegun saw this remarkable run of success as proof of Atlantic's ability, after twenty years in the business, to adapt to changing times. His
partner, Jerry Wexler, however, saw it as an unmistakable sign that the
roof was about to cave in, and with the support of Nesuhi Ertegun, he
managed to convince Ahmet that Atlantic's value would never be higher
and that the time had come to cash in on their investment by selling the
company. In the last week of October, *Billboard* reported that the Holly-

wood entertainment conglomerate Warner Bros.–Seven Arts had reached an agreement in principle to purchase Atlantic for a combination of cash and stock worth $17 million. Once the sale went through, the article stated, Atlantic would operate as an autonomous division of Warner Bros. It would continue to be run by Ahmet Ertegun, Jerry Wexler, and Nesuhi Ertegun, "with the same management, personnel, distributors, international licensees, and artists as heretofore."

At Stax, the ramifications of this prospective purchase were unclear. Under the "key man" clause of the agreement that Jim Stewart and Jerry Wexler had signed in 1965, the sale would give Stax the option of withdrawing from its distribution deal with Atlantic in six months' time. Stax had no good reason to exercise that option, but at the very least, Stewart and Al Bell (who had recently been rewarded with an equity stake in the company) hoped to renegotiate the percentages of the deal. Another possibility that Stewart and Bell considered was that Warner Bros. might purchase Stax as well, thereby consolidating its hold on the wellsprings of southern soul.

Around the middle of November, five weeks after his throat operation, Otis began to sing—gingerly at first, then with growing confidence. His voice *felt* good, better than it had in years. Encouraged, he reserved a block of studio time at Stax the following week. Dick Fraser flew him to Memphis in the new Beechcraft, and Otis phoned Steve Cropper from the airport to tell him, "I've got something I need you to hear." When the two of them got together, "something" turned out to be a medium-tempo ballad called "The Dock of the Bay." It was one of more than a dozen songs that Otis had sketched out during his convalescence from the surgery, but this one was special. Otis regarded it as the song that inaugurated his idea of the "new Otis Redding." In its contemplative mood and acoustic instrumental texture, "The Dock of the Bay" bore some affinities to "A Day in the Life," the final track on *Sgt. Pepper,* on which the Beatles had dropped the curtain on the gaudy self-assertion of their Pepper Band personas in order to expose the deep well of ambivalence and vulnerability that lay behind the mask of the crowd-pleasing entertainer. In his own way, Otis was attempting something similar.

A few weeks before the start of these November sessions, in an effort to keep pace with the growing demands for studio time from Stax's expanding roster of acts, Jim Stewart had finally relented and hired a full-time recording engineer. Ron Capone was a Louisiana native in his thirties who had made his home in Memphis, where he learned his craft at a studio called Pepper Tanner that specialized in the production of advertising jingles. Capone was also a capable drummer who had played with members of the Mar-Keys at club dates around town. He was an amiable man, and Otis warmed to him quickly. Most important, he was well versed in the use of the four-track system, and he did not share Jim Stewart's superstition that mono recording was in and of itself a key to the "Stax sound."

The sessions that began that week had the same focused intensity as the sessions for *Otis Blue*; the difference was that they continued for days on end, driven by Otis's pent-up energy, his backlog of new material, and the shared excitement at how good his voice sounded after his throat surgery. "His voice was so clear, we just couldn't get over it," Steve Cropper recalled. "We just couldn't record enough. And when the band would leave at night, we'd break and go have a little dinner somewhere, and come back to the studio and start recording." Whereas the daytime sessions involved the entire Stax band, the night sessions centered on Otis, Cropper, and Ron Capone, who would run the board and play drums while Otis sang and Cropper overdubbed instrumental parts, making four-track demos that could then be refined and rerecorded by the full group the following day. When Otis learned that Don Covay was passing through Memphis, the two of them spent an evening together that yielded a pair of cowritten songs. All told, in addition to "The Dock of the Bay," they cut around a dozen new tracks. These included the titles "Hard to Handle," "Direct Me," "Love Man," "The Happy Song," "You Made a Man Out of Me," "Nobody's Fault but Mine," "Think About It," "Champagne and Wine," and Otis's new manifesto, "I'm a Changed Man." Most were medium- to uptempo songs with markedly stronger, wittier, sexier lyrics than Otis's previous work. And many were collaborations, with Covay, Steve Cropper, Al Bell, Deanie Parker, Alan Walden, and others, most of whom helped out on the lyrics.

In addition to the new material, Steve Cropper and Ron Capone encouraged Otis to go back and recut his vocals on some of the tunes he had recorded earlier in the year, using the four-track to overdub his "new" voice. But the song that set the tone for the whole enterprise was "The Dock of the Bay." The basic track was one of the first things they recorded, with acoustic guitar, bass, drums, and horns. On the initial take, Otis forgot the words to the last verse and then tried to whistle a melody in the coda that served mainly to demonstrate, as Ron Capone announced over the intercom, "You're not going to make it as a whistler." It didn't take long for them to get the song down, and when they did, according to Cropper, "We knew when we cut it that it was the best thing he'd ever done. We just looked at each other and said we got it, this is it, we did it."

At some point during these November sessions, Otis called Jerry Wexler in New York. As Wexler recounted the conversation, "He said, 'I want you to do my next album.' And I said, 'Otis, that could be very political. I don't want any problems with Jim Stewart and everybody.' I said to Otis, 'Well, why do you want me to produce you? You're going great with Jim and Steve Cropper and your own thing.' He said, 'I want to get my sound a little thicker the way you do with Aretha.' We had another sound, we had more broadness and more impact, it had more shadings and more dynamics. I said, 'Otis that would be great, but what about the problems with Stax and Jim Stewart?' He said we'll work on that, don't worry about it, and left it there."

Tom Dowd recalled a similar conversation with Otis around this time, but there is no way to know exactly what he had in mind. Having already recorded more than enough good new material to fill both sides of an album, Otis's overtures to Wexler and Dowd would most likely have pertained to the album after that. But he was also talking with Steve Cropper about renting a house in Memphis so that he could spend more time there writing and recording. He may have envisioned recording like Aretha with Wexler and Dowd in New York, using musicians imported from Memphis or Muscle Shoals. Or he may have envisioned prevailing on Jim Stewart to allow Wexler and Dowd to work with him at Stax. Wexler's concern about the "politics" of the situation was further compounded by the uncertainty surrounding the pending sale of Atlantic to Warner Bros. But Otis had made it clear during the Stax-Volt European tour that he was not about to let Jim Stewart come between him and the way he wanted his music to sound.

On the first weekend in December, Otis tested his voice in live performance by playing a private party at a country club in New Orleans and a theater show in Newark, New Jersey. Dick Fraser flew him and the Bar-Kays to these dates in the new Beechcraft, but because the plane had not yet been modified to provide enough seating for the entire group, several of the band members took commercial flights. For the first time in a long time, Otis's road manager, Speedo Sims, did not accompany him on this trip, as he was still suffering from the aftereffects of the hallucinogenic drug he had been given in San Francisco. In addition, he and Otis had had a falling-out over Otis's unfulfilled promise to give Speedo a share of the publishing royalties on "Respect"—a long-standing issue that took on new life now that Aretha Franklin had turned the song into a million-selling hit. For two years, Otis had been proposing various schemes to reward Speedo for his role in writing the song, but when Speedo began to press the matter, Otis reacted angrily. Both of them regarded the breach in their relationship as temporary, but for the time being, Otis was on his own.

The dates in New Orleans and Newark went well, and Otis returned to Memphis the following Monday. As the sessions entered their third week, his mood became progressively more intense. "That was our first real insanity at Stax," Booker Jones recalled. "We were in the studio until two or three in the morning, and then back at ten A.M., recording all the time. Through it all, he was electric. . . . Obviously," Jones concluded, "there was some type of premonition going on."

That same week, *Soul* magazine published a short press release from Stax that ran under the headline "Otis to Become a Pilot." "He is currently taking flying lessons and is expected to qualify for a pilot's license by the end of the year," the magazine reported. "The singer has looked into the possibility of constructing a landing strip on his ranch home, but was dismayed to learn it would cost over $40,000." The press release was typically overstated; while Otis was indeed interested in learning to fly, he had barely gotten started on the forty to sixty hours of instruction it would take to earn a pilot's license, which in any case would not qualify him to fly a Beech 18.

His love for people showed up in his songs. He was always trying to get back to his baby or he missed her—she was the greatest thing in the world. . . . Otis didn't get to be with his wife
and children as much as he wanted. He had a definite thing for
them.

—STEVE CROPPER

On Friday, December 8, Otis came by Stax in the morning
to look in on Steve Cropper, who was setting up to overdub guitar
parts on some of the tracks they had recorded that week. After hanging
around the studio for a while, Otis stuck his head through the door of the
control room. "See you on Monday," he said. That afternoon, Dick Fraser
flew Otis and most of the Bar-Kays to Nashville, where they were booked
to play a fraternity dance in the Vanderbilt Memorial Gym. As an opening act, Otis invited Carl Sims (no relation to Speedo), a young singer
from Memphis who had performed with the Bar-Kays in local clubs. In
Speedo's absence, the Bar-Kays invited a friend named Matthew Kelly
to serve as Otis's valet, while two members of the group drove a rental
car from Memphis to Nashville with the band's equipment. The rest of
the weekend's itinerary consisted of a Saturday-night date in Cleveland
at Leo's Casino, a 700-seat club known for its integrated clientele and its
role as an out-of-town showcase for Motown acts, followed by a Sunday-
night date in Madison, Wisconsin, at a club called the Factory.

The fraternity dance at Vanderbilt ended early, before 11:00, and Otis
decided they should leave at once for Cleveland in hopes of catching the
last set by the Temptations, who were playing at Leo's that night. Though
the flight took two and a half hours, the club was close to Cleveland's
lakefront commuter airport, and they caught the end of the show. Otis and

the band spent Saturday afternoon taping a syndicated television program called *Upbeat* at the local ABC affiliate in Cleveland, performing live versions of "Respect" and "Try a Little Tenderness." The Bar-Kays wore pale orange uniforms and deadpan expressions as they played behind Otis, who was clearly enjoying himself. His rendition of "Respect" conformed to his own arrangement of the song, but in deference to Aretha Franklin, he added her stop chorus of "R-E-S-P-E-C-T / Tell you what it means to me." "Try a Little Tenderness" was very capably done, with trumpeter Ben Cauley adding a Spanish tinge to the horn lines. Otis closed the show by performing "Knock on Wood" as a duet with Mitch Ryder, a white Detroit soul singer who sounded desperately out of his league.

James Alexander remembered their appearance at Leo's that Saturday night as one of the best gigs they ever played, but when Otis called home on Sunday morning to check in with Zelma, she felt he sounded "depressed." They discussed household matters, and Otis said he would phone her when he got to Madison. "I was about to hang up," Zelma recalled, "and I heard his voice and I put the phone back to my ear and he said, 'Most of all, you know what I want you to do? I want you to be real good for me and I want you to take care of my children.' I said, 'Otis, I always take care of your children and I'm always good!' I tried to turn it into a joke, but he was very serious."

They gathered at the airport around noon. James Alexander and Carl Sims were nominated to return the rental cars to Cleveland's main airport, Hopkins, after which they would board a commercial flight to Milwaukee. The plan called for Dick Fraser to drop everyone off in Madison, then fly back to Milwaukee to pick up Alexander and Sims. They took off a few minutes later. The weather in Cleveland was rainy, with the temperature around forty degrees. The weather in Madison was more concerning, with the temperature near the freezing mark and reports of fog, low overcast, and cold rain.

The 400-mile trip took about two hours and fifteen minutes in the Beech. Their route took them over Ann Arbor, Lake Michigan, and Milwaukee. The flight was uneventful, though most of it was through heavy clouds. Shortly after 3:00 (they had passed into the Central Time Zone), Dick Fraser spoke with the tower in Madison and received a weather update informing him that visibility on the ground had declined to less than a mile. On that basis, Fraser initiated an instrument approach to the main runway at Truax Field, as Dane County Municipal Airport was known. The city of Madison lies on a strip of land between a pair of large lakes, Mendota and Monona. The airport was due north of Lake Monona, about six miles from the downtown. None of this was visible from the Beech, however, because the whole region lay under a thick blanket of clouds that reached as low as a hundred feet above the ground in some places. In keeping with the standard procedure for an instrument landing, Fraser set his autopilot to follow the radio signals that would control the orientation and glide path of the plane and bring it to the edge of the runway at a height of two hundred feet.

At 3:25, Fraser radioed the Madison tower and requested permission to land. The Beech was now on its final approach, about four miles south of the airport and twelve hundred feet over Lake Monona, descending through the dense overcast. With the controls still set on autopilot, Fraser focused his attention on monitoring his altitude and position and looking for the first sign of a break in the cloud cover that would allow him to catch sight of the flashing runway lights ahead. With one hand on the control yoke, he pulled a lever on the center console to lower the landing gear. As the wheels came down with a thump, the Beech went into a sudden, vertigo-inducing stall, with its nose pitching straight down toward the surface of Lake Monona and the whole airplane rolling to the left. Ben Cauley had been dozing in his seat, directly behind Otis, who sat in the copilot's seat on the right side of the cabin. He woke up to hear the "bump" of the landing gear engaging, followed by a "spinning sensation of falling" that made it hard for him to breathe. Cauley heard his saxophonist Phalon Jones, who was sitting across the aisle, say, "Oh no." It took the free-falling plane about ten seconds to hit the surface of the lake below. The force of the impact shattered the fuselage and tore the passenger seats from their anchors. "When I came to I was on top of all this water," Cauley recalled. "The only thing I could think was, 'We're in the wrong place.'"

Bernard Reese, a bakery executive who lived on the eastern shore of Lake Monona, was standing in his yard when he saw an airplane plummet out of the low overcast and hit the water with a powerful impact about half a mile away. While the plane rested on the surface, Reese ran into his house and called the police. By the time he went back outside, the plane had disappeared. A police boat reached the scene seventeen minutes after the call came in. The officers on board found Ben Cauley clutching a seat cushion, alive and in shock. Amid the debris that floated on the surface, they retrieved the bodies of Dick Fraser and the Bar-Kay guitarist Jimmy King. They also retrieved an attaché case that caught their eye. After determining that there were no more survivors in the freezing water, they returned to shore, anxious to get Cauley to a hospital. Other boats remained in the area until nightfall, when the search was suspended.

Phil Walden, Joe Galkin, Jerry Wexler, Ahmet Ertegun, and Tom Dowd were all attending a radio convention that weekend at the Riviera Hotel in Las Vegas, where Wexler had accepted an award as music executive of the year. On Sunday afternoon, Wexler and Ertegun left the convention and boarded a flight to New York. Joe Galkin was holding forth at the craps table of the Riviera's casino when Tom Dowd heard him being paged. Knowing that Galkin was oblivious to all else when he was gambling, Dowd took the call. It fell to him to inform Phil and Joe that Otis's plane had gone down. Jerry Wexler and Ahmet Ertegun heard the news after they landed in New York. When he arrived home at his town house on the Upper East Side, Ahmet sat down on a sofa with his wife, Mica, and wept.

Booker T. and the MGs had played a college gig the night before in Terre Haute, Indiana, and were waiting to board their flight from Indianapolis to Memphis, which was delayed by fog and rain. Dave Porter, who was singing with the group, called his wife to update her on their status. She told him she had heard on the radio that Otis's plane had crashed. Booker Jones, Steve Cropper, Duck Dunn, and Al Jackson learned about the death of their friend and inspiration in an airport lounge, where they had been speculating a few minutes before about whether they could get in touch with Dick Fraser and prevail on him to fly them to Memphis if their commercial flight was canceled.

Andrew Love heard the news report on WDIA. He immediately called Wayne Jackson. "I said Wayne, they're all dead. Otis and the Bar-

Kays." Jackson recalled "standing there for a long time. I don't know how long. Fifteen or twenty minutes. And Andy and I didn't say a word. I had a feeling, a pivotal feeling, as though nothing would ever be the same again." Jim Stewart had a similar feeling when Joe Galkin called him on Sunday evening: "The day that Otis Redding died took a lot out of me. I was never the same person. The company was never the same to me after that. Something was taken out and never replaced. The man was a walking inspiration."

Zelma, as always, was home with the children in Round Oak when the phone rang. A man whose voice she didn't recognize told her that Otis's plane was missing and hung up before she could ask who was calling. Her initial reaction was that it was a nasty prank of some sort, but she decided to call Dick Fraser's wife to see what was going on. "They're all gone, Zelma," Diane Fraser told her. "Dick's gone. Otis is gone." Karla remembers Zelma screaming and dropping the phone and running out of the house. Karla ran after her in her bare feet, a five-year-old girl wondering what could possibly have happened to upset her mother that way.

Phil Walden reacted at first by going into his managerial mode, booking his flights back to Macon and worrying about how to break the news to his father, who was touring in the Caribbean with Percy Sledge. He then returned to his room at the Riviera and "totally went to pieces." The hotel doctor was called to administer a sedative so that Phil could get some sleep. On Monday morning, with Otis's body still missing, Phil arranged for one of his employees, a young road manager named Twiggs Lyndon, to accompany Zelma and the Rev. Redding to Madison that day. They arrived shortly after divers recovered Otis's body from the bottom of the lake. They had found him at the back of the Beech's shattered cabin, still strapped in his seat. He had a wound on his forehead and assorted cuts and bruises that led the coroner to determine that he had probably been knocked unconscious by the initial impact of the crash and then drowned when the plane sank. The possessions found on his body included a gold watch, a billfold containing three hundred dollars in cash, and a small bag of marijuana. Twiggs Lyndon and Phil Walden prevailed on the coroner to disregard the pot. Otis's body was flown back to Macon the following day.

The attaché case the police reported finding at the scene of the crash had contained several thousand dollars in cash receipts from the shows at Vanderbilt and Leo's Casino; the case was returned, but the money vanished without a trace. Many years later, a policeman who had taken part in the investigation told a reporter for the *Madison Capital Times*, "You want something for the record on that attaché case? You won't get it."

Otis's funeral was originally scheduled for Friday, December 15, at the City Auditorium, Macon's great temple of black music, the use of which was offered to the Redding family by the city's newly elected Republican mayor, Ronnie Thompson, a former white gospel singer whom Phil Walden had befriended during his recent campaign. But the service was postponed until the following Monday to accommodate the large number of music celebrities who wished to attend. Encased in a glass-covered casket, Otis's body lay in state in the City Auditorium on Monday morning while thousands of Maconites filed by. The service began at noon, under overcast skies, with the Rev. C. J. Andrews of the Vineville Baptist Church presiding. The arrival of the stars—James Brown, Wilson Pickett, Joe Tex, Solomon Burke, Percy Sledge, Sam Moore, Dave Prater, Johnny Taylor, Joe Simon, Rufus Thomas, Carla Thomas, Arthur Conley, Don Covay—was greeted with gasps and cheers by some of the 4,500 mourners who filled the auditorium and the even greater number who lined the streets outside. (It was reported that Aretha Franklin was coming, but she never made the trip.) The members of Booker T. and the MGs were there as part of the Stax contingent, with Booker Jones seated at the organ, where he accompanied Joe Simon on the gospel hymn "Jesus Keep Me Near the Cross" and Johnny Taylor singing "God Is Standing By." Zelma Redding broke down during Simon's performance ("Be my glory ever / Till my raptured soul shall find / Rest beyond the river"), wailing and stamping her heels on the hardwood floor while a pair of uniformed nurses tried to console her.

His voice breaking, Jerry Wexler began his eulogy, "Otis Redding was a natural prince." Wexler then paused as he struggled to regain his composure. "When you were with him, he communicated love and a tremendous faith in human possibility, a promise that great and happy events were coming. In some magic way, his recordings had the same inspirational quality. His performances were original and powerful, and he sang his songs with the emotion of great lyric poetry." After naming some of the many people whose lives were touched by Otis in his twenty-six years on earth, Wexler ended by saying, "Otis sang, 'Respect when I come home.' And Otis has come home."

To the strains of "These Arms of Mine," the casket was carried out of the auditorium by Earl Sims, Sylvester Huckabee, Arthur Conley, Joe Tex, Hamp Swain, Johnny Taylor, Joe Simon, and Clark Walden, standing in for his brother Alan, who was too distraught to serve as a pallbearer. In a scene out of his usual publicity playbook, James Brown was mobbed by fans on the street outside the auditorium and required the police to intervene. Then a long line of limousines made its way out of the city and across the Jones County line to the Big O Ranch, where Otis was buried in the yard of the home he loved.

On the Sunday before Otis's funeral, two of the four Bar-Kays who died in the crash, Jimmy King and Carl Cunningham, along with their friend Matthew Kelly, were buried in Memphis, where the Booker T. Washington Warriors marching band performed "When Day Is Done" in their honor. The services for Phalon Jones and Ronnie Caldwell, whose bodies were recovered later than those of their bandmates, were held a few days after that.

PARANOIA IS A fearful delusion that leads people to attribute far greater power or agency to their adversaries than they actually possess. In 1964, the historian Richard Hofstadter published a celebrated essay in *Harper's* magazine in which he characterized the "paranoid style" in postwar American politics as a primarily right-wing phenomenon, citing McCarthyism and Goldwater Republicanism to illustrate his case. Hofstadter's essay was based on a lecture he delivered at Oxford University on November 21, 1963. The events of the following day would significantly enlarge his thesis. The national trauma of John F. Kennedy's assassination introduced the center and left of the American political spectrum to the satisfying intrigues of conspiracy theory and helped to establish paranoid thinking as a generalized phenomenon in American public life—to the point where it sometimes seemed that *no one* died by fate or accident during the 1960s, and that every public tragedy was perceived as the work of unseen hands.

There were people in Macon, and throughout the music industry, who needed to make sense of Otis Redding's senseless death, and for those familiar with the details of Otis's career, his relationship with the Waldens became the focus of their paranoia. Within days of the tragedy, a malicious rumor arose that Phil Walden had played some part—*must* have played some part—in Otis's death. It was said that Otis had been planning to fire Phil as his manager, prompting Phil to cash in on a life insurance policy he held in Otis's name; or that Phil had gotten involved, or had gotten Otis involved, with "Mafia interests" in the music business who had some score to settle with him; or that Otis's vague plan to "unionize" the soul fraternity had been seen as a dire threat to the white power structure of the entertainment industry. The details didn't matter. The point was that "someone" had wanted Otis dead and had fatally tampered with his plane. To describe these rumors as "unfounded" was beside the point. Otis was a black singer from the South whose successful career had been aggressively managed by a white man—indeed, an entire white family—who had profited handsomely from his success. To some people, this was not a biographical fact, this was a cautionary tale. This was what happened to a black man who was foolish or arrogant enough to place his trust in a white man in America in 1967.

It did not help that the official investigation into the crash of Beechcraft 390R was perfunctory. Across the country, there were more than six hundred fatal accidents involving privately owned planes in 1967, and the National Transportation Safety Board, which had been established only in April of that year, did not have the resources to delve deeply into most of them. The NTSB report on the fate of Otis's Beech listed the probable cause as "undetermined," citing "miscellaneous acts [and] conditions." But according to Jim Lowe's son Henry, a teenager at the time, his father felt he knew exactly what had happened as soon as he heard the circumstances of the accident. In Jim Lowe's expert opinion, Dick Fraser was a southern-trained pilot flying an unfamiliar airplane in northern winter conditions, making an instrument approach to an unfamiliar airport in a region of the country, the Great Lakes, that was notorious for icing conditions in the fall and winter months. The Beechcraft Model 18 was a sturdy, thick-winged plane, known for its ability to "carry a lot of ice." This may have given Fraser a false sense of confidence as he flew through dense clouds and declining temperatures on his way to Madison that day. Given the exceptionally low visibility and cloud ceiling, Fraser was correct to rely on the autopilot to fly the plane during its final approach to the airport so that he could focus intently on sighting the runway ahead. What Fraser did not know enough to take into account, however, was the capacity of the autopilot to mask the effects of ice building up on the Beech's airframe, silently correcting for the increased drag and aerodynamic instability until things reached the point, most likely caused by the lowering of the landing gear, where it couldn't correct anymore. At that moment, the autopilot would have automatically disengaged, sending the plane into a sudden, asymmetrical stall. At an altitude of barely 1,000 feet, there would have been no time for Fraser to recognize what was happening, much less compensate for it. He was not alone in this. NTSB records show that of the six other fatal accidents involving Beech 18s on final approach between 1967 and 1983, *all* of them involved icing conditions, and all but one of them took place in the Great Lakes region.

Otis on the dock

The night after he finished that song, he called me and told me,
"I got it. This is my first million-seller."

—PHIL WALDEN

EVEN BEFORE THE FUNERAL, AL BELL IN MEMPHIS AND JERRY Wexler in New York had spoken with Steve Cropper about the need to get a new record out as soon as possible. The grim reality was that tragedy sold in the music business. Buddy Holly's posthumous single, ominously titled "It Doesn't Matter Anymore," had reached #13 on the *Billboard* charts after his death in a plane crash in 1959—his best showing in more than a year. Sam Cooke's "Shake" was his most successful pop single since "Chain Gang." Otis's death was a commercial opportunity, and in the long run, the ability of Stax and Atlantic to capitalize on that opportunity would work to the benefit of Otis's bereaved family as well.

"It seemed impossible," Steve Cropper recalled. "It was hard just to go into the studio. Otis *was* Stax, and we were in pieces. But we did it." In the week before the funeral, Cropper put the finishing touches on "(Sittin' on) The Dock of the Bay." There was no question in his mind that this was the right record to release; he knew how proud Otis had been of the track and how certain he had been that it was the song that would bring him the full measure of success. Cropper felt the same way about it, but in this he was alone at Stax. True to form, Jim Stewart showed no enthusiasm for the record. "It was just too far over the border for Jim," Duck Dunn recalled. "It had no R&B in it whatsoever. And I agreed with him. I thought it might even be detrimental." Phil and Alan Walden had expressed similar reservations when Otis played them a tape of the song shortly before he died. "I felt it was too pop for him," Phil admitted. For Jerry Wexler, however, the anomalous quality of "The Dock of the Bay," beginning with its somber, contemplative mood, made it "the perfect record" to release in the wake of his death.

Cropper maintained that he and Otis had discussed the possibility of having the Staple Singers, the noted family gospel group that had recently signed with Stax, sing backup on the track. Though it is hard to imagine what they might have added to this very solitary song, the idea was dropped after Otis's death. Instead, Cropper picked up on a jokey touch that Otis (who was taken with the use of sound effects on *Sgt. Pepper*) had tried on an earlier take, when he imitated the sound of a seagull at the start of the song. Cropper obtained a recording of gull calls and wave sounds from the jingle studio where Ron Capone had worked, made them into a tape loop, and mixed them onto the track. He sent the finished version to New York the week after Otis's funeral. Reprising a familiar point of contention between Stax and Atlantic, Jerry Wexler sent it back, asking Cropper to bring Otis's vocal up in the mix. Cropper made some adjustments, and the single was set to go.

Otis's death inspired an outpouring of publicity that far exceeded the sum of what was written about him during his life. It began with obituaries in newspapers and magazines ranging from the *New York Times* to the newly founded *Rolling Stone,* and it continued with detailed accounts of Otis's funeral that ran in African American papers nationwide. After attending the service in Macon, the *Chicago Defender*'s entertainment columnist Lee Ivory wrote glowingly of the Waldens, crediting them with "showing me what love there can be between white and black men in the God-forsaken red clay country of mid-Georgia." *Jet* magazine outdid its usual standards of sensationalism by illustrating Ben Cauley's first-person account of the plane crash with appalling photographs of Otis's body, still strapped in his seat, being hoisted out of the lake and lying on the floor of the Dane County morgue. *Esquire* published a belated and characteristically catty overview of the Monterey Pop Festival in its January 1968 issue; written by the rock critic Robert Christgau, the piece began with an account of Otis's performance ("the dancing, the chuckling, the running around, the whole image of masculine ease on which his career is based"), along with a two-page color photograph whose caption identified Otis as "the high point" of the festival. The *Saturday Evening Post* ran a feature on the soul scene in Memphis by the journalist Stanley Booth, a graduate of Macon's Lanier High School, whose story chronicled Otis's last sessions at Stax and the funerals of the Bar-Kays. Back home in Macon, the *Telegraph* published a column by its editor William Ott, who noted the irony that while Otis was the city's most famous resident, "to most Maconites over twenty-five, he and his music were strangers." Ott then joined the many people who were prepared to put words into Otis's mouth, writing that "Otis Redding never blamed the town for the occasional cutting insult he suffered from ignorant people who judge others by the color of their skins. He knew that prejudice can be found anywhere, north and south, and that every race has its bad actors."

Additional tributes appeared in the weeks and months ahead. *Melody Maker* eulogized Otis as "the man who introduced soul music to Britain," while Norman Jopling wrote a heartfelt piece in the *Record Mirror* that placed him among the ranks of the "legendary singers [with] the gift, like great writers, of reaching out and grabbing your emotions." The most perceptive posthumous appraisal came from Jon Landau, who followed his *Crawdaddy* review of *Dictionary of Soul* with an article in *Eye* magazine in the spring of 1968. Landau chronicled Otis's career with a precision that reflected his budding friendship with Phil Walden, who had sought him out after reading his piece in *Crawdaddy*. Picking up on a theme of that earlier review, Landau drew a contrast with the pretensions of many contemporary rock groups, celebrating Otis as an unabashed "entertainer" who was "openly and honestly concerned with pleasing crowds and being successful," and whose "music was always deliberately simple: direct, honest, unintellectual, and concise." He concluded by once again singing the praises of *Dictionary of Soul*, which he extolled as "one of the finest pop albums of the decade."

Ultimately, Otis Redding didn't need anyone else to write his epitaph. He had done that himself, with a newfound grace and eloquence. "(Sittin' on) The Dock of the Bay" was released as a single in January 1968. Having contributed to the verses, harmonized the bridge, and, in Otis's absence, produced the final track, Steve Cropper justly claimed a cowriting credit. In one of the crassest acts of his crassly opportunistic career, Al Bell arranged to have "Sweet Lorene," the nondescript tune he had written with Otis more than a year before, placed on the B-side of the single, thereby endowing himself with a share of the record's publishing royalties. Within days of its release, "(Sittin' on) The Dock of the Bay" assumed the trajectory of a runaway radio hit, rising into the Top 10 by the middle of February. A month later, having already sold more than a million copies, it crested at #1 in both Pop and R&B: the first posthumous #1 record in the history of the *Billboard* charts. Atlantic followed it with a hastily assembled album called *The Dock of the Bay* that included Otis's recent singles "Tramp," "The Glory of Love," and "I Love You More than Words Can Say," supplemented with an outtake ballad called "Open the Door," his updated version of "The Hucklebuck," and a pair of tracks,

"Nobody Knows You When You're Down and Out" and "Ole Man Trouble," from *Otis Blue*. The album sleeve, once again designed by Atlantic's Loring Eutemey, was beautifully produced. It featured a fine front-cover photograph of Otis at Monterey, a candid back-cover photograph of Otis playing the guitar (thereby acknowledging his role as a music *maker* for the first time), and erudite liner notes by Jon Landau, who added to his litany of praise by describing Otis as "the best one man campaign soul music ever had." Together with the *History of Otis Redding* greatest hits collection, *The Dock of the Bay* rose into the Top 10 on the LP charts and remained among the bestselling albums in the country for six months.

When Jerry Wexler described "(Sittin' on) The Dock of the Bay" as "the perfect record," he wasn't just referring to its commercial appeal. Like the sort of "divine invention" that Louise Redding ascribed to her brother as a child, the song seems to have emerged fully formed, without precedent in Otis's work, setting an evocative mood and then elaborating on that mood in a concerted and unexpected way. The instrumentation of the opening bars signals an immediate departure: the track begins in a hush of softly strummed acoustic guitar, washed by the sound of waves in a way that faintly suggests the static of an AM radio. "Sittin' in the morning sun, I'll be sittin' when the evening's done," Otis sings over the gentle, bobbing rhythm of bass, piano, and drums, introducing himself as a man on the edge, sitting on a dock, moored but not rooted in place, looking out to sea as the ships roll in and the "*ti-i*-ide" rolls away. All at once, with a confident grace, Otis seems to have mastered the use of metaphor, and in the second verse, he applies his new technique to a more personalized form of narrative than he had ever attempted before: "I left my home in Georgia, headed for the Frisco Bay," he sings, quietly joined by the chorus of horns that had provided him with his main source of musical companionship since the early days of his career. "I've got nothing to live for, looks like nothing's gonna come my way." The reference to home in Georgia gives the lyric an autobiographical cast, but the opposite was really the case, for this was the song on which, more than any other, Otis drew on the possibilities of fictional imagination. This Georgia boy with "nothing to live for" is the antithesis of the real-life Otis Redding, a man who had *everything* to live for at the time he wrote those words. "Looks like nothing's gonna change," he sings in the bridge of a song whose very existence was a testament to change, a declaration of the "new" Otis Redding, even as he halfheartedly resolves to "remain the same." After invoking a loneliness that "won't leave me alone," Otis sings the refrain a final time, his every word shadowed by Steve Cropper's lacy, loving filigrees on guitar, ending his somber masterpiece in the guise of a man at rest, if not at peace, indulging in the one activity he had never allowed himself in real life: "Sittin' at the dock of the bay . . . *wasting time.*" And then, like the great artist he was, Otis saved the best for last. Instead of his customary coda of rising horns, driving rhythm, and vocal pyrotechnics, the instruments evaporate, leaving only the pulse of the rhythm and the whisper of the acoustic guitar to accompany the sound of his whistling, a musical metaphor for contentment and nonchalance, applied here to the sort of syncopated countermelody that would normally be carried by the horns, stepping up and then winding down through a series of bluesy flatted thirds.

Like the songs that Otis drew inspiration from on *Sgt. Pepper,* "(Sittin' on) The Dock of the Bay" is something much more compelling than autobiography. Instead, it is the work of a musical artist adopting a new form of identity to reach for a larger truth. Like John Lennon in "A Day in the Life," or Sam Cooke in *his* transcendent epitaph, "A Change Is Gonna Come," Otis was shedding his usual persona of self-assurance and self-assertion in order to convey the uncertainty and ambivalence of life as it is actually lived. "It's unwise ever to assume that they're doing only one thing or expressing themselves in only one style," the critic Richard Poirier wrote of the songs on *Sgt. Pepper,* which "remind the listener that one kind of feeling about a subject isn't enough." The same could be said of "(Sittin' on) The Dock of the Bay." At the age of twenty-six—the same age as John Lennon when he wrote "A Day in the Life," the same age as Sam Cooke when he *began* his secular career—Otis was verging on a similar form of artistic maturity. Having made his name, in Jon Landau's words, by "doing something simple perfectly," he was preparing to introduce a new emotional complexity into his work.

NEEDLESS TO SAY, this was not to be. "The Dock of the Bay" was by far the most ambitious of the dozen or so songs that Otis recorded in the weeks before his death. But in the summer of 1968, Atlantic released eleven tracks from those final sessions on an album titled *The Immortal Otis Redding* that ranks with the best of *Otis Blue, The Soul Album,* and *Dictionary of Soul* in the canon of Otis's work. Befitting the title, there was a decidedly elegiac quality to the album's opening and closing tracks. *The Immortal Otis Redding* begins with "I've Got Dreams to Remember," Otis's poignant collaboration with Zelma, upgraded with a rerecorded vocal and, for the first time on one of his records, an overdubbed female backup chorus whose seamless interplay with Otis's singing turns the title line into a male-female dialogue ("rough dreams! . . . bad dreams!" he cries in response to a trio of voices he would never hear). Ten tracks later, the album ends with a delicately restrained medley of the gospel standards "Amen" and "This Little Light of Mine," on which Otis revisited his church roots as never before, paying homage to his own father with the lines "One thing my *pappy* used to say . . . Even in your home, son, you've got to let it shine."

An aesthetic of restraint and relaxation was the hallmark of many of the tracks from those last sessions, even the uptempo numbers, where Ron Capone's capable engineering served to highlight the subtleties in Otis's reconditioned voice and the superlative interplay in the band's accompaniment. (Among other things, Capone got a brighter and more balanced sound from Al Jackson's drums.) With its high, bluesy melody, "Hard to Handle" comes off as a swaggering sexual boast worthy of Muddy Waters or James Brown. "*Ba*-by, here I am, I'm a man on the scene," Otis announces over a hypnotic groove of jolting piano, snapping snare, and choppy, whirling guitar. He then goes on to dismiss his competition with the admonition "Boys will come a dime by the dozen / But that ain't nothing but *drugstore* loving / Pretty little thing let me light your candle / 'Cause, mama, I'm sure hard to handle." As the sequel to "Fa-Fa-Fa-Fa-Fa (Sad Song)," "The Happy Song" (equipped with the inane subtitle "Dum-Dum") applies a stomp rhythm and a joyful blast of brass to a vignette of domestic bliss inspired by Otis's weeks of convalescence at home: "Bring my breakfast to the table / When I go to work she knows I'm able / Do my job, I come back in / You want to see my baby's face: she just grin, grin, grin." Written in collaboration with Don Covay, "Think About It" is a delicate cameo of heartbreak that silhouettes Otis's singing against a muted background of groaning bass and rueful piano as he reminds his lover on her way out the door, "I'm the one who saved you from a long lonely life / I'm the one who gave you your first taste of paradise." "Champagne and Wine" is another collaboration, this one written with Alan Walden and Roy Johnson (a Walden agency client best known as the composer of the raucous Beatles cover "Mr. Moonlight"). It has Otis romancing a former flame ("the one girl that I can't forget") with the assurance "I'm a man now—a full-grown man." Otis enlists a chorus of laughing, swooning horns to strike a similar pose of self-conscious maturity in "You Made a Man Out of Me," while on "Nobody's Fault but Mine," his attempts at self-recrimination ("But I was such a doggone fool / Trying to be so doggone cool") are animated by Al Jackson's stumbling beat and Steve Cropper's acerbic lead guitar, which endow the song with one of the fattest, funkiest grooves that Stax would ever produce.

The release of *The Immortal Otis Redding* was the result of an awkward new arrangement between Atlantic and Stax. In the winter of 1968, after months of negotiations had failed to yield an acceptable offer for the purchase of Stax by Warner Bros., Jim Stewart decided to exercise his option to terminate the agreement he had signed with Jerry Wexler in 1965. That spring, with the concurrence of his partners Estelle Axton and Al Bell, Stewart sold his record label to Gulf & Western Industries, a New York–based conglomerate that already owned ABC-Paramount Records, for approximately $1 million in cash and $3 million worth of convertible debentures that were based on Stax's future earnings.

Stewart, Axton, and Bell considered the offers they received from Warner Bros. insultingly low, but the economic reality of the situation was that Otis Redding was dead, while Stax's other bestselling artists, Sam and Dave, had always been under contract to Atlantic—a fact that Stewart had failed to mention to the musicians and songwriters at Stax who had turned the duo into such a successful recording act. In the long run, however, the question of who owned the rights to Sam and Dave paled beside a provision that only came to Stewart's attention after the sale of Atlantic went through, when he discovered that the letter of agreement he had signed with Wexler in 1965 stipulated in no uncertain terms ("absolutely and forever, without any limitations or restrictions") that Atlantic owned the rights to *all* of the recordings it had distributed for Stax, dating back to the start of the relationship between the two labels in 1961. That Stewart was blindsided by this revelation affirmed his claim that he had never bothered to read the contract or have it reviewed by a lawyer. Stax loyalists would ascribe this blunder to Stewart's honorable, trusting nature—thereby casting Jerry Wexler in the role of a wily New York Jew. But Stewart was, after all, a former bank officer, and his failure to understand, much less negotiate, the terms of the distribution deal that had underwritten his company's three-year run of remarkable success was only the crowning example of the stubborn, if well-intentioned, ineptitude that had characterized his career as a record executive from the start.

Despite his feelings of embarrassment and betrayal, Stewart recognized that it was still in Stax's best interest to maintain the terms of the Atlantic deal where Otis Redding was concerned. With this in mind, the agreement terminating the relationship between the two labels included a provision that gave Atlantic the option of issuing any *unreleased* tracks that Otis had recorded in the year before his death, with Stax receiving its usual royalty. *The Immortal Otis Redding* was the first and the best of the three albums that Atlantic would cull from that trove of unissued (and in some cases unfinished) material over the next two years. Though its sales did not equal those of *The Dock of the Bay*, they exceeded 300,000 copies, which was still far more than any album Otis had released while he was alive. Atlantic also issued a series of tracks from the album as singles during the second half of 1968. "The Happy Song" and "Amen" both became solid Top 40 hits, while "I've Got Dreams to Remember" rose to #6 R&B in November. That same month, Atlantic reached into its vaults and released a live album taken from the recordings that were made at the Whisky a Go Go in 1966. Carefully edited and equalized to minimize the impact of the out-of-tune horn section, *Otis Redding in Person at the Whisky a Go Go* included Otis's last Top 40 single, a two-year-old cover of the James Brown classic "Papa's Got a Brand New Bag."

All told, Stax and Atlantic would sell 2.6 million singles and 1.3 million albums by Otis Redding in the United States during the year that followed his death—more than double his sales totals for any previous year. That *The Dock of the Bay* and *The Immortal Otis Redding* were composed almost entirely of original songs made their success even more unprecedented in the world of R&B.

He wasn't just a magnificent talent. He was a magnificent man.

—PHIL WALDEN

BY THE TIME *THE IMMORTAL OTIS REDDING* WENT ON SALE IN THE summer of 1968, the outlines of the world in which Otis Redding had made his mark were already beginning to fade. The first strains of "(Sittin' on) The Dock of the Bay" drifting out of radios and jukeboxes across America coincided with the first shocking reports of the Tet Offensive in Vietnam, which demolished the Johnson administration's claims that the United States was winning the war in Southeast Asia. The resulting political crisis would unfold over the course of 1968 like a Shakespearean tragedy, with abdications, assassinations, insurrections, and intrigues that would culminate in the election of Richard Nixon as president and the collapse of the New Deal coalition that had dominated national politics since the 1930s. The year that began with the wistful ambivalence of Otis Redding's ballad would end with the abject paranoia of Marvin Gaye's "I Heard It Through the Grapevine," a song so preternaturally in tune with its times that it became the most successful R&B single of the decade, spending seven weeks at #1.

In April of 1968, four months after he buried his son, Otis Redding Sr. died of heart failure at the age of fifty-five. For members of the Redding family, it came as no surprise. "We were all so shattered, in so many different ways," Louise Redding recalled of the months after her brother's death. "My father had to have a lot of medication. I had never seen him cry before, because he was kind of stoic. I knew then that it wouldn't last. He was broken." Having endured a lifetime of hard work and harsh oppression as a sharecropper and manual laborer in the Jim Crow South, the loss of his beloved Sonny was more than Otis Sr. could bear.

Otis had died leaving a simple will that named his wife and children as the sole beneficiaries of his estate and his father as its administrator. During his brief tenure in that role, the Rev. Redding had turned to Sen. Leroy Johnson for legal counsel. (Johnson helped to endear himself to the family by pushing a unanimous resolution through the Georgia Senate praising Otis as one "who rose from poverty and obscurity to become one of the most famous entertainers in the United States.") Unsurprisingly, Johnson recommended that the estate conduct an audit of Otis's accounts at Redwal Music and Walden Artists and Promotions.

Relations between Otis's parents and Phil Walden had never been close. Though it had little bearing on Otis's career, his father had mistrusted Phil in the way that a black man of his generation had every reason to mistrust a white man in Phil's position, and Phil had responded with the same sense of offended honor that characterized his reaction to Otis's own involvement with Leroy Johnson. In years to come, he would go out of his way to discredit the Rev. Redding, a man he had hardly known, telling one interviewer, falsely, that he was "illiterate to say the least," and suggesting on several occasions that Otis was actually much closer to "Pops" Walden than he was to his own father.

At the same time, both Phil and Alan Walden felt a genuine sense of responsibility for Zelma and her children. Following the Rev. Redding's death, Phil arranged for Otis's estate to be administered by Don Pinson, a former schoolmate of his who worked as a trust officer at the Macon branch of the Savannah-based Citizens & Southern National Bank. Though Pinson had no knowledge of the music business, he proved to be a competent enough administrator. Otis had died at the absolute peak of his earning power, and his estate left his family in sound financial shape. His 1967 income had come to well over half a million dollars, and the millions of singles and albums he sold in 1968 would generate nearly that much in recording and publishing royalties. And though Otis had subscribed to a superstition about life insurance that was shared by many African Americans of his time, his family was the beneficiary of a $250,000 indemnity as well.

Don Pinson's only significant mistake in his management of the estate would come in 1972, when he went along with the Waldens' plan to sell

Redwal's interest in the publisher's share of Otis's songwriting catalog to Joe Galkin's Time Music for the sum of $100,000. In typical fashion, Galkin turned around and resold this share to Jim Stewart for three times that amount. It was a costly mistake on Pinson's part, and it helped to inspire a 1977 lawsuit that the Citizens & Southern Bank brought against Time Music, Stax, and its publishing company, East Memphis Music, on behalf of the Redding estate, which won a summary judgment of $300,000 in unpaid royalties. Joe Galkin's testimony in this lawsuit was a disturbing collection of lies, in which he grossly underestimated the extent of Otis's record sales and brazenly insisted that "Otis Redding had only one hit ["(Sittin' on) The Dock of the Bay"] in all the years he was alive." Galkin himself died in 1978, having spent the last years of his life living in Miami and hosting his friends on a fishing boat he named *The Big O.*

For Zelma Redding, the loss of the husband she had loved so loyally and relied upon so intently for financial and emotional support thrust her into a world of affairs of which she knew almost nothing. "Otis took care of his own business," she later said. "My job was to take care of my family. At the time of his death, I didn't know anything about Redwal Music, why it was formed or who owned it." Consumed by her own grief and the need to care for her children, Zelma felt overwhelmed by the sudden onset of financial responsibility, and twice in the year after Otis's death she was hospitalized for her nerves.

But, as Malcolm X had noted, "Negroes born in Georgia had to be strong simply to survive," and Zelma Redding was nothing if not a survivor. By the time she sat down with a reporter from *Jet* magazine in the summer of 1968 for her first published interview, the reality of her situation had begun to sink in. "We all talk about it as if he is just away working somewhere as he used to. But in our hearts, we know he's not." Surveying the granite headstone inscribed with her name next to Otis's that now stood in the front yard of her home, Zelma declared, "I'm going to spend the rest of my life here. Those are my long-range plans. There's nothing to do in Macon, but I'm going to be here. I'm going to live here until I die."

Later that year, after the Waldens offered her a nominal salary of $125 a week as a vice president of Redwal Music, Zelma returned to school, earned her high school equivalency degree, and enrolled at a local business college in order to learn for herself how business was done. She went on to start a booking agency of her own, followed by a series of ventures in Macon that included a nightclub, a record shop, a cleaning service, and, together with her daughter Karla, a shoe boutique on Cherry Street in the heart of the downtown. True to her word, she never remarried, remaining in the house she shared with Otis in Round Oak, maintaining the property much as it was when he was still alive. Over the years, Zelma would find her true calling in her fierce stewardship of Otis's creative legacy, seeing to it that her family earned every dollar from his music that they were due. "I wanted what my husband worked for and lost his life for," she explained. She remains a prominent and respected figure in the Macon community, sitting on the boards of civic organizations, and presiding, with Karla, over the Otis Redding Foundation, which sponsors music education programs and an arts-oriented charter school. "I love being Mrs. Otis Redding," Zelma would come to say. "I love that job."

THE SAME MONTH that the Rev. Redding died of a broken heart in Macon, the Rev. Dr. Martin Luther King Jr. was murdered at the Lorraine Motel in Memphis. King's death was a cataclysm for the entire country, setting off waves of rioting, arson, and looting in cities from coast to coast. But its impact was especially strong in Memphis, which now joined Dallas and Birmingham in the popular imagination as another southern city where the murderous undercurrents in America's political psyche had exploded to the surface with a force that changed the world.

Dr. King had come to Memphis to lend his support to a strike by the city's black sanitation workers union, whose members had walked off the job in February 1968 to protest their subsistence wages and their deplorable working conditions. What began as a local labor dispute was transformed into a national cause célèbre by the intransigence of the city's white supremacist mayor, Henry Loeb, and the brutality of his police force, whose officers attacked the picketing workers with billy clubs and mace. Loeb epitomized the racial paternalism that local blacks referred to as the "plantation mentality" of Memphis. Having once served as the city's commissioner of public works, he spoke of the sanitation workers as *his* men, and claimed to have enjoyed the trust of "their fathers before them." Yet Henry Loeb was a far cry from stereotypical southern racists such as George Wallace and Lester Maddox. The scion of a prominent Jewish business family, he was a tall, Kennedyesque figure who had been educated at Andover Academy and Brown University, commanded a PT boat in World War II, and publicly converted to Episcopalianism on his way to winning a second term as mayor on a law-and-order platform in 1967. As a onetime Democrat who had deserted the party on account of its support for organized labor and civil rights, Loeb was the latest incarnation of that old phenomenon, the "New South," whose region-wide backing of George Wallace's third-party candidacy would deliver the presidency to Richard Nixon and the states of the former Confederacy to the Republicans for generations to come.

On the night before he was murdered, Dr. King addressed a crowd of strikers and their supporters who had braved tornado warnings to come and hear him speak at an auditorium in Memphis. While thunder and lightning rocked the building, King stood at the podium and contemplated his own death. "Like anybody I would like to live a long life," he declared. "Longevity has its place, but I'm not concerned about that now. I just want to do God's will. And He's allowed me to go up the mountain. And I've looked over. And I have *seen* the promised land! I may not get there with you," King cried. "But I want you to know, *tonight*, that we, as a people, will get to the promised land."

King's "Mountaintop" speech was the final biblical flourish of the church-bred, church-led movement that began in Montgomery in the fall of 1955. The speech would be replayed often in the days and weeks ahead, and every year after that on the commemorations of Dr. King's birth and death. But in Memphis, its eloquence was matched by a more prosaic form of rhetoric that originated with the sanitation workers themselves, who paraded along the downtown streets of the city, day after day during the two-month strike, with placards hanging from their necks that read simply: I AM A MAN. Those four words came as a blunt reminder of just how elemental the struggle for African American freedom and dignity that arose in the South had been. They harkened back to W. E. B. Du Bois's assertion at the dawn of the Jim Crow era that "the history of the American Negro is the history of this strife—this longing to attain self-conscious manhood." Seventy years later, Dr. King's last words combined with the image of those determined men on the streets of Memphis to fulfill the promise of his *first* speech as a civil rights leader, delivered in Montgomery on the eve of the boycott, when he envisioned the day when future historians would write, "There lived a race of people, of black people, of people who had the moral courage to stand up for their rights, and thereby injected a new meaning into the veins of history and of civilization."

Martin Luther King Jr. was an embattled figure at the time of his death: despised as ever by racist whites in all parts of the country, dismissed as an accommodationist by Black Power advocates who hoped to threaten and posture their way to social change, and shunned by the white liberal establishment for his outspoken opposition to the war in Vietnam. Yet, like nothing that had come before—not the thousands of lynchings, the tens of thousands of murders, the hundreds of thousands of rapes—King's death was the last straw for untold numbers of African Americans, many of whom had rejected his unshakable commitment to nonviolent protest, yet still revered him in a corner of their hearts as the greatest moral leader that black America had produced. For thirteen years, King had prevailed on the patience of his people ("How long? Not long!") while he and his fellow activist ministers in the SCLC subjected the conscience of white America to the moral suasion of soul force. Their work remained unfinished. But by emboldening black Southerners to overcome their well-founded fears of white oppression, exploitation, and violence in order to confront the social reality of Jim Crow, they had succeeded in undermining the essential social fantasy of white supremacy and black inferiority on which the white South, and much of white America, had constructed its sense of nationhood.

Coming on the heels of Otis's death and the bitter divorce from Atlantic, Dr. King's assassination punctured the bubble of interracial harmony that had prevailed at Stax since the label's founding in 1960. The leak was small at first, but it would prove to be irreparable. Everyone who worked at the label had a vivid recollection of how it felt when the news arrived, late on a Thursday afternoon, that King had been shot at the Lorraine Motel. The familiarity of the Lorraine, whose restaurant and pool had been one of the few places in Memphis where black and white musicians could congregate in public, only added to the shock. Some of those present, like Isaac Hayes and David Porter, jumped in their cars and drove to the motel, drawn by a need to bear witness to the event. Others, including all the white musicians, headed for their homes and braced for trouble ahead. Before he left, Jim Stewart loaded all the company's master recordings into the trunk of his car.

Stax remained closed in the tense week that elapsed between King's death and the settlement of the sanitation workers' strike, and the studio was untouched by the sporadic arson and looting that took place along McLemore Avenue. But everyone agreed that things were never the same there. In Rufus Thomas's view, "The whole complexion of everything changed. It had to." "That was the turning point for relations between the races in the South," Booker Jones recalled. "Emotionally, Memphis was riding on Dr. King's visit to heal some really deep wounds, and not only were the wounds not healed, but it was made worse by the assassination. There was a fissure that was inevitable. It was inevitable because that's the song of the South." In Duck Dunn's view, "It became really hard to go on. We were so sad and confused. I didn't know what to say to anybody, because it always seemed as if the words came out wrong."

Steve Cropper agreed with the prevailing impression that everything changed in the aftermath of the King assassination, but his perspective on it was very different. "You know Memphis was a refuge for black people, it really was," Cropper told an interviewer in 1984. "Blacks were blacks and whites were whites and everybody was cool. We all loved each other." "The black people were perfectly happy with what was going on," he continued. "I don't think anywhere in the universe was as racially cool as Memphis was until Martin Luther King showed up. That just set it off for the world, basically. What a shame. There must be something political about that. Let's go to the one place in the South where everybody is getting along and blow that fuse. That's the only way I can see it."

No white musician of his generation had collaborated more closely, sympathetically, or successfully with black musicians, singers, and song-writers than Steve Cropper did in his work with Otis Redding, Wilson Pickett, Sam and Dave, Don Covay, and his fellow MGs. Cropper regarded these men as his friends and musical brothers. He had worked with them on a daily basis, traveled with them in and out of the South, and spent long hours in their company. Their experience together exemplified the model of cooperative effort toward a common goal that the sociologist Gordon Allport proposed as a corrective to racial prejudice. In one of his many moving tributes to Otis, Cropper told *Hit Parader* in the summer of 1968, "My original feeling for Otis wound up to be my final feeling for Otis. He was a pure man. Anything you say about him has to be good."

Yet friends and family are capable of their own forms of self-delusion. That Cropper could believe that Memphis was truly a "refuge" for black people until 1968, that blacks and whites in the city "loved each other," and that everything was fine there "until Martin Luther King showed up" was not simply an expression of his ignorance or insensitivity. Rather, it was a demonstration of the power of segregation to insulate white people from the social reality of black people's lives—a barrier that did not necessarily yield to professional friendship or the pursuit of common goals. And Cropper's view was common, as Garry Wills reported in *Esquire* a few months after the King assassination: "The odd thing is that white Memphis really does think that—as citizen after citizen will tell you—'race relations are good.' Its spokesmen cannot stop saying 'how much we have done for the Negro.'"

The attitude Wills described was the essence of the "plantation mentality"—a presumption of white authority and black subordination, a pretense of white generosity and black gratitude—and it was by no means confined to Memphis. As the civil rights movement crested in the mid-1960s and the more overt forms of legalized segregation came to an end, white Americans in all parts of the country took comfort in an attitude that allowed them to feel as if they were making a concession or conferring a benefit of some kind by treating African Americans with a bare modicum of respect and decency and obeying the laws designed to redress the denial of their civil rights. But as Phil Walden had discovered when Otis first summoned the nerve to question the benevolence of Phil's management, this sense of self-congratulation could be a fragile thing indeed.

Nowhere was this paternalism more pervasive than in the music business, which had been capitalizing on the skilled labor and artistic genius of African American singers, musicians, and composers for generations. And nowhere in the music business was it more pervasive than at R&B labels like Stax, where Jim Stewart, Estelle Axton, Steve Cropper, Duck Dunn, and Wayne Jackson owed their careers to the black artists who had inspired them, schooled them, accepted them (as Booker Jones once said of his early days at Stax, "I didn't have apprehensions, other than the normal daily apprehensions of associating with whites"), and ultimately *allowed* them to profit handsomely from the fruits of their talent and success. Had it not been for Rufus and Carla Thomas, Booker Jones, Al Jackson Jr., Otis Redding, and Sam and Dave, there is every reason to think that Jim Stewart would have lived out his life as a bank clerk, Estelle Axton as a bookkeeper and a housewife, while Steve Cropper, Duck Dunn, and Wayne Jackson could have looked forward to performing in the honky-tonks and country clubs of a city that by the early 1960s had little white music scene to speak of.

Yet the story of Stax has always been told in terms of the opportunities the label created for the African American artists it recorded, rather than the other way around. The same could be said of Atlantic and, especially, Motown, where Berry Gordy ran his company like an upscale plantation store. But Gordy and Jerry Wexler and their celebrated production teams were remarkable arbiters, curators, marketers, and, in the case of Motown, manufacturers of talent in ways that the owners of Stax were not. Rufus Thomas was already an established star in Memphis when he first walked in the door. Otis Redding was delivered to the label, unsolicited, by Joe Galkin. Sam and Dave were sent to them, unsolicited, by Jerry Wexler. Considering Jim Stewart's initial indifference toward Otis and Sam and Dave, his intolerance of Wilson Pickett and Don Covay, his rejection of Aretha Franklin, and his consistent misjudgment of records that proved to be hits, Stax's saving grace as a record label was Stewart's willingness to defer to the talent of his singers and session men, allowing performers like Otis Redding the freedom to produce themselves. But it wasn't as if Otis was ever paid or credited for the production work on his records, and while Stewart was scrupulously honest, the percentages he offered his artists were as tight-fisted as those across the recording industry. By the late 1960s, the notion that black musical artists should be grateful for the opportunity to succeed on the basis of their talents was rapidly losing its hold. Not with Aretha Franklin on the cover of *Time* magazine. And not with Dr. Martin Luther King Jr. lying dead on the balcony of the Lorraine Motel.

The most dramatic expression of the shift in the racial climate of the record business that was catalyzed by the assassination of Dr. King came at the convention of the National Association of Television and Radio Announcers in Miami in August 1968. There, with Coretta Scott King as the keynote speaker and Bill Cosby as the emcee, the tensions that Jerry Wexler had noted the year before in Atlanta resurfaced with a vengeance when a consortium of black gangsters from New York calling themselves the "Fair Play Committee" commandeered the convention with their demands for cash "reparations" from the white power structure of the recording industry. Wexler himself was due to be honored for his work with Aretha Franklin, who had headlined a NATRA benefit at Madison Square Garden a few weeks before. Instead, he was the target of death threats, and was hastily escorted out of the opening-night ceremonies by his friend King Curtis, only to be hung in effigy in the lobby of the convention hall. The same fate awaited NATRA's executive director, Del Shields, who came to Miami with $250,000 in pledges he had collected from a number of white-owned labels to fund the establishment of a broadcasting school for black deejays and announcers. Instead, Shields was forced to flee his own convention after his refusal to share this bounty with the members of the Fair Play Committee led to threats on his life as well. Phil Walden was similarly menaced, as was Marshall Sehorn, Allen Toussaint's white partner in Sea-Saint Recording Studios, who was beaten unconscious in his hotel room as a "message" to the music business. Stax's Al Bell was yet another prominent NATRA member who disappeared suddenly in the middle of the convention. Bell would later insist that he had merely taken time off for rest and relaxation, but his associates at Stax insisted that he, too, was the target of an extortion attempt. Subsequent developments at Stax lent credence to this view.

The main figures in the Fair Play Committee were a pair of self-styled "black mafia" enforcers, Johnny Baylor and Dino Woodward. A few months after the Miami convention, as the racial climate in Memphis deteriorated, Al Bell "invited" Baylor and Woodward to Stax, ostensibly to deal with a local street gang that had begun to harass the label's artists and employees. After quickly neutralizing the street gang, these two gun-toting hoodlums then made themselves at home in Soulsville U.S.A., where they were both awarded "management" positions. Their arrival coincided with the further consolidation of Al Bell's power at the label. Toward the end of 1968, Bell brought in a Detroit-based producer named Don Davis to give the Memphis Sound more of a Motown flavor. When Davis scored a major hit with Johnny Taylor's "Who's Making Love," he was promptly appointed the label's new head of A&R. With Bell's encouragement, he then began subcontracting more and more of Stax's recording to studios in Detroit, Philadelphia, and Muscle Shoals.

In the meantime, flush with his gains from the Gulf & Western purchase, Jim Stewart was transforming himself into a parody of a corporate record executive at the dawn of the Aquarian Age: growing his hair, mustache, and goatee; dressing in Nehru jackets; and moving his family into a garish suburban mansion whose amenities included no fewer than four swimming pools, a tennis court, and a separate "party house." Stewart stayed on as the nominal president of Stax, but Al Bell ran the company, churning through untold amounts of Gulf & Western's credit and capital. Under his leadership, the record label that had exemplified the integrationist spirit of the 1960s became explicitly identified with the separatist ideology of Black Power. In the process, with Stewart's acquiescence, Bell wound up alienating nearly all of the people who had poured their lives into Stax over the preceding decade, beginning with Estelle Axton, who was forced out in the spring of 1969 and had to retain a lawyer in order to get her due. Booker Jones moved to Los Angeles a few months after that. The MGs continued to record together for another year, until Steve Cropper negotiated his departure in 1970.

Having largely dispensed with its signature sound, Stax thrived commercially during this period with hits by Johnny Taylor, the newly secularized Staple Singers, and most notably Isaac Hayes, who released a series of lushly orchestrated, million-selling albums on which he portrayed a cartoon-like caricature of black ghetto masculinity that prefigured the aesthetic of gangsta rap. In 1970, Stewart and Bell repurchased Stax from Gulf & Western with the help of a loan from Deutsche Grammophon, whose Polydor subsidiary took over distribution for the label. With sales booming, yet another change in corporate sponsorship came two years later, when Bell negotiated a distribution deal with Clive Davis of CBS Records that allowed him to buy out Jim Stewart's interest and assume sole ownership of the company. Bell also scored a promotional coup in 1972 by teaming up with the Rev. Jesse Jackson to produce a major black music festival in Los Angeles called Wattstax. But the quality of the label's output languished under Bell's increasingly grandiose leadership, causing sales to fall off and the relationship with CBS to sour after Clive Davis was fired for the misappropriation of funds.

By 1974, the Stax payroll had tripled, huge sums of money had been funneled to Johnny Baylor for protection and payola, and a mountain of debt had accumulated. As creditors began lining up at the door—led by Isaac Hayes, who filed a multimillion-dollar lawsuit for unpaid royalties—Al Bell somehow convinced Jim Stewart to indemnify the company with his personal wealth. It was the final chapter of their deeply dysfunctional relationship, and the last of the many wrongheaded decisions on the part of Stewart, who lost his mansion and most of his money when Stax was declared bankrupt by a federal judge in the summer of 1976. The studios and offices on McLemore Avenue were padlocked, and Soulsville was no more.

Though Jerry Wexler's hard-nosed personality caused him to downplay its impact, everyone close to him agreed that he was deeply shaken by his experience at the NATRA convention in the summer of 1968. ("That was the end of rhythm and blues in the South," he later said.) Freed from the need to oversee the operations of Atlantic by the sale to Warner Bros. and Ahmet Ertegun's new enthusiasm for the role, Wexler bought a house and a boat in Miami and focused his attention almost exclusively on record production in the years ahead, working with a diverse roster of artists, including Aretha Franklin, Dusty Springfield, Donny Hathaway, Willie Nelson, King Curtis, and Dr. John. In 1969, after hearing Duane Allman's playing on a Wilson Pickett album that was recorded at Fame in Muscle Shoals, Wexler purchased the young guitarist's contract from Rick Hall. He then turned Allman over to Phil Walden, who made him the centerpiece, along with his brother Greg, of the Allman Brothers Band.

With Wexler's help, Walden simultaneously started an independent record label called Capricorn, which was based in Macon and distributed by Atlantic. Frank Fenter came over from London to replace Alan Walden as Phil's business partner, and the fortunes of Capricorn soared on the popularity of the new commercial genre known as Southern rock: a hybrid style that combined elements of rhythm and blues, country blues, the double-lead-guitar format of the Butterfield Blues Band, and the free-form improvisational playing of the San Francisco groups. At its peak in the mid-1970s, Capricorn had the Allman Brothers, Marshall Tucker, Elvin Bishop, and Wet Willie under contract. Having struck out on his own, Alan Walden also achieved some success in the Southern rock genre as the first manager of the Alabama group Lynyrd Skynyrd.

"The Miami convention signaled the end for me," Phil Walden would say of his decision to withdraw from the world of soul music as the 1960s came to an end. "A lot of people we had considered friends were suddenly calling us blue-eyed devils. It really just turned me off. It was shake-down time, and I didn't care to be shaken down." At the time of Otis's death, Phil and his brother were running one of the largest booking agencies in the country that specialized in black talent. Reconstituted as Paragon and headed by Phil's protégé Alex Hodges, the agency would gradually shed its black artists and reorient itself toward the far more lucrative market in Southern rock.

Capricorn bands like the Allman Brothers and Wet Willie paid homage to the integrationist spirit that had characterized soul music in the 1960s, and in 1970, the label signed Johnny Jenkins to a recording contract and promoted him, without success, as a Hendrix-like hoodoo man. For the most part, however, black musicians were a token presence in the world of Southern rock, which conformed to the traditional pattern of white musicians emulating and adapting black musical styles and marketing them successfully to mainstream white audiences. To the long line of brazen cultural contradictions embraced in American popular music, Southern rock would add the spectacle of avowedly redneck bands like Lynyrd Skynyrd and Black Oak Arkansas singing the praises of a fictional black bluesman called Curtis Lowe and a "good ole boy" named Luther King on concert stages bedecked with Confederate battle flags.

It was typical of Phil Walden to ascribe his disenchantment with the world of black music to the racial politics of the time, but there was one dimension of it that had nothing to do with his offended honor and pride. Since the summer of 1962, Otis Redding had been the be-all and end-all of Phil's professional life, and after Otis died, his heart wasn't in it anymore. "Otis had so much warmth," Phil told an interviewer in 1971. "He was so good, just really so good. It's hard to believe people are like that. And to see it all go like *that* one day, and to see it happen to the one real nice guy in the whole thing, the one guy who had both feet on the ground, the one guy who had a sense of obligation." Phil continued, "I don't think I ever really want to have that close of a relationship with anybody ever again. That transcended the whole management thing. I mean, I *loved* that guy."

HE WAS NOT alone in that. Popular music in the 1960s was graced by the talents of an incomparable generation of African American singers, many of whom also excelled as songwriters, producers, arrangers, and instrumentalists. Beginning with the progenitors, Ray Charles and Sam Cooke, the decade saw the flowering of James Brown, Jackie Wilson, Smokey Robinson, Solomon Burke, Martha Reeves, Curtis Mayfield, Marvin Gaye, Otis Redding, Wilson Pickett, Gladys Knight, Stevie Wonder, and Aretha Franklin, to name only some of the most prominent. Together, these artists injected "a new meaning" into the veins of musical history by inventing and exalting a new idiom of pop romanticism, cured of its false innocence and sentimentality—a synthesis of sacred and profane emotional expression that was rooted in the human realities of sex and love. In the way they presented and conducted themselves in the public eye, these performers demolished the savage stereotypes with which American society and its complicit popular culture had once conspired to keep black people firmly in their "place." By extending the reach of their music in its boldest, richest, and most undiluted form to countries around the world, the soul singers of the 1960s fulfilled the cultural destiny that W. E. B. Du Bois had envisioned for his fellow African Americans some seventy years before: "He would not bleach his Negro soul in a flood of white Americanism, for he knows his Negro blood has a message for the world."

Thanks to the power and fidelity of their recordings and the proliferation of digital access to music, each of these iconic singers has remained a familiar and unmistakable presence in the minds of succeeding generations of listeners—even now, fifty years after they first took their places in the pantheon of soul music and long after most of them have passed from the scene. Yet, while each of these artists was identified by his or her signature sound, a unique mixture of timbre, timing, and vocal personality, none was more distinctive, more immediately recognizable, more emotionally compelling, than the voice with which Otis Redding made himself known to the world. For all the feelings of excitement, enchantment, catharsis, lust, and longing that the members of this constellation of African American singing stars inspired, perhaps none of them, not even Sam Cooke, was quite as beloved—not merely admired or desired, but truly and surely *loved*—as Otis Redding was. And the feeling was mutual. In song after song, on record after record, from the start to the finish of his tragically abbreviated career, Otis was soul music's greatest apostle of devotion. Of all the emotions that the black singers of his generation derived from their collective upbringing in the church and the myriad joys and sorrows of their lives in the world—the carnal rapture of Ray Charles, the sublime sensuality of Sam Cooke, the elegant anguish of Marvin Gaye, and the transcendent glory of Aretha Franklin—Otis's special distinction turned on his desire to have and to hold. He sang of yearning and tenderness, security and respect, of one more day, and a lover's prayer. He had the capacity to reduce human emotion to its absolute essence, to bring things down to a level of simplicity that nevertheless defied simplification. *Hold on*, he implored his listeners. Got to. Hold on. Got to. Can't stop. *Got* to. Hold on.

ACKNOWLEDGMENTS

It is amusing for me to recall that I once considered writing this book without the cooperation of Zelma Redding and her family. Though it took considerable time and effort on my part to gain their blessing, Zelma, her daughter, Karla Redding-Andrews, and her sons, Dexter Redding and Otis Redding III, have added immeasurably to the quality and accuracy of my work. Knowing as I do the depth of Zelma's love for her late husband and her devotion to his legacy, my fondest hope is that she will consider this book worthy of the trust she has shown in me.

Another indispensable source was Otis's eldest sister, Louise Redding McClain, who provided me with essential information and insight into her parents, her family, and Otis's childhood. My sense is that meeting Louise was as close to meeting Otis Redding as I will ever come, and I cherished the opportunity.

On my repeated visits to Macon, I have enjoyed the company and hospitality of a great many people who were closely connected with Otis Redding and the world in which he grew up. Phil Walden's former secretary and Capricorn vice president Carolyn Brown Killen was an early source of encouragement and advice. Alice Bailey received me royally and introduced me to Otis's former friends and neighbors from Tindall Heights, Richard Atkins and Geneva Jones. The late Eddie Ross spoke with me about singing with Otis in their childhood gospel group. Charles Huckabee, William Ellis, and C. Jack Ellis shared their memories of coming of age with Otis in Bellevue. Delores Cook and Robert Scott recalled their service as teachers at Ballard-Hudson High School. Artralia Andrews provided helpful information about her father-in-law, the Rev. C. J. Andrews. Clinton Brantley Jr. shared his memories of his father, Ish Mosley spoke with me on several occasions about playing with the Pinetoppers, and Terry Jenkins enlightened me about his brother Johnny. Ray "Satellite Papa" Brown recalled the days of the *Teenage Party*, Jimmy Barber his service with Roye Mathis's band. Walter Johnson showed me around his House of Johnson barbershop on Poplar Street. Year after year, Peyton Carswell and Newton Collier served as my sounding boards and guides to the social and racial geography of Macon.

Robert Albritten welcomed me to Otis's birthplace in his capacity as the mayor of Dawson, where the late Nathaniel James shared his memories of the Reddings, the Rosemans, Monroe Myrick, and the Laings. Ken Laing gave me a tour of his family's former plantation and showed me the remains of the sharecropper's shack where Otis may well have been born.

Grady Gaines of the Upsetters and the late Eddie Kirkland spoke with me about Otis's early musical career in Macon, while their respective managers, Susan Criner and Hedy Langdon, were instrumental in putting me together with these two eminent figures.

Members of the Walden family were a constant source of support from the start of my work on this book. Katherine Walden spoke with me at length about her memories of Phil and Otis, and then proved to be the sort of correspondent every writer dreams of, responding to my endless questions with eloquent, invariably fascinating e-mails. Alan Walden regaled me with vivid anecdotes about his experiences with Otis and provided heartfelt encouragement on the need to do justice to the memory of his friend. Alan's daughter Jessica Walden helped to orient me in Macon, and Phil's daughter Amantha Walden became a friend as well as a source during the course of my work, sharing both her enthusiasm and her clear-eyed perspective on her family.

I was also privileged to speak with many of Phil Walden's loyal friends. In Macon, these included Lee Martin and his wife, Susan; Bobby Wallace and his wife, Harriet; Steven Chanin; Mike Cass; George Hart; and the late, great Seaborn Jones. Phil's high school girlfriend, the late Violet Neblet Dubose, invited me to her home in Gray. Jimm Roberts in Orlando and Bill Hall in Los Angeles gave me hours of their time on the phone, providing valuable insights into Phil's personality. Several of Phil's associates at Capricorn were also kind enough to speak with me, including Jim Hawkins, Bunky Odom, Ira Sokoloff, Roger Cowles, and Mike Bone.

Jackie Avery, James McEachin, and the late Don Henry spoke with me about their experiences working with Otis in Los Angeles in 1960. Frank Kavelin provided useful information about his father, Al, and the early days of Lute Records.

James Newton showed me around his hometown of Tifton and shared important information about Tifco Records. The late Bobby Smith gave me his version of the Confederate Records story. Wayne Pierce recounted his part in the "Shout Bamalama" recording session. The late Tom Wells shared his impressions of the Macon music scene.

Anyone who presumes to write about southern soul music owes a debt to Peter Guralnick, who wrote the proverbial book on the subject in 1986. Peter was a source of encouragement and occasional commiseration throughout my work. Similarly, anyone who presumes to write about Stax Records owes a debt to Rob Bowman, who has served as Stax's house historian for the past twenty years, and also to Robert Gordon, who has written with great insight and generosity of spirit about Stax and the wider music scene in his beloved hometown of Memphis. Readers of their work will note that my own perspective on Stax differs significantly from those of all three of these writers at times, but I am grateful to them for holding up their ends of the conversation.

A special perspective on the interplay of music and race in Memphis came from the anthropologist Laura Helper-Ferris, who has written a fascinating dissertation on the subject. Tim Sampson and Deanie Parker at the Stax Foundation Museum gave freely of their time, while the former Stax publicists Eddie Braddock and the late Alan Abrams shared their memories with me. The Memphis attorney Michael Pleasants answered my questions about the litigation that surrounded the demise of the label, and Nancy Morrow helped with my legal research. I am also beholden to the artist Pinkney Herbert, who first explained to this jaded New Yorker that if you want to speak with someone in Memphis, you simply call them up.

Numerous people were eager to entertain me with their memories of Joe Galkin, including Gwen Kesler, Steve Begor, Jack McIntyre, Philip Rawls, John Rys, and Larry King. Dick Alen, Jack Bart, Maurice Seller, and David Spero responded to my questions about Otis's touring days.

Jerry Wexler was the first person I interviewed for this book, in a short but memorable phone call (of course) shortly before he died. Jerry Greenburg, Paul Marshall, Ted Nussbaum, and Dick Kline provided me with valuable information about Atlantic Records, and Haig Adishian spoke with me about the album covers he designed.

In addition to Don Henry, Earl "Speedo" Sims, Bobby Holloway, Leroy Hadley, Jai Johnny Johnson, Tony Dorsey, Egbert "Woody" Woodson, Loretta Williams, and Carl Sims were valuable sources of reminiscence and information about their service with the Otis Redding Show.

Henry Lowe spoke with me in detail about his father Jim Lowe's professional relationship with Otis and his commentary on the causes of the plane crash that took Otis's life. Tracy Toth shed light on the circumstances of the accident from the perspective of a professional pilot who had extensive experience flying a Beech 18 in and out of Truax Field in Madison.

Michael Mauldin in Atlanta and Jeff Jampol in Los Angeles were instrumental in putting me together with Zelma Redding and her family. Jeff and his associate Kenny Nemes have also served as savvy facilitators throughout the writing and production of this book.

Daniel Underwood and Rodney Lowe were a welcome source of distraction and conversation on my many visits to Macon.

Muriel Jackson at the Washington Memorial Library provided me with the same stoic attention she has given to the many other writers who have sought to chronicle aspects of Macon's musical history. John Hornyak and Kelly Darr familiarized me with the holdings of the Grammy Foundation Living History Project, while Kay Peterson did the same for the Smithsonian Rock 'n' Soul Collection. Guy Hall helped me navigate the National Archive in Morrow, Georgia. Chuck Perkins and Otto Zielke allowed me to sift through their personal archives of material on Capricorn Records. Jared Wright was a great resource in his capacity as an archivist at the now-defunct Georgia Music Hall of Fame and later for the Redding Family.

A full cast of characters, including Tom Vickers, Lance Freed, Linda Chelgren, Dale Pollack, Lianne Halfon, David Bradley, Thomas Pope, Billy Bob Thornton, Malcolm Leo, the late Gil Freisen, Ben Myron, and Joe Eszterhas aided and abetted my persistent efforts to find the background interviews that were done in connection with the multiple attempts to make a biographical film about Otis Redding during the 1980s and '90s, while Tom Epperson turned out to be the one person connected with these projects who held on to the precious biographical materials they generated.

Many gifted music writers, historians, and researchers contributed to my own research, including Pete Daniel, Jim Delehant, Candice Dyer, Tony Fletcher, Norman Jopling, Harvey Kubernik, Jon Landau, Preston Lauterbach, David Less, John Ridley, Tim Riley, and Holly George Warren. Several friends and mentors at Cornell, including Larry Moore, Glenn Altschuler, and Kenneth McClane, read chapters of the book in manuscript and gave me invaluable feedback.

The vicissitudes of the modern publishing world have caused me to have multiple editors on this book. The idea that I should write "something about soul music" was suggested by my original editor, John Glusman, and my original publisher, Shaye Areheart. In a very real sense, I never stopped writing this book for them. John was followed by Sean Desmond and Dominick Anfuso, who nursed and nudged the work along, and finally by Matt Inman, who patiently wrestled both the manuscript and its headstrong author into their current form. In addition to Matt, Ellen Folan, Julie Cepler, and Angeline Rodriguez at Crown Archetype have all played vital roles in the production and promotion of the book, while Chris Brand and Lauren Dong were responsible for the splendid cover and interior design, respectively.

My agent, Richard Pine, has calmly held my hand and had my back at every step of the way.

Through it all, my constant source of delight and companionship, strength and support, inspiration and intimidation, has been my partner, Lisa Corinne Davis. It is to her and her alone that I lovingly dedicate this book.

NOTES

MONTEREY

1   **"I was pretty sure that I'd seen God . . ."**: B. Weir in Notes to *Monterey International Pop Festival* CD; Rhino Records (1992).

1   **7,500 fans . . . :** The often-cited figures of 35,000 to 50,000 were based on total admissions over the course of the three-day festival. The official seating capacity of the fairgrounds arena was 7,000. See Ralph J. Gleason, *San Francisco Chronicle*, June 19, 1967.

1   **self-styled "psychedelic city-state"**: W. Hinckle, *Ramparts*, March 1967.

1   **a gleam in the eye . . . :** On the genesis of the festival, see Kubernik (2011), Taylor (1987), and Adler (1999).

3   **"At times, our audience was more outrageous . . ."**: P. Kantner in Taylor (1987): 58.

4   **"from another planet . . ."**: W. Jackson in Bowman (1999): 123.

5   **Wexler told his young protégé . . . :** P. Walden in *Shake!* DVD (2002).

5   **Redding had teasingly pretended that he hadn't given the matter much thought.:** Jackson (2005): 147; P. Walden in Graham (2004): 190.

6   **"the best gig I ever put on . . ."**: Graham (2004): 176.

7   **"This is a song that a girl took away . . ."** and **"This is the Love Crowd . . ."**: O. Redding in *Shake!* DVD (2002).

8   **"he had the audience spinning . . ."**: R. Goldstein, *Village Voice*, June 29, 1967.

9   **"I've got to go . . ."**: Otis took this line from Sam Cooke, *Live at the Copa*, RCA Records (1964).

17   **a panel of artists, critics, and music business professionals . . . :** *Rolling Stone*, Nov. 27, 2008.

GEORGIA ON MY MIND

20   **blackface minstrelsy . . . :** On the history of minstrelsy, see Toll (1974), Lott (1993), and Wondrich (2003).

21   **"Never was there such an excitement . . ."**: *New York Herald,* June 30, 1855.

23   **"Since the beginning of the nation . . ."**: Ellison (1986): 110.

25   **a twenty-year-old African American woman named Mary Turner . . . :** See Myers (2006) and Armstrong (2008).

26   **Also lost in the narrative:** See Woodward (1974), Williamson (1984), and Hale (2005).

27   **a heroic crusade called Redemption** . . . : See Godshalk (2005) and Lemann (2006).

28   **a now-forgotten novelist named Thomas Dixon** . . . : See Williamson (1984): 140–79.

28   **the psychological concept of "projection":** Freud (1979): 132.

29   **this "rape complex . . .":** Cash (1991): 114.

30   **"It is like history written with lightning . . .":** W. Wilson, in Williamson (1984): 176.

30   **According to the most conservative estimates** . . . : See Brundage (1993) and Ginzberg (1988).

31   **"What was strikingly new and different . . .":** Litwack (1998): 287.

31   **"Northern Fever":** Grossman (1989): 3.

31   **the Great Migration** . . . : See Grossman (1989), Lemann (1992), and Wilkerson (2010).

32   **jailed as vagrants** . . . : Grossman (1989): 492.

32   **"I suppose the worst place there is better . . .":** Ibid.: 493.

LAURA

33   **It's the most important thing about me** . . . : O. Redding to BBC, *Dreams to Remember* DVD (2007).

33   **"Negroes born in Georgia . . .":** Malcolm X (1965): 89.

33   **Born in 1877** . . . : Genealogical information on the Fambros and Reddings is derived from US Census records, 1880–1940.

34   **"How curious a land is this . . .":** Du Bois (1999): 81.

35   **In the eyes of southern society** . . . : On sharecropping, see Raper (1936), Johnson (1967), and Powdermaker (1968).

37   **James Williams was charged** . . . : G. Freeman (1999).

37   **a black hoodlum named John "Cocky" Glover** . . . : Manis (2004): 63–70.

37   **"seen enough of the white man's brutality . . .":** Halasa (1990): 29.

39   **the Laings were known as fair-dealing landlords** . . . : N. James, author interview.

39   **According to family lore** . . . : R. Redding in *GMHF Archive* (2007).

40   **Radio sets had been unknown** . . . : US Census, 1930, 1940.

40   **"Two things which shaped me for the rest of my life . . .":** Charles (1978): 8.

40–41 **"The feel of power, even in an old automobile . . .":** Raper (1936): 174.

GALLANTRY'S LAST BOW

42   **There was a Land of Cavaliers and Cotton Fields called the Old South** . . . : Opening credits, *Gone with the Wind*.

42   **the world premiere of *Gone with the Wind*** . . . : See Bridges (1999), Hale (1999), and Storace (1991).

42   **"the biggest event to happen in the South . . .":** J. Carter to Barbara Wal-
      ters, ABC-TV Special, Dec 14, 1976.

43   **"a high ritual for the reassertion of the legend . . .":** Cash (1991): 420.

43   **"Tonight, we want to give you a glimpse . . .":** Bridges (1999): 51. P. Storace
      (1991) notes that the Rev. King was "censured by the Atlanta Baptist Minis-
      ters Union for his decision to participate in the event."

44   **Carl Vinson, longtime chairman of the House Naval Affairs Commit-
      tee . . . :** See Cook (2004).

45   **Otis Sr. quickly found work as a laborer . . . :** *A Pictorial History of Robins
      Air Force Base* (1982).

SONNY

49   **As far back as I can remember he was always singing . . . :** R. Redding in
      Myron (1994): 1.

49   **"Perhaps never in history . . .":** Wright (1941): 93.

50   **The African American novelist John Oliver Killens . . . recounted an inci-
      dent . . . :** See Killens (1954): 163–76; Gilyard (2011): 7–8.

52   **"My mother was very serious about her religion . . .":** L. Redding, author
      interview.

53   **"he was going to have to change his life . . .":** R. Redding in *GMHF Archive*
      (2007).

53   **"My father had no positive examples in his family . . .":** L. Redding, author
      interview.

54   **"Whenever he came on the scene, he just took over . . .":** Ibid.

54   **"He was always in the spotlight about something . . .":** R. Redding in
      Myron (1994): 5.

54   **the family of Carter and Inez Jones . . . :** G. Jones, author interview.

54–55 **"Everybody in that house could sing . . .":** R. Redding in *GMHF Archive*
      (2007).

GEORGIA TOM

56   **"Blues are songs of despair, but gospel songs are songs of hope . . .":**
      M. Jackson (1969): 71.

56   **"I am now satisfied that the future music of this country . . .":** A. Dvořák,
      New York Herald, May 28, 1893.

57   **"Pick up four colored boys or young men anywhere . . .":** J. W. Johnson
      (1942): 35.

59   **Dorsey was born in Villa Rica . . . :** See Harris (1992) and Reagon (1992).

61   **writing . . . "about hope and love . . .":** T. Dorsey in Heilbut (1975): 35.

61   **"He was our Irving Berlin. . . .":** M. Jackson in Heilbut (1975): 29.

SISTER ROSETTA AND THE JUKEBOX KING

64   **"I started out singing spiritual songs in my father's church . . .":** O. Redding to BBC, *Dreams to Remember* DVD (2007).

64   **Family members recall that one of Otis's favorite songs . . . :** R. Redding in Myron (1994): 43.

65   **Though Roberta Martin had never played a note of gospel . . . :** See Reagon (1992): 255–309.

65   **Rosetta Tharpe was more like the gospel version . . . :** See J. A. Jackson (2004) and Wald (2007).

66   **"It was the best thing that ever happened to me . . .":** R. Penniman in White (1984): 17; also see Brantley (1978).

66   **"O-o-h Sistuh! Rosetta 'n' Her Gitar . . .":** *Billboard,* April 9, 1949.

67   **"The police were running around [yelling] . . .":** J. A. Jackson (2004): 107.

67   **"There was a calypso song out then called 'Run, Joe' . . .":** O. Redding (1967).

70   **"If you really want to do something . . .":** L. Jordan in Coleman (2006): 45.

MACON MUSIC

71   **"Mr. Brantley is who I'd call the father of rock 'n' roll in Macon . . .":** Dimmons (1978).

71   **"The Air Force Leads the Way" . . . :** *Chicago Defender,* June 18, 1949.

72   **"They had what they called 'party houses' down on Fifth Street . . .":** J. Hancock in S. Freeman (2007): 17.

72   **The sovereign figure of this demimonde . . . :** See Brantley (1978), Dimmons (1978), and Lauterbach (2011).

73   **"I'd hire ten or fifteen policemen to do the shows . . .":** C. Brantley in Oppy (1977).

73   **"We toured with Clint Brantley out of Macon . . .":** E. Kirkland in Murray (2002): 173.

76   **"The Rosemans were very proud people . . .":** L. Redding, author interview.

76   **"My father was more like a teacher than anything . . .":** R. Redding in Myron (1994): 11.

76   **"He was always planning, devising . . .":** L. Redding, author interview.

77   **"But where had I got this notion of doing something in the future . . .":** Wright (1989): 168.

77   **"You were born into a society which spelled out with brutal clarity . . .":** Baldwin (1998): 293.

78   **"The church was the main area of social life in which Negroes could aspire . . .":** Frazier (1974): 48.

78   **"That was their Juilliard . . ."** J. Avery, author interview.

78 **Still another young Maconite with a church background . . . :** See White (1984) and Chalmers (2010).

79 **"he was a clown more than a musician . . .":** White (1984): 28.

BROWN V. BOARD

80 **"The South was now undergoing a new convulsion . . .":** Baldwin (1998): 199.

80 **Her obituary notice . . . :** The *Telegraph*, Feb. 18, 1951.

80 **Robins was a very different place . . . :** See *A Pictorial History of Robins Air Force Base* (1989).

81 **"My father was always a worker . . .":** L. Redding, author interview.

81 **Rodgers recalled his brother's performance . . . :** R. Redding in Myron (1994): 9.

81 **"He was onstage every day he went to school . . .":** L. Redding, author interview.

82 **As the name implied, Ballard-Hudson was a merger . . . :** See Brown (2002) and Large (2004).

82 **Though Macon's booster spirit had convinced . . . :** Schrag (1965): 162.

83 **One teacher compared the sound of the many course sections . . . :** R. Scott in Large (2004).

83 **"It was a very close feeling of affection and responsibility . . .":** D. Cook in Large (2004).

83 **"he liked to go to school, but he didn't like to buckle down.":** R. Redding in Duke (1999): 23.

84 **"We didn't even talk about *Brown v. Board of Education* . . .":** D. Cook in Large (2004).

84 **"non-segregation in our schools will never work . . .":** See Grant (1993): 372–79.

84 **"If we have to choose between integrated schools and no schools at all . . .":** M. Griffin in Grant (1993): 377.

84 **"These are not bad people . . .":** D. Eisenhower in Dudziak (2000): 130.

84 **"In the summer of 1954, a river of interracial sexual fantasies . . .":** Daniel (2000): 194.

BROTHER RAY

86 **"Now soul I find easy to define . . .":** R. Charles in *New Musical Express*, May 24, 1963.

86 **Born in Albany, Georgia, in 1930 . . . :** See Charles (1992) and Lydon (2004) for the details of Charles's biography and musical upbringing.

89 **"We all idolized him . . . all the cats who really knew music . . .":** M. Gaye in Ritz (1991): 79.

89–90 **"wasn't what you would call religious . . .":** See Charles (1992).

1955

91 **"Our music makes the feet of the whole world dance . . .":** Wright (1941): 130.

91 **"mass acceptance of rhythm & blues . . .":** *Billboard*, Feb 4, 1956.

92 **"an environment of switchblade knives, marijuana . . .":** E. Vandiver in "Let Us Not Be Deceived," *University of Georgia Vandiver Papers*, series I.A, box 9, folder 4.

92 **"We hold these truths to be self-evident . . .":** J. Eastman in *New York Post*, June 19, 1956.

93 **"A cocky, self-assured boy . . .":** *The Murder of Emmett Till* DVD (2003).

94 **cheerfully greeted the black reporters . . . :** *Time*, Oct. 3, 1955.

94 **"I just decided it was time a few people got put on notice . . .":** J. W. Millem in Huie (1956).

95 **"When people saw what had happened to my son . . .":** M. T. Bradley in *The Murder of Emmett Till* DVD (2003).

95 **she steeled her nerves, she later said . . . :** See Houck (2005).

95 **he did toy with the idea of athletic glory . . . :** R. Atkins, author interview.

97 **flatly refusing to wear the overalls his parents bought for him . . . :** R. Redding in Myron (1994): 36.

97 **Radio broadcasting was emerging as yet another new arena . . . :** See Cantor (1992) and Barlow (1999).

100 **Hamp Swain's "King Bee" program on WBML . . . :** H. Swain in *GMHF Archive* (2007).

100 **"We were the 'mayors' back then . . .":** J. Steinberg in Barlow (1999): 134.

SPECIALTY

104 **Born Arthur Goldberg in 1917 . . . :** See Wolff (1995), Broven (2010), and Guralnick (2005).

106 **But that was not an issue for Fats Domino . . . :** See Coleman (2006).

106 **"He would just talk loud and boss everybody around . . .":** R. Hall in Guralnick (2005): 248.

107 **As for Little Richard . . . :** See White (1984).

107 **"What the *fuck* is this? . . .":** E. Palmer in Scherman (1995): 90.

108 **having been banned from Macon . . . :** White (1984): 41.

BELLEVUE

109 **"My brother in his younger days was a very nice person. . . .":** R. Redding in Duke (1990): 4.

110 **"The only time he got really upset . . .":** L. Redding, author interview.

111 **"never kept a job for more than five minutes . . .":** R. Redding in Duke (1990): 23.

112 "Most of the girls and boys I'd grown up with . . .": Killens (1965): 69.

112 Beginning in the 1960s with pioneering work . . . : see Hannertz (1969) and Anderson (1999).

112 "These two orientations—decent and street . . .": Anderson (1999): 33.

112–113 Otis Sr. had begun to study with a local minister . . . : L. Redding, author interview.

113 "nothing like it is today. . . .": R. Redding in Myron (1994): 4.

113 "to be fought for and held and challenged . . .": Anderson (1999): 66.

114 "the dilemma of the decent kid": Anderson (1999): 98.

114 There were plenty of adults in Macon like the Rev. Moses Dumas . . . : See S. Freeman (2001): 11.

114 And then there were people like Alice Bailey . . . : A. Bailey, author interview.

114 "We would fight early in the morning . . .": R. Redding in Myron (1994): 4.

115 Ulf Hannerz has characterized the "streetcorner sociability" . . . : Hannerz (1969): 105.

115 "a bit of a hero, a bit of a villain, and a bit of a fool . . .": Hannerz (1969): 112.

115 "ghetto-specific masculinity . . .": Hannerz (1969): 78.

116 Herbert Ellis went on to sell bootleg liquor . . . : W. Ellis and C. J. Ellis, author interviews.

HILLVIEW SPRINGS

117 "The guy who got the most applause . . .": S. Huckabee in *The Commercial Advertiser*, Dec. 18, 1967.

117 Their group was sometimes joined by a sax player . . . : I. Mosley, author interview.

117 Williams had grown up in the city . . . : The *Telegraph*, June 9, 1950; P. Welch in *Mid-Georgia Archives* (undated).

118 In Welch's account, Otis launched into a headlong rendition . . . : See S. Freeman (2001): 13.

118 "I won the talent show for fifteen Sunday nights straight . . .": Redding (1967).

118 "When he won that first talent show . . .": R. Redding in Myron (1994): 20.

119 "That's the strategy Richard used . . .": C. Connors in *Modern Drummer*, August 2010.

120 "He was like the black Billy Graham . . .": B. Blackwell in Guralnick (2005): 127.

120 "The moral aspects of the thing just fell out into the water.": R. Harris in Heilbut (1975): 86.

120 His replacement Sam Cook . . . : See Wolff (1995) and Guralnick (2005).

121 "the greatest singer I ever heard.": R. Harris in *Rejoice*, June–July 1991: 23.

124   **Little Richard was performing outdoors at a sports stadium . . . :** See White (1984): 91; *Jet*, Dec. 19, 1957; and *Jet*, Jan. 16, 1958.

TEENAGE PARTY

126   **"Week in and week out . . .":** H. Swain in *GMHF Archive* (2007).

126   **After filing a claim against his former protégé . . . :** Brantley (1978): 2.

127   **"We were not really too surprised . . .":** C. Connors in White (1984): 92.

128   **"His impressions of Richard were word perfect . . .":** H. Nash in White (1984): 56.

128   **The first live radio broadcast of *Teenage Party* . . . :** See Malcolm X. Abram, *The Telegraph*, Oct. 30, 2000.

129   **"The group behind him just wasn't making it . . .":** J. Jenkins in Guralnick (1986): 136.

130   **Johnny Jenkins was nineteen years old . . . :** J. Jenkins in *GMHF Archive* (1994).

130   **"I'd go through there playing and singing . . .":** J. Jenkins in *GMHF Archive* (1994).

132   **According to the notice . . . :** The *Telegraph*, Aug. 1, 1958.

133   **Jenkins's left-handed theatrics would eventually give rise to a local legend . . . :** See Walden (1987): 3-3; S. Freeman (2001): 31.

134   **"I was never interested in being no musician . . .":** J. Jenkins in *GMHF Archive* (1994).

134   **"He talked very fast, very un-southern, and un-black . . .":** Walden (1987): 3-1.

ATLANTIC

135   **"We were making black records, with black musicians and black singers . . .":** J. Wexler in Fox (1986): 127.

136   **"We wanted to make the kind of records we wanted to buy . . .":** Ertegun (2001): 36.

136   **"the southern market, and the extension of the southern market . . .":** A. Ertegun in *Tom Dowd and the Language of Music* DVD (2003).

139   **"It was Horace Silver as musical director of Art Blakey's Jazz Messengers . . .":** Williams (1962): 233.

PHIL

142   **"The pragmatic philosophy of some Negroes . . .":** Killens (1965): 64.

142   **Though Phil Walden was born in the textile town of Greenville . . . :** P. Walden in *GMHF Archive* (1992 and 2002); author interviews with Katherine Walden, Alan Walden, Bobby Wallace, Lee Martin, and Seaborn Jones.

143 he developed a lifelong fascination with . . . the Jekyll Island Club . . . : K. Walden, author interview.

144 "It had a rawness and a realness . . .": P. Walden in *Georgia Music* Summer 2006: 27; *GMHF Archive* (2002); and Walden (1987): 1–3.

144 "hanging over the edge . . .": P. Walden in *GMHF Archive* (1992).

144 "I had never been around that many black people in my life . . .": P. Walden in *GMHF Archive* (2002).

145 "Lanier was never intended to produce . . .": Schrag (1965): 164.

146 "too cool for school . . .": B. Wallace, author interview.

147 Atlantic Records' Jerry Wexler once described Walden . . . : J. Wexler in Fox (1986): 128.

147 "I think that vicarious attitude was in a lot of us white boys . . .": S. Jones, author interview.

147 "Up until then our high school used white bands . . .": A. Walden in Myron (1994).

148 After rehearsing the group for several weeks . . . : V. Nesbit, author interview.

149 a group of undergraduates led by Lanier's own John Birch . . . : See Campbell (1995).

149 The most charismatic of these newcomers . . . : See Manis (2004): 184–91.

149 "I left because I said there is no way you can breathe in Georgia . . .": G. M. Bryan in Manis (1988): 188.

150 A poll conducted by the student newspaper . . . : Manis (2005): 223.

150 had recently abolished a covenant . . . : See Wikipedia: https://en.wiki pedia.org/wiki/Phi_Delta_Theta.

151 Walden recalled that the first time he booked Welch's band . . . : P. Walden (1987): 1–4.

151 "When I initially started booking bands . . .": P. Walden in *GMHF Archive* (2002).

151 "I thought my entire world revolved around Johnny Jenkins's guitar . . .": P. Walden in the *Telegraph*, Sept. 8, 1996.

OTIS AND PHIL

152 "I do not want you to see so much of the physical . . .": Du Bois (1904).

152 In his coming-of-age novel *Youngblood* . . . : Killens (1954): 377.

153 he and Otis "really hit it off instantly.": P. Walden in *GMHF Archive* (2002).

153 "Even when a white man asked us an innocent question . . .": Wright (1941): 128.

154 "You didn't trust a white man if you were a black man . . .": P. Walden in *GMHF Archive* (2002).

155 "For black men and women to know white folks . . .": Litwack (1998): 412–13.

155 literary critic Fred Hobson has applied the term *racial conversion narratives . . .* : Hobson (1999).

156 "the sex-race-sin cycle": L. Smith (1994): 121.

156 "how the plaster walls of our parlor rang . . .": K. Lumpkin in Hobson (1999): 41.

156 "It was proper—indeed, it was Southern . . .": Boyle (2001): 23, 34.

157 the same unpopular if self-evident conclusion . . . : See Myrdal (2009).

157 "It is one of the many paradoxes of our way of life . . .": L. Smith (1994): 212.

158 A 1961 poll showed that the student body had reversed itself . . . : Manis (2004): 223.

158 "an out-and-out racist . . .": P. Walden in Gillett (1971).

159 "Wherever M. L. King Jr. has been there has followed in his wake . . .": E. Vandiver in Branch (1989): 267.

159 "I didn't know there were that many niggers *in* college.": Branch (1989): 301.

ZELMA

160 "She not only loved him, she worshipped him.": L. Redding, author interview.

160 "For some reason, girls used to love him, always": R. Redding in *GMHF Archive* (2007).

160 "He would fall in love with someone one week . . .": C. Huckabee, author interview.

161 "You don't know me, and I'm not your *baby* . . .": Z. Redding (1972).

161 "I'm a plain Jane . . .": Z. Redding in Bradley (1982): 6.

162 "The police of Los Angeles fall just a stone's throw short . . .": Buntin (2009): 262.

162 Most nights, Henry's group was fronted by Bobby Day . . . : D. Henry, author interview.

162 "He could imitate anybody . . .": J. Avery, author interview.

165 One such figure was James McEachin . . . : J. McEachin, author interview.

165 a plaintive ballad called "These Arms of Mine": J. Avery, author interview.

167 Al Kavelin signed his two new artists . . . : Ibid.

168 Don Henry was under the impression . . . : D. Henry, author interview.

LOVE TWIST

169 "A two-toned Cadillac purred to a stop . . .": *Time*, October 20, 1961.

169 "Just back from L.A. California: Otis 'Rockin' Redding": The *Telegraph*, Aug. 14, 1960.

169 "When he first came back and was telling people about it . . .": R. Redding in *GMHF Archive* (2007).

169 The daughter of a local businessman . . . : K. Walden, author interview.

170 borrowing a few hundred dollars . . . : L. Martin, author correspondence.

170 "I'd answer the phone in one voice . . . : Walden (1987): 1–9.

171 "The side is done in Coasters style . . .": *Billboard,* Oct. 10, 1960: 40.

171 "We went through changes of him being out in the streets . . .": Z. Redding in Duke (1990).

172 "One-two-three-four . . .": *Time,* Jan. 20, 1961.

172 "The students at the university have demonstrated . . .": Ibid.

172 In Macon, the local chapter of the Ku Klux Klan . . . : Manis (2004): 211.

173 As Phil described it, he had "overspent" his resources . . . : Walden (1987): 1–11; P. Walden in *GMHF Archive* (2002).

174 "the ancient Southern love of the splendid gesture": Cash (1991): 21.

175 James Newton was a part-time musician . . . : J. Newton, author interview.

175 "selling jazz in Georgia is about as easy . . ." : G. Statiris in the *IAJRC Journal,* vol. 20 (1987).

176 "He was saying, 'I'm gonna be a star . . .'": Z. Redding in Guralnick (1986): 140.

177 "So one word led to another . . .": Z. Redding in Myron (1994): 9.

177 On one occasion, when Otis was badly beaten up . . . : Z. Redding in Myron (1994): 19.

178 the recording date was "absolute chaos": Walden (1987): 2-2.

179 "America's newest adult dance craze": *Billboard*, Oct. 20, 1962: 44.

JOE

180 "He changed my life. I was really his son . . .": P. Walden in *GMHF Archive* (1992). On Joe Galkin, see Wexler (1993) and Rauls (2008); G. Kesler and K. Walden, author interviews.

181 "It's a goddamn smash!": Wexler (1993): 168.

182 "obnoxious Hebe": Wexler (1993): 167. For Wexler and Galkin, see Gillett (1974), chapter 8.

182 A key to his success was his relationship with Southland Records . . . : G. Kesler, author interview.

183 meeting Joe Galkin "really changed my life. . . .": P. Walden in *GMHF Archive* (1992).

184 His response was to turn to Bobby Smith . . . : B. Smith, author interview.

186 Bobby Smith would later insist . . . : Ibid.

187 the new flag "will show that we in Georgia intend to uphold . . .": Coski (2005): 254.

187 "It didn't sound too good to me from the start . . .": B. Robinson in Gillett (1974): 13.

187   **"the worst record I ever heard . . .":** Ibid.: 190.

188   **Toward this end, Galkin contacted Jerry Wexler in New York . . . :** See P. Walden in Bowman (1999): 41; Walden (1987): 2–12; J. Wexler in Vickers (1984); J. Wexler in *Grammy Foundation* (1999): 37.

SATELLITE

189   **"I can't place too much importance . . .":** P. Walden in *Shake!* DVD (2002).

190   **"I just wanted music, anything to be involved with music":** J. Stewart in Lisle (1998).

190   **"I had scarcely seen a black person till I was grown . . .":** Ibid.

195   **"I hear my record's doing good":** J. Wexler in Bowman (1997): 19.

196   **"literally blew me away":** S. Cropper in *Rock 'n' Soul* (1999): 13.

STAX

197   **"You didn't think of it. It's like if you've got a wart . . .":** B. Linder in Helper-Ferris (1997): 234.

197   **Memphis in the early 1960s . . . :** See Helper-Ferris (1997); Green (2007).

198   **"This is a white man's country.":** See Green (2007): 38–41.

201   ***Having Fun with Morris*:** See Helper-Ferris (1997), chapter 6.

201   **"We learned what you had to do to make people dance.":** Jackson (2005).

204   **Moman's heavy drinking and domineering personality . . . :** See Gordon (2013): 59–61.

THESE ARMS OF MINE

207   **"It was different, but I don't think anyone jumped up and down.":** J. Stewart in Bowman (1997): 42.

207   **"We're a recording studio. We have our own . . .":** S. Cropper in *Dreams to Remember* DVD (2007).

208   **he proposed that they use the remaining studio time . . . :** J. Wexler in Vickers (1984).

208   **the world wasn't waiting for another Little Richard . . . :** J. Stewart in Vickers (1984).

208   **"Just play me those church things . . .":** Cropper (2004): 100.

208   **"We're not going to do the one about the record . . .":** S. Watts, *New York Times*, April 26, 1964.

209   **"I never sang like that in my in whole life . . .":** E. Presley in *Jet*, Aug. 1, 1957.

209   **In Steve Cropper's recollection . . . :** Cropper (2004): 100; also *Rock 'n' Soul* (1999): 105.

210   **Galkin asked Stewart for a half share, after expenses . . . :** Author's copy of signed contract between Joe Galkin and Jim Stewart, Aug. 16, 1962.

210 **Over time, Johnny Jenkins would perfect his own account . . . :** J. Jenkins in *GMHF Archive* (1994).

210 **Phil Walden presented Otis with a management contract . . . :** Author's copy dated Aug. 23, 1962.

211 **Smith's response was to walk downstairs . . . :** B. Smith, author interview.

212 **Smith opted for a cash payment . . . :** Ibid.

THAT'S WHAT MY HEART NEEDS

213 **"If you want to be a singer, you've got to concentrate on it . . .":** O. Redding (1967).

215 **Little Richard was no less determined to make an impression . . . :** See White (1984) and Guralnick (2005).

216 **Syd Nathan, the owner of King Records, was so adamantly opposed . . . :** See Brown (1986): 132 and Smith (2012): 108–15.

218 **"The side features a strong, soulful, blues-touched ballad vocal . . .":** *Billboard*, Nov. 24, 1962: 26.

218 **Stewart would later insist . . . :** See Gordon (2013): 76.

219 **"Then what are you doing on this *bus*?":** Gillett (1974): 192; Walden (1987): 5-2.

220 **"I knew it was best not to count on just making it as a popular musician . . .":** B. Jones in *Ebony*, April 1969: 97.

223 **"They stopped supporting me and threw all the attention on [Otis]. . . .":** J. Jenkins in Schuster (1996) and *GMHF Archive* (1994).

THE HOT SUMMER REVUE

224 **"It was my first time out on the road . . .":** Walden (1987): 5–4.

224 **Phil took it upon himself to sign Otis to a second management contract . . . :** Author's copy, May 7, 1963.

225 **Davis would wait nearly four years . . . :** See *S. Davis v. P. Walden,* Superior Court of Bibb County, No. 30401, April 1967.

225 **selling a car with a lien . . . :** *The State v. Otis Redding,* Civil Court of Bibb County, No. 93686, April 1963.

226 **"a wonderful experience. The first step in my new education. . . .":** P. Walden in *GMHF Archive* (2002); Gillett (1974): 188.

226 **In his seminal work *The Nature of Prejudice* . . . :** Allport (1978): 278.

227 **it is "only the type of contact that leads people to *do* things together . . .":** Ibid.: 276.

227 **"they were as curious about *me* as I was about them . . .":** P. Walden in *GMHF Archive* (2002).

228 **"You know, that was forbidden fruit . . .":** Walden (1987): 5-5; also see Morris (2000): 79–81.

228 "I was terrified of it . . .": Walden (1987): 9-6; see also A. Walden in Myron (1994): 69–72.

228 "a moral issue . . . as old as the Scriptures . . .": J. F. Kennedy, "Report to the American People on Civil Rights," June 11, 1963. jfklibrary.org.

PAIN IN MY HEART

230 "We were never the same once we met Tom Dowd": B. Jones in Gordon (2012).

230 "the Lost Tribes of the Sinai": Wexler (1993): 184.

230 "I had this feeling that a puff of smoke could come along . . .": Wade and Picardie (1990): 144.

231 "Motown scared the shit out of me.": A. Ertegun in *The Language of Sound* DVD.

231 In February 1963, EMI contacted Marshall . . . : P. Marshall, author interview.

231 Wexler blew a fuse of his own . . . : Wexler (1993): 172; T. Dowd in Blair (1999) and Ertegun (2002): 158.

232 "We must rise to the majestic heights . . .": M. L. King, www.american rhetoric.com/speeches/mlkihaveadream.

232 "One ever feels his twoness—an American, a Negro . . .": Du Bois (1999): 11.

233 "one day, down in Alabama . . .": M. L. King, www.americanrhetoric.com/speeches/mlkihaveadream.

234 the two brothers managed to convince their parents . . . : R. Redding in *GMHF Archive* (2007).

235 When he and Avery met again in Gulfport . . . : J. Avery, author interview.

236 "My beginning of learning what the record business meant . . .": S. Burke in *Grammy Foundation* (2003).

238 "After about probably the third single . . .": J. Stewart in Cooper (1993): 8–9.

THE APOLLO

239 "I knew absolutely nothing about the business . . .": A. Walden in *Soul*, Nov. 24, 1966: 8.

239 According to Alan, Phil called him into the office . . . : A. Walden, author interview.

240 "long letters detailing everything from how I wanted Otis to dress . . .": Walden (1987): 6-1.

241 "the greatest array of recording stars to appear on one stage . . .": *Amsterdam News*, Nov. 16, 1963: 16.

241 "We liked him immediately . . .": J. Wexler in Clark (1967).

242 **"They would boo their mama off the stage.":** R. Thomas in Cantor (1992): 37.

242 **"Otis told me he was up from home . . .":** B. E. King in Hirshey (2006): 296.

242 **"He was inept on stage . . .":** Wexler (1993): 196.

242 **Bobby Shiffman characterized Otis's Apollo debut . . . :** Schiffman (1996).

243 **including his fellow guest at the Hotel Theresa . . . :** R. Redding in Myron (1994): 58.

243 **According to Sylvester Huckabee, who stayed on after Otis left . . . :** S. Huckabee in Duke (1990): 67–68.

244 **the fact that he didn't even mention it to Alan Walden . . . :** A. Walden, author interview.

SECURITY

245 **"The black brothers are the mainstay of our pop music today . . .":** N. Montague in *Billboard*, May 24, 1964.

245 **But the first issue of the magazine in which the charts were merged . . . :** *Billboard*, Nov. 30, 1963.

250 ***Pain in My Heart* was reviewed that month in *Billboard* . . . :** *Billboard*, March 21, 1964.

252 **"Slow, drawling, bluesy material from Otis . . .":** *Disc*, April 25, 1964.

252 **"stodgy, uninspired backing . . .":** *New Musical Express*, April 17, 1964.

BERRY, BROWN, AND BURKE

253 **"Otis was like a sponge. . . .":** P. Walden in *GMHF Archive* (2002).

255 **As Alan explained it . . . :** see A. Walden in Duke (1990); Myron (1994): 10; M. Smith (2002).

255 **"Pops, we need you.":** A. Walden in Duke (1990).

255 **"His emphasis on ego breaks all bounds":** M. Dehn in *Sound & Fury*, June 1966.

256 **"Something was always wrong . . .":** Guralnick (2005): 437–38.

256 **"Of all the attributes of soul singing . . .":** Wexler (1993): 152.

257 **"Hair and teeth. A man's got those two things . . .":** Brown (1986): 88.

259 **"big-city thinking . . .":** J. Brown in Guralnick (1986): 231.

260 **On one occasion, Burke, Otis, and Joe Tex were driving . . . :** R. Redding in Duke (1990).

ROY STREET

261 **"Part of what protects a person is . . . how many people can be counted on . . .":** Anderson (1999): 73.

262 **"I've waited forty-one years for this . . .":** C. Evers in *New York Times,* July 8, 1964: 19.

263 **"We wanted to show them . . .":** S. Huckabee in Duke (1990): 22.

263 **The shoot-out on Roy Street could have ended Otis Redding's career . . . :** see S. Huckabee in Duke (1990); Walden (1987): 6–7; Bibb Superior Court, No. 10353, August Term, 1965.

264 **"It taught him a very good lesson. . . . He changed completely. . . .":** Z. Redding in *Blues & Soul,* no. 96: 14.

264 **Solomon Burke recalled hearing a deputy sheriff . . . :** Guralnick (1986): 271.

267 **Instead, he had come to think of Otis as a streetwise "big brother" . . . :** S. Cropper in *Modern Guitars,* Jan. 13, 2009.

268 **"Otis Redding did more to change my sound than anybody. . . .":** S. Cropper in *Guitar Player,* May 1978: 21.

SOUL BALLADS

269 **"I want to fill the silent vacuum that was left . . .":** O. Redding in *Chicago Defender,* Aug. 1967: 4.

270 **"Cooke's business manager, Allen Klein, hired a private investigator . . .":** Guralnick (2005): 643–45.

270 **"He talked about him a lot . . .":** S. Cropper in Hirshey (2006): 339.

270 **"Get that thing off your head.":** R. Redding in Myron (1994): 47; Z. Redding in Bradley (1982).

273 **"Eclectic, Reminiscent, Amused . . .":** Trow (1978).

273 **"The arrangers were out of ideas, the songwriters out of material . . .":** Wexler (1993): 171.

275 **"A lot of artists, they had a record that was real good in four cities . . .":** D. Alen in Broven (2010): 452.

275 **"Galkin would call three or four times a day . . .":** A. Walden in Duke (1990).

276 **"Music people all over the country are hailing 1965 . . .":** The *Telegraph,* Jan. 3, 1965.

276 **Otis received his first coverage in a national publication . . . :** *Jet,* Jan. 21, 1965: 61.

276 **In February, a preliminary court hearing ended . . . :** Bibb Superior Court, No. 10353, August Term, 1965.

277 **When questioned on the witness stand . . . :** A. Walden in Myron (1994): 24; S. Huckabee in Duke (1990).

277 **the McGees had retained a prominent Macon attorney . . . :** The *Telegraph,* Feb. 11, 1965; Bibb Superior Court Civil Division, Nos. 27942 and 27943, April Term, 1965.

I'VE BEEN LOVING YOU TOO LONG

281 "I'd never really worked with a singer who could reach down . . .": J. Stewart in *Rock 'n' Soul* (1992).

282 "There's not a lot to it, but the way Otis interpreted it . . .": J. Butler in *Grammy Foundation* (1999): 35.

284 A twenty-nine-year-old native of Baltimore . . . : E. Sims, author interview.

284 "a very emotional experience . . .": Walden (1987): 6-2.

284 Alan recalled interrupting his brother . . . : A. Walden, author interview.

286 "Joe promoted Otis day and night . . .": J. Stewart in Carroll (1993).

286 "more Redding's soul brother than his manager.": Wexler (1993): 197.

287 the singer's "obstreperous" personality.: Wexler (1993): 175.

288 Dowd configured the system . . . : R. Capone in Bowman (1995): 316–17.

288 "the microphones never moved from day to day.": S. Cropper in *Mix*, June 2002: 68.

289 "Watching the way they made records organically . . .": J. Wexler in Buskin (1999): 32.

289 There he began to enact his version of the Jerk . . . : W. Jackson in *Rock 'n' Soul* (1999): 139.

289 "it was the first time we had a chance to work with somebody . . .": S. Cropper in *Rolling Stone*, Dec. 21, 1968: 13.

289 "They'd be the first to say that they learned as much from Jerry . . .": T. Dowd in Wexler (1993): 173.

290 "He was from such a different culture . . .": D. Hood in *Bass Player*, August 1999: 54.

OTIS BLUE

291 "[Otis] would come in the door with the whole recording in his mind . . .": W. Jackson in *Soul Deep* DVD.

291 Both men would later insist that they never bothered to read the letter . . . : See Gordon (2013): 175–77.

293 "He's probably the most positive person you'll ever meet.": P. Ramone in *Tom Dowd and the Language of Music* DVD (2003).

294 "You could feel the excitement when he was coming.": W. Jackson in Wexler (1993): 197.

294 "The Stax studio would light up. . . .": D. Dunn in Wexler (1993): 196.

294 At Otis's suggestion, Sims had recently tried to record "Respect" . . . : E. Sims, author interview.

295 Phil Walden compared the after-hours scene in Otis's hotel suite . . . : Walden (1987): 12–3.

296 "I happened to think my husband was a very handsome man . . .": Z. Redding, author interview.

296 "I told him, don't bring nothing home . . .": Z. Redding in Duke (1990): 29.

297 "Otis was a very strong individual . . .": T. Dowd in Bowman (2008).

297 "When he came in there and did 'Respect' . . .": D. Dunn in *Rock 'n' Soul* (1998).

301 "They asked me if I'd heard the new Rolling Stones song, but I hadn't. . . .": O. Redding (1967).

301 Richards had originally conceived of the riff . . . : K. Richards in *Rolling Stone*, Dec. 7, 2000: 63.

MY GIRL

303 John Lennon: Otis Redding is one.: J. Lennon in beatlesinterviews.org, Aug. 18, 1965.

303 "A woman of about 65, dressed in black suit and hat . . .": T. Reston, *Atlanta Constitution*, July 19, 1965: 13.

303 "We'll cut it to even less than that. . . .": Walden (1987): 8–1.

305 "What can I tell ya? I'm fucking rich!": J. Galkin in Walden (1987): 2–9.

305 "It was like a shopping center.": Walden (1987): 8–5.

305 "You could see his confidence grow in the way he tilted his head.": Walden (1987): 5-3, 8-5.

305 Otis's "ability to learn something from a one-time explanation.": P. Walden in Duke (1990) and Myron (1994).

306–7 "Black people teach you how to live.": Walden in Hedgepath (1988).

308 From that point on, the particulars of Bell's résumé . . . : See Bowman (1997): 80–87 and Gordon (2013): 113–19.

308 "the way the Irish used whiskey . . .": A. Bell in Gordon (2013): 114.

308 "Jerry Wexler taught me all I know . . .": A. Bell in Gillett (1974): 198.

309 "He was our Otis for promotion.": B. Jones in Bowman (1997): 84.

309 "In the past three or four years established R&B artists . . .": J. Wexler in *Billboard*, Oct. 9, 1965: 1.

310 The *Record Mirror* ran a long article by staff writer Norman Jopling . . . : Jopling (1966).

310 "I've had eleven hits altogether . . .": O. Redding in *New Musical Express*, Dec. 31, 1965.

311 "There may be a little jealousy on my part.": P. Walden in Myron (1994).

311 "Otis really taught Daddy a lot about being human . . .": P. Walden in Gillett (1971).

312 "We don't use that word around here.": Walden (1987): 6-6; see also Bane (1982): 223.

312 "Otis told Daddy, 'I want a farm . . .'": Walden (1987): 6-5.

312 "The Negro buys land only when some white man will sell it to him.": Raper (1936): 122.

313 "He told them that Otis Redding was considering buying this property . . .": Walden (1987): 6-5.

I CAN'T TURN YOU LOOSE

314 'If you can't march to it, it ain't no good.': W. Jackson in *Dreams to Remember* DVD.

314 "Got to go make that dollar": P. Walden (1987): 10-6; A. Walden, author interview.

315 "Otis wouldn't have a *song* . . .": J. Avery, author interview.

315 "Otis worked it up with the horns in about ten minutes . . .": S. Cropper in *Rolling Stone,* April 15, 2005: 100.

316 "It was more the conviction he played with . . .": J. Keltner in *Modern Drummer,* October 1987.

316 "Otis never tried to tell Al Jackson anything.": A. Walden, author interview.

319 "It got to the point where the guys felt they were being used.": J. Stewart in Bowman (1997): 63; Gordon (2013): 129; Guralnick (1986): 176.

319 "a big pill to swallow.": S. Cropper in *Get Ready to Rock* (2014).

320 "We had that policy to preserve the sound that we had developed": A. Bell in Bowman (1997): 64.

321 "I called Ahmet in Europe and told him . . .": Wexler (1993): 179.

THE SOUL ALBUM

322 "I can tell you that from the musicians' standpoint . . .": S. Cropper in *Dreams to Remember* DVD.

322 Though the *Amsterdam News* reported . . . : *Amsterdam News,* Jan. 1, 1966: 12.

323 "Real stomper and shouter.": Schiffman (1996).

323 "Anything that Jim Stewart said wouldn't sell . . .": R. Thomas to Barney Hoskyns (1985).

324 Jim Stewart and Estelle Axton played host to Brian Epstein . . . : Bowman (1997): 96; Gordon (2013): 138.

326 a newly recorded ballad called "Good to Me" . . . : see Walden (1987): 7-4.

THE WHISKY

330 "Ladies and gentlemens, holler as loud as you wanna. . . .": O. Redding in Kahn (2010).

333　**"Word got out that this was a super hot show. . . .":** R. Cooder in Lewis (2010).

333　**According to Rodgers Redding . . . :** R. Redding in *GMHF Archive* (2007).

334　**"He'd get up, stomp his foot, wave his arm . . .":** R. Cooder in Lewis (2010).

334　**"Picture a calliope, spouting blasts of sound . . .":** Johnson (1966).

334　**according to one account, he wrapped Sellers's trombone . . . :** A. Walden in Myron (1994): 28.

335　**"He wasn't the best paymaster in the world. . . .":** D. Henry, author interview.

337　**Dylan's drummer, Mickey Jones, had introduced himself . . . :** Jones (2007): 143–45.

337　**Dylan's guitarist, Robbie Robertson, had already suggested . . . :** Robertson (2011).

337　**"too many damn words":** Walden (1987): 9-5.

SUMMER 1966

338　**"Not since the great days of Sun Records . . .":** *Billboard*, Aug. 20, 1966: 6.

339　**But Jim Stewart disliked the song . . . :** See Gordon (2013): 140 and Bowman (1997): 99.

341　**"You can't describe the feeling that artists like me had for the Big O. . . .":** P. Sledge in *Mojo*, December 1994.

341　**"What are you trying to do to me?":** O. Redding in Walden (1987): 11-2.

342　**Halfway through the evening . . . :** *The Telegraph*, July 17, 1966.

342　**Otis's performance earned a glowing notice in the *New York Times* . . . :** *New York Times*, Aug. 18, 1966.

343　**"the most dynamic voice I'd encountered since Billie.":** J. Hammond in Werner (2004): 91.

OTIS AND PHIL REDUX

344　**"We were completely aboveboard. . . .":** P. Walden in *GMHF Archive* (2002).

345　**"hatemonger" comparable to Josef Stalin . . . :** Branch (2006): 486.

345　**"We've been saying 'freedom' for six years . . .":** S. Carmichael in ibid.

345　**"While believing firmly that power is necessary . . .":** M. King in Branch (2006): 487.

346　**mobs of rock-throwing residents brandishing Confederate flags . . . :** Branch (2006): 506–12.

347　**"The seal of the great State of Georgia lies tarnished":** I. Allen in Meyers (2008): 337.

347　**"Georgia is a sick state":** M. King in ibid.

347　**"The way we made our reputation was . . .":** P. Walden in *GMHF Archive* (2002).

349   **"I didn't pay him a damn bit of mind":** Walden (1987): 7-2.

349   **"Otis got real distant all of a sudden. . . .":** Walden (1987): 10-8.

349   **"He went through about a three-month deal with a Black Muslim group . . .":** Walden (1987): 10-8; P. Walden in Duke (1990).

350   **Though the Waldens liked to describe Otis as their "partner" . . . :** A. Walden in Dyer (2008): 152.

350   **"I was never interested in how much we were making. . . .":** P. Walden in *GMHF Archive* (2002).

351   **Otis's band member Don Henry described the younger Grogan . . . :** D. Henry in Epperson and Thornton (1990).

351   **"a fascinating black Machiavelli . . .":** Lesher (1970).

351   **"I had worked so hard on this career . . .":** Walden (1987): 10-8.

352   **"the Southerner's native tendency . . .":** Cash (1991): 232.

353   **"Those traditions were so ingrained into every fiber . . .":** P. Walden in Duke (1990).

READY STEADY GO!

354   **"I loved England from head to toe. . . .":** O. Redding (1967).

354   **Tensions between Otis and Phil came to a head . . . :** Walden (1987): 10-9; and P. Walden in Duke (1990).

354   **gregarious former actor with a passion for R&B . . . :** Harry (1966).

355   **"Bobby is the greatest . . .":** O. Redding in *Melody Maker*, Sept. 17, 1966.

355   **"I'll tell you what happens. . . .":** Ibid.

355   **a taping of the television show *Ready Steady Go!*:** See Melly (1972): 187–89; M. Ward (1967).

358   **"You just felt your heart being opened . . .":** P. Gabriel in Easlea (2013).

358   **"one could almost believe the stories that he recorded it . . .":** Jopling (Jan. 14, 1967).

358   **"Otis should receive a mention in the *Financial Times* . . .":** Millar (1966).

DICTIONARY OF SOUL

360   **"I don't know of another man now . . .":** S. Cropper in Delehant (1967).

361   **"For a long time now, the public has been thrilled . . .":** Stax flyer in *Rock 'n' Roll Hall of Fame Archive*.

365   **"If I had to pick the best record that Stax ever made . . .":** J. Stewart in *Dreams to Remember* DVD (2007).

369   **"this is the first of Otis Redding that I have ever heard . . .":** Ward (1967).

369   **"I have become convinced that Otis Redding's performances . . .":** Landau (1967).

369   **"cleverly produced album, with Otis continually stuttering . . .":** Jopling (Jan. 14, 1967).

THE FILLMORE

370   "It was the best gig I ever put on . . .": Graham (2005): 176.

371   "He was always asking us and other musicians . . .": B. Weir in Graham (2005): 200.

371   "There was an ultimate musician that everyone wanted to see. . . .": Graham (2005): 173.

372   "They thought it was, like, voodoo rites . . .": Graham (2005): 173.

372   "To this day . . . no musician ever got *everybody* out . . .": Graham (2005): 174.

372   "Janis wanted to *be* Otis Redding . . .": J. MacDonald in Glatt (2016): 85.

373   "There was this woman leaning against the front of the stage . . .": Graham (2005): 174.

373   "He has created a style of heavily emotional . . .": R. Gleason in *San Francisco Chronicle*, Dec. 22, 1967.

KING & QUEEN

376   "I had never experienced so much feeling . . .": R. Hawkins in Wexler (1993): 210.

376   "Omelet"—a nickname that Wexler insisted was facetious . . . : see Wexler (1993): 196.

376   "Otis was never cocky about his material. . . .": J. Wexler in Clark (1969).

378   With Jerry Wexler, every story seemed to start with a phone call. . . . : See Wexler (1993) and Doblin (2015).

378   "the first gospel star to switch fields . . .": Heilbut (2012).

379   "I just don't see her recording in this environment. . . .": See Ritz (2014): 146.

379   "Thank you, Jesus.": Wexler (1993): 204.

379   Wexler, with Tom Dowd in tow, wasted little time . . . : See Doblin (2015).

380   "I always heard that he patted her on the butt . . .": D. Penn in ibid.: 171.

382   "That's the most non-singing bitch . . .": A. Walden, author's interview.

382   Otis sat down with Jim Delehant . . . : O. Redding (1967).

384   "Be sure and get yourself a white man . . .": L. Armstrong in Bergreen (1997): 376.

384   Soviero responded by filing a half-million-dollar lawsuit . . . : *Billboard*, Feb. 18, 1967: 12.

385–86 Otis's contribution . . . was written for him by Deanie Parker . . . : Bowman (1997): 124.

HIT THE ROAD, STAX

387   "I guess you could call me the father-figure of the show.": O. Redding in *Melody Maker*, March 25, 1967: 9.

388 "I think rock 'n' roll is drifting toward the blues. . . ." O. Redding in *Soul Deep* DVD (2005).

391 "To anyone who isn't a Redding fanatic . . .": N. Jopling (March 25, 1967).

391 "God bless Sam and Dave for reminding us . . .": Millar (1967).

392 "We're not going to let those songs just lie there onstage.": D. Dunn in *Bass Player*, December 1994.

393 "We're trying to make a recording here": J. Stewart in Walden (1987): 7-2.

393 "These people are fans of mine and I'm going to entertain them": O. Redding in Walden (1987): 7-3.

393 "clearly an imperfect term for a phenomenon . . .": Peter Fryer, *Encounter*, October 1967: 7.

393 "You don't know what it's like for a bunch of kids . . .": W. Jackson in Bowman, *Stax/Volt* DVD.

393 "I was taking pictures of *clouds*": A. Love in Bowman, *Stax/Volt* DVD.

393 Having determined that a cabdriver in Stockholm . . . : W. Jackson (2005): 130.

395 "Some things were said. . . .": S. Cropper in Gordon (2013): 152.

395 "Everybody came back with a totally different attitude . . .": S. Cropper in Calemine (2008); see also S. Cropper and W. Jackson in *Soul Deep* DVD (2005).

395 "I think we maybe took for granted the music we were making . . .": D. Dunn in mikevisceglia.com (2003).

R-E-S-P-E-C-T

397 "This is a song that a girl took away from me.": O. Redding in *Shake!* DVD (2002).

400 "It was the greatest rhythm and blues music ever made": A. Ertegun in Dobkin (2015): 223.

400 "I thought that all of a sudden, music had jumped up another level. . . .": D. Hood in Dobkin (2015): 225.

401 "the new Negro national anthem": P. Garland in *Ebony*, October 1967: 47.

402 "Thanks to her example . . . women vocalists of all races were allowed a freedom . . .": Heilbut (2012).

402 joint panel of the Recording Industry Association . . . : RIAA press release, March 2001.

402 Ten years later, *Rolling Stone* would place the record . . . : *Rolling Stone*, April 7, 2011.

404 "Good. Loved by audiences. Duet with Carla Thomas very cute": Schiffman (1996).

404 James Alexander also recalled that Brown's constant ragging . . . : J. Alexander in Vickers (1984).

THE LOVE CROWD

405   **"It was power, but not raw power. . . ."**: J. Wexler in Vickers (1984).

405   **"I'd sure like to go with you . . ."**: O. Redding in Walden (1987): 10-6.

405   **Phil received a phone call from Andrew Oldham . . .** : P. Walden in *Shake!* DVD (2002).

407   **"Phil Walden knew immediately that Otis was right for Monterey . . ."**: L. Adler in *Monterey Pop* (2002).

407   **"I was wary . . . so I called Jerry Wexler . . ."**: P. Walden in Duke (1990).

407   **"I think it's going to work . . . But it could backfire."**: J. Wexler in Walden (1987): 13-1.

410   **"It changed my life . . . It was our first announcement that something new was happening . . ."**: B. Jones in Gordon (2013): 156. See also Bowman (1997): 123.

410   **Wexler . . . "considered the musical tastes of the Flower Children . . ."**: Wexler (1994): 245.

411   **"Our set was a disaster"**: C. Hillman in Kubernik (2001): 126.

411   **"This really frightens me . . ."**: J. Wexler in Walden (1987): 13-3.

412   **Phil watched as Otis took a "huge hit" . . .** : Walden in Duke (1990).

412   **"Otis stirred the crowd to its greatest excitement . . ."**: P. Johnson, *Los Angeles Times,* June 19, 1967: 17.

412   **"He had the audience tied and spinning . . ."**: R. Goldstein, *Village Voice,* June 29, 1967.

BUSES TO PLANES

413   **"Phil Walden was in heaven. . . ."**: A. Oldham in Kubernik (2011): 142.

413   **"He is looking for a 'soul pilot'"**: *Jet,* July 7, 1966.

414   **"Otis's manager has contacted Sen. Richard Russell . . ."**: McClure (1967).

414   **NATRA had been formed . . .** : See Barlow (1999).

415   **"the highest ranking Negro recording executive . . ."**: *Chicago Defender,* Aug. 12, 1967.

415   **Five hundred people were invited . . .** : *Jet,* Aug. 31, 1967.

415–16 **"a big ball, with good feeling. . . ."**: Wexler in Vickers (1984): 11.

416   **Wayne Jackson of the Mar-Keys was so unnerved by the hostility . . .** : Jackson (2005): 146.

416   **uninvited presence of H. Rap Brown . . .** : See *Billboard,* Aug. 19, 1967: 1; *Chicago Defender,* Aug. 31, 1967: 17; P. Walden in Duke (1990).

416   **"If America don't come around, we're gonna burn it down"**: H. Brown in Maryland State Archives, MSA SC 2221-12-8-3, July 24, 1967.

416   **"a gathering of twenty-five major black artists behind closed doors . . ."**: O. Redding in *Billboard,* Aug. 19, 1967.

416   **"a union of all black entertainers"**: Brown (1986): 176.

417   **guests of honor at the city's Bud Billiken Parade . . . :** *Chicago Defender*, Aug. 9, 1967; Aug. 17, 1967.

417   **"First, I want to become an international recording and performing star. . . .":** *Chicago Defender*, Aug. 9, 1967.

417   ***Billboard* would shortly report . . . :** *Billboard*, Sept. 2, 1967: 24.

418   **"It's not the cliché of the raw country boy . . .":** J. Wexler in Vickers (1984): 2.

419   **In the course of this visit, Speedo Sims was dosed . . . :** E. Sims, author interview.

419   **"His show is too polished to achieve any deep musical expression":** S. Toomagian, *Downbeat*, Nov. 16, 1967.

419   **"total emotional explosion. . . .":** R. Gleason in *San Francisco Examiner*, Aug. 28, 1967.

WHAT MAKES THESE GUYS SO SPECIAL

420   **"I think it tended to sadden him, to chasten him a great deal . . .":** J. Wexler in Clark (1969).

420   **"I'd like to say something to the R&B singers who were around ten years ago. . . .":** O. Redding (1967).

421   **"It would be an honor to play on the same stage with you anytime . . .":** M. Balin in Gleason (1969): 279.

421   **"Otis came in one night and he had that *Sgt. Pepper* album . . .":** Z. Redding in Bradley (1982): 111.

421   **"The summer of 1967 was spent listening to *Sgt. Pepper*. . . .":** P. Williams, *Mademoiselle*, November 1968.

422   **"I'm trying to figure out what they're doing here . . .":** O. Redding in P. Walden, *GMHF Archive* (2002).

422   **"They're *manufacturing* a record . . .":** O. Redding in Walden (1987): 9-8.

423   **Within a few weeks, they located a well-equipped model . . . :** On the Beech 18, see Parmerter (2004) and Stekel (2010). On the history of Otis's Beech H-18, see FAA Aircraft Records for BA623.

424   **Every September, *Melody Maker* announced the results . . . :** *Melody Maker*, Sept. 23, 1967.

424   **"Basically, I like any music that remains simple. . . .":** *Soul*, Sept. 18, 1967.

425   **His initial reaction, Zelma recalled . . . :** Z. Redding, author interview.

426   **Arnold examined Otis and found that he had developed polyps . . . :** Information about Dr. Arnold and the diagnosis and treatment of Otis's throat condition comes from Dr. Scott Kessler, otolaryngologist at Mount Sinai Hospital in New York.

426   **"I'll *never* sing again.":** Walden (1987): 14-3.

427   **"I really got to realize what having a husband was all about. . . .":** Z. Redding in Bradley (1982): 7.

427   "[i]t was like the Lord intended for us to spend some time together . . .":
         Ibid.: 8.

427   "I said Otis, you're not going to live with that beard": Ibid.: 24.

                        THE DOCK OF THE BAY

428   "When I heard some of the songs he was writing . . .": Z. Redding in Gu-
         ralnick (1986): 323.

428   the Turkish Tycoon of Soul . . . : *Time*, July 8, 1967.

428   In the last week of October, *Billboard* reported . . . : *Billboard*, Oct. 28,
         1967: 1.

429   "I've got something I need you to hear.": S. Cropper in *Rolling Stone*, July
         12, 2007: 109.

430   "His voice was so clear, we just couldn't get over it. . . .": S. Cropper in *Rock
         'n' Soul* (1999): 101.

431   "You're not going to make it as a whistler": See "(Sittin' on) the Dock of the
         Bay" [Take 1] on *Remember Me*, Stax/Volt Records (1991).

431   "We knew when we cut it that it was the best thing he'd ever done . . .":
         S. Cropper in *Rock 'n' Soul* (1999): 101. See also Hirshey (2005): 343.

431   "'I want you to do my next album.'": J. Wexler in Vickers (1984): 4–5; Wex-
         ler (1993): 202; Hirshey (2006): 344; Buskin (1999): 29–30.

431   Tom Dowd recalled a similar conversation . . . : T. Dowd in *Hittin' the Note*,
         Summer 1994.

431   talking with Steve Cropper about renting a house in Memphis: S. Cropper
         in *Rock 'n' Soul* (1999): 99.

432   Speedo Sims, did not accompany him . . . : E. Sims, author interview, and
         Z. Redding in Duke (1990): 37.

432   "That was our first real insanity at Stax. . . .": B. Jones in R. Gordon, Sep-
         tember 2012.

432   *Soul* magazine published a short press release . . . : *Soul*, Dec. 11, 1967.

                           DECEMBER 10

433   "His love for people showed up in his songs. . . .": S. Cropper in *Rock 'n' Soul*
         (1999): 103.

433   "See you on Monday": S. Cropper in Wexler (1993): 201; S. Cropper in
         Vickers (1984).

434   appearance at Leo's . . . as one of the best . . . : J. Alexander in *Rock 'n' Soul*
         (2000): 79.

434   she felt he sounded "depressed": Z. Redding in Bradley (1982): 22.

435   At 3:25, Fraser radioed the Madison tower . . . : This account of the cir-
         cumstances of the plane crash is based on the NTSB report, historical re-
         ports of the weather conditions along the plane's flight path, Henry Lowe's

description of Jim Lowe's comments on the causes of the accident, and Tracy Toth's interview with the author.

435   "spinning sensation of falling": B. Cauley in *Jet*, Dec. 28, 1967.

435   "We're in the wrong place.": Ibid.

435   Bernard Reese, a bakery executive . . . : Moe (1997).

436   Phil Walden, Joe Galkin, Jerry Wexler . . . : Katherine Walden, author interview.

436   Booker T. and the MGs had played a college gig the night before . . . : S. Cropper in *Rock 'n' Soul* (1999): 104.

436   Andrew Love heard the news report on WDIA: See Gordon (2013): 169; Jackson (2005): 167; and W. Jackson in *Rock 'n' Soul* (1999): 125.

437   "The day that Otis Redding died took a lot out of me.": J. Stewart in Bowman (1997): 134.

437   Zelma, as always, was home with the children . . . : Z. Redding, author interview.

437   "totally went to pieces . . .": P. Walden in Duke (1990).

438   "You want something for the record on that attaché case? . . .": See Moe (1997).

438   His voice breaking, Jerry Wexler began his eulogy . . . : J. Wexler, audiotape in *Rock 'n' Roll Hall of Fame Archive*; see also *Chicago Defender*, Dec. 20, 1967: 8 and Dec. 27, 1967: 11.

439   historian Richard Hofstadter published a celebrated essay . . . : *Harper's*, December 1964.

440   this was a cautionary tale.: The African American writer Ben Caldwell made this accusation the basis of a play called *The King of Soul or The Devil and Otis Redding* (Bantam Press, 1969).

440   In Jim Lowe's expert opinion . . . : Henry Lowe, author interview; see also Tracy Toth, author interview, Parmerter (2004), Stekel (2010), and the NTSB Report CHI68A0053, 14 CFR, Part 91.

EPITAPH

442   "The night after he finished that song he called me . . .": P. Walden in *Shake!* DVD (2002).

443   "It seemed impossible . . .": S. Cropper in Hirshey (2005): 333; see also Bowman (1997): 134.

443   "It was just too far over the border for Jim": D. Dunn in Guralnick (1986): 323.

443   "I felt it was too pop for him . . .": P. Walden in *GMHF Archive* (2002).

443   "the perfect record" to release . . . : J. Wexler in Vickers (1984): 9.

443   Cropper maintained that he and Otis had discussed . . . : S. Cropper in *Rock 'n' Soul* (1999): 103.

444   obituaries in newspapers and magazines . . . : See *New York Times*, Dec. 11,

1967; *Rolling Stone,* Jan. 20, 1968; *Los Angeles Sentinel,* Dec. 14, 1967; *Chicago Defender,* Dec. 12, 1967; *Amsterdam News,* Dec. 16, 1967.

444 **the *Chicago Defender*'s entertainment columnist . . . :** L. Ivory, *Chicago Defender,* Dec. 28, 1967.

444 **"what love there can be . . .":** Ibid.: 14.

444 ***Jet* magazine outdid its usual standards of sensationalism . . . :** *Jet,* Dec. 28, 1967.

444 ***Esquire* published a belated . . . :** Christgau (1968).

444 **The *Saturday Evening Post* ran a feature . . . :** Booth (1991).

444 **Back home in Macon, the *Telegraph* published a column:** Ott (1967).

445 **"the man who introduced soul music to Britain":** *Melody Maker,* Dec. 16, 1967; Jopling (Dec. 23, 1967).

445 **"the gift, like great writers, of reaching out . . .":** Jopling (Dec. 23, 1967).

445 **"one of the finest pop albums of the decade.":** Landau (April 1968).

447 **"It's unwise ever to assume that they're doing only one thing . . ."** Poirier (1967).

EPILOGUE

452 **"He wasn't just a magnificent talent . . .":** P. Walden in *GMHF Archive* (2002).

452 **"We were all so shattered, in so many different ways. . . .":** L. Redding, author interview.

453 **Otis had died leaving a simple will . . . :** *Jet,* Jan. 4, 1968; P. Walden in Walden (1987): 8-4 maintained that Otis did not leave a will.

453 **pushing a unanimous resolution through the Georgia Senate . . . :** *Chicago Defender,* March 20, 1968: 13.

453 **"illiterate to say the least":** P. Walden in Gillett (1971).

453 **subscribed to a superstition about life insurance . . . :** Z. Redding in Duke (1990): 36; P. Walden in Myron (1994): 35. The superstition centered on the fear that life insurance put a "price" on one's life.

454 **[sale of] Redwal's interest . . . :** *Billboard,* March 25, 1972: 48.

454 **$300,000 in unpaid royalties . . . :** *Billboard,* Feb. 19, 1977: 74.

454 **Galkin's testimony in this lawsuit . . . :** See Vandevanter (1976); *Citizens & Southern National Bank of Georgia v. Union Planters National Bank of Tennessee et al.,* Civil Action No. C-75-539, U.S. District Court for the Western District of Tennessee, Western Division.

454 **"Otis took care of his own business. . . .":** Z. Redding in *Citizens & Southern National Bank of Georgia v. Union Planters National Bank of Tennessee et al.,* Civil Action No. C-75-539, U.S. District Court for the Western District of Tennessee, Western Division.

454 **"as if he is just away working somewhere . . .":** Z. Redding in Higgens (1968).

455 **"I love being Mrs. Otis Redding . . .":** Z. Redding interviewed on CNN, Dec. 14, 2009.

457 **his *first* speech as a civil rights leader . . . :** Branch (1988): 76; *King: A Filmed Record* DVD (2013).

458 **Isaac Hayes and David Porter, jumped in their cars . . . :** See Green (2007): 285.

458 **"The whole complexion of everything changed. . . .":** R. Thomas in *Soul Deep* DVD (2005).

458 **"That was the turning point for relations between the races . . .":** B. Jones in Guralnick (1986): 355.

458 **"Emotionally, Memphis was riding on Dr. King's visit . . .":** B. Jones in Gordon (2012).

458 **"It became really hard to go on. . . .":** D. Dunn in *Bass Player,* December 1994: 48.

458 **"You know Memphis was a refuge for black people . . .":** S. Cropper in Vickers (1984): 3–5. See also S. Cropper in *Rock 'n' Soul* (1999): 108.

459 **"My original feeling for Otis . . .":** Cropper (1968).

459 **"The odd thing is that white Memphis really does think . . .":** G. Wills in *Esquire,* August 1968.

460 **"I didn't have apprehensions . . .":** B. Jones in Hoskyns (2001).

463 **"That was the end of rhythm and blues in the South. . . ."** J. Wexler in Gordon (2013): 184.

464 **"The Miami convention signaled the end for me. . . .":** P. Walden in Hoskyns (1998): 189.

465 **To the long line of brazen cultural contradictions . . . :** See M. Butler (1999): 46–47.

465 **"Otis had so much warmth . . . He was so good . . .":** P. Walden in Gillett (1971).

BIBLIOGRAPHY

BOOKS AND ARTICLES

Allport, Gordon W. *The Nature of Prejudice*. New York: Basic Books, 1979.

Altschuler, Glenn C. *All Shook Up*. New York: Oxford U. Press, 2003.

Anderson, Elijah. *Code of the Street*. New York: Norton, 1999.

Andrews, William L., ed. *The Concise Oxford Companion to African American Literature*. New York: Oxford University Press, 2001.

Armstrong, Julie Buckner. "The People Took Exception to Her Remarks." *Mississippi Quarterly*, January 2008.

Baldwin, James. *The Price of the Ticket*. New York: St. Martin's Press, 1985.

————. *Collected Essays*. New York: Library of America, 1998.

Bane, Michael. *White Boy Singin' the Blues*. New York: Da Capo, 1982.

Barfield, James. *Historic Macon*. San Antonio: Historical Publishing Network, 2007.

Barlow, William. *Voice Over: The Making of Black Radio*. Philadelphia: Temple University Press, 1999.

Beifuss, Joan Turner. *At the River I Stand*. Memphis: St. Luke's Press, 1990.

Bergreen, Laurence. *Louis Armstrong: An Extravagant Life*. New York: Broadway Books, 1997.

Blair, Jackson. Interview with Tom Dowd. *Mix*, October–November 1999.

Bond, Beverly G., and Janann Sherman. *Beale Street*. Charleston: Arcadia, 2006.

Booth, Stanley. *Rhythm Oil*. New York: Da Capo, 1991.

Boyer, Horace Clarence. *How Sweet the Sound*. Washington, DC: Elliot & Clark, 1995.

Boyle, Sarah Patton. *The Desegregated Heart*. Charlottesville: University of Virginia Press, 2001.

Bowman, Rob. *Soulsville U.S.A.* New York: Schirmer Trade Books, 1997.

————. Notes. *The Complete Stax/Volt Singles 1959-1968*. Atlantic Records, 1991.

————. *Stax Records: A Historical and Musicological Study*. PhD. dissertation, Memphis State University, 1993.

————. Notes. *Booker T. & the MGs Anthology: Time Is Tight*. Stax, 1998.

————. Notes. *Dreams to Remember* DVD. Reeling in the Years Productions, 2007.

————. Notes. *Stax/Volt Revue Live in Norway* DVD. Reeling in the Years Productions, 2007.

————. Notes. *Otis Blue* (Reissue). Rhino Entertainment, 2008.

Branch, Taylor. *Parting the Waters*. New York: Simon & Schuster, 1989.

———. *Pillar of Fire*. New York: Simon & Schuster, 1998.

———. *At Canaan's Edge*. New York: Simon & Schuster, 2006.

Bridges, Herb. *Gone with the Wind: The Three-Day Premiere in Atlanta*. Macon: Mercer University Press, 1999.

Broven, John. *Record Makers and Breakers*. Urbana: University of Illinois Press, 2010.

Brown, Geoff. *Otis Redding*. New York: Mojo, 2001.

Brown, James. *The Godfather of Soul*. New York: Thunder's Mouth Press, 1986.

Brown, Titus. *Faithful, Firm, and True*. Macon: Mercer University Press, 2002.

Brundage, W. Fitzhugh. *Lynching in the New South*. Urbana: University of Illinois Press, 1993.

Bryan, G. McLeod. *These Few Also Paid a Price*. Macon: Mercer University Press, 2001.

Buntin, John. *L.A. Noir*. New York: Crown, 2009.

Buskin, Richard. *Inside Tracks*. New York: Avon, 1999.

Butler, Charles Elvis. *People, Cars, Hounds and Wings*. Macon: Graphic Resource, 2009.

Butler, Mike. "Luther King Was a Good Ole Boy." *Popular Music & Society* 23, 2 (1999).

Butler, Jerry. *Only the Strong Survive*. Bloomington: University of Indiana Press, 2000.

Calemine, James. "The Steve Cropper Interview." Swampland.com, 2008.

Campbell, Will D. *The Stem of Jesse*. Macon, GA: Mercer University Press, 1995.

Cantor, Louis. *Wheelin' on Beale*. New York: Pharos Books, 1992.

Cash, W. J. *The Mind of the South*. New York: Vintage, 1991.

Chalmers, Robert. "Legend: Little Richard." *GQ* (UK), October 2010.

Charles, Ray, and David Ritz. *Brother Ray*. New York: Da Capo, 1992.

Christgau, Robert. "Anatomy of a Pop Festival." *Esquire*, January 1968.

Clark, Sue Cassidy. Jerry Wexler Interview. Sue Cassidy Clark Collection. Rock 'n' Roll Hall of Fame Archive, 1967.

Coleman, Rick. *Blue Monday*. New York: Da Capo, 2006.

Cook, James F. *Carl Vinson*. Macon, GA: Mercer University Press, 2004.

Cooper, Carol. "Suite Otis." *The Definitive Otis Redding*. Rhino Records, 1993.

Coski, John M. *The Confederate Battle Flag*. Cambridge, MA: Harvard University Press, 2005.

Cropper, Steve. "The Otis Redding I Knew." *Hit Parader*, June 1968.

———. "50th Anniversary of Rock: Otis Redding." *Rolling Stone*, April 15, 2004.

———. Interview. *Get Ready to Rock*. www.getreadytorock.com, October 18, 2014.

Daniel, Pete. *Lost Revolutions*. Chapel Hill: University of North Carolina Press, 2000.

Darden, Robert. *People Get Ready!* New York: Continuum, 2004.

Day, Jeffrey. "Otis Redding's Music Bridged Racial Boundaries." *Macon Telegraph and News*, February 3, 1987.

Delehant, Jim. "The Stax Story: Steve Cropper." *Hit Parader,* September and October 1967.

Doblin, Matt. *I Never Loved a Man the Way I Love You.* New York: St. Martin's, 2015.

Dollard, John. *Caste and Class in a Southern Town.* New York: Doubleday Anchor, 1949.

Dorrell, Robert Nathan. "Percy Welch." *Macon Telegraph and News,* March 12, 1984.

Douglas, Susan J. *Listening In.* Minneapolis: University of Minnesota Press, 1999.

Dovidio, John F., ed. *On the Nature of Prejudice.* Oxford: Blackwell, 2005.

Du Bois, W. E. B. *The Souls of Black Folk.* New York: Norton, 1999.

———. "On the Development of a People." *International Journal of Ethics,* April 1904.

———. "Georgia: Invisible Empire State." *The Nation,* January 21, 1925.

Dudziak, Mary L. *Cold War Civil Rights.* Princeton, NJ: Princeton University Press, 2000.

Duval, Tommy. "Ballard-Hudson High School." *Remembering the Civil Rights Movement.* Mercer University: http://faculty.mercer.edu/davis_da/fys102/Ballard_Hudson.html.

Dyer, Candice. *Music from Macon.* Macon, GA: Indigo, 2008.

Early, Gerald. *One Nation Under a Groove.* Ann Arbor: University of Michigan Press, 1995.

Easlea, Daryl. *Without Frontiers: The Life and Music of Peter Gabriel.* London: Omnibus, 2013.

Ellison, Ralph. *Going to the Country.* New York: Random House, 1986.

———. *Shadow and Act.* New York: Vintage, 1995.

Ertegun, Ahmet, et al. *What'd I Say: The Atlantic Story.* New York: Orion, 2001.

Foley, Barbara. "In the Land of Cotton." *African American Review,* Summer 1998.

Forte, Dan. "Steve Cropper and Duck Dunn." *Guitar Player,* May 1978.

Fox, Ted. *In the Groove.* New York: St. Martin's, 1986.

———. *Showtime at the Apollo.* New York: De Capo, 1993.

Franklin, John Hope, and Moss, Alfred A. *From Slavery to Freedom.* 8th ed. New York: McGraw-Hill, 2000.

Frazier, E. Franklin, and Eric C. Lincoln. *The Negro Church in America.* New York: Schocken, 1994.

Frederickson, George M. "Panic in the New South." *NY Review of Books,* December 6, 1984.

Freeman, Gregory. *Lay This Body Down.* Chicago: Chicago Review Press, 1999.

Freeman, Scott. *Otis!* New York: St. Martin's, 2001.

———. "James Brown Is Soul Brother No. 1." *Atlanta Creative Loafing,* January 10, 2007.

Freud, Sigmund. *Case Histories II.* London: Penguin, 1979.

Gambaccini, Paul, et al. *British Hit Singles.* 8th ed. Enfield: Guinness, 1991.

————. *British Hit Albums.* 5th ed. Enfield, UK: Guinness, 1992.

George, Nelson. *The Death of Rhythm and Blues.* New York: Penguin, 2004.

————. *Where Did Our Love Go?* Urbana: University of Illinois Press, 2007.

Georgia Humanities Council. *The New Georgia Encyclopedia.* georgiaenclyclopedia .org.

Gillett, Charlie. *Making Tracks.* New York: Dutton, 1974.

————. Interview with Phil Walden. *Rock's Back Pages.* Audio, 1971.

Gilyard, Keith. *John Oliver Killens.* Athens: University of Georgia Press, 2011.

Ginzburg, Ralph. *100 Years of Lynchings.* Baltimore: Black Classic Press, 1988.

Glatt, John. *Live at the Fillmore East and West.* New York: Lyons Press, 2016.

Gleason, Ralph J. *The Jefferson Airplane and the San Francisco Sound.* New York: Ballantine, 1969.

Godshalk, David Fort. *Veiled Visions.* Chapel Hill: University of North Carolina Press, 2005.

Goosman, Stuart L. *Group Harmony.* Philadelphia: University of Pennsylvania Press, 2005.

Gordon, Robert. *It Came from Memphis.* New York: Pocket Books, 1995.

————. *Respect Yourself.* New York: Bloomsbury, 2013.

Graham, Bill, and Robert Greenfield. *Bill Graham Presents.* New York: Da Capo, 2004.

Grant, Donald. *The Way It Was in the South.* New York: Birch Lane Press, 1993.

Green, Laurie B. *Battling the Plantation Mentality.* Chapel Hill: University of North Carolina Press, 2007.

Greenberg, Steven. "Otis Redding and the Integrationist Dream." *The Definitive Otis Redding.* Rhino Records, 1993.

Greenfield, Robert. *The Last Sultan.* New York: Simon & Schuster, 2011.

Grossman, James R. *Land of Hope.* Chicago: University of Chicago Press, 1989.

Guralnick, Peter. *Sweet Soul Music.* New York: Harper & Row, 1986.

————. *Dream Boogie.* New York: Little, Brown, 2005.

Hale, Grace Elizabeth. *Making Whiteness.* New York: Vintage, 1999.

————. "On the Meaning of Progress." *The American South in the Twentieth Century.* Edited by C. S. Pascoe, K. T. Leathem, and A. Ambrose. Athens: University of Georgia Press, 2005.

Hall, Jacquelyn Dowd. *Revolt Against Chivalry.* New York: Columbia, 1993.

————. "The Long Civil Rights Movement." *Journal of American History,* March 2005.

Hall, Rick. *The Man from Muscle Shoals.* Monterey, CA: Heritage Builders, 2015.

Hamasa, M. *Elijah Muhammad, Religious Leader.* New York: Chelsea, 1990.

Hannerz, Ulf. *Soulside.* New York: Columbia University Press, 1969.

Harris, Michael. *The Rise of Gospel Blues.* New York: Oxford University Press, 1992.

Harry, Bill. "Atlantic 67." *Record Mirror,* December 24, 1966.

Hedgepeth, William. "Phil Walden Reinvents Himself." *Southern Magazine,* March 1988.

Heilbut, Anthony. *The Gospel Sound.* Garden City, NJ: Anchor/Doubleday, 1975.
———. Notes. *How Sweet It Was* DVD. Shanachie Entertainment. 2010.
———. *The Fan Who Knew Too Much.* New York: Knopf, 2012.
Helper-Ferris, Laura. "An Ethnography of Race Relations and Crossover Audiences for Rhythm & Blues and Rock 'n' Roll in 1950s Memphis." PhD diss., Rice University, 1997.
Henderson, David. *'Scuse Me While I Kiss the Sky.* New York: Bantam, 1981.
Herring, Jeanne. *Macon, Georgia.* Charleston, SC: Arcadia, 2000.
Higgins, Chester. "Wealthy, Faces Lonely Future." *Jet,* July 18, 1968.
Hirshey, Gerri. *Nowhere to Run.* New York: Times Books, 1984.
Hoare, Ian, et al. *The Soul Book.* New York: Dell, 1976.
Hobson, Fred. *But Now I See.* Baton Rouge: Louisiana State University Press, 1999.
Hook, John. *Shagging in the Carolinas.* Charleston: Arcadia, 2005.
Hoskyns, Barney. *Say It One Time for the Broken Hearted.* New York: Bloomsbury, 1987.
———. "Booker T. and the MGs." *Mojo,* August 2001.
Houck, Davis W., ed. "From Money to Montgomery." *Rhetoric & Public Affairs,* Summer 2005.
Hughes, Charles. *Country Soul.* Chapel Hill: University of North Carolina Press, 2015.
Hughes, Langston. *The Ways of White Folks.* New York: Knopf, 1934.
Huie, William Bradford. "Approved Killing in Mississippi." *Look,* January 24, 1956.
Inscoe, John C. *Georgia in Black and White.* Athens: University of Georgia Press, 1994.
Jackson, Jarma A. *Singing in My Soul.* Chapel Hill: University of North Carolina Press, 2004.
Jackson, John A. *American Bandstand.* New York: Oxford, 1997.
Jackson, Mahalia. *Movin' On Up.* New York: Avon, 1969.
Jackson, Wayne. *In My Wildest Dreams.* Nashville: Privately published, 2005.
Johnson, Charles S. *Growing Up in the Black Belt.* New York: Schocken, 1967.
Johnson, James Weldon, and J. Rosamund. *American Negro Spirituals.* New York: Viking, 1942.
Johnson, Pete. "Otis Redding's Southern-Style Blues Band." *Los Angeles Times,* April 2, 1966.
———. "First Pop Music Festival Draws Large Crowds." *Los Angeles Times,* June 19, 1967.
———. "Stax Horns into the Pop Market for Sound Success." *Los Angeles Times,* June 22, 1969.
Jones, Mickey. 2007. *That Would Be Me.* Bloomington: Author House, 2007.
Jopling, Norman. "Two-Sided Bluester." *Record Mirror,* May 1, 1965.
———. "Otis R. The Man Who Sings As Though He Means It." *Record Mirror,* January 22, 1966.

————. *Record Mirror,* January 14, 1967.

————. *Record Mirror,* March 25, 1967.

————. "The Life and Music of Otis Redding." *Record Mirror,* December 23, 1967.

Kahn, Ashley. Liner Notes. *Otis Redding Live on the Sunset Strip.* Stax, 2010.

Keil, Charles. *Urban Blues.* Chicago: University of Chicago Press, 1966.

Kempton, Arthur. *Boogaloo.* Ann Arbor: University of Michigan Press, 2005.

Killens, John Oliver. *Youngblood.* New York: Dial Press, 1954.

————. *The Black Man's Burden.* New York: Pocket Books, 1965.

Kirby, Jack Temple. *Rural Worlds Lost.* Baton Rouge: Louisiana State University Press, 1987.

Kubernik, Harvey, and Kenneth Kubernik. *A Perfect Haze.* Solena Beach, CA: Santa Monica Press, 2001.

Kubernik, Harvey. "Otis Redding Was King of the Sunset Strip." *Goldmine,* June 28, 2010.

Landau, Jon. "Dictionary of Soul." *Crawdaddy,* December 1967.

————. "Otis Redding: The King of Them All." *Eye Magazine,* April 1968.

————. "Soul Roll." *Rolling Stone,* December 21, 1968.

Large, Maggie. "Worlds Apart: The Segregation of Macon Schools." The *Telegraph,* May 17, 2004.

Lauterbach, Preston. *The Chitlin Circuit.* New York: Norton, 2011.

Lemann, Nicholas. *The Promised Land.* New York: Vintage, 1992.

————. *Redemption.* New York: Farrar, Straus & Giroux, 2006.

Lesher, Steven. "Leroy Johnson Outslicks Mr. Charlie." *New York Times Magazine,* November 8, 1970.

Levine, Lawrence W. *Black Culture and Black Consciousness.* New York; Oxford, 2007.

Lewis, Randy. "When Otis Redding Caught the Groove." *Los Angeles Times,* May 20, 2010.

Lhamon, W. T. *Deliberate Speed.* Washington, DC: Smithsonian Institution Press, 1990.

Liebow, Elliot. *Tally's Corner.* Lanham, MD: Rowman & Littlefield, 2003.

Lincoln, C. Eric, and Lawrence H. Mamiya. *The Black Church and the African American Experience.* Durham, NC: Duke University Press, 1990.

Lisle, Andrea. "Jim Stewart." *Memphis Downtowner,* July 1998.

Litwack, Leon. *Trouble in Mind.* New York: Vintage, 1998.

Lomax, Alan. *The Land Where the Blues Began.* New York: Pantheon, 1993.

Lott, Erick. *Love and Theft.* New York: Oxford, 1993.

Lubiano, Wahneema, ed. *The House That Race Built.* New York: Vintage, 1998.

Lydon, Michael. *Ray Charles.* New York: Routledge, 2004.

Maley, Dan. "Blessed Return." The *Telegraph,* September 8, 1996.

Manis, Andrew M. *Macon Black and White.* Macon, GA: Mercer University Press, 2004.

Marsh, Dave, ed. *Sam and Dave*. New York: Avon, 1998.

Mayes, Elaine. *It Happened in Monterey*. Culver City, CA: Britannia Press, 2004.

McClure, Don. "Redding Enjoying His Greatest Year." The *Telegraph*, July 9, 1967.

McGill, Ralph. *The South and the Southerner*. Athens: University of Georgia Press, 1992.

McKee, Margaret, and Fred Chisenhall. *Beale Black and Blue*. Baton Rouge: Louisiana State University Press, 1981.

McWhorter, Diane. *Carry Me Home*. New York: Touchstone, 2002.

Melly, George. *Revolt into Style*. London: Penguin, 1972.

Meyers, Christopher C., ed. *The Empire State of the South*. Macon: Mercer University Press, 2008.

Millar, Bill. "Otis Redding at Tiles." *Soul Music Monthly*, October 1966.

———. "Otis Redding et al." *Soul Music Monthly*, April 1967.

Moe, Doug. "The Riddle of Otis Redding." *Madison Capital Times*, December 6, 1997.

Moore, Allan, ed. *The Oxford Companion to Blues and Gospel Music*. Cambridge, UK: Cambridge University Press, 2002.

Morris, Willie. *North Toward Home*. New York: Vintage, 2000.

Murray, Albert. *Stompin' the Blues*. New York: McGraw-Hill, 1976.

Murray, Charles Shaar. *Crosstown Traffic*. New York: St. Martin's, 1989.

———. *Boogie Man*. New York: St. Martin's Griffin, 2002.

Myers, Christopher C. "Killing Them by the Wholesale: A Lynching Rampage in South Georgia." *Georgia Historical Quarterly*, Summer 2006.

Myrdal, Gunnar. *An American Dilemma*. New Brunswick: Transaction, 2009 (orig. 1944).

Oldham, Andrew Loog. *Stoned*. New York: St. Martin's, 2000.

———. *2Stoned*. London: Vintage, 2002.

Oliver, Paul. *Blues Fell This Morning*. Cambridge: Cambridge University Press, 1990.

Oppy, Jane. "Clint Brantley: Star Dust." The *Telegraph*, May 17, 1977.

Ott, William. "Home Forever." The *Telegraph*, December 17, 1967.

Palmer, Robert. *A Tale of Two Cities: Memphis Rock and New Orleans Roll*, Brooklyn: I.S.A.M. Monograph No. 12, Brooklyn College of the City University of New York, 1979.

———. *Deep Blues*. New York: Penguin, 1981.

———. *Blues & Chaos*. New York: Scribner, 2009.

Parmerter, Robert, K. *Beech 18: A Civil and Military History*. Twin Beech 18 Society, 2004.

Pictorial History of Robins Air Force Base. Macon, GA: University Press of the South, 1982.

Pleasants, Henry. *The Great American Popular Singers*. New York: Simon & Schuster, 1974.

Poirier, Richard. "Learning from the Beatles." *Partisan Review*, Fall 1967.

Posner, Gerald. *Motown*. New York: Random House, 2002.

Powdermaker, Hortence. *After Freedom*. New York: Athenaeum, 1968.

Rachlin, Harvey. *The Encyclopedia of the Music Business*. New York: Harper & Row, 1981.

Raper, Arthur F. *Preface to Peasantry*. Chapel Hill: University of North Carolina Press, 1936.

Rauls, Phillip. "Joe Galkin: Music Business Power Broker." phillipraulsphololog .blogspot.com, March 16, 2008.

Reagon, Bernice Johnson. *We'll Understand Better By and By*. Washington, DC: Smithsonian Institution Press, 1992.

Redding, Otis. Interviewed by Jim Delehant. *Hit Parader*, August 1967.

Redding, Zelma. "Zelma Redding Remembers." *Blues and Soul* no. 95, October 20, 1972.

———. "Testimonial." *The Definitive Otis Redding*. Rhino Records, 1993.

Reed, Teresa. *The Holy Profane*. Lexington: University of Kentucky Press, 2003.

Ritz, David. *Divided Soul: The Life of Marvin Gaye*. New York: Da Capo, 1991.

———. *Respect: The Life of Aretha Franklin*. Boston: Little, Brown, 2014.

Robertson, Robbie. Interview. *The Blues Mobile Radio Show*. bluesmobile.com, October 17, 2011.

Rubin, Richard. "The Ghosts of Emmett Till." *New York Times*, July 31, 2005.

Salvatore, Nick. *Singing in a Strange Land*. Urbana: University of Illinois Press, 2006.

Sanjek, Russell. *American Popular Music and Its Business*. New York: Oxford, 1998.

Scherman, Tony. *Backbeat*. Washington, DC: Smithsonian Institution Press, 1999.

Schiffman, Frank. *Apollo Theater Collection 1933–1985*. Washington, DC: National Museum of American History, 1996.

Schrag, Peter. *Voices in the Classroom*. Boston: Beacon, 1965.

Selvin, Joel et al. *Peppermint Twist*. New York: Macmillan, 2012.

Shaw, Arnold. *The World of Soul*. New York: Cowles, 1970.

———. *Honkers & Shouters: The Golden Years of Rhythm and Blues*. New York: Collier, 1978.

Shuster, Fred. "Johnny Jenkins." *Los Angeles Daily News*, August 28, 1996.

Smith, Lillian. *Killers of the Dream*. New York: Norton, 1994.

Smith, Michael B. "Alan Walden's Career in Rock and Soul." *Gritz Magazine*, January 2002.

Smith, R. J. *The One*. New York: Gotham, 2012.

Sokol, Jason. *There Goes My Everything*. New York: Vintage, 2007.

Southern, Eileen. *The Music of Black Americans*, New York: Norton, 1997.

Stekel, Peter. *Final Flight*. Birmingham, AL: Wilderness Press, 2010.

Stewart, Jim. "Testimonial." *The Definitive Otis Redding*. Rhino Records, 1993.

Storace, Patricia. "Look Away, Dixie Land." *New York Review of Books*, December 19, 1991.

Sugrue, Thomas J. *Sweet Land of Liberty*. New York: Random House, 2008.

Taylor, Derek. *It Was Twenty Years Ago Today.* New York: Fireside, 1987.

Thomas, Tracy. "Stones Knock Otis Out." *New Musical Express,* December 31, 1965.

Trawick, Gertrude. "He's Never Regretted Missing Law School." The *Telegraph,* June 23, 1970.

Toll, Robert C. *Blacking Up.* New York: Oxford, 1974.

Trow, George W. S. "Eclectic, Reminiscent, Amused, Fickle, Perverse." *The New Yorker,* May 29 and June 5, 1978.

Tuck, Stephen G. N. *Beyond Atlanta.* Athens: University of Georgia Press, 2001.

Vandevanter, Peter. "Suit Filed by Widow of Singer." The *Telegraph,* April 13, 1976.

Wade, Dorothy, and Justine Picardie. *Music Man.* New York: Norton, 1990.

Wald, Gayle. *Shout, Sister, Shout!* Boston: Beacon Press, 2007.

Walden, Alan. "Testimonial." *The Definitive Otis Redding.* Rhino Records, 1993.

Walden, Phil. Video interview. *Shake! Otis at Monterey* DVD. Criterion Collection, 2002.

Ward, Brian. *Just My Soul Responding.* London: Routledge, 2004.

Ward, Ed. "Otis Redding." *Crawdaddy,* March 1967.

Ward, Miranda. "Otis Redding in London." *Hit Parader,* February 1967.

Werner, Craig. *A Change Is Gonna Come.* New York: Plume, 1999.

———. *Higher Ground.* New York: Crown, 2004.

Wexler, Jerry. "Otis Redding Eulogy." Audiotape. Rock 'n' Roll Hall of Fame Archive, 1967.

———. "Otis, The Man." *Blues and Soul* 95, October 20, 1972.

Wexler, Jerry, and David Ritz. *Rhythm and the Blues.* New York: Knopf, 1993.

Whitburn, Joel. *Pop Singles Annual 1955-1986.* Menomonee Falls: Record Research, 1987.

———. *Top 40 Albums.* Menomonee Falls, WI: Record Research, 1987.

———. *Top R&B Singles 1942-1988.* Menomonee Falls: Record Research, 1988.

———. *Billboard Hot 100: The Sixties.* Menomonee Falls: Record Research, 1990.

———. *Across the Charts: The 1960s.* Menomonee Falls: Record Research, 2008.

White, Charles. *The Life and Times of Little Richard.* London: Omnibus, 1984.

Wilkerson, Isabel. *The Warmth of Other Suns.* New York: Random House, 2010.

Williams, Martin T. *The Art of Jazz.* New York: Jazz Book Club, 1962.

Williamson, Joel. *The Crucible of Race.* New York: Oxford, 1984.

Wirtz, Billy C. "Take My Hand, Lead Me Home." *Georgia Music,* Summer 2008.

Wolf, Jaime. "The Big O and the Real Sound of Soul." *The Definitive Otis Redding.* Rhino Records, 1993.

Wolff, Daniel. *You Send Me.* New York: William Morrow, 1995.

Wolk, Douglas. *James Brown Live at the Apollo.* London: Bloomsbury, 2012.

Wondrich, David. *Stomp and Swerve.* Chicago: A Cappella, 2003.

Woodward, C. Vann. *The Strange Career of Jim Crow.* New York: Oxford, 1955.

Wright, Richard. *Black Boy.* New York: Harper Perennial, 1989.

———. *Native Son*. New York: Harper Perennial, 1993.

———. *12 Million Black Voices*. New York: Basic Books, 2008.

X, Malcolm, with Alex Haley. *The Autobiography of Malcolm X*. New York: Grove, 1965.

FILMS AND DVDS

Atlantic Records: The House That Ahmet Built. Rhino Entertainment, 2007.

Dreams to Remember: The Legacy of Otis Redding. Reeling in the Years, 2007.

Eyes on the Prize: America's Civil Rights Years. PBS Films, 2010.

How Sweet It Was. Shanachie Entertainment, 2010.

King: A Filmed Record. Kino Lorber Films, 2013.

Monterey Pop. Pennebaker Hegedus Films, Criterion Collection, 2002.

The Murder of Emmett Till. Firelight Media, 2003.

Rejoice and Shout. Magnolia Pictures, 2011.

Respect Yourself: The Stax Records Story. Concord Music Group, 2007.

Sam Cooke, Legend. ABKCO Music & Records, 2003.

Shake! Otis at Monterey. Pennebaker Hegedus Films, Criterion Collection, 2002.

Soul Deep: The Story of Black Popular Music. BBC Films, 2005.

Stax/Volt Revue: Live in Norway. Reeling In the Years, 2007.

The Story of Gospel Music. BBC Video. 1996.

Tom Dowd and the Language of Music. A Mark Moorman Film, Palm Pictures, 2003.

UNPUBLISHED INTERVIEWS AND MANUSCRIPTS

The unpublished interviews listed below derive from five main sources:

Grammy Foundation Living History Project (1999–2000)

Smithsonian Rock 'n' Soul Project (1992–2000)

Archives of the Georgia Music Hall of Fame (GMHF)

Mid-Georgia Genealogical and Historical Collection in the Washington Memorial Library, Macon Georgia

A series of interviews that were done in conjunction with two commercial film projects that were produced by A&M Films and Universal Pictures between 1982 and 1994. These film-related materials consist of a 1982 interview of Zelma Redding by the screenwriter David Bradley; six interviews conducted in 1984 by the music journalist Tom Vickers; a sixty-three-page manuscript written in 1987 by Phil Walden; six interviews conducted in 1990 by the director Bill Duke and the screenwriters Billy Bob Thornton and Tom Epperson; and five interviews conducted in 1994 by the producer Ben Myron. All are used by permission.

Adler, Lou. Unknown interviewer. *Grammy Foundation Living History Project,* 1999.

Alexander, James. Interviewed by Tom Vickers. A&M Films, undated 1984.

———. Interviewed by David Less and John Mechan. *Smithsonian Rock 'n' Soul Project,* 2000.

Bell, Al. Interviewed by Jeff Scheftel. *Grammy Foundation Living History Project,* 2000.

Brantley, Clint. Interview. Mid-Georgia Collection. Washington Memorial Library, 1978.

Burke, Solomon. Interviewed by John Sutton Smith. *Grammy Foundation Living History Project,* 2003.

Butler, Jerry. Interviewed by Jeff Scheftel. *Grammy Foundation Living History Project,* 1999.

Cauley, Ben. Interviewed by Pete Daniel and David Less. *Smithsonian Rock 'n' Soul Project,* 1999.

Cropper, Steve. Interviewed by Tom Vickers. A&M Films, September 18, 1984.

———. Interviewed by David Less. *Smithsonian Rock 'n' Soul Project,* December 10, 1999.

Dimmons, Albert. Interview. Mid-Georgia Collection, Washington Memorial Library, 1978.

Dunn, Donald "Duck." Interviewed by David Less. *Smithsonian Rock 'n' Soul Project,* 1998.

Ertegun, Ahmet. Interviewed by Tom Vickers. A&M Films, undated 1984.

Hayes, Isaac. Interviewed by John Hornyak. *Grammy Foundation Living History Project,* 2001.

Huckabee, Sylvester and Hamp Swain. Interviewed by Bill Duke. A&M Films, January 21, 1990.

Henry, Don. Interviewed by Tom Epperson and Billy Bob Thornton. A&M Films, March 19, 1990.

Jackson, Wayne, and Andrew Love. Interviewed by David Less and Pete Daniel. *Smithsonian Rock 'n' Soul Project,* 1999.

Jenkins, Johnny. Audio Interview by Rob Blout. *Georgia Music Hall of Fame Archive,* 1994.

Jones, Booker T. Interviewed by Tom Vickers. A&M Films, September 26, 1984.

———. Interviewed by Robert Gordon, Country Music Hall of Fame, September 13, 2012.

Jones, Seaborn. Interviewed by Tom Vickers. A&M Films, October 12, 1984.

Redding, Zelma. Interviewed by David Bradley, A&M Films, December 9, 1982.

———. Interviewed by Bill Duke. A&M Films, January 21, 1990.

Redding, Rodgers. Interviewed by Bill Duke. A&M Films, January 21, 1990.

———. Interviewed by Ben Myron. Universal Pictures, November 27, 1994.

———. Video Interview by Ellen Fleurov. *Georgia Music Hall of Fame Archive,* 2007.

Sims, Earl "Speedo." Interviewed by Tom Vickers. A&M Films, undated 1984.
———. Interviewed by Bill Duke. A&M Films, undated, 1990.
———. Interviewed by Ben Myron. Universal Pictures, November 28, 1994.
Stewart, Jim. Interviewed by Tom Vickers. A&M Films, undated, 1984.
———. Interviewed by Pete Daniel, Peter Guralnick, David Less, and Charlie McGovern, *Smithsonian Rock 'n' Soul Project*, May 19, 1992.
———. Interviewed by Robert Gordon, 2012.
Swain, Hamp. Interviewed by Tom Vickers. A&M Films, undated, 1984.
———. Video Interview by Ellen Fleurov, *Georgia Music Hall of Fame Archive*, 2007.
Thomas, Carla. Interviewed by Pete Daniel and David Less. *Smithsonian Rock 'n' Soul Project*, 1999.
Thomas, Rufus. Interviewed by Tom Vickers. A&M Films, undated, 1984.
———. Audio Interview by Barney Hoskyns, *Rock's Back Pages: Audio*, 1985.
———. Interviewed by David Less, Pete Daniel, Charles McGovern, and Peter Guralnick, *Smithsonian Rock 'n' Soul Project*, 1992.
Walden, Alan. Interviewed by Bill Duke. A&M Films, 1990.
———. Interviewed by Ben Myron. Universal Pictures. November 26, 1994.
———. Interviewed by Jessica Walden. Macon: Story Corps, February 10, 2011.
Walden, Peggy. Interviewed by Ben Myron, Universal Pictures. November 29, 1994.
Walden, Phil. "Notes for the Otis Redding Story." May 17, 1987.
———. Interviewed by Bill Duke. A&M Films, undated, 1990.
———. Audio Interview by Joseph Johnson. *Georgia Music Hall of Fame Archive*, 1992.
———. Unknown Audio Interviewer. *Georgia Music Hall of Fame Archive*, 2002.
Walden, Phil; Alan Walden; Carolyn Killen; and Rodgers Redding. Interviewed by Ben Myron, undated, 1990.
Welch, Percy. Interview. Mid-Georgia Historical Archive, Washington St. Memorial Library.
Wexler, Jerry. Interviewed by Tom Vickers. A&M Films, October 8, 1984.
———. Unknown Interviewer. *Grammy Foundation Living History Project*, 1999.

AUTHOR INTERVIEWS

Interviews with the sources listed below were conducted in person, on the telephone, and/or by e-mail. Many of these sources were contacted multiple times.

Acree, Paul. *Photographer and friend of Phil Walden*
Adishian, Haig. *Graphic artist for Atlantic Records*
Adkins, Richard. *Schoolmate of Otis Redding in Tindall Heights*
Albritten, Robert. *Mayor of Dawson, Georgia*
Alen, Dick. *Talent agent*

Andrews, Artralia. *Daughter-in-law of the Rev. C. J. Andrews*

Avery, Jackie. *Songwriter and member of the Shooters*

Bailey, Alice. *Friend of Otis Redding in Tindall Heights*

Barber, Jimmy. *Guitarist for Roye Mathis*

Bart, Jack. *Manager of James Brown*

Bone, Mike. *Associate of Phil Walden*

Booth, Stanley. *Music journalist*

Braddock, Eddie. *Publicist for Stax Records*

Brantley, Clint Jr. *Son of Clint Brantley*

Brown, Ray "Satellite Papa." *Macon disk jockey*

Burkhardt, Kent. *Atlanta disk jockey and associate of Otis Redding*

Carswell, Peyton. *Macon club owner*

Cass, Mike. *Schoolmate of Phil Walden*

Chernin, Stephen. *High school classmate of Phil Walden*

Collier, Newton. *Tindall Heights resident and trumpeter for Sam and Dave*

Cook, Delores. *English teacher at Ballard-Hudson High School*

Cowles, Roger. *Associate of Phil Walden and Frank Fenter*

Delehant, Jim. *Editor of* Hit Parader *magazine*

Dorsey, Tony. *Trombonist for the Otis Redding Revue*

Dubose, Violet Neblet. *High school girlfriend of Phil Walden*

Ellis, C. Jack. *Neighbor of Otis Redding in Bellevue*

Ellis, William. *Friend of Otis Redding in Bellevue*

Fowley, Kim. *Artist at Lute Records*

Gaines, Grady. *Leader of the Upsetters*

Hadley, Leroy. *Guitarist for the Otis Redding Revue*

Hall, Bill. *Friend and associate of Phil Walden*

Hart, George. *Friend of Phil Walden*

Hawkins, Jim. *Recording engineer and associate of Phil Walden*

Henry, Don. *Saxophonist and advance man for the Otis Redding Revue*

Holloway, Bobby. *Saxophonist and bandleader for the Otis Redding Revue*

Huckabee, Charles. *Friend of Otis Redding in Bellevue*

James, Nathaniel. *Resident of Dawson, Georgia*

Jenkins, Terry. *Brother of Johnny Jenkins*

Johnson, Jai Johnny. *Drummer in the Otis Redding Revue and the Allman Brothers Band*

Johnson, Leroy. *Georgia state senator and attorney for Otis Redding*

Jones, Geneva. *Daughter of Carter Jones and neighbor of Otis Redding in Tindall Heights*

Jones, Seaborn. *Friend of Phil Walden*

Kavelin, Frank. *Son of Al Kavelin, owner of Lute Records*

Kesler, Gwen. *Manager of Southland Records*

Kessler, Dr. Scott. *Otolaryngologist at Mount Sinai Hospital, New York*

King, Larry. *Associate of Joe Galkin*

Kirkland, Eddie. *Bluesman and associate of Otis Redding*

Kline, Dick. *Publicity director at Atlantic Records*

Laing, Ken. *Son of Will Laing and resident of Dawson, Georgia*

Landau, Jon. *Music journalist*

Lowe, Henry. *Son of Jim Lowe, owner of Lowe Aviation*

Lyndon, John. *Brother of Twiggs Lyndon*

Marshall, Paul. *Attorney for Atlantic Records*

Martin, Lee. *Friend and college roommate of Phil Walden*

McClain, Louise Redding. *Sister of Otis Redding*

McEachin, James. *Actor and producer of the Shooters*

McIntyre, Jack. *Associate of Gwen Kesler and Joe Galkin*

Mordaunt, Richard. *Filmmaker, 1967 Stax/Volt Tour*

Mosley, Ish. *Saxophonist with the Pinetoppers*

Newton, James. *Owner of Tifco Records*

Norwood, Anderson. *Member of the Heartbreakers*

Nussbaum, Ted. *Attorney for Atlantic Records and Joe Galkin*

Odom, Bunky. *Associate of Phil Walden*

Pennebaker, D. A. *Filmmaker, Monterey Pop*

Pierce, Wayne. *Member of the Rockin' Capris*

Rauls, Phillip. *Associate of Joe Galkin*

Redding-Andrews, Karla. *Daughter of Otis Redding*

Redding, Zelma. *Widow of Otis Redding*

Roberts, Jimm. *Photographer and friend of Phil Walden*

Roseman, LaJuene. *Great-granddaughter of Willie Roseman*

Roseman, Lorenz. *Grandson of Willie Roseman*

Ross, Eddie. *Childhood friend of Otis Redding in Tindall Heights*

Scott, Robert. *Music teacher at Ballard-Hudson High School*

Seller, Maurice. *Former owner of Tiles Club, London*

Sims, Carl. *Singer with the MGs and Otis Redding*

Sims, Earl "Speedo." *Road manager for Otis Redding*

Smith, Bobby. *Owner of Confederate Records*

Spero, David. *Son of Herman Spero, producer of* Upbeat *television show*

Toth, Tracy. *Professional airline pilot and Beech 18 owner*

Walden, Alan. *Manager of Otis Redding*

Walden, Amantha. *Daughter of Phil Walden*

Walden, Jessica. *Daughter of Alan Walden*

Walden, Katherine. *Wife of Phil Walden*

Wallace, Bobby. *Friend and associate of Phil Walden*

Wells, Thomas. *Guitarist in Atlanta*

Williams, Loretta. *Singer with the Otis Redding Revue*

Woodson, Elbert "Woody." *Drummer with the Otis Redding Revue*

PHOTOGRAPHY CREDITS

INDEX

Also by Jonathan Gould

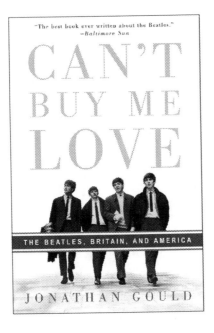

"Can't Buy Me Love provides a thrilling account of how four nowhere kids from Liverpool translated their love of American rock and blues into a body of popular music unmatched in the nearly forty years since they ended their careers as Beatles. Writing with a scholar's attention to history and a musician's interest in songcraft, Gould meticulously charts the group's evolution from three-chord sprints like 'She Loves You' to multipartite, symphonic masterpieces like 'A Day in the Life.' If you've ever wanted to know why the Beatles' music is great and how better to appreciate it, look no further than this brilliant book."

—*People*

THREE RIVERS PRESS

Available wherever books are sold

Printed in the United States
by Baker & Taylor Publisher Services